The Who's Who of
STOKE CITY

Compiled by Tony Matthews

The Who's Who of STOKE CITY

First published in Great Britain in 2005 by
The Breedon Books Publishing Company
Limited
Breedon House, 3 The Parker Centre,
Derby, DE21 4SZ.

A catalogue record for this book is available from the British Library.

ISBN 1 85983 474 4

Printed and bound by Cromwell, Trowbridge, Wiltshire.

Contents

Acknowledgements

I would like to thank the following people for their help in the production of this work:

Steve Caron, who kindly agreed to produce the book; editor Michelle Grainger and co-ordinator Susan Last, all from Breedon Books, Derby.

David Barber (from the Football Association), Zoe Ward (Premier League) for clarifying personal records of several players and to Lee Biddle, 'Stokies' Julian Boodell, especially Paul Bradbury, Roy Price, Wade Martin and Peter Wyatt, all of whom have generously supplied several pictures from their own private collections (some of which had been used in my publications)

Thanks, also, to my friend of many years Tommy Tams (ex-Stoke City FC) for his help towards this project, to Hazel Bailey (Stoke City FC) and to my step-daughter Cathie Smith for her terrific efforts in typing up hundreds of words.

And there's a special thank you (again) to my darling wife, Margaret, who has had to watch TV on her own or graft hard and long in the garden while I've been seated in front of my computer screen, typing in word after word with hundreds of programmes, scrapbooks and reference books scattered on the floor.

If I've missed anyone, thank you all, too – your efforts are much appreciated.

Important Notice

The majority of pictures used in this book have come from within the club, from certain supporters, families of current and ex-players, from scrapbooks, albums and libraries. I have been unable to establish clear copyright on some of these pictures and, therefore, both the publishers and myself would be pleased to hear from anyone whose copyright has been unintentionally infringed.

Introduction

I am certain that all supporters of Stoke City Football Club, young and old, male and female, have, at some time or another, been involved in an argument concerning a player, whether from the past or present!

In pubs, clubs, cafes, bars and restaurants, schools, colleges and universities, at home, in the office, out walking or shopping, at a ground, in a car, on a train, bus or plane, even on the beach, discussions have taken place about one or more players, even managers, who have been associated with the Potters through the years.

Some of these discussions have turned into heated arguments with questions being asked but no definite answer given. As a result, wagers have been laid as to who is right and who is wrong!

The questions are varied: When did he join the club? Where did he come from? How many goals did he score? Who did he join after leaving the club? Did he play international football? Was he a defender or midfielder? Did he play in a Cup Final?

This Who's Who will answer most, if not all, of these questions, as well as offering the fan loads more information besides. It will also satisfy that laudable curiosity without a shadow of doubt.

You will find multitudinous authentic personal details of each and every player who has appeared for the club in a competitive match over a period of almost 122 years... since the Potters' first FA (English) Cup game against Manchester in November 1883 to the last League encounter at Sunderland in May 2005.

And apart from players' records in all the major League and Cup competitions, details of appearances made and goals scored in Birmingham League and Southern League competitions (1908–1919) are also included.

There are also details of players who guested for the club during the two World Wars and the club's managers, assistant managers, chairmen, secretaries and coaches are listed too.

The date and place of birth and death are given, if known, although occasionally it has only been possible to ascertain a year with regards to when the player was actually born and died. By checking several documents (i.e. public census), I have, in some cases, been able to ascertain that a player was deceased at a given time.

Following on from my two previous books on the club, *The Encyclopaedia of Stoke City 1868 to 1994* and *The A-Z of Stoke City*, I have been aided and abetted by several statisticians up and down the country regarding personal details of players.

I have also been in touch with the families and friends of former players and have been lucky to acquire a considerable amount of extra information. Some of this has proved to be quite interesting, although details of some of the players, especially those who appeared for the club before the Great War, is still rather limited.

I have included in each player's write-up (if possible) details of the junior and non-League clubs he served, any transfer fees involved (these have been taken from matchday programmes and various newspapers) and any honours won at club and international level.

All the player's individual senior appearance and goal-scoring records with the Potters are up to the end of the 2004–05 season and given directly under the player's name, alongside his preferred playing position. A plus sign (i.e. 100+3 apps) indicates the number of substitute appearances that player made

Throughout virtually all this book, the name of the club is referred to as the Potters, Stoke or Stoke City. Very few abbreviations have been used but among the more common ones are the obvious: FC (Football Club), apps (appearances), 'sub' (substitute), c. (circa, about).

Where a single year appears in the text (when referring to an individual player's career) it indicates, in most cases, the second half of a season, i.e. 1975 is the second half of the 1974–75 season. However, when the figures such as 1975–80 appear, this means seasons 1975–76 to 1979–80 inclusive and not 1974–80.

This is not a story or history book. It is a reference book – and a lot of the information printed on the following pages has been read before, certainly in the A-Z of Stoke City. Yet, like a dictionary, a book of this nature always needs updating and that's what I've done this time round, especially as an awful lot of players have come and gone since my last major publication on the club some eight years ago.

I know someone somewhere will criticise my efforts. That's a way of life. But I can honestly say that if someone can do better, good luck. I've put a lot of hard work into this book over the last 12 months and I am proud of what I have achieved.

If you spot any discrepancies, errors and/or omissions I would appreciate it if you could contact me (or the publishers) so that any amendments can be made in future publications regarding Stoke City FC. If you have anything to add this too would be appreciated, as people tend to reveal unknown facts from all sources when football is the topic of conversation.

ADAM, Jimmy

Winger: 24 apps. 7 goals.

Born: Glasgow, 13 May 1931.
Career: Blantyre Celtic (amateur, September 1946), Aldershot (amateur, August 1948, professional, August 1951), Spennymoor United (August 1952), Berwick Rangers (briefly, later 1953), Hibernian (briefly, March–April 1953), Luton Town (July 1953), Aston Villa (£3,000, August 1959), POTTERS (£5,000, July 1961), Falkirk (July 1963), South Melbourne, Australia (June 1964), later Australian staff coach and physical education instructor, became Victoria State coach and assistant coach to the Australian national team (1965–66), Stourbridge (August 1967), Oxford United (assistant-trainer, November 1968, then manager for four weeks).

■ A direct, fast-raiding winger, able to occupy both flanks, Jimmy Adam played his early football as an amateur in Scotland. He appeared in only one League game for Aldershot and 137 for Luton (22 goals) before helping Villa win the Second Division Championship. He partnered Tommy Thompson on the left for Stoke but lost his place to Don Ratcliffe, who switched flanks.

ADAMS, Elijah

Centre-forward: 2 apps.

Born: Longton, Stoke-on-Trent, 1888.
Died: Stoke-on-Trent, c.1965.
Career: Newchapel United, Biddulph Mission, Goldenhill Wanderers, Tunstall Park, Kidsgrove Wellington, Audley (1909), POTTERS (September 1910), Burlsem Port Vale (June 1912), Audley Town (October 1913). Did not play after World War One.

■ A useful reserve centre-forward, Eli Adams had just two senior outings for Stoke, both in March 1911. He won a Birmingham Senior Cup winner's medal with Vale in 1912–13, when he was the club's leading scorer.

ADAMS, Michael Richard

Midfield: 10 apps. 3 goals.

Born: Sheffield, 8 November 1961.
Career: Gillingham (professional,

November 1979), Coventry City (£75,000, July 1983) Leeds United (£110,000, January 1987), Southampton (£250,000, March 1989), POTTERS (March 1994), Fulham (July 1994, then player-manager, February 1996), Brighton & Hove Albion (manager, February 1999), Leicester City (manager, April 2002, sacked, 2004), Coventry City (manager, January 2005).

■ Hard working midfielder Micky Adams played in well over 500 competitive games as a professional before taking over as manager at Fulham in 1996. An England youth international, he spent only four months at The Victoria Ground. He subsequently guided Fulham to promotion from The Third Division in 1996–97 and with it won the 'Manager of the Year' award. After taking Brighton up from the Third and Second Divisions in successive seasons, he then lifted Leicester into the Premiership, but lost his job with the Foxes owing to a poor start to the 2004–05 season following relegation. He replaced Peter Reid in the hot seat at Highfield Road.

ADAMS, Neil James

Outside-right: 38+1 apps. 4 goals.

Born: Stoke-on-Trent, 23 November 1965.
Career: POTTERS (1983, professional, July 1985), Everton (£150,000, July

1986), Oldham Athletic (on loan, January–February 1989, signed permanently for £100,000, June 1989), Norwich City (£250,000, February 1994), Oldham Athletic July 1999, retired, July 2001).

■ An orthodox outside-right (or wide midfielder in present-day terms), Neil Adams began his career at The Victoria Ground and did well before moving to Goodison Park in 1986. He won a First Division Championship medal with the Merseysiders in 1987 and later helped the 'Latics' win the Second Division title. An England under-21 international (one cap gained), Adams had 497 senior appearances and 66 goals under his belt when he retired in 2001. He missed the first penalty of his career, the unlucky 13th in a League Cup tie against Swansea in his last season with Oldham.

AISTON, Samuel James

Outside-left: 3+4 apps.

Born: Newcastle, 21 November 1976.
Career: Newcastle united (juniors, April 1993), Sunderland (free, July 1995), Chester City (on loan, February–May 1997 and November 1998–January 1999), POTTERS (on loan, August–October 1999), Shrewsbury Town (on loan, December 1999–February 2000, signed permanently, free, July 2000).

■ An England schoolboy international, capped in 1992, skilful left-winger Sam Aiston made 24 appearances for

Sunderland but was never a regular in the side, and after a series of loan spells, including one at Stoke, he eventually settled down at Gay Meadow. After relegation from the Football League he then contributed greatly to Shrewsbury's promotion campaign from the Conference in 2004, making over 30 appearances.

AKINBIYI, Adeola Peter

Striker: 58+8 apps. 19 goals.

Born: Hackney, London, 10 October 1974.
Career: Norwich City (apprentice, April 1992, professional, February 1993), Hereford United (on loan, January–February 1994), Brighton & Hove Albion (on loan, November–December 1994), Gillingham (£250,000, January 1997), Bristol City (£1.22 million, May 1998), Wolverhampton Wanderers (£3.5 million, September 1999), Leicester City (£5 million, July 2000), Crystal Palace (£2.2 million, February 2002), POTTERS (on loan, March–May 2003, signed permanently, free, September 2003), Burnley (March 2005).

■ A Nigerian international, capped once against Greece in November 1999 – just after he had scored a hat-trick for Wolves against Grimsby Town – Ade Akinbiyi is a lively, all-action striker

who certainly makes defenders hop around. Having worked hard at his game, he arrived at Stoke an experienced campaigner with over 350 competitive games and almost 100 goals under his belt, including 29 for Gillingham, 25 for Bristol City and 16 for Wolves, for whom he top-scored in 1999–2000. He did well during his loan spell at The Britannia Stadium. When he returned on a full-time contract he took time to regain peak fitness, but then showed the form that had eluded him since the early days of his career when he switched clubs for huge fees. It was perhaps a surprise when he left the club for Burnley in 2005.

ALLEN, Anthony

Left-back: 470+3 apps. 4 goals.

Born: Stoke-on-Trent, 27 November 1939.
Career: Broom Street School (Stoke) and Wellington Road School (Hanley), Stoke Boys' Brigade, POTTERS (amateur, April 1955, professional, November 1956), Bury (£10,000, October 1970), later Hellenic FC, South Africa, then Stafford Rangers (mid-1970s). Now lives and works in the Potteries.

■ Tony Allen, with his distinctive blonde hair, was a splendid left-back who occupied the left-half position later in his career. Sure-footed with fine tackling skills and temperament, he appeared in over 470 games for Stoke, 121 in succession between mid-March 1960 and the end of March 1963. He helped the team win the Second Division Championship in 1962–63 and reach the League Cup Final the following year when they lost

over two legs to East-Midland rivals Leicester City. An England youth international in 1958, he won seven under-23 and three full caps, the latter all coming in 1959 when he partnered West Brom's Don Howe in games against Wales (at Cardiff), Sweden and Northern Ireland (at Wembley), and he also twice represented the Football League. Some newspaper pundits said that Allen's club form deteriorated because he had made his senior international debut too early – he was a month short of his 20th birthday when he lined up against the Welsh. It may have done for two months – but that was all!

ALLEN, Paul Kevin

Midfield: 19 apps. 1 goal.

Born: Aveley, Essex, 28 August 1962.
Career: West Ham United (apprentice, April 1978, professional, August 1979), Tottenham Hotspur (£400,000, June

1985), Southampton (£550,000, September 1993), Luton Town (on loan, December 1994), POTTERS (on loan, January–May 1995), Swindon Town (free, October 1995), Bristol City (free, January 1997), Millwall (free, August 1997), Purfleet FC (June 1998).

■ A member of the famous footballing family, unlike most of his relatives Paul Allen was a right-sided midfielder who could also fill in as a full-back if required. He made almost 200 appearances for the Hammers and followed up with over 370 for Spurs but failed to settle at Southampton. He did well during his loan spell at Stoke before winding down his senior career with Swindon, Bristol City and Millwall. Capped three times by England at under-21 level, he won the FA Cup with West Ham in 1980 at the age of 17 years 256 days, making him the youngest recipient of a medal this century. He then added a second Cup winners' medal to his collection with Spurs in 1991 and helped Swindon win the Second Division Championship in 1995. When he left The Den in 1997, Allen had accumulated an exceptionally fine club record of 43 goals in 744 League and Cup appearances. Other footballing members of the Allen family are: Martin's uncle, Les, a forward with Chelsea, Spurs and QPR (1954–69); Les's son Clive, a striker with QPR, Arsenal, Crystal Palace, Tottenham Hotspur, Bordeaux, France, Manchester City, Chelsea, West Ham United, Millwall, Carlisle United, and England (1978–96); Les's brother, Dennis, a forward with Charlton Athletic, Reading and Bournemouth (1956–71); Dennis's son, Martin, a midfielder with QPR, West Ham United, Portsmouth and Southend United (1983–97) and currently manager of Brentford and Clive's brother, Bradley, a forward with QPR, Charlton Athletic, Colchester United, Grimsby Town, Peterborough United and Bristol Rovers (1988–2003).

ALLINSON, Ian James Robert

Forward: 7+4 apps.

Born: Stevenage, Herts, 1 October 1957.

Ian Allinson

Career: Alleyne's School, Hitchin Boys, local Hertfordshire non-League football, Colchester United (apprentice, April 1973, professional, October 1975), Arsenal (free, August 1983), POTTERS (free, June 1987), Luton Town (£15,000, October 1987), Colchester United (December 1988), Baldock Town (player-manager, May 1990), Stotford FC (manager), later with Stevenage Borough (player-coach, mid-1990s).

■ A winger or inside-forward, Ian Allinson played for Stoke during the opening months of the 1987–88 season.

He looked an excellent free signing by manager Mick Mills but never settled in the Potteries. He scored 92 goals in 401 appearances for Colchester (two spells), played in 105 games for Arsenal (23 goals) and gained a Full Member's Cup runners'-up medal with Luton in 1988. He was at Layer Road when Colchester lost their Football League status.

ALMOND, Henry John

Forward: no apps.

Born: Westminster, London, 17 April 1850.
Died: at sea, 1910.
Career: Charterhouse School (April 1863–May 1868), POTTERS (August 1868–February 1869).
Harry Almond helped form Stoke (City) Football Club in 1868. The son of William Almond of Westminster, he played for his 'House' team, Gownboys, at Charterhouse School and for the school first XI (Old Carthusians) in season 1867–68. During his last year at Charterhouse, he assisted in the formation of the Stoke (City) club.

■ After ending his educational studies and skippering Stoke in their first few games (he scored the first ever Potters' goal against E W May's 15 in a friendly on 17 October 1868), Almond completely forgot about football. He became a very successful Civil Engineer, going abroad to work in Costa Rica for the Venezuela-based La Guayra and Caracus Railway Company.

ALMOND. John

Outside-left: 3 apps.

Born: Prescot, 4 October 1915.
Died: Before 2000.
Career: Prescot Cables (1932), POTTERS (March 1935), Tranmere Rovers (£250, December 1935), Shrewsbury Town (August 1937), guest for Crewe Alexandra during World War Two. Did not play after the hostilities.

■ John Almond was a reserve who failed to dislodge England international Joe Johnson from the outside-left position. His only goal for Stoke came on his League debut in a 2–1 defeat at Wolves in April 1935. He played

regularly for Shrewsbury Town in the Birmingham & District League for two seasons (1937–39).

ANDERSON, John Hugh Todd

Inside-forward: 24 apps. 2 goals.

Born: Renfrewshire, 11 January 1937.
Career: Johnstone Burgh (from 1953), POTTERS (professional, January 1957), Bangor City (May 1961–64).

■ Diminutive Scottish inside-forward Jock Anderson possessed good ball skills but never quite fulfilled the promise he had displayed north of the border. After National Service he left The Victoria Ground on a free transfer and moved into non-League football.

ANDRADE, Jose Manuel Gomes

Striker: 8+10 apps. 2 goals.

Born: Gaboverde, Portugal, 1 June 1970.
Career: Academica del Coimbra, Portugal, POTTERS (on loan, March–May 1995, signed permanently, August 1997), Academica del Coimbra (January 1998).

■ A 6ft striker, slight of build, Jose 'Zay' Andrade broke his leg during the League game at Swindon in a 1–0 win in April 1995 and returned to Portugal during the summer to regain fitness. He returned to Stoke two years later, but, although a big hit with the supporters, he failed to settle in England and was released after five months.

ANDREW, Ronald Edward Harold

Defender: 129 apps. 2 goals.

Born: Bebington, Cheshire, 5 January 1936.
Career: Ellesmere Port Town, POTTERS (professional, May 1954), Port Vale (free, July 1964, retired, May 1965).

■ Ron Andrew was a dogged but natural centre-half (or right-back) who joined the Potters initially as reserve to Ken Thomson, but he eventually established himself in the first team in 1959. He remained in the side for three seasons, but then lost his place following the signing of Wolves defender Eddie Stuart. Andrew subsequently moved across the country to arch rivals Port Vale after 10 years dedicated service at The Victoria Ground, during which time he made surprisingly few appearances for such a consistent defender.

ANDREWS, Keith Joseph

Midfield: 16 apps.

Born: Dublin, 13 September 1980.
Career: Wolverhampton Wanderers (apprentice, April 1996, professional,

September 1997), Oxford United (on loan, November–December 2000), POTTERS (on loan, August–October 2003), Walsall (on loan, March–May 2004).

■ A combative midfielder possessing a firm tackle, good passing technique and terrific work-rate, Keith Andrews had found it hard going to establish himself as a regular in the Wolves side and chose to maintain his match fitness with a succession of loan spells. He served the Potters well during the first three months of the 2003–04 season before returning to Molineux.

ANTONIO, George (nee George Rowlands)

Inside-forward/wing-half: 98 apps. 15 goals.

Born: Whitchurch, 20 October 1914.
Died: Oswestry, 2 July 1997.
Career: Oswestry Technical College, Oswestry Town (1932), POTTERS (£200, February 1936), guest for Aldershot, Ipswich Town, Leeds United, Leyton Orient, Norwich City, Nottingham Forest, Notts County, Wrexham and York City during World War Two, Derby County (£5,000, March 1947), Doncaster Rovers (£1,000, October 1948), Mansfield Town (free transfer, October 1949–May 1951), Oswestry Town (player-manager, July 1951), Wellington (player-coach, July 1954, player-manager, January 1955–May 1957), Stafford Rangers (player-manager, September 1957), Berriew (briefly as player), Oswestry Town (player-coach, July 1958, player-manager, June 1959–June 1962), thereafter ran a sports outfitters business in Oswestry.

■ George Antonio gave Stoke City excellent service for 10 years, being one of the few players to represent the club before, during and after World War Two. Brought up by an Italian family, he was signed by manager Bob McGrory who just pipped Bolton Wanderers for his signature. He went on to appear in almost 100 League and Cup games for the Potters before transferring to the FA Cup holders, Derby, in 1946. After leaving The Baseball Ground he had decent spells with Doncaster (34 League outings) and Mansfield Town (67). In his prime, Antonio was selected to play for Wales, but before he could pull on the famous red jersey it was discovered that he had been born a mile or so 'over the border' on the English side and, therefore, missed out on a full international cap.

ARCHIBALD, Robert Franklin

Outside-left: 276 apps. 40 goals.

Born: Strathaven, Lanarkshire, 6 November 1894.
Died: Scotland, January 1966.
Career: Rutherglen Glencairn (1910), Albion Rovers (professional, April 1912), Third Lanark (1913), Albion Rovers (briefly), Aberdeen (August 1914), Third Lanark (August 1920), POTTERS (£2,000, June 1925), Barnsley (free, May 1932, retired, May 1937), returned to Scotland (Glasgow) where he became an Insurance Agent, scouting from time to time for Bradford City.

■ A diminutive left-winger, Bobby Archibald joined Stoke at the age of 30. After scoring on his debut in a 3–0 home win over Stockport County he quickly became an established member of the side and went on to appear in almost 280 senior games for the club, gaining a Third Division North Championship medal at the end of his second season. After giving the Potters superb service for seven full seasons he moved to Oakwell, being replaced by future England international Joe Johnston. He had a fine career, which included over 200 appearances in Scottish football (113 for Aberdeen alone), and during World War One he also played (and served) in France, Belgium, Denmark, Italy and South America. Archibald was called 'Steve' by his colleagues because he resembled the champion jockey Steve Donoghue. NB: Archibald's brother, John, kept goal for Albion Rovers, Chelsea, Reading, Newcastle United, Grimsby Town and Darlington, and his daughter became an airline stewardess with Icelandic Airways.

ARMITAGE, Leonard

Centre or inside-forward: 200 apps. 19 goals.

Born: Sheffield, 20 October 1899.
Died: Wortley, near Sheffield, May 1972.
Career: Sheffield Forge & Rolling Mills FC, Walkley Amateurs, Wadsley Bridge, Sheffield Wednesday (amateur, October 1914, turned professional after World War One, August 1919), Leeds United (August 1920), Wigan Borough (March 1923), POTTERS (March 1924), Rhyl, Port Vale (December 1932, retired through injury, May 1934).

■ At schoolboy level Yorkshireman Len Armitage was regarded as a 'terrific talent', and after gaining a winners' medal with Sheffield in the Final of the English Schools Shield in 1914 several top-class managers sought his signature! In the end he joined his home-town club, Sheffield Wednesday, and then, after World War One, became one of the first players to sign for the reconstructed Leeds United side, scoring the Elland Road club's first-ever League goal. After a spell at Wigan he moved to Stoke in 1924. Originally an out-and-out centre-forward, Armitage was as 'strong as a bull' and was utterly fearless. He had a tremendous 'engine', being able to cover acres of ground during every game he played in. He helped Stoke win the

Third Division North title in 1926–27 and represented the FA XI against South Africa two years later. At the end of the 1931–32 season – with 200 appearances under his belt for the Potters – he left The Victoria Ground for non-League Rhyl and within four months had moved back to Stoke-on-Trent to sign for City's arch rivals, Port Vale. Armitage, who retired with a serious knee injury, was the grandson of a Yorkshire cricketer.

ARROWSMITH, Arthur

Inside-forward: 48 apps. 9 goals.

Born: Finchfield, Wolverhampton, 23 May 1880.
Died: Wolverhampton, June 1954.
Career: Compton FC, Coventry City (July 1904), POTTERS (August 1906), Wolverhampton Wanderers (July 1908), Willenhall Swifts (April 1909).

■ Arthur Arrowsmith, a junior international inside-forward who represented the Birmingham Association against Scotland's Juniors in 1906, joined Stoke in readiness for the 1906–07 campaign. He had an excellent first season at The Victoria Ground, scoring seven goals in 34 League games before losing his way and eventually moving to his home-town club, Wolves.

ARTHERN, Thomas

Inside-forward: 1 app.

Born: Stoke-on-Trent, 1868.
Died: Before 1945.
Career: Hanley Town, POTTERS (August 1891), Congleton (season 1892–93).

An unknown reserve, Tom Arthern (some reference books state Atherton) made only one League appearance for Stoke, lining up against Wolves (home) in the Football Alliance in September 1891.

ASABA, Carl Edward

Forward: 44+31 apps. 10 goals.

Born: Westminster, London, 28 January 1978.
Career: Dulwich Hamlet (amateur, July 1993), Brentford (professional, August 1994), Colchester United (on loan, February–May 1995), Reading (£800,000, August 1997), Gillingham (£600,000, August 1998), Sheffield United (£92,500, March 2001), POTTERS (free, August 2003).

■ A 6ft 2in, 13st 4lb striker, Carl Asaba has an eye for goal, and prior to joining the Potters he had netted over 100 goals in almost 300 League and Cup games since leaving Dulwich Hamlet in 1994. Strong and mobile with good control, he had a decent first season with the Potters, netting eight times in 40 senior games, including a penalty on his home debut against Wimbledon (won 2–1).

ASHWORTH, Samuel Bolton

Defender: 39 apps.

Born: Fenton, Stoke-on-Trent, 12 March 1877.
Died: Stoke-on-Trent, 30 December 1925.
Career: Stoke Alliance (April 1893), Fenton Town (August 1894), Stafford Wednesday (December 1895), Stafford Rangers (March 1896), Stoke Nomads (April 1898), POTTERS (August 1901), Oxford City (August 1902), Reading (September 1903), Manchester City (August 1903), Oxford City (again, while on holiday), Reading (August 1904), Everton (September 1904), Burlsem Port Vale (October 1905), North Staffs Nomads (August 1906), Sheffield FC (1907), Richmond Association (1908), Northern Nomads (1910–11), a surveyor and architect by profession, he later became chief architect to the Stoke-on-Trent Education Committee, a position he held until his death at the age of 48. He was also a Stoke director from 1920.

■ An amateur defender, Sam Ashworth failed to make an impression with Sheffield Wednesday (his first major club) and had to wait until he was 24 before making his Football League debut for Stoke against Liverpool in September 1901. He only spent a season at The Victoria ground but later performed superbly well with several of his other clubs at various levels. An FA Cup winner and League Championship runner-up with Manchester City (season 1903–04), he also represented the Football League as an Everton player. He was one of 17 Manchester City players (including Welsh international Billy Meredith) who were involved in a soccer scandal, which eventually resulted in Ashworth being accused of earning money over and above the normal expenses allowed for amateurs. He was found guilty, fined £25 and ordered never to play for City again (although by the time the enquiry had ended he was elsewhere, playing for Port Vale).

ASPREY, William

Defender: 341 apps. 26 goals.

Born: Wolverhampton, 11 September 1936.
Career: POTTERS (amateur, May 1953, professional, September 1953), Oldham Athletic (£19,000, January 1966), Port Vale (£2,000, December 1967, retired as a player, December 1968), Sheffield Wednesday (coach, February 1969), Coventry City (coach-assistant manager, February 1970), Wolverhampton Wanderers (coach), Rhodesia national soccer director of coaching (summer 1975–January 1978), then coach in the Middle East (February–April 1978), Oxford United (coach, May 1978, manager, July 1979–December 1980), Syria (national team coach), POTTERS (assistant manager, February 1982, manager, December 1983–May 1985), later ran a hotel on England's south coast.

■ Bill Asprey was signed by Potters boss Frank Taylor from under the nose of his counterpart at Molineux, Stan Cullis. A Wolves supporter as a lad, he developed quickly at The Victoria Ground and made his League debut as a 17-year-old against his former club Oldham Athletic. After establishing himself in the first team during the 1957–58 season, he went from strength to strength, performing superbly well either as a full-back, his preferred position, occasionally as a central defender and from time to time as a makeshift attacker. Indeed, in January 1961 he netted a hat-trick while wearing the number eight shirt against Charlton Athletic. When he left the club in 1966 Asprey had amassed a fine record of 341 appearances and 26 goals. He had helped Stoke win the Second Division title in 1963 and reach the League Cup Final the following year. He made 80 League appearances for Oldham and, after a brief spell with Port Vale, took up coaching in the Middle East. In 1979 he took over as manager of Oxford and returned to The Victoria Ground as assistant to Richie Barker in 1981. Two years later he replaced Barker in the 'hot seat' and held the position for two seasons before poor results coupled with his own ill-health saw him replaced by Mick Mills. Stoke won only 14 out of 67 League games when Asprey was in charge.

AXCELL, Arthur Charles

Utility: 3 apps.

Born: Leigh-on-Sea, Essex, 1882.
Died: Leigh-on-Sea, c.1965.
Career: Leigh Ramblers (1899), Fulham (amateur, April 1903, professional, January 1904), Burton United (July 1905), POTTERS (December 1906), Burton United (June 1907), Southend United (seasons 1908–10).

■ Basically signed as cover for left-winger John Miller at The Victoria Ground, Charlie Axcell was, in fact, a jack of all trades who occupied seven different positions during his career, lining up as a full-back, a wing-half and in all five forward-line berths. He made his League debut for the Potters three days before Christmas 1906, in a 2–0 home defeat by Preston North End. He worked as a fisherman at Leigh-on-Sea before joining Fulham, for whom he made 18 appearances and scored four goals.

BACOS, Desmond Patrick

Inside-forward: 1+1 apps.

Born: Wynberg, Johannesburg, 13 November 1950.
Career: Highlands Park, South Africa (semi-professional, August 1967), Chelsea (trialist, 1969), Grinaker Rangers, South Africa (1970), Hellenic, South Africa (April 1973), Los Angeles Aztecs, NASL (season 1976–77), POTTERS (£1,000, October 1977), Highlands Park (May 1978), Grinaker Rangers (late 1978), Hellenic (1979), Grinaker Rangers (1980), Dion Cosmos, South Africa (1982), Grinaker Rangers (player-manager, 1985), Mondeor FC, South Africa (player-coach, season 1987–88).

■ Signed in anticipation by Stoke manager George Eastham who had seen him perform well in South Africa, Des Bakos failed to make any impression at The Victoria Ground. He appeared in two away League games against Cardiff City and as a second-half substitute against Southampton (both lost).

BADDELEY, Amos

Inside-left: 101 apps. 56 goals.

Born: Fegg Hayes, Stoke-on-Trent, June 1887.
Died: North Staffordshire, c.1955.
Career: Fegg Hayes, POTTERS (professional, November 1906), Blackpool (August 1908), POTTERS (July 1909), Walsall (July 1912, retired, June 1913), Abertillery (player-manager, August 1913), Ebbw Vale (player-manager, season 1914–15). Did not figure after World War One.

■ Amos Baddeley was 19 years of age when he followed his brother, George Baddeley, to The Victoria Ground in 1906. But when the club folded in the summer of 1908 he went off to play for Blackpool, returning to the Potters for a second spell in 1909, having made 34 appearances for the Seasiders. After re-establishing himself in the first team, Baddeley, who was only 5ft 6in tall, went on to score a goal every two games for the club before transferring to Walsall in 1912. One of Baddeley's goals is said to have been the fastest ever scored from kick-off at the start of a game by a Stoke player. He achieved the feat playing against West Bromwich Albion reserves in a Birmingham & District League game at The Victoria Ground on 30 October 1909 when he found the net after just eight seconds – but Stoke still lost the game 3–1.

BADDELEY, George

Half-back: 225 apps. 19 goals.

Born: Fegg Hayes, Stoke-on-Trent, 8 May 1874.
Died: West Bromwich, 3 July 1952.
Career: Fegg Hayes Church of England School, Ball Heath, Burslem Swifts (1894), Pitshill FC (1897), Biddulph FC (1899), POTTERS (professional, May 1900), West Bromwich Albion (£250, June 1908, retired, May 1914), later became a publican in West Bromwich.

■ Strong in all aspects of half-back play, George Baddeley captained the Potters for several years before spending six seasons with West Bromwich Albion, with whom he gained a Second Division Championship medal in 1911 and an FA Cup runners'-up medal a year later. When he played his last League game for the Baggies, against Sheffield Wednesday in April 1914, Baddeley was almost 40 years of age – the oldest player ever to appear in a senior game for the Black Country club. Baddeley, known as 'Stodger', twisted his knee in his 99th consecutive game for Stoke, against Liverpool on Boxing Day 1905. He made his League debut for Stoke in September 1901 against Bury at The Victoria Ground (lost 2–1) and played his last game at senior level against Leicester Fosse at home in April 1908 (lost 1–0).

BADDELEY, Samuel

Centre or right-half: 203 apps. 9 goals.

Born: Norton-in-the Moors, July 1884.
Died: Stoke-on-Trent, 1960.
Career: Ball Green (1899), Endon FC (1901), Norton FC (1902), Endon FC (season 1904–05), Burslem Port Vale (professional, October 1905), POTTERS (September 1907), Kidsgrove Wellington (May 1915). Did not play after World War One.

■ Another member of the Baddeley family, Sam was a strong-tackling, highly competitive and consistent defender who joined Stoke when Burslem Port Vale were in financial trouble. A very consistent player, he spent eight years at The Victoria Ground and was a regular in the side from 1908 to 1913, making 56 first-team appearances in the 1910–11 season. He made his Football League debut at left-half in place of Albert Sturgess against Glossop (away) in February 1908. He was a key member of Stoke's Southern League Division Two (Western) Championship-winning side in 1910.

BADDELEY, Thomas

Goalkeeper: 8 apps.

Born: Bycars, Stoke-on-Trent, 2 November 1874.
Died: Hartshill, Stoke-on-Trent, 24 September 1946.
Career: Burlsem Swifts (September 1890), Burlsem Port Vale (professional, September 1893), Wolverhampton Wanderers (£50, October 1896), Bradford Park Avenue (July 1907), POTTERS (free, March 1910), Whitfield Colliery (April 1911, retired, May 1912).

The fourth member of the Baddeley clan to play for the Potters, goalkeeper Tom Baddeley had done exceedingly well with both Port Vale (74 appearances) and Wolves (315 appearances). He was then a founder-member of the Bradford club (43 games played) and had already gained five full England caps (between February 1903 and April 1904) and represented the Football League on four occasions before joining Stoke at a time when regular custodian Jack Robinson was indisposed. Baddeley, who was of medium height for a goalkeepers, just 5ft 9in tall, feared no one. He could throw a ball out right-handed up to 50 yards (an unusual feature for a 'keeper of his era), had outstanding agility, was brilliant at closing down opponents and was certainly a good shot-shopper… one of the best of his time.

BAILEY, Horace Peter

Goalkeeper: 1 app.

Born: Derby, 3 July 1881.
Died: Biggleswade, 1 August 1960.
Career: Derby County (reserves, 1899–1902), Ripley Athletic (seasons 1903–05), Leicester Imperial (briefly), Leicester Fosse (January 1907), Derby County (April 1910), POTTERS (November 1910), Birmingham (February 1911, retired, May 1913), worked for many years as a rating officer for the Midland Railway Company.

■ Horace Bailey – known as 'H.P.' – was capped five times by England at senior level and on four occasions by the amateur team, and he also won an Olympic Gold medal for Great Britain in soccer in 1908. A small man, standing only 5ft 8in tall, he had a massive pair of hands, could kick long and true and could deal very capably, and often brilliantly, with all manner of shots (and headers). An amateur throughout his career, he actually played for Derby County while working full-time as a rating officer with the Midland Railway Company based in the town. He was recruited (for one match) by Stoke after the ageing Jack Robertson had been taken ill and reserve Baxter was unavailable. One of the most famous 'keepers in the land, he stood between the posts in a Birmingham League game when the Potters beat Wrexham in a 6–2 win in November 1910, before returning to St Andrew's.
* Bailey had the misfortune to concede 12 goals while playing for Leicester Fosse against Nottingham Forest in a First Division game in 1908.

BAILEY, Thomas Henry

Wing-half: 35 apps. 1 goal.

Born: Burton-on-Trent, June 1888.
Died: c.1955.
Career: Overseal Swifts (1905), Burton United (1907), Lincoln City (trialist, April 1908 – one game), Walsall (August 1908), Stoke Priory (September 1911), POTTERS (September 1912), Hanley Swifts (May 1915). Did not play after World War One.

■ Originally a centre-forward, Tom Bailey arrived at The Victoria Ground as a half-back and gave the Potters good service, especially during the last two pre World War One campaigns, helping the team win the Southern League Division Two Championship 1915.

BAINES, Paul

Inside-forward: 1+1 apps.

Born: Tamworth, 15 January 1972.
Career: POTTERS (professional, July 1990, released, May 1992), Tamworth (trialist, July–August 1992), Walsall (trialist, September 1992), later played for Tamworth and Atherstone United (on loan).

■ A reserve at The Victoria Ground, Paul Baines made just two League appearances for Stoke, in the away defeats at Birmingham City and Cambridge United in April 1991.

BAIRD, William

Centre-forward: 3 apps.

Born: Glasgow, 1876.
Died: Scotland, c.1950.
Career: Greenock Morton (from 1894), POTTERS (August 1896), St Bernard's (October 1896).

■ A reserve centre-forward, strong and willing, Bill Baird had three League outings for Stoke during the early stages of the 1896–97 season, lining up against Aston Villa, Wolves and Bolton Wanderers. He never settled in the area and quickly returned to Scotland.

BAKER, Charles

Inside-forward: 38 apps. 13 goals.

Born: Stafford, 10 February 1868.
Died: Stafford, 1940.
Career: Stafford Rangers (1886), POTTERS (professional, April 1889), Wolverhampton Wanderers (free, August 1891), POTTERS (free, January1893), Southampton St Mary's (free, August 1894), Stafford Rangers (free, April 1896, retired, May 1900, to continue his trade as a shoemaker).

■ Charlie Baker, described as being a 'neat dribbler', had two spells with Stoke, gaining a Football Alliance Championship-winning medal in 1891. A smart forward with neat ball control, he averaged a goal every three games for the Potters. He was presented with a gold medal on his departure from The Dell after scoring 17 times in 42 games for the Saints in their first two seasons in the Southern League.

BAKER, Frank

Outside-left: 174 apps. 33 goals.

Born: Stoke-on-Trent, 22 October 1918.
Died: Stoke-on-Trent, December 1989.
Career: Port Vale (amateur, from 1934), POTTERS (June 1936), Stafford Rangers (May 1951), Leek Town (season 1952–53), became a fish and chip shop proprietor in Fenton.

■ Stoke City manager Bob McGrory pipped Wolves boss Major Frank Buckley for Baker's signature in the summer of 1936. A former delivery van driver for a laundry firm, he played as an amateur with Port Vale in their Cheshire League team before giving the Potters excellent service over the next 13 years or so either side of World War Two. He also turned out occasionally during the hostilities, occupying both wing positions. Baker, who replaced England international Joe Johnson on Stoke's left-wing, was 33 when he retired from competitive League football, having suffered four broken legs during his career.

BALLHAM, Joseph Lewis

Outside-right: 45 apps. 14 goals.

Born: Stoke-on-Trent, 1864.
Died: Stoke-on-Trent, 1935.
Career: Stoke Locomotive, POTTERS (August 1886), Burslem Port Vale (August 1888, while still under contract with Stoke for another month), POTTERS (September 1890, retired through injury, April 1892).

■ Another player who had two separate spells with Stoke, Joe Ballham was an orthodox winger, quick and clever, who gained a Football Alliance Championship-winning medal in 1891, scoring six goals in 20 games.
His brother, Edgar, also played for Port Vale (February 1890).

BAMBER, John Belfield

Centre-half: 24 apps. 1 goal.

Born: Preston, June 1912.
Career: Preston North End (1928, professional, July 1929), Fleetwood Town (July 1931), POTTERS (May 1932, retired, September 1939), worked in

Swynnerton as a joiner in a reserved occupation before moving back to Preston in 1942, the year teamed up with the Hertfordshire Yeomanry on duty in Normandy with the Second Army. He did not play football after the war.

■ Jack Bamber was a member of Stoke's playing staff for seven years, during which time he appeared in only 24 first-team games. He had played for the 'A' team at Deepdale before assisting Fleetwood and came to The Victoria

Ground as reserve to Arthur Turner. In fact, Bamber skippered Stoke's second XI on several occasions.

BAMBER, John David

Striker: 49 apps. 12 goals.

Born: Whiston, Lancashire, 1 February 1959.
Career: St Helens FC (April 1975), Winsford United (August 1977), Manchester University (for two years, 1977-79), Blackpool (professional, September 1979), Coventry City (£50,000, June 1983), Walsall (£20,000, March 1984), Portsmouth (free, December 1984), Swindon Town (£12,500, November 1985), Watford (£105,000, June 1988), POTTERS (£190,000, December 1988), Hull City (£130,000, February 1990), Blackpool (£35,000, November 1990, retired through injury, May 1995), now runs his own damp-proofing business in Blackpool.

■ A 6ft 3in striker, good in the air, strong and capable on the ground, 'Big Dave' Bamber was born deep in Rugby League territory. In his nomadic career he netted 188 goals in 523 senior appearances, including 149 in 437 League games. His best return came with Blackpool with a haul of 89 goals in 179 outings covering two spells. He gained a degree in economics at Manchester University.
*Alan Ball sold Bamber three times during his managerial career.

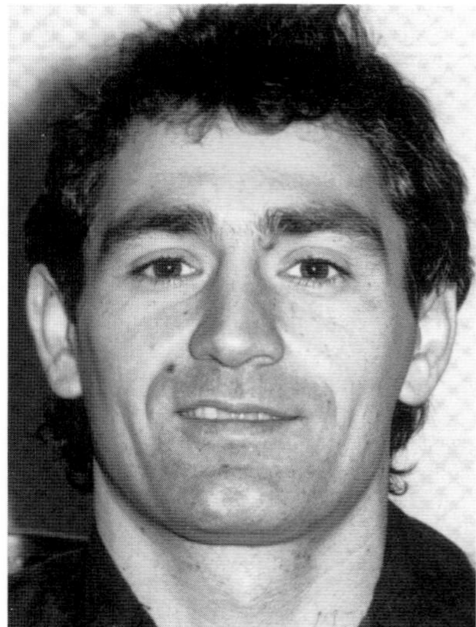

BANGOURA, Sambegou

Striker: new signing.

Born: Guinea, 3 April 1982.
Career: Lokeren, Belgium, Standard Liege, Belgium (May 2001), POTTERS (£3m, August 2005, on three-year contract).

■ Striker Sambegou Bangoura joined the Potters for a club-record fee. Tall and strong with good pace and skill, he had to wait before making his debut in English football owing to injuries.

BANKS, Gordon, OBE

Goalkeeper: 246 apps.

Born: Tinsley, Sheffield, 30 December 1937.
Career: Sheffield & District Schools, Millspaugh Steelworks FC (two spells), Rawmarsh Welfare, Chesterfield (amateur, April 1954, professional, September 1955), Leicester City £7,000, May 1959), POTTERS (£52,000, April 1967), Fort Lauderdale Strikers, NASL (free, March 1977), POTTERS (coach,

Gordon Banks

May 1978), Port Vale (senior coach, December 1978, reserve-team coach, October–December 1979), Telford United (general manager, season 1980–81), Leicester City (on 'Lifeline' fund-raising committee, 1986), also ran his own Sports Promotion Agency.

■ Gordon Banks was by far the finest goalkeeper in the world during the period 1968–71; some people in football even classed him as being the greatest 'keeper ever. That tremendous save from Pele's downward header in the 1970 World Cup Finals in Mexico is still, to this day, being shown on TV all over the world – and is, in a lot of people's minds, the greatest save ever made in top-class football. At the time Banks was a Stoke player, having joined the club in as a 29-year-old in 1967. He played in 23 League games for Chesterfield and earned an FA youth Cup runners'-up medal before transferring to Filbert Street. For Leicester he added a further 293 League outings to his tally and played for them against Stoke in the 1964 League Cup Final and in two losing FA Cup Finals (against Spurs in 1961 and Manchester United two years later). He won the first of his 73 full England caps in April 1963 (against Scotland), having already played twice for the under-23 side. He later represented the Football League on six occasions. A year before moving to The Victoria Ground he gleefully collected his World Cup winners' medal from the Queen after England had defeated West Germany 4–2 after extra-time in the Final at Wembley. His haul of international caps when he switched from Filbert Street to the Potteries stood at 37 – making him Leicester City's most-capped player at that time. He, therefore, added 36 more to his collection with the Potters and is now Stoke's most-capped player at full international level. Awarded the OBE in the Queen's Honours List in 1970, Banks won the League Cup with the Potters in 1972 when he was also named both 'Footballer of the Year' and 'Sportsman of the Year'. In 1977 he was voted the NASL 'Goalkeeper of the Year' when serving with Fort Lauderdale Strikers'. This came five years after he had been involved in an horrific car smash, which cost him the sight in his right eye and forced him into an early retirement from League football in this country. This accident took place five miles from Ashley Heath on 22 October 1972 when his Ford Granada crashed head on with an Austin van. An immensely likeable man, Banks coached at The Victoria Ground after retiring and he also assisted on the coaching side at Vale Park before becoming General Manager of Telford United.

NB: When Fort Lauderdale lured him over to America, Banks's first thoughts were that he was joining a circus act and admitted to seeing bill-boards revealing 'Roll-up, roll-up – come and see the greatest one-eyed goalkeeper in the world!'

BANKS, Steven

Goalkeeper: 16 apps.

Born: Hillingdon, Middlesex, 9 February 1972.

Career: West Ham United (apprentice, April 1988, professional, March 1990), Gillingham (free, March 1993), Heart of Midlothian (free, August 2005), Blackpool (£60,000, August 1995), Bolton Wanderers (£50,000, March 1999), Rochdale (on loan, December 2001–February 2002), Bradford City (on loan, August–September 2002), POTTERS (free, December 2002), Wimbledon (free, August 2003), Gillingham (free, March 2004), Heart of Midlothian (August 2005).

■ Steve Banks was already a vastly experienced goalkeeper when he joined the Potters, having amassed 317 senior appearances with his previous clubs. He spent just eight months at The Britannia Stadium before joining Wimbledon.

BANNISTER, Gary

Striker: 12+6 apps. 2 goals.

Born: Warrington, 22 July 1960.

Career: Warrington junior football, Coventry City (apprentice, July 1976, professional, May 1978), Sheffield Wednesday (£100,000, August 1981), Queen's Park Rangers (£200,000, August 1984), Coventry City (£300,000, March 1988), West Bromwich Albion (£250,000, March 1990), Oxford United (on loan, March–May 1992), Nottingham Forest (August 1992), POTTERS (May 1993), FC Seiko, Hong Kong (summer 1994), Lincoln City (September 1994), Darlington (player-coach, August 1995, retired due to a back injury, May 1996), Porthleven FC, Cornwall (coach), now runs a bed and breakfast business in Cornwall.

■ A very positive, all-action goalscorer, as keen as mustard with the knack of scoring goals out of nothing, Gary Bannister had a fine career spanning 20 years, netting a total of 206 goals in 621 League and Cup matches. He made his debut for Stoke against Millwall (home) in August 1993 but spent only one season at The Victoria Ground before trying his luck in Japan. An England under-21 international, capped as a Queen's Park Rangers player, he helped Darlington reach the 1996 Play-off Final at Wembley.

BARKER, Christopher Andrew

Defender: 4 apps.

Born: Sheffield, 2 March 1980.

Career: Maltby Juniors (Rotherham), Alfreton (July 1996), Barnsley (professional, August 1998), Cardiff City (£600,000, July 2002), POTTERS (on loan, August–September 2004).

■ A solid left-sided defender, strong and versatile, Chris Barker made 130 appearances for Barnsley and over 90 for Cardiff before joining the Potters on loan. After four outings he returned to Ninian Park to link up with former 'Stokie' Graham Kavanagh, helping the Bluebirds win the 2003 Play-off Final against QPR at the Millennium Stadium. His bother, Richard Barker, has played for Rotherham United.

BARKER, William

Centre-forward: 1 app.

Born: Stoke-on-Trent, 31 May 1924.

Career: local junior and non-League football, POTTERS (professional, October 1948, retired through injury, May 1950).

■ Bill Barker's career ended with a broken leg, suffered in the 1949–50 season after he had played in just one

League game for the Potters against Manchester City at Maine Road in October 1949. He was always a reserve-team player at The Victoria Ground.

BARNES, Paul Lance

Striker: 13+17 apps. 5 goals.

Born: Leicester, 16 November 1967.
Career: Notts County (apprentice, April 1982, professional, November 1985), POTTERS (£30,000, March 1990), Chesterfield (on loan, November 1990), York City (£50,000, July 1992), Birmingham City (£350,000, March 1996), Burnley (£350,000, September 1996), Huddersfield Town (£50,000, January 1998), Bury (£40,000, March 1999), Nuneaton Borough (on loan, March–May 2001), Doncaster Rovers (May 2001), Hinckley Athletic (August 2004).

■ Paul Barnes, who started his playing career at Meadow Lane, moved to Stoke at the age of 22. Despite being a natural goalscorer he never really established himself in the first team, but after leaving the club he did extremely well at Bootham Crescent. He struck 85 goals in 179 outings for the 'Minstermen', and hit the headlines in 1995 when he netted twice at Old Trafford in a League Cup win over Manchester United. Barry Fry secured his services for Birmingham and then he became Burnley's record signing in 1996. When he moved out of the Football League in 2001, Barnes' first-class career had realised 461 appearances and 158 goals. He then top scored in the Conference for Doncaster in 2002–03 with 26 goals.

BARR, Robert

Centre-forward: 3 apps.

Born: Kilmarnock, April 1865.
Died: Scotland, c.1935.
Career: Hurlford, STOKE (August 1888), Abercorn (July 1889), Preston North End (August 1894), Bury (May 1896–April 1897), later returned to Hurlford.

■ Bob Barr had just three senior outings with Stoke in the first season of League football (1888–89). He scored on his debut for PNE against Wolves in September 1894 and helped the Deepdale club win the Lancashire Combination title in 1896.

BARRETT, Scott

Goalkeeper: 60 apps.

Born: Ilkeston, 2 April 1963.
Career: Notts County (junior, April 1979), Derby County (apprentice, August 1979), Ilkeston Town (1981), Wolverhampton Wanderers (professional, September 1984), POTTERS (£10,000, July 1987), Colchester United (on loan, January–February 1990), Stockport County (on loan, March–May 1990), Colchester United (free, July 1991), Gillingham (free, August 1992), Cambridge United (free, August 1995), Kingstonian (on loan, August–September 1998), Leyton Orient (free, January 1999, appointed goalkeeping coach at Brisbane Road, May 2001).

■ Introduced to League football by Wolves manager Tommy Docherty in 1984, goalkeeper Scott Barrett made 35 appearances for the Molineux club before joining the Potters in 1987. On his day he was an excellent 'keeper but did have his moments of inconsistency. He made over 400 senior appearances during his career, won the GM Vauxhall Conference and FA Trophy with Colchester in 1992 (when he was an ever-present) and also participated in BBC TV's *Question of Sport* quiz programme that same year.

BARRON, Paul George

Goalkeeper: 1 app.

Born: Woolwich, London, 16 September 1953.
Career: Erith Grammar School, Borough Road College (Isleworth), Kent Schoolboys, Kent Youth, Welling United (1971), Wycombe Wanderers (1973), Slough Town (August 1975), Plymouth Argyle (professional, July 1976), Arsenal (£70,000, July 1978), Crystal Palace (£140,000 + Clive Allen and Kenny Sansom, August 1980), West Bromwich Albion (£60,000, December 1982), POTTERS (on loan, January–February 1985), Queen's Park Rangers (£35,000, March 1985), Reading (on loan, December 1986), Welling United (August 1988–May 1989), Cheltenham Town (August 1990), Welling United (November 1990–January 1991), ran his own fitness club in Birmingham (for two years) and had a spell with Cheltenham Town (1993), Aston Villa (coach), Middlesbrough (coach, then fitness/specialist coach at The Riverside Stadium).

■ Goalkeeper Paul Barron, 6ft 2in tall and 13st 6lb in weight, qualified as a P.E. instructor before becoming a professional footballer. He spent one season at Home Park, failed to establish himself in the first team at Highbury, played in 90 League games for Palace and took over from Tony Godden at The Hawthorns. A safe handler of the ball and a good shot-stopper, his only League outing for the Potters was against Leicester City at Filbert Street in January 1985 (0–0 draw). During his career Barron played in more than 300 first-team matches.

* His father, George, was an amateur with Tottenham Hotspur.

BASNETT, Alfred Frederick

Inside-forward: 2 apps.

Born: Stoke-on-Trent, 1924.
Died: Stoke-on-Trent, 24 June 1966.
Career: POTTERS (semi-professional,

November 1941, professional, August 1945), served in RAF and guested for Northampton Town during World War Two, Northwich Victoria (1946–49).

■ Alf Basnett was a competent inside-forward who played in just two senior games for the Potters, both in the FA Cup in 1946 against two Lancashire clubs, Burnley and Bolton Wanderers. He had an excellent strike record during the hostilities, scoring 58 goals in 121 regional games, but surprisingly was not retained when peacetime football resumed. His brother, Albert Edward Basnett, also played for Stoke City during World War Two as a semi-professional in February 1942 to May 1945 (scoring twice in three starts).

BATEMAN, George Henry

Outside-left/full-back: 6 apps.

Born: Wolstanton, Stoke-on-Trent, March 1865.
Died: Stoke-on-Trent, c.1948.
Career: Burslem Port Vale (amateur, August 1882, professional, August 1885), POTTERS (September 1886), Burlsem Port Vale (May 1887), POTTERS (July 1890), Northwich Victoria (April 1893–May 1895).

■ A solid, strong-kicking full-back, George Bateman had two spells with the Potters deputising for the England international Alf Underwood. Bateman was a pioneer of the Port Vale club and appeared in their first ever match, a 5–1 defeat at Stoke in a Staffordshire Cup encounter in December 1882. He helped the Valiants win the 1883 North Staffs Charity Cup and the 1885 Burslem Challenge Cup while also sharing the former in 1885. In 1866 he joined the Potters, despite signing a contract to play for the Vale only. The incident went to the Burlsem County Court in November 1866 and Vale won the case but reached an agreement with Stoke whereby Bateman was allowed to play for the Potters until the end of the season. Bateman, who appeared in almost 150 first-team games for the Vale at all levels, made his debut for the Potters at outside-left (in place of in the injured Billy Dunn) against Darwen in the Football Alliance in December 1890 (won 6–2).

BAXTER, John

Goalkeeper: 6 apps.

Born: Wigan, 24 December 1889.
Career: Burslem FC (1905), Liverpool Road FC (1906), Congleton White Star (1908), Tunstall Park (1909), Derby County (trialist, July 1910), POTTERS (amateur, August 1910), Macclesfield (June 1911). Did not play after World War One.

■ With Tom Baddeley due to retire, Stoke chose Jack Baxter as their reserve goalkeeper to Jack Robertson for the 1910–11 campaign. He remained an amateur throughout his career and made just six first-class appearances for Stoke, his debut coming against the welsh club Aberdare (away) in a Southern League game.

BEACHILL, Arthur

Full-back: 136 apps.

Born: Monk Bretton, Yorkshire, 21 May 1905.
Died: Stoke-on-Trent, 12 April 1943.
Career: Monk Bretton FC (1921), Frickley Colliery (1923), Rotherham County (professional, May 1924), POTTERS (May 1926), Millwall (May 1934), Wellington Town (August 1935–September 1939).

■ A rugged full-back and contemporary of Bob McGrory, Billy Spencer and Charlie Scrimshaw, Arthur Beachill made almost 140 senior appearances for the Potters spread over a period of eight years. He was described in the press as the man who, week after week, played a painstaking game, unhurried and fluent with distribution in both feet. Initially a mill worker, he kept himself superbly fit, enjoyed walking and played bowls, and it was a shock to his family and friends when he died after suffering a heart attack in Stoke, while returning home from Hyde & Sons Foundry, where he was carrying out essential munitions work.

BEAGRIE, Peter Sydney

Forward/wide-midfield: 61 apps. 8 goals.

Born: Middlesbrough, 29 November 1965.
Career: Guisborough, Middlesbrough (amateur, April 1983, professional, September 1983), Sheffield United (£35,000, August 1986), POTTERS (£210,000, June 1988), Everton (£750,000, November 1989), Sunderland (loan, September 1991), Manchester City (£1.1m, July 1997), Bradford City (£50,000, July 1997), Everton (loan, March–April 1998), Wigan Athletic (free, February 2001), Scunthorpe United (July 2001).

■ Renowned for his back-flip somersault after scoring a goal, soccer journeyman Peter Beagrie has had a wonderful career. Capped twice by England at both 'B' and under-21 levels, he's now netted over 80 goals in almost 750 first-class appearances. He made his League debut as a substitute for Middlesbrough against Oldham in October 1984 and hit his first goal on the last day of that season against Shrewsbury. He had already played in over 130 games before moving to The Victoria Ground in 1988. With his brilliant left foot, he loved to tease and torment his opponent by hugging the touchline and could deliver pin-point acurate crosses for his strikers. Unfortunately, at times, he could be

Peter Beagrie

frustrating to watch, but on his day he was a superb footballer who was fast-approaching his 40th birthday when he was voted into the PFA League Two team by the players in 2004–05.

BECKETT, Roy Wilson

Defender: 15 apps. 1 goal.

Born: Stoke-on-Trent, 20 March 1928.
Career: Milton Youth Club (1942), Burslem Albion (April 1943), POTTERS (juniors, August 1943, professional, April 1945), Northwich Victoria (May 1953).

■ Roy Beckett was a registered player at The Victoria Ground for 10 years, mainly acting as a dependable and reliable reserve. Indeed, he donned six different numbered shirts, two, four, five, seven, eight and nine, while making 15 senior appearances.

BECKFORD, Jason Neil

Midfield: 5 apps.

Born: Manchester, 14 February 1970.
Career: Burnage High School, Manchester School of Excellence, Manchester City (apprentice, April 1986, professional, August 1987), Blackburn Rovers (on loan, March–April 1991), Port Vale (loan, September–October 1991), Birmingham City (£50,000, January 1992), Bury (on loan, April–May 1994), POTTERS (trialist, july 1994, signed on a free transfer, August 1994), Millwall (free, December 1994), Northampton Town (free, as player-assistant manager, May 1995–May 1996).

■ Jason Beckford, an England schoolboy and youth international, was a right-sided attacking midfield player who was never really a regular member of the first team with any of his clubs. In fact, he made only 63 League and Cup appearances in nine years as a professional footballer, although a spate of injuries certainly didn't help his cause (in 1992 he had an operation to produce a synthetic cartilage in his right knee). His brother, Darren, a striker, played for Manchester City, Bury and Port Vale as well as Oldham Athletic, Norwich City and Hearts.

BEBBINGTON, Richard Keith

Outside-left: 123+1 apps. 22 goals.

Born: Cuddington near Nantwich, Cheshire, 4 August 1943.
Career: Northwich Victoria (trialist), POTTERS (amateur, 1958, professional, August 1960), Oldham Athletic (£26,000, plus George Kinnell, August 1966), Rochdale (in exchange for Ronnie Blair, July 1972), Winsford (June 1973, retired, May 1974).

■ Keith Bebbington, a speedy left-winger, versatile and mobile, was nurtured through the junior and intermediate ranks at The Victoria Ground before making his senior debut against Luton Town (away) in September 1962. Two years later he appeared for Stoke in the 1964 League Cup Final against Leicester City and in 1965 became Stoke's first used substitute when he replaced Dennis Viollet in a League game at Arsenal. Often faced with strong competition from other players for a wing place, at times he switched flanks, and after leaving the club he spent six years at Boundary Park, making 250 appearances for the Latics.

BEESTON, Carl Frederick

Midfield: 258+13 apps. 17 goals.

Born: Stoke-on-Trent, 30 June 1967.
Career: POTTERS (apprentice, June

1983), Clayton Parkway (briefly), POTTERS (professional, July 1985), Hereford United (on loan, January–March 1997), Southend United (trialist, July 1997), Hednesford Town (free, September 1997).

■ Carl Beeston was an enterprising but injury-prone midfield player, gifted no doubt with a neat first touch, who spent 14 years with Stoke, during which time he appeared in more than 270 first-team matches. Glandular fever forced him to miss the 1986–87 campaign, but he recovered and gained an England under-21 cap against the USSR the following season. Then, five years on, he helped the Potters win the Second Division Championship – after missing the Autoglass Trophy triumph at Wembley in 1992 through suspension, served for a second red card. After failing to regain his first-team place at The Victoria Ground, he was loaned out to Third Division side Hereford United, and after nine games as a trialist with Southend he dropped down a level to join non-League side Hednesford. Beeston's son, also named Carl, has played for Hyde United, Crewe Alexandra and Newcastle Town.

BENBOW, Leonard

Centre-forward: 23 apps. 4 goals.

Born: Hanley, Stoke-on-Trent, 1874.
Died: Stoke-on-Trent, 1946.
Career: Burslem Port Vale (briefly), Oswestry United, Shrewsbury Town, Nottingham Forest (1897), POTTERS (July 1900), Northampton Town (August 1901–May 1906).

■ Len Benbow was a whole-hearted centre-forward with a determined approach, who spent just one season at The Victoria Ground, during which time he scored four goals (two in the FA Cup, two in the League). He made over 50 senior appearances for Forest, gaining an FA Cup winners' medal in 1898 playing against Derby County.

BENNETT, Edward

Forward: 3 apps. 4 goals.

Born: Stoke-on-Trent, 1862.
Died: Stoke-on-Trent, 1940.
Career: Stoke St Peter's, POTTERS (amateur, August 1882), Leek Welfare (August 1887).

■ One of Stoke's earliest utility forwards, Ted Bennett's haul of four goals in his three FA Cup appearances included the club's first hat-trick in a 10–1 victory over Caernarvon Wanderers in October 1886.

BENSON, Harold Lewis

Full-back: 91 apps.

Born: Hartshill, Stoke-on-Trent, 22 January 1883.
Died: Stone, c.1953.
Career: Shelton Albion, Porthill FC, POTTERS (professional, May 1901), Northampton Town (April 1907), Port Vale (December 1908, released, May 1911), later worked as an office clerk in Stafford.

■ Harold Benson spent six seasons with the Potters as a reliable, strong-tackling full-back. He made his League debut against Everton (home) in March 1902 when both Sam Meredith and Charlie Burgess were absent through injury.

BENT, Junior Antony

Winger: 1 app.

Born: Huddersfield, 1 March 1970.
Career: Huddersfield Town (apprentice, April 1986, professional, December 1987), Burnley (on loan, November–December 1989), Bristol City (£30,000, March 1990), POTTERS (on loan, March 1992), Shrewsbury Town (on loan, October–November 1996), Blackpool (free, August 1997, released, January 2001).

■ Yorkshireman Junior Bent (5ft 5in tall) was an out-and-out winger, fast

and exciting, who preferred to raid mainly down the right. His only League game for Stoke came in the 1–0 defeat at Torquay United. He made 221 appearances in his seven years with Bristol City and 120 for Blackpool, being a huge hit with the supporters of both of those clubs.

BENTLEY, Anthony

Utility-forward: 51 apps. 15 goals.

Born: Stoke-on-Trent, 20 December 1939.
Career: POTTERS (amateur, April 1955, professional, December 1956), Southend United (£1,500, May 1961, retired, May 1971).

■ Tony Bentley did well at schoolboy level before making his senior debut for the Potters at outside-right against Barnsley in February, at the age of 18. He went on to play in over 50 games for the Potters. After being successfully converted into a full-back, he gave Southend excellent service, amassing more than 400 senior appearances, while skippering the Shrimpers many times and receiving two testimonials. On retirement in 1971, Bentley turned down an offer from Port Vale and quit football to go into catering and teaching in the Folkestone area.

BENTLEY, Arthur

Inside-forward: 5 apps.

Born: Longton, Stoke-on-Trent, 1871.
Died: before 1960.
Career: Sandbach Ramblers (1890), POTTERS (July 1896), Sandbach Ramblers (May 1897).

■ A stockily built inside-forward, Arthur Bentley spent one season with the Potters as a reserve, making only a handful of League appearances before moving back to his former club.

BENTLEY, Frank William

Defender: 5 apps. 1 goal.
Born: Butt Lane, Staffordshire, 9 October 1884.
Died: Stoke-on-Trent, October 1958.
Career: Butt Lane FC, POTTERS (June 1907), Tottenham Hotspur (July 1908), Brentford (August 1912–April 1914). Did not play after World War One.

■ A centre-half with a solid frame, Frank Bentley played for the Potters (mainly as a reserve) for one season before leaving The Victoria Ground for Spurs, for whom he appeared in 43 senior games, followed by 40 for Brentford in the Southern League.

BENTLEY, William John

Left-back: 49+4 apps. 2 goals.

Born: Longton, Stoke-on-Trent, 21 October 1947.

Career: St Gregory's School (Hanley), POTTERS (apprentice, April 1964, professional, October 1964), Blackpool (£30,000, January 1969), Port Vale (July 1977, caretaker manager, December 1979), Stafford Rangers (free, May 1980), later Fenton British Legion (player-manager), Foley FC (player-manager).

■ During his career, hard-tackling left-back Bill Bentley appeared in almost 500 competitive games (439 in the Football League, 296 for Blackpool and 95 for the Vale). After gaining England youth honours, he made his senior debut for the Potters at the age of 18 in a First Division game against Aston Villa (home) in April 1966 (won 2–0). He played alongside England international Jimmy Armfield at Bloomfield Road and in 1971 won the Anglo-Italian Cup with the Seasiders.

BENTON, John David

Goalkeeper: 9 apps.

Born: Newcastle-under-Lyme, Staffordshire, 1878.
Died: Stoke-on-Trent, c.1942.
Career: Newcastle Swifts (1894), North Staffordshire Regiment (1896), Glentoran (1901), Transvaal Police team, South Africa (1903), POTTERS (March 1904), Glentoran (November 1905), POTTERS (September 1908, retired through injury, April 1910, trainer until 1918).

■ Jack Benton represented the Irish League on three occasions as a Glentoran player. He then travelled to South Africa where he assisted the Transvaal Police team and joined the Potters on his return to England in 1904. He made his League debut against Sheffield Wednesday at Hillsborough (replacing Tom Wilkes) before being replaced between the posts by Jack Whitley. Benton then languished in the reserves, and when Welsh international Richmond Roose rejoined the club in November 1905 he chose to return to Glentoran. He came back to Stoke in 1908 and took his senior appearance tally up to nine before retiring in 1910 through injury. He remained with the club as trainer until 1918, having taken the job on a temporary basis initially in 1908.

BERNARD, Michael Peter

Wing-half or defender: 167+10 apps. 11 goals.

Born: Shrewsbury, 10 January 1948.
Career: POTTERS (apprentice, April 1964, professional, January 1965), Everton (£140,000, April 1972), Oldham Athletic (July 1977, retired with a knee injury, May 1979), became a Dee Valley publican (Chester), then Football in the Community Officer at Crewe Alexandra and later worked in the club's Commercial Department, now employed as a lawnmower repairer and general maintenance gardener in Swindon.

■ Hard-tackling and resourceful, Mickey Bernard accumulated a fine record with Stoke City. Capped three times by England at under-23 level, he gained a League Cup winners' medal with the Potters in March 1972, a month before transferring to Goodison Park. Linking up with Colin Harvey and Howard Kendall in midfield, he continued to produce some quite outstanding performances and helped the Blues reach the 1977 League Cup Final against Aston Villa.

BERRY, George Frederick

Defender: 261+8 apps. 30 goals.

Born: Rostrop, West Germany, 19 November 1957.
Career: Holy Trinity & St Thomas of Canterbury Schools, Blackpool, Bipsham FC, Blackpool (junior, 1971), Handsworth Wood Boys School, Birmingham, Ipswich Town (trialist), Wolverhampton Wanderers (apprentice, April 1974, professional, November 1975), POTTERS (August 1982), Doncaster Rovers (on loan, August 1984), Peterborough United (July 1990), Preston North End (August 1991), Aldershot (March 1992), Stafford Rangers (August 1992, later becoming their Commercial Manager when members of the GM Vauxhall Conference), in 1996 he was appointed full-time by the PFA, working alongside Chief Executive Gordon Taylor, Pat Nevin and Brendan Batson. In 1998 he took a position with PFA Enterprizes Ltd (Manchester branch) and later had his own programme on BBC Radio Stoke.

■ A strong-tackling, determined and wholehearted central defender, who became a firm favourite with the Stoke fans following his transfer from Wolves in 1982, George Berry was born in Germany to a Welsh mother (from Mountain Ash, Glamorgan) and Jamaican father. After returning to

England he attended school initially in Blackpool and then in Handsworth, Birmingham, before joining the Molineux club. He appeared in 160 games for Wolves, helping them win the Football League Cup in 1980. Two years later he signed for Stoke and quickly became a star performer at The Victoria Ground, the fans loving his combative style and all-round endeavour. A third of his 30 goals for the Potters came from the penalty spot. Berry won five full caps for Wales – his first, ironically, against West Germany in 1979. He was the second black player to represent the Principality (after Ted Parris in 1932). In Berry's testimonial programme (August 1990) his Wolves colleague John Richards wrote 'George's infectious and audible enthusiasm was an example to any player, young and old.'

BERTSCHIN. Keith Edwin

Striker: 93+10 apps. 33 goals

Born: Enfield, Middlesex, 25 August 1956.
Career: Mount Grace School, Enfield, South Mimms FC, Barnet (semi-professional, August 1972), Ipswich Town (professional, October 1973), Birmingham City (£135,000, July 1977), Norwich City (£200,000, August 1981), Jacksonville Teamen, NASL (on loan, summer 1982), POTTERS (£50,000, November 1984), Sunderland (£32,500, March 1987), Walsall (£30,000, July 1988), Chester City (£5,000, November 1990), Aldershot (free, August 1991), Solihull Borough (February 1992), Evesham United (October 1993), Barry Town (March 1994), Tamworth (trialist, August 1994), Worcester City (August 1994–May 1995), also assisted Oldbury Town and Atherstone Town, became a financial advisor and worked for Pro-Sport, a company that provided materials (including peat and sand) for top-line golf courses like the Belfry, Troon, Sunningdale and Hoylake as well as the pitches at Stoke's Britannia Stadium, Stockport County and QPR.

■ Keith Bertschin scored with his first kick in League Football – for Ipswich Town against Arsenal at Highbury in April 1976. After that he continued to do well as a marksman and netted well over 150 goals in 450 games during the next 16 years or so Lively, good in the air and decisive on the ground, his record at The Victoria Ground was impressive – a goal every three games. As an Ipswich player he represented England at both youth and under-21 levels, winning three caps in the latter

category. He gained a Third Division Championship medal with Sunderland in 1988 and won the Welsh Cup with Barry Town in 1994.

BESWICK, David

Goalkeeper: 9 apps.

Born: Stoke-on-Trent, 3 February 1910.
Career: Mount Pleasant FC (August 1925), POTTERS (amateur, April 1928, professional, March 1929), Walsall (November 1933–May 1935).

■ Reserve-team goalkeeper at The Victoria Ground during the early 1930s, initially to Dick Williams and then to Norman Lewis, Dave Beswick did well when called into the first team.
* He was not associated with the famous pottery family.

BESWICK, John Ewart

Defender: 63 apps. 2 goals

Born: Macclesfield, 5 April 1897.
Died: Stoke-on-Trent, February 1978.
Career: Longton High School, Congleton Town (1914), POTTERS (amateur, April 1921), POTTERS (August 1925).

■ No relation to Dave, Jack Beswick was an intelligent and determined 6ft 1in centre-half, a first-class header of the ball, who thought hard and long about his game, giving nothing away. He had two spells at The Victoria Ground but retired through injury at the end of his second. One of the most distinguished amateurs to serve the club, he was a member of the famous Longton pottery family (Samuel Macadam Beswick was his elder brother). He was a key member of the Potters' Third Division North Championship-winning side in 1926–27.

BETTANY, Frederick

Inside or centre-forward: 2 apps.

Born: Stoke-on-Trent, 1862.
Died: by 1950.
Career: Tunstall Park (1884), POTTERS (August 1885); Newcastle Town, Staffs (April 1886)

■ Both of Fred Bettany's senior outings for the Potters were in the FA Cup, against Crewe Alexandra (home and away) in October–November 1885.

BEVANS. Stanley

Forward: 15 apps. 1 goal.

Born: Kingsley, 16 April 1934.
Career: Cheadle, POTTERS (professional, April 1951), Macclesfield Town (November 1955), Heanor Town (1957), Freehay Rovers (1958), Bolton Social Club (1960).

■ Bevans, who was at The Victoria Ground for five-and-a-half years, averaged three appearances a season as a reserve forward. He was one of the youngest players ever to appear in a Stoke shirt, aged 17 years and five months when he made his debut against Tottenham Hotspur (home) in September 1951.

BIGGINS, Wayne

Striker: 168+13 apps. 61 goals.

Born: Sheffield, 20 November 1961.
Career: Lincoln City (schoolboy forms, February 1977, apprentice, July 1978, professional, November 1979), King's Lynn (May 1981), Matlock Town (June 1982), Burnley (£7,500, February 1984), Norwich City (£40,000, October 1985), Manchester City (£150,000, July 1988), POTTERS (£250,000, August 1988), Barnsley (£200,000, October 1992, under the freedom of contract agreement), Glasgow Celtic (free, November 1993), POTTERS (£125,000, March 1994), Luton Town (on loan, January–March 1995), Oxford United (free, July 1995), Wigan Athletic (November 1995, released, May 1997).

■ The recipient of an Autoglass Trophy winners' prize with Stoke in 1992 and a

Wayne Biggins

Third Division Championship winners' medal with Wigan in 1997, striker Wayne Biggins netted 150 goals in more than 500 appearances at club level during his 15 years in major League and Cup football. An eager-beaver type of player, always on the go and putting defenders under pressure, he was a good header of the ball, used both feet and certainly proved his worth during his two spells with the Potters, where he became a firm favourite with the fans. He played under manager John Deehan at three different clubs

BILEY, Alan Paul

Striker: 8 apps. 1 goal.

Born: Leighton Buzzard, 26 February 1957.
Career: Luton Town (apprentice, April 1973, professional, March 1975), Cambridge United (free, July 1975), Derby County (£350,000, January 1980), Everton (July 1981), POTTERS (on loan, March–April 1982), Portsmouth (£100,000, August 1982), Brighton & Hove Albion (£45,000, March 1985), New York Express, NASL (May 1986), Cambridge United (non-contract, November–December 1986), Waterford, Ireland (player-assistant manager, June 1987), played for Brest, France, Panionios, Greece (late 1987), Swindon Town (briefly, 1988), Dulwich Hamlet, Whyteleafe FC, Welton Rovers (November 1989), then with Fisher Athletic, also played in Holland and Nigeria, Ely Town (player-manager), Potton United (briefly), Diss Town, Spalding United, Barton Rovers, Wooton Blue Cross (August 2003), Kettering Town (January 2004), now runs his own gym and health club.

■ Much travelled striker Alan Biley was positive and highly effective inside the box, especially in the lower Divisions. He netted 156 goals in 382 League matches, including a club record 82 for Cambridge. A Fourth Division Championship winner in 1977 and Third Division winner six years later with Portsmouth, he had finished runner-up in that section with Cambridge under Ron Atkinson in 1978. He netted his only goal for the Potters in a 4–3 League defeat at Southampton in March 1982.

BIRCH, Percy

Goalkeeper: 3 apps.

Born: Stoke-on-Trent, 1860.
Died: before 1950.
Career: Stoke Priory (1880), POTTERS (September 1883), Cobridge(April 1886).

■ Tall goalkeeper Percy Birch was among the first batch of players to sign professional forms for the club, earning 2s 6d (12p) a match. He starred in the Potters' first-ever match in the FA (English) Cup competition against Manchester in November 1883 and then appeared in the home and away Cup games versus Crewe Alexandra in October–November 1887.

BITHELL, Brian

Wing-half: 17+1 apps.

Born: Winsford, 5 October 1956.
Career: POTTERS (apprentice, April 1972, professional, October 1973), Port Vale (on loan, September 1977), Wimbledon (£5,000, December 1977), Stafford Rangers (1978), Congleton (1980), Rhyl (1981).

■ Brian Bithell graduated via the Stoke youth scheme (set up when George Eastham was manager in the early 1970s). He was in and out of the side for two seasons, and following a loan spell with Port Vale and a sending-off at West Brom he was sold to Wimbledon in 1977. A wing-half with good balance, he made only six senior appearances for the Dons before drifting in non-League football.

BLACKIE, Sidney

Centre-forward: 2 apps.

Born: Gateshead, 1907.
Died: before 1990.
Career: Gateshead schoolboy football, Hebden Bridge (1923), POTTERS (professional, August 1924), Southend United (free, July 1926–May 1927).

■ Reserve centre-forward Sid Blackie deputised for Len Armitage in successive League games against Leicester City and Port Vale in January 1925.

BLAKE, Noel Lloyd George

Defender: 89+3 apps. 3 goals.

Born: Jamaica, 12 January 1962.
Career: Alderlea School, Wilhemena Boys, Sutton Coldfield Town (amateur, April 1978), Walsall (non-contract player, March–April 1979), Aston Villa (professional, August 1979), Shrewsbury Town (on loan, March–April 1982), Birmingham City (£55,000, September 1982), Portsmouth (£150,000, August 1984), Leeds United (free, July 1988), POTTERS (£175,000, February 1990), Bradford City (on loan, February 1992, signed permanently, free, July 1992), Dundee (free, December 1993), Exeter City (free, player-assistant manager, August 1995, coach-caretaker manager, January 1999, player-manager, May 2000, retired as a player, May 2001, continued as manager to October 2001), Barnsley (coach, July 2003), POTTERS (Academy manager-coach, July 2004).

■ A fiercely competitive defender, Noel Blake was built like a heavyweight boxer. Commanding in the air, strong and fearless on the ground, he was a match for any bustling centre-forward and never shirked a tackle. Having been

dismissed by the Blues (after much-publicised misdemeanours with manager Ron Saunders), he made nearly 100 first-team appearances for the Potters (signed by Alan Ball who had been his boss at Fratton Park) and later teamed up with his former Stoke City playing colleague Peter Fox at Exeter. When he quit competitive football, Blake's record was impressive: 694 League and major Cup appearances and 40 goals. He returned to Stoke 11 years after leaving to play in Scotland.

BLOOR, Alan

Defender: 470+4 apps. 19 goals

Born: Longton, Stoke-on-Trent, 16 March 1943.
Career: Uttoxeter Road Council Primary & Queensbury Road senior schools, Stoke-on-Trent Schoolboys, POTTERS (amateur, May 1958, professional March 1960), Port Vale (player-youth team manager, June 1978, caretaker manager August 1979, manager, September 1979, resigned, December 1979, became successful in a carpet business in his native Longton.

■ Nicknamed 'Bluto', Alan Bloor was a local lad who certainly made good. After winning England youth recognition and skippering his country at this level, he signed professional forms for the Potters on his 17th birthday but had to bide his time as manager Tony Waddington would not be rushed into introducing him to first-team action. Indeed, it was not until 1961–62 that Bloor eventually entered League Football, and it was not until 1965 that he established himself in the first XI. But from then on he never looked back. He went from strength to strength and in the next 12 seasons, mainly as partner to Denis Smith, he was an inspiring figure in Stoke's defence. He eventually amassed a total of 474 first-team appearances for the club. He was a member of Stoke's 1972 League Cup and 1973 Watney Cup winning teams and during his time at The Victoria Ground received praise from many of the country's top managers, including Sir Matt Busby, Ron Greenwood and Bill Shankly. After serving the Potters as a professional for 18 years, Bloor moved across town to join rivals Port Vale. Unfortunately, he did not have a happy reign as manager!

BOARDMAN, Albert

Goalkeeper: 4 apps.

Born: Stoke-on-Trent, February 1870.
Career: Burlsem Port vale, POTTERS (June 1894), Dresden United (July 1897).

■ Albert Boardman was a capable goalkeeper whose last appearance for Stoke was in the left-back position against Nottingham Forest in September 1896 when he deputised for flu victim Jack Eccles at the eleventh hour, after his replacement, Peter Durber, failed to receive the postcard requesting him to play. Stoke turned up at Nottingham with only 10 men, but Boardman arrived 37 minutes after the kick-off with manager-secretary Billy Rowley. Stoke lost the game 4–0.

BONNYMAN, Philip

Midfield: 7 apps.

Born: Glasgow, 6 February 1954.
Career: Anniesland Wanderers (1970), Glasgow Rangers (junior, 1972), Hamilton Academical (professional, January 1974), Carlisle United (£22,500, March 1976), Chesterfield (£150,000, March 1980), Grimsby Town. (£60,000, August 1982), POTTERS (on loan, March–April 1986), Darlington (free, July 1987), Dunfermline Athletic (free, June 1989, retired, May 1990), Hamilton Academical (Football in the Community officer), now living in Glasgow.

■ Experienced midfielder Phil Bonnyman was 32 years of age when he joined the Potters on loan from Grimsby in the 1985–86 season. A fine passer of the ball, he read the game superbly and retired with more than 500 club appearances under his belt. He was a record signing by Chesterfield in 1980.

BOOTE, George

Goalkeeper: 1 app.

Born: Stoke-on-Trent, 1878.
Died: Stoke-on-Trent, 1940.
Career: St Peter's Bards, POTTERS, Lonsdale Rovers (May 1902).

■ George Boote – signed as cover for Tom Wilkes – was one of four different goalkeepers utilised by Stoke in four matches. He played in the 1–1 home

League draw with Nottingham Forest in the First Division on 5 October 1901 – his only senior appearance for the club. Always a reserve at The Victoria Ground, he was allowed to leave the club in 1902 when Leigh Richmond Roose arrived.

BOUGHEY, Darren John

Outside-right: 5+5 apps.

Born: Newcastle-under-Lyme, Staffs, 30 November 1970.
Career: POTTERS (apprentice, May 1987, professional, July 1989), Wigan Athletic (on loan, January 1991), Exeter City (on loan, March–May 1991), Macclesfield Town (April 1992), Stafford Rangers (September 1992).

■ Darren 'Dodger' Boughey graduated through the junior ranks at Stoke and went on to make 10 first-team appearances for the club before moving into non-League football in 1992. He was granted a testimonial match in August 2001, Stafford Rangers against West Bromwich Albion.

BOULD, Stephen Andrew

Defender: 204+7 apps. 7 goals

Born: Stoke-on-Trent, 16 November 1962
Career: POTTERS (apprentice, May 1978, professional, November 1980), Torquay United (on loan, October–December 1982), Arsenal (£390,000, June 1988), Sunderland (£500,000, July 1999, released, May 2000).

■ After making over 200 appearances for the Potters, Steve Bould became Tony Adams's long-standing partner at the heart of the Arsenal defence, and when he finally retired from competitive football in 2000 he had amassed well over 600 appearances at club level. He made the number five shirt his own at The Victoria Ground in 1983 and was a regular in the senior side until his tribunal-set transfer to Arsenal in the 1988. A strong, determined player, powerful in the air, keen and assured on the ground, he suffered back problems as a Stoke player, and he went through the same pain as well as being plagued by a number of thigh and leg injuries while at Highbury. Nevertheless, he still gained two First Division Championship medals (1989 and 1991) and a European Cup-winners' Cup medal in 1994. Capped twice by England at senior level and once for the 'B' team, he was, without doubt, a great competitor.

BOULLEMIER, Lucien Emile

Right-half: 7 apps.

Born: Penkhull, Stoke-on-Trent, 1877.
Died: Newcastle-under-Lyme, 9 January 1949.
Career: Stoke Alliance, Chesterton White Star, Stone Town, POTTERS, Burslem Port vale (June 1897), Philadelphia Hibernians, US (August 1903), Northampton Town (August 1905), Port Vale (November 1905), later with Northern Nomads and North Staffs Nomads.

■ The son of the famous Parisian ceramic artist Anton Boullemier who was employed by Mintons, Lucien Boullemier was a useful wing-half who, besides his outings for Stoke during the 1896–97 season, was also employed as a potter by Royal Worcester. He was also a very good opera singer, a respected actor and successful artist, and after his brief association with Port Vale he went over to America to pursue his artistic career. On his return after a year he continued playing football with Northampton. In season 1905–06 he was back with the Vale for one game.
NB: Lucien's brother, Leon Antony Boullemier, kept goal for Stoke's reserve team, Burslem Port Vale, Lincoln City, Brighton & Hove Albion and Northampton Town.

BOULTON, Ernest

Centre-forward: 11 apps. 6 goals.

Born: Hanley, Stoke-on-Trent, 1889.
Died: c.1959.
Career: Grenadier Guards (from 1907), POTTERS (September 1910, retired through injury, October 1912).

■ Ernie Boulton played for the Potters in the Southern League and Birmingham League games during the second half of the 1910–11 season, deputising initially for Billy Smith and then taking over as leader of the attack when key players were injured. Unfortunately, his career was cut short through injury, Boulton being forced to retire at the age of 23.

BOURNE, Albert

Full-back: 1 app.

Born: Burslem, Stoke-on-Trent, 1862.
Died: before 1960.
Career: Local church football, POTTERS (August 1888), Tunstall Rovers (April 1889).

■ Albert Bourne's only senior game for the Potters was against Warwick County in the first qualifying round of the FA Cup in October 1888, when he deputised for Tommy Clare. Never a candidate for regular first-team duty, he stayed at the club for just the one season.

BOURNE, George Frederick

Full-Back: 109 apps. 1 goal.

Born: Burslem, Stoke-on-Trent, 7 October 1932.
Died: Stoke-on-Trent, 7 October 2004.
Career: Middleport County Modern School, Park Road Youth Club, Thomas

Hughes (Pottery), Burslem Albion, POTTERS (amateur, June 1950, professional, May 1951, retired through injury, May 1956), later worked many years in the building industry before establishing his own window cleaning business, also coached a local junior team.*

■ George Bourne signed professional forms for the Potters after completing his National Service in 1951. Originally a forward, he was successfully converted into a solid right-back at The Victoria Ground and developed into a exceptionally fine defender who went on make over 100 appearances for the Potters. A broken leg (suffered in November 1955) effectively ended his career at the age of 24. He was awarded a testimonial and given a club grant, reported in the press as being £855… nowhere near the princely sum received by players these days!

BOWERS, Ian

Full-back: 41+5 apps. 22 goals

Born: Audley, Staffs, 16 January 1955.
Career: POTTERS (apprentice, May 1971, professional, June 1973), Shrewsbury Town (on loan, March–April 1978), Crewe Alexandra (£8,000, July 1979), Audley & District F.C. (August 1983), later with Bignall End Swan FC.

■ A competent full-back in his own right, 'Danny' Bowers graduated through the junior ranks at Stoke before turning professional at the age of 18. He made his League debut two years later along with Peter Shilton against Wolves, and went on to appear in almost 50 senior games for the Potters. After making 175 League appearances for the 'Alex', he quit League soccer at the age of 28.

BOWMAN, John William

Wing-half: 4 apps.

Born: Middlesbrough, 23 April 1879.
Died: Sudbury, Middlesex, 26 January 1943.
Career: Shelton Juniors, Hanley St Jude's, Burslem Port Vale (February 1899), POTTERS (August 1899), Queens Park Rangers (July 1901), Norwich City (manager, May 1905–June 1907), Croydon Common (manager, April 1912–May 1916), Queen's Park Rangers (director, 1920s, then manager, March–November 1931), ran a sports shop in Harlesden, Middlesex, supplying a number of football clubs with kit.

■ Jack Bowman, who was discovered playing junior football in 1899, moved to the Potters after a short spell at Port Vale. He was a reserve at The Victoria Ground but after leaving played in over 100 games for QPR. He was Norwich City's first-ever manager but left after two years of a three-year contract. Tee-total and a non-smoker, he was a member of the Burslem Water Polo Club, which won the Northern Counties Championship, was captain of the North Staffs Harriers, taking part in races from 100 yards to 10 miles, and was also an exceptionally fine swimmer.

BOWYER, Francis

Inside-forward: 435 apps. 149 goals

Born: Chesterton, Stoke-on-Trent, 10 April 1922.
Died: Torquay, 11 November 1999.
Career: Birches Head School, POTTERS (amateur, June 1937, professional, April 1939), Macclesfield Town (June 1960, retired, May 1962).

■ Frank Bowyer joined Stoke soon after leaving his local school. He developed quickly, but unfortunately World War Two disrupted his career at the outset and it was not until February 1948, at the age of 26, that he finally made his debut in the Football League

and FA Cup competitions. However, during the hostilities, Bowyer did extremely well for the Potters, scoring 62 goals in 162 competitive matches, and thereafter, up until 1960, he added over 430 more senior appearances to his tally, netting almost another 150 goals. One of the finest marksmen in Stoke's history, he finished only three goals short of Freddie Steele's club record of 140 League goals. A quality player, possessing an excellent shot in both feet, Bowyer went on tour with the FA to Canada in the summer of 1950. After 23 years' service with Stoke, Bowyer moved into non-League football with Macclesfield Town.

BOX, Arthur

Goalkeeper: 39 apps.

Born: Hanley, Stoke-on-Trent, September 1884.
Died: Stoke-on-Trent, c.1950.
Career: Wellington Road School, Hanley Villa, Northwood Mission (junior), POTTERS (trialist, March 1904), Burlsem Port Vale (August 1904), POTTERS (July 1907), Birmingham (£100), Leek Victoria, Croydon Common (1910–11), Crewe Alexandra (August 1911, retired, May 1921).

■ Arthur Box was a squarely built goalkeeper who spent two years with Stoke. Initially a trialist at The Victoria Ground, he was not considered good enough at first and moved to Port Vale, scoring their winning goal from the penalty spot against Manchester United in March 1906. He returned to Stoke in 1907 when Vale faced a financial crisis that eventually led to the club's liquidation.

BOXLEY, David

Inside or centre-forward: 8 apps. 4 goals

Born: Cradley Heath, 17 June 1890.
Died: West Midlands, 1941.
Career: Cradley St Luke's, POTTERS (March 1919), Dudley Town (August 1920), Old Hill Wanderers (1921), Smethwick Town (1923).

■ David Boxley scored a goal every two League games for Stoke in the first season after World War One. Signed as cover for the three inside-forward berths, he made his debut for the club against Manchester City in the Lancashire Secondary Competition in April 1919 and his League debut followed in September 1919 in a 3–1 home win over Hull City.

BRACEWELL, Paul William

Midfield: 135+6 apps. 6 goals

Born: Heswall, Wirral, Cheshire, 19 July 1962.
Career: POTTERS (apprentice, July 1978, professional, February 1980), Sunderland (£225,000, July 1983), Everton (£250,000, May 1984), Sunderland (loan, August 1989, signed for £250,000, September 1989), Newcastle United (£250,000, June 1992), Sunderland (£50,000, player-coach, May 1995), Fulham (£75,000, player-coach, October 1997, retired as a player, May 1999, later coach-assistant manager, then manager, May 1999–July 2000), Halifax Town (manager, season 2000–01), England under 16 to under 20 coach (from summer, 2002–04), Walsall (assistant manager-coach, February–May 2004).

■ Paul Bracewell played in three losing FA Cup Finals with Everton (those of 1985, 1986 and 1989) and a fourth with Sunderland (1992 against Liverpool). He also made his first and last appearances for the Merseysiders against Liverpool at Wembley – his debut came in the 1984 Charity Shield and his last outing was in the 1989 FA Cup Final. Very skilful, he gained three full and 13 under-21 caps for England between 1983–85, won the League title in 1985, collected two First Division Championship medals in 1993 and 1996, twice won promotion from the Second Division, in 1990 as runners-up and in 1999 as champions, and helped Everton win the European Cup-winners' Cup in 1985. A steadying influence on the game, Bracewell was a gritty, determined performer who had a simple yet efficient approach when it came to passing the ball, never looking hurried, always in control. He was nurtured through the ranks at Stoke and after more than 140 appearances for the club followed Alan Durban to Sunderland. The first signing made by Kevin Keegan when he took over as manager of Fulham, Bracewell (referred to on the field as 'Brace') appeared in 720 club games during his 21-year career (27 goals) and is one of the few players to have won titles with four different clubs.
* Potters coach Tony Lacey rated Bracewell highly at The Victoria Ground and at one stage believed he could have become England's most talented midfielder.

BRADBURY, William

Half-back: 31 apps.

Born: Sudbury, Derbyshire, 5 August 1884.
Died: Stoke-on-Trent, 30 September 1966.
Career: May Bank FC (1900), Newcastle Swifts (1901), Port Vale (professional, May 1903), Fegg Hayes (July 1907), POTTERS (free, September 1911), Leek Alexandra (seasons 1912–15). Did not play after World War One.

■ Bill Bradbury was a sturdy defender who made his senior debut for Port Vale in a League game against Bristol City on Boxing Day 1903. After that he was used essentially as a stopgap for four seasons before moving to Fegg Hayes when Vale faced a financial crisis, which led to the club's liquidation. He made 12 senior appearances for Stoke's rivals. He joined the Potters a week or so into the 1910–11 season and made his first appearance at left-half in a 2–0 away win over West Bromwich Albion reserves in the Birmingham League. He moved to Leek Alexandra following the arrival of Scotsman Jock Grieve from Watford.
* His brother, also named Bill, played for Aberdare, Oldham Athletic, Scunthorpe United and Rochdale between 1911 and 1922.

BRADLEY, James Edwin

Wing-half: 256 apps. six goals.

Born: Goldenhill, Stoke-on-Trent, May 1881.
Died: Goldenhill, 17 June 1961.
Career: POTTERS (amateur, February 1898, professional, May 1998), Liverpool (1905), Reading, POTTERS (August 1913, retired, May 1915, later part-time coach at The Victoria Ground), also worked for the Stoke-on-Trent Highways Department.

■ Jimmy Bradley, a model of consistency who tackled with great judgement, had two separate spells at The Victoria Ground, making over 250 League and Cup appearances for the club. A regular in the side right up until his transfer to Liverpool after refusing to go to Plymouth Argyle, he did very well on Merseyside, gaining a League Championship medal with the 'Reds' in 1906. A great practical joker, he played for Reading for a short time before returning to Stoke after his contract was terminated at Elm Park following a row when he threw the whole Reading kit into the bath. Back at Stoke, he helped the Potters win the Championship of the Southern League Division Two in 1915. Bradley, who represented the Football League, was unlucky not to win a full England cap, being passed over in favour of Robert Hawkes of Luton Town in season 1907–08.
* His younger brother, Martin Bradley, played for Sheffield United, Grimsby Town and Bristol Rovers before World War One.

BRAMMER, David

Midfield: 42+2 apps. 1 goal.

Born: Bromborough, 28 February 1975.
Career: Wrexham (apprentice, April 1991, professional, July 1993), Port Vale (£350,000, March 1999), Crewe Alexandra (£500,000, August 2001), POTTERS (free transfer, June 2004).

■ Hard-working midfielder Dave Brammer made 168 appearances for Wrexham, 84 for Port Vale and 103 for

Crewe before moving to The Britannia Stadium. He skippered the side at Gresty Road and in 2001 helped Vale win the LDV Vans Trophy. Positive in his play, he quickly bedded into the Potters style and produced some excellent displays during the 2004–05 season.

BRIDGETT, George Arthur

Outside-left: 7 apps.

Born: Forsbrook, Staffs, 11 October 1882.
Died: Newcastle-under-Lyme, Staffs, 26 July 1954.
Career: Stoke St Peter's School, Burslem Park Boys, Trentham, POTTERS (August 1902), Sunderland (November 1902), South Shields (manager, July 1912), North Shields (player-manager, August 1914), Port Vale (guest, April 1917, signed permanently, November 1923), Sandbach Ramblers (May 1924, retired, May 1926).

■ A fleet-footed and markedly unselfish outside-left, outstandingly quick and dangerous with a terrific shot (he once sent the ball straight through the net when scoring for Sunderland against Stoke), Arthur Bridgett won 11 caps for England between 1905 and 1909 (never finishing on the losing side). Unfortunately, from the clubs point of view, he spent only a few months with Stoke during the early part of the 1902–03 season when he appeared in just seven League games. He was a player that Stoke certainly let slip through their fingers as he became an exceptionally fine footballer, playing in well over 320 senior matches for Sunderland and scoring 112 goals. As a religious man, he would never play football on a holy day.

BRIDGWOOD, Gerald

Winger: 106+5 apps. 8 goals

Born: Stoke-on-Trent, 17 October 1944.
Career: POTTERS (amateur, April 1960, professional, October 1961), Shrewsbury Town (£12,000, February 1969–May 1974), became a publican and played for both Telford United and Burton Albion until retiring in 1979.

■ Gerry Bridgwood was a product of the youth scheme at The Victoria Ground and was given his senior debut at the age of 16 against Brighton & Hove Albion at home in April 1961 – thus becoming the second youngest player in Stoke's history at that time behind Peter Bullock. A winger with good pace and neat footwork, he did not gain a regular place in the first XI until 1966, and his best season with the Potters came in 1966–67 when he made

26 appearances. He helped the team reach the Final of the League Cup in 1964 but did not play in the two-leg showdown against Leicester City.

BRIGHAM, Harold

Full-back: 119 apps.

Born: Selby, Yorkshire, 19 November 1914.
Died: 1978.
Career: Bolton Wanderers (junior) Frickley Colliery FC, POTTERS (professional, May 1936), guest for Chester and Wrexham during World War Two, Nottingham Forest (£4,000, November 1946), York City (July 1948), Gainsborough Trinity (May 1950).

■ Potters boss Bob McGrory beat off a number of big-named clubs to land the

signature of Harry Brigham. At the time the press described the rock-hard Yorkshire-born defender, as 'the most coveted player in the Midland League'. He quickly bedded himself into the Stoke side and went on to appear in almost 120 senior games for the club, plus another 101 during the hostilities. He was 32 when he left The Victoria Ground to join Nottingham Forest

BRIGHT, David John

Striker: 0+1app.

Born: Bath, Avon, 5 September 1972
Career: Schoolboy football, POTTERS (apprentice, September 1989), Stromsnasbruck IF, Norway (on loan, February 1991), Newcastle Town (on

loan, March 1991), Tamworth (on loan, April–May 1991), POTTERS (professional, July 1991), Clevedon Town (August 1992–May 1995).

■ Reserve striker David Bright's only game for Stoke City's first team was as a second-half substitute in the home League game against Reading in November 1990.

BRIGHTWELL, David John

Defender: 1+1 apps.

Born: Lutterworth, 7 January 1971.
Career: Manchester City (apprentice, August 1986, professional, April 1988), Chester City (on loan, March–April 1991), Lincoln City (on loan, August 1995), POTTERS (on loan, September–October 1995), Bradford City (£30,000, December 1995), Blackpool (on loan, December 1996), Northampton Town (free, July 1997), Carlisle United (free, July 1998), Hull City (free, June 2000), Darlington (free, February 2001, retired, June 2002).

■ A 6ft tall defender, David Brightwell, the son of the Olympic athletics Robbie Brightwell and Ann Packer and younger brother of Ian, started his career at Maine Road as a 15-year-old. His two outings for the Potters were against Birmingham City (away) in the League and Salernitana (home) in the Anglo-Italian Cup. When he retired in 2002 Brightwell had a total of 303 club appearances under his belt, including 87 with Carlisle, 53 with Manchester City and 45 for Northampton.

BRIGHTWELL, Ian Robert

Defender: 3+2 apps.

Born: Lutterworth, 9 April 1968.
Career: Manchester City (apprentice, May 1984, professional, May 1986), Coventry City (free, July 1998), Walsall (free, February 2000), POTTERS (free, March 2002), Port Vale (free, August 2002, retired, May 2003, but re-signed as player-coach, June 2003, retired, again, May 2004 to pursue his own business interests outside the game).

■ Ian Brightwell, brother of David, represented England as a youth team player before gaining four under-21 caps. He made 382 appearances during his 14-year stay with Manchester City but failed to make headway at Highfield Road before adding 95 more outings to his tally with Walsall. He spent just over four months with the Potters, prior to his service with rivals Port Vale.

Ian Brightwell

BRINDLEY, Horace

Outside-left: 4 apps.

Born: Newcastle-under-Lyme, Staffs, 1 January 1885.
Died: 1971.
Career: Knutton Villa (1902), POTTERS (July 1904), Norwich City (January 1906), Blackpool (June 1907), Crewe Alexandra (August 1908), Queens Park Rangers (August 1910), Sutton Town (January 1911), Lincoln City (May 1911), Chester (August 1914). Did not play after World War One.

■ Horace Brindley was only 19 years of age when he joined Stoke. He appeared in only four League games for the Potters, making his first against Derby County (away) when both George Brown and Tom Coxon were unavailable. He made over 250 appearances in total, at various levels.

BRITTLETON, James Thomas

Full-back: 123 apps. 5 goals.

Born: Winsford, Cheshire, 23 April 1879.
Died: Winsford, 22 February 1955.
Career: Winsford Celtic, Winsford United, Stockport County), Sheffield Wednesday, POTTERS (1920), Winsford (August 1924, retired, April 1926).

Surprisingly, Tom Brittleton was over 41 years of age when he moved to Stoke. He had made 353 League appearances for the Hillsborough club and had starred in their 1907 FA Cup Final win over Everton, as well as gaining five full England caps. A well built, sturdy full-back or right-half who had exceptional kicking ability, he played his early football as a centre-half with Sheffield Wednesday. He left The Victoria Ground after starring in over 120 League and Cup games for Stoke. In his long career,

Brittleton – also a keen fisherman – made 512 appearances in the Football League. He had his last outing for Stoke shortly after his 46th birthday and, therefore, held the title of the club's oldest player for 40 years, until Stanley Matthews came along and played his last match at the age of 50 in 1965.
* His son, John, played for Aston Villa and Chester.

BROAD, James

Forward: 116 apps. 67 goals

Born: Stalybridge, Cheshire, 10 November 1891.
Died: Chelmsford, 22 August 1963.
Career: St Mark's, West Gorton (August 1907), Stalybridge Celtic (September 1908), Manchester City (professional, November 1909), Oldham Athletic (August 1913), served with Royal Scots Guards (from 1915), guest for Blackburn Rovers and Greenock Morton during World War One, Millwall Athletic (April 1919), POTTERS (£2,000, June 1921), Sittingbourne (guest, early 1924), Everton (£1,400, November 1924), New Brighton (December 1925), Watford (September 1926), Caernarfon Town (June 1927), Taunton United (September 1928), Fleetwood (August 1931, retired, November 1931), Chelmsford City (groundsman, December 1931–34), also coached Spanish sides CF Barcelona and La Coruna, Las Palmas (Canary Islands), Geneva in Switzerland and several clubs in Italy, Turkey, South Africa, Norway and Holland, all between 1924 and 1939.

■ Jimmy Broad was a fine goalscorer and a footballing nomad who played all over the country during a career spanning 24 years. The son of a Manchester City trainer, he began his exploits as a goalkeeper in non-League circles but developed into a clever forward and great finisher who had the knack of being in the right place at the right time. He scored for every club he served, including five in 10 starts for Oldham and 39 in 54 appearances for Millwall. One of England's early 'exports', his first appointment abroad was in the summer of 1924 with Barcelona.
* His brothers Wilf (with Manchester City and Millwall) and Tommy were also professional footballers.
NB: Broad, wearing a kilt, turned up at Millwall immediately after World War One and asked for a trial. His request was granted and in an early game for Millwall reserves he scored all his side's goals in an 8–1 win over Spurs second XI. He was signed up immediately!

BROAD, Thomas Higginson

Outside-right: 89 apps. 4 goals

Born: Stalybridge, 31 July 1887.
Died: June 1966.
Career: Redgate Albion (1902), Denton Wanderers (early 1903), Openshaw Lads' Club (September 1903), Manchester City (trialist, April 1904), West Bromwich Albion (September 1905), Chesterfield Town (February 1908), Oldham Athletic (£250, May 1909), Bristol City (May 1912), Manchester City (March 1919), POTTERS (£500, May 1921), Southampton (July 1924), Weymouth (September 1925), Rhyl Athletic (June1926, retired, May 1928), later worked at a seaside fun fair.

■ A Junior international (capped against Scotland in April 1906), Tommy Broad was blessed with pace and power. He was described in the press as being in the 'tearaway class' but nonetheless had a very interesting and nomadic career that saw him appear in well over 350 games (35 goals scored). He perhaps produced his best form at The

Victoria Ground after taking over on the right-wing from John Spencer. With his brother Jimmy at centre-forward he delivered plenty of inviting crosses, although their combined efforts failed to keep the Potters in the top flight. Unfortunate to miss out on full international honours, he represented the Football League in 1910 and in 1925, and at the age of 37 he became the oldest player ever to appear in a senior game for Southampton. He also starred for Oldham in their promotion-winning campaign of 1909–10.

BROADHURST, Joseph

Right-half: 1 app.

Born: Stoke-on-Trent, 1862.
Died: before 1950.
Career: Leek, POTTERS (September 1887), Leek (August 1888), Arcadians (1890).

Joe Broadhurst's only senior appearance for the Potters was in an FA Cup tie against West Bromwich Albion (away) in January 1888, when he deputised for Will Holford in a 4–1 defeat.

BRODIE, David

Wing-half: 218 apps. 3 goals

Born: Paisley, Scotland, 9 November 1863.
Died: Stoke-on-Trent, 1938.
Career: Paisley, Abercorn, POTTERS (December 1889), Burlsem Port Vale (August–September 1897).

■ Recruited from Scottish football, wing-half David Brodie helped the Potters win the Football Alliance in 1890 and spent eight years with the club before moving across the city to sign for neighbouring Burslem Port Vale. A strong, forceful player, he enjoyed a battle and was always totally committed to playing football at whatever level. He had a run of 98 consecutive appearances for the Potters between September 1891 and September 1894.

BROOKE, Garry James

Midfield: 6+2 apps.

Born: Bethnal Green, London, 24 November 1960.
Career: Winns Junior & Sidney Chaplin Junior High Schools, Waltham Forest District Boys, McEntre Seniors, Essex County Boys, Tottenham Hotspur (apprentice, June 1977, professional, October 1978), GAIS Gothenburg, Sweden (on loan, April–October 1979),

Norwich City (£50,000, May 1985), Groningen, Holland (December 1986), Wimbledon (March 1988), POTTERS (on loan, March–April 1990), Brentford (August 1990), Baldock Town (January 1991), Colchester United (on loan, January 1991), Reading (trialist, February 1991), Wivenhoe Town (April 1991), St Albans City (September 1991), Romford.

■ Gary Brooke, a stocky, strongly-built midfield player, had a loan spell at The Victoria Ground at the end of the 1989–90 season. He scored twice on his League debut for Spurs in 1978 and was named as a substitute by Spurs in three FA Cup Final matches. He scored 18 goals in 101 competitive games for Spurs and starred in the UEFA Cup with Groningen.

BROOKE, Percy

Full-back: 12 apps.

Born: Kidsgrove, May 1893.
Died: 1970.
Career: Kidsgrove Wellington, POTTERS (professional, December 1919), Aberdare (July 1921), Swindon Town, Accrington Stanley, Blackburn Rovers.

■ Percy Brooke spent a season and a half at The Victoria Ground where he acted as reserve to Tom Brittleton, Alec Milne and Billy Twemlow. After leaving the Potters he represented the Welsh League and went on to skipper Aberdare and Swindon.

BROOKES, Gilbert Henry

Goalkeeper: 14 apps.

Born: Churchill near Kidderminster, 2 April 1895.

Died: Kidderminster, 1952.
Career: Kidderminster Harriers, Shrewsbury Town, POTTERS (£300, May 1922). Swansea Town (May 1923), Luton Town (May 1924), Merthyr Town (August 1925), Kidderminster Harriers (1927–28).

■ Giant goalkeeper Gilbert Brookes (6ft 1in tall) played in a third of Stoke's League games in the 1922–23 season, stepping in as a replacement for the injured Les Scott. During his career he appeared in129 League games, 42 being with Luton.

BROOKES, Issac

Goalkeeper: 17 apps.

Born: Bilston, May 1861.
Died: before 1950.
Career: Staffordshire County CC, POTTERS (registered between November 1890–April 1901 and March 1892), later with Northwich Victoria.

■ Ike Brookes was a well-respected cricketer during the 1890s, being the wicketkeeper for Staffordshire County. He was persuaded to play in goal for Stoke in an emergency during the period from November 1890 to March 1902 – and he did well in a total of 17 Football Alliance and FA Cup games, helping the Potters win the 'Alliance' Championship in his first season.

BROOKES, John

Left-half: 2 apps.

Born: Stoke-on-Trent, 8 February 1927.
Career: POTTERS (amateur, April 1945, professional, December 1946), Eccleshall Town (May 1951).

■ Reserve half-back John Brookes made two League appearances for the club during his four and a half years at The Victoria Ground, his debut coming against Sunderland (away) in December 1950, followed by a home game with Aston Villa. He replaced Jock Kirton in both matches.

BROOKFIELD, Arthur

Outside-right: 10 apps. 2 goals

Born: Stoke-on-Trent, 1870.
Died: before 1950.

Career: Longton Atlas FC, POTTERS (January–September 1895), Crewe Alexandra (October 1895–May 1897)

■ Deputising for Willie Naughton at outside-right, Arthur Brookfield scored twice on his League debut for the Potters in a 6–0 home win over Bolton Wanderers. He spent just eight months at The Victoria Ground.

BROOMHALL, Arthur

Goalkeeper: 1 app.

Born: Stoke-on-Trent, 1860.
Died: before 1950.
Career: POTTERS (September 1886), Burlsem Port Vale (July 1888), Hanley Town (June 1890).

■ Arthur Broomhall's only first-team game for the Potters was in the FA Cup tie against Crewe Alexandra in November 1886 when he replaced Billy Rowley. He let in half-a-dozen goals that day as Stoke went out of the competition 6–4 after extra-time. He appeared in 20 first-team matches for Port Vale.

BROUGH, Henry Burton

Right-half or inside-right: 85 apps. 1 goal.

Born: Guisborough, 12 December 1896.
Died: Longton, Staffs, March 1975.
Career: Sheffield Schoolboys, Kilnhurst (August 1911), Huddersfield Town (professional, May 1913), Manchester United (briefly), York City (May 1922), POTTERS (February 1923, retired through injury, April 1926), continued to live in the Potteries for the rest of his life.

■ Harry Burton spent three and a half seasons at The Victoria Ground during the mid-1920s. His only goal for the club was scored against Coventry City in September 1924. He skippered the Sheffield schoolboys' side and his performances as an inside-right attracted the attention of several leading clubs, but it was two years before he became a professional with Huddersfield. He made 60 appearances for the Terriers.

BROUGH, Joseph

Centre-forward or half-back: 1 app.

Born: Burslem, Stoke-on-Trent, 9 November 1886.
Died: Stockton Brook, 5 October 1968.
Career: Burslem Park Boys, Smallthorne FC (1903), Burslem Port Vale (amateur, October 1906, professional, February 1907), POTTERS (September 1907), Tottenham Hotspur (July 1908), Liverpool (August 1910), Bristol City (January 1912), Port Vale (April 1913, retired, June 1922), served in the Army during World War One (1917–19).

■ One League outing was all wing-half Joe Brough managed during his brief association with Stoke, who he joined

when Port Vale were facing a financial crisis. A stocky player, he later returned to the Vale and went on to score 111 goals in over 200 first-team matches, including 15 in 85 Football League and FA Cup matches. He also helped the Valiants win both the Staffordshire Junior and Senior Cups and share the Staffordshire Infirmary Cup. Unfortunately, poor health hampered his stay with Spurs.

BROWN, David Carre

Inside or centre-forward: 52 apps. 17 goals

Born: Broughty Ferry near Dundee, 26 November 1887.
Died: Scotland, 1970.
Career: Dundee St Joseph's (1909), Dundee (March 1911), Greenock Morton (1912), Peebles Rovers (July 1913), Dundee (March 1914), guest for Glasgow Rangers (1917), Port Vale (1918), Nottingham Forest and Birmingham during World War One, POTTERS (£1,200, October 1919), Notts County (July 1921), Kilmarnock (August 1922), Darlington (£80, August 1923), Crewe Alexandra (June 1926), Barrow (June 1927, retired, March 1928), Darlington (honorary reserve team manager, July 1933–May 1935).

■ Stoke management team thought that David Brown would be the answer to their scoring problems, but sadly he never really hit it off in the Potteries and, after netting a goal every three games, he was transferred to Notts County. A good ball player with a strong right-foot shot, he netted 74 times in only 97 League games for Darlington, when he helped them win the Third Division North title in 1924–25, and scored 27 in 59 outings for Crewe.
* Several years ago there was a real case featuring a 'bent' policeman whose surname had the hyphen between Carre and Brown!

BROWN, George Gerald

Outside-left: 8 apps.

Born: Nottingham, August 1883.
Died: c.1955.
Career: Dulwich Hamlet (1898), Woolwich Arsenal (1902), POTTERS

(September–December 1904), Norwich City (July 1905), Millwall Athletic (August 1906), Gainsborough Trinity (May 1907), Sheffield United (September 1908–January 1909).

■ George Brown was an amateur who played on the left-wing throughout his career. He was a reserve with Arsenal, never really settled in the Potteries area, scored once in 19 Southern League games for Norwich, hit one goal in 25 outings for Millwall, had 18 outings for Gainsborough and two for Sheffield United. He was a coal miner before taking up football.

BROWN, Horace Robert

Utility: 4 apps.

Born: Stoke-on-Trent, 1860.
Died: Stoke-on-Trent, c.1940.
Career: Stoke Priory, POTTERS (August 1883), Stoke St Peter's (August 1886).

■ One of the many versatile players in Stoke's early years, Horace Brown appeared in four FA Cup ties for the club over a period of three years (November 1883–October 1886) as well as starring in several friendly matches. In fact, he played outside-right in the first-ever Stoke Cup game against Manchester in November 1883 and later featured at centre-half and left-back.

BROWN, James Frederick

Inside or centre-forward: 29 apps. 11 goals

Born: Brierley Hill, 23 February 1886.
Died: May 1939.
Career: Jubilee Park Junior School (Tipton), Great Bridge Celtic (1902), Kidderminster Harriers (August 1903), POTTERS (April 1907), West Bromwich Albion (£210, May 1908), Kidderminster Harriers (May 1910), Willenhall Swifts (May 1914, retired, April 1919), later worked in the carpet trade.

■ Fred Brown was a quick-moving, ever-relaxed player, whose only drawback was that he lacked courage and conviction in 50-50 situations. Nevertheless, he had a useful career, mainly in non-League football.

BROWN, John Edward Pursoe

Outside-right or left: 15 apps. 7 goals

Born: Liverpool, 1888.
Died: c.1958.
Career: Orrell (1906), Manchester City (September 1908), POTTERS (May 1910), Hanley Swifts (August 1911), Port Vale (June 1912–May 1914). Did not play after World War One.

■ Jackie Brown, who was able to play on both flanks as well as inside-forward, made six League appearances for Manchester City but stayed just the one term at The Victoria Ground, where he was mainly reserve to Amos Baddeley and the amateur Edwin Griffiths.
* Some reference books state that Brown started his career with Hanley Swifts.

BROWN, Henry Roy

Utility: 74 apps. 14 goals

Born: Stoke-on-Trent, 20 December 1923.
Died: Watford, 8 November 1989.
Career: POTTERS (amateur, September 1939, professional, August 1942), Watford (£3,500, July 1953), Chelmsford City (August 1957).

■ A useful utility player, Roy Brown appeared in 10 World War Two games for the Potters before establishing

himself as a member of the first-team squad in 1946. A professional at The Victoria Ground for 11 years, he made his senior debut at centre-half against Preston North End in September 1946. He scored 40 goals in 142 League games in his four seasons with Watford. His brother, Doug Brown, was appointed trainer at Stoke in 1963–64.

BULLER, Joseph

Left-half: 7 apps.

Born: Chilton, County Durham, 1909.
Deceased.
Career: Chilton Colliery (1925), Spennymoor United (1927), Hartlepool United (professional, May 1930), POTTERS (£250, April 1932), Aldershot (£100, August 1936, retired, September 1939).

■ A miner in County Durham before becoming a professional footballer, Joe

Buller spent four seasons at The Victoria Ground, yet, owing to the form and presence of Harry Sellars and Arthur Tutin and later Frank Soo, his senior outings were limited. Just short of First Division quality, he made 86 league appearances for Hartlepool and 22 for Aldershot.

BULLOCK, Albert

Outside or inside-right: 5 apps. 1 goal.

Born: Stoke-on-Trent, c.1884.
Died: Stoke-on-Trent, 1951

Career: Bucknall, POTTERS (March 1909), Stafford Rangers (November 1909).

■ A reserve inside-forward with Stoke, Albert Bullock scored on his debut for the Potters in a 2–1 home defeat by Shrewsbury in the Birmingham & District League in April 1909. He was a useful marksman for Bucknall at non-League level.

BULLOCK, Matthew

Midfield: 4+4 apps.

Born: Stoke-on-Trent, 1 November 1980.
Career: POTTERS (apprentice, April 1997, professional, November 1997, released, June 2000).

■ A right-sided midfielder, Matthew Bullock gained England youth-team

honours in 1998 and was handed his senior debut by Potters manager Gary Megson as a substitute against Bournemouth a year later. He slipped out of first-team contention following the arrival of new boss Gudjon Thordarson.

BULLOCK, Peter Leonard

Forward: 46 apps. 15 goals.

Born: Stoke-on-Trent, 17 November 1941.
Career: POTTERS (amateur, July 1957, professional, November 1958), Birmingham City (£10,000, March 1962), Southend United (February 1965), Colchester United (October 1965), Exeter City (July 1968), Stafford Rangers (November 1968), Walsall (December 1968–May 1969).

■ The youngest footballer ever to appear for Stoke City in a Football League game, Peter Bullock was just 16 years and 153 days old when he made his debut against Swansea Town on 19 April 1958. This was the first of almost 50 senior appearances he made for the club as an inside or centre-forward. Capped by England at both schoolboy and youth international levels, Bullock's career suffered a set back when he broke a leg while on tour with Stoke in Morocco in 1959. He took time to recover and after regaining full fitness he went on to have a useful career, although from time to time injuries severely handicapped his progress. After leaving the Potters he did well with Birmingham City and Colchester United, for whom he netted 33 goals in 95 League games.
NB: Bullock's brother, Michael, played for Birmingham City as well as Oxford United, Leyton Orient and Halifax Town, while his elder brother, Brian, was an amateur with West Bromwich Albion, who was also on Stoke's books in the 1950s. When Michael was manager of Halifax he signed Peter's son, Simon, as a player.

BURGESS, Charles

Defender: 195 apps.

Born: Church Lawton, 25 December 1883.
Died: Hartshill, Stoke-on-Trent, 11 December 1956.
Career: Butt Lane Swifts, POTTERS (March 1901), Manchester City (July 1908, retired through injury, May 1911).

■ Charlie Burgess was a cool and solid defender who tackled tigerishly but was never flustered, always playing a cool, calculated game of football. He was a farmer at Field Farm and played his early soccer with Butt Lane Swifts before signing for Stoke, while perched on the top of a haystack in one of his father's barns. When Stoke went bust in 1908 Burgess moved to Manchester City, but a knee injury hampered his performances, forcing him to retire at the age of 27. He made almost 200 appearances for the Potters but only 32 for City.

BURNS, William Samuel

Centre-forward: 3 apps. 2 goals.

Born: Durham, 1907.
Died: before 2000.
Career: Crook Town (1927), POTTERS (amateur, October 1930), Stockport County (August 1931), Rotherham United (January 1932).

■ Centre-forward Bill Burns deputised for Wilf Kirkham during his brief stay with the Potters. An amateur throughout his career, he was only 5ft 5in tall and less than 9st.

BURROWS, Henry

Outside-left: 272+9 apps. 79 goals.

Born: Haydock, 17 March 1941.
Career: St Joseph's School (Wigan), Aston Villa (amateur, April 1956, professional, March 1958), POTTERS (£27,000, March 1965), Plymouth Argyle (August 1973–May 1974), non-League football until 1979, Aston Villa Old Stars (1979–82), later became a publican at Mow Cop, Stoke, and in the early 1990s ran a post office in Abbots Bromley.

■ Harry Burrows bided his time at Villa Park before making the outside-

Harry Burrows

left position his own during the 1961–62 season, having acted as reserve to the Irish international Peter McParland. Fast and direct with a fair amount of skill and a cracking left-foot shot, Burrows was an old-fashioned winger with an eye for goal. He attended the same school as his Villa colleague Walter Hazelden before signing for Villa, spotted by scout Peter Downes. Nicknamed 'The Blast', Burrows gained one England under-23 cap and helped Villa win the Second Division Championship and the Football League Cup in successive years (1960 and 1961). He also played in the 1963 losing League Cup Final against the Blues. He scored 73 goals in 181 appearances for Villa, finishing as top-scorer in 1961–62 and 1962–66, before transferring to the Potters in 1965. He did a shade better at The Victoria Ground than he'd done at Villa Park. An instant hit with the Potters fans, he was twice joint top-scorer at The Victoria Ground, helped the Potters retain their First Division status and was a very consistent performer during his eight years with the club. He spent just the one season at Home Park, helping Argyle win promotion from Division Three while taking his overall appearance tally in League Football past the 400 mark. NB: Burrows scored a hat-trick for Stoke against his former club, Aston Villa, in a First Division League game in 1966–67.

BURTON, Deon John

Striker: 13+2 apps. 4 goals

Born: Ashford, Kent, 25 October 1976.
Career: Portsmouth (apprentice, April 1993, professional, February 1994), Cardiff City (on loan, December 1996–January 1997), Derby County (£1 million, August 1997), Barnsley (on loan, December 1998), POTTERS (on loan, February–May 2002), Portsmouth (on loan, August 2002, signed for £75,000, December 2002), Walsall (on loan, September 2003), Swindon Town (on loan, October–November 2003), Brentford (free, July 2004).

■ A Jamaican international with almost 50 caps to his credit, Deon Burton is a capable striker who can also perform as an attacking midfielder. He did well at Portsmouth (first time round – 13 goals in 69 outings) before starting his mini tour of England and Wales. He was an inspired signing by the Potters and his crucial goal in the Play-off semi-final against Cardiff City kept the club's hopes alive, and they eventually went on to gain promotion.

BURTON, Matthew

Inside-left or outside left: 9 apps. 2 goals.

Born: Grassmoor, 1897.
Died: before 1980.
Career: Chesterfield, guest for Everton during World War One, POTTERS (January 1920), Wrexham (June 1921), New Brighton, Rhos FC, Connah's Quay, Shotton.

■ Matt Burton had a quiet time at The Victoria Ground, unable to hold down a regular place in the first team despite his competitiveness. He was joint top-scorer for Wrexham with 12 first-team goals in 1921–22, when they reached the semi-final of the Welsh Cup (beaten by Ton Pentre).

BURTON, Richard Arnold

Defender: 2 apps.

Born: Stoke-on-Trent, April 1889.
Died: before 1975.
Career: North Staffs Nomads, POTTERS (May 1913), North Staffs Nomads (July 1914).

■ A reserve centre-half with Stoke in season 1913–14, Dick Burton's two senior outings were both in the Southern League, away to Aberdare in November and Pontypridd in April, when he deputised for Joey Jones and Charlie Parker respectively.

BUSBY, Vivian Dennis

Forward: 38+22 apps. 11 goals

Born: Slough, 19 June 1949.

Career: Terries FC (High Wycombe), Wycombe Wanderers (semi-professional, July 1966), Luton Town (free, professional, January 1970), Newcastle United (on loan, December 1971–February 1972), Fulham (£25,000, August 1973), Norwich City (£50,000, September 1976), POTTERS (£50,000, November 1977), Sheffield United (on loan, January–February 1980), Tulsa Roughnecks, NASL (on loan, March–November 1980), Blackburn Rovers (£40,000, February, 1981), Tulsa Roughnecks (briefly, summer 1982), York City (player-coach, August 1982, then assistant manager, 1984–May 1987), Sunderland (assistant manager, June 1987), Manchester City (scout, December 1991–January 1993), Hartlepool United (manager, February–November 1993), scout afterwards for West Bromwich Albion and Southampton, Sheffield United (assistant-coach, December 1995–97), later York City (coach, then caretaker-manager, December 2004–February 22005), also worked as a football analyst for a local radio station in the North-East of England.

■ Yet another soccer nomad, Viv Busby served with 16 different professional clubs (as player, coach, assistant manager, manager and scout) between 1966 and 1997. He scored 73 goals in more than 300 League appearances during a varied playing career
He was striker-partner to Malcolm Macdonald at Luton and Newcastle and gained an FA Cup runners'-up medal with Fulham in 1975. Useful if not brilliant, he acted as a foil to the far-better equipped striker most of the time, but he certainly gave a good account of himself wherever he played. He made his debut for the Potters against his former club in November 1977 and struck his first goal for the club in a 4–0 home win over Charlton Athletic on Boxing Day of that same year. He worked under former Stoke City players Denis Smith at Sunderland (1987–91) and Howard Kendall at Bramall Lane (1995–97). In fact, he and Smith moved to Roker Park from York in a £20,000 deal.
* His younger brother, Martin, played for Burnley, Queen's Park Rangers and Portsmouth in the 1970s.

BUSSEY, Walter

Inside or centre-forward: 197 apps. 49 goals.

Born: Eckington, 6 December 1904.
Died: Exeter, January 1982.
Career: Denaby United (1920), Aughton Celtic (1921), Dinnington Main (1922), Anston Athletic (1923), POTTERS (amateur, March 1924, professional, November 1925), Blackpool (May 1933), Swansea Town (July 1934), Exeter City (August 1936, retiring in September 1939).

■ Walter Bussey spent nine seasons at The Victoria Ground. A workmanlike striker who could play in all three central forward positions, he was highly thought of by Potters manager Tom Mather. He gained a regular place in the side in 1926–27, helping the team win the Third Division North title, and he played in the first game of the 1932–33 campaign when Stoke won the Second Division Championship. Bussey appeared in almost 200 senior games for the Potters before switching to Bloomfield Road. He made 79 and 80 appearances respectively for Swansea and Exeter as World War Two broke out.

BUTLER, John Edward

Right-back: 314+5 apps. 9 goals.

Born: Liverpool, 7 February 1962.
Career: Prescot Cables, Wigan Athletic (professional, January 1982), POTTERS (£75,000, December 1988), Wigan Athletic (free, June 1995, released, May 1997).

■ A very consistent and wholly dependable defender, John Butler was Stoke City's regular right-back for most of his six and a half years at The Victoria Ground, although occasionally he was asked to play in other positions. He made 302 appearances for Wigan and, following his transfer to Stoke in 1988, went straight into the side against Manchester City on Boxing Day.
He retained his position, producing some excellent performances, and went on to amass well over 300 senior appearances for the Potters, whom he helped win the Autoglass Trophy at

Wembley in 1992 and the Second Division Championship a year later. At the age of 33 he returned to Wigan and in 1997 helped the Latics win the Third Division title. When he retired from competitive football his personal appearance record at club level stood at 687 (27 goals).

BUXTON, Lewis Edward

Defender: 15+2 apps.

Born: Newport, Isle-of-Wight, 10 December 1983.
Career: Portsmouth (apprentice, April 2000, professional, April 2001), Exeter City (on loan, October–November 2002), AFC Bournemouth (on loan, March–May 2003 and again, October 2003–May 2004), POTTERS (December 2004).

■ Lewis Buxton made his League debut for Portsmouth in 2001, and when he arrived at The Britannia Stadium (halfway through the 2004-05 campaign) he had amassed more than 70 appearances at senior level for his three previous clubs. Able to play at right-back or centre-half, he had his first outing for the Potters against Preston North End on Boxing Day and proved to be a key member of the side thereafter. Strong and confident, he stands at 6ft 1in tall and weighs 13st 10lb.

CAIN, Thomas

Goalkeeper: 14 apps.

Born: Sunderland, October 1872.
Died: summer, 1952.
Career: Hebburn Argyle, POTTERS (professional, November 1893), Everton (April 1894), Southampton St Mary's (October 1895), Grimsby Town (£20, April 1896) Hebburn Argyle (October 1896), West Stanley (January 1897, retired through injury, December 1899).

■ Tom Cain, almost 6ft tall and weighing over 12st, was a reasonable 'keeper but weak under pressure. He spent barely six months at The Victoria Ground before joining Everton, for whom he made just 11 senior appearances in 18 months. He had a nightmare debut for Southampton, conceding seven goals at Clapton, but thankfully he overcame this setback and helped Saints have a satisfactory season.

CAIRNS, Robert Seggie

Wing-half: 196 apps. 11 goals.

Born: Glenboig near Glasgow, 27 May 1929.
Career: Annathill Boys, Royal Albert (1945), Third Lanark (1948), Ayr United (1950), POTTERS (December 1953), Macclesfield Town (July 1961).

■ Wing-half Bobby Cairns joined the Potters along with Joe Hutton just before Christmas 1953. Neat and constructive with a splendid right foot, he was certainly more of a playmaker than a goalscorer and acted as the team's penalty taker for a short while. He had appeared in almost 200 League and Cup games for Stoke before a niggling knee injury saw him leave The Victoria Ground for non-League Macclesfield at the age of 32.

CALLAGHAN, Aaron Joseph

Centre-half: 11+6 apps.

Born: Dublin, 8 October 1966.
Career: POTTERS (apprentice, February 1983, professional, November 1984), Crewe Alexandra (on loan, November 1985), Oldham Athletic (£10,000, November 1986), Crewe Alexandra (£15,000, May 1988), Preston North End (August 1992), St Patrick's, Dublin (during season 1993–94).

■ Facing stiff opposition from a number of players, Irish-born defender Aaron Callaghan never really established himself in the first XI at Stoke. Capped by the Republic of Ireland at youth, under-17 and under-21 levels, he starred for his country in the four-nations European under-21 tournament in Dourgess, France, in May 1986 and was immediately chased by Oldham Athletic, finally joining before the end of the year.

CAMERON, John

Centre-forward: 4 apps.

Born: Glasgow, 1868.
Died: Edinburgh, 1939.
Career: Renton (August 1888), POTTERS (September 1891), Hibernian (November 1891), later with Musselburgh Thistle.

■ One of many Scots who came south to play in English football during the 1890s, Jock Cameron starred for Renton for three years, scoring over 30 goals. He failed to settle in the Potteries and after barely six weeks he returned home to sign for Hibernian.

CAMPBELL, Kenneth

Goalkeeper: 35 apps.

Born: Cambuslang, Glasgow, 6 September 1892.
Died: Macclesfield, 28 April 1977.
Career: Rutherglen Glencairn (Glasgow), Cambuslang Rangers, Liverpool (May 1911), Partick Thistle (£1,750, April 1920), New Brighton (June 1922), POTTERS (March 1923), Leicester City (November 1925), New Brighton (November 1929, retired, June 1931), remained in the area and ran a successful

sports shop in Wallasey for more than 60 years.

■ Kenny Campbell was a very popular and unassuming Scottish international goalkeeper who gained eight full caps for his country, between 1920–22, and represented the Scottish league as a Partick player. Signed to replace the former Sunderland 'keeper Les Scott, he did well for the Potters but never really settled in the area, and in 1925 he was transferred to Leicester. After more than 80 appearances for the Foxes he returned to New Brighton and retired two seasons later. Campbell, who amassed over 400 League and Cup appearances during his career, was a Scottish Cup winner with Partick in 1921 and an FA Cup runner-up with Liverpool, against Burnley, in 1914.

CAPES, Adrian

Inside or centre-forward: 19 apps. 2 goals.

Born: Burton-on-Trent, 18 April 1873.
Died: Smallthorne, Stoke-on-Trent, 29 September 1955.
Career: Burton Wanderers (September 1894), Nottingham Forest (July 1896), Burton Swifts (September 1897), Burslem Port Vale (November 1900), POTTERS (November 1905, with Harry Croxton), Port Vale (December 1908, retired with knee injury, April 1911), became a publican in Smallthorne and was also training supervisor-coach with Port Vale (July 1911–August 1919, continuing to work with the club's backroom staff until May 1934).

■ Adrian Capes was a very useful, all-purpose attacking forward who played with his brother, Arthur, at Nottingham Forest. His scoring record wasn't brilliant with Stoke, where he struggled to adapt to a different style of play and system. However, during his career he netted over 100 goals in almost 280 League games, producing his best form without doubt with Port Vale, for whom he claimed 69 goals in 181 first-team matches, and 89 in 243 outings all told. He hardly missed a match for five years up to 1905. He gained a Kettering District Charity Cup winners' medal with Burton Wanderers in 1895.

CAPES, Arthur John

Utility forward: 65 apps. 20 goals.

Born: Burton-on-Trent, 1875.
Died: Burton-on-Trent, 26 February 1945.
Career: Burton Wanderers (September 1894), Nottingham Forest (July 1896), POTTERS (June 1902), Bristol City (June 1904), Swindon Town (August 1905).

■ Arthur 'Sailor' Capes was a quality forward, able to play in a variety of front-line positions. He netted 20 goals in two seasons for the Potters, having joined the club four years after gaining an FA Cup winners' medal with Forest when he netted twice in the 4–1 Final victory over Derby County. Described occasionally as 'an artisan or unpolished and workmanlike' player, Capes was awarded one England cap against Scotland in April 1903, and he also represented the Football League. He scored over 100 goals in more than 380 League appearances during his career. Like his brother, he also gained a winners' medal for victory in the Kettering District Charity Cup Final of 1895.
* The Capes brothers signed for Forest together: one would not join without the other.

CAPEWELL, William

Left-back or left-half: 61 apps.

Born: Stoke-on-Trent, February 1878.
Died: Stoke-on-Trent, c.1955.
Career: POTTERS (May 1895), Reading (July 1896), POTTERS (August 1899, retired through injury, May 1902).

■ Billy Capewell was a tenacious footballer who had two spells with the Potters. He did far better the second time round, having his best season in 1900–01 when he missed only one game when partnering Peter Durber at full-back.

CARR, Clifford Paul

Right-back: 134+9 apps. 1 goal.

Born: Hackney, London, 19 June 1964.
Career: Fulham (apprentice, July 1980, professional, August 1982), POTTERS (£45,000, July 1987), Shrewsbury Town (non-contract, August 1991), Telford United (September 1991), Mansfield Town (October 1991), Chesterfield (August 1992–May 1993), worked for the Severn Trent Water Board in the mid-1990s, was President of the Junior Potters during his final year at The 'Vic'.

■ Diminutive right-back Cliff Carr joined Fulham on leaving school and quickly made the grade at Craven Cottage, rising to first-team captain and also representing England at under-21 level. After more than 150 appearances for the London club he was signed by Potters boss Mick Mills in 1987. It took him some time to settle in at The

Victoria Ground following Stoke's poor start to the 1989–90 season, and there was speculation within the camp that he was to leave quickly. But Carr battled on and eventually established himself in the side, becoming very popular with the supporters. Unfortunately, he never quite matched up to the manager's requirements, yet still made over 140 senior appearances for the club. He later teamed up with former Stoke player Mick Kennedy at Chesterfield.

CARRUTHERS, Martin George

Striker: 80+39 apps. 20 goals.

Born: Nottingham, 7 August 1972.
Career: Aston Villa (apprentice, July

1988, professional, July 1990), Hull City (loan, October 1992), POTTERS (£100,000, July 1993), Peterborough United (November 1996), York City (loan, January 1999), Darlington (March 1999), Southend United (loan, August 1999, signed for £50,000, September 1999), Scunthorpe United (£20,000, March 2001), Macclesfield Town (July 2003), Boston United (free, August 2004), Lincoln City (free, September 2004), Cambridge United (on loan, January–February 2005), Bristol Rovers (July 2005).

■ Martin Carruthers failed to make an impact under two managers at Villa Park, Josef Venglos or Ron Atkinson, and was subsequently transferred to The Victoria Ground where, generally, he did well after a tentative start. In later years he prospered even more, and ended the 2004–05 season with over 130 goals to his credit in more than 500 senior appearances at club level. A determined 6ft tall striker, quick off the mark with a work-rate second to none, during his time with Stoke he was linked with Burnley and Fortuna Sittard but chose to continue to play in the reserves, hoping for a first-team call up.

CARTLIDGE, Arthur Edwin

Goalkeeper: 45 apps.

Born: Stoke-on-Trent, 12 June 1880.
Died: Stoke-on-Trent, 20 August 1940.
Career: Penkhull Victoria, Market Drayton (1897), POTTERS (professional, May 1899), Bristol Rovers (£75, April 1901), Aston Villa (£100 April 1905), POTTERS (£315, April 1911), South Shields (May 1912, retired, May 1915)

■ Arthur Cartlidge, who had two spells with Stoke, stood a shade over 6ft tall, weighed around 14st, was well built with a safe pair of hands and possessed a strong right-foot kick. He made just three League appearances as understudy to Tom Wilkes during his first half spell at The Victoria Ground. He then left and played in more than 250 games for Bristol Rovers, helping them win the Southern League Championship in 1905. Four years later he was transferred to Villa Park, added a further 55 appearances to his tally and won a League Championship medal in 1910 before returning to Stoke.
* His cousin, Francis Arthur Cartlidge, born in 1899, was a centre-forward with Port Vale for two seasons in 1920–22.

CATON, William Clifford

Inside-forward: 22 apps. 2 goals.

Born: Stoke-on-Trent, 11 September 1924.
Career: Middleport (1939), POTTERS (junior, September 1940, professional, September 1941), guest for Wrexham and the Italian club Benevento during World War Two, Carlisle United (£3,000, April 1950), Chesterfield (October 1952), Worcester City (March 1953), Crewe Alexandra (July 1954), Stafford Rangers (May 1956), Mossley (1957), Gresley Rovers (1958), Congleton Town (1960), Burslem Albion (1961, later became a committee member, chairman and then president of the Stoke-on-Trent club), later worked as a publican in Newcastle (Staffs).

■ Bill Caton was the only Stoke City player to be signed by the great Bill Shankly, in 1950 when 'Shanks' was the manager of Carlisle United. Caton had struggled to secure a regular first-team place at The Victoria Ground and averaged only three first-team outings a year. It's on record that Caton was an expert with penalties and from the 31 he took as a player, 29 were converted! He could also throw a ball a vast distance and had 22 outings for the Potters during World War Two. He scored 16 goals in 64 League games for Chesterfield and eight in 38 for Crewe.

CHADWICK, Luke Harry

Midfield: new signing.

Born: Cambridge, 18 November 1980.
Career: Manchester United (apprentice, May 1997, professional, February 1999), Reading (loan, February–May 2003), Burnley (loan, July 2003, May 2004), West Ham United (free, August 2004), POTTERS (loan, July 2005).

A 2001 Premiership winner with Manchester United, for whom he made 39 senior appearances, Luke Chadwick also did well at Reading and Burnley before having a hard season with the Hammers, who were subsequently relegated. An England Youth international, he went on to gain 13 caps at under-21 level and made his debut for the Potters against Sheffield Wednesday in August 2005.

CHADWICK, Richard

Right-back: 1 app.

Born: Stoke-on-Trent, 1860.
Died: Stoke-on-Trent, 1929.
Career: Church football, POTTERS (August 1886), Longton Albion (May 1888).

■ Dick Chadwick's only senior appearance for the Potters was in the FA Cup tie against Caernarvon Wanderers in October 1886, which resulted in a comprehensive 10–1 victory.

CHADWICK, Wilfred

Inside-forward: 8 apps. 2 goals

Born: Bury, Lancashire, 7 September 1900.
Died: Bury, February 1975.
Career: Bury Juniors, Nelson (season 1920-21), Rossendale (August 1921), Everton (February 1922), Leeds United (November 1925), Wolverhampton Wanderers (August 1926), POTTERS (£250, May 1929), Halifax Town (October 1930–May 1931).

■ Wilf Chadwick was a soccer wanderer and during a lengthy career served with eight different clubs at various levels. He was top-scorer at Goodison Park in 1923–24 with 30 goals and, in all, netted 55 times in his 109 appearances for the Merseysiders.

Afterwards, he struck 44 goals in 101 appearances for Wolves and at League level claimed 104 goals in 251 outings. A clever and sometimes very creative player, he also struck 35 goals in only 23 games for Rossendale.

CHALLINOR, John

Full-back: 46 apps.

Born: Middlewich, Cheshire, 5 August 1916.
Died: 1981.
Career: Witton Albion (semi-professional, 1934), POTTERS (trialist, October 1936, signed professional, November 1936), Linfield, Northern Ireland (April 1946).

■ Resilient full-back Jack Challinor was captured from under the nose of West Bromwich Albion, who had given him a trial only months before he agreed to sign for the Potters in 1936 – brought in as cover for Charlie Scrimshaw and Bill Winstanley. In the end it was he and another full-back, Harry Brigham, who battled it out between them for a first-team place. In fact, Challinor waited 10 months (until September 1937) before making his League debut against Chelsea at Stamford Bridge when he replaced broken-leg victim Scrimshaw. He remained a registered player at The Victoria Ground until 1945, at which point he travelled over to Northern Ireland to play for the Belfast-based club, Linfield.

CHALMERS, John

Centre-forward: 43 apps. 19 goals.

Born: Beith, Renfrewshire, 16 October 1886.
Died: Glasgow, 1959.
Career: Rutherglen Glencairn, Glasgow Rangers (August 1904), POTTERS (January 1906), Bristol Rovers (October 1908), Clyde (November 1908), Woolwich Arsenal (October 1910), Greenock Morton (£500, March 1912, retired, November 1914), went to work in a steel factory.

■ Centre-forward Jack Chalmers was a reserve at Ibrox Park (3 appearances, two goals) before doing very well in his two and half years with the Potters, but then, along with several other players, he was forced out The Victoria Ground when the club folded in 1908. He quickly joined Bristol Rovers and scored on his debut. He later netted 23 goals in 52 first-class matches for Arsenal when he partnered the game's first £1,000 player, Alf Common, up front.

CHAMBERLAIN, Mark Valentine

Winger: 123+2 apps. 18 goals.

Born: Stoke-on-Trent, 19 November 1961.
Career: Port Vale (apprentice, April 1977,

Mark Chamberlain

Lee Chapman

professional April 1979), POTTERS (£135,000, August 1982), Sheffield Wednesday (£300,000, September 1985), Portsmouth (£200,000, August 1988), Brighton & Hove Albion (August 1994), Exeter City (August 1995), Fareham Town (player-manager-coach, March 1997, later Director of Football, from June 2000).

■ Mark Chamberlain, younger brother of Neville, spent 20 years in top-class football. He started his career as a junior with Port Vale and made his League debut against Scunthorpe United in August 1978. He went on to appear in 110 first-team matches for the Valiants (20 goals scored). During the first 15 years of his senior career he played as a direct, fast-raiding winger. Clever, with excellent ball control, he loved to run at defenders and could centre on the run and with great precision. He scored on his full international debut for England in a 9–0 win over Luxembourg at Wembley in December 1982 and added a further seven caps to his tally as a Potter, having already represented his country at schoolboy, youth and under-21 levels. Former Potters boss Alan Ball signed him for Portsmouth, and he teamed up with another ex-Stoke colleague, Peter Fox, when he joined struggling Exeter City. At the end of the 1996–97 season, when he moved to Fareham, Chamberlain had taken his League appearance tally to an impressive 518 and had netted 69 goals.

CHAMBERLAIN, Neville Patrick

Forward: 7 apps.

Born: Stoke-on-Trent, 22 January 1960.
Career: Port Vale (apprentice, April 1976, professional, January 1978), POTTERS (£40,000, September 1982), Newport County (on loan, November–December 1983), Plymouth Argyle (on loan, March–May 1984), Newport County (July 1984), Mansfield Town (July 1985), Cambridge United (briefly), Doncaster Rovers (August 1987), Stafford Rangers (May 1988), Worksop Town (1989), Stafford Rangers (again, 1990), then Worksop Town, Shepshed Charterhouse, Matlock Town, Leek Town, Shamblers FC, Rocester, Kynpersley Victoria (retired, May 1993), Alsager Town (assistant manager, 1993–94), thereafter Hanley Town (manager).

■ Like his younger brother, Mark, Neville Chamberlain also did extremely well at Vale Park, scoring 41 goals in 158 senior appearances for the Valiants and finishing as top-scorer in successive seasons, 1979–81, having made his League debut as a 17-year-old apprentice against Rotherham United in December 1977. Unfortunately, he never hit the high spots at The Victoria Ground, playing in only seven competitive games for the Potters. But after leaving in 1984 things changed for the better, and he went on to take his career appearance-tally past the 350 mark at senior club level before drifting into non-League football with Stafford Rangers in 1988. He was his brother Mark's agent during his time in non-League football.

CHAPMAN, Lee Roy

Striker: 103+4 apps. 38 goals.

Born: Lincoln, 5 December 1959.
Career: POTTERS (apprentice, June 1976, professional, June 1978), Plymouth Argyle (on loan, December 1978), Arsenal (£500,000, August 1982), Sunderland (£200,000, December 1983), Sheffield Wednesday (£100,000, August 1984), Niort, France (£350,000, June 1988, Nottingham Forest (£350,000, October 1988), Leeds United (£400,000, January 1990), Portsmouth (£250,000, August 1993), West Ham United (£250,000, September 1993), Southend United (on loan, January 1995), Ipswich Town (£70,000, January 1995), Leeds United (on loan, January 1996), Swansea City (free, non-contract, March–May 1996), Stafford Rangers (briefly in season 1996–97), retired to open a his own restaurant/wine bar in the Chelsea district of London. He is married to TV's Men Behaving Badly *actress Lesley Ash.*

■ Striker Lee Chapman first hit the headlines as a junior with the Potters. He developed fast and went on to win caps for England at 'B' and under-21 levels. He later gained Second and First Division Championship medals with Leeds in 1990 and 1992 respectively, having earlier collected League Cup and Simod Cup prizes with Forest, both in 1989. His scoring record for Stoke was impressive – a goal every three games – and in his playing career in England at club level Chapman revealed a fine set of statistics – 253 goals in 679 competitive appearances, including 197 strikes in 552 League games.
* Lee Chapman's father, Roy, was a utility forward with Aston Villa, Lincoln City, Mansfield Town, Port Vale and Chester, and he also managed several clubs including Stockport County, Stafford Rangers and Stourbridge. Lee's mother, Margaret, was also associated with football, being the secretary of Stoke City's manager Frank Taylor during the 1950s.

CHARNLEY, William

Outside-right: 2 apps.

Born: Kirkham near Preston, April 1895.
Died: Edinburgh, c.1970.
Career: Great Eccleston, Aberdeen (briefly, 1918), POTTERS (July 1919), Musselburgh (seasons 1920–25).

■ Will Charnley moved south to the Potteries in readiness for the 1919–20 season. He was given just two League outings by the club – in successive home wins over Hull City and Blackpool – before returning to Scotland. He drifted out of football in the mid-1920s after suffering a spate of injuries.

CHRISTIE, David

Half-back: 135 apps. 3 goals.

Born: Forfar, January 1867.
Died: Scotland, c.1945.
Career: Forfar Athletic (August 1885), POTTERS (August 1889), Dresden United (May, 1895, retired, April 1900).

■ Stoke had several Scottish-born players at the club during the late 1890s/early 1900s, and David Christie was undoubtedly one of the best. A powerfully-built half-back, able to occupy all three middle line positions, he was comfortable on the ball, had good technique and was never hurried.

He spent six years at The Victoria Ground and made almost 140 senior appearances for the Potters. He returned to Scotland after retiring.

CLAMP, Harold Edwin

Wing-half: 62 apps. 22 goals.

Born: Coalville, Leicestershire 14 September 1934.
Died: Wolverhampton, 10 November 1995.
Career: Coalville State School, Wolverhampton Wanderers (amateur, 1949, professional, April 1952), Arsenal (£12,000, November 1961), POTTERS (September 1962), Peterborough United (October 1964), Worcester City (August 1965–May 1966), thence out of football until joining Lower Gornal (Dudley) in September 1967, retiring in 1969, played in charity matches for the Wolves Old Stars until 1984 while running his own business, he was a regular visitor to both The Victoria Ground and Molineux right up until his death in 1995.

■ Capped five times by England at schoolboy level, Eddie 'Chopper' Clamp developed into a forceful wing-half with a biting tackle and never-say-die attitude. An FA Youth Cup finalist in 1953, he won two League Championship medals with Wolves in 1958 and 1959 and an FA Cup winners' medal in 1960, later adding a Second Division prize to his collection with Stoke in 1963. During his two years at The Victoria Ground he played in front of Bill Asprey and behind Stanley Matthews, and between them they formed a pretty useful combination, especially with first Dennis Viollet and then Peter Dobing lining up the inside-right position. Clamp won four full caps for his country in the space of 28 days (during May and June 1958), forming the half-back line with Wolves team-mates Billy Wright and Bill Slater in each one. He appeared in 241 senior games for Wolves (25 goals scored) and during his career amassed well over 350 first-class appearances at club and international levels. His mother was employed as the laundry-lady at Molineux in the 1950s.

CLARE, Thomas

Full-back: 251 apps. 6 goals.

Born: Congleton, Cheshire, March 1865.
Died: Ladysmith, Vancouver, Canada, 27 December 1929.
Career: Talke Rangers (1880), Goldenhill Wanderers (1882), Burslem Port Vale (February 1884), POTTERS (July 1884), Port Vale (guest, November 1884, signed permanently as player-coach, July 1897), Manchester City (trialist, March 1898), Burlsem Port Vale (April 1898, appointed player-coach, August 1898, retired as a player, April 1899, re-signed as player-coach, August 1900, continued as coach then manager-secretary, July 1905–May 1906). Emigrated to Canada.

■ Tom Clare was, according to the record books, the first player to sign as a full-time professional for Stoke, and he was also the club's first captain in the Football League. An inspirational player, he was a splendid header of the ball, was quick off the mark, strong and purposeful in the tackle and ever-reliable, always working for his team. He made his senior debut in a Potters jersey in 1885 and went on to amass over 250 League and Cup appearances up to 1897. He represented Staffordshire on several occasions and gained four full England caps as a Stoke player. He played in only one League game for Manchester City, against Newcastle United in March 1898. After returning to Vale he unfortunately broke his leg in October 1898 and after that was never the same player. He appeared in 23 first-class matches for Vale, with whom he won the Staffordshire Cup in 1898.

CLARK, Andrew

Left-back: 59 apps.

Born: Leith, Midlothian, 12 August 1881.
Died: before 1960.
Career: Hamilton Academical (1897), Buckheaven United (1898), Heart of Midlothian (1899), POTTERS (May 1901), East Fife (March 1903), Plymouth Argyle (August 1903), Leeds City (May 1906–May 1907), Plymouth Argyle (August–September 1907), Brentford (October 1907), Southend United (1908–09).

■ A forceful, strong-running left-back, Andy Clark spent four years playing competitive football in Scotland before moving down to the Potteries. He partnered firstly Sam Meredith and then Charlie Burgess in the Stoke defence before returning to his homeland with East Fife. He later did well in the Southern League with Plymouth (for whom he made 145 senior appearances), Brentford and Southend.

CLARK, John Brown

Defender: 18 apps. 1 goal.

Born: Edinburgh, 22 September 1964.
Career: Dundee United (amateur, September 1979, professional, July 1981), POTTERS (£150,000, January 1994), Falkirk (£100,000, September 1994), Dunfermline Athletic (February 1996), later Cowdenbeath (manager, briefly).

■ A rugged, well-built utility defender, John Clark's family never settled in Stoke and he spent less than eight months at The Victoria Ground, during which time he appeared in 18 games. A Scottish youth international, Clark netted 36 goals in 324 outings for Dundee United, who Stoke played in a Testimonial Match for the Scotsman at Tannadice Park in 1994.

CLARKE, Clive Richard

Left-back or midfield: 242+22 apps. 10 goals.

Born: Dublin, 14 January 1980.
Career: POTTERS (apprentice, April 1996, professional, January 1997).

■ Named club captain for 2003–04, Clive Clarke played in 46 of Stoke's games that season, producing some outstanding performances, mainly at left-back but also in midfield. He struck two superb goals from distance, against Gillingham and Sheffield United. Prior to that he had been nurtured along at The Britannia Stadium and represented the Republic of Ireland at youth team level, and has since gained 11 under-21 and two senior caps for his country.

CLARKE, George

Half-back: 165 apps. 4 goals.

Born: Nantwich, Cheshire, 3 December 1894.

Died: Willaston near Nantwich, 30 July 1960.
Career: Nantwich Town, POTTERS (£125, May 1914), Crewe Alexandra (May 1925, retired, summer 1927 to become as a scout for the 'Alex').

■ George Clarke remained a part-time footballer throughout his career, occupying a half-back position. He spent 11 years at The Victoria Ground, although he didn't actually enter first-team games until after World War One, having suffered a broken leg while playing army football as a member of the Liverpool Scottish Regiment, serving

in France during the hostilities. He cost Stoke an agreed fee (from Nantwich) plus the proceeds of a game between the two sides. In 1922 he helped Stoke win promotion to the First Division, but after breaking his leg again (in a Cup tie against Leeds United) he was never the same player and eventually left The Victoria Ground for Gresty Road.

CLARKE, Wayne

Striker: 9 apps. 3 goals.

Born: Willenhall, 28 February 1961.
Career: Wolverhampton Wanderers (apprentice, April 1976, professional, March 1978), Birmingham City (£80,000, August 1984), Everton (£500,000, March 1987), Leicester City (£500,000, July 1989), Manchester City (£500,000, January 1990), Shrewsbury Town (on loan, October–December

1990), POTTERS (on loan, March–May 1991), Wolverhampton Wanderers (on loan, September 1991), Walsall (free, August 1992), Shrewsbury Town (free, July 1993), Telford United (free, player-manager, August 1995, resigned November 1996), later worked as a postman in the Telford area.

■ A former England Schoolboy and youth international and West Midland representative player, Wayne Clarke was a natural goal-scorer. Like his three brothers – Allan, Derek and Frank – he joined Wolves as teenager and netted over 30 goals in more than 160 first-team matches for the Molineux club before transferring to St Andrew's. Continuing to pester defences, he notched a further 43 goals in 105 outings for the Blues and then joined Everton. While at Goodison Park he gained a League Championship medal (1987) and had the pleasure of scoring in the FA Charity Shield game win over Coventry City at Wembley, but when Tony Cottee arrived at the club Clarke quickly departed to Leicester. His loan spell with Stoke realised a goal every three games, and when he pulled out of competitive soccer in 1995 he had accumulated over 500 senior games and scored more than 130 goals.

CLARKSON, Ian Stewart

Right-back: 91+5 apps.

Born: Solihull, 4 December 1970.

Career: Chapel Fields Primary & Tudor grange schools, Birmingham City (apprentice, June 1987, professional, December 1988), POTTERS (£50, September 1993), Northampton Town (free, August 11996), Kidderminster Harriers (free, November 2000).

■ After almost 100 first-team appearances for Stoke, efficient and steady right-back Ian Clarkson was given a free transfer by manager Lou Macari and was quickly snapped up by Northampton. A Blues supporter since he was 10, he played in 172 games for the St Andrew's club before moving to The Victoria Ground, where he joined a band of former Blues players already with the Potters. Clarkson returned to Stoke with the Cobblers for a Coca-Cola Cup game in 1996.

CLAWLEY, George W.

Goalkeeper: 96 apps.

Born: Scholar Green, Staffs, 10 April 1875.
Died: Southampton, 16 July 1920.
Career: Crewe Alexandra (August 1893), POTTERS (£10, September 1894), Southampton St Mary's (June 1896), POTTERS (May 1898), Tottenham Hotspur (July 1899), Southampton June 1903–May 1907), became landlord of the Wareham Arms Hotel, Southampton.

George Clawley, 6ft 2in tall and 12st 7lb in weight, always wore a cap. He was one of the finest 'keepers of his era, possessing all the physical requirements for a player in his position. He had two separate spells at The Victoria Ground and appeared in almost 100 games for Stoke. Unfortunately, he broke a leg in his first season at White Hart Lane but recovered in time to gain an FA Cup winners' medal in 1901 against Sheffield United and play in an England international trial in March 1903. Clawley, who was a big favourite with supporters everywhere he went, won three Southern League Championship medals with Southampton (1897, 1898 and 1904, the second as skipper). He also represented both the Hampshire County FA and the Southern League during the 1890s as a Saints player. Clawley had appeared in 163 games for Southampton and 187 for Spurs on announcing his retirement in 1907. Although he died in Southampton, he was buried in a churchyard in Kidsgrove.

CLEGG, Donald

Goalkeeper: 2 apps.

Born: Huddersfield, 2 June 1921.
Career: Imperial Chemical Industries FC (Huddersfield), Huddersfield Town (professional, May 1940), Bury (£1,500, July 1948), POTTERS (free, June 1950), Rossendale (July 1951, retired, April 1956).

Stoke City's goalkeeping strength at the start of the 1950–51 season was exceptionally good with Dennis Herod,

Norman Wilkinson and Don Clegg all ready to claim the number one position. It was Clegg who started off the campaign, being given just two League outings by manager Bob McGrory before he was dropped following two defeats! Clegg served his local club before making 15 League appearances for the 'Shakers'.

CLENNELL, Joseph

Inside-left: 35 apps. 9 goals.

Born: New Silksworth, 18 February 1889.
Died: February, 1965.
Career: Silksworth United, Seaham Harbour FC, Blackpool (professional, July 1910), Blackburn Rovers (£600, April 1911), Everton (£1,500, January 1914), Cardiff City (October 1921), POTTERS (February 1925), Bristol Rovers (September 1926), Rochdale (March-October 1927), Ebbw Vale (player-manager, November 1927), Barry Town (player-manager-coach, August 1928), Distillery (manager from 1929), Bangor (player-manager), Great Harwood (player-manager), Accrington Stanley (coach, season 1934–35).

A player with a terrific shot, Joe Clennell could also dribble through the opposition in great style, although he did have a tendency to overdo the clever stuff at times, much to the annoyance of his colleagues (and manager). Only a little chap, difficult to knock off the ball, he was plagued by injuries during the latter stages of his Goodison Park career and was allowed to move to Cardiff in 1921 – having gained a League Championship medal in 1915 when he scored 15 goals in 36 games. Often described as a 'little demon and a terror for his size', he was something of a veteran when he joined the Potters, but still gave the club good value for money before moving on to Bristol Rovers. Clennell, who appeared in over 350 competitive games (309 in the Football League, scoring 112 goals) was sadly killed in a car crash, nine days after his 76th birthday.

CLIFFORD, Hugh

Half-back: 34 apps. 2 goals.

Born: Glasgow, May 1866.
Died: Scotland, 1942.
Career: Renton, Carfin Shamrock, POTTERS (professional, September

1890), Celtic (1893); later with Manchester City (July 1895–March 1896).

■ After playing for Stoke, half-back Hugh Clifford illegally signed for Celtic in 1893 and was banned from English football for two years. In fact, he walked out of The Victoria Ground in a temper and threatened to quit football altogether. After his ban had been served, Clifford played in a handful of games for Manchester City.

CLOWES, John Alan

Inside-forward: 4 apps. 2 goals.

Born: Alton, 5 November, 1929.
Career: Crewe Alexandra, POTTERS (June 1950), Shrewsbury Town (June 1952), Wellington Town (1954), POTTERS (August 1955), Wellington (March 1956–May 1957), also played for Macclesfield town (briefly).

■ Jack Clowes was a useful reserve inside-forward who scored twice on his League debut for Stoke in a 3–2 win over Wolverhampton Wanderers at Molineux in April 1951.

COATES, Richard James

Centre-forward: 1 app.

Born: Born in Hanley, April 1889.
Died: Cheshire, c.1960.
Career: Mardy (1909), POTTERS (July 1912), Annfield Plain (May 1913). Did not play after World War One.

■ Dick Coates was a short, stocky reserve centre-forward, who had one Southern League outing for Stoke against Coventry City (home) in January 1913.

COLCLOUGH, Ephraim

Forward: 3 apps.

Born: Blurton, Stoke-on-Trent, 7 June 1875.
Died: Hove, Sussex, 1914.
Career: Blurton Swifts, Burslem Swifts (1897), POTTERS (January 1899), Watford (July 1900), Brighton & Hove Albion (August 1901–May 1902).

■ Described as a 'versatile forward', Ephraim Colclough's three League outings for Stoke were spread over a nine-month period: April 1899 to January 1900. He replaced Jack Farrell in his first two and Sam Higginson in his last.

COLEMAN, Neville James

Outside-right: 126 apps. 52 goals.

Born: Prescot, Lancashire, 29 January 1930.
Career: Gorleston (1951), POTTERS (August 1953, professional, January 1955), Crewe Alexandra (February 1959, retired, May 1961).'Tim' Coleman holds the record for scoring most goals in a game for Stoke City – netting seven times in an 8–0 victory over Lincoln City in a Second Division fixture at The Victoria Ground on 23 February 1957.

■ After this flourish Coleman failed to hit the target again for the Potters that season – but during his six years with the club he amassed a pretty useful set of statistics: over 50 goals in more than 125 senior appearances. He did his National Service in the RAF and actually assisted in providing the cost of buying himself out of the forces in the summer of 1955, when he immediately signed professional forms for the Potters and established himself in the first XI the very next season. He scored 16 goals

in 73 League outings for Crewe before pulling out of competitive football in 1961.

COLLINS, Lee David

Defender: 4 apps.

Born: Birmingham, 10 September 1977.
Career: Birmingham & District schoolboy football, Aston Villa (apprentice, April 1994, professional, July 1996), POTTERS (free, February 1999, released, May 1999).

■ Under the eye of Brian little at Villa Park, Lee Collins was then snapped up by his former manager for Stoke in 1996. A tall, commanding defender, he made his League debut in place of Larus Sigurdsson against Millwall at The New Den in March 1999 and added a further three appearances to his tally before his release.

COMMONS, Kristian Arran

Left-back or midfield: 22+24 apps. 5 goals.

Born: Mansfield, 30 August 1983.
Career: POTTERS (apprentice, August 1999, professional, January 2001), Nottingham Forest (tribunal set fee, August 2004).

■ Now described as being a utility player, having also appeared in a League game at centre-forward for the Potters against West Bromwich Albion in May

2004, Kris Commons recovered from a knee ligament injury to produce his best at Stoke in what was to be his last season with the club before his transfer to Nottingham Forest.

CONNOR, Harold

Centre-forward: 4 apps. 2 goals.

Born: Liverpool, 26 December 1929.
Career: Peterborough United (September 1947), Marine Crosby (1951), POTTERS (amateur, March 1953), Marine Crosby, New Brighton, Skelmersdale United.

■ Harry O'Connor played for Peterborough United in the Midland League before serving with and playing for the RAF (Halton). He joined the Potters as a 23-year-old, as reserve to Bill Finney, but his senior outings were

restricted to just four, scoring the first of his two goals after just 10 minutes of his debut against Sunderland. The last amateur to play senior football for Stoke City, Connor was also a very fine athlete, especially on the track over middle distances (400–800 yards). In later years he chose to live in retirement in Maidstone, Kent.

CONNOR, Paul

Striker: 23+25 apps. 10 goals.

Born: Bishop Auckland, 12 January 1979.
Career: Middlesbrough (apprentice, April

1995, professional, July 1996), Hartlepool United (on loan, February–March 1998), POTTERS (free, March 1998), Cambridge United (on loan, November 2000–January 2001), Rochdale (£100,000, March 2001), Swansea City (free, March 2004).

■ An Auto-Windscreen Shield winner with the Potters in 2000, Paul Connor is a willing, hard-running striker who works the front-line superbly well. His total first-team appearances for the Potters were virtually split between him starting a game and coming on as a substitute. He failed to make the senior side at Middlesbrough but certainly did well with Rochdale, for whom he scored 33 goals in 108 competitive matches.

CONROY, Gerald Anthony Francis

Forward: 302+31 apps. 66 goals.

Born: Dublin, 2 October 1946.
Career: Glentoran, POTTERS (£10,000, March 1967), Bulova, Hong Kong (free, June 1979), Crewe Alexandra (free, January 1980, retired, June 1981).

■ Terry Conroy was a very popular player at The Victoria Ground, and was certainly the fans' favourite son from the day he joined the Potters from Glentoran in 1967. Starting off in the reserves, he was not introduced to first-team action by manager Tony Waddington until September 1967 – six months after joining. The red-headed Dubliner, known as 'White Legs', wore the number seven shirt in practically all of his 302 starts for Stoke, and besides his tally of goals he certainly created another 100 or so for his colleagues. A brilliant dribbler, he had pace, a terrific bodyswerve and fierce shot in either foot, and, above all, he had great stamina. He ran his socks off for the Potters week after week and was rewarded for his bold efforts with a League Cup winners' medal in 1972 when he starred and scored in that famous 2–1 victory over Chelsea at Wembley. Capped by the Republic of Ireland on 26 occasions, the first Stoke City player to represent this country against Czechoslovakia in 1969, he left The Victoria Ground for a spell in Hong Kong on a free transfer in the summer of 1979, having spent 12 happy years in the Potteries. He returned to England and served with Crewe Alexandra, scoring five goals in 37 League outings before hanging up his boots in 1981 to concentrate on his business in the area. He turned out in a few charity matches from time to time and attends Stoke home games whenever possible. Now Commercial Executive at The Britannia Stadium, he contributes regularly to the club's matchday programme.

COOK, Jeffrey William

Forward: 25+8 apps. 5 goals.

Born: Hartlepool, 14 March 1953.
Career: Hellenic FC, South Africa (1973), POTTERS (November 1977), Bradford City (on loan, February–April 1979), Plymouth Argyle (on loan, December

Terry Conroy

1979–January 1981, signed for £25,000, October 1981), Halifax Town (August 1983, released, March 1985), Worksop Town (1986), North Ferriby United (1987), Ferryhill Athletic (1988), Hartlepool Town (as player-coach and assistant manager, 1993–94).

■ Jeff Cook spent five years in South Africa before joining Stoke at the age of 24 in 1977. He made his debut for the Potters in a League game at Ninian Park on Bonfire Night, 24 hours after joining the club, and netted his first goal on his home debut three weeks later against Blackpool. A useful competitor, perhaps lacking in skill, he scored 26 times in 65 outings for Plymouth and teamed up with ex-Potter Viv Busby at Hartlepool in the early 1990s.

COOKE, Andrew Roy

Striker: 78+24 apps. 23 goals.

Born: Shrewsbury, 20 January 1974.
Career: Newtown (Wales), Burnley (professional, May 1995), POTTERS (£350,000, December 2000), Buskan Icons, Korea (free, July 2003), Bradford City (free, January 2004).

■ A prolific marksman at Turf Moor (62 goals scored in 202 appearances for Burnley), Andy Cooke continued to find the net on a regular basis for the Potters.

Totally committed, his honest, hard-working performances certainly made him a huge favourite with the fans. He top-scored for the club in his last season when he battled on gamely despite niggling injuries and managerial changes. At the end of the campaign he chose to leave The Britannia Stadium for a career in Korean football – one of the few Brits to attempt such a venture.

COPE, William Arthur

Full-back: 31 apps.

Born: Burslem, Stoke-on-Trent, 25 November 1884.
Died: Hartshill, Stoke-on-Trent, 18 February 1937.
Career: Mount Pleasant (1901), Burlsem Port Vale (professional, August 1904), POTTERS (July 1907) Oldham Athletic

(£300, June 1908), West Ham United (£150, May 1914), Wrexham (July 1922, retired, May 1923), returned to live and work in the Potteries.

■ Billy Cook was a fine full-back whose game was characterised by some beefy clearances despite the fact that he wore only a size 4 boot. When he first arrived at The Victoria Ground (signed from Port Vale who were facing a financial crisis) he seemed short on pace but as time went by he developed into a sound player with a fine tackle. He made 77 League and Cup appearances for the Valiants, skippered West Ham United before World War One and was 38 when he played his last League game for Wrexham against Durham City in April 1933.

COPESTAKE, Joseph

Utility defender: 2 apps.

Born: Fenton, Stoke-on-Trent, June 1859.
Died: Stoke-on-Trent, c.1932.
Career: Newcastle-under-Lyme, Stoke Town, POTTERS (August 1885), Stoke Town (April 1886), Newcastle-under-Lyme (season 1888–89).

■ Joe Copestake played in two FA Cup ties for Stoke, both against Crewe Alexandra in October/November 1885, his only senior outings for the club.

CORRIGAN, Thomas Joseph

Goalkeeper: 9 apps.

Born: Manchester, 18 November 1948.
Career: Sale FC, Manchester City (professional, January 1967), Seattle Sounders, NASL (June 1982), Brighton & Hove Albion (September 1983), Norwich City (on loan, September 1984), POTTERS (on loan, November–December 1984), retired, April 1985, later goalkeeping coach with several Premiership clubs, including Liverpool (2003) and West Bromwich Albion (from December 2004).

■ Joe Corrigan, at 6ft 5in, was one of the tallest goalkeepers in the game between 1967 and 1985, and is certainly one of the tallest footballers ever to don a Stoke shirt. An England international (capped nine times at senior level between 1976 and 1982, and once by the under-23's), he appeared in 592 first-team games for the Maine Road club (476 in the League) before moving over to the States to assist the Seattle Sounders in the NASL. He returned to England in 1983 and the following term had loan spells with both Norwich and Stoke. Replacing Peter Fox, he made his debut for the Potters against Liverpool and played his last game for the club against Manchester United on Boxing Day 1984, both games being at The Victoria Ground. As a Manchester City player, 'Big Joe' twice won the League Cup (1970 and 1976) and collected an FA Cup runners-up medal in 1981, playing against Spurs.

COTTON, Harold Henry

Goalkeeper: 2 apps.

Born: Crewe, 5 April 1882.
Died: Crewe, 1959.
Career: Nantwich, Burslem Port Vale (May 1901), Crewe Alexandra (July 1905), POTTERS (£50, October 1908), Eccleshall (May 1909).

■ Six foot goalkeeper Harry Cotton – who made 139 League and Cup appearances for Port Vale, was signed as cover for Bert Miller and Fred Rathbone during the 1908–09 season when he was given just two League outings when Miller was absent. An ironsmith by trade, Cotton was certainly a sporting fellow who enjoyed fishing, cricket, swimming and athletics, as well as soccer.

COTTON, John

Full-back: 2 apps.

Born: Stoke-on-Trent, 2 March 1930.
Career: POTTERS (amateur, April 1948, professional, May 1952), Crewe Alexandra (October 1955).

■ Both of reserve full-back Jack Cotton's League appearances for the Potters were made in April 1954, in a draw at West Ham and a home defeat by Hull City. After leaving Stoke he played 14 times for Crewe in the Third Division North.

COUPAR, Peter Angus

Centre-forward: 17 apps. 6 goals.

Born: Dundee, 1863.
Died: America, c.1940.
Career: Dundee Our Boys FC, Dundee (1885), POTTERS (August 1889), Dundee (January 1890), Newton Heath (June–September 1892), later emigrated to America.

■ Workmanlike centre-forward Peter Coupar was hoping to make a name for himself in English League football following his transfer from Dundee. But unfortunately he never settled in at the Potteries and returned home after just five months. He was later re-united with his brother (James) at Newton Heath but failed to get a game with the Lancashire club.

COWAN, Thomas

Full-back: 18 apps.

Born: Belshill, Scotland, 28 August 1969.
Career: Netherdale Boys Club, Clyde (professional, July 1988), Rangers (February 1989), Sheffield United (£350,000, August 1991), POTTERS (on loan, October–November 1993), Huddersfield Town (£150,000, March 1994), Burnley (£20,000, March 1999), Cambridge United (on loan, February–March 2000, signed permanently, August 2000), Peterborough United (on loan, January–February 2002), York City (free, July 2002), Dundee (free, August 2003), Carlisle United (free, November 2003), Shrewsbury Town (January 2005), Shrewsbury Town (May 2005).

■ Despite his lack of height (5ft 9in), Tom Cowan could match anyone in the

air and was no mean tackler when competing for the ball on the ground. He made 33 appearances in Scottish football, prior to his transfer to Bramall Lane in 1991, and certainly proved a capable loan signing for the Potters. He later had 165 outings with Huddersfield.

COWDEN, Stuart

Wing-half: 1 app.

Born: Alsager, 1926.
Career: POTTERS (amateur, April 1943, professional, August 1945), Witton Albion (June 1946).

■ 'Ted' Cowden's only competitive game for Stoke City was against Burnley in the third round, first leg FA Cup clash with Burnley at The Victoria Ground in January 1946, when he stood in for Jock Kirton in a 3–1 win. He also played in 41 World War Two games, but after failing to gain a regular place in the senior side (when peactimne football returned in effect in 1945) he was transferred to Witton Albion at the end of the season.

COX, Walter

Right-half: 1 app.

Born: Stoke-on-Trent, September 1860.
Career: Talke Rangers, Burslem Swifts, Stoke St Peter's, POTTERS (player-secretary-manager, June 1883–April 1884).

■ Sturdy wing-half Wally Cox played in Stoke's first-ever FA Cup tie against Manchester in October 1883. He handed over his secretary-manager duties to Harry Lockett (See MANAGERS).

COXON, Thomas

Outside-left: 38 apps. 6 goals

Born: Hanley, Stoke-on-Trent, 10 June 1883.
Died: Cleethorpes, 30 January 1942.
Career: Bradeley, Burslem Port Vale (professional, August 1902), POTTERS (£200, October 1903), Middlesbrough (September 1905), Burslem Port Vale (May 1906), POTTERS (May 1907), Grimsby Town (May 1908), Leyton (£50, August 1910), Grimsby Rovers

(September 1912). Did not play after World War One.

■ Tom Cull was a clever, stocky left-winger who caused defenders plenty of problems with his trickery. Regarded as one of he fastest wingers in Division Two in 1903, he rejoined the potters in 1907 when Port vale faced a financial crisis. He scored 16 goals in 46 League and Cup games for the Vale, claimed six in 63 outings for the Mariners and notched one goal in 11 League games for Middlesbrough.

CRANSON, Ian

Defender: 277+4 apps. 12 goals.

Born: Easington, 2 July 1964.
Career: Ipswich Town (apprentice, July 1980, professional, July 1982), Sheffield Wednesday (£450,000, March 1988), POTTERS (£450,000, July 1989, retired, November 1996), returned to the POTTERS as coach in 2002.

■ Ian Cranson was a vastly experienced professional when he joined the Potters from Sheffield Wednesday for a club record fee in 1989, having previously made 165 appearances for Ipswich Town and 35 for the 'Owls'. Capped five times by England at under-21 level while at Portman Road, he went to Hillsborough, also for £450,000, but never really settled in Yorkshire. He suffered his fair share of injuries during his career, but when fit Cranson was a terrific defender who put his heart and soul into the game. He helped the Potters win the Autoglass Trophy in 1992 and the Second Division title the following year. In 1996, after a tedious, long-term injury, he decided to quit football on medical advice, having netted 15 goals in 481 club games during a fine career.

CROOKS, Garth Anthony, OBE

Forward: 154+10 apps. 53 goals.

Born: Stoke-in-Trent, 10 March 1958.
Career: St Peter's Comprehensive School (Penkhull near Stoke), POTTERS (apprentice, July 1974, professional, March 1976), Tottenham Hotspur (£600,000), West Bromwich Albion (£100,000, July 1985), Charlton Athletic (March 1987), Manchester United (on loan, November 1983–January 1984), retired through injury, May 1990, having already been appointed as Chairman of the PFA (1988), now works for the media, covering Premiership football on radio and TV.

■ They say that Stoke City manager Tony Waddington signed Garth Crooks after watching him kick a ball against a wall outside The Victoria Ground. Whether that story is true or not, Crooks went on to become an exceptionally fine goalscorer in a career that spanned 15 years. He made his League debut against Coventry City in April 1976, and as a 'Potter' was capped four times by England at under-21 level, netting a hat-trick on his first outing against Bulgaria at a foggy Filbert Street in 1979. On leaving Stoke in the summer of 1980 (after rather heated relations with manager Alan Durban) he went on to score 75 goals in 175 outings for Spurs, gaining successive FA Cup winners' medals in 1981 and 1982 as well as collecting a League Cup runners'-up prize in 1983. He then moved to West Bromwich Albion, whose manager Johnny Giles was strengthening his squad following a rather disappointing 1984–85 season. But at that point injuries started to

disrupt Crooks's game and he was out of action for three weeks. He battled on until 1990 before hanging up his boots in favour of reporting on and analysing football matches and players for radio and TV. He scored 129 league goals in 375 matches during his career. Chairman of the PFA in 1988–89, he was awarded the OBE in October 1999 for services to the Institute of Professional Sport.

CROOKS, Paul

Forward: 0+3 apps.

Born: Durham, 12 October 1966.
Career: Bolton Wanderers (apprentice, April 1983), POTTERS (professional, July 1986), Caernarfon Town (August 1987), Carlisle United (briefly, 1988), Rhyl (1989), Bangor City, Blaenau Festiniog Amateurs (after being reinstated as an amateur).

■ Paul Crooks never made an impact at The Victoria Ground and appeared in only three senior games for the Potters (all as substitute) before switching to non-League football.

CROSSLEY, Mark Geoffrey

Goalkeeper: 12 apps.

Born: Barnsley, 16 June 1969.
Career: Nottingham Forest (apprentice, June 1985, professional, July 1987),

Millwall (on loan, February 1998), Middlesbrough (free, July 2000), POTTERS (on loan, November 2002, and again January–May 2003), Fulham (£500,000, August 2003).

■ Goalkeeper Mark Crossley, 6ft tall and weighing almost 16st, made 393 appearances for Nottingham Forest, 13 for Millwall and 31 for Middlesbrough

before having two separate loan spells at The Britannia Stadium, where he replaced, initially, Neil Cutler and then Steve Banks. He represented both England and Wales as a Forest player, capped by the former on three occasions at under-21 level in 1990 and by the latter in one 'B' and eight full internationals. He played in the 1991 FA Cup Final defeat by Tottenham Hotspur, helped Forest win the Zenith Data Systems Cup a year later and in 1994 appeared in 37 League games as the East Midland club reached the Premiership. Powerfully built, brave and an excellent shot-stopper, he was signed by Middlesbrough as cover for Aussie star Mark Schwarzer and joined Fulham as reserve to the Dutch international Edwin van der Saar.

CROSSTHWAITE, Harold

Outside-right: 31 apps.

Born: Stockport, 9 August 1890.
Died: Stockport, 28 November 1939.
Career: Heywood United, Stockport

County (July 1912), POTTERS (£1,250, March 1920), Stockport County (£750, July 1921), Stalybridge Celtic (May 1923, retired, May 1925).

■ Diminutive right-winger Harry Crossthwaite was quick and clever and, despite lacking a goalscoring touch, created plenty of chances for his colleagues. He joined the Potters on transfer-deadline day in 1920 and took over from Jack Stirling, remaining at The Victoria ground until the summer of 1921 when he returned to Edgeley Park. He scored 19 goals in a combined total of 142 League and Cup appearances in his two spells with Stockport, gaining a Third Division North Championship winners' medal in 1922.

CROWE, Dean Anthony

Striker: 33+34 apps. 13 goals

Born: Stockport, 6 June 1979.
Career: POTTERS (apprentice, June 1995, professional, September 1996), Northampton Town (on loan, February–March 2000), Bury (on loan, March–April 2000 and August–September 2000), Luton Town (free, September 2001), York City (on loan, September–October 2003), Oldham Athletic (free, March 2004). Leek Town (May 2004).

■ Despite being only 5ft 5in tall, 'Deano' Crowe is, nevertheless, a very

effective striker whose career record speaks for itself – over 32 goals scored in more than 149 competitive matches (up to May 2005). He did pretty well with the potters and was a big hit with the fans, but when Brian Little moved in as manager his outings were spasmodic and he eventually moved on to pastures new.

CROXTON, Henry

Inside-right: 24 apps. 1 goal.

Born: Biddulph, Staffs, February 1880.
Died: before 1960.
Career: Burslem Park (1888), Port Vale (March 1901), POTTERS (November 1905 with Adrian Capes), Port Vale (December 1908, retired, February 1911).

■ Basically a reserve during his three years with the Potters, Harry Croxton had his best season with the club in 1905–06 when he made 18 senior appearances and scored his only goal, in a 4–0 home League win over Wolves in early January. He made a total of 128 League and FA Cup appearances for the Valiants and netted seven goals, gaining a Staffordshire Cup winners' medal in 1910.

CULL, John Ernest

Outside-right: 80 apps. 10 goals.

Born: Aston, Birmingham, 18 November 1900.

Died: Birmingham, c.1979.
Career: Aston Magna, Shrewsbury Town (1917), POTTERS (£1,000, September 1925), Coventry City (April 1931), Shrewsbury Town again (August 1932), Crewe Alexandra (August 1933), Accrington Stanley (June 1934), Gateshead (July 1935), Aldershot (January–May 1936), retired to work in a steel factory.

■ Jack Cull played local junior football before entering a more established and competitive game at the age of 17. He helped the Potters win the Third Division North title in 1927, but he had to battle hard to retain his place in the side and injuries didn't help his cause. Standing 5ft 7in tall, he could occupy either wing and in all netted 32 goals in a total of 182 League appearances.

CUNLIFFE, Jack

Outside-left: 28 apps. 3 goals.

Born: Wigan, 4 February 1930.
Died: Tunstall, Stoke-on-Trent, 15 November 1975.
Career: Bolton Wanderers (amateur), Leeds United (trialist), Port Vale (professional, December 1950), POTTERS (£2,000, plus Peter Ford and Harry Oscroft, September 1959), Macclesfield Town (September 1960), Stafford Rangers (1963), Buxton (April 1964, retired, May 1965).

■ 'Dickie' Cunliffe played amateur football for Bolton, and after a trial on the left-wing for Leeds he joined Port Vale as a 20-year-old in 1950. A firm favourite with the fans at Vale Park, he scored 51 goals in 283 League appearances for the Valiants, gaining a Third Division North Championship medal and playing in the semi-finals of the FA Cup in 1953–54. He followed up in 1958–59 with a Fourth Division Championship medal before moving down to The Victoria Ground in 1959 and served the Potters for just one season. He was only 45 when he died.

CURTIS, Alan Thomas

Forward: 3 apps.

Born: Rhondda, Glamorgan, 16 May 1954.
Career: Porth Grammar school, Swansea City (professional, July 1972), Leeds United (£350,000, May 1979), Swansea City (£165,000, December 1980), Southampton (£75,000, November 1983), POTTERS (on loan, March 1986), Cardiff City (free, late March 1986), Swansea City (free, October 1989), Barry Town (free, July 1990), Haverfordwest County (retired, May 1994), Swansea City (Football in the Community officer and also Youth coach, Youth Development Officer to May 2005), now employed as a financial advisor for a Life Assurance Company in South Wales.

■ Alan Curtis was almost 32 when he joined Stoke on a months' loan. A Welsh international, capped 35 times at senior level, he made his debut in the centenary match in 1976. He also represented his country in one under-21 and one under-23 international, and in a long and distinguished career in the Football League he netted 116 goals in 570 appearances. He reached the 500 mark in his last outing for Cardiff in 1989. His stay at Elland Road was severely disrupted after twice damaging his right knee, first against Middlesbrough on Boxing Day 1979 and then versus Wolves in October 1980. He was subsequently transferred to Southampton to ease the Yorkshire club's financial plight. He won three Welsh Cup winners' medals, two with Swansea in 1981 and 1982 and one with Cardiff City in 1988. When he joined Swansea for a third time, Curtis said 'I keep turning up at The Vetch Field like a bad penny.' He is the nephew of Roy Paul, also a Welsh international, who won the FA Cup with Manchester City in 1956.

CUTLER, Neil Anthony

Goalkeeper: 77+5 apps.

Born: Cannock, Staffs, 3 September 1976.
Career: West Bromwich Albion (apprentice, June 1992, professional, September 1993), Chester City (on loan, March 1996), Crewe Alexandra (free, July 1996), Chester City (on loan,

August–September 1996, signed permanently, July 1998), Aston Villa (November 1999), Oxford United (on loan, December 2000–January 2001), POTTERS (free, July 2001), Swansea City (on loan, February–March 2003), Stockport County (free, July 2004), Rotherham United (free, August 2005).

■ Unable to break into West Bromwich Albion's first team despite some impressive displays in reserve and friendly matches, Neil Cutler – who was capped by England at schoolboy and youth team levels – finally made his

League debut in 1996 with Chester City. He failed to get a senior game with Crewe and returned to Chester in 1998 where he established himself in the side, producing excellent form. So much so that Aston Villa secured his services as cover for David James and he appeared in the 4–0 home Premiership win over Middlesbrough in February 2000. He did well in his first season with the Potters, helping them gain promotion from the Second Division.

DA COSTA, Hugo Alexandre

Defender: 2+2 apps.

Born: Tramagal, Portugal, 4 November 1973.
Career: Benfica (professional, March 1992), POTTERS (trialist, June 1996, on loan/non-contract, August 1996), Benfica (October 1996).

■ Hugo Da Costa joined Stoke after impressing manager Lou Macari during summer trials at The Victoria Ground. Tall, dark haired, strongly-built with good ball distribution, he deputised for both Ian Cranson and John Dreyer before returning to Benfica.

DADASON, Rikhardur

Striker: 22+27 apps. 12 goals.

Born: Reykjavik, Iceland, 26 April 1972.
Career: Fram, Iceland (professional, April 1990), Knattspyrufelag Reykjavik, Iceland

(August 1996), Kalamata, Iceland (December 1996), Knattspyrufelag Reykjavik (May 1997), Viking Fotballklubb, Norway (June 1998), POTTERS (free, October 2000), Lillestrom Sportsklubb, Norway (July 2002).

■ One of the tallest players ever to appear for the Potters in the Football League, 6ft 4in striker Rikki Dadason was already an experienced Icelandic international with five youth, 10 under-21 and almost 40 senior caps to his credit when he arrived at The Britannia Stadium. He had also scored 100 goals in 201 League games in Iceland and Norway, including 49 in just 69 outings for Viking. Although used half the time as a substitute, he had an excellent first season with Stoke, scoring eight goals in 35 games, including a dramatic late winner in the League Cup against Barnsley that set up a mouth-watering fourth-round home tie with Liverpool. Unfortunately, it was a case of 'what might have been' for the talented Icelander the following season when he struggled with a serious knee, which restricted him to just 14 outings. Having taken his tally of full caps to 51, he left the club when new boss Steve Cotterill took over in 2002.

DALE, James Joseph

Wing-half: 4 apps.

Born: Motherwell, July 1869.
Career: Carluke, Bellshill, Sunderland (briefly, during season 1893–94), POTTERS (June 1894), Southampton St Mary's (October 1895–April 1896).

Scotsman Jimmy Dale was a solid wing-half who was signed as a cover for fellow countryman David Christie. He spent just over a season with the Potters before making five appearances for Southampton.

DALY, Gerard Anthony

Midfield: 25+5 apps. 2 goals

Born: Cabra, Dublin, 30 April 1954.
Career: Bohemians, Manchester United (£20,000, April 1973), Derby County (£175,000, March 1977), New England Teamen (on loan, two spells, May 1978

and May 1979), Coventry City (August 1980), Leicester City (on loan, January 1983), Birmingham City (August 1984), Shrewsbury Town (October 1985), POTTERS (£15,000, March 1987), Doncaster Rovers (free, July 1988), Telford United (free, assistant player-manager-coach, December 1989, then full-time manager, August 1990–September 1993).

■ Republic of Ireland international Gerry Daly emerged as one of Tommy Docherty's bright young players at Old Trafford, a brilliant, energetic midfielder whose skilful displays made him an instant hit with the fans. Born in the same Dublin suburb as Johnny Giles, he made over 140 appearances in almost four years for Manchester United before joining Derby. He helped the Reds regain their First Division status in 1975 and played in the 1976 FA Cup Final defeat by Southampton. An astute penalty taker, he missed only one in 17 at United and only three in his entire career, Daly made over 550 League and Cup appearances at club level, scoring almost 100 goals. In League action alone his record was 88 goals in 472 outings. The recipient of 47 full caps for the Republic of Ireland (13 goals scored), Daly also played once for his country's under-21 side. Signed as a short-term replacement for the sidelined Tony Kelly, he was unfortunately injured on his debut and, in fact, his whole spell at The Victoria Ground was dogged by bad luck and injury. As player-manager of Telford he was a thorn in Stoke's side over two FA Cup campaigns! He was succeeded at Telford by another ex-Potter, Wayne Clarke.

DANIELS, George

Half-back: 2 apps.

Born: Winsford, Cheshire, June 1913.
Career: Leeds United (amateur, 1931), Altrincham (amateur), POTTERS (professional, July 1933), Torquay United (October 1935), Crystal Palace (May 1937), Hartlepool United (June 1939), Carlisle United (briefly, retired during World War Two).

■ Reserve half-back George Daniels made just two League appearances for Stoke during a his two-year stay with the club, taking the place of Arthur Tutin in games against Middlesbrough (home) and Blackburn Rovers (away) in the latter stages of the 1933–34 season.

DANIELSSON, Einar Thor

Midfield: 4+5 apps. 1 goal.

Born: Iceland, 19 January 1970.
Career: Knattspyrufelag Reykjavik, Iceland, POTTERS (on loan, November 1999–January 2000).

■ Signed on loan by Potters boss Gudjon Thordarson during his home country's close season, Einar Danielsson, who had already been capped 18 times by Iceland, played on the left of midfield during his two-month stay at The Britannia Stadium. He made a dream start by scoring a wonderful individual goal on his debut in a 4–0 away win over Wycombe Wanderers. A fine crosser of the ball, he certainly had the skill but lacked determination.

DAVIES, Lloyd

Outside-left and defender: 37 apps. 3 goals.

Born: Cefn Mawr near Ruabon, 23 February 1877.
Died: Cefn Mawr, 10 October 1957.
Career: Rhosymedre St John's (August 1898), Druids FC, Ruabon (August 1899), POTTERS (professional, July 1903), Wellington Town (free, May 1904), Swindon Town (£100, May 1905), POTTERS (£100, December 1905), Northampton Town (£200, May 1908), Reading (August 1920), Northampton Town (coach, 1921), after quitting football, despite the threat of bankruptcy, he ran a successful tobacconist shop in Cefn Mawr for many years.

■ Lloyd Davies, the youngest of six brothers, five of whom played senior football with four of them representing Wales at senior level, started out as an orthodox left-winger but was successfully converted into a defender after joining the Potters in 1903. Able to play as a full-back or centre-half, he had two spells at The Victoria Ground, and after leaving the Potters second time round he became the great Herbert Chapman's first-ever signing (for Northampton). Davies was also the first Northampton player to win a full cap, representing Wales against Scotland in 1908. He later returned to Northampton as coach shortly after the club had gained entry in to the Football League. A totally committed player, Davies was a Welsh Cup finalist in 1901 (with Druids), won 18 full caps for Wales (four as a Stoke player), represented the Southern League against the Irish League in 1914 and collected a Southern League Championship medal and runners'-up prize in 1909 and 1911 respectively with Northampton, for whom he made over 300 Southern League appearances.
NB: Davies's son, Ronald, was a reserve with Manchester United in the 1940s.

DAVIES, Harold Augustus

Inside-forward: 410 apps. 101 goals.

Born: Gainsborough, 29 January 1904.
Died: Blurton, Stoke-on-Trent, 23 April 1975.
Career: Bamfords Athletic (1920), POTTERS (June 1922), Huddersfield Town (May 1929), POTTERS (February 1932), Port Vale (February 1938, £250, plus Tom Ward, retired, April 1939), remained in Stoke-on-Trent until his death.

■ Harry Davies averaged a goal every four games for Stoke, whom he served in two separate spells in the 1920s and 1930s. An inside-forward, he had loads of ability and always looked the part on the field, often taking the ball in precarious positions and then opening up the play with either a splendidly struck pass, a swift turn of foot or a delicate manoeuvre. A class act, he gave the fans plenty to cheer about. Davies came to Stoke's attention while playing intermediate football in Uttoxeter. The son of the former Hull City and Wolves player of the same name, he made his League debut in the Staffordshire derby against West Bromwich Albion in September 1923. He held his place in the side until his transfer to Huddersfield, who recruited him to replace Clem Stephenson who had become manager at Leeds Road. Davies had helped Stoke climb back into the Second Division in 1927 by netting 15 vital goals. Twice selected to represent Staffordshire FA, in 1929 he came very close to winning a full England cap, being chosen as a reserve in a trial match at Sheffield, but in the summer (after leaving Stoke) he went on tour to

South Africa with the FA party, playing in two matches. With the 'Terriers', Davies had two successful seasons, playing in the losing 1930 FA Cup Final against Arsenal. He returned to Stoke early in 1932 after finding himself languishing in the reserves at Leeds Road and was instrumental in seeing the Potters win the Second Division Championship in 1933. He remained a permanent fixture in the Potters' first XI, and pushed his appearance total past the 400 mark and his goal-haul over 100, reaching the century mark with a strike in a 3–1 win over Birmingham in February 1936. After a season in the second team at The Victoria Ground (Jimmy Westland had taken over at inside-left), Davies moved to Port Vale in a deal that brought Tom Ward to Stoke. Besides being a fine footballer, Davies was also an extremely good billiards player and recorded seven three-figure breaks in his time, with a high of 135.

DAVIES, Harold Donald

Outside-right or left: 1 app.

Born: Pendleton, 13 March 1892.
Died: Munich, Germany, 6 February 1958.
Career: Lancashire Wanderers (1908), Smithills FC (1910), Northern Nomads (August 1912), POTTERS (amateur, October 1913), Port Vale (amateur, July 1914), Northern Nomads (season 1919–20), became a prominent journalist and broadcaster who lost his life in the Munich air disaster.

■ Harry Davies could play on either wing. An England amateur international, he was quick over short distances but perhaps lacked the ability required at a higher level. He appeared in one Southern League game for Stoke, in a 5–1 home win over Treharris in November 1913.

DAVIES, William Charles

Winger: 17 apps.

Born: Forden near Welshpool, 2 April 1883.
Died: 1960.
Career: Rhayader & Llandrindod Wells Schools, Knighton FC, Shrewsbury Town (1903–05), POTTERS (December 1905), Crystal Palace (October 1907), West Bromwich Albion (August 1908), Crystal Palace (September 1910–April 1915). Did not play after World War One.

■ A strong, bold performer who possessed exquisite ball control and excelled with pin-point crosses, Billy Davies was one of the first footballers to emerge from the newly-formed Mid-Wales League. Like Lloyd Davies, he was a Welsh international who gained four full caps between 1908–14, but alas none with the Potters who beat off approaches from the FA Cup holders Aston Villa to secure his signature in 1905. When in the first team at The Victoria Ground, he certainly made an impression, and moreso with Palace where he linked up with Jimmy 'Ginger' Williams to form the only 'Welsh left-wing' in top-class football. He netted 23

goals in 208 games during his two spells with the London club.

* Davies would have gained another cap (versus England in 1913) but the notice informing him that he had been selected to replace Ted Vizard (Bolton) did not arrive in time for him to get to the ground in Bristol.

DAVIES, William

Inside-forward: 31 apps. 16 goals.

Born: Longton, Stoke-on-Trent, April 1886.
Died: Stoke-on-Trent, 1942.
Career: Newcastle Rangers (Staffs), POTTERS (July 1907, retired through injury, May 1909).

■ Nicknamed 'Longton Billy' by his friends and colleagues, Davies was a useful inside-forward, serving Stoke for two seasons, during which time his goals per games ratio was excellent. Unfortunately, a serious knee injury (suffered in an FA Cup tie versus Sheffield Wednesday) forced him into early retirement at the age of 23. He was a very popular fellow around the Potteries.

DAVIS, Samuel Storey

Full-back: 2 apps.

Born: Marsden near Whitburn Colliery, Tyne and Wear, 25 May 1900.
Died: 1988.
Career: Marsden Council School,

Whitburn FC, POTTERS (amateur, November 1923, professional, January 1924), Tranmere Rovers (May 1925), Accrington Stanley (August 1926), Spennymoor United (September 1926–May 1928).

■ A reserve full-back, shaky at times, Sammy Davies – a member of the Marsden School XI – made only two first-team appearances for the Potters, replacing the injured Tom Brittleton in home and away League games against South Shields in March 1924. A tedious knee injury disrupted his career and in all he played in only nine League games during his career.

DAWSON, Thomas

Defender: 24 apps.

Born: Springwell, County Durham, 15 December 1901.
Died: Washington, County Durham, 30 November 1977.
Career: Washington Colliery (1919), Chopwell Institute (Northern League), POTTERS (professional, June 1924), Clapton Orient (free, May 1932), Gateshead (August 1933, retired, May 1934; remained at the club as first assistant trainer and then head trainer).

■ One-time miner in the North East, Tommy Dawson was a versatile defender with good heading ability and a strong right-foot. He spent eight years at The Victoria Ground and made only 24 first-team appearances due to the strength of the team at the club. He did, though, skipper the reserves for six of those eight seasons and could well have been a regular with any other club if he had chosen to move on. He had 20 senior outings for both Orient and Gateshead.
* Two of Tommy's relatives also played professionally: Edward Dawson for Manchester City, Bristol City and Gateshead (1934–48) and George Dawson, who played 123 League games for Preston North End (1912–21).

DE GOEY, EDUARD FRANCISCUS

Goalkeeper: 55 apps.

Born: Gouda, Holland, 20 December 1966.
Career: FC Gouda, Holland, Sparta Rotterdam, Holland (April 1984), Feyenoord, Holland (July 1990), Chelsea (£2.25 million, July 1997), POTTERS (free, August 2003).

■ Giant goalkeeper Ed De Goey, who was 6ft 6in in height and once tipped the scales at 15st, represented Holland in 17 under-21 and 31 full internationals, reaching the peak of his form in the late 1990s. He made 145 League appearances for Sparta and 201 for Feyenoord before

embarking on a career in the Premiership. Commanding in the box and a fine shot-stopper, he was the first choice at Stamford Bridge for virtually three seasons, until losing his place to the Italian Carlo Cudicini in 2000 after 179 outings for the Blues, with whom he won the League Cup, European Cup-winners' Cup and Super Cup (all in 1998) and the FA Cup and Charity Shield two years later. After almost two years of non-activity he moved down the League ladder to Stoke at the age of 33.

DEAKIN, Jack

Centre-half: 2 apps.

Born: Stoke-on-Trent, August 1873.
Died: Stoke-on-Trent, c.1950.
Career: Dresden United, POTTERS (August 1898), Hanley Swifts (July 1899).

■ Jack Deakin played twice in Stoke's defence in the 1898–99 season, deputising for Alf Wood.

DENNY, Jay

No appearances.

Born: Los Angeles, US, 1986.
Career: POTTERS (apprentice, professional, released, May 2005).

■ Jay Denny was named as a substitute for the Potters several times during the 2004–05 season but failed to make a first-team appearance. A member of the USA under-20 squad, he also played for his country at under-17 level against Japan in Florida.

DEPLEDGE, Joseph

Defender: 5 apps.

Born: Sheffield, 15 April 1897.
Died: c.1965.
Career: Rotherham United, POTTERS (£130, March 1923), Mansfield Town (free, May 1924).

■ Joe Depledge joined Stoke as a reserve defender in 1923. He made just five first-team appearances

during his 14-month stay at The Victoria Ground. He helped Mansfield win the Midland League Championship in 1925.

DEVINE, John Anthony

Midfield: 16 apps. 1 goal.

Born: Dublin, 11 November 1958,
Career: St John Bosco Juniors (Dublin), Arsenal (amateur, January 1974, apprentice, November 1974, professional, October 1976), Norwich City (free, June 1983), POTTERS (free, November 1985), IK Start, Norway (August 1986–March 1988), Chelmsford City (non-contract, April–May 1988), East Bengal, India (player-coach, June 1988–January 1989), Shelbourne, Northern Ireland (February–April 1989), Shamrock Rovers (1989–90).

■ Manager Mick Mills brought capable midfielder Devine to The Victoria Ground on a free transfer as a straight replacement for Alan Hudson in 1985, but the Dubliner's career at Stoke was ruined when he sadly broke his leg in five places during a game at Brighton on 15 March 1986. He regained full fitness and played on in Norway, India and with Shamrock Rovers until his retirement in 1990. He joined Arsenal as a 15-year-old and made 103 senior appearances for the Gunners before adding a further 69 to his tally with the Canaries. While at Highbury he played in two losing FA Cup Finals and gained a League Cup winners' medal with Norwich in 1985. He was also capped 12 times by the Republic of Ireland, having played twice for the under-21 side and also for his country's youth team (as captain). He was a keen guitarist and vocalist (he recorded 'The Morning After The Night before' but it was not released) and married the runner-up in the Miss Universe contest in 1981, who, seven years later, presented the Eurovision Song contest.

DEVLIN, Mark Andrew

Utility: 46+19 apps. 2 goals

Born: Irvine, Ayrshire, 18 January 1973.
Career: Kilmarnock Boy's Club, POTTERS (apprentice, April 1989, professional, April 1991), Raith Rovers (trialist, during 1991–92), Exeter City (October 1997), Northwich Victoria (January 1999).

■ Scottish youth international utility player Mark Devlin was introduced to first-team football by Potters boss Alan Ball while still an apprentice. This was in February 1991 when he came on as a substitute against Chester City. He had to work hard to get in the first team but when selected he knitted well into the Potters' style of play, but unfortunately he couldn't hold down a regular place in the side. His manager at Exeter was the former Stoke City goalkeeper Peter Fox.

DICKIE, George

Outside-right: 1 app.

Born: Montrose, Scotland, March 1905.
Career: Forres Mechanics, POTTERS (August 1925), St Johnstone (October 1925).

■ Reserve winger George Dickie's only League game for Stoke came in September 1925 when he deputised for Bert Ralphs in a 7–2 defeat at Oldham Athletic.

DICKIE, William Cunningham

Half-back: 40 apps.

Born: Kilmarnock, Scotland, 2 May 1893.
Died: Sittingbourne, Kent, 15 January 1960.
Career: Riccarton FC (1909), Kilbirnie Ladeside (1910), Kilmarnock (May 1912), guest for Chelsea, Everton, Southport and Wrexham during World War One, Chelsea (signed, £500, June 1919), POTTERS (£2,000, April 1921), Sittingbourne (May 1922), Sheppey United (season 1923–24), Sittingbourne (coach, seasons 1924–26).

■ A block cutter by trade, and a Sergeant Instructor during World War One, Bill Dickie was a tall, fair-haired, wholehearted Scottish defender, whose best position was centre-half. As a guest player for Chelsea he gained a London Victory Cup winners' medal in April 1919 when Fulham were defeated 3–0 in the Final. Unfortunately, Dickie could not hold down a first-team place at any of his three major clubs and made only 40 appearances for Chelsea.

DICKINSON, Carl

Defender: 0+1 app.

Born: 1 March 1987.
Career: Derby County (Academy), POTTERS (junior, April 2002, apprentice, April 2003, professional, March 2004).

■ Carl Dickinson made his senior debut for the Potters as a second-half substitute in the League game against Coventry City in December 2004, which they won 1–0.

DICKSON, William Alexander

Centre-forward: 134 apps. 48 goals

Born: Crail, Fife, 27 August 1866.
Died: Stoke-on-Trent, 1 June 1910.
Career: Dumfries Schools, Dumbarton (briefly), Dundee, Dundee Strathmore (1885), Sunderland (July 1888), Aston Villa (August 1889), POTTERS (July 1892, retired through injury, May 1897, then coach and later directors, 1907, also a licensee in the Potteries.

■ Billy Dickson, a striker of the highest quality, hit four goals in his only international outing for Scotland in a 10–2 win over Ireland in 1888. He skippered Aston Villa on several occasions, played in the 1892 FA Cup Final defeat by West Bromwich Albion and struck 34 goals in 64 senior games for the Birmingham-based club before moving to Stoke.
NB: Dickson's brother, Charles, played for Preston North End, Newcastle United and Loughborough in the 1890s.

DINNING, Anthony

Midfield: 8 apps.

Born: Wallsend, Tyne & Wear, 12 April 1975.

Career: Newcastle United (apprentice, May 1991, professional, October 1993), Stockport County (free, June 1994), Wolverhampton Wanderers (£600,000, September 2000), Wigan Athletic (£750,000, September 2001), POTTERS (on loan, March–May 2002), Walsall (on loan, November–December 2003), Blackpool (on loan, January–March 2004), Ipswich Town (loan, August–September 2004), Bristol City (free, October 2004), Port Vale (loan, March–May 2005).

■ When he arrived at Stoke on loan from Wigan in 2002, Tony Dinning was already a vastly experienced professional with over 250 senior appearances under his belt. He contributed well in his eight games for the Potters before returning to The JBB Stadium. A second Division Championship winner with Wigan in 2003, he helped the Latics win the LDV Vans Trophy when Blackpool beat Southend United 2–0 at The Millennium Stadium the following season.

DIXON, Lee Michael

Right-back: 88 apps. 5 goals.

Born: Manchester, 17 March 1964.
Career: Manchester & District Schools, Burnley (apprentice, May 1980, professional, July 1982), Chester City (free, February 1984), Bury (free, July

Lee Dixon

1985), POTTERS (£40,000, July 1986), Arsenal (£400,000, January 1988, retired, June 2002), became a soccer analyst on TV.

■ Lee Dixon followed Steve Bould to Highbury from Stoke. A fine attacking player with strength, ability and courage, he made his debut for the Potters in the home League game against Birmingham City in August 1986, was an ever-present in his first season and all his senior games for the club were consecutive. He spent over 14 years with the Gunners, amassed 621 appearances (28 goals scored) and won medals galore, for two League Championships, two Premiership titles, three FA Cup wins, victory in the European Cup-winners' Cup Final and two FA Charity Shield successes. He also gained 21 full and 4 'B' caps for England, and when he retired his career appearance record (at club and international level) stood at 860 (40 goals).

DIXON, Robert Hewitson

Goalkeeper: 200 apps.

Born: Easington near Whitehaven, 30 August 1904.
Died: Stoke-on-Trent, c.1980.
Career: West Stanley, POTTERS (January 1923), West Ham United (March 1929, retired, April 1932), returned to Stoke where he became licensee of The Prince of Wales pub in Sandford Hill while also renting out holiday caravans at Lytham St Anne's.

■ Bob Dixon was a courageous goalkeeper who was spotted by an eagle-eyed scout plying with West Stanley, the club that produced another fine 'keeper in Dick Herron. Dixon, who was recruited as cover for Les Scott, bided his time in the reserves, establishing himself as the first choice within a year. Despite fierce competition from Scottish international Kenny Campbell, who was signed in March 1923, he went on to accumulate exactly 200 senior appearances for the club, helping the Potters win the Third Division North Championship in 1926–27 when he missed only one game, while also keeping 18 clean sheets. Dixon, who was born within sight of the coal-face, understudied England 'keeper Ted Hufton at Upton Park, having one decent spell in the senior side (65 outings in all) before he was forced to quit the game with a knee injury. At this juncture he returned to Stoke to become a publican. Just before World War Two Dixon turned down a coaching job in Turkey. His wife, Daisy, played football and cricket for England Ladies.

DOBING, Peter Alan

Forward: 367+5 apps. 94 goals.

Born: Manchester, 1 December 1938.
Career: Crewe Rangers (during season 1953–54, Blackburn Rovers (amateur, April 1954, professional, December 1955), Manchester City (July 1961), POTTERS (£37,500, August 1963, retired through injury, May 1973), became a pottery worker in Longton, later ran his own business selling crockery to hotels and restaurants and still lives in Stoke.

■ Signed by manager Tony Waddington for what was to prove a bargain fee a week or so after Stoke had gained promotion to the First Division, Peter Dobing was, without doubt, a quality player. He could occupy a number of positions in the forward-line and became a firm favourite with the fans at The Victoria Ground. His father was a Rugby League professional, but it

Peter Dobing

was at soccer that Dobing junior excelled. He scored 104 goals in 205 League and Cup games for the Ewood Park side, collecting an FA Cup runners'-up medal in 1960. He followed that up by netting 32 times in 94 competitive games for Manchester City and then did the business with the Potters. Dobing, who was capped seven times at under-23 level by England and also represented the Football League on three occasions (scoring a hat-trick against the League of Ireland in Dublin), captained Stoke to victory in the 1972 League Cup Final at Wembley, having earlier collected a runners'-up medal in the same competition in his first season at The Victoria Ground. He gave Stoke City football club 10 years' excellent service. Unfortunately, Dobing's disciplinary record left a lot to be desired, and in 1970 he served a nine-week suspension, which was an English record at the time, although that ban didn't affect Dobing (or Stoke) as the player was suffering from a broken leg at the time! Besides being a footballer, Dobing was also a very competent cricketer and once came on as 12th man for Lancashire against Yorkshire in the County Championship.

Alan Dodd

DODD, Alan

Defender: 409+7 apps. 4 goals.

Born: Stoke-on-Trent, 20 September 1953. Career: POTTERS (apprentice, April 1969, professional, October 1970), Wolverhampton Wanderers (£40,000, November 1982), POTTERS (January 1985), Elfsborg, Sweden (July 1985), GAIS Gothenburg, Sweden, Elfsborg (again), Port Vale (on loan, December 1986), Cork City, Landskrona Bols, Sweden, later with Rocester, Goldenhill Wanderers, Rocester again (as player-coach, season 1992–93), Ball Haye Green Working Men's Club.

■ When he was declared ready for first-team action, Alan Dodd had to fight for a place in Stoke's League side with the likes of Denis Smith and Alan Bloor, but he battled on gamely and professionally and eventually established himself in the side in 1973. He amassed a fine set of statistics for the club: over 400 appearances in two spells, including a consecutive run of 102 in the League between January 1976 and April 1978, having joined the junior ranks at The Victoria Ground on leaving school in 1969. He made his first-team debut in November 1972 and became a class player with a lot of skill, being strong in both aerial and ground confrontations. Despite his producing some superb displays for the Potters, he never gained full England honours, collecting just six under-23 caps for his bold and brave efforts. Nevertheless, as a club-man 'Doddy' was quite magnificent. After more than 13 years at Stoke he moved to Molineux in 1982 and helped Wolves win promotion to the First Division, but after 99 outings for the Black Country team he returned to Stoke under manager Bill Asprey early in 1985, initially on a monthly contract. He played two games for Port Vale.

DONALDSON, O'Neill McKay

Striker: 2 apps.

Born: Birmingham, 24 November 1969. Career: Hinckley Town (1989), Shrewsbury Town (free, November 1991), Doncaster rovers (free, August 1994), Mansfield Town (on loan, December 1996–January 1995), Sheffield Wednesday (£50,000, January 1994), Oxford United (on loan, January–February 1998), POTTERS (on loan, March–May 1998).

■ A pacy, enthusiastic 6ft striker, O'Neill Donaldson scored 18 goals in 68 competitive games during his senior career, which spanned seven years. He had his best spell at Gay Meadow (4 goals in 29 outings) and was recruited by the Potters as cover for Dean Crowe and Peter Thorne

DONOWA, Brian Louie

Outside-right or left: 4+1 apps. 1 goal.

Born: Ipswich, 24 September 1964.
Career: Ipswich Boys, Norwich City (apprentice, September 1980, professional, September 1982), POTTERS

(on loan, January 1986), Deportivo La Coruna, Spain (£40,000, February 1986), Willem II Tilburg, Holland, Ipswich Town (August 1989), Bristol City (£50,000, August 1990), Birmingham City (£50,000, August 1991), Burnley (on loan, January 1993), Crystal Palace (on loan, March 1993), Shrewsbury Town (on loan, January–February 1994), Walsall (on loan, October–November 1986), Peterborough United (free, December 1996), Walsall (free, August 1997), Ayr United (December 1997), later with Forest Green Rovers.

■ A fast-raiding winger, Louie Donowa came to Stoke on a month's loan and scored on his debut in a 3–2 win at Millwall when he replaced Mickey Adams on the right-flank. Capped three times by England at under-21 level, he gained a Milk Cup winners' medal with the Canaries in 1985. After spells in Spain and Holland he moved back to the East coast with Ipswich and, thereafter, travelled around the country, eventually moving into non-League football after amassing more than 350 first-team appearances.

DORIGO, Anthony Robert

Left-back: 39+2 apps.

Born: Melbourne, Australia, 31 December 1965.
Career: Birmingham junior football, Aston Villa (apprentice 1981, professional January 1982), Chelsea (£475,000, July 1987), Leeds United (£300,000, May 1991), Torino (free, June 1997), Derby County (free, October 1998), POTTERS (free, July 2000, retired, May 2002), entered media work with TV companies, covering football matches in the English Premiership and Italy's Serie 'A', also involved with property development in Portugal.

■ Tony Dorigo has three different passports – Australian, Italian and British. An efficient and steady defender, he won seven England under-21 caps while with Aston Villa, who gave him a trial after he had pestered the club to answer his letters! He made his League debut as a 'sub' on the last day of the 1983–84 season against Ipswich Town and gained a regular place in the side the following season. After joining Chelsea for a record fee he skippered the England under-21s and added four

more intermediate caps to his tally. He also played in seven 'B' and 15 full internationals for England, helped Chelsea win both the Second Division title (1989) and the Full Member's Cup (1990), scoring one of the finest goals ever seen at Wembley, the winner in the Final of the latter competition against Middlesbrough. In his spell with Leeds, Dorigo (nicknamed 'Aussie') gained both First Division Championship and FA Charity Shield medals in 1992. He added know-how and experience to the Potters' defence and certainly gave a good account of himself during his time at The Britannia Stadium. He retired in 2002 with well over 650 senior appearances under his belt, including 30 in Italy's Serie 'A'.

DOWD, Henry William

Goalkeeper: 3 apps.

Born: Salford, Manchester, 4 July 1938.
Career: Blackley Imperial Chemical Industries FC, Manchester City (professional, July 1960), POTTERS (on loan, October–November 1969), Charlton Athletic (on loan, August–September 1970), Oldham Athletic (December 1970, retired, June 1974), later worked in the brewery trade and was area manager for JW Lees (Middleton).

Harry Dowd had a fine career that spanned 14 years, from 1960 to 1974. He appeared in more than 200 first-team games during his time at Maine Road, which incorporated a loan spell with Stoke when he deputised for Gordon Banks. He won the Second Division Championship (1965–66) and the FA Cup (1969) with Manchester City, for whom he made 219 senior appearances, scoring one goal in the 1–1 draw against Bury in February 1964 when he was switched to the wing following an injury. He retired after playing in 131 games for the Oldham and helped the Latics win the Third Division Championship in 1973–74.

DOWDS, Peter

Utility: 24 apps.

Born: Johnstone, Renfrewshire, 12 December 1867.
Died: Glasgow, 2 September 1895.

Career: Broxburn Shamrock, Celtic (February 1889), Aston Villa (May 1892), POTTERS (July 1893), Celtic (May 1894–September 1895).

■ Rather stone-faced, Peter Dowds was a quality footballer. Unhurried in his ways, he was able to play in any outfield position, but preferred to line-up as a wing-half or centre-half. He took over from John Proctor in 1893–94. He was an artist with the ball, always in control of the situation, always displaying a full range of tricks and graces and very creative in the process. Capped once by Scotland against Ireland in 1892, he had two good spells with Celtic, notching 19 goals in 49 games and gaining a Scottish Cup winners' medal in 1892. A heavy drinker, he died following a chest complaint.

DOWNING, Keith Gordon

Midfield: 22+2 apps.

Born: Oldbury, West Midlands, 23 July 1965.
Career: Oldbury & Warley junior football, Chelsea (apprentice, season 1981–82), Mile Oak Rovers, Tamworth (amateur, August 1982), Notts County (free, professional, May 1985), Wolverhampton Wanderers (free, August 1987), Birmingham City (free, July 1993), POTTERS (August 1994), Cardiff City (free, August 1995), Hereford United (free, October 1995, retired, May 1997), became a representative for a Dudley publishing company, returned to Hereford United as player-coach (June 1998), Wolverhampton Wanderers (Youth team manager-coach, March 1999).

■ Nicknamed 'psycho', Keith Downing was a hard-working, impetuous midfielder who was often in trouble with referees for his over-robust style of play. But that was his nature; he was totally committed to playing football and gave his all each and every time he took the field. He had an unsuccessful spell with Chelsea as a teenager and was almost 20 when he signed professional forms for Notts County in 1985. He appeared in 228 games for Wolves, helping them win both the Third and Fourth Division Championships (in

successive seasons) and the Sherpa Van Trophy. In his 12 months at Stoke he was certainly committed but, after leaving, slowly wound down his career with spasmodic outings for Cardiff and Hereford, although he did help the Bulls reach the Third Division play-offs in 1996 (under his former Molineux boss, Graham Turner).

DOYLE, Joseph Brian

Full-back: 19 apps.

Born: Manchester, 15 July 1930.
Died: Cheshire, 22 December 1990.
Career: Salford Docks (1945), Lostock Green (1949), POTTERS (professional, March 1951), Exeter City (April 1954), Bristol Rovers (August 1957–June 1959), Carlisle United (coach, early 1960s), Workington (manager, July 1968, retired, May 1969), Blackpool (coach, season 1971–62), Stockport County (manager, March 1972–May 1974).

■ A strong-tackling, resourceful full-back, Brian Doyle played in less than 20 first-team games for Stoke during the early 1950s, yet after leaving The Victoria Ground he made 104 senior appearances for the 'Grecians' and 43 for Bristol Rovers before retiring two months before his 39th birthday. As a manager, he saw Workington finish 12th in the Fourth Division but failed miserably at Edgley Park as Stockport ended up as the bottom club in the Football League in 1974.

DOYLE, Michael

Defender: 128 apps. 6 goals

Born: Manchester, 25 November 1946.
Career: Manchester City (apprentice, April 1962, professional, May 1964), POTTERS (£50,000, June 1978), Bolton Wanderers (£10,000, January 1982), Rochdale (August 1983, retired, May 1984), became sales manager for the sports company Slazenger, also commentated on local radio, now lives in Ashton-under-Lyne.

■ Mick Doyle had a fine playing career that spanned 20 years from 1964 to 1984. For Manchester City he appeared in 562 competitive games (448 in the League), gained five full caps for England, collected eight more at under-23 level and twice represented the Football League. He was the recipient of winners' medals for triumphs in both the Second and First Division League Championships (1966 and 1968 respectively), the FA Cup (1969), two League Cup Finals (1970 and 1976), the European Cup Winners' Cup (also in 1970) and two FA Charity Shields (1968 and 1973). He also received a collection of runners'-up prizes as well. Manager Alan Durban, who had played against

Doyle on a number of occasions, was responsible for bringing the respected defender to The Victoria Ground and it was money well spent. In a little over three seasons with the Potters he made almost 130 senior appearances before falling out with boss Richie Barker after a game against Manchester United. He never wore a Stoke jersey again, and early in 1982 he was transferred to Bolton Wanderers. In his first two games for the Trotters he conceded an own goal and was then sent off! Doyle finished his career with Rochdale and finally hung up his boots with more than 700 senior appearances under his belt (627 in the Football League).

DRAYCOTT, William Levi

Utility: 2 apps.

Born: Newhall near Derby, 15 February 1869.
Died: c.1950.
Career: POTTERS (July 1899), Burlsem Port Vale (July 1890), POTTERS (June 1891), Burton Wanderers (June 1894), Newton Heath (May 1896), Bedminster (May 1899), Bristol Rovers (August 1900), Wellingborough (July 1901), Luton Town (August 1902–April 1903).

■ Bill Draycott, who failed to make the senior side during his first spell with the Potters, moved to neighbours Port Vale as a right-winger and helped them share the Staffordshire Charity Cup success in 1891. He was re-signed to boost the squad at The Victoria Ground, but his debut at inside-right was one to forget as Stoke crashed 9–3 to Darwen. Over the next three years Draycott, a hard worker, had only one more outing (at left-half) before leaving the club for Burton Wanderers. During his career he appeared in well over 200 first-team matches, including 95 for Newton Heath and 70 in the Southern League.

DRYDEN, Richard Andrew

Defender: 12+3 apps.

Born: Stroud, Gloucestershire, 14 June 1969.
Career: Bristol Rovers (apprentice, June 1985, professional, July 1987), Exeter City (on loan, September–October 1988, signed for £10,000, March 1989), Notts County (£250,000, August 1991), Plymouth Argyle (on loan, November–December 1992), Birmingham City (£165,000, March 1993), Bristol City (£140,000, December 1994), Southampton (£150,000, August 1996), POTTERS (on loan, November 1999, and again March–May 2000), Northampton Town (on loan, September–October 2000), Swindon Town (on loan, November–December 2001), Luton Town (free, February 2001), Scarborough (August 2002), Tamworth (assistant manager-coach, 2004–05).

■ A forgotten man at Southampton, Richard Dryden arrived at The Britannia Stadium with well over 300 senior appearances to his credit (105 for Exeter). A vastly experienced defender, he did a sound job in the Potters' back four, helping the team win the Auto-Windscreen Shield, and, in fact, manager Gudjon Thordarsson was all set to sign him on a permanent basis but an injury put paid to that.

DREYER, John Paul

Defender: 42+18 apps. 4 goals.

Born: Alnwick, Northumberland, 11 June 1963.

Career: Wallington FC, Oxford United (professional, January 1985), Torquay United (on loan, December 1985–January 1986), Fulham (on loan, March–May 1988), Luton Town (£140,000, June 1988), POTTERS (free, July 1994), Bolton Wanderers (on loan, March-April 1995), Bradford City (£25,000, November 1996), Cambridge United (July 2000), Stevenage Town (August 2001).

■ The versatile John Dreyer occupied every defensive position and played in midfield during a 16-year period. A real dogged footballer, totally committed, he gave the potters excellent service for eight months, and when he lost his place in the first team to Icelander Larus Sigurdsson he eventually moved on. He amassed 544 competitive appearances, 250 of them with Luton.

DUBERRY, Michael Wayne

Defender: 25 apps.

Born: Enfield, Middlesex, 14 October 1975.
Career: CHELSEA (trainee, April 1992, professional, June 1993), Bournemouth (loan, September–October 1995), Leeds

United (£4 million, July 1999), Stoke City (loan, October 2004–January 2005, signed free, March 2005).

■ After producing some exquisite displays in Chelsea's second and third teams, defender Michael Duberry became a regular in the first XI at Stamford Bridge in 1997 and continued to perform splendidly, earning himself three England under-21 caps, later adding two more to his collection. Standing 6ft 1in tall and weighing 13st 6lb, he made over 100 senior appearances for the London club, gaining winners' medals in the League Cup, European Cup-winners' Cup and Super Cup, all in 1998. He did well initially at Elland Road, but then suffered a series of injuries before being relegated from the Premiership in 2004. He was recruited to The Britannia Stadium following an injury to veteran defender Gerry Taggart.

DUNN, William

Outside-left: 71 apps. 21 goals

Born: South Bank near Middlesbrough, April 1865.
Died: Scotland, c.1955.
Career: East Stirlingshire, POTTERS (November 1889), Hednesford Town (January 1893), Walsall Town Swifts (November 1893), Blyth (March 1894), South Bank (August 1894), Newton Heath (May 1897), Reading (July 1898, retired, April 1900).

■ Left-winger Billy Dunn (who occasionally played inside) was described as 'A man of many parts'. He drew up an excellent scoring record for Stoke, helping the team win the Football Alliance title in 1891 when he missed only one game and secured 11 goals. He lost his place on the left-wing to Joe Schofield and later had two League outings for Walsall and 10 for Newton Heath.

DURBER, Peter

Left-back or half-back: 65 apps.

Born: Wood lane, Stoke-on-Trent, April 1873.
Died: Stoke-on-Trent, 1946.
Career: Wood Lane FC, Audley, POTTERS (May 1896), Southampton (May 1898), POTTERS (June 1900), Glossop (August 1901), Northampton Town (July 1902), returned to Stoke-on-Trent where he became a licensee.

■ After two seasons with Stoke, during which time he played very well alongside his full-back partner Tom Clare while also having a handful of games at wing-half plus one at centre-forward (against West Bromwich Albion in October 1897), Peter Durber moved, with others, to Southampton. He became a huge favourite with the fans at The Dell, enjoying a lot of success on the south coast, making an appearance in the 1900 FA Cup Final and having an England trial in that same year (South against North). In fact, a lot of people were surprised he didn't win a full cap as he was a polished performer, a strong tackler and a player who was never afraid to get 'stuck in'. After 52 games for the Saints, Durber rejoined Stoke in the summer of 1900 and made 35 more appearances for the Potters before moving north to Glossop.

DYER, Bruce Antonio

Forward: new signing.

Born: Ilford, Essex, 13 April 1975.
Career: Watford (apprentice, May 1981, professional, April 1993), Crystal Palace (£1.1m, March 1994), Barnsley (£700,000, October 1998), Watford (free, July 2003), POTTERS (free, July 2005).

Signed by the Potters at the age of 30 with an excellent career record behind him of 136 goals in 485 competitive games for his four previous clubs, plus 11 England under-21 caps, the experienced Bruce Dyer, 6ft tall and over 13st in weight, is a honest, hardworking forward who holds the ball up well. He played his first game in a Potters shirt against Millwall (as a substitute).

DYKE, Archibald Samuel

Outside-right or left: 44 apps. 3 goals.

Born: Newcastle-under-Lyme, Staffs, 9 September 1886.
Died: Stoke-on-Trent, 1955.
Career: Chesterton, Newcastle Congregational, Newcastle PSA (1907), POTTERS (August 1909), Port Vale (July 1912), POTTERS (August 1913), Aston Villa (£500, February 1914), guest for Port Vale (September 1916, signed permanently, August 1919), Stafford Rangers (March 1920), Coventry City (October 1920), Blackpool (September 1921), Congleton Town (October 1921, retired, April 1922).

■ Archie Dyke was a clever winger, able to occupy both flanks, who had two spells at The Victoria Ground. He made only 13 appearances in the Football League during a lengthy career but did play consistently well at intermediate level.

DYSON, Paul Ian

Centre-half: 123 apps. 5 goals

Born: Kings Heath, Birmingham, 27 December 1959.
Career: Coventry City (apprentice, April 1976, professional, 1978), POTTERS (£150,000, July 1983), West Bromwich Albion (£60,000, March 1986), Darlington (March 1989), Crewe Alexandra (August 1989), Telford United (May 1990), Solihull Borough (manager, 1996–03).

■ A well-built, sturdy centre-half, Paul Dyson, who was capped by England at under-21 level as a Coventry City player, joined the Potters after making 166 senior appearances for the Sky Blues. A player who relied on positional sense rather than pace, he was good in the air and possessed a timely tackle. Nicknamed 'Dyce', he replaced Dave Watson at the heart of the Potters and served them for three seasons, making over 120 appearances before transferring to The Hawthorns when he was sold by Mick Mills, who replaced him with Steve Bould. After a good spell at The Hawthorns, Dyson moved to Darlington in 1989 and later assisted Crewe Alexandra, Telford United and Solihull Borough, taking over as player-manager of the latter club in 1996. He amassed over 400 senior appearances for his four major clubs.

EARDLEY, Frank

Inside-forward: 3 apps. 2 goals.

Born: Hanley, Stoke-on-Trent, June 1885.

Died: Stoke-on-Trent, c.1954.
Career: Tunstall Park, Goldenhill Wanderers (1907), POTTERS (July 1908), Port Vale (June 1910), Hanley Town (September 1911), Meir Social (season 1912-13). Did not play after World War One.

■ Frank Eardley scored twice for the Potters and four times for Port Vale, for whom he made his debut against Stoke reserves in a North Staffs League game in October 1910. Basically a reserve with both clubs, he spent all of his career in Stoke.

EARDLEY, William George

Outside-right: 10 apps. 1 goal.

Born: Tunstall, Stoke-on-Trent, December 1871.
Died: Stoke-on-Trent, c.1955.
Career: Burslem Port Vale (May 1894), Newcastle Swifts (June 1895), Port Vale September 1895), POTTERS August 1896–May 1897), later with Goldenhill United.

■ Right-winger Billy Eardley (no relation to Frank) was quick over the ground but liable to sulk if things weren't going his way. He spent just one season at The Victoria Ground, scoring once in his 10 League games for the Potters, when he deputised for Freddie Johnson. He played all his football in the North Staffordshire area.

EASTHAM, George Edward, OBE.

Inside-forward (midfield): 226+13 apps. 5 goals.

Born: Blackpool, 23 September 1936.
Career: Revoe Primary & Arnold Grammar Schools (Blackpool), Bipsham church team (Blackpool), Highfield Youth Club, Blackpool (trialist), Bolton Wanderers (trialist), Ards, Northern Ireland (amateur, April 1954, professional, September 1956), Newcastle United (£9,000, May 1956), Arsenal (£47,500, November 1960), POTTERS (£30,000, August 1966), Cape Town Spurs, South Africa (on loan, player-coach, February 1971), Hellenic FC, South Africa (player-manager, February 1971), POTTERS (October 1971, assistant player-manager, December 1972, retired as a player, March 1977, continued as manager until January 1978), emigrated to South Africa where he started his own sportswear business in Johannesburg called 'Hat Trick', he was also vice-president of the Arsenal supporters' club.

■ George Eastham was an exceptionally talented inside-forward who netted his fair share of goals as well as making scores more for his colleagues. He commenced his career with local sides in Blackpool, and after unsuccessful trials with two First Division clubs he joined Ards at the age of 17, signed by his father, the former Bolton Wanderers, Brentford, Blackpool, Swansea Town, Rochdale, Lincoln City and England international player, who was player-manager. A gifted schemer, able to pass the ball inch-perfect, he then struck 34 goals in 129 outings for Newcastle and while at St James' Park was involved in the famous court case, which finally broke the 'retain and transfer' system. He was successful in that long-winded case and quickly moved to Arsenal. He did exceedingly well at Highbury and scored 41 goals in 223 competitive games for the Gunners before Tony Waddington stepped in and brought him to Stoke in 1966, shortly after England had won the World Cup, when Eastham was in Alf Ramsey's squad. He went on to claim five goals in almost 240 appearances for the Potters, his most valuable strike being the winner in the 1972 League Cup Final against Chelsea when, at the age of 35 years and 161 days, he became the oldest player to receive a winners' medal. Just prior to that Wembley triumph he had returned to The Victoria Ground after developing his coaching qualities during a six-month period in South Africa with Cape Town Spurs and Hellenic. After retiring as a player, he became assistant manager and when Waddington was dismissed Eastham took over the 'hot seat' at The Victoria Ground, retaining the position for barely a year before Alan Durban moved in. Eastham emigrated to South Africa where he set up his own business and in his spare time coached football to the black youngsters in the townships around Johannesburg, while also venturing across to Cape Town to do likewise. Eastham was awarded an OBE in 1975.

EASTWOOD, Cecil Milner

Half-back: 48 apps.

Born: Tadcaster near Doncaster, June 1894.
Died: Cheshire, c.1968.
Career: Castleford Town (1914), served in the Army during World War One, Plymouth Argyle (£500, with two other players, Billy Cook and Joe Little, August 1920), Preston North End (free, June 1924), POTTERS (free, June 1926), Stockport County (August 1928, retired, March 1929).

■ Cecil Eastwood could play in any of the three half-back positions and was a vital cog in the Stoke side during their 1926–27 Third Division North Championship-winning season. He played initially in Rugby League with Castleford and made 116 appearances for Plymouth, with whom he gained three successive Second Division runners'-up medals. After two years with Preston he teamed up with Stoke in 1926, but unfortunately, during his second season at The 'Vic', Eastwood found himself playing more in the reserves than in the first team, and this led to him leaving the club for Stockport.

EBANKS, Michael Wayne Anthony

Full-back: 12 apps.

Born: Longbridge, Birmingham, 2 October 1964.
Career: Turves Green Primary & Secondary Modern Schools (Birmingham), Southern Cross FC, West Bromwich Albion (apprentice June 1980, professional, April 1982), POTTERS (on loan, August 1984), Port Vale (on loan, March 1985, signed permanently, June 1985–May 1987), Cambridge United (trialist, August 1987, then non-contract, September–November 1987), Oldbury United (December 1987–May 1990), later joined the Staffordshire Police Force, and played for the force soccer team.

■ A reserve at The Hawthorns, full-back Wayne Ebanks made only a handful of first-team appearances for the Albion. After his loan spell with the Potters (signed by Richie barker during a mini injury crisis), he played in 48 senior games for Port Vale and three for Cambridge before drifting into non-League soccer, eventually becoming a police officer and occasionally covering games at Vale Park.

ECCLES, John

Full-back: 193 apps. 1 goal.

Born: Newcastle-under-Lyme, 31 March 1869.
Died: Small Heath, Birmingham, 2 February 1932.
Career: Newcastle Congregational, Wolstanton Brotherhood FC, Stoke St Peter's, Titbury Town, London Road FC (briefly, 1889), Middleport, POTTERS (March 1890), Burslem Port Vale (reserve side, 1901–02), POTTERS (trainer, from August 1902), Birmingham (1912–15).

■ Despite his slight frame, full-back Jack Eccles was a resolute defender who had to battle for a first-team place early on, along with the formidable duo of Tommy Clare and Alf Underwood. But he hung in there and went on appear in almost 200 senior games for the Potters. He spent just 11 years at The Victoria Ground, during which time he twice represented the Football League and must have been mighty close to winning a full England cap. Eccles was said to have been a dour man, although he did produce 14 children, of whom Joe played top-class football for Aston Villa, Coventry City and West Ham United. His bother, George, who was born in 1874, played for Port Vale, Wolves, Everton, Preston North End, West Ham United and Bolton Wanderers.

EDGE, Alfred

Forward: 69 apps. 28 goals
Born: Hanley, Stoke-on-Trent, 1866.
Died: Stoke-on-Trent, April 1941.
Career: Goldenhill (August 1882), POTTERS (September 1884), Newton Heath L & Y Railway (£100, May 1891), Notts Jardines (briefly, July 1892), POTTERS (free, October 1892), Northwich Victoria (August 1893), Ardwick (January–May 1894).

■ One of Stoke's first professionals, the moustachio'd Alf Edge was an exceptionally fine footballer; a versatile forward with loads of skill quick over short distances and who never gave up the ghost. He spent six excellent seasons with the Potters, played in the club's first-ever League game versus West Bromwich Albion in 1888 and gained a Football Alliance Championship-winning medal in 1891. He then moved to Newton Heath (now Manchester United) where things went wrong and resulted in a suspension after he had signed for Notts Jardines without knowledge of the Lancashire club. Following a subsequent FA inquiry, the ban was lifted and he quickly rejoined the Potters for a second spell. This lasted for just a few months before he switched to Northwich Victoria and later Ardwick (now Manchester City), for whom he made his debut against his former club, Northwich. Awarded a gold medal by the Stoke directors for his services to the club, he holds the record for scoring the most goals in an FA Cup tie for Stoke, claiming five in a 10–1 home win over Caernarvon Wanderers in October 1886.

ELDER, Alexander Russell

Left-back: 94+6 apps. 1 goal.

Born: Lisburn, Northern Ireland, 25 April 1941.
Career: Glentoran (amateur, August 1956, semi-professional, May 1958), Burnley (professional, January 1959), POTTERS (£50,000, August 1967), Leek Town (free, July 1973, retired as a player, May 1975).

■ Alex Elder's Football League debut for Burnley was as an 18-year-old against Preston North End during the

Alex Elder

Lancashire club's League Championship-winning season of 1959–60, the first of 330 senior appearances he made for the Clarets, whom he served for eight years. A wartime baby, Elder broke his left ankle in 1963, but recovered, was appointed captain and remained a regular in the side until his departure to Stoke in 1967. He spent five seasons at The Victoria Ground, adding another 100 appearances to his tally at senior level, producing some fine displays when partnering first Bill Bentley and then Jackie Marsh at full-back. He won six caps for Northern Ireland while at Stoke, having earlier collected 34 with Burnley. He left the Potteries in 1973 on a free transfer and signed for Leek Town near his home.

ELLIOTT, Frank Frederick George

Goalkeeper: 23 apps.

Born: Lambeth, London, 23 July 1929.
Career: Welsh schoolboy football and rugby), Merthyr Tydfil (August 1946), Swansea Town (semi-professional, September 1949), POTTERS (trialist, November 1952, professional, December 1952), Fulham (March 1954), Mansfield Town (July 1956–May 1958).

■ Fred Elliott took over the goalkeeping duties at The Victoria Ground in 1953 when Bill Robertson was unavailable. He played non-League football for Merthyr during the mid-to-late '40s and won Welsh Cup winners' medals with both Merthyr and Swansea. Moving to The Victoria Ground initially on trial, he was transferred to Fulham after failing to hold down a regular place in the Potters side. Strong and well proportioned, he made 25 League appearances for the 'Cottagers' and 63 for Mansfield Town.

ELLIS, Anthony Joseph

Striker: 75+18 apps. 20 goals.

Born: Salford, 20 October 1964.
Career: Poets Corner FC, Horwich RMI (August 1985), Bolton Wanderers (trialist, March 1986), Northwich Victoria (April 1986), Oldham Athletic (professional, August 1986), Preston North End (£23,000, October 1987), POTTERS (December 1989), Preston North End (exchange deal involving Graham Shaw, August 1992), Blackpool (£165,000, July 1994), Bury (December 1997), Stockport County (£25,000, February 1999), Rochdale (free, November 1999), Burnley (free, July 2001), Mossley (free, February 2002), Leigh Railway Mechanics Institute (September 2002).

■ Tony Ellis, a real snapper-up of half chances, had a wonderful career that spanned 16 years, during which time he appeared in 613 competitive games and scored 203 goals. Never shifting lower in

the country than Stoke-on-Trent, he was registered, in effect, with eight different League clubs and certainly played his best football with Preston, for whom he struck 87 goals in 194 outings. He spent two-and-a-half years with the Potters, linking up well with Wayne Biggins. Unfortunately, for all his efforts he never gained a winners' medal in any major League or Cup competition.

ELLIS, John Albert

Half-back or forward: 3 apps.

Born: Manchester, August 1889.
Died: Manchester, c.1961.
Career: Salford United (1908), Witton Albion (1910), POTTERS (semi-professional, January 1914), served in Army during World War One, guest for Manchester United (December 1916–April 1919), Stalybridge Celtic (July 1919), Witton Albion (October 1923), Eccles United (August 1924, retired, May 1925).

■ The versatile Jack Ellis, who could play in any forward position as well as a wing-half, joined Stoke at the age of 24. Unfortunately, he never really made an impact at The Victoria Ground and appeared in relatively few first-team matches, all in 1913–14. Described as 'crafty and tricky', he left the club when the War in Europe forced the termination of competitive football. He later emerged with Stalybridge Celtic. He scored 13 goals in 74 regional matches as a guest for Manchester United during World War One.

EUSTACE, John Mark

Midfield: 3+2 apps. 6 goals.

Born: Solihull, 3 November 1979.
Career: Coventry City (apprentice, April 1996, professional, November 1996), Dundee United (on loan, February–April 1999), Middlesbrough (on loan, January 2003), POTTERS (free, August 2003).

■ A tough-tackling, energetic and purposeful midfielder, John Eustace made almost 100 appearances for Coventry City (some as captain), 13 for Dundee United and one in the Premiership for Middlesbrough before joining the Potters prior to the start of

the 2003–04 campaign. He quickly made his mark with some strong efficient performances, but he suffered a long-term groin injury at Christmas and was out of first-team contention for virtually a year, making his return in December 2004 against his former club Coventry.

EVANS, Arthur Walter

Goalkeeper: 9 apps.

Born: Stoke-on-Trent, April 1868.
Died: Stoke-on-Trent, c.1945.
Career: Church football, POTTERS (August 1893), Barlaston Swifts (July 1894–May 1900).

■ Archie Evans had nine outings for the Potters during the early part of the 1893–94 season when he took over from Billy Rowley. His spell at The Victoria Ground ended when Tom Cain had taken over between the posts.

EVANS, Gareth John

Inside-forward: 7 apps. 2 goals.

Born: Coventry, 14 January 1967.
Career: Coventry City (apprentice, April 1983, professional, January 1985), Rotherham United (October 1986), Hibernian (February 1988), POTTERS (on loan, September–October 1990), Northampton Town (on loan, December 1990), Partick Thistle (July 1997–May 1998).

■ Rejected by Coventry as a teenager, inside-forward Gareth Evans broke through with Rotherham United, for whom he scored 13 goals in 63 League games. He did well during his loan spell with the Potters, scoring twice in a League Cup clash against West Ham and the winner against Bolton in a Third Division encounter at Burnden Park. He went on to appear in more than 150 games for Hibs, with whom he gained a Skol Cup winners' medal in 1992.

EVANS, John

Outside-left: 12 apps.

Born: West Bromwich, 12 July 1900.
Died: Wednesbury, June 1976.
Career: West Bromwich Standard (1919), Ewells FC (1920), Walsall (professional, June 1921), Shrewsbury Town (free, May 1922), Sheffield United, free, May 1923), POTTERS (free, July 1924), Nantwich Victoria (free, May 1925), Shrewsbury Town (free, 1926–27), Stalybridge Connaughts (1927–29).

■ Jack Evans was born and bred in the Black Country and played intermediate football before becoming a professional with Walsall and making his League debut against Barrow in February 1922. He played in two First Division games for Sheffield United before spending a season at The Victoria Ground where he deputised on the left-wing for Welshman Dai Nicholas.

EVANS. John Edward

Forward: 62 apps. 19 goals.

Born: Fenton, Stoke-on-Trent, April 1868.
Died: Stoke-on-Trent, c.1942.
Career: Newcastle Swifts, POTTERS (September 1891), Bury (April 1895), Port Vale, (October 1896, retiring, May 1899), later worked in a pottery factory.

■ Ted 'Jammer' Evans was the first Stoke player ever to be sent off – dismissed in a League game against Everton on Merseyside on 12 November 1892. The result was a 2–2 draw. Evans was a real tough guy, a forward who loved to dribble his way through a defence and was a regular in the Potters' side for more than three seasons, during which time he produced some fine performances. He won the Staffordshire Cup with Port Vale in 1898.

EVANS, Raymond Leslie

Full-back: 105 apps. 2 goals.

Born: Edmonton, Middlesex, 20 September 1949.
Career: Edmonton Boys, Middlesex Schools, Tottenham Hotspur (apprentice, July 1965, professional, May 1967), Millwall (£40,000, January 1975), Fulham (£35,000, March 1977), St Louis Stars, NASL (on loan, summer 1977), California Surf, NASL (on loan, summer 1978), POTTERS (£120,000, August 1979), Seattle Sounders (free, March 1982, retired, June 1984), remained in Seattle where he became a soccer coach and still lives there today.

■ Ray Evans made 203 first-team appearances for Spurs (136 in the Football League) and 89 for Fulham before joining the Potters. He signed professional forms at White Hart Lane just as Spurs lifted the FA Cup! He made his debut in the local derby against Arsenal in March 1969 and never looked back. An England youth international, he was a strong, purposeful footballer who operated like an engine down the right-hand touchline, his overlapping being a feature of many of his performances. He unfortunately missed out on Spurs' three successive Cup Final victories: the League Cup in 1971 and 1973 and the UEFA Cup in 1972, but he did make the second UEFA Cup Final in 1974, although only receiving a runners'-up medal. After spells with Millwall and Fulham and two trips to America, he signed for Stoke in 1979. He quickly adapted to manager Alan Durban's style of play at The Victoria Ground and went on to make over 100 appearances for the Potters, skippering the side at times before an unfortunate training-ground incident blighted his stay at the club. He helped Seattle reach the Super Bowl Final and after spending a short time playing in the American Indoor Soccer League he announced his retirement in 1984 to became a coach in the States where he still resides. He made over 600 appearances for his four English and three American clubs.

EYRES, John

Inside-forward: 65 apps. 23 goals.

Born: Northwich, Cheshire, 20 March 1899.
Died: Cheshire, 1975.
Career: Northwich Victoria, Witton Albion, POTTERS (£250, June 1922),

Walsall (£100, May 1929), Brighton & Hove Albion (July 1931), Bristol Rovers (May 1932), York City (August 1934), Gainsborough Trinity (July 1935, retired, May 1936).

■ John Eyres was associated with Stoke for a period of seven years without really establishing himself in the first team. He had spells with his home-town club and Witton Albion before joining Stoke in 1922. After scoring, on average, a goal every three games for the Potters, he was transferred to Walsall for a modest fee, which Eyres received himself as part of an arranged benefit. After that he became something of a soccer nomad before retiring in 1936 with over 300 senior appearances under his belt (267 in the Football League, 85 goals scored).

FARMER, Albert

Half-back: 6 apps.

Born: Stoke-on-Trent, 1864.
Died: before 1945.
Career: Everton (season 1887–88), POTTERS (August 1888), Newton Heath, Manchester (July 1890).

■ Albert Farmer was a gritty half-back whose senior appearances were equally divided between League and FA Cup competitions during his two seasons with the club in 1888–90. He had a few games for Everton before moving to The Victoria Ground but was never a serious contender for a regular place in the Potters' side. He failed to make the first XI with Newton Heath.

FARMER, George David

Left-half: 1 app.

Born: Stoke-on-Trent, April 1862.
Career: Tunstall (1883), POTTERS (August 1886–March 1887), Burslem Swifts (from August 1887).

■ George Farmer (no relation to Albert) played in one FA Cup tie for Stoke against Crewe Alexandra in November 1886 when he deputised for George Bateman.

FARMER, John

Goalkeeper 185 apps.

Born: Biddulph, Staffs, 31 August 1947.
Career: Chatterley Boys' Club, POTTERS (apprentice, August 1963, professional, January 1965), West Bromwich Albion (on loan, July 1972), Leicester City (on loan, December 1974), Northwich Victoria (August 1976–May 1978).

■ A sensational find when he emerged into the side having originally played for a local boy's team, Farmer had gone to a rugby playing school but the lack of football did not hinder his early progress. After performing well in the Potters' second and third teams, he made his League debut at the age of 18, against Arsenal in January 1966, and remains, to this day, one of the youngest goalkeepers ever to play for the club. Inside two years (November 1967) he made his international debut for the England under-23 side against Wales in a 2–1 win. On his day, Farmer was certainly one of the best 'keepers in the game but he did lose confidence several times during his Stoke career, especially when he knew the manager was looking to sign Gordon Banks! Tony Waddington pounced and brought the World Cup winner to The Victoria Ground, but Farmer stayed loyal to the club (turning down the opportunity of a move to other clubs) and he became a capable reserve to England's number one. After Banks's accident he got another chance, but as Stoke mounted their biggest ever challenge for Division One honours he was deposed by Peter Shilton. Farmer assisted West Bromwich Albion as a guest during their Scandinavian tour in 1972 and played a couple of games for Leicester City on loan before moving to Northwich Victoria. He had the distinction of playing in both of Stoke's ties in European competition away at Kaiserslautern and home and away against Ajax. He is now employed as a factory manager with Smiths Crisps at Cheadle near Stockport.

FARRELL, John

Centre-forward: 42 apps. 12 goals.

Born: Tunstall, Stoke-on-Trent, August 1873.
Died: Stoke-on-Trent, 22 February 1947.
Career: Dresden United (1890), POTTERS (professional, October 1894), Southampton St Mary's (£40, April 1895), POTTERS (August 1898), Southampton St Mary's (May 1899), New Brighton Tower (June 1900), Northampton Town (July 1901), West Ham United (August 1902–May 1904), returned to Tunstall where he became a licensee.

■ Jack Farrell spent two seasons at The Victoria Ground, three years apart. He played his early football from the age of 17 with Dresden United, and he also had two spells with Southampton, for whom he scored 54 goals in 97 appearances. He netted seven goals in 17 league games in his first season with the Potters and claimed five in 25 second time round when he partnered Willie Maxwell in attack. When he joined Saints in 1895, newspapers described his arrival as a 'great catch at £40'. A fast and tricky player, very reliable with a level-headed approach, Farrell won two Southern League Championship medals with Saints in 1897 and 1898 and played in the 1900 FA Cup Final defeat by Bury. On retiring, he returned to Tunstall where he became a publican.

FARRELL, Stephen Edward

Midfield: 0+2 apps.

Born: Kilmarnock, 8 March 1973.
Career: POTTERS (apprentice, April 1989, professional, July 1991), St Mirren (free transfer, May 1992).

■ Midfielder Steve Farrell made just two substitute League appearances for Stoke in season 1989–90. Having skippered the club's youth team, it was thought that he would make the grade in the senior side but sadly that didn't materialise, and he left The Victoria Ground at the end of the 1991–92 season. He failed to make any impression in Scotland.

FARROW, Desmond Albert

Defender: 8 apps.

Born: Peterborough, 11 February 1926.
Career: Leicester City (amateur, 1942), Queen's Park Rangers (professional, November 1944), POTTERS (£4,000 plus George Mountford, 1952), Peterborough United (free transfer, May 1955).

■ Rugged defender Des Farrow, an amateur with Leicester, was one of manager Frank Taylor's early signings for Stoke City, arriving in a cash/player deal involving George Mountford in 1952 after scoring seven goals in 118 League games for QPR. Unfortunately, he failed to impress at The Victoria Ground and made only eight Second Division appearances in three years before joining his home-town club Peterborough United, who were then members of the Midland League.

FENTON, Graham Anthony

Inside-forward and midfield: 4+3 apps.

Born: Wallsend-on-Tyne, 22 May 1974.
Career: Aston Villa (apprentice, June 1990, professional, February 1992), West Bromwich Albion (on loan, January–February 1994), Blackburn Rovers (£1.5 million, November 1995), Leicester City (£1.1 million, August 1997), Walsall (free transfer, March 2000), POTTERS (free, August 2000), St Mirren (free, September 2000), Blackpool (free, August 2001), Darlington (on loan, September–October 2002), Blyth Spartans (June 2003).

■ A very skilful and active footballer, Graham Fenton made his senior debut for Aston Villa in 1993, and when he entered non-League football a decade later he had made over 150 first-team appearances. He was a League Cup winner with Villa in 1994 and helped Leicester reach the Final of the same competition in 2000. He also gained one England under-21 cap.

FERNS, William

Half-back: 4 apps.

Born: Glasgow, Scotland, September 1871.
Died: Scotland, c.1950.
Career: Queen's Park, Corinthians, POTTERS (April 1894), Corinthians (August 1895).

■ There are references to this footballer's name being spelt as Fearns. A typically stern Scottish half-back, he played in four League games for Stoke midway through the 1896–97 season, having signed for the club in April 1984. He remained an amateur throughout his career and either side of his service with the Potters played for the famous Corinthians.

FIELDING, Alec Ross

Outside-right: 109 apps. 12 goals.

Born: Trentham near Stoke-on-Trent, 7 January 1880.
Died: Stoke-on-Trent, 1952.
Career: Silverdale Council School (Stoke), Stoke Priory (1888), Florence Colliery, POTTERS (amateur, March 1902), Nottingham Forest (September 1902), POTTERS (March 1903), West bromwich Albion (September 1908), POTTERS (February 1909), Burton United (August 1909, retired, May 1913), returned to work on his father's estate.

■ Right-winger Ross Fielding was a ebullient winger with excellent dribbling skills and a wonderful body-swerve. He had three spells with Stoke and, overall, notched up more than a century of appearances. He was signed by West Bromwich Albion in 1908 while out hunting on his father's estate in North Staffordshire. Rather slim and fragile-looking, he weighed barely 10st.

FIELDING, Arthur John

Inside-forward: 3 apps.

Born: Trentham near Stoke-on-Trent, 17 March 1888.
Died: before 1960.
Career: Dresden Athletic, Florence Colliery, Dresden Victoria, Florence Colliery, Bolton Wanderers (1906), Florence Colliery, POTTERS (August 1908), Burslem Port Vale (June 1910), Florence Colliery (season 1911–12).

■ Archie Fielding, younger brother of Ross, played briefly for Bolton Wanderers reserves before going to work in a coal mine. He then assisted Florence Colliery before joining Stoke at the age of 25. He made only three Birmingham & District League appearances for the Potters during the season (as deputy for Owen and Gorman) and left the club in June 1910 to sign for Burslem Port Vale, staying for one season when he suffered an injury before going back to Florence Colliery for a fourth spell.

FINNEY, Charles William Thomas

Centre-forward: 62 apps. 15 goals.

Born: Stoke-on-Trent, 5 September 1931.
Career: Stoke-on-Trent Schoolboys, Edensor Youth Club, Crewe Alexandra (amateur, 1947), POTTERS (part-time professional, May 1949, professional, October 1951), Birmingham City (£7,000, November 1955), Queen's Park Rangers (£1,500, May 1957) Crewe (free transfer, July 1958), Rochdale (free, September 1959), Cheltenham Town (free, November 1959, retired, August 1960).

■ An amateur under the managership of the former Stoke City centre-half Arthur Turner at Crewe Alexandra, Bill Finney moved to The Victoria Ground in 1949 as a part-time professional, and it was not until the autumn of 1951 (aged 20) that he signed full-time forms. He was handed his League debut in the away game at Old Trafford in October 1952, when he scored with a stunning left-footer as Stoke beat Manchester United 2–0 in front of almost 29,000 fans. Come November 1955, and with Potters boss Frank Taylor looking elsewhere for a central striker, Finney's stay at The Victoria Ground ended when he was re-united with his former manager, Turner, at Birmingham City, having netted practically a goal every four games for Stoke. He later played as a goal-maker rather than goal-taker and when he retired in 1960 he had 113 League appearances to his credit (16 goals).

FLYNN, Michael Anthony

Defender: 11+2 apps.

Born: Oldham, 23 February 1969.
Career: Oldham Athletic (apprentice, April 1985, professional, February 1987), Norwich City (£100,000, December 1988), Preston North End (£125,000, December 1989), Stockport County (£125,000, March 1993), POTTERS (on loan, January–March 2002), Barnsley (free, March 2002), Blackpool (free, January 2003).

■ When he joined the Potters on loan

in 2002 defender Mike Flynn had already appeared in a total of 667 League and Cup games, including 460 for Stockport County. A powerful and determined defender, able to withstand challenges from the heftiest of forwards, he partnered the Belarus star Sergei Shtanyiuk at the heart of the Potters' defence as they cemented themselves in a Play-off position, finally finishing fifth. In 2004 Flynn helped Blackpool win the LDV Vans Trophy at the Millennium Stadium as well as reaching the career milestone of 750 appearances.

FLYNN, Sean Michael

Midfield: 110+12 apps. 9 goals.

Born: Birmingham, 13 March 1968.
Career: Halesowen Town (August 1988), Coventry City (£20,000, December 1991), Derby County (£250,000, August 1995), POTTERS (on loan, March–May 1997), West Bromwich Albion (£260,000, August 1997), Tranmere Rovers (free, July 2000), Halesowen Town (June–July 2002), Kidderminster Harriers (August 2002–September 2003), Evesham United (October 2003), Redditch United (July 2004).

■ Never-say-die midfielder Sean Flynn was a purposeful, aggressive and a thoroughly honest competitor. On loan to the Potters from Derby, he had already made 105 senior appearances for Coventry and 65 for the Rams, and when he slipped into non-League football in 2003 he had gone past the 350 mark.

FOLEY, Stephen

Midfield: 134+1 apps. 13 goals.

Born: Liverpool, 4 October 1962.
Career: Liverpool (apprentice, April 1979, professional, September 1980), Fulham (on loan, december 1983), Grimnsby Town (free transfer, August 1984), Sheffield United (free, August 1985), Swindon Town (£40,000, June 1987), POTTERS (£50,000, January 1992), Lincoln City (free, July 1994), Bradford City (free August 1995, released, October 1995)

■ Steve Foley was a grafter, a player who strove hard and long, preferring to

occupy a position on the right side of the pitch, where he produced some excellent perfomances at senior level. Indeed, after being released without a game by Liverpool and making his League debut on loan with Fulham he bedded in at Grimsby, playing in 40 games before appearing in 79 matches for Sheffield United and 190 for Swindon, scoring 29 goals for the latter club. Signed by Potters boss Lou Macari halfway through the 1991–92 season, Foley gained an Autoglass Trophy winners' medal that same season and a year later helped the team clinch the Second Division title. He was only three short of a career appearance tally of 450 by the time he left the Potters for Lincoln in 1994.

FORD, Tony, OBE

Outside-right/midfield: 135 apps. 14 goals.

Born: Grimsby, 14 May 1959.
Career: Grimsby Town (apprentice, July 1975, professional, May 1977), Sunderland (on loan, March–May 1986), POTTERS (£35,000, July 1986), West Bromwich Albion (£145,000, March 1989), Grimsby Town (£50,000, November 1991), Bradford City (on loan, September–October 1993), Scunthorpe United (free transfer, August 1994), Barrow (free, August 1998), Mansfield Town (free, October 1996, later player-assistant manager), Rochdale (free, July 1999), Barnsley (£70,000 paid in compensation to Rochdale, November 2001, as assistant manager-coach, sacked, October 2002, reappointed as Rochdale assistant-boss, December 2003, under former Potters' player Steve Parkin).

■ Tony Ford – football's version of a 'Model T Ford' – has been associated with professional football for almost 30 years and as a player he accumulated more than 900 League appearances (1,000 plus in all competitions), the second highest tally behind another former Stoke City player Peter Shilton. After giving Grimsby Town splendid service for 11 years he joined the Potters after they had just finished 10th in the Second Division. He continued to produce some sterling performances while playing on the right hand side of the park, and after two useful campaigns he was signed by his former teammate at The Victoria Ground Brian Robson, manager of West Bromwich Albion. A player who loved to pump up and down the pitch, he again gave a good, honest account of himself at The Hawthorns, making a further 128 appearances for the Baggies. He then returned to Blundell Park and took his total of appearances for the Mariners to an impressive 469. He was later appointed assistant manager-coach by ex-Potter Steve Parkin at Barnsley. Capped twice by England 'B' (against Switzerland and Norway) as a West Bromwich player, he had earlier helped Grimsby twice gain promotion, helping them win the Third Division title in 1980 and the Football League Group Cup in 1982. In fact, when he made his Football League debut for Grimsby on 4 October 1975 as substitute against Walsall he became the youngest player ever to appear for the Mariners in a first-team game, aged 16 years and 143 days. Ford was awarded the OBE in 2000 for services to football.

* In November 2001 Ford became the costliest-ever 47-year-old footballer when Barnsley were forced to pay Rochdale £70,000 for his services because he was still registered as a player at Spotland. He was sacked after just 11 months at Oakwell.

FORD, Peter Leslie

Centre-half: 14 apps.

Born: Etruria, Stoke-on-Trent, 10 August 1933.
Career: Cannon Street Youth Club, West Bromwich Albion (amateur, 1952), POTTERS (professional, May 1953), Port Vale (£2,000 co-ordinated three player-exchange deal involving Harry Oscroft and Dickie Cunliffe, September 1959), Macclesfield Town (August 1963), later with Stafford Rangers, Macclesfield Town (again), Hanley Town (manager), Milton United (coach).

■ For six seasons during the 1950s Peter Ford acted as understudy to centre-half Ken Thomson and played in 14 League games for the Potters. He played for Cannon Street youth Club and was an amateur with West Bromwich Albion prior to signing professional forms for the Potters in 1953. He had to wait almost four years before making his senior debut against Swansea Town away from home in April 1957. A loyal and dedicated club man, he battled on regardless and eventually left The Victoria Ground in 1959 to sign for rivals Port Vale in a deal that saw City's Harry Oscroft move across town in exchange for Dickie Cunliffe, plus a cash adjustment. Ford went on to make over 125 appearances for the Valiants before drifting into non-League football with Macclesfield Town.

FORD, Stephen Derek

Inside-forward: 1+1 apps.

Born: Shoreham-on-Sea, Sussex, 17 February 1959.
Career: Lewes (semi-professional, 1979), POTTERS (£2,000, June 1981), Stafford Rangers (April 1983), later with AEL Sports Club, Limasol (Cyprus), Finn Harps, Ireland, South China, Hong Kong.

■ Stephen Ford failed to settle down in the Potteries and, after just two senior games for the club, reverted back to non-League football with Stafford Rangers. In later years he played in Cyprus, Ireland and Hong Kong.

Reg Forester

FORESTER, Reginald

Wing-half: 8 apps.

Born: Penkhull, Staffs, 12 May 1892.
Died: Newcastle-under-Lyme, 9 December 1959.
Career: Kidsgrove Wellington. Manchester City (October 1912), POTTERS (£300, September 1913), served in Army during World War One, Macclesfield Town (July 1922), Congleton Town (1924–25), later worked in pottery.

■ Reg Forester was one of the few players to serve the Potters before, during and after World War One. He appeared in a dozen or so games for Manchester City's reserve team before signing for Stoke at the age of 21. He was given just one outing in the Southern League before war broke out and during the hostilities served as a sergeant in the Machine Gun Corps, being involved in the action in Mesopatamia and Russia. He was not demobbed until 1919 when he returned to The Victoria Ground, adding another seven League outings to his tally before leaving the club in 1922 to sign for Macclesfield Town. Prior to taking up football, Forrester trained as artist with Mintons and on retiring became decorating manager of Johnson Brothers (Imperial Pottery) in Hanley.

FORREST, James

Centre-forward: 6 apps. 3 goals.

Born: Glasgow, September 1878.
Died: Scotland, 1955.
Career: Motherwell, POTTERS (August 1902), Bradford City (May 1903), Hamilton Academical (January 1906–June 1907).

■ Jack Forrest was one of the many Scots who crossed the border to try to establish themselves in English League football in the late 1890s/early 1900s. He played in only six first-team matches, yet scored three goals, two on his debut in a 3–0 home win over Wolves in September 1902. He went on to score 24 goals in 58 games for Bradford.

FORRESTER, Thomas

Forward: 1 app.

Born: Stoke-on-Trent, June 1864.
Died: before 1945.
Career: Trentham, POTTERS (August 1888), Stoke St Peter's (September 1889), later with Ardwick, Manchester City (October 1892–May 1894).

■ No relation to Reg, Tom Forrester was a utility forward who could play in any position. He spent just two seasons with Stoke, appearing in the FA Cup tie against Warwick County in October 1888 when he deputised for Bob McSkimming in a changed and seemingly weakened team, which lost 2–1.

FORRESTER, William

Outside-left: 1 app.

Born: Stoke-on-Trent, August 1869.
Died: before 1938.
Career: Hanley Town, POTTERS (August 1891), Hanley Town (March 1892).

■ Billy Forrester appeared in one Football League game for the Potters – a 3–0 defeat at Accrington in January 1892 when he replaced Billy Dunn.

FORSYTH, Richard Michael

Midfield: 102+6 apps. 18 goals.

Born: Dudley, 3 October 1970.
Career: Kidderminster Harriers, Birmingham City (£50,000, July 1995), POTTERS (£20,000, July 1996), Blackpool (free transfer, July 1999), Peterborough United (free, July 22000), Cheltenham Town (£15,000, October 2002), Northwich Victoria (June 2004).

■ In 1994 Richard Forsyth was playing in the GM Vauxhall Conference with Kidderminster Harriers. The following year he was battling it out in midfield for Birmingham City in the Football League. A well-built, strong tackling player with a powerful right-foot shot, he went on to make 41 appearances during his season at St Andrew's, but when Trevor Francis replaced Barry Fry as manager Forsyth left St Andrew's for Stoke City. He spent three seasons with the Potters, making over 100 senior appearances, generally performing well in centre-field and scoring his fair share of goals. Prior to teaming up with Blues, he helped the Harriers win the Conference and also represented the FA XI, as well as playing in three semi-professional international matches for England. Forsyth, who could also occupy a full-back role, reached the milestone of 300 League and Cup appearances at senior level in 2004.

FORSTER, Arthur

Full-back: 7 apps.

Born: Fenton, September 1869.
Died: Chirk, 1912.
Career: Hanley Town, POTTERS (June 1893), Oswestry Town (May 1895), Chirk (1897–98).

■ Reserve full-back Archie Forster made just seven League appearances for Stoke during his two seasons with the club, his debut coming in a 6–2 defeat at Everton in April 1894 when he was called up at the 11th hour to replace Tommy Clare.
* Some reference books have this player listed as Foster.

FOSTER, Emmanuel

Goalkeeper: 1 app.

Born: Wolstanton, 4 December 1921.
Career: Mow Cop, POTTERS (March 1943), Stafford Rangers (May 1947).

■ Goalkeeper Manny Foster's only game at senior level for Stoke was against Bolton Wanderers (away) in a First Division game on 11 September 1946. That day over 25,000 fans saw the Potters lose 3–2. Understudy at the time to Dennis Herod, he was passed over when cricketer-footballer Arthur Jepson took over the green jersey in Herod's lengthy absence and became surplus to requirements at the end of the season. Joining the club halfway through World War Two, he made 27 appearances during the hostilities.

FOWLER, Lee Edward

Full-back or central defence: 55+10 apps.

Born: Eastwood, Nottingham, 26 January 1969.
Career: POTTERS (apprentice, April 1985, professional, July 1988), Preston North End (May 1992), Doncaster Rovers (December 1993), Telford United (May 1994).

■ Lee Fowler started off as a trainee at The Victoria Ground in 1985 and stayed with the club for seven years, having his best spell in the first team in 1991–92 when he played in 16 of the first 17 League games. He wore six different numbered shirts for the Potters.

FOX, Peter David

Goalkeeper 477 apps.

Born Scunthorpe, 5 July 1957.
Career: Sheffield Wednesday (apprentice, July 1973, professional June 1975), West Ham United (November 1977), Barnsley (on loan, December 1977), Team Hawaii, NASL (on loan, three months), POTTERS (£15,000, March 1978), Linfield, Ireland (on loan, February 1993), Exeter City (free transfer, player-coach, July 1993, later manager, June 1995–May 2000), Rochdale (scout, 2001),

Blackpool (joint-goalkeeping coach, 2004).

■ In a time when loyalty seems to mean less and less to professional footballers Peter Fox's commitment to Stoke City shone through. He spent 15 years at the club and broke the record number of appearances for a goalkeeper. It was ironic that Lou Macari as Stoke boss did not seem to really fancy Foxy yet in 1992–93, despite a number of loan signings, Foxy kept the jersey for Autoglass Trophy games and won a medal at Wembley. The following promotion season it was Foxy again that he turned to in the vital 10 games to win the Championship of the Second Division. Fox started his career at Hillsborough and, at 15 years 8 months, he is still the youngest player ever to appear for Wednesday in a first-team match which was against Orient on 31 March 1973. After loan spells at West Ham and Barnsley and several outings with Team Hawaii, he joined the Potters in 1978, signed by Alan Durban. At first he slotted in as deputy to Roger Jones but soon gained a first-team place. Unfortunately, a number of back injuries interrupted his career at The Victoria Ground. Had he remained injury-free then he would surely have broken the 500-appearance barrier for the club. After leaving the Potteries he assisted Linfield in the Irish League for a time before becoming player-coach to Alan Ball at Exeter City in 1993, having been freed by Macari. Later in charge at St James' park, he was replaced in the Grecians hot-seat by another former Stoke City player, Noel Blake, who had previously been his assistant.

FRANKLIN, Cornelius

Centre-half: 162 apps.

Born Stoke-on-Trent, 24 January 1922. Died: Stoke-on-Trent, 9 February 1996. Career: Stoke-on-Trent Schools, Stoke Old Boys, POTTERS (amateur, April 1936, professional, January 1939), Independiente Santa Fe, Bogota (May 1950), Hull City (February 1951), Crewe Alexandra (February 1956), Stockport County (October 1957), Wellington Town (player-coach, July 1959), GKN Sankeys, Wellington (player, July 1960), manager July–August 1961, retired, December 1962), Apoel Tel Aviv, Nicosia (coach, February–November 1963), Colchester United (manager, November 1963–May 1968), later a licensee in Oswaltwistle (from January 1969) and then Sandon.

■ At his peak, Neil Franklin was one of the greatest centre halves in England (perhaps the world). Relying on skill, he marshalled a defence like a general and was magnificent in heading and positioning. Like so many local players to emerge in the years of World War Two, which interrupted competitive football in this country, Franklin was 17 years old when the League was closed down in 1939 and 24 when it came to life again in 1946. He developed strongly through one of Stoke's nursery teams, Stoke Old Boys, and made 186 appearances for the Potters during the war, also playing three times for England in wartime internationals. He soon established himself as a regular in the League side and was a consistent performer in both the Potters and England teams after football returned. He went on to win a total of 27 full caps in consecutive international matches,

Neil Franklin

which was a record at the time. He also played once for England 'B' and had five games with the Football League as his professional career resumed in earnest after the hostilities. However, in May 1950 Franklin was tempted to fly to Colombia (then outside the jurisdiction of FIFA) to play for Independiente Santa Fe in Bogota. His salary in Colombia and lifestyle far exceeded what was offered in the Football League, which was bound by a maximum wage. He made the decision prior to England's attempts in the closing stages of the World Cup of that summer in Brazil and his trip (accompanied by George Mountford among others) effectively ended his international career. Walter Winterbottom and the FA begged him not to go but Franklin, like many professionals of today, wanted to improve his family's circumstances. The transfer was not a success and he failed to settle in Bogota, returning to England inside two months. Unfortunately, he was not welcomed home with open arms at Stoke and had to serve a suspension from League football. By February 1951 Stoke had sold him to Hull City, then managed by Franklin's old England team-mate Raich Carter, a man who had always coveted the centre-half's talents. After Hull he served Crewe Alexandra and Stockport County before venturing into management, first as player-manager at non-League side Wellington Town. He later had successful spells in charge of Apoel in Cyprus and Colchester United. Franklin was certainly a great player, who would be in many experts' all-time best teams. Indeed, many believe that Billy Wright, for one, would never have accumulated so many England caps as he did had Franklin decided to stay at home instead of going to South America. After his footballing days were over, Franklin became a publican and was a regular spectator at The Victoria Ground for many years.

* Franklin scored only four goals (all for Crewe, three of them headers) in a total of 323 League appearances.

FRASER, Stuart James

Goalkeeper: 0+1 app.

Born: Cheltenham, 1 August 1978.
Career: Cheltenhaam Town (apprentice, August 1994), POTTERS (professional, July 1996), Exeter City (free transfer, July 2000).

■ Second-choice goalkeepoer at Cheltenham and also at The Britannia Stadium, Stuart Fraser's only League outing for the Potters was as a substitute for Carl Muggleton in the closing stages of the final game of the 1998–99 season against promoted Walsall (won 2–0). He underwent a hernia operation while at St James' Park, where his manager was the former Stoke City defender Noel Blake.

FRASER, William

Outside-right: 3 apps.

Born: Glasgow, June 1868.
Died: Glasgow, September 1923.
Career: Renton, POTTERS (August 1891), Renton (December 1891), Glasgow United (1893–May 1895).

■ All of Bill Fraser's League appearances for the Potters were made in September 1891, at a time when the right-wing position was causing some concern. He failed to impress and moved back to his native homeland before the turn of the year.

GABBIADINI Marco

Striker: 3+6 apps. 1 goal.

Born: Nottingham, 20 January 1968.
Career: York City (apprentice, April 1984, professional, September 1985), Sunderland (£80,000, September 1987), Crystal Palace (£1.8 million, September 1991), Derby County (£1 million, January 1992), Birmingham City (on loan, October 1996), Oxford United (on loan, January–February 1997), Panionios, Greece (August 1997), POTTERS (free, December 1997), York City (free, February 1998), Darlington (free, July 1998), Northampton Town (free, June 2000), Hartlepool United (free, July 2003, retired through injury, January 2004).

■ Blonde striker Marco Gabbiadini – his father was Italian – emerged as a teenager with York City and followed manager Denis Smith (ex-Stoke City) to Sunderland. He averaged 20 goals a season at Roker Park, helped the

Wearsiders win the Third Division title in 1988 and gained one 'B' and two under-21 caps for England. After four rather unhappy months at Selhurst Park he scored the winner at Portsmouth on his debut for Derby, but needed a few weeks to rid himself of the Palace experience before settling down to score 68 goals for the Rams until he was released in 1997, having helped Jim Smith's side gain promotion to the Premiership. On some days Gabbiadini looked a world-beater and on others his control deserted him, but he always had enthusiasm and continued to find the net (albeit only once for the Potters), and when he eventually retired with a knee injury in 2004 he had scored a total of 272 goals in 780 senior appearances for his English clubs alone.

GADSDEN, Herbert

Goalkeeper: 76 apps.

Born: Bulwell, Notts, 12 September 1893.
Died: Mansfield, 1973.
Career: Standen Hill Victoria, POTTERS (October 1912–April 1915), served in the Army during World War One, Mansfield Invicta (seasons 1919–22), then Notts Rangers (retired 1930).

■ All of Bert Gadsden's first-team appearances for the Potters during the three seasons prior to World War One were made consecutively. Recruited from Notts & Derbyshire League football following the departure of Arthur Cartlidge, he immediately established himself in the side, producing many fine displays. He was in goal for the Potters when they achieved their record FA Cup win of 11–0 versus Stourbridge in 1914. Gadsden did not rejoin Stoke after World War One, signing for Mansfield Invicta instead. * His brother, Ernest (born in December 1895), was a left-back with Mansfield Town, Nottingham Forest, Norwich, Blackpool, Portsmouth and Halifax Town during the 1920s.

GALLACHER, Patrick

Inside-forward: 4 apps.

Born: Bridge of Weir, Renfrewshire, 21 August 1909.
Died: Greenock, 4 January 1992.
Career: Linwood Council School, Linwood St Connel's, Bridge of Weir FC, Sunderland (amateur, August 1927, professional, September 1928), POTTERS (£5,000, November 1938), served in the RAF from September 1939, Weymouth (player-manager, 1945–46), ran a business in London before returning to Scotland to work in engineering.

■ Scottish international inside-forward 'Patsy' Gallacher cost Stoke manager Bob McGrory a record fee when

recruited from Sunderland in 1938. Already the holder of League Championship and FA Cup winners' medals in 1936 and 1937 respectively, Gallacher was a fine footballer, an all-rounder, quick-thinking and a fine dribbler who could also head the ball with power. Capped against Ireland in 1935, Gallacher made 307 appearances for the Roker Park club, scoring 108 goals. Unfortunately, he played in only four League games for the Potters before joining the RAF.

GALLAGHER, Paul

Striker: new signing.

Born: Glasgow, 9 August 1984.
Career: Blackburn Rovers (apprentice, August 2000, professional, February 2003), POTTERS (July 2005).

■ A Scottish international at three different levels: full (one appearance),'B' (one game) and under-21 (4 caps), Paul Gallagher scored five goals in 43 Premiership outings for Blackburn Rovers before joining the Potters at the start of the 2005–06 season. A striker with a snappy finish and good pace, he made his debut for Stoke against Norwich City (as a substitute).

GALLIMORE, Anthony Mark

Full-back: 6+5 apps.

Born: Crewe, 21 February 1972.
Career: POTTERS (June 1988), Carlisle United (on loan, October–November 1991 and February 1992, signed permanently for £15,000, March 1993), Grimsby Town (£125,000, March 1996), Barnsley (free, August 2003), Rochdale (August 2004).

■ Full-back Tony Gallimore was a strong tackler who played with coolness and competency. He served the Potters for almost five years, during which time he appeared in just 11 senior games, acting as a reserve to the more established defenders. He did superbly well at Brunton Park, playing in 164 games for Cumbrians, gaining a Third Division Championship medal in 1995. He replaced Gary Croft at Grimsby and helped the mariners win the Auto-Windscreen Shield in 1998. He added a further 318 senior appearances to his tally during his seven years at Blundell Park and in 2004, having switched to Barnsley, he reached the career milestone of 500 games with the Tykes.

GALLIMORE, George

Forward: 85 apps. 17 goals.

Born: Ashwood Villa, East Vale, Longton, Stoke-on-Trent, April 1884.
Died: Stoke-on-Trent, 1949.
Career: East Vale (1900), POTTERS (professional, May 1903), Sheffield United (July 1908), Birmingham (April 1910), Leek Town (August 1911), East Vale (July 1912–May 1914), served in Army during World War One. Did not play after the hostilities.

■ George Gallimore was an adventurous, dribbling utility forward, unpredictable at times, often over-running the ball, but on his day was a fine footballer. He joined Stoke at the age of 19, although he may well have escaped the clutches of the Potters after signing for Hanley Swifts on the wrong registration form! But that mishap was quickly sorted out and he enjoyed five good years at The Victoria Ground before transferring to Sheffield United – when Stoke went bust.

GAYLE, Howard Anthony

Forward: 4+2 apps. 2 goals.

Born: Liverpool, 18 May 1958.
Career: Bedford FC (Merseyside Sunday League, 1973), Liverpool (apprentice, June 1974, professional, November 1977), Fulham (on loan, January–March 1980), Newcastle United on loan, November 1982), Birmingham City (on loan, January 1983), Sunderland (£70,000, August 1984), Birmingham City (signed permanently, June 1985), Dallas Sidekicks, NASL (summer 1986), POTTERS (free, March 1987), Blackburn Rovers (£5,000, August 1987), Carlisle United (trialist, January–February 1992), Wrexham (trialist, March–April 1992), Halifax Town (July 1992), Accrington Stanley (September 1993–May 1995).

■ Howard Gayle, with a crop of thick, curly, black hair, was a purposeful forward with pace and a lot of skill, although at times he tended to over-run the ball. He scored twice in six outings for Stoke at the end of the 1986–97 season before moving to Ewood Park. After playing in one of the semi-final legs Gayle was named as a substitute by Liverpool when they met, and subsequently beat, Real Madrid in the 1981 European Cup Final. He was not called into action yet still received a winners' medal. He was also capped three times by England at under-21 level and gained a League Cup runners'-up medal with Sunderland in 1985. During his career Gayle netted 47 goals in a total of 247 appearances in the Football League, having his best spell with Blackburn (29 goals in 116 games).

GAYLE, John

Striker: 19+14 apps. 4 goals.

Born: Turves Green, Birmingham, 30 July 1964.
Career: Turves Green Boys' School, Highgate United (1980), Mile Oak Rovers (1982), Tamworth (1983), Bromsgrove Rivers (1985), Burton Albion (August 1987), Wimbledon (£30,000, March 1989), Birmingham City (£175,000, November 1990), Walsall (on loan, August–September 1991), Coventry City (£100,000, September 1993), Burnley (£70,000, August 1994), POTTERS (£70,000, January 1995), Gillingham (on loan, March–May 1996), Northampton Town (£25,000, February 1997), Scunthorpe United (free, July 1998), Shrewsbury Town (free, November 1999), Torquay United (free, December 2000), Moor Green (July 2001–May 2003).

■ Standing 6ft 4in tall and weighing well over 13st, John Gayle was one of the tallest and heaviest strikers in League football during the 1990s. A real beefy player, he made his Football League debut for Wimbledon in 1989 and two years later scored a stunning goal for Birmingham when they won the Freight Rover Trophy at Wembley. Unfortunately, he never fitted in at Highfield Road or, indeed, at his next club Burnley and it was no surprise when his former boss at St Andrew's, Lou Macari, bought him to Stoke in 1995. He failed to hold down a regular place in the first team at The Victoria Ground, and after a loan spell with Gillingham he joined Northampton Town. He scored 49 goals in 32 senior appearances between 1989 and 2001.

GEE, Frederick

Wing-half or inside/centre-forward: 21 apps. 5 goals.

Born: Handsworth, Birmingham, 23 June. 1872.
Died: Birmingham, c.1943.
Career: Grove County School (Handsworth), Edgbaston Park (1886), POTTERS (August 1888), Pershore Swifts (1890–91), later with King's Heath

■ Fred Gee played in just 21 games for the Potters in his two seasons. A busy little player, he made his debut on the last day of the first-ever league season against Accrington, away, in April 1889 when he deputised for Ed Smith in the half-back line.

GEMMILL, James

Inside-forward: 11 apps. 2 goals.

Born: Glasgow, 17 November 1880.
Died: Glasgow, 1952.
Career: Maryhill (Glasgow, 1896), Clyde (professional, August 1897), Sunderland (November 1900), POTTERS (July 1907), Leeds City (December 1907), Sunderland (May 1910), Third Lanark (April 1912). Did not play after World War One.

■ Jimmy Gemmill was a an astute forward, much abused (and bruised), who played the majority of his football with Sunderland, for whom he made 227 appearances and scored 46 goals during his two spells at Roker Park, gaining a League Championship medal in 1901–02, when he missed only one game. He did well initially with Clyde, never settled in the Potteries despite half-a-dozen excellent performances, including those in the Second Division against Gainsborough Trinity (won 5–0) and Glossop (won 4–0), and played in 73 matches and netted 14 goals for Leeds City.
His son, Jimmy Gemmill junior (born in Sunderland in 1911), played for Bury and Southport either side of World War Two.

GIBBONS, Ian Kenneth

Outside-right: 0+1 app.

Born: Stoke-on-Trent, 8 February 1970.
Career: Local junior football, POTTERS (apprentice, April 1986, professional, February 1988), Hilberry FC (June 1988), Florence Colliery (1990), later with Newcastle Town (two spells), Coalville Wanderers, Eastwood and Rochester.

■ One of the few men to make only one substitute appearance for Stoke, winger Ian Gibbons's only outing was against Crystal Palace in April 1988. He was still playing non-League football in 2005.

GIBLIN, Edmund John

Left-half: 1 app.

Born: Stoke-on-Trent, 29 June 1923.
Career: Tunstall Boys' Club (1940), POTTERS (February 1943, professional April 1944), Stafford Rangers (August 1948).

■ Initially an amateur signing by Stoke in 1943, wing-half Ted Giblin's only senior appearance was at left-half against Manchester United at Old Trafford in October 1947. Giblin was born a mile from Stoke's Victoria Ground.

GIDMAN, John

Full-back: 9+4 apps.

Born: Liverpool, 10 January 1954.
Career: Merseyside schoolboy and junior football, Liverpool (apprentice, June 1969), Aston Villa (professional, August 1971), Everton (£650,000, October 1979), Manchester United (£450,000, August 1981), Manchester City (free, October 1986), POTTERS (August 1988), Darlington (player-assistant manager, February–May 1989), Kings Lynn (manager, early 1990s), now a café/bar owner in Marbella, Spain.

■ Attack-minded right-back John Gidman had an excellent career. After failing to make the breakthrough at Anfield, he took time to establish himself in the first XI with Aston Villa, but once in he stayed and appeared in 243 games, scoring nine goals. He also gained England recognition at full, 'B' and under-23 levels, having earlier represented his country as a youth-team player. He helped Villa win the FA youth Cup in 1972 and the League Cup in 1977, against his future club Everton, but missed the 1975 League Cup Final win over Norwich with an eye injury following a firework accident on Bonfire Night in 1974. He was also sent-off in the Nou Camp Stadium playing for Villa against Barcelona in the UEFA Cup in 1978. He quickly settled into his stride at Goodison Park, making an impressive debut against Manchester United in 1979. He held his position, injuries aside, until leaving for Old Trafford, duly collecting an FA Cup winners' medal when United beat Everton in the 1983 Final. He was 34 when he joined the Potters, his career slowly coming to an end, but he still gave some useful performances. He made over 500 senior appearances during his career (432 in the Football League) and is now enjoying life on Spain's Costa del Sol.

GLEGHORN, Nigel William

Midfield: 208 apps. 31 goals.

Born: Seaham, 12 August 1962.
Career: Deneside Junior & Northlea Senior Schools, Seaham Red Star (April 1978), Ipswich Town (£5,000 as a professional, August 1985), Manchester City (£47,500, August 1988), Birmingham City (September 1989) POTTERS (£100,000, October 1992), Burnley (free, July 1997), Brentford (on loan, November–December 1977),

Northampton Town (on loan, February–March 1998), Altrincham (June 1988), Witton Albion (November 2001), Nantwich Town (player-manager-coach, 2002–04), also worked with England under-14s and was scout for the under-21s, now employed as a senior sports lecturer at South Trafford College, Manchester.

■ Nigel Gleghorn, 'Gleggy' to his pals, possessed a fine left foot and gave Stoke excellent service on the left-side of midfield for almost four years. He played locally in Seaham before becoming a professional with Ipswich, for whom he made 84 appearances before transferring to Manchester City. He spent one season at Maine Road, playing in 39 first-team matches before making his next move to Birmingham. He did very well at St Andrew's, amassing 176 appearances while scoring 43 goals and gaining a Freight Rover Trophy winners' prize at Wembley in 1991. Then, at the end of his first campaign at The Victoria Ground, he added a Second Division Championship-winning medal to his collection. In the summer of 1996, after more than 200 appearances for Stoke, he teamed up with his former colleague Vince Overson at Burnley. Gleghorn, who was also a capable stand-in goalkeeper, had trials for Middlesex as a batsman-wicketkeeper and represented Durham under-18s and under-21s, and at one time held the record for the highest score in the Durham Coast League (135).

GODFREY, Thomas

Right-back: 10 apps.

Born: Stenhousemuir, October 1904.
Died: Redditch, December 1983.
Career: Stenhousemuir (professional, August 1921), POTTERS (August 1927), Walsall (April 1929), Swindon Town (1931–32).

■ Scotsman Godfrey was a sturdy half-back who played for Stoke for a couple of seasons in the late 1920s. He played for his home-town club before acting in the main as a reserve to Len Armitage at The Victoria Ground. He made 42 appearances for Walsall.

GODLEY, William

Inside-forward: 3 apps. 1 goal.

Born: Durham, 8 September 1879.
Died: Berkshire, c.1953.
Career: Brandon Juniors, Croxdale FC, Middlesbrough (professional, December 1902), POTTERS (April 1904), Plymouth Argyle (September 1905), Reading (August 1906), New Brompton (July 1908), Reading (seasons 1909–11).

■ Bill Godley's only senior goals for Stoke was against Grimsby Town in a first-round FA Cup tie at The Victoria Ground in February 1905. He was reserve to Hall, Holcroft and Sheridan and later played in the Southern League with Plymouth, New Brompton and Reading, amassing over 100 appearances at that level.

GODWIN, Verdi

Inside or centre-forward: 23 apps. 2 goals.

Born: Blackburn, 11 February 1926.
Career: Blackburn Rovers (amateur, April 1943, professional, March 1946), Manchester City, June 1948), POTTERS (£3,000, June 1949), Mansfield Town (player/cash exchange deal, January 1950), Middlesbrough (November 1951), Grimsby Town (January 1952), Brentford (March 1953), Southport (July 1954), Barrow (August 1955), Tranmere Rovers (August 1956), Kings Lynn (August 1957), Macclesfield Town (May 1958), Netherfield FC (May 1960), New Brighton (July 1961, retired, April 1964), continued in the game as scout for Blackpool, Chelsea, Plymouth Argyle, Liverpool (two spells), Vancouver Whitecaps, Bolton Wanderers and Wimbledon up to 1985.

■ Verdi Godwin was a useful utility forward whose first-team outings were limited at The Victoria Ground. He made just 143 League appearances during his career (netting 28 goals), having perhaps his best spells with Blackburn (six goals in 27 outings) and Mansfield (nine in 31). He was responsible more than anyone else for spotting the talent of Steve Heighway, Paul Mariner and Tony Waiters, all of whom became full internationals, and he also arranged for the Whitecaps to release Peter Beardsley to Carlisle in 1979.

GOODFELLOW, Marc David

Winger: 25+46 apps. 9 goals.

Born: Swadlincote, Derbyshire, 20 September 1981.

Career: POTTERS (apprentice, April 1998, professional, January 1999), Bristol City (£50,000, January 2004).

■ An exciting player, fast and direct, over two-thirds of his senior outings for the Potters were made as a substitute, virtually all in the second-half of matches. He spent six years at the club and was a regular performer in the side during the last two when he made 43 League appearances before his transfer to Ashton Gate.

GOODWIN, David

Centre-forward: 24+4 apps. 3 goals.

Born: Nantwich, Cheshire, 15 October 1954.
Career: POTTERS (apprentice, August 1970, professional, June 1972), Workington (on loan, October–November 1976), Mansfield Town (November 1977), Bury (September 1980), Rochdale (August 1981), Crewe Alexandra (August 1982), Macclesfield Town (March 1983), later with Alsager United, Kidsgrove Athletic and Hanley Town.

■ Dave Goodwin was, on his day, a pretty useful striker, who always gave a good account of himself. After leaving The Victoria Ground he went on to appear in almost 100 League games before dropping down the ladder with Macclesfield Town in 1983.

GORMAN, James John

Inside-forward: 17 apps. 7 goals.

Born: Stourbridge, 7 April 1882.
Career: Old Hill Wanderers (1898), Woodside Albion (1900), Halesowen (1902), Wolverhampton Wanderers (April 1906), POTTERS (April 1907), Croydon Common (July 1909), Dudley Town (May 1910), later with Cradley Heath, did not play after World War One, also served with the Police Force, based in Halesowen.

■ A proper down-to-earth Black Country-born inside-forward with a splendid physique and enormous willpower, Jim Gorman spent two full seasons with the Potters, partnering Sam McAllister in attack from October 1908 onwards. He suffered a knee injury playing in the second XI during the 1907–08 campaign, from which he took some time to recover. A year after leaving The Victoria Ground he returned to the Black Country.

GRAVER, Andrew Martin

Centre-forward: 42 apps. 14 goals.

Born: Craghead, County Durham, 12 September 1927.
Career: Quaking House Juniors (1942), Willington FC (1945), Annfield Plain (April 1947), Newcastle United (professional, September 1947), Lincoln City (£3,000, September 1950), Leicester City (£27,500 plus Eric Littler, December 1954), Lincoln City (£13,000, June 1955), POTTERS (£12,000, November 1955), Boston United (£1,000, September 1957), Lincoln City (£2,500, October 1958), Skegness Town (July 1961), Ilkeston Town (July 1962, retired through injury, November 1963), Lincoln City (Youth team coach, June 1964–October 1965, then scout for four years), later worked as a financial consultant in Lincoln.

■ Andy Graver was already an established marksmen when he moved to The Victoria Ground, having scored

111 goals in 187 League games for Lincoln, but unfortunately he never really bedded down with Stoke, and, after averaging a goal every three games, he was sold for a £1,000. He then had a third spell at Sincil Bank before rounding off his career in non-League football. Graver, who still lives in Lincoln and played alongside that prolific marksman Arthur Rowley at Filbert Street, netted 159 goals in 325 League games over a period of 14 years (1947–61). He scored a double hat-trick (six goals) for Lincoln in an 11–1 League win over Crewe in September 1951 and gained a Third Division North Championship medal that season, his only prize at senior level. His playing career ended after he fractured his right ankle playing for Ilkeston reserves at the age of 36. He was nicknamed 'homing pigeon' following his third move to Lincoln. His father, Fred Graver, played for Grimsby Town and Leeds United in the 1920s and brother, Alf, was also registered with Lincoln but did not make the first team.

GREAVES, Thomas

Centre-forward: 13 apps. 5 goals.

Born: Hanley, Stoke-on-Trent, 12 April 1888.
Died: Stoke-on-Trent, c.1960.
Career: Goldenhill Villa, POTTERS (July 1908), Hanley Swifts (May 1910), POTTERS (guest, World War One).

■ The Potters picked up robust centre-forward Tommy Greaves from local football as cover for the club's three main strikers. He stayed at The Victoria Ground for two seasons before moving to his home-town club. After retiring he became a referee.

GREENACRE, Christopher Mark

Striker: 51+32 apps. 9 goals.

Born: Halifax, 23 December 1977.
Career: Manchester City (apprentice, April 1994, professional July 1995), Cardiff City (on loan, August–September 1997), Blackpool (on loan, March–April 1998), Scarborough (on loan, December 1998–February 1999), Mansfield Town (free, November 1999), POTTERS (free, July 2002), Tranmere Rovers (August 2005).

■ Chris Greenacre made his League debut with Manchester City in 1997, but after limited first-team chances at Maine Road he joined Mansfield after loan spells with three other clubs. A penalty-box striker with an eye for goal, he netted 58 times in 134 games for the Stags before his switch to the Potters. Unfortunately, a pre-season ankle injury delayed his debut until October 2002, but after that he quickly made up for lost time with some early goals. He then had to battle for a place in the starting line up in 2003–04, owing to the rise in form of Ade Akinbiyi, and likewise the following season when he was used mainly as a substitute.

GREENHOFF, James

Inside-forward: 338 apps.97 goals.

Born: Barnsley, 19 June 1946.
Career: Barnsley & Yorkshire Schoolboys, Leeds United (apprentice, June 1961, professional, August 1963), Birmingham City (£70,000, 1968), POTTERS (£100,000, August 1969), Manchester United (£120,000, November 1976), Crewe Alexandra (December 1980), Toronto Blizzard (player-coach, March 1981), Port Vale (August 1981), Rochdale (player-manager, March 1983–March 1984), Port Vale (part-time coach, March 1984, assistant manager-coach, April 1984, left club, May 1984), later coached youngsters at a Butlins holiday centre (late 1980s), worked for a Staffordshire-based paint company and ran his own insurance business – Greenhoff Peutz & Co, now lives in Alsager (North Staffs).

■ Jimmy Greenhoff – Stoke City's first £100,000 signing – was a quality footballer who gave the Potters supreme service over a number of years. A big favourite with the fans, he had the power to turn a match round with one fleeting movement, either with his own scoring ability or with his distinctive knack of laying on a chance for a colleague. Excellent at screening the ball, with his back to goal and defenders behind him, he was certainly a very skilful player and highly talented with a fierce shot in both feet. He was also useful with his head and scored some cracking goals, a few of them terrific volleys. He netted almost 100 goals in just under 340 first-team matches and helped the Potters win their first major trophy, the League Cup, in 1972. After leaving The Victoria Ground he achieved further success at Old Trafford, claiming United's fortuitous winning goal in the 1977 FA Cup Final versus Liverpool when Lou Macari's effort rebounded off him and bounced over the line past a helpless Ray Clemence. Then, two years later, he was on the losing side as Arsenal pipped the Reds with a last-minute winner. He bagged 36 goals in 123 games for the Reds before moving to Gresty Road. Previously a League Cup and Fairs Cup winner with Leeds United, as well as being a runner-up in the latter competition during his time at Elland Road, the blonde-haired Greenhoff represented the Football League and appeared in both 'B' and under-23 internationals for England. But unfortunately a full cap eluded him, despite being rated as one of the League's finest strikers during the mid-1970s. Greenhoff scored in two FA Cup semi-finals for different clubs on the same ground (Goodison Park). His first goal was for Stoke City against Arsenal in 1972 and his second for Manchester United against Liverpool in 1979. He also netted in another semi-final for United versus Leeds at Hillsborough in

Jimmy Greenhoff

1977. His terrific volleyed goal for the Potters in a 3–0 League win over his former club Birmingham City at St Andrew's in December 1974 was duly voted 'Goal of the Season' on ITV.
* He and his brother, Brian Greenhoff, played in the same Manchester United team during the 1970s.

GREGG, Henry, MBE

Goalkeeper: 2 apps.

Born: Magherafelt, County Derry, Northern Ireland, 25 October 1932.
Career: Linfield Rangers (1947), Linfield Swifts (1948), Coleraine (1950), Doncaster Rovers (£2,000, October 1952), Manchester United (£23,000, December 1957), POTTERS (player-coach, December 1966), Shrewsbury Town (manager, July 1968–October 1972), Swansea City (manager, November 1972–January 1975), Crewe Alexandra (manager, January 1975–May 1978), Kitan Sports Club (summer 1978), Kuwait (manager-coach for August–December 1978), Manchester United (coach, November 1978–June 1981), Swansea City (coach, February 1982, assistant manager, July 1984), Swindon Town (coach-assistant manager, 1984–86), Carlisle United (manager, May 1986–November 1987), later ran a hotel in his native Magherafelt.

■ A hero of the Munich air crash when he went back into the wreckage to help out his colleagues and surviving passengers, goalkeeper Harry Gregg made almost 250 senior appearances for Manchester United before being replaced between the posts by David Gaskell. An agile, daring and courageous 'keeper, never afraid to dive in among flying boots, he is remembered as one of United's best-ever goalkeepers. Gregg played in the 1958 FA Cup Final defeat by Bolton when he was controversially bundled over the line by the England centre-forward Nat Lofthouse. An Irish schoolboy and amateur international, he also represented the Irish League and went on to earn a total of 25 full caps for his country, appearing in the 1958 World Cup Finals in Sweden. He was succeeded between the Irish posts by Pat Jennings. He was appointed player-coach by Stoke City boss Tony Waddington but appeared in only two League games, against Leicester City away and Blackpool at home in the 1966–67 season, when he deputised for John Farmer. A severe shoulder injury ended his career. He later worked under former United star and future Potters manager Lou Macari at Swindon, but left the County Ground after a clash of personalities! Gregg's son, John, was on Barnsley's books and was capped by Northern Ireland at under-18 level.

GREGORY, David Harry

Forward: 24+1 apps. 4 goals.

Born: Peterborough, 6 October 1951.
Career: Chatteris Town (January 1973), Peterborough United (professional, August 1973), POTTERS (£50,000, June 1977), Blackburn Rovers (on loan, July–August 1978), Bury (£30,000, September 1978), Portsmouth (£60,000, December 1978), Wrexham (free, August 1982), Peterborough United (free, August 1986), King's Lynn (free, July 1987), Holbeach United (1988), Watton United (1989), Spalding United (1990–91), now a self-employed ceramic tile manufacturer, he also played for Peterborough Old Stars.

■ David Gregory, a utility forward, spent 14 years in League football (1973–87), during which time he scored for each of the clubs he served, including four for the Potters. During his League career he netted 108 times in 481 outings.

GREWER, James

Defender: 84 apps. 1 goal.

Born: Dundee, February 1865.
Died: c.1930.
Career: Middlesbrough Ironopolis (May 1893), POTTERS (August 1894), Gravesend (1898–1902).

■ Jimmy Grewer played 84 times in Stoke's first XI between June 1894 and December 1897, being the first Potters player to pass the 75 appearance mark in the centre-half position. A powerful defender, born in Dundee in February 1865, he joined the Potters from Sunderland, Albion having previously been associated with Middlesbrough Ironopolis. He left The Victoria Ground for Gravesened & Northfleet, retiring in 1902. He died *c.*1950.

GRIEVE, James

Left-half: 24 apps. 1 goal.

Born: Edinburgh, April 1887.
Died: Edinburgh, May 1955.
Career: Hibernian, Belfast Distillery, Watford POTTERS (£200, August 1911), South Shields (March 1912), Edinburgh Thistle (1914). Did not play after World War One.

■ Having moved south from Scotland, Jock Grieve was suspended sine die by the FA after being sent off as a Watford player, but on appeal that decision was later over-turned and he moved to the Potteries. A tough campaigner, he played across the middle of the park with Jimmy McGillivray and Joey Jones for most of his stay at The Victoria Ground. His only goal was a consolation penalty against Coventry City in a 3–2 Southern League defeat in September 1911.

GRIFFIN, Andrew

Left-back: 58+6 apps. 2 goals.

Born: Billinge near Wigan, 7 March 1979.
Career: POTTERS (apprentice, April 1995, professional, September 1996), Newcastle United (£1.5 million, January 1998), Portsmouth (free, June 2004).

■ Left-back Andy Griffin made his League debut for the Potters following injuries to Nigel Worthington and the

sale of John Dreyer during the first part of the 1996–97 season. Born in Rugby League territory, he joined Stoke on leaving school and made rapid progress into the first XI, much to the delight of his manager and coaches. In February 1997 Griffin was called up to the England under-18 squad and he went on to appear in over 60 games for the potters before his big-money transfer to Premiership side Newcastle. He went on to play for his country in two under-21 internationals and helped the Geordies qualify for European competition under boss Sir Bobby Robson.

GRIFFITHS, Arthur Alexander

Outside-left: 4 apps.

Born: Tonypandy, South Wales, 1 January 1908.
Career: Barry Town (May 1927), Torquay United (March 1932), Newport County (August 1932), Barry Town (1933–34), Cheltenham Town (1934–35), Barry Town (1935–36), Newry Town (1936–37), Glenavon (August 1937), Rochdale (January 1938), POTTERS (July 1938), served in World War Two, played non-League football, thereafter, until 1948.

■ No relation to any of the other Griffiths players, Archie Griffiths took over from Frank Baker on Stoke's left-wing for four games halfway through the 1938–39 season. A useful reserve-team player, he left The Victoria Ground when World War Two broke out and after the conflict played non-League football prior to his retirement at the age of 40.

GRIFFITHS, Arthur Edwin

Outside or inside-right: 121 apps. 51 goals.

Born: Hartshill, Stoke-on-Trent, 2 February 1885.
Died: 1944.
Career: Goldenhill Wanderers, Hartshill, POTTERS (September 1905) Oldham Athletic (August 1908), POTTERS (July 1909), Wrexham (August 1912–April 1915), served in the Army during World War One, guest for Oldham Athletic (1917), did not play after the hostilities.

■ Arthur Griffiths had two spells at The Victoria Ground as a goalscoring winger or inside-forward. His first ended when he joined the exodus of players who left the club when the Potters went out of the League at the end of the 1907–08 campaign. He quickly returned to bigtime football, however, by signing for Oldham, for whom he had 25 outings prior to his return to Stoke in 1909. Three years later he went to Wrexham. He top-scored for the Potters in 1909–10 with 38 goals and on his 'second' debut for the club netted a hat-trick in an 11–1 Southern League win over Merthyr Town (September 1909). Army officer Griffiths spent 20 months serving in the trenches in France during the Great War.

GRIFFITHS, Edwin

Outside or inside-right: 7 apps.

Born: Hanley, Stoke-on-Trent, 11 February. 1883.
Died: Stoke-on-Trent, c.1950.
Career: Charterhouse School, Old Carthusians, North Staffs Nomads, POTTERS (August 1908–May 1909), North Staffs Nomads (to 1915). Did not play after World War One.

■ Ed Griffiths remained an amateur throughout his career. An orthodox right-winger, he spent just the one season with the Potters, playing in the opening five games and two more later in the campaign.

GRIFFITHS, Peter James

Outside-right: 47+17 apps. 5 goals

Born: Barnstaple, Devon, 14 August 1957.
Career: Bideford Town POTTERS (November 1980), Bradford City (on loan, March–April 1984), Port Vale (July 1984), Salisbury United (June 1986), Newcastle KB, Australia (May 1987), later with Stafford Rangers, Northwich Victoria, Matlock Town, Milton United, Nantwich Town.

■ Efficient right-winger Peter Griffiths was being chased by a number of clubs while playing in the North Devon League during the late 1970s, but chose the Potters in the end and did well during his three and a half years at The Victoria Ground. A loan spell with Bradford preceded his departure to Port Vale in 1984.

GRIMES, Augustine Ashley

Forward/midfield: 7+8 apps. 1 goal.

Born: Dublin, 2 August 1957.
Career: Stella Maris, Bohemians, Manchester United (trialist, August 1972), Bohemians (professional, 1975), Manchester United (£20,000, March

1977), Coventry City (August 1983), Luton Town (1984), Osasuna, Spain (August 1990), POTTERS (coach, August 1991, non-contract player-coach from January 1992, retired as a player, May 1992), Celtic (coach, 1993–94), POTTERS (assistant manager-coach, 1994–95).

■ Almost one third of Ashley Grimes's 107 first-team appearances for United were made as a substitute. A player with a useful left-foot, he was a hard-working midfielder who was sadly plagued by illness and injury during his time at Old Trafford. He didn't have much joy at Highfield Road but appeared in successive League Cup Finals with Luton, gaining a winners' medal against Arsenal in 1988, coming on as a substitute. He was never a regular in the first XI at Stoke, but when called to action he never let the side down. The recipient of 17 full caps for the Republic of Ireland, he was also honoured by his country at under-21 level. A close friend of Lou Macari's, Grimes played with the Scottish international at Old Trafford and was then on Macari's coaching staff at both The Victoria Ground and Celtic.

GROBBELAAR, Bruce David

Goalkeeper: 4 apps.

Born: Durban, South Africa, 6 October 1957.
Career: Inyazura Police, Salisbury Callies, Matabeland Highlanders, Hamilton High School, Bulawayo, Chibuku Shumba (Salisbury), Salisbury Callies (again), Durban City, Amazulu (guest), Vancouver Whitecaps, NASL, West Bromwich Albion (trialist, July–September 1978), AFC Bournemouth (trialist), Crewe Alexandra (non-contract, December 1979–May 1980), Vancouver Whitecaps (June 1980), Liverpool (£250,000, March 1981), Southampton (August 1994), POTTERS (on loan, March–April 1993), Plymouth Argyle (August 1996), Oxford United (September 1997), Sheffield Wednesday (September 1997), Oldham Athletic (non-contract, December 1997–February 1998), later coach of Manning Rangers (South Africa).

■ Bruce Grobbelaar played his early football in Canada and after an unsuccessful trial with West Bromwich

Albion (under manager Ron Atkinson) he joined Crewe Alexandra on loan, making his League debut in 1979. He continued to impress in the NASL with the Whitecaps and in 1981 Liverpool paid £250,000 to bring him to Anfield. With the 'Reds' he did exceedingly well and went on to win medals galore, as well as amassing 628 senior appearances for the Merseysiders, gaining full caps for Rhodesia and Zimbabwe and representing the Football League. Transferred to Southampton in 1984, he then joined the Potters on a months' loan and made four League appearances before signing for Plymouth Argyle carrying on his shoulders the burden that he was under suspicion for match-fixing. In January, February and March 1997 Grobbelaar, along with fellow 'keeper Hans Segers, striker John Fashanu and a Malaysian businessman, Heng Suan Lim, appeared at Winchester Crown Court accused of match-rigging. The jury could not reach a decision and a re-trial was ordered for later in the year. The four men were subsequently found not guilty of all charges against them.

GROVES, Frederick

Inside or centre-forward: 46 apps. 13 goals.

Born: Lincoln, 6 August 1892.
Died: Lincoln, 8 December 1980.
Career: South Bar FC (Lincoln League), Lincoln City (professional, August 1909), Worksop Town (July 1910), Sheffield United (£100, June 1911), Huddersfield Town (£50, August 1912), Worksop Town (May 1913), Pontypridd (September 1914), Tranmere Rovers (August 1919), POTTERS (£750, November 1921), Crystal Palace (August 1924), Rhyl Athletic (July 1926), Sutton Town (July 1927, retired, June 1929).

■ Fred Groves developed his skills in local junior football before joining the professional ranks at Sincil Bank in 1909. After a useful career with Worksop Town (twice), Sheffield United, Huddersfield, Portsmouth and Tranmere, when he played in all four Divisions of the Football League, he signed for Stoke in 1921 and made his debut within four hours against Notts County. A hard-working forward with a powerful right-foot shot, Groves had a mixed stay at The Victoria Ground, never really establishing himself in the side. He made a total of 78 appearances at League level and scored 23 goals.

GUDJONSSON, Bjarni

Midfield: 143+18 apps. 16 goals.

Born: Iceland, 26 February 1979.
Career: IA Akranes, Iceland (professional, March 1996), Newcastle United (£500,000, July 1997), KRC Genk, Belgium (£175,000, November 1998), POTTERS (£250,000, March 2000), Vfl Bochum, Germany (free, July 2003), Coventry City (on loan, January–May

2004, signed permanently, July 2004), Plymouth Argyle (December 2004), Watford (August 2005–06).

■ Bjarni Gudjonsson surprisingly found himself 'out in the cold' at Newcastle and failed to make a senior appearance. He then tried his luck in Belgium before transferring to Stoke, signed by his father, Gudjon Thordarson. He took some time to settle down at The Britannia Stadium but did help the Potters win the Auto-Windscreen Shield in 2000. However, after his father left he finally won over the club's supporters, and, switching to the right side of midfield after a spell in the centre, he produced some positive performances, his crossing and free-kicks creating several scoring opportunities. He also loved to shoot on sight and netted some fine goals. However, when new boss Tony Pulis elected to utilise other players in the same position, Gudjonsson's slipped out of contention and moved to Germany when his contract expired at the end of the 2002–03 campaign. An Icelandic international, by 2005 he had been capped 15 times at senior level, on 20 occasions by the under-21 side and also as a youth team player. With his brother Thordar he helped Genk win their first ever Belgium League title in 1999.

GUDJONSSON, Thordar

Midfield: 0+2 apps.

Born: Akranes, Iceland, 14 October 1973.
Career: KA Akranes, Iceland (professional, October 1990), IA Akranes (May 1991), Vfl Bochum, Germany (September 1994), KRC Genk, Belgium (August 1997), UD Las Palmas, Spain (August 2000), Derby County (on loan, March 2001), Preston North End (on loan, February 2002), Vfl Bochum (July 2002), POTTERS (January 2005).

■ An Icelandic international and the son of former Potters' manager Gudjon Thordarson and brother to Bjarni, Thordar Gudjonsson arrived at The Britannia Stadium on loan from Bochum, having already played in more than 250 club and international matches around Europe. A member of Genk's first-ever Belgian League Championship-winning side (with Bajrni) in 1999, he is a skilful if somewhat lightweight player of whom it was said 'was one of Stoke City's best-ever loan signings'. Already an experienced Icelandic international when he arrived at The Britannia Stadium, having gained almost 60 full caps as well as representing his country in four youth and 10 under-21 matches, he made just two substitute appearances for the Potters before returning to Bochum.

GUNNARSSON, Brynjar Bjorn

Midfield: 155+6 apps. 20 goals.

Born: Reykjavik, Iceland, 16 October 1975.
Career: Knattspyrnufelag Reykjavik, Iceland (professional, January 1995), Moss FotballKlub, Norway (April 1998), Orgryte IS, Sweden (briefly), POTTERS (£600,000, January 2000), Nottingham Forest (free transfer, February 2003), POTTERS (on loan, March 2004), Watford (free, July 2004). Reading (August 2005).

■ On his day Brynjar Gunnarsson was superb, one of the best defensive midfield players to come out of Iceland. But, after two wonderful seasons, he lost his way, failed to maintain his form and his performances became rather inconsistent. When he returned for a second spell he was used sparingly and added just three more appearances to his tally. An Icelandic international, capped 50 times at senior level, on eight occasions by the under-21 side and also

as a youth-team player, he is 6ft 1in tall and weighs almost 12st. When he joined Watford he linked up with fellow countryman Heidar Helguson.

GUNLAUGSSON, Arnar Bergmann

Midfield: 26+3 apps. 6 goals.

Born: Akranes, Iceland, 6 March 1973.
Career: IA Akranes, Iceland (professional, April 1990), Feyenoord, Holland (March 1993), 1 FC Nurnberg, Germany (August 1994), IA Akranes (August 1995), FC Sochaux, France (briefly), IA Akranes (1997), Bolton Wanderers (£100,000, August 1997), Leicester City (£2 million, February 1999), POTTERS (on loan, March–May 2000, signed, free, February 2002), Dundee (July 2002).

■ An Icelandic international who gained four youth and six under-21 caps before going on to win 30 more at senior level, Arnie Gunlaugsson was a strong, left-sided, midfield player who could also be used as an emergency striker. Very popular at The Reebok Stadium and Filbert Street, he certainly

filled the 'hole' in front of the Potters defence and attack and generally gave a good account of himself during his two spells at The Britannia Stadium. He was a League Cup winner with Leicester in 2000, and during his time in England he appeared in 122 competitive matches scoring 25 goals.

GUPPY, Stephen Andrew

Outside-left: 0+4 apps.

Born: Winchester, 29 March 1969.
Career: Colden Common (1987), Wycombe Wanderers (professional, September 1989), Newcastle United (£150,000, August 1994), Port Vale (£225,000, November 1994), Leicester City (£950,000, February 1997), Glasgow Celtic (£350,000, August 2001), Leicester City (free, January 2004), POTTERS (on loan, September–November 2004).

■ During the early 1990s Steve Guppy was one of the best wingers in the game. Long striding with a smashing left foot, he delivered teasing crosses for his strikers and his corner-kicks and free-kicks were usually of quality and precision. He made 58 senior appearances for Wycombe, 128 for Port Vale, 185 (in two spells) for Leicester, 49 for Celtic but only one for Newcastle (as a substitute). He gained two FA Trophy winning medals and helped Wycombe win the GM Conference, was a League Cup winner with Leicester in 2000 and assisted Celtic to their Scottish Premiership triumph in 2002. Also honoured by England at semi-professional, under-21, 'B' and full team levels, collecting one cap in each category, he had four outings as a substitute during his brief association with the Potters.

GYNN, Michael

Midfield: 19+9 apps.

Born: Peterborough, 19 August 1961.
Career: Peterborough United (apprentice, August 1977, professional, April 1979), Coventry City (£60,000, August 1983),

POTTERS (free, August 1993–May 1994), then, in turn, with Hednesford Town, Kettering Town, King's Lynn, Stamford, Corby Town, Stafford Rangers, Warboys Town, Soham Town Rangers, Stratford Town, Wisbech Town, and he retired in 2003.

■ An industrious midfielder, adept at marking tightly, Mickey Gynn played in 179 competitive games for his home-town club before joining Coventry in 1983. He stayed at Highfield Road for 10 years, making 291 senior appearances for the Sky Blues and gaining an FA Cup winners' medal (as a substitute for the injured Brian Borrows) in 1987. He stayed only a season at The Victoria Ground before drifting into non-League football in 1994, continuing to play until well over the age of 40. At 5ft 3in tall he is one of the smallest players ever to appear at senior level for the Potters and, indeed, in a major Cup Final.

HACKETT, Gary Stuart

Winger: 73+11 apps. 7 goals

Born: Stourbridge, 11 October 1962.
Career: Stourbridge & Dudley Schools, Lye Town (briefly), Bromsgrove Rovers (1981), Shrewsbury Town (£5,000, July 1983), Aberdeen (£80,000, July 1987), POTTERS (£110,000, March 1988), West

Bromwich Albion (£70,000, March 1990), Peterborough United (£40,000, September 1993), Chester City (free, August 1994), Bromsgrove Rovers (August 1995, later assistant manager), Stourbridge (player-coach, August 1997), Stourport Swifts (2000–01), Redditch United (player-coach, 2001–02), Bromsgrove Rovers (joint manager, 2002–03), Stourbridge (joint manager, from July 2003), also played for the Belbroughton and Halesowen Cricket Clubs.

■ Predominantly a touch-line winger, able to play on both flanks, Gary Hackett had good, close ball control, could deliver the perfect cross and (when he used it) a powerful shot. Injured on his Potters debut against Plymouth, he then had one and a half very successful seasons at The Victoria Ground, playing in every League game in 1988–89. He then lost his form and eventually moved to West Bromwich Albion, signed by ex-Potters midfielder Brian Talbot. During a fine career Hackett amassed over 400 senior appearances and was a Welsh Cup winner with Shrewsbury in 1984.

HAINES, Wilfred Henry

Outside-right: 3 apps.

Born: Stone, Staffs, 4 June 1882.
Died: Stoke-on-Trent, c.1963.
Career: Mount Pleasant Alliance, Newcastle Swifts (1903–05), POTTERS (August 1905), Hanley Swifts (May 1906), Stafford Rangers (June 1907), Birmingham £250 (July 1908), Leek United (August 1909), West Ham United (briefly, 1910), Stafford Rangers (June 1910, retired, April 1915).

■ Short and stocky outside-right Wilf Haines was a reserve with both Stoke and Birmingham and made just three senior appearances for each club.

HALES, Herbert

Outside-left: 1 app.

Born: Kettering, Northants, 21 November. 1908.
Died: Gainsborough, Lincs, 1982.
Career: Desborough Town (April 1925), Nottingham Forest (trialist, March 1929, signed, April 1929), Northampton Town (trialist, August 1929), Peterborough & Fletton United (November 1929), POTTERS (December 1930), Preston North End (July 1931), Chesterfield (July 1933), Stockport County (December 1934), Rochdale (July 1935), Burton Town (August 1937), Kidderminster Harriers (August 1938, retired during World War Two).

■ Herby Hales was a busy outside-left with a sound understanding of the game. A player who loved to hug the touchline, he was reserve to Bob Archibald at The Victoria Ground and his only senior appearance was against Bradford City in a home League game on Boxing Day in 1930. At the end of the season he was transferred to Preston for whom he played over 60 times. He accumulated over 160 career appearances (League and Cup) and scored 25 goals

HALES, Leonard

Inside-forward: 20 apps. 4 goals.

Born: Crewe, February 1872.
Died: Northwich, 1946.
Career: Crewe Alexandra (April 1889), POTTERS (on loan, December 1898, signed permanently, August 1901, retired through injury, April 1902), later went into business in Northwich.

■ Amateur inside-forward Len Hales had two spells with the Potters, his first on loan and his second for an entire season. He was injured during his latter weeks at Stoke and was forced to retire at the age of 30.

HALL, Ellis

Defender: 49 apps. 4 goals.

Born: Ecclesfield near Sheffield, 22 June 1889.
Died: County Durham, 1949.
Career: Ecclesfield Bible Class FC (July 1904), Hull City (January 1906), Millwall Athletic (December 1907), Hastings St Leonard's (May 1908), POTTERS (July 1909), Huddersfield Town (June 1910), South Shields (September 1912), Hull City (World War One guest, March–April 1916), Goole Town (World War One guest, 1916–17), Hamilton Academical (April 1919), Halifax Town (August 1922), Rochdale (May 1925), Consett (August 1926, retired through ill-health, September 1927).

■ Ellis Hall was a rock solid centre-half, powerful in the air and strong on the ground, who was described in some circles as being a 'rare spoiler'. He had a long and reasonably successful career, and was 38 when he retired in September 1927. Unfortunately, he failed to impress with Hull. Despite making his League debut at the age of 16, he played in just one League game for Millwall versus Crystal Palace and made his debut for the Potters in an 11–0 win over Merthyr Town. Hall appeared in almost 50 competitive matches for the club, gaining a Southern League Division Two (Western) Championship medal in 1910. He went on to star in 117 Scottish League games for Hamilton and 115 in the Northern section for Halifax. His brothers, Harry (Hull City) and Ben (Derby County), were both professional footballers.

HALL, John Henry

Centre-forward: 55 apps. 18 goals.

Born: Hucknall, Notts, 3 July 1883.
Died: Nottingham, 17 July 1938.
Career: Hucknall Boys Club (1898), Newark Town (1900), Nottingham Forest (trialist, during season 1902–03), Mansfield Town (trialist, 1903–04), POTTERS (professional, October 1904), Brighton & Hove Albion (June 1906), Middlesbrough (April 1908), Leicester Fosse (May 1910), Birmingham (£750, December 1910), Hucknall Town (May 1915, retired, May 1918), Feyenoord, Holland (coach, 1919–21).

■ Despite standing only 5ft 9in tall, Jack Hall was a terrific marksman who was good in the air and strong and powerful on the ground. In a varied career, which took him all over the country, he scored over 150 goals at club level, including 48 in 103 appearances for Birmingham and 30 in 62 for Middlesbrough. He partnered Fred Rouse in the Potters' attack and scored on his debut in a 2–1 home League win over Sheffield United. After the Great War he did well as a coach with Feyenoord.

HALL, Laurence

Striker: 0+1 apps.

Born: Nottingham, 26 March 1984.
Career: POTTERS (apprentice, May 2000, professional, March 2002).

■ After making excellent progress in the intermediate and reserve teams when he hit excellent goalscoring form, strong athletic striker Laurence Hall made his senior debut for the Potters in the LDV Vans Trophy game against Blackpool in the 2001–02 season. This was his only first-team outing for the club before his release in 2003.

HALL, Marcus Thomas

Defender: 84+3 apps. 1 goal.

Born: Coventry, 24 March 1976.
Career: Coventry City (apprentice, April 1992, professional, July 1994), Nottingham Forest (free, August 2002), Southampton (free, August 2002), POTTERS (free, December 2002), Coventry City (free, February 2005).

■ Marcus Hall spent 10 years with Coventry, for whom he made 157 senior appearances (the first as an 18-year-old) and gained one 'B' and eight under-21 caps for England. He played only once for Forest and was at The City Ground for just 23 days before being reunited with his former boss Gordon Strachan at Southampton. Understudying Wayne Bridge, he failed to break into the Saints first team and within four months moved back to the Midlands to sign for the Potters, recruited to replace the injured Clive Clarke. Tall and pacy, his swashbuckling runs down the left flank certainly benefited the team, and he made 27 appearances in his first half season with the club, 38 the following season and another 22 in 2004–05. He has also slotted in very well at centre-half.

HALL, Victor

Outside-right: 1 app.

Born: Ashton-under-Lyme, 1886.
Died: 1966.
Career: Macclesfield (1906), POTTERS (on loan, November–December 1910).

■ Amateur half-back Vic Hall spent a fortnight on loan at The Victoria Ground and played once in Stoke's first team – in a 4–0 Birmingham League home win over Walsall in November 1910 when he played on the right-wing – then he moved into the centre-forward position to replace Jack Peart.

HALL, Wilfred

Goalkeeper: 57 apps.

Born: Haydock Park, 14 October 1934.
Career: Earlstown FC, POTTERS (professional, October 1953), Worecester City (on loan, March 1954–January 1955), Ipswich Town (£2,000, June 1960), Macclesfield Town (June 1963), Stafford Rangers (May 1965), Altrincham (August 1966), Stafford Rangers (April 1968, retired, May 1970).

■ Wilf Hall was born in sight of Haydock Park racecourse. Despite his height (only 5ft 8in tall), he was well built with good reflexes and a safe pair of hands. Cover for Bill Robertson, he had 45 games on loan with Worcester City before finally making his League debut in a 0–0 home draw with Luton Town. In the summer of 1960 he was transferred to Ipswich Town and stayed at Portman Road for three seasons, making just 16 League appearances (as deputy to Roy Bailey).

HALLAM, Clifford Charles

Inside-forward: 33 apps. 2 goals.

Born: Longton, Stoke-on-Trent, 17 January 1902.
Died: Fenton, Stoke-on-Trent, 20 March 1970.
Career: Sandford Hill Primitives, Port Vale (September 1922), Sandbach Ramblers (August 1923), Sandbach Ramblers (September 1923), POTTERS (August 1924), Crystal Palace (June 1927), Sandbach Ramblers (August 1928), Stafford Rangers (1931), Hednesford Town (1932–33).

■ Charles Hallam spent three years at The Victoria Ground and most of his senior outings came at inside-left when he deputised first for Johnny Eyres and then Joe Clennell. He played in 10 League games when the Potters won the Third Division North Championship in 1926–27 and later scored twice in his two games for Palace.

HALLS, John

Defender/midfield: 58+2 apps.

Born: Islington, London, 14 February 1982.
Career: Arsenal (apprentice, April 1998, professional, July 2000), Colchester United (on loan, January–February 2002), KSK Beveren, Belgium (on loan, August 2002), POTTERS (on loan,

October–November 2003, signed permanently, December 2003).

■ An adaptable player who can perform adequately well at full-back or in midfield, John Halls was an FA youth Cup winner with Arsenal in 2000 and also gained England youth-team honours during his time at Highbury. He made six appearances in Belgium football before joining the Potters on a two and a half year contract halfway through the 2003–04 season after a successful loan spell, during which time he made his debut for the club in a 2–1 win over Nottingham Forest in October 2003.

HAMNETT, Abraham Samuel

Outside-right: 9 apps.

Born: Runcorn, Cheshire, 2 February 1882.
Died: Cheshire, c.1956.
Career: Birkenhead FC, POTTERS (October 1908), Annfield Plain (April 1909), Crewe All Saints (seasons 1912–14).

■ Enterprising right-winger Sam Hamnett played for Stoke in the Birmingham & District League during the second half of the 1908–09 season when he deputised in the main for Vic Horrocks.

HAMNETT, Robert

Outside-right: 5 apps. 2 goals.

Born: Manchester, 8 April 1889.
Died: Chester, 1967.
Career: Fenton FC, Stoke, POTTERS (December 1913), Burslem United (May 1914), Ashton Rangers (1915). Did not play after World War One.

■ No relation to Abe, Bob Hamnett, also an outside-right, appeared in a handful of Southern League games for Stoke between January and April 1914 scoring two goals, both against Mardy (away) in a 2-1 win. He joined the club on a short-term basis from local junior football.

HAMPSON, Eric

Defender: 8 apps.

Born: Norton, Staffs, 11 November 1921.
Career: Summerbank (1937), POTTERS (professional, May 1939), Fulham (World War Two guest), Stafford Rangers (July 1952, later appointed team manager).

■ Eric Hampson joined Stoke as a professional after serving with local intermediate side Summerbank. During World War Two he guested for Fulham in two friendly matches and also made 26 appearances for the Potters. He stayed at The Victoria Ground until 1952 having played most of his football in the reserves. He was given just eight League appearances by manager Bob McGrory, his debut coming against Manchester City on New Year's Day in

Eric Hampson

1949 when he took over at right-back from Billy Mould. His other outings were all at right-half.

HAMPTON, Peter John

Left-back: 152+4 apps. 4 goals.

Born: Oldham, 12 September 1954.
Career: Leeds United (apprentice, September 1969, professional, September 1971), POTTERS (£165,000, August 1980), Burnley (August 1984), Rochdale (August 1987), Carlisle United (December 1987, retired, May 1989, later trainer-physiotherapist at Brunton Park until 1997).

■ An England youth international left-back with pace, good ball control and excellent temperament, Peter Hampton appeared in over 150 League and Cup games for the Potters during his four-year stay at The Victoria Ground. A Lancastrian, he joined Leeds at the age of 15 and made 68 First Division appearances for the Yorkshire club. He played in 355 League games during his senior career.

HANDYSIDE, Peter David

Defender: 88 apps. 1 goal.

Born: Dumfries, Scotland, 31 July 1974.
Career: Grimsby Town (apprentice, July 1990, professional, November 1992), POTTERS (free transfer, July 2001), Barnsley (free, August 2003–May 2004).

■ After making 236 senior appearances at the heart of the Grimsby defence, Peter Handyside moved south to join Stoke City shortly before his 27th birthday in 2001. Solid in the tackle, he proved to be the Potters' best signing that summer, and as initial partner to Sergei Shtaniuk he gave the club splendid service for two seasons before his switch to Oakwell where he became captain.

HANSSON, Mikael

Right wing-back: 77+6 apps. 3 goals.

Born: Norrkoping, Sweden, 15 March 1968.
Career: Soderkopings, Sweden (professional, 1987), IFK Norrkoping, Sweden (August 1990), POTTERS (free transfer, December 1999–May 2002), returned to Swedish football (from August 2002).

■ A regular in the Potters side for virtually two seasons, Mikael Hansson gained one full cap for Sweden and was a member of Stoke's Auto-Windscreen Shield-winning side in 2000. A player with electrifying pace, he was particularly effective when driving forward down the right flank, although some of his crosses were not the greatest. However, his influence on the team was such that when he was on

song the Potters rarely lost. He appeared in almost 250 League games in his native Sweden (204 for Norrkoping) before moving to England.

HARBEY, Graham Keith

Full-back: 26+2 apps.

Born: Chesterfield. 29 August 1964.
Career: Derby County (apprentice, April 1981, professional, August 1982), Ipswich Town (£65,000, July 1987), West Bromwich Albion (£80,000, December 1989), POTTERS (£80,000, July 1992), Exeter City (trialist, June 1994), Gresley Rovers (trialist, July 1994, signed, August 1994), Burton Albion (August 1995–May 1997), Brailsford FC (seasons 1997–99).

Blonde-haired, clean-kicking left-back Graham Harbey made 50 appearances for Derby, 77 for Ipswich and 113 for West Bromwich Albion before joining the Potters in readiness for the 1992–93 season. Harbey's transfer fee to Stoke was fixed by an independent tribunal.

HARBOT, James Willie

Full-back: 2 apps.

Born: Bolton, 16 August 1907.
Died: Lancashire, 1992.
Career: Royal Navy Depot, Chatham (1929), Gillingham (amateur, August 1931), Charlton Athletic (professional, May 1932), Barrow (August 1933).

POTTERS (May 1934), Torquay United (July 1937), Chorley (May 1938), did not play after World War Two.

■ Lancastrian Jimmy Harbot played amateur football for the Royal Naval and Gillingham before signing professional forms for Charlton in 1932. Then a forward, he was quickly converted into a hard-tackling full-back, but starred in only one League game for the Addicks, scoring in a 1–1 draw at Manchester United in September 1932. He spent just one season at Holker Street before switching to The Victoria Ground. Basically a reserve, he was freed at the end of the 1936–37 campaign after making just two senior outings for the Potters, his only League game coming in that record breaking 10–3 home win over West Bromwich Albion in February 1937. In his long career Harbot made only 42 League appearances, spending most of his time playing second-grade football. He played under three managers at Charlton.

HARDING, William

Right-half: 5 apps.

Born: Hanley, Stoke-on-Trent, 13 July 1883.
Died: Stoke-on-Trent, 1967.
Career: Wolstanton RS, POTTERS (July 1908), Ribbendale FC (January 1909).

■ Bill Harding made all his first-team appearances for the Potters in the Birmingham & District League at the start of the 1908–09 season before losing his place to Sam Baddeley who switched from centre-half to right-half.

HARDMAN, Harold Payne

Outside-left: 55 apps. 10 goals.

Born: Kirkmanshulme, Manchester 4 April 1882.
Died: Sale, Cheshire, 9 June 1965.
Career: South Shore High School, Blackpool, South Shore Choristers FC, Blackpool (amateur, July 1900), Northern Nomads (making guest appearances between 1901–03), Everton (amateur, May 1903), Manchester United (amateur, August 1908), Bradford City (amateur, January 1909), POTTERS (amateur, February 1910, retired, August 1913), Manchester United (Director from August 1912, then Chairman, September 1951–June 1965).

■ Outside-left Harold Hardman, who chose to remain an amateur throughout his playing days, had a remarkable footballing career. An Olympic Games Gold medal winner in 1908 when England beat Denmark 2–0 in the Final, he went on to gain four full caps for his country plus another 20 at amateur level, playing brilliantly when France were defeated 16–0 in Paris in 1906. An FA Cup winner with Everton in 1906, he gained a runners'-up medal with the same club in the same competition 12 months later and made four senior appearances for Manchester United in 1908, having starred in over 200 first-team matches prior to arriving at Old Trafford. He actually joined the Board of Directors at United in 1912 while still a registered player with Stoke. He went on to serve the Old Trafford club almost continuously for the next 53 years, holding office as Chairman for the last 14 until his death at the age of 83 in 1965. A quite remarkable man, he was a qualified solicitor and was able to withstand the rigours of professional football without the benefit of full-time training. A tiny, bird-like figure, he could also be regularly found at the 'other' Old Trafford watching cricket. Hardman, Manchester City's Sam Ashworth (another ex-Potter) and the Reverend Kenneth Hunt of Wolverhampton Wanderers were the only amateurs to win FA Cup medals in the 20th century. Hardman was also an FA councillor, president of the Lancashire FA and was also associated strongly with the Central League. Thankfully, he chose not to travel with the Manchester United party to Yugoslavia for the game against Red Star Belgrade in February 1958 when, of course, on the homeward journey the plane crashed at Munich airport, killing many star players and other distinguished personnel.

HARGREAVES, Frederick James

Centre-forward: 15 apps. 11 goals.

Born: North Yorkshire, 8 June 1884.
Died: 1960.
Career: Burton United (August 1903), Leeds City (July 1905), POTTERS (November 1908–May 1909).

■ Fred Hargreaves was a fine amateur centre-forward who scored twice on his Birmingham & District League debut for Stoke against Wrexham in December 1908. A serious leg injury caused him to quit competitive football in the summer of 1909, although he did play at a lower level until the outbreak of World War One. He scored 14 goals in 56 League games for Burton and 12 in 63 for Leeds City, playing in that club's first-ever League game against Bradford City in September 1905.

HARGREAVES, Henry

Outside-right: 38 apps. 4 goals.

Born in Wolstanton, 21 August 1893.
Died: France, 1916.
Career: Newcastle Town (May 1909) POTTERS (semi-professional, August 1912, until his death at the age of 23).

■ No relation to Fred, Harry Hargreaves was a local man who played on the right-wing throughout his career. Regarded as one of the quickest players of his time, especially over 20–30 yards, he averaged a goal every four games for the Potters. He was killed while serving in the Army in France in 1916.

HARPER, Kevin Patrick

Midfield: 0+1 app.

Born: Oldham, 15 January 1976.
Career: Hutchison Vale Boys' Club, Hibernian (apprentice, August 1992, professional, August 1993), Derby County (£300,000,September 1998), Walsall (on loan, December 1999–February 2000), Portsmouth (£300,000, March 2000), Norwich City (on loan, September–November 2003), Leicester City (loan, September 2004), POTTERS (on loan, February–March 2005).

■ Kevin Harper, a right-sided midfield player, made his debut for the Potters as a substitute against Millwall at The New Den in February 2005, helping the team win 1–0. A Scottish international at

schoolboy and 'B' team levels, he has also played in seven under-21 games and made 115 senior appearances for Hibs, 41 for Derby, nine for Walsall, 128 for Pompey and two for Leicester before signing for the Potters. A First Division Championship winner with Portsmouth in 2003, he then served them in the Premiership.

HARRIS, George

Inside-left: 23 apps. 5 goals.

Born: Rocester, Staffs, 1878.
Died: Staffordshire, June 1940.
Career: Uttoxeter Town (1896), POTTERS (professional, November 1900), Reading (May 1904), Southampton (May 1905, retired, May 1907), became a licensee in Tutbury near Burton-on-Trent, played for Tutbury Town (briefly during season 1908–09).

■ George Harris made his Stoke debut in a 6–1 League defeat at Sunderland in November 1900, and at the halfway stage of the following campaign he had established himself in the first team. But after that he struggled to get a game in the first XI and was subsequently transferred to Reading. He did well at Elm Park (11 goals in 28 games) and this form led to him taking part in an England international trial. He made 48 appearances for Southampton (nine goals) but then surprisingly announced his retirement from first-team football to take over a pub.

HARRISON, Mark Simon

Goalkeeper: 8 apps.

Born: Derby, 11 December 1960.
Career: Derby County (junior), Nottingham Forest (junior), Southampton (apprentice, professional, December 1978), Port Vale (February 1980), POTTERS (on loan, June–July 1981, signed permanently in a £150,000 deal that also involved Mark Chamberlain, August 1982), Cape Town City, South Africa (November 1983), then Hellenic, South Africa, Kettering Town, Stafford Rangers, Telford United, Clyde FC, South Africa (maanager), later with Bristol City (youth team coach), Everton (goalkeeping coach), Barrow (assistant manager-coach), Stafford Rangers (player-manager to June 1995), Oxford United (reserve team coach, August 1995–May 1997).

■ Mark Harrison's chances of keeping goal for Stoke on a regular basis were severely restricted owing to the presence of Peter Fox. He was a junior at both the Baseball Ground and with Nottingham Forest and an apprentice with Southampton, turning professional at The Dell on his 18th birthday. He failed to break into the Saints' first team and moved to Port Vale. Harrison's fee was levelled out at £15,000 when he moved to Stoke, but owing to a troublesome knee injury (and of course the expertise of Fox) he was given only eight senior outings by the Potters before moving over to South Africa in 1983. He received an insurance pay out for the injury received while at Stoke.

HARTSHORNE, Arthur

Full-back: 56 apps.

Born: Moxley near Darlaston, 15 December 1880.
Died: c.1945.
Career: Moxley White Star, Wolverhampton Wanderers (December 1900), Burslem Port Vale (June 1902), POTTERS (£500, joint deal involving Teddy Holdcroft, April 1903), Aston Villa (April 1905), Southampton (May 1905), Northampton Town (May 1906).

■ Full-back Arthur Hartshorne and his colleague Teddy Holdcroft joined the Potters in 1903 for a combined fee of £750 from hard-up neighbours Port Vale. A well-built player who occasionally looked overweight, he could be quite brilliant at times and his performances belied his bulky frame. Nonetheless, he was a fine defender, strong and resourceful, who made 30 appearances for the Valiants and played over 50 games for the Potters. He spent just two weeks with Aston Villa before signing for Southampton, for whom he made 30 appearances. Never happy on the south coast, he joined Northampton after one season at The Dell.

HASLEGRAVE, Sean Matthew

Midfield: 132+10 apps. 8 goals.

Born: Stoke-on-Trent, 7 June 1951.
Career: POTTERS (apprentice, June 1976, professional, November 1968) Nottingham Forest (£35,000, July 1976), Preston North End (September 1977), Crewe Alexandra (August 1981), York City (July 1983), Torquay United (August 1987, retired, May 1989, joined Plainmoor coaching staff).

■ Sean Haslegrave made almost 600 senior appearances (491 in the Football League) during his 13-year career. He

bided his time at The Victoria Ground before gaining a regular first-team place in 1971. He lost out to George Eastham and there were many other good midfielders at the club, but he, nevertheless, remained loyal to the Potters, whom he served for 10 years before transferring to Forest. He proved to be a tireless worker, statute and constructive.

HASSALL, Charles

Goalkeeper: 1 app.

Born: Hanley, Stoke-on-Trent, June 1863.
Died: Staffordshire, c.1930.
Career: Jude's FC, POTTERS (September 1888), Leek Town (April 1889).

■ Solidly-built goalkeeper Charlie Hassall played in one FA Cup tie for Stoke, deputising for Billy Rowley against Warwick County in October 1888 (lost 1–2). He spent only one season with the club before moving to Leek Town.

HAWE, Richard

Half-back: 3 apps.

Born: Goldenhill, Stoke-on-Trent, June 1883.
Died: c.1940.
Career: Goldenhill Juniors, Goldenhill St Joseph's, Tunstall Park, Goldenhill Wanderers (two spells), Goldenhill Villa, Goldenhill United (1906), POTTERS (July 1908), Goldenhill United (April 1911).

■ Raven-haired Dick Haw was one of several half-backs recruited by Stoke for the 1908–09 season and was given just three outings, all in the Birmingham & District League, before his release in 1911. Besides Stoke, he assisted a number of other local teams and in fact spent all his playing days in the Stoke area.

HAWKINS, Albert Crop

Right-half: 4 apps.

Born: Fenton, Stoke-on-Trent, 10 August 1893.
Died: before 1980.
Career: Stoke St Peter's, POTTERS (September 1912), Stoke United (April 1914). Did not play after World War One.

■ Crop Hawkins preferred the right-half position, although during his career he also lined up at full-back and centre-half. He remained an amateur throughout his career.

HAWORTH, Jack

Centre-forward: 6 apps. 2 goals.

Born: Nelson, Lancashire, 9 March 1883.
Died: c.1955.
Career: Colne, POTTERS (February 1904), Netherfield (December 1904), Darwen Institute (season 1905–06).

■ Fair-haired Jack Haworth scored on his debut for Stoke against Sunderland in March 1904. Short and stocky, he was a smart footballer who arrived at The Victoria Ground following an injury to Sam Higginson.

HAY, James

Full-back: 80 apps. 3 goals

Born: Lanark, Renfrewshire, June 1876.
Died: Barnsley, 1940.
Career: Renfrew Victoria (from 1896), Barnsley (July 1901), Chesterfield (May 1908), POTTERS (July 1909, retired through injury, December 1911), became a licensee in Barnsley.

■ Tough Scottish full-back, cool under pressure and a player who feared no one, Jimmy Hay joined the Potters at the age of 33 and stayed at The Victoria Ground for two and a half years. In that time he made 80 senior appearances and scored two of his three goals in a 6–2 home win over Birmingham reserves in a Birmingham & District League game in January 1911. He made his debut in the Southern League fixture against Merthyr Town when the Potters won 11–0 on the opening day of the 1909–10 season, partnering Ernie Mullineux. His younger brother, John Hay, also a full-back, played for Bathgate, Bradford City and St Bernard's either side of World War One.

HEAMES, William Thomas Henry

Outside-left: 19 apps. 3 goals.

Born: Middleport, Stoke-on-Trent, July 1869.
Died: c.1939.
Career: Middleport Athletic, Middleport Alma, POTTERS (August 1893), Burslem Port Vale (August 1897, refused to re-sign and was released, May 1904).

■ Averaging a goal every three games for Stoke during the latter part of the 19th century, Billy Heames was an out-and-out left-winger with good pace and temperament. He spent seven seasons with the Vale, during which time he amassed 254 appearances and scored 28 goals, gaining a Staffordshire Cup winners' medal in 1898.

HEATH, Adrian Paul

Forward: 115+3 apps. 17 goals

Born: Knutton, Stoke-on-Trent, 17 January 1961.
Career: POTTERS (apprentice, June 1977, professional, January 1979), Everton (£700,000, January 1982), Espanyol, Spain (£600,000, August 1988–July 1989) Aston Villa (£360,000, August 1989), Manchester City (£300,000, February 1990), POTTERS (£50,000, March 1992), Burnley (free transfer, August 1992), Sheffield United (free, December 1995), Burnley (non-contract, March 1996, then manager, from late March 1996–97), Sheffield United (assistant manager-coach), Sunderland (coach-scout, seasons 2000–03), Coventry City (coach, 2004, assistant manager, June 2005).

■ Capped eight times by England at under-21 level and once by the 'B' team,

Adrian Heath was a sharp-shooting, nippy, all-action striker with good close control, who scored 150 goals in 604 competitive games, including 120 in 525 League matches in England alone. Known as 'Inchy' due to his size, he gave the Potters excellent service for five years, making his debut at the age of 17. A record signing by Everton in 1982, he certainly played his best football at Goodison Park, gaining two League Championship medals (1985 and 1987), an FA Cup winners' medal (1984) and a European Cup-winners' Cup medal (1985), while also starring in four Charity Shield triumphs, plus one shared with Liverpool (1986) when he scored at Wembley. In December 1984, when in prime form, he was on the verge of an England team place but an injury suffered in a challenge with Sheffield Wednesday's Brian Marwood ended his chances. He never settled down at Villa Park and he failed as manager at Turf Moor. He was with former Stoke midfielder Howard Kendall at both Everton and Sheffield United.

HEATH, Philip Adrian

Winger: 166+13 apps. 19 goals.

Born: Longton, Stoke-on-Trent, 24 November 1964.
Career: POTTERS (apprentice, November 1980, professional, October 1982), Oxford United (£80,000, June 1988), Cardiff City (March 1991), Port Vale (trial), Aldershot (August 1991), Aylesbury United (season 1992–93), retired to concentrate on his pottery business in Bourton-on-the-Water and Burford in the Cotswolds' also manager of Chipping Norton Town (mid to late 1990s).

■ Fast-raiding winger Phil 'Steady' Heath spent eight years at The Victoria Ground. Naturally right-footed, he had plenty of skill, showed a lot of endeavour, was pretty quick over short distances and at times caught the eye of scouts from both Derby County and Everton. He was a regular performer in the Potters' side for several seasons, but his best return in terms of goals scored came in his last campaign, 1987–88, when he weighed in with a total of nine. He made 204 League appearances during his career.

HEATH, Robert

Midfield: 14+10 apps. 1 goal.

Born: Newcastle-under-Lyme, 31 August 1978.

Career: POTTERS (apprentice, August 1994, professional, July 1996), Stafford Rangers (January 2001).

■ Always on the fringe of the Potters' first team, the career of hard-working midfielder Robert Heath, who could also play at full-back, was blighted by injury. His only goal for the club came in a 5–1 League Cup win at York in August 2000.

HEGGARTY, Archibald

Outside-right: 22 apps. 1 goal.

Born: Belfast, August 1884.
Died: Belfast, 1951.
Career: Belfast Distillery (1908), POTTERS (July 1912), Tottenham Hotspur (May 1913), Belfast Crusaders (October 1913), did not appear after World War One.

■ Irishman Archie Heggarty spent just one season at The Victoria Ground in 1912–13. A useful right-winger with good pace and a fair amount of skill, he had done very well with Distillery and, to a certain extent, produced some excellent displays in the Football League. After failing to make the first team at Spurs he returned to his homeland.

HELME, James Albert

Inside-left: 4 apps. 1 goal.

Born: Altrincham, Cheshire, 1887.
Died: Altrincham, 1945.
Career: Altrincham (1912), POTTERS (February 1921), Altrincham (July 1921).

■ An amateur throughout his career, Jack Helme played for Stoke during the latter stages of the 1920–21 season, deputising for Arty Watkin and Albert Whitehurst. His goal was scored in a 3–2 home League win over Barnsley.

HEMMING, Christopher Andrew John

Defender: 96+9 apps. 2 goals.

Born: Newcastle-under-Lyme, 13 April 1966.
Career: POTTERS (apprentice, May 1982, professional, April 1984), Wigan Athletic (on loan, January–February 1989), Hereford United (£25,000, August 1989), Merthyr Tydfil (July 1991), then Macclesfield Town, Stafford Rangers.

■ Ginger-haired utility defender Chris Hemming hit the national sporting headlines when he had a pace-maker fitted at the peak of his career and then stunned everyone by bouncing back to

continue his career as a professional footballer. Having graduated through the junior ranks, he made his League debut for the Potters on his 18th birthday against Tottenham Hotspur at White Hart Lane in 1984 – this being the first of more than 100 appearances for the club. His two League goals were scored in a 2–2 home draw with Leicester in September 1984 and a 3–1 home victory over Barnsley in March 1988.

HENDRY, William Henry

Centre-forward: 16 apps. 1 goal.

Born: Dundee, Scotland, 16 June 1864.
Died: Sussex, April 1901.
Career: Dundee & Invergowrie Schools, Dunblane Thistle (1882), Dundee Wanderers (August 1885), West Bromwich Albion (August 1888), POTTERS (March 1889), Preston North End (January 1890), Sheffield United (February 1891), Bury (August 1895), Brighton United (September 1898, retired, May 1900, due to ill-health).

■ Billy Hendry had the qualities of speed, good headwork and whole-hearted endeavour. He made his debut for West Bromwich Albion against Stoke in the first-ever League game in September 1888, but was never at home in the Black Country and after moving on did reasonably well with the Potters and even better with Sheffield United, where he was converted into a solid centre-half. He skippered the Blades for a time and helped them win promotion to the First Division in 1893, making 20 appearances (2 goals). Hendry died of consumption at the age of 26.

HENRY, Anthony

Midfield: 67+3 apps. 11 goals.

Born: Houghton-le-Spring, Lancashire, 26 November 1957.
Career: Manchester City (apprentice, July 1974, professional, December 1974), Bolton Wanderers (£125,000, September 1981), Oldham Athletic (£21,000, March 1983), POTTERS (£40,000, December 1987), Mazda FC, Japan (June 1989), Shrewsbury Town (August 1991), Witton Albion (1992–94), now a financial advisor with the Prudential Insurance Company at Bicton near Shrewsbury.

■ Stoke manager Mick Mills signed midfielder Tony Henry from Oldham halfway through the 1987–88 season. He did a useful job as the playmaker in the centre of the park, although he never really won the support of the fans. He skippered the team occasionally and made 70 appearances for the first team. Henry, who could also play in defence, had earlier gained an FA Cup runners'-up medal with Manchester City in 1981. He initially signed a two and a half year contract with Stoke but left the club prematurely, choosing to play in Japan. In his League career Henry made over 480 appearances and netted 80 goals.

HENRY, Karl Levi Daniel

Midfield: 60+48 apps. 1 goal.

Born: Wolverhampton, 26 November 1982.
Career: POTTERS (apprentice, May 1998, professional, November 1999), Cheltenham Town (on loan, January–March 2004).

■ Voted Stoke's 'Young Player of the Year' for the 1999–2000 season, Karl Henry developed quickly at The Britannia Stadium and established himself in the first team in 2003 after rapid progress through the Academy and reserve ranks. An England under-21 international, he has also figured in his country's under-18 and under-20 squads and skippered the Potters Academy side. His composure with the ball is one of his major assets, and as well as playing positively in midfield he has also been used to good effect at right-back and central defender. He scored his first goal for Stoke in the 4–2 Boxing Day defeat at Bradford City in 2002.

HERBERT, William Edward

Inside or outside-right: 67 apps. 28 goals.

Born: Canning Town, London, 12 November 1888.
Died: London, 1963.
Career: Walthamstow Grange (1905), Barnet Alston (1908), Woolwich Arsenal (August 1909), Glossop North End (August 1910), Gravesend United (September 1911), POTTERS (December 1912), Bolton Wanderers (November 1919), Wigan Borough (September 1921–May 1923).

■ Billy Herbert, a true 'Cockney', played inside or outside-left during a useful career. He joined Stoke when the Potters were in the Southern League and made his debut for the club on Christmas Day in 1912 against the club he supported as a lad, West Ham United. He remained at The Victoria Ground until he moved north to Bolton. One of the few players to don a Stoke jersey at senior level before, during and after the 1914–18 hostilities, Herbert was certainly a fine attacker who enjoyed running with the ball. He won a Southern League Championship medal with the Potters in 1915 and during World War One football scored 64 goals in 135 outings to add to his peacetime record with Stoke.

HERD, David George

Centre-forward: 43+5 apps. 11 goals.

Born: Hamilton, Lanarkshire, 15 April 1934.
Career: Princes Road school (Moss Side, Manchester), Stockport County (amateur, July 1949, professional, April 1951), RAF (national service), Arsenal (£9,500, August 1954), Manchester United (£35,000, July 1961), POTTERS (free transfer, July 1968), Waterford (December 1970, retired, knee injury, February

1971), Lincoln City (manager, March 1971–December 1972), later became a garage proprietor in Manchester.*

■ David Herd played alongside his father, George, for Stockport County before moving to Arsenal. At Highbury he began to score regularly, and in the next seven seasons he netted 107 goals in 166 First Division matches and 14 FA Cup games for the Gunners. In 1961 he was transferred to Manchester United and two years later scored at Wembley when Leicester City were defeated 3–1 in the FA Cup Final. Twice a League Championship winner with the 'Reds', in 1964–65 and again in 1966–67, Herd was capped five times by Scotland at senior level having earlier represented his country in two under-23 and four amateur internationals. During his time at Old Trafford he scored 144 times in 263 senior appearances (114 of his goals coming in the top flight). Potters boss Tony Waddington enticed Herd (then aged 34) to The Victoria Ground on a free transfer in 1968, and over the next two and a half years he scored 11 goals in almost 50 first-team outings for Stoke. A knee injury had niggled him for some time before he moved to Waterford.

NB: In November 1966 Herd scored an unusual hat-trick for Manchester United against Sunderland, scoring against three different goalkeepers, Jim Montgomery, his replacement Charlie Hurley and then John Parke. Herd also kept goal for United, replacing the injured Harry Gregg during a League game against Liverpool in November 1963.

HEROD, Dennis John

Goalkeeper: 215 apps. 1 goal.

Born: Basford, 27 October 1923.
Career: Trent Vale FC (April 1937), POTTERS (junior, April 1940, professional, January 1941), Stockport County (£750, July 1953, retired, May 1955), later ventured into the greengrocery business and occasionally turned out for his adopted club, Newcastle Town.

■ Dennis Herod had the distinction of scoring a vital goal for Stoke in a 3–2 League win against Aston Villa in an away First Division match on 16 February 1952, this after being put out to 'grass' (on the wing) following an injury. One of a bevy of young talent to

emerge during and immediately after World War Two, Herod signed as a junior at The Victoria Ground in 1940 and played in 120 wartime games when free from service with the armed forces in Europe. Although on the small side for a 'keeper at 5ft 9in, he was exceptionally sound in his ground work and quite fearless and acrobatic when he was called into action. He was wounded in battle during the hostilities, and on being demobbed Herod became first choice 'keeper at Stoke, beating off the challenges of Norman Wilkinson and Arthur Jepson. Besides his wartime appearances, he made well over 200 in peacetime football during his 13 years' association with the Potters, which came to an end in 1953 when he moved to Stockport. After retiring he continued to make the occasional visit to The Victoria Ground, his last in 1996.

HERRON, Richard

Goalkeeper: 46 apps.

Born: West Stanley, County Durham, January 1890.
Died: France, April 1917.
Career: West Stanley, POTTERS (March 1911–April 1917).

■ Dick Herron was another useful goalkeeper who was registered with the Potters for six years before his tragic death on a French battlefield. One of the shortest 'keepers to play for the club at 5ft 7in, Herron was born near the coal face in County Durham. Known as 'Invincible Dick', he played for his home-town club before moving down to the Midlands to join Stoke in March 1911. He was quickly embedded into the first XI (replacing Jack Robinson) and went on to appear in almost 50 peacetime games plus another 74 during the first part of the war.

HESHAM, John Frank

Outside-right: 17 apps. 1 goal.

Born: Hyde, Manchester, 11 December 1880.
Died: France, 17 November 1915.
Career: Gorton St Francis FC (from 1897), Manchester City (January 1901), Accrington Stanley (1903), POTTERS (May 1904–June 1906), Leyton (briefly in season 1906–07), Oldham Athletic (August 1907), Preston North End (£25, September 1909), Croydon Common (November 1909), Crewe Alexandra (July 1910), Newton Heath Alliance (September 1913–November 1915).

■ Right-winger Frank Hesham had a useful career, which ended after 18 years when he was sadly killed while serving with the Royal Garrison Artillery in France. He deputised for that great, Welsh, wing wizard Billy Meredith at Manchester City. Hesham was described as 'an earnest and conscientious player, full of dash and judgement'. Arriving at Stoke with a good reputation, having scored well with his first two major clubs, he never really fitted into the 'plan of attack' at The Victoria Ground and departed after just the one season.

HICKSON, Geoffrey Geoffrey

Goalkeeper: 11 apps.

Born: Crewe, 26 September 1939.
Career: Coventry City (junior, August 1954), Liverpool (briefly, later 1954), Blackburn Rovers (amateur, September 1955), POTTERS (professional, August 1957), Crewe Alexandra (July 1962), Port Vale (on loan, August–November 1968), Southport (December 1968), Shrewsbury Town (on loan, March–April 1969), Cape Town Spurs, South Africa (1969–70).

■ Geoff Hickson's tally of 11 League appearances for the Potters covered a 16-month period between 1959 and 1961. Reserve to Wilf Hall and Bill Robertson, he had to wait almost two years before making his debut, which came against Sunderland at Roker Park in December 1959. He did well, never letting the side down, but after conceding five goals at Liverpool he was replaced by new signing Tommy Younger (ironically ex-Liverpool) and went into the reserves. Hickson wasn't happy and was desperate for first-team football so he left Stoke in 1962, moving to his home-town club Crewe Alexandra. After more than 100 games for the Alex he had 17 games on loan with Port Vale. Some people said that Hickson was 'given away' by the club far too quickly.

HIGGINS, Mark Nicholas

Defender: 44+2 apps. 1 goal.

Born: Buxton, Derbsyhire, 29 September 1958.
Career: North West Derbyshire Schoolboys, Everton (apprentice, April 1975, professional August 1976, retired through injury, June 1984), Manchester

United (December 1985), Bury (on loan, January 1987, signed permanently, February 1987), POTTERS (£150,000, September1988–December 1990), Burnley (trialist, January 1991, retired through injury, March 1991).

■ Capped by England at youth-team level, Mark Higgins was a valuable member of Everton's defence for a number of years until sidelined by a niggling groin injury in 1983. He was ready to quit the professional game on medical advice after some 200 appearances for the Merseysiders, but following a hernia operation and a two-year break he bounced back and joined Manchester United in 1985. He regained full fitness at Old Trafford, and after a handful of League outings for the 'Reds' and a spell with Bury he moved to Stoke at the age of 30 in 1988. Potters boss Mick Mills gambled on Higgins and to a certain extent the gamble paid off with the defender chalking up 46 appearances in his first two seasons at The Victoria Ground. Unfortunately, he didn't figure in the first team at the start of the 1990–91 campaign and in December his three-year contract was cancelled, allowing him to switch to Burnley. Sadly, after just two months at Turf Moor injury again forced Higgins out of the game and within a short time he had decided to hang up his boots.
* Mark's father, John Higgins, played in 202 games at centre-half for Bolton Wanderers (1952–61), gaining an FA Cup winners' medal in 1958.

HIGGINSON, Samuel

Forward: 124 apps. 23 goals.

Born: Tunstall, Stoke-on-Trent, July 1880.
Died: Stoke-on-Trent, 1945.
Career: Tunstall Casuals, Goldenhill Wanderers, POTTERS (trialist, July 1899, signed permanently, August 1899), Reading (June 1904), Bradford City (October 1908), POTTERS (February 1909, retired, March 1909).

■ Sam Higginson could play in a number of attacking positions with centre-forward being his best. He served with two local clubs prior to joining Stoke in 1899, having impressed in a series of pre-arranged practise matches. He spent five seasons at The Victoria Ground, during which time he scored, on average, a goal every five games, which was well below expectations. On his day Higginson was without doubt a clever footballer, a good mover and tidy passer of the ball, but unfortunately his finishing sadly let him down far too many times.

HILAIRE, Vincent Mark

Outside-left: 17 apps. 3 goals.

Born: Forrest Hill, London, 10 October 1959.
Career: Crystal Palace (apprentice, April 1975, professional, October 1976), San Jose Earthquakes, NASL (on loan), Luton Town (July 1984), Portsmouth (November 1984), Leeds United (July 1988), POTTERS (on loan, November–December 1989), Oldham Athletic (on loan, January 1990), POTTERS (November 1990), Exeter City (September 1991), Waterlooville (player and joint manager, August 1992), Bangor Town (May 1994), later worked for Cable TV (Portsmouth).

■ Vince Hilaire, who represented England at youth-team level, went on to add nine under-21 caps to his tally and also played in one 'B' international. He helped Crystal Palace win the Second

Division title in 1979 and during a fine career scored 67 goals in 499 League appearances as a professional. Recruited by Stoke initially on loan when Peter Beagrie was sidelined, he returned to the club on a permanent basis and did well down the left hand side of midfield before an injury suffered in a 1–0 defeat at Southend knocked him back. Hilaire and his former Palace team-mate Billy Gilbert were joint managers of Waterlooville.

HILL, Clinton Scott

Defender: 41+4 apps. 1 goal.

Born: 19 October 1978.
Career: Tranmere Rovers (apprentice, April 1995, professional, July 1997), Oldham Athletic (July 2002), POTTERS (£120,000, July 2003).

■ A strong, dominating, no-nonsense centre-back, Clint Hill made his Football League debut for Tranmere Rovers as an 18-year-old. He went on to appear in 170 senior games for the Birkenhead club (20 goals), performing superbly well during their FA Cup and League Cup exploits. He suffered a fractured leg after joining Oldham and took time to regain full fitness. As tough as they come, he loves to get forward for dead-ball situations, and over the years he has scored his fair share of goals. A hamstring injury and a severe bout of

flu disrupted his first season with the Potters, but he bounced back again to give the club excellent service.

HILL, James

Forward: 35 apps. 13 goals.

Born: Paisley, Scotland, June 1865.
Died: Glasgow, July 1940.
Career: St Mirren (July 1886), Burnley (December 1889), POTTERS (January 1897), New Brighton Tower (May 1898), Wellingborough (1899–1900), returned to Scotland for the 1900–01 season.

■ Jimmy Hill was already an experienced footballer when he joined Stoke in 1897. He had previously given good service to St Mirren and was approached by New Brighton Tower before moving to the Potteries. Hill was a versatile forward but with perhaps the left-wing being his best position. He was tricky and possessed a powerful right-foot shot, which he used to good effect when cutting inside his full-back. Ironically, he left The Victoria Ground for New Brighton Tower. A consistent goalscorer throughout his career, he netted 41 times in 162 games for Burnley, who he joined on Christmas Eve in 1889. In fact, he was the first player to top the 150 appearance mark for the Clarets.

HILL, Thomas

Centre-forward: 5 apps. 2 goals.

Born: Market Drayton, 20 June 1871.
Died: Leicester, 1933.
Career: Market Drayton (from 1893), POTTERS (August 1897), Leicester Nomads (December 1897, retired through injury, April 1899).

■ A well built centre-forward who was a Stoke player for a relatively short period of time, Tommy Hill never settled in at the Potteries. His two goals were scored against Liverpool (home), which ended as a 2–2 draw, and in the 4–1 defeat at Derby.

HINGERTY, James

Centre-forward: 24 apps. 8 goals.

Born: Walsall, December 1875.
Died: Wednesfield, 1958.
Career: North Staffs Regiment, POTTERS (January 1897), Rushden (March 1898).

■ Jim Hingerty found it difficult to adapt to competitive League football but in a brief career with Stoke his strike record was impressive.

HINKS, Charles William

Outside-left: 1 app.

Born: Manchester, September 1880.
Died: Cheshire, 1957.
Career: Darwen (1899), Stockport County (September 1901), Manchester City (April 1902), POTTERS (September 1903), Altrincham (1904–05).

■ Charlie Hinks played in only two League games during his career, his first for Stockport against Barnsley in March 1902 and his second for the Potters, whom he helped beat Liverpool 5–2 at home in a First Division match a month after signing.

HOBSON, James Walter Francis

Half-back: 1 app.

Born: Smallthorne, Staffs, June 1889.
Died: Stafford, 1961.
Career: Smallthorne Amateurs, POTTERS (October 1910), Audley (May 1911), Rocester (season 1912–13), did not play after World War One.

■ Reserve half-back Frank Hobson's only senior appearance for the Potters was against Stafford Rangers in a Birmingham & District League game in

April 1911 when he deputised for Bill Bradbury in a 4–0 victory.

HOCKADAY, David

Defender: 7 apps.

Born: Billingham, 9 November 1957.
Career: Billingham Synthonia, Blackpool (professional, June 1975), Swindon Town (free transfer, August 1983), Hull City (£50,000, September 1990), POTTERS (on loan, March–April 1993), Shrewsbury Town (free, May 1993, released, May 1995).

■ A well-built defender who could also play in midfield, Dave Hockaday made 178 appearances for Blackpool and followed up with a further 308 for Swindon Town, with whom he gained a Fourth Division Championship medal in 1988. He then had 83 outings for Hull City before his loan spell at Stoke in 1993. After that he played in 61 games for the 'Shrews' before his departure from Gay Meadow in 1995.

HODGKIN, Ernest

Defender: 29 apps. 1 goal.

Born: Grassmore near Chesterfield, 1891.
Died: County Durham, 1967.
Career: Mansfield Mechanics (from 1909), Sunderland (professional, September 1911), POTTERS (April 1912), Billingham (May 1913). Did not play after World War One.

■ Ernie Hodgkin, at 5ft 7in tall and less than 12st, was one of the smallest and lightest central defenders of his era, yet he never shirked a tackle, always battled hard and long against some of the toughest forwards around and never gave less than 100 percent effort out on the park. He lined up at both left-half and centre-half for the Potters, deputising in the latter position for Joey Jones. In February 1913 he was suspended by the Stoke directors for one month for a breach of club discipline. He left The Victoria ground at the end of the season.

HODGKINS, Thomas Reginald

Defender: 5 apps.

Born: Nuneaton, Warwickshire, 7 January 1903.
Died: Coventry, July 1927.
Career: Hinckley United, POTTERS (September 1925–July 1927).

Reg Hodgkins joined the Potters in 1925 with a reputation for being a fearless defender. He was well proportioned with a strong tackle and certainly looked the part. He did well in reserve-team matches before making his senior debut (in place of Ewart Beswick) against Barnsley at home in March 1926. Unfortunately, injuries upset his rhythm and he managed only a handful of League outings in two seasons at The Victoria Ground. In the summer of 1927 Hodgkins was admitted to Coventry Hospital for an appendix operation. Sadly, he never left his bed and three weeks later passed away, aged 24.

HOEFKENS, Carl

Defender: new signing.

Born: Belgium, 6 October 1978.
Career: Germinal Ekeren, Belgium, Lierse FC, Belgium (August 2000), POTTERS (June 2005).

■ A versatile defender, able to play at right-back or centre-half, Carl Hoefkens joined the Potters on a two-year deal in the summer of 2005 having previously appeared in some 140 League and Cup games for Lierse in Belgium. He made his debut for Stoke against Sheffield Wednesday.

HOEKSTRA, Peter

Winger: 73+15 apps. 12 goals.

Born: Asser near Groningen, Holland, 4 April 1973.
Career: PSV Eindhoven (professional, May 1991), Ajax Amsterdam (December 1995), Groningen (August 2000), POTTERS (free transfer, July 2001, retired, June 2004).

■ A Dutch international capped five times at senior level, Peter Hoekstra, at 6ft 3in, was one of the tallest wingers in League football during the early 2000s. Highly skilful, on his day no defence was safe when he had the ball at his feet. He produced many superb displays and was a huge favourite with the Potters faithful. One of his best performances in

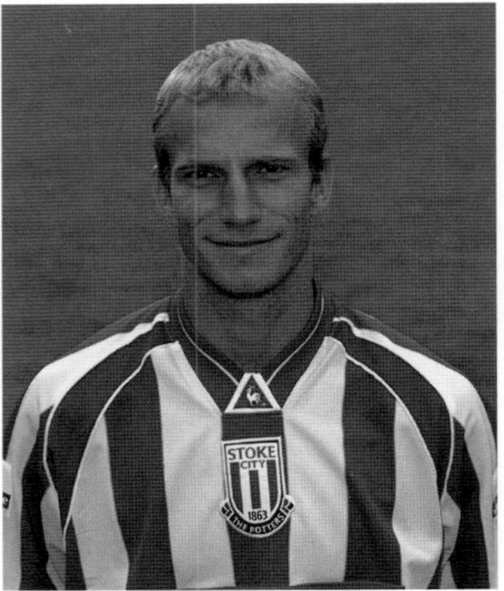

a Stoke City shirt came against Reading in December 2003 when he scored a hat-trick (including a penalty) in a 3–0 home win, and his 20-yard rocket in this same game was voted 'Goal of the Season'. He announced his retirement from the game at the age of 31 having appeared in 250 League games in Dutch and English football, scoring 47 goals.

HOLDCROFT, Hugh Edward

Inside-forward: 43 apps. 11 goals.

Born: Tunstall, Stoke-on-Trent, 12 July 1882.
Died: Norton, Staffs, 4 February 1952.
Career: Burslem Port Vale (October 1901), POTTERS (£500, joint deal involving Arthur Hartshorne, March 1903, retired, September 1908).

■ Long-striding inside-forward Teddy Holdcroft scored a goal every four games for Stoke during the early part of the 20th century. Earlier, he had played 18 times in defence for Port Vale before transferring to The Victoria Ground in 1903. In 1905 he was taken ill with heart trouble, which kept him out of the game for three years until a specialist consultant advised him to continue light training in 1908. However, he failed to regain his first-team place and retired from first-level football at the age of 26.

HOLFORD, Thomas

Centre-half: 269 apps. 33 goals.

Born: Hanley, Stoke-on-Trent, 28 January 1878.

Died: Blurton, Stoke-on-Trent, 6 April 1964.
Career: Granville's Night School (1892), Cobridge (1896), POTTERS (professional, May 1898), Manchester City (July 1908), Port Vale (player-manager, May 1914), served in the Royal Artillery during World War One, guest for Nottingham Forest, September 1918–March 1919, retired as a player, May 1923, appointed trainer, returned as a player in an emergency in 1924, team manager in June 1932–September 1935, then scout until 1950, serving as trainer again from July 1939–July 1946.

■ Known as 'Dirty Tommy', Holford joined the Potters on £1 a week and made the first of his 269 senior appearances for the club against

Sheffield United away in September 1898, resulting in a 1–1 draw. Between March 1903 and February 1906 he played in 105 consecutive League games, having firmly established himself in the centre of the defence and having gained his one and only England cap against Ireland in February 1903, which was won 4–0. A versatile performer who would and could play anywhere, Holford, who was only 5ft 5in tall, excelled in distribution and was a hard worker, but occasionally he tended to give the ball far too much air when clearing his lines. Nevertheless, he was a very fine and competitive footballer who served the Potters supremely well for a decade before leaving the club when it went bust in 1908. He proceeded to make 141 first-team appearances for Port Vale, having his last outing in 1924 at the age of 46. He occupied every position except goal for the Valiants, whom he helped win the North Staffordshire Infirmary Cup in 1920 and share the prize two years later. Holford was the cousin of Wilf Kirkham.

HOLFORD, William Wilfred

Half-back: 4 apps.

Born: Cobridge, March 1862.
Died: Stoke-on-Trent, May 1930.
Career: Cobridge Swifts, Boothen Victoria, Stoke Priory, POTTERS (July 1886, retired through injury, April 1889).

■ Bill Holford, elder brother of Tom Holford, was a useful half-back whose first-team outings for Stoke were all in the FA Cup between November 1886 and September 1888. During his last season at The Victoria Ground he suffered a serious knee injury, which forced him into an early retirement.

HOLMES, Andrew John

Defender: 11 apps.

Born: Stoke-on-Trent, 7 January 1969.
Career: Parkway Clayton FC, POTTERS (apprentice, April 1985, professional, January 1987), Doncaster Rovers (free transfer, July 1990, retired, April 1991), took employment in the family's picture-framing business, combining this with occasional outings for Leek Town.

■ Andy Holmes's career with Stoke was plagued by injury, and he appeared in less than a dozen senior games before his departure. A rugged defender, he came through the ranks at The Victoria Ground under the guidance of Tony Lacey, but a leg and serious back injuries kept him out of action for 18 months. With such a wealth of defensive cover at the club, Holmes was allowed to leave for Belle Vue, but a broken leg interrupted his progress with Rovers, and although he regained full fitness again he was forced to quit top-class football on medical advice at the age of 22.

HOLMES, William Hall

Centre-forward: 9 apps. 4 goals.

Born: Stone, 1889.
Died: Wales, 1933.
Career: Leek Alexandra, Darlaston, POTTERS (March 1913), Mid-Rhondda (August 1914, retired soon after World War One).

■ A well-built centre-forward, Bill Holmes did well enough during his short stay at The Victoria Ground but failed to hold down a regular place in the first XI.

HOLSGROVE, Paul

Midfield: 11+1 apps. 1 goal.

Born: Cosford near Wolverhampton, 26 August 1969.
Career: Aldershot (apprentice, September 1985, professional, February 1987), West Bromwich Albion (trialist, 1989), Wokingham (July 1990), Luton Town (£25,000, January 1991), Heracles, Spain (free transfer, November 1991), Millwall (free, August 1992), Reading (free, August 1994), Grimsby Town (on loan, September–October 1997), Crewe Alexandra (free, November 1997), POTTERS (free, January 1998), Brighton & Hove Albion (free, early July 1998), Hibernian (£150,000, late July 1998), Darlington (free, March 2000), Bury Town (May 2000–May 2001).

■ A tall, powerful midfielder, son of the former Wolves and Derby County defender John Hoslgrove, Paul had a nomadic playing career that spanned 16 years, during which time he served with 13 different clubs. An accurate passer of the ball with a terrific engine, he surprisingly played in only 162 first-team matches with his English employers. His only goal for the Potters earned a point from a 1–1 home draw with Ipswich Town in February 1998.

HOLT, Harold

Defender: 1 app.

Born: Aberystwyth, July 1889.
Died: Ruabon, c.1956.
Career: Aberystwyth Town, POTTERS (November 1910), Wrexham (February 1911), Mold (May 1911–March 1913).

The only first-team appearance Welsh amateur centre-half Harold Holt made for the Potters was against West Bromwich Albion reserves in an away Birmingham & District League game in January 1911 when he deputised for George Latham.

HOPE, Richard

Inside-forward: 2 apps.

Born: Gorbals, Glasgow, 17 January 1890.
Died: Glasgow, 1969.
Career: Glasgow St Peter's (from 1910), POTTERS (August 1914), Port Glasgow (October 1914). Did not play after World War One.

A Scottish inside-forward, Richard Hope came to Stoke in an attempt to establish himself in English football. He failed to impress and after two Southern League outings, both in September 1914, he returned home. He scored over 20 goals for Glasgow St Peter's.

HORNE, Brian Simon

Goalkeeper: 2 apps.

Born: Billericay, Essex, 5 October 1967.
Career: Millwall (apprentice, April 1984, professional, October 1985), Watford (on loan, 1991), Sunderland (on loan, March–April 1992), Middlesbrough (on loan, August–September 1992), POTTERS (on loan, October 1992), Woking (on loan, November 1992), Portsmouth (free transfer, December 1992), Hartlepool United (free, August 1994), Dover Athletic (August 1995).

An England youth international who went on to gain five under-21 caps, Brian Horne kept goal in almost 200 games for Millwall and made 244 League appearances during his career. A fine shot-stopper, he had to work hard at his game and certainly did the lions proud with some excellent displays during his time at The Den. He deputised for Ronnie Sinclair in the Potters goal.

HORROCKS, Victor

Wing-half or forward: 21 apps. 8 goals.

Born: Goldenhill, Stoke-on-Trent, 10 October 1884.
Died: Hartshill, Stoke-on-Trent, 7 January 1922.
Career: Burslem Boys Club, Goldenhill Wanderers, POTTERS (March 1903), Talke United (April 1903), Sandyford (August 1904), Goldenhill United (February 1905), Port Vale (April 1905), Goldenhill United (May 1907), POTTERS (September 1908), Port Vale (September 1911), Congleton Town (1912–13).

Vic Horrocks was another local player who could occupy either wing-half position or any of the three central striking berths, with centre-forward perhaps his best role. He made 38 appearances in his two spells with the Valiants but never really established himself in the Potters side, although he did score a smart hat-trick in a 7–0 win over Wellington in a Birmingham League game at The Victoria Ground in October 1908.

HOULDSWORTH, Frederick Charlton

Goalkeeper: 2 apps.

Born: Henley-on-Thames, 29 May 1911.
Died: Framlingham, Suffolk, 1994.
Career: Army football, Swindon Town (amateur, July 1934), POTTERS (£750, April 1935), Ipswich Town (May 1935), Reading (1938–45). Did not play after World War Two.

Fred Houldsworth, 5ft 9in tall and 11st 3lb in weight, played for the Army while serving in the Surrey Corps and also represented the British Army against the Belgian Army in 1932. He began his soccer career in earnest as an amateur with Swindon before transferring to Stoke in 1935. Reserve to Ken Scattergood and Norman Lewis, he played in only two League games for the Potters before switching to Portman Road. A keen club cricketer, he retired to become an umpire at Framlingham College where he was employed.

HOWE, Thomas

Full-back: 56 apps. 2 goals.

Born: Wolverhampton, 26 May 1890.
Died: Cannock, c.1957.
Career: Sunbeam Motors, POTTERS (professional, May 1921–May 1926), Featherstone Rovers (February 1927).

Reserve to Bob McGrory, Tom Howe was at The Victoria Ground for five years and had a couple of decent runs in the first team, the best being in 1923–24. After his release from Stoke he spent eight months out of the game before joining Featherstone Rovers.

HOWITT, Robert Gibb

Half-back: 150 apps. 16 goals.

Born: Glasgow, 15 July 1929.
Died: Carluke, Lanarkshire, 31 January 2005.
Career: Partick Thistle (semi-professional, August 1947, professional, January 1949), Sheffield United (July 1955), POTTERS (£8,000, April 1958, retired, May 1962), Greenock Morton (coach, August 1962), Motherwell (manager, March 1965–March 1973) later POTTERS (scout, based in Scotland).

Bobby Howitt, a hardworking, purposeful half-back, was never the most popular player around The Victoria Ground yet always gave 100 percent out on the field. His professional career began north of the border with Partick, and he also represented the Scottish League before being launched into League football in England by Sheffield United in 1955. He scored 33 goals in 98 competitive games for the Blades prior to joining the

Potters three months short of his 29th birthday. In his five seasons at The Victoria Ground he appeared in exactly 150 first-team games and gained a Second Division Championship medal in 1962–63. As manager he guided Motherwell to victory in the Summer Cup of 1965 and then brought the Scottish club down to Stoke for an Anglo-Scottish Cup tie in the early 1970s. Howitt died at the Roadmeetings Hospital, Carluke, following a lengthy struggle with Alzheimer's Disease.

HOWSHALL, John Henry

Left-half: 1 app.

Born: Normacot, Longton, Stoke-on-Trent, 12 July 1912.
Died: Shelton, Hanley, Stoke-on-Trent, 24 December 1962.
Career: Dresden Juniors (August 1927), Longton Juniors (1928), Dresden Juniors (1929), POTTERS (amateur, October 1931, professional, November 1931), Chesterfield (June 1934), Southport (June 1935), Bristol Rovers (£350, June 1937), Accrington Stanley (July 1938), Carlisle United (October 1938), during World War Two, served in the RAF and played football on a regular basis for the various units, Northwich Victoria (August 1946), Wigan Athletic (July 1947–May 1948).

■ A member of the playing staff at The Victoria Ground for three seasons, Jack Howshall made only one League appearance for the Potters, lining up against Wolverhampton Wanderers in September 1933 when he replaced Harry Sellars. His father, Sam Howshall, played for Burslem Port Vale, Stoke and Merthyr Town during the early 1900s, and two of Jack's three brothers, Tom and Tony Howshall, both played for Southport. The former also guested for the Potters during World War Two, and Tony's son, Gerry Howshall, was a wing-half with West Bromwich Albion during the 1960s.

HOWSHALL, Samuel

Outside-left: 1 app. 2 goals.
Born: Cobridge, Stoke-on-Trent, July 1883.
Died: Stoke-on-Trent, 1964.
Career: Newcastle Swifts, Burlsem Port Vale (May 1903–May 1905), Salisbury Town, Clapton Orient, POTTERS (August 1908), Merthyr Town (May 1909).

■ Reserve left-winger Sam Howshall, father of Jack, scored twice in his only senior outing for Stoke against Stourbridge in a Birmingham & District League game in September 1908.

HUDSON, Alan Anthony

Midfield: 161+1 apps. 9 goals.

Born: Chelsea, 21 June 1931.
Career: London Schools, Chelsea (schoolboy forms, July 1965, apprentice, April 1966, professional, June 1968), POTTERS (£240,000, January 1974), Arsenal (£200,000, December 1976), Seattle Sounders, NASL (£120,000,

Alan Hudson

October 1978), Hercules CF Alicante, Spain (1980), Chelsea (£23,500, August 1983), POTTERS (January 1984, retired, May 1985), later opened a night club in Stoke-on-Trent, penned a column in the Sporting Life and worked for the media in general. After recovering from a serious illness he now lives in East London.

■ Alan Hudson's progress as a teenager was severely hampered by a bone infection that caused him to miss a lot of football. He signed for Chelsea as a 14-year-old and after serving his apprenticeship turned 'pro' in 1968, making his League debut in February 1969 when the Blues crashed to an embarrassing 5–0 defeat at Southampton. The following season he gained a regular place in the side and literally shot to stardom overnight, gaining the first of his 10 England under-23 caps in March 1970. Unfortunately, injury ruled him out of that season's FA Cup Final win over Leeds United, but he returned to full fitness and was a key member of Chelsea's victorious European Cup-winners' Cup team against Real Madrid the following year. And then in 1972 he was a losing finalist in the League Cup Final against his future club Stoke City. In 1978 he was a loser with Arsenal in the FA Cup Final against Ipswich Town. Rewarded with two full England caps against West Germany and Cyprus in 1975, Hudson was at times quite masterful with the ball, swaying and weaving his way past defenders to create scoring opportunities for his colleagues. Certainly one of the most gifted footballers of his generation, he was an inside-forward who at times could make the ball talk. He had two spells at The Victoria Ground a decade apart, and in both instances he produced some outstanding performances. During his career he made over 350 senior appearances and in 1974–75 was voted the most 'Exciting Young Player' in England. Hudson was awarded a goal that never was playing for Chelsea against Ipswich Town in a League game at Stamford Bridge in September 1970. His shot struck the outside netting and angle woodwork but referee Roy Capey signalled a goal. Despite the protests of the Ipswich players and officials, the goal stood and Chelsea went on to win 2–1.

HUGHES, Dennis

Outside-right: 1 app.

Born: Stoke-on-Trent, 9 April 1931.
Career: POTTERS (professional, September 1948), Congleton Town (May 1950).

■ Dennis Hughes's only one League appearance for Stoke City was on the right-wing against Huddersfield Town at home in August 1950 when he deputised for Johnny Malkin (before Harry Oscroft was switched from the opposite flank). He stayed at The Victoria Ground for two seasons before moving into non-League football.

HULSE, Robert Arthur

Centre-forward: 2 apps.

Born: Crewe, 5 November 1948.
Career: Nantwich Victoria (1965), POTTERS (April 1967–May 1968), emigrated to Australia in the summer of 1969 but returned to England within two years.

■ Bob Hulse had a short career in League football, playing twice for the Potters in the First Division in the late 1960s. He is the father of the current striker by the same name who has played for Crewe Alexandra, West Bromwich Albion and Leeds United.

HURST, Sir Geoffrey Charles, MBE

Striker: 123+5 apps. 37 goals.

Born: Ashton-under-Lyne, Lancashire, 8 December 1941.
Career: Chelmsford Schools, Halstead FC (August 1955), Chelmsford City (1956–57), West Ham United (apprentice, July 1957, professional, April 1959), POTTERS (£75,000, August 1972), Cape Town Spurs, South Africa (on loan, May–August 1973), West Bromwich Albion (£20,000, August 1975), Cork Celtic (February, 1976), Seattle Sounders (April–August 1976), Telford United (player-manager, 1976–May 1979), England (assistant-coach, August 1977–July 1982), Chelsea (coach, May 1979, then manager, September 1979–April 1981), Al-Kuwait Club, Middle East (coach, seasons 1982–84), was a key member of the England coaching set-up looking after the under-21 side before running a pub in Whitmore and then taking a Directorship in a motor insurance company (Motorplan), he was also a useful cricketer, playing briefly for Essex.

■ Geoff Hurst was the first player to score a hat-trick in a World Cup Final when his treble saw off West Germany in 1966. A big, strong, positive centre-forward, good in the air, excellent on the ground and able to withstand the toughest of challenges, he had a fine career serving three major Football League clubs: West Ham, Stoke and West Brom. He joined the Hammers in 1957 and turned professional the following year. He made his senior debut as a wing-half in 1960 (having already won England youth honours) before being converted into a striker by manager Ron Greenwood at Upton Park. Hurst never looked back after that, scoring 252 goals in 502 outings for the London club, 37 in 128 games for the Potters and two in 12 starts for the Baggies. He won 49 full caps for England between 1966 and 1972 (netting 24 goals), had four outings for the under-23 side, represented the Football League and helped the Hammers win the FA Cup and European Cup-winners' Cup in successive seasons in 1964 and 1965, and also played in the 1966 League Cup Final defeat by his future club West Bromwich Albion.
NB: Hurst's father, Charles, was a professional footballer with Oldham Athletic, Bristol Rovers and Rochdale.

HUTCHINSON, Colin

Utility forward: 9 apps.

Born: Lanchester near Consett, County Durham, 20 October 1936.
Career: Crook Hall FC, POTTERS (amateur, April 1952, National Service in the RAF, turned professional, November 1953), Crewe Alexandra (on loan, March–April 1958), Stafford Rangers (May 1958, later manager, early 1960s), Nantwich Town (manager), Droylesden

(manager), was seen regularly in the directors' box at The Victoria Ground in his free hours outside the running of a successful stationery business in Newcastle, Staffordshire.

■ Colin Hutchinson was a reserve at The Victoria Ground for six years during the 1950s, and in that time he was given nine League outings, lining up at outside-right, inside-right and inside-left, and made his debut as a 17-year-old against Middlesbrough in August 1954. Unfortunately, he broke his leg, which set him back as a player and he never recaptured his true form.

HUTCHINSON, William

Outside-right: 1 app.

Born: Stoke-on-Trent, July 1870.
Died: Stoke-on-Trent, July 1943.
Career: Fenton RS, POTTERS (August 1888), Long Eaton (August 1989).

■ Bill Hutchinson was Stoke's reserve right-winger during the club's first League season of 1888–89. A well-built footballer, he played once for the first team, deputising for George Lawton in a 2–1 defeat at Derby County in January 1889.

HUTSBY, Henry

Full-back: 37 apps.

Born: Norton Bridge, 4 January 1886.
Died: Stafford, 30 December 1971.
Career: Alleyne's Grammar School, Stafford FC, Stafford Wednesday, Stafford Excelsior, Stafford Wesleyans, Northern Nomads, Stone Town, POTTERS (amateur with Albert Pitt, July 1908, professional, December 1908), Wrexham (briefly, 1909–10), Stafford Rangers (1911–15). Did not play after World War One.

■ A good, competent full-back from a footballing family, Harry Hutsby made 32 of his 37 senior appearances for the Potters in his first season. A very useful club cricketer, he later returned to Stafford where he died.

HUTTON, Joseph

Inside-forward: 37 apps. 8 goals.

Born: Dundee, 18 November 1927.
Career: Albion Rovers (1947), Leytonstone (1949), Reading (October 1950), Ayr United (1952), POTTERS (December 1953), Gillingham (£3,000, August 1957), Millwall (August 1958), Poole Town (August 1959, retired through injury, May 1962).

■ Joe Hutton joined Stoke at the same time as Bobby Cairns. A diminutive inside-forward (5ft 4in tall and 10st in weight), he made a fine start to his career at The Victoria Ground, scoring on his debut in a 5–0 drubbing of Swansea Town, but his outings were restricted after that due to the form of Bowyer, King and Kelly. He scored 22 goals in 103 League games, all told.

HYSLOP, Thomas

Inside or centre-forward: 49 apps. 30 goals.

Born: Mauchline, Ayrshire, 22 September 1874.
Died: Glasgow, July 1936.
Career: Elderslie FC, Ayrshire, Millwall Athletic (trialist, then guest), Army football, Sunderland (January 1894), POTTERS (March 1895), Glasgow Rangers (July 1896), POTTERS (August 1898), Rangers (August 1899), Partick Thistle (July 1900–May 1902).

■ An ex-Scots Guardsman, Tom Hyslop was a tall, rangy centre or inside-forward, fast over the ground with a powerful right-foot shot. Sunderland bought him out of the Army on 25 January 1894, and he went on to score 10 goals in 19 games before leaving Roker Park for Stoke with the League Championship already destined for Sunderland (Hyslop had played in 12 games that season and subsequently collected a winners' medal). He was an instant success at The Victoria Ground, being the first 'Stokie' to score a hat-trick on his debut, doing so in a 4–1 home win over Derby County three days after signing. He was also the first 'Potter' to score a penalty, obliging against his former club, Sunderland, in March 1896. Hyslop stayed with the Potters for just over a season before switching to Ibrox Park where he added two Scottish Cup winners' medals to his collection, being part of a superb Rangers vanguard along with four other Scottish internationals, Low, McPherson, Millar and Scott. Hyslop gained two full caps for his country, one with Stoke in 1896 (being the first Scotsman to be honoured as a Potter), the other with Rangers, both against England. He scored 31 times in 43 games for Rangers and during his career claimed a total of 82 goals in more than 125 club and international appearances. Hyslop was, without doubt, a very fine footballer.

IRVINE, Robert James

Goalkeeper: 31 apps.

Born: Carrickfergus, 17 January 1942.
Career: Linfield, POTTERS (£6,000 in June 1963), Altrincham (free transfer, May 1966).

■ Northern Ireland international goalkeeper Bobby Irvine won eight full caps, one at under-23 level and two as a schoolboy. Signed to replace fellow countryman Jimmy O'Neill, he played in the first seven League games of the 1963–64 season but then lost his place to another new signing, Lawrie Leslie. Out of the side until April 1964, when he came back for three more League games he also appeared in the second leg of the League Cup Final against Leicester City, gaining a runners'-up prize. His career at The Victoria Ground effectively came to an end five months prematurely after a penalty incident in a third-round FA Cup tie against Walsall, a game the Saddlers won 2–0. City manager Tony Waddington was livid with Irvine's antics and never picked him again. The Irishman left on a free transfer. Irvine's brother, Willie, played centre-forward for Burnley, Preston North End, Brighton and Halifax Town.

IRVINE, Samuel

Midfield: 77 apps. 12 goals.

Born: Glasgow, 7 January 1956.
Career: Shrewsbury Town (apprentice, April 1972, professional, January 1974), POTTERS (£60,000, June 1978, retired through injury, September 1980), later entered the licensing trade, sold insurance and worked as a laboratory

technician and groundsman, the latter from 1995.

Scottish-born midfield player Sammy Irvine played for Shrewsbury Town

under manager Alan Durban, who then bought him to The Victoria Ground after he had taken over as boss of the Potters. Unfortunately for Stoke, Irvine was involved in a horrific car crash in February 1980, and although he recovered from his injuries he was forced to quit football and became a license.e

IWELLUMO, Christopher Robert

Striker: 52+51 apps. 23 goals.

Born: Coatbridge, 1 August 1978.
Career: Ayr United (schoolboy 'S' form), Kilmarnock (schoolboy 'S' form, 1993), St Mirren (apprentice, August 1994, professional, August 1996), Aarhus Fremad, Denmark (free transfer, July 1998), POTTERS (£25,000, March 2000), York City (on loan, November 2000–January 2001), Cheltenham Town (on loan, February–March 2001), Brighton & Hove Albion (March 2004), Alemannia Aachen, Germany (June 2004), Colchester United (July 2005).

Giant striker, 6ft 3in tall and 13st 8lb in weight, Chris Iwellumo scored on his debut for St Mirren, aged 16 years. Excellent in the air and a fighter to the last (appreciated by the fans), he grafted

hard and long despite his high proportion of substitute appearances. He suffered knee and foot injuries during his time with the Potters yet still managed a useful return in respect of goals per games. Known as 'Big Un', he claimed 'Goal of the Season' in 2002–03 with a stunning volley against Sheffield Wednesday at The Britannia Stadium. He reached the milestone of 200 career appearances in 2004 before leaving for Brighton. Iwellumo is a qualified teacher.

JACKSON, George

Midfield: 8+2 apps.

Born: Stretford, Manchester, 10 February 1952.
Career: POTTERS (apprentice, April 1967, professional, July 1969), Cape Town City, South Africa (May 1972, retired through injury, November 1972), POTTERS ('B' team coach, mid-1970s).

George Jackson had a relatively short career as a midfielder, staring in only eight first-team games for the Potters during the second half of the 1971–72 season before a niggling injury forced him out of the English game. Having made his League debut on New Year's Day in 1972 (at Huddersfield), he went to play for Cape Town City in South Africa, but sadly another serious leg injury resulted in him calling it a day at the age of 20. He later returned to The Victoria Ground as 'B' team coach.

JACKSON, John

Centre-forward: 4 apps. 3 goals.

Born: Newcastle-under-Lyme, 7 January 1923.
Died: Endon, Staffs, June 1992.
Career: Alsager FC, POTTERS (professional, May 1941), Congleton Town (guest, during the hostilities), Northwich Victoria (May 1952), Congleton Town (April 1954), Leek Town (1955–56).

Johnny Jackson had a superb record with Stoke, three goals scored in four League games in 1947, including two in a 3–0 home win over Grimsby Town. Owing to World War Two, he had to wait six years before making his senior debut in a 1–1 draw with Manchester City at Maine Road when he deputised for Freddie Steele. He did, however, manage to net seven goals in 34 World War Two games for the Potters.

JACKSON, Wilbert

Half-back: 73 apps. 1 goal.

Born: Luddendon Foot village, Yorkshire, 4 August 1904.
Died: Shipley, Yorkshire, 9 May 1956.
Career: Ludden Foot FC, Hebden Bridge, POTTERS (April 1924), Southend United (January 1934), Congleton Town (June 1934), POTTERS (assistant manager, July 1935), Wrexham (manager, November 1950), Bradford City (manager, February 1955–March 1961), POTTERS (scout, seasons 1961–67), Bradford City (scout, 1969–70).

Wilbert Jackson – known as Peter and nicknamed 'Jammy Legs' – spent 10 years in the Potteries. In that time he appeared in over 70 first-team games and scored one goal in a vital victory over Southampton in March 1933, when the Championship of the Second Division was in the Potters' sights. A sturdy competitor, he had his best season in 1930–31 when he made 22 appearances. A dedicated club man and very conscientious, he gave a good account of himself at whatever level he played. On leaving The Victoria Ground he moved south to Southend United, and after a spell in non-league football he returned to Stoke as assistant manager to Bob McGrory. From that point on Jackson's

managerial career blossomed. He guided Wrexham to the third spot in the Northern Section and applied a steadying hand and brought an air of confidence to Bradford City, seeing them enter the newly-formed Third Division in 1958. His twin sons, Peter and David, both played for Bradford City, Peter going on to become manager of the Terriers in 1997–99 and again from 2003.

JACOBSEN, Anders

Defender: 39+5 apps. 2 goals.

Born: Norway, 18 April 1968.
Career: IK Start, Norway, Sheffield United (December 1998), POTTERS (free transfer, August 1999), Notts County (free, September 2000), Skeid Oslo, Norway (July 2001).

■ A cultured and thoughtful central defender, strong in the tackle, he spent just the one season with the Potters where he produced some excellent performances before leaving to become the linchpin of Notts County's defence.

JAMES, Charles

Defender: 13 apps.

Born: Longton, Stoke-on-Trent, September 1882.
Died: before 1960.
Career: Halmerend FC (Staffs), POTTERS (July 1908), Florence Colliery FC (May 1914). Did not play after World War One.

■ Reserve defender Charlie James spent six seasons at The Victoria Ground, during which time he appeared in only 13 first-class matches, lining up in both full-back positions as well as right-half and centre-half. A hard-working player, he was unfortunate to concede four penalties in season 1913–14, all for handball. The Press said 'He just couldn't resist the temptation' to touch the ball, yet he never considered being a goalkeeper.

JAMES, Robert Mark

Midfield: 56 apps. 7 goals.

Born: Gorseinon near Swansea, 23 March. 1957.
Died: Llanelli, 18 February 1998.
Career: Bishop Vaughan School, Swansea Schoolboys, Cardiff City (schoolboy forms), Swansea City (amateur), Arsenal (month's trial), Swansea City (amateur, March 1973, professional, April 1973), POTTERS (£160,000 July 1983), Queen's Park Rangers (£100,000, October 1984), Leicester City (June 1987), Swansea City (January 1988), Bradford City (August 1990), Cardiff City (August 1992), Llanelli (player-manager, July 1994), Weston-Super-Mare (1995–96).

■ A Welsh international midfielder with power and stamina and a real work-horse, Robbie James made over 50

appearances for Stoke during his short spell with the club. Signed by Richie Barker, he was then sold to QPR for £100,000, the money received being invested in striker Keith Bertschin. Capped 47 times at senior level and on three occasions by the under-21s, he gained a League Cup runners'-up medal with QPR in 1986 and in all won four Welsh Cup Finals with Swansea. He top-scored with 14 goals in 1981–82 when the Vetch Field side brushed shoulders with the big boys in the First Division. James, who made almost 400 League appearances during his career and scored 99 goals, was perhaps annoyed with himself for missing two penalties! He collapsed and died a month before his 41st birthday, while playing for Llanelli in the Welsh League.

JARRETT, Jason Lee Mee

Midfield: 0+1 app.

Born: Bury, 14 September 1979.
Career: Blackpool (apprentice, April 1996, professional, July 1998), Wrexham (free transfer, October 1999), Bury (free, July 2000), Wigan Athletic (£75,000, March 2002), POTTERS (January 2004).

■ Jason Jarrett made his debut for the Potters as a second-half substitute against Queen's Park Rangers (away) in January 2005, having amassed well over 175 senior appearances with his four previous clubs, including more than 100

for Wigan, whom he helped win the Second Division Championship in 2003. An 6ft tall, energetic player, he packs a powerful right-foot shot but admitted that he needs to work more on direction!

JARVIS, George Henry

Utility: 33 apps. 10 goals.

Born: Glasgow, 3 December 1889.
Died: Glasgow, 1962.
Career: Glasgow Royal, Cambuslang Rangers (May 1907), Celtic (August 1912), guest for several Scottish League clubs (1915–18), POTTERS (£300, August 1919), Clydebank (£50, December 1920).

■ A strong-limbed utility player preferring a forward role, George Jarvis came down from Scotland to try his luck in English football immediately after World War One. He made a big impact and averaged a goal every three games in his first season (1919–20) while occupying six different positions, four in the front-line! Unfortunately, Jarvis became homesick and left The Victoria Ground halfway through the following season after taking his appearance tally up to 33. During World War One he guested for at least six other Scottish League sides, including Clyde, Hamilton Academical and Partick Thistle.

JEPSON, Arthur

Goalkeeper: 32 apps.

Born: Selston, Notts, 12 July 1915.
Died: Kirkby-in-Ashfield, 1997.
Career: Newark Town, Mansfield Town (November 1934), Grantham Town (March 1935), Burslem Port Vale (June 1938), guest for Nottingham Forest, Notts County, Watford and Swansea Town during World War Two, POTTERS (£3,750, September 1946), Lincoln City (December 1948), Northwich Victoria (August 1950), Gloucester City (October 1951), Hinckley United (player-manager, 1953–54, retired as a player in 1956), Coventry City (scout, late 1950s), Middlesbrough (scout, 1960–62), Hinckley Athletic (manager, July 1963–March 1964).

■ Arthur Jepson was certainly better known in sporting circles as an all-round cricketer rather than a goalkeeper! In 390 matches for Nottinghamshire CCC between 1938 and 1959, when he starred as a hard-hitting, lower order batsman, he scored 6,369 runs (avg. 14.31) and as a right-arm fast-medium bowler took 1,051 wickets (avg. 29.08) with a best return of 8-45. A close fielder, he claimed 201 catches and achieved his best seasonal haul of wickets (115) in 1947. He later became a County and Test Match umpire. As a footballer, between 1934–50 he appeared between the posts in more than 300 League and Cup games at various levels. Jepson joined the Potters after making 92 first-team appearances for arch-rivals Port Vale. In March 1947 he suffered a serious spinal injury that put him into temporary retirement, but he bounced back and stayed another two years. He eventually retired from playing football at the age of 41.

JOHN, William Ronald

Goalkeeper: 76 apps.

Born: Briton Ferry near Neath, 29 January 1911.
Died: Port Talbot, 12 July 1973.
Career: Briton Ferry Schoolboys, Swansea Town (amateur, February 1927), Manchester United (trialist, February 1928), Walsall (professional, May 1928), POTTERS (April 1932), Preston North End (June 1934), Sheffield United (December 1934), Manchester United (£600, June 1936), Newport County (March 1937), Swansea Town (July 1937, retired, December 1939), became a hotel manager, returned to the game and played as a guest for Blackburn Rovers, Bolton Wanderers, Burnley and Southport during World War Two, a pub landlord in Swansea after the hostilities, he later worked for British Steel. He was also a fine batsman/wicketkeeper for Briton Ferry CC.

■ 'Roy' John started out as a centre-forward, then performed at left-back before finally settling down in goal, a position in which he excelled, appearing for Wales in 13 full internationals plus one in wartime against England in November 1939. A useful goalscorer for both his school team and Briton Ferry Athletic before joining Swansea, he was converted into a left-back. After an unsuccessful trial with Manchester United he went on to amass 93 appearances for the Saddlers. He had the pleasure of saving a penalty on his debut for the Potters against Bradford Park Avenue and gained a Second Division Championship medal in 1932–33. He kept goal for Stoke in front of 84,569 fans when Manchester City won a sixth-round FA Cup tie 1–0 at Maine Road in March 1934. He starred for a Welsh XI against the RAF in 1942, his last game at any level.

JOHNSON, Edward

Winger: 1 app.

Born: Birmingham, 9 June 1862.
Died: Stoke-on-Trent, 30 June 1901.

Career: Saltley College (from August 1880), POTTERS (September 1881, retired through injury, April 1885), Stoke St Peter's (committee member, 1886–89), then Staffordshire FA (committee member until ill-health forced him to give up his position in 1898).

■ Teddy Johnson was Stoke's first full international, capped by England against Ireland in February 1884 when he scored two goals in an 8–1 victory. He also represented the Birmingham FA and played in a second international against Wales in March 1880 while with Saltley College, and after joining Stoke he played for Staffordshire. A fast, dashing winger, fine dribbler and marksman, he occasionally flawed his performances by holding on to the ball for far too long – much to the annoyance of his colleagues. He played in Stoke's first-ever FA Cup tie against Manchester two months after joining the club, this being his only senior/competitive appearance for the Potters before he was forced into early retirement after damaging his back when falling out of a trap as the horse reared up. He was only 39 when he died.

JOHNSON, Frederick James

Outside-right: 196 apps. 20 goals.

Born: Stoke-on-Trent, February 1877.
Died: Stoke-on-Trent, 14 May 1943.
Career: Stoke St Peter's (1889), POTTERS (April 1895, retired, May 1903).

■ An excellent right-winger, 6ft tall with a receding hairline, Fred Johnson first made the grade in local football, actually signing for the St Peter's club at the age of 12. He made his debut for the Potters on Christmas Day in 1895 against Preston North End – the first of almost 200 senior appearances for the club. A player with good pace and crossing ability, he represented the Football League against the Irish League during his Stoke days, which ended in 1903 when he retired. Two years earlier he was granted a benefit game, Stoke against the famous Corinthians amateur side at The Victoria Ground. The result was a 3–3 draw. As a youngster Johnson, shortly before he joined the Potters, scored a hatful of goals when St Peter's beat Bucknall St Mary's 44–0 in an hour-long game.

JOHNSON, Joseph Arthur

Outside-left: 193 apps. 57 goals.

Born: Grimsby, 4 April 1911.
Died: West Bromwich, 8 August 1983.
Career: Grimsby Schools, Cleethorpes Royal Saints (August 1926), Scunthorpe & Lindsey United (professional, April 1928), Bristol City (£1,200, May 1931), POTTERS (£2,500, April 1932), West Bromwich Albion (£6,500, November 1937), guest for Crewe Alexandra, Leicester City and Notts County during World War Two, Hereford United (free, May 1946), Northwich Victoria (August 1948, retired, May 1950), later ran the Dartmouth Park café-restaurant in West Bromwich during the late 1950s-early '60s.

■ Joe Johnson was an excellent outside-left who received much praise for some quite superb displays in the Stoke side of the 1930's. He loved to start his runs deep in his own half of the field and often cut sharply from the left to shoot at goal. In fact, he drew up a very fine record as a goal-scoring winger, and along with Stanley Matthews he steered the Potters to the Second Division Championship in 1932–33. Capped by England on five occasions between November 1936 and May 1937 (scoring two goals against Sweden and Finland), Johnson made almost 200 appearances for Stoke, 184 at League level, netting close on 60 goals. He added almost 150 more games to his total while with Albion (47 goals). He went on to amass another 60 appearances in non-League football, eventually retiring with well over 450 senior outings under his belt (120 goals scored).

JOHNSON, Paul

Left-back: 33+1 apps.

Born: Stoke-on-Trent, 25 May 1959.
Career: POTTERS (apprentice, September 1974, professional, May 1976), Shrewsbury Town (£20,000, May 1981), York City (£2,000, July 1987–May 1989), POTTERS (Community Development Officer to 1995), also played for Macclesfield Town (early 1990s).

■ Introduced to League football by manager Alan Durban, Paul Johnson looked set for a bright future in the

game, but when Peter Hampton arrived from Leeds United his days were numbered at The Victoria Ground, and in 1981 he was transferred to Shrewsbury Town. He went on to top the 200 appearance mark during a fine spell at Gay Meadow.

JOHNSON, Paul Anthony

Midfield: 54+6 apps.

Born: Blurton, Stoke-on-Trent, 19 September 1955.
Career: POTTERS (apprentice, April 1971, professional, June 1973), Chester (free transfer, August 1982–April 1983), California Lasers, NASL, later with Altrincham, Buxton, Stafford Rangers and Leek Town.

■ Paul Johnson was a firm favourite with the Stoke City crowd but often took some stick on away grounds because of his build (12st 2lb for a man of 5ft 6in tall). He was a determined midfielder, nevertheless, who appeared in 60 senior games for the Potters plus another 270 at reserve-team level.

JOHNSON, Richard Kemp

Centre-forward: 83 apps. 25 goals.

Born: Gateshead, June 1895.
Died: Liverpool, 3 January 1933.
Career: Felling Colliery, World War One guest for Sunderland (1918–19), Liverpool (January 1920), POTTERS (£1,200, February 1925), New Brighton (September 1929), Connah's Quay (August 1931, retired, May 1933).

■ A centre-forward with speed and superb ball control, Dick Johnson's career was marred by a knee injury. Nevertheless, he scored regularly during his four and a half years with the Potters after netting 28 goals in 78 games for Liverpool, whom he helped win the Second Division Championship in 1923. A lively player with a receding hairline, he was good on the ground and in the air, and he added a Third Division North Championship medal to his collection with Stoke in 1927. When he left The Victoria Ground for New Brighton he received a fee as his accrued share.

JOHNSON, Richard Mark

Midfield: 4+5 apps.

Born: Newcastle, Australia, 27 April 1974.
Career: Watford (apprentice, May 1990, professional, May 1992), Northampton Town (on loan, February–March 2003), Colchester United (free transfer, October 2003), POTTERS (free, November 2003), Queen's Park Rangers (free, February 2004).

■ An Australian international, capped once, central midfielder Richard Johnson made 278 senior appearances for Watford, whom he helped win the Second Division title in 1998, but after leaving Vicarage Road he failed to settled down with any other club. Committed to the game, the first of his nine outings for the Potters came as a second-half substitute in the 3–1 defeat at Gillingham shortly after arriving at The Britannia Stadium.

JOHNSON, Samuel

Left-half: 40 apps.

Born: Kidsgrove, 19 October 1901.
Died: York, 1982.
Career: Goldenhill Wanderers, POTTERS (October 1924), Swindon Town (May 1926), York City (July 1929), Southport (August 1933 – one game), Crystal Palace (briefly), Scarborough (August 1934, retired, May 1937), became a publican in York, returned to York City (trainer, 1945–1964).

■ Sammy Johnson spent two seasons with the Potters as a tough-tackling left-half. He made his League debut against Portsmouth at home in March 1925 and the following season played in 30 of Stoke's 41 League games. Cliff Eastwood took over his position for the 1926–27 season. After being converted into a left-back, he appeared in 137 senior games for York City.

JOHNSTON, Leslie Hamilton

Inside-forward: 92 apps. 22 goals.

Born: Glasgow, 16 August 1920.
Died: Clayton, Staffs, October 2001.
Career: Clydebank, Clyde (December 1941), Hibernian (£10,000, February 1947), Clyde (£10,000, October 1947), Celtic (£12,000, October 1948), POTTERS (£9,000, October 1949), Shrewsbury Town (£2,000, July 1953), Hinckley Athletic (free transfer, September 1954), Leek Town (1956) Clover Dairies FC, Wolstanton United, continued to play regularly in 5-a-side games until he was 50, he also qualified as a referee.

■ Les Johnston served the Potters for four years, during which time he claimed a very respectable record, scoring on average a goal every four games and setting up plenty more for his colleagues despite having a few annoying injury problems. Stoke manager Bob McGrory paid a club-record fee for the Scottish international, who had already gained two full caps against Belgium and Switzerland in 1948. He also appeared as a substitute in a wartime international, scoring against England in a 6–1 win in April 1945 in front of 133,000 fans at Hampden Park. It was reported that Johnston, who was described as a 'strolling player', had had more money spent on him in transfer fees than any other footballer in the game at that time. When he joined

Celtic from Clyde he became the first Scottish-born player to be transferred to a Scottish club for a five-figure fee.

JOHNSTON, Ezekiel

Goalkeeper: 43 apps.

Born: Belfast, 1870.
Died: Belfast, 1942.
Career: Glentoran (1889), Burnley (February 1894), Glentoran (April 1895), POTTERS (November 1896), Belfast Celtic (March 1898, retired, May 1905), remained in Belfast in engineering.

■ Goalkeeper Zeke Johnston went straight into the Stoke team against Derby County a week after joining the Potters, signed when the team was slipping deep into trouble at the foot of the First Division table. Retaining his place during the second-half of that season, he produced some excellent displays and helped the team avoid relegation. Another relegation dog-fight took place the following season and in the end the Potters escaped via the Test Match system (today's play-offs), by which time Johnston had been replaced by Tom Wilkes, recruited from Aston Villa. Johnston, rather disappointed, quickly departed. Later in 1902 he saved three people from drowning in a Belfast river.

JONES, Alfred

Outside-left: 5 apps. 1 goal.

Born: Hanley, Stoke-on-Trent, 17 March 1902.
Died: Stoke-on-Trent, c.1976.
Career: Port Vale (August 1920), Crewe Alexandra (March 1921), Congleton Town (November 1922), POTTERS (May 1924), Congleton Town (August 1925–May 1928).

■ Amateur Alf Jones was one of six players used on the left-wing by Stoke in 1924–25 when the position was causing some concern in the camp. He scored his only goal in the 2–0 home win over Hull City in November.

JONES, David Douglas

Goalkeeper: 1 app.

Born: Blaenau Festiniog, North Wales, 8 September 1914.

Died: Cheshire, 1997.
Career: Blaenau Festiniog (1931), Everton (professional, May 1935), Colwyn Bay (1936), POTTERS (April 1939), Carlisle United (August 1939), POTTERS (guest, October 1939–May 1940 and February 1941), Rochdale (August 1948), Northwich Victoria (December 1948, retired, May 1950).

■ During the final week of the 1938–39 season Stoke manager Bob McGrory was in a predicament with two of his senior goalkeepers, Norman Wilkinson and Doug Westland, both unavailable. He decided to gamble by bringing the Welsh amateur international Doug Jones to The Victoria Ground to bridge the gap! Jones made his debut against Leeds United at Elland Road on the last day of the League programme (6 May) and performed tremendously well in a 0–0 draw before 18,000 fans. This was his only appearance for the Potters, and during the summer Leeds asked about his availability but instead of joining the Yorkshire club Jones chose Carlisle United instead. World War Two, however, disrupted his career, and although he made 20 guest appearances for Stoke during the hostilities he resumed his career at Brunton Park in 1946, going on to appear in 66 League games in two seasons for the Cumbrians. He was almost 36 when he retired.

JONES, Gerald

Outside-left: 7 apps.

Born: Middleport, Stoke-on-Trent, 30 December 1945.
Career: POTTERS (April 1962, professional, June 1963), Stafford Rangers (June 1967), Macclesfield Town (August 1970–72).

■ Reserve left-winger Gerry Jones deputised for first Keith Bebbington and then Harry Burrows for Stoke in the mid-1960s.

JONES, John Love

Inside-forward: 13 apps. 3 goals.

Born: Rhyl, 29 April 1885.
Died: Rhyl, 21 December 1913.
Career: Rhyl (May 1903), POTTERS (November 1905), Crewe Alexandra (November 1907), Middlesbrough (March 1909), Portsmouth (June 1911, until his death).

■ Stoke signed 19-year-old inside-forward Love Jones three days after seeing him play exceedingly well for Rhyl against Birkenhead. He made a superb start to his League career by scoring on his Potters debut against Newcastle United, one of the strongest teams in the land at that time. A player who favoured the open game, he held his place in the side (injuries apart) for the rest of the season, and he also gained the first of two full caps for Wales when he replaced Archie Green against Scotland in March 1906 (his second followed in 1910). Jones then lost his place in the side and struggled somewhat over the next season and a half. He also failed to hold down a regular first-team place with Crewe, then did fractionally better with Middlesbrough before scoring 19 goals in 41 Southern league games for Portsmouth. In August 1913, when still a registered player at Fratton Park, he fell ill with tuberculosis and returned home to Rhyl where he sadly died a few months later, aged 28.

JONES, Joseph Thomas

Defender: 129 apps. 12 goals.

Born: Rhosymedre near Wrexham, 9 January 1888.
Died: Stoke-on-Trent, 23 July 1941.
Career: Cefn Albion (May 1906), Wrexham (July 1910), Treharris (April 1911), POTTERS (with George Smart, September 1910), Crystal Palace (£150, June 1920), Coventry City (July 1922), Crewe Alexandra (May 1924, retired, April 1925).

■ One of the select band of players who appeared for Stoke before, during and after the World War One, Joey Jones, known as 'The Old Warhorse', spent 10 years with the Potters, making almost 130 senior appearances plus 133 more during the hostilities. A solid, uncompromising, yet bustling-type of defender, particularly good in the air, he was a tower of enthusiasm who dominated many a game by sheer spirit and was a very consistent performer. A Welsh international, he gained 10 of his 15 full caps as a Stoke player, skippering both club and country, and helped the Potters finish runners'-up in successive World War One seasons of Lancashire Section football in 1917–18 and 1918–19 before leaving The Victoria Ground for Crystal Palace. Jones, who sadly lost the sight in one eye after heading the laced-up part of one of those old-fashioned leather footballs, appeared in more than 250 senior games during his career. He later ran a snooker hall in Stoke-on-Trent, but during the years preceding his death he worked in a bookshop for the blind.

JONES, Kenwyne

Striker: 13 apps. 3 goals.

Born: Trinidad, 5 October 1984.
Career: W-Connection, Trinidad, Southampton (professional, May 2004), Sheffield Wednesday (loan, December 2004–January 2005), POTTERS (loan, February–May 2005).

■ Trinidad & Tobago striker Kenwyne Jones, who was strong and mobile, scored with a header on his debut against Millwall away in February 2005, earning the Potters a 1–0 win. He arrived at the Britannia Stadium in prime form, having notched seven goals in seven games for Sheffield Wednesday. Unable to get a game in Southampton's attack, owing to the presence of Kevin Phillips, Peter Crouch and Anders Svensson, he was loaned out 'to gain experience' and what an impact he made.

JONES, Roger

Goalkeeper: 112 apps.

Born: Upton-on-Severn, 8 November 1946.
Career: Portsmouth (apprentice, August 1963, professional, November 1964), AFC Bournemouth (£5,000, May 1965), Blackburn Rovers (£30,000, January 1970), Newcastle United (£100,000 in joint transfer involving Graham Oates, March 1976), POTTERS (free, February 1977), Derby County (£25,000, July 1980), Birmingham City (on loan, February–March 1982), York City (August 1982, retired, May 1985), entered coaching, first at York (June 1985), Loggerheads FC (player-coach, 1986–88), Sunderland (assistant-coach, November 1988–May 1993), later worked in the building trade.

■ A very consistent goalkeeper with good reflexes, Roger Jones served with eight different League clubs during a lengthy career that spanned 23 years. He made almost 800 appearances, all told, helping the Potters win promotion from the Second Division in 1978–79, keeping a club-record 20 clean sheets in the process. He also gained a Third Division Championship medal with Blackburn in 1975, a Fourth Division prize as captain of York City in 1984, when former Stoke defender Denis Smith was in charge at Bootham Crescent, and was capped by England at under-23 level during his time at Ewood Park. He continued to play non-League football until he was 41.

JONES, Roy

Centre-half: 7 apps.

Born: Stoke-on-Trent, 29 August 1924.
Career: POTTERS (amateur, July 1942, semi-professional, October 1943, professional, August 1946), Congleton Town (free transfer, May 1950).

■ Roy Jones changed his name by deed poll from Roy Shufflebottom in 1948. He made his first-team debut for the Potters in November 1943 against West Bromwich Albion in the League North game at The Hawthorns and after the hostilities became a full-time professional with the club. However, his senior outings were limited owing to the form and brilliance of the England pivot Neil Franklin. He left The Victoria Ground at the end of the 1949–50 season.

JONES, Thomas James

Inside or outside-left: 29 apps. 9 goals.

Born: Newcastle-under-Lyme, November 1876.
Died: Stoke-on-Trent, c.1940.
Career: Newcastle Boys (1890), Congleton Hornets (1895), Newcastle Swifts (1897), POTTERS (May 1899), Crewe Alexandra (November 1900).

■ Tommy Jones played local junior football for nine years before spending 18 months at The Victoria Ground. A reserve forward, he made his senior debut against the reigning League champions Aston Villa (away) just before Christmas 1899.

JORDAN Alfred Ralph

Right-half: 2 apps.

Born: Belfast, 1900.
Died: Belfast, 1969.
Career: Willowfield FC, POTTERS (professional, November 1923), Hull City (June 1924), Bristol Rovers (August 1926–May 1927).

■ Signed as cover for George Clarke, Alf Jones made his debut for Stoke in a 1–1 home draw with Sheffield Wednesday in December 1923. He made just nine League appearances for Hull but failed to make the first team with Bristol Rovers. His elder brother, David Jordan, also played for Hull City as well as Ards, Wolves and Crystal Palace.

JORDAN, Frank

Versatile forward: 10 apps. 2 goals.

Born: Berkshire, 1888.
Died: August 1962.
Career: Reading, POTTERS (August 1911), Merthyr Town (May 1912).

■ Frank Jordan scored twice in 10 Southern League games for Stoke in the 1911–12 season when he occupied four different positions in the front-line.

JUMP, Stewart Paul

Defender: 52+9 apps. 1 goal.

Born: Crumpshall near Manchester, 27 January 1952.
Career: POTTERS (apprentice, April 1968, professional, July 1969), Crystal Palace (£70,000, December 1973), New York Cosmos (on loan, April–August 1976), Fulham (on loan, January–February 1977), then played for Tampa Bay Rowdies, Houston Hurricane and Minnesota Kicks, NASL (March 1978–April 1985).

■ Stewart Jump graduated through the junior ranks at The Victoria Ground and made his senior debut in 1970. Basically a reserve defender, he was always hovering on the edge of the first team, yet had a good 1971–72 campaign when he played in 30 matches. Jump made over 80 League appearances for the London club, and after a loan spell with Fulham he spent seven years in the NASL. When the US celebrated its bicentennial in May 1976 he lined up for Team America against England, this being the highlight of his career.

KAMARA, Christopher

Defender or midfield: 71 apps. 7 goals.

Born: Middlesbrough, 25 December 1957.
Career: Portsmouth (apprentice, January 1974, professional, January 1976), Swindon Town (£20,000, August 1977), Portsmouth (£50,000, August 1981), Brentford (exchange deal involving David Crown, October 1981), Swindon Town (£14,500, August 1985), POTTERS (£27,500, July 1988), Leeds United (£150,000, January 1990), Luton Town (£150,000, November 1991), Sheffield United (on loan, November–December 1992), Middlesbrough (on loan, February–March 1993), Sheffield United (free transfer, July 1993), Bradford City (free, as player-assistant manager, July 1994, retired as a player, May 1995, then manager from November 1995–December 1997), POTTERS (manager, January–March 1998), now works in the media (reporting on football for Sky Sports and also for radio).

■ Chris Kamara, who was initially a tall, aggressive striker and developed into a tough-tackling defender or midfielder, amassed more than 770 appearances at club level (641 in the Football League) during his 20 years in the game. He was signed by Potters manager Mick Mills in 1988 after being involved in an unsavoury incident while playing for Swindon at Shrewsbury, which ultimately led to a court appearance (Lou Macari was the Swindon boss at the time). He left Stoke for Elland Road after 18 months and at the end of that 1989–90 season gained a

Second Division Championship medal with the Yorkshire club. This followed his Fourth Division Championship triumph with Swindon four years earlier. Kamara, likeable off the pitch and as tough as iron on it, also collected a runners'-up medal in the Associate Member's Cup Final with Brentford in 1985. As manager at Valley Parade he went to Wembley for the 1996 Play-off Final and was successful against Notts County (2–0). Unfortunately, he failed as boss of the Potters.

KASHER, Joseph W.R.

Defender: 55 apps. 1 goal.

Born: Willington, County Durham, 14 January 1894.
Died: Middlesbrough, 8 January 1992.
Career: Hunwick Juniors (1910), Willington (1911), Crook Town (1913), Petty Officer in the Royal Naval Division (World War One), Sunderland (professional, May 1919), POTTERS (£1,200, October 1922), Carlisle United (part-time professional, May 1924), Accrington Stanley (£1,000, June 1925, retired, May 1927), became a hotelier in Accrington.

■ Between 1910 and 1915, sturdy, well-built defender Joe Kasher (6ft 2in tall) played non-League football in the north-east of England. After joining the Royal Naval for the Great War (when he played regularly for his unit), he was eventually drafted to France where he was held prisoner for two years. After gaining his freedom he joined Sunderland as a professional and appeared in 90 games for the Wearsiders before his transfer to Stoke. Strong in heading, he certainly had that military look about him on the field, where he marshalled his fellow defenders accordingly. Kasher left the Potters after failing to agree terms for a new contract. Rather disgusted, 'big Joe' returned home to Willington where he played part-time for Carlisle United in the North-Eastern League, later assisting Accrington Stanley for whom he made 47 appearances during his two years at Peel Park before retiring to take over The Park Hotel next to Stanley's ground. Kasher was almost 98 years of age when he died in 1992.

KAVANAGH, Graham Anthony

Midfield: 245+10 apps. 46 goals.

Born: Dublin, 2 December 1973.
Career: Home Farm (junior forms, April 1989), Middlesbrough (professional August 1991), Darlington (on loan, February–March 1994), POTTERS (on loan, September 1996, signed permanently for £250,000, October 1996), Cardiff City (£1 million, July 2001), Wigan Athletic (March 2005).

■ A strong-running left-sided midfielder with good vision and positional sense, Graham Kavanagh was recruited by Potters' boss Lou Macari from Premiership club Middlesbrough on a month's loan in mid-September 1996 – around the same time his fellow countryman Gerry McMahon was acquired from Spurs. Prior to that he had done well at Ayresome Park and, although having several other players to contend with for a first-team place, managed 47 senior outings for the Teessiders. Following the arrival of manager Bryan Robson, however, 'Boro's midfield department became somewhat overloaded and as a result Kavanagh was allowed to depart to Stoke. He did exceedingly well during his five years with the Potters. He played in more than 250 first-team matches, netted almost 50 goals and helped the team win the Auto-Windscreen Shield in 2000. After representing the Republic of Ireland at schoolboy and youth-team levels, Kavangah then appeared in one 'B' and nine under-21 internationals as well as a handful of senior matches. He reached the career milestone of 450 League and Cup appearances in 2004–05 before moving to premiership-bound Wigan Athletic.

KAVANAGH, Jason Colin

Right wing-back: 9 apps.

Born: Meriden, Warwickshire, 23 November 1971.
Career: Birmingham City (schoolboy forms), FA School of Excellence, Derby County (apprentice, June 1988, professional, December 1988), Wycombe Wanderers (on loan, November 1996, signed for £25,000, December 1996), POTTERS (free transfer, March 1999), Cambridge United (free, December 1999), Burton Albion (free, July 2000), Mickleover Sports (December 2002), now works as a financial advisor.

■ England schoolboy and youth international right wing-back Jason Kavanagh had pace and stamina and made 127 appearances for Derby and 104 for Wycombe before joining the Potters towards the end of the 1998–99 season. He remained at the club for just two months and entered non-League football with Nigel Clough's Burton Albion in 2000.

KAY, Thomas

Goalkeeper: 77 apps.

Born: Mossley Common, Manchester, November 1892.
Died: Stoke-on-Trent, 1940.
Career: Walkden FC (Lancashire Combination), Bolton Wanderers (reserve, 1913–14), Rochdale (August 1913), POTTERS (£300, April 1919, retired due to poor health, July 1922).

■ Stoke recruited goalkeeper Tom Kay as they prepared to renew their acquaintance with the Football League after a break of 11 years. He gave the club excellent service until the summer of 1922 when he retired from football after suffering a bout of poor health. He

Graham Kavanagh

played in 71 successive games for the Potters and kept a total of 25 clean sheets.

KEARTON, Jason Brett

Goalkeeper: 17 apps.

Born: Ipswich, Australia, 9 July 1969.
Career: Brisbane Lions, Australia, Everton (free transfer, October 1988), POTTERS (on loan, August–November 1991), Blackpool (on loan, January–March 1992), Notts County (on loan, January–March 1995), Preston North End (on loan, April–May 1996), Crewe Alexandra (free, October 1996), Brisbane Lions (free, August 2001).

■ Signed by Everton as cover for Neville Southall, tall, blonde goalkeeper

Jason Kearton was given very little chance to show his worth at Goodison Park owing to the consistency and form of his Welsh international counterpart. He actually made his League debut on loan with Stoke and also assisted Blackpool before making his first appearance for the Merseysiders as a substitute against QPR in December 1993. An FA Cup winner with Everton in 1995, he was voted Crewe's 'Player of the Year' in 2000 and made over 200 appearances under manager Dario Gradi at Gresty Road before returning to Australia.

KEEN, Kevin Ian

Midfield: 169+34 apps. 12 goals.

Born: Amersham, 25 February 1967.
Career: West Ham United (apprentice, May 1982, professional, March 1984), Wolverhampton Wanderers (£600,000,

July 1993), POTTERS (£300,000, October 1994), Macclesfield Town (August 2000, player-assistant manager, January 2001, caretaker manager, October–November 2001, retired as a player, June 2002), gained his UEFA 'A' coaching badge in 2002.

■ A hardworking right-sided midfield player with good pace and excellent vision, Kevin Keen arrived at The Victoria Ground when the Potters engine-room needed stoking up. He did a useful job for six years, certainly in 1998–99 when he blossomed under manager Brian Little's style. He was released at the end of Gudjon Thordarson's first season in charge. A former England schoolboy and youth international, he made 279 appearances for the Hammers (30 goals scored) and followed up with 54 for Wolves. After leaving The Britannia Stadium he went on to take his career appearance tally to 554 (44 goals) before retiring in 2002 having had a brief flirtation in management with Macclesfield.

* His father, Mike Keen, led Queens Park Rangers to the double in 1966–67, victory in the League Cup Final at Wembley and the Third Division title.

KELLY, Anthony Gerald

Midfield: 41+3 apps. 4 goals.

Born: Huyton near Liverpool, 1 October 1964.
Career: St Colombus School (Liverpool), Liverpool & Merseyside Boys, Liverpool (apprentice, April 1980, professional, September 1982), Derby County (briefly, August 1983), The Eagle FC, Liverpool, Wigan Athletic (November 1983), POTTERS (£80,000 April 1986), West Bromwich Albion (£60,000, July 1987), Chester City (on loan, September–October 1988), Colchester United (on loan, October–November 1988), Shrewsbury Town (on loan, January 1989, signed permanently for £30,000, March 1989), Bolton Wanderers (August 1991), Port Vale (non-contract, September 1994), Millwall (non-contract, October 1994), Peterborough United

(December 1994), Wigan Athletic (July 1995–March 1996), Sligo Rovers (player-manager-coach, seasons 1997–99), later worked as a scheme leader for under privileged children with special needs in Huyton; also football coach at same venue (with 20 kids), POTTERS (North-west, scout, 2004–05).

■ A busy, aggressive midfield player, Tony 'Zico' Kelly failed to make the grade with Liverpool, and after a brief association with Derby County he was finally handed his Football League debut by Wigan in 1984. He then won the Freight Rover Trophy with the Springfield Park club at Wembley a year later. Joining the Potters after making 137 senior appearances for the Latics (22 goals), he had a good first-half to the 1986–87 season, being a key figure in the midfield set-up as they forced their way into the promotion reckoning. Alas, Kelly became rather 'overweight' and consequently lost his place in the side, moving to The Hawthorns during the summer of 1987, signed by former 'Stokie' Brian Talbot. He made a total of 419 League appearances during his nomadic career.

KELLY, Charles

Inside-forward: 28 apps. 5 goals.

Born: Sandbach ,Cheshire, 14 June 1894.
Died: Birkenhead, 1969.
Career: Sandbach Ramblers, POTTERS (April 1923), Tranmere Rovers (July 1926).

■ Charlie Kelly was basically a reserve at The Victoria Ground during the mid-1920s, deputising in the main for Harry Davies. His best season came in 1924–25 when he netted four times in 17 League outings, two of his goals coming in a 2–0 away win at Clapton Orient when he was outstanding. He made only one senior appearance for Tranmere.

KELLY, Christopher

Defender: 20 apps. 1 goal.

Born: Tunstall, Stoke-on-Trent, July 1887.
Died: York, c.1960.
Career: Goldenhill Wanderers, POTTERS (July 1908), Denaby United (August 1909), Leeds City (July 1910–May 1912).

■ A well-built centre-half who could also perform adequately as a full-back, Chris Kelly gave the Potters excellent service alongside Sam Baddeley during the 1908–09 season. He moved on following the arrival of Ellis Hall and later appeared in four League games for Leeds City.

KELLY, George Lawson

Inside-forward: 73 apps. 37 goals.

Born: Aberdeen, 29 June 1933.
Career: Aberdeen, POTTERS (£4,000, March 1956), Cardiff City (£20,000, March 1958), Stockport County (July 1959–May 1960).

■ A well-proportioned Scottish inside-forward, tall and rangy, George Kelly scored a goal every two games for the Potters over a period of two years. He was only 22 when he moved south having appeared in just two League games for the Dons. It was perhaps 'good business' on the part of Stoke boss Frank Taylor when he was sold to Cardiff. Kelly, who was appropriately nicknamed 'Spider' and 'Grace', was a six-yard-box finisher, a real poacher, seemingly always on hand to tap home a vital goal. He actually combined playing football with tennis, then an amateur sport, yet he never let his diabetes affect him in any way, and along with another Stoke City player, Johnny King, formed a wonderful double-pairing on the court and almost qualified for the Wimbledon Championships.

KELLY, Nyrere Anthony Okpara

Forward: 41+27 apps. 8 goals.

Born: Meriden, Warwickshire, 14 February 1966.
Career: Bristol City (apprentice, May 1982, non-contract, September 1982), Dulwich Hamlet, Cheshunt, Enfield, Gimonas Cycle, Sweden (on loan), St Albans City (July 1989), POTTERS (£20,000, January 1990), Hull City (on loan, January–February 1992), Cardiff City (on loan, October–November 1992), Bury (£10,000, September 1993), Leyton Orient (£30,000, July 1995), Colchester United (on loan, October 1996), St Albans City (February 1997–May 1998).

■ No relation to Anthony Gerard Kelly, this 'Tony' Kelly was born in the heart of England. A fast-raiding utility forward, able to play on both flanks, he failed to make the breakthrough at Ashton Gate and then served with four non-League clubs and a spell in Swedish football before finally making headway with the Potters in 1990 at the age of 24. Positive and willing, he made his debut for Stoke in the Potteries derby against Port Vale away in February 1990, resulting in a 0–0 draw. His first goal for the club earned victory at Swansea in a League Cup encounter seven months later. When he returned to St Albans in 1997 Kelly's record in the Football League stood at 169 appearances and 21 goals.

KENDALL, Howard

Wing-half: 91 apps. 10 goals.

Born: Ryton-on-Tyne, 22 May 1946.
Career: Ryton & District schools, Preston North End (apprentice, June 1961, professional May 1963), Everton (£80,000, March 1967), Birmingham City (£350,000 deal involving Bob Latchford and Archie Styles, March 1974), POTTERS (£40,000, August 1977), Blackburn Rovers (player-manager, July 1979–May 1981), Everton (non-contract, player-manager, May

1981), Atletico Bilbao, Spain (coach, June 1987), Manchester City (manager, December 1989), Everton (November 1990–December 1993), FC Xanti, Greece (manager, May–November 1994), Notts County (manager, January–April 1995), Sheffield United (manager, December 1995–June 1997), Everton (manager, June 1997–May 1998), then scout for and coach to several clubs (1990s).

■ Howard Kendall's uncle, Harry Taylor, played for Newcastle United, but it was his father who inspired him to become a footballer. He was selected to play for England against Wales in a schoolboy international in 1961, did well and almost immediately was signed as an apprentice by Preston. In 1964, after skippering England youngsters to victory in the Little World Cup, he became the youngest player since 1879 to appear in an FA Cup Final, aged 17 years and 345 days, for Preston against West Ham United. His game got better and better and after more than 100 League outings for the Deepdale club he joined Everton. He quickly gained the first of six under-23 caps against Wales and represented the Football League, but that senior cap always eluded him, despite Kendall being regarded as one of the finest attacking midfielders in the country during the 1969–72 period. In 1968 he collected a second runners'-up medal when Everton lost in the FA Cup Final, but in 1970 he was a key performer when the First Division Championship came to Goodison Park, Kendall forming a terrific partnership in midfield with Alan Ball and Colin Harvey. Moving to St Andrew's in 1974 as part of a complicated deal involving Bob Latchford, he had three and a half excellent seasons with Birmingham who entrusted him with the captaincy. After a wonderful spell with the Potters, being an ever-present in 1977–78 and missing just two League games the following season, he spent two seasons as player-manager at Ewood Park, helping Rovers win the Third Division title before returning to Goodison Park. He brought a great deal of success to Everton, two League Championships (1985 and 1987), an FA Cup Final triumph (1984), two runners'-up prizes (1985 and 1986), European Cup-winners' Cup glory (1985) and a hat-trick of Charity Shield successes (1984, 1985 and 1986). After spells in Spain and at Maine Road he surprisingly returned to Everton for a third spell, and after serving in Greece, at Meadow Lane and Bramall Lane he was taken on a fourth time (third as manager) in 1997. Kendall, who is still regarded as a great hero by Everton fans, appeared in 613 games and scored 65 goals, making his 600th appearance as player-manager of Blackburn in March 1981.

NB: Kendall is one of a handful of men to have featured in an FA Cup Final as a player (with Preston) and manager (of Everton).

KENNEDY, John

Inside-forward: 70 apps. 12 goals.

Born: Edinburgh, June 1873.
Died: Edinburgh, August 1940.
Career: Hibernian (professional, April 1892), POTTERS (March 1898), Glossop North End (June 1900), Edinburgh St Bernard's (July 1903–May 1904).

■ Inside-forward Jack Kennedy was one of a plethora of Scots who ventured south to try their luck in English football during the 1890s. A strong, muscular player, he made his League debut in a 2–1 home win over Sheffield Wednesday a week after moving to The Victoria Ground and scored the first of his 12 goals a month later in the 2–1 Test Match defeat at Newcastle. He had two outings at centre-half halfway through the following season but was not a success as the Potters lost both matches, conceding six goals in the process. A Scottish international, capped against Wales in 1897, Kennedy also represented the Scottish League and gained a runners'-up medal when Hibs but lost the 1896 Scottish Cup Final. He scored seven goals in 39 League games for Glossop.

KENNEDY, Michael Francis Martin

Midfield: 64+1 apps. 3 goals.

Born: Salford, 9 April 1961.
Career: Halifax Town (apprentice, May 1977, professional, January 1979), Huddersfield Town (£50,000, August 1980), Middlesbrough (£90,000, August

1982), Portsmouth (£100,000, June 1984), Bradford City (£225,000, January 1988), Leicester City (in exchange for Jimmy Quinn, March 1989), Luton Town (£150,000, August 1989), POTTERS (£180,000, 1990), Chesterfield (free transfer, May 1992–May 1993), Wigan Athletic (free, July 1993, retired through injury, May 1994), later coached in Northern Ireland.

■ Capped twice by the Republic of Ireland at senior level and once by the under-21s, tough-tackling midfielder Mick Kennedy started his career in 1977 as a junior with Halifax Town and continued playing until 1994, eventually retiring at the age of 33. With almost 450 League appearances under his belt, as well as being a promotion winner with Portsmouth in 1987 and helping Bradford reach the play-offs a year later, he joined the Potters, signed by former Pompey boss Alan Ball. He spent two years at The Victoria Ground before leaving the club in May 1992 for Chesterfield having had, according to the press, 'a torrid time under manager Lou Macari'. During his senior career he struck 30 goals in 631 competitive appearances. He went on to coach youngsters in Ireland, producing several who went on to enter League football.

NB: Kennedy attracted censure during his Pompey days for some ill-judged verbal revelling.

KEVAN, David John

Midfield: 96+6 apps. 2 goals.

Born: Newton Stewart, Wigtown, Scotland, 31 August 1968.
Career: Notts County (apprentice, May 1985, professional, August 1986), Cardiff City (on loan, September 1989), POTTERS (on loan, January 1990, signed for £75,000, February 1990), Maidstone United (on loan, February 1991), AFC Bournemouth (March 1994, retired through injury, January 1995), returned as youth team coach with the POTTERS (late 1990s).

■ A hard-working midfield player, David Kevan, an unused substitute at under-21 level for Scotland, was forced to quit the game through injury at the age of 27. He appeared in 89 League games for Notts County, despite having his progress hampered when Neil

Warnock took over as manager at Meadow Lane. Signed by Alan Ball, he quickly made his debut for the Potters in the local derby with Port Vale, but then faded from the scene. However, following a loan spell at Maidstone, Lou Macari resurrected his career, and in 1992 he gained an Autoglass Trophy winners' medal at Wembley, missing only two senior games during that season. He later returned to coach and work with the youth team at Stoke.

KIERNAN, Thomas

Inside-forward: 30 apps. 7 goals.

Born: Coatbridge near Dumfries, Scotland, 22 October 1918.
Died: Dumfries, Summer 1991.
Career: Celtic, POTTERS (£8,000, September 1947), Luton Town (£7,000, November 1948–May 1950), later returned to Scotland.

■ Inside-forward Tom Kiernan was recruited to The Victoria Ground by manager Bob McGrory in 1947 for a club-record fee. Introduced to 'bolster up' the side, he was a regular in the first team at Parkhead (17 goals in 32 games) and represented the Scottish League, but sadly he never quite fitted the bill at Stoke, and after 15 months' service he switched his allegiance to Luton Town.

KING, John William

Inside-left: 371 apps. 113 goals.

Born: Wrenbury near Nantwich, Cheshire, 9 August 1932.
Career: Crewe Alexandra (amateur, August 1947, professional, October 1949), POTTERS (£8,000, September 1953), Cardiff City (£12,000, May 1961), Crewe Alexandra (June 1962, retired, May 1967).

■ Johnny King was a natural goalscorer. Short and chunky with a wonderful left foot, he was deceivingly quick over a short distance and possessed a splendid shot (in both feet). At Crewe he partnered Frank Blunstone who later became an England international outside-left, and when Blunstone switched to Chelsea King made his way to the Potters. Standing at just 5ft 7in tall, he quickly settled into the City attack and became a huge favourite with the fans. A regular marksman season after season, he had his best return in 1954–55 when he struck 20 goals, including a hat-trick against Bury, the time the Potters played on Christmas Day. One of only a handful of players to have netted over 100 League goals for the Potters, King went on to chalk up a career record of

172 goals in 543 League games, including 43 in 178 outings for the Alex, whom he helped gain promotion from the Fourth Division in 1963. He also starred for an FA XI as a Crewe player. In partnership with Stoke reserve of the mid-1950s George Kelly, King formed a fine double partnership at tennis and at one stage the pair were on the brink of making the Wimbledon Championships.

KINNELL, George

Defender: 109+2 apps. 8 goals.

Born: Cowdenbeath, 22 December 1937.
Career: Crossgates Primitives (1956), Aberdeen (professional, March 1959), POTTERS (£27,000, November 1963), Oldham Athletic (joint £26,000 deal with Keith Bebbington, August 1966), Sunderland (£20,000, November 1966), Middlesbrough (£20,000, October 1968–May 1969).

■ George Kinnell, cousin of the legendary former Scottish international wing-half Jim Baxter, made more than 100 first-team appearances for the Potters covering a period of three years. Strong, fearless and able to occupy any position across the back line, he was occasionally used in attack where it was hoped his strength would upset opposing defenders! The recipient of a League Cup runners'-up prize in 1964, he later teamed up with his former Stoke colleague Jimmy McIlroy at Oldham but stayed only three months

at Boundary Park before transferring to Sunderland. During his club career Kinnell appeared in 378 competitive games and scored 48 goals.

KIPPE, Frode

Defender: 40+4 apps. 1 goal.

Born: Oslo, Norway, 17 January 1978.
Career: Kilbotn FC, Norway, Lillestrom, Norway, Liverpool (£700,000, January 1999), POTTERS (on loan, December 1999–March 2000 and October 2000–May 2001), Lillestrom (March 2002).

■ A giant 6ft 4in Norwegian 'B' and under-21 international defender (27 caps gained in the latter category), Frode Kippe's second loan spell with the Potters was hampered by a spate of tedious knee injuries that restricted his appearances considerably. In his first spell he produced some excellent displays and gained an Auto-Windscreen Shield winners' medal in 2000. It was perhaps surprising that he never made the grade at Anfield, having only two substitute outings for Liverpool.

KIRK, Stephen David

Full-back: 12 apps.

Born: Kirkcaldy, Fife, 3 January 1963.
Career: East Fife (apprentice, April 1979, professional, February 1980, POTTERS (£5,000, May 1980), Partick Thistle (£2,000, June 1982), East Fife (free transfer, September 1982), Motherwell (free, August 1986–May 1996).

■ All of Steve Kirk's senior appearances for the Potters came during the second half of the 1981–82 season when in the main he partnered Peter Hampton at full-back. He left the club after failing to command a regular place in the side. He appeared in almost 250 League games for Motherwell and 135 outings for East Fife.

KIRKBY, John

Full-back: 1 app.

Born: North America, 29 November 1929.
Died: Wrexham, August 1953.
Career: Banks o'Dee FC, POTTERS (free transfer, December 1946), Wrexham (£500, August 1951, until his death).

■ Jack Kirby was the first overseas footballer to play for Stoke City. A stocky full-back, he appeared in just one First Division game for the club, partnering Cyril Watkin against Middlesbrough away in April 1949, ending 1–1. He was only 23 when he collapsed and died while playing in a reserve-team game for Wrexham against Crewe Alexandra.

KIRKHAM, Wilfred Thomas

Centre-forward: 51 apps. 31 goals.

Born: Cobridge, Stoke-on-Trent, 26 November 1901.
Died: Bournemouth, 20 October 1974.
Career: Cobridge Church, POTTERS (trialist, 1918), Congleton Town (1919), Burslem Port Vale (amateur, April 1920, released, October 1920), Shelton United (November 1920), Sheffield Teacher Training College (1921, for two years), Port Vale (trialist, August 1923, signed professional September 1923), POTTERS (£2,800, May 1929), Port Vale (January 1932), attained the position as headmaster at Cobridge School as a Vale player, Kidderminster Harriers (July 1933, retired, May 1934).

■ An outstanding goalscorer with Port Vale, Wilf Kirkham (described as a dashing centre-forward) always seemed to do well against Stoke and it was perhaps no surprise when the Potters manager and directors decided that they wanted him at The Victoria Ground. The Victoria Ground fans thought that the 27-year-old would continue his marksmanship. He did well enough, but in truth never really settled down in his new surroundings despite his return of 30 goals in only 51 League games. Vale's top-scorer on four occasions, in 1924–25, 1925–26, 1926–27 (when he struck a club record 38 goals) and 1932–33, he registered a total of 12 hat-tricks and twice scored four goals in a game. He ended with a haul of 164 goals (in 276 games) for the Valiants, a record that still stands today. In the summer of 1933 the North Staffordshire Education Authority decided that professional football was incompatible with his new post as headmaster at Cobridge School and as a result Kirkham moved into non-League football with Kidderminster Harriers.
The cousin of Tom Holford, Kirkham moved to the south coast later in life.

KIRTON, John

Wing-half: 249 apps.

Born: Aberdeen, 4 March 1916.
Died: Stoke-on-Trent, 12 March 1996.
Career: St Marcher's FC (Aberdeen),

Banks o' Dee FC, POTTERS (professional, November 1935), Bradford City (July 1953), Hinckley Athletic (March 1954), Downings FC (July 1956, retired, May 1960).

■ Jock Kirton's career was interrupted by seven years of World War Two, but he still managed to attain a terrific record for the Potters by appearing in almost 250 peacetime matches and 65 during the war. A splendid wing-half, he was enticed down to Stoke by fellow Scot Bob McGrory in 1935, having earlier won schoolboy caps for his country. Arthur Tutin and Frank Soo

were in charge of the two wing-half berths when Kirton arrived at The Victoria Ground, but he bided his time and eventually gained a regular first-team place, lining up behind Frank Baker down Stoke's left-hand flank. After 18 years at the club, Kirton moved on to Bradford City and finally quit League football at the age of 36. He was 80 when he died in the Stoke City General Hospital in 1996.

KNOTT, Percy

Goalkeeper: 30 apps.

Born: Hartshill, Stoke-on-Trent, 7 July 1899.
Died: South Africa, April 1972.
Career: Hartshill White Star, POTTERS (amateur, August 1920, professional, October 1920), Queen's Park Rangers (September 1927), emigrated to South Africa in 1961.

■ Percy Knott was reserve to Tom Kay during the second and third seasons

after World War One. Signed from local junior football, he made his League debut in February 1921 – the first of 30 games for the Potters in a seven-year stay with the club. He spent the last five as a permanent reserve to Bob Dixon, Kenny Campbell, Jim Lee and Les Scott.

KOLAR, Martin

Midfield: new signing.

Born: Czechoslovakia, 18 September 1983.
Career: RSC Anderlecht, Belgium (professional, 2002), POTTERS (loan, August 2005).

■ Exciting and skilful, attacking left-sided midfielder Martin Kolar made a splendid start with the Potters and quickly became a firm favourite with the fans. He made his debut in English football against Sheffield Wednesday and scored his first goal against Norwich City. Prior to joining Stoke he made over 40 appearances in three seasons of Belgian League football.

KRISTINSSON, Birkir

Goalkeeper: 22 apps.

Born: Vestmannaeyjar, Iceland, 15 March 1964.
Career: IA Akranes, Iceland (League debut, 1987), Fram Reykjavik, Iceland (May 1988), Sportsklubben Brann Bergen, Norway (September 1996), IFK Norrkoping, Sweden (March 1997),

Birmingham City (trialist), Bolton Wanderers (briefly, 1998), IB Vestmannaeyjar, Iceland (February 1999), Lustenau, Austria (February 2000), POTTERS (free transfer, November 2000), IB Vestmannaeyjar (November 2001).

■ Icelandic international (capped 70 times between 1988 and 1999) Birkir Kristinsson was 36 when asked to help out the Potters during a goalkeeping crisis in 2000. He performed well and held his place until the arrival of Gavin Ward. He was the first Stoke City shareholder to appear in a first-team match at competitive level. He had already appeared in over 200 League games in four different countries before joining the Potters, gaining an Icelandic Cup winners' medal with Fram in 1990.

LACEY, Anthony John

Right-back or midfield: 3+2 apps.

Born: Leek, Staffordshire, 18 March 1944.
Career: Leek Church School Old Boys, St Luke's College (Exeter University), POTTERS (professional, October 1965), Port Vale (on loan, February 1970, signed permanently for £2,500, April 1970), Rochdale (free transfer, May 1975), Stafford Rangers (August 1977), returned to POTTERS (1980, as youth-team coach, then reserve-team coach, two spells as caretaker-manager and finally Youth Development Officer, left club in 1996).

■ Tony Lacey studied at Exeter University before turning to soccer. He made his League debut for the Potters against the reigning champions Manchester City at the age of 24 in September 1968 and spent four and a half years at The Victoria Ground before joining neighbours Port Vale, for whom he scored nine goals in 215 first-team matches. He later returned to the Potters where he remained for a further 16 years, initially as coach. In that time he nurtured some excellent footballers.

LATHAM, Frederick

Goalkeeper: 5 apps.

Born: Crewe, Cheshire, 11 July 1876.
Died: Crewe, June 1949.
Career: Crewe Alexandra, POTTERS (May 1896), Tottenham Hotspur (trialist, April–May 1897), Crewe Alexandra (August 1897, retired, 1904).

■ Following the success they had with ex-Crewe Alexandra 'keeper George Clawley, Stoke returned to their Gresty Road neighbours to sign Fred Latham in 1896. He started off well and played in five League games before Billy Rowley was recalled. Left out in the cold, he returned to Crewe where he ended his career.

LATHAM, Captain George, MC

Full-back or wing-half: 8 apps.

Born: Newtown, Monmouthshire, 1 January 1881.
Died: Newtown, 9 July 1939.
Career: New Road School (Newtown), Newtown FC (season 1897–98), fought in the Boer War (to 1901), guest for Caledonian FC (South Africa), Everton (trialist, 1900), Newtown (August 1901), Liverpool (May 1902), Southport Central (June 1909), POTTERS (September 1910, retired, March 1911), Cardiff City (April 1911, as head trainer until May 1932), Chester (trainer, August 1932–June 1937).

■ Having retired in 1911, George Latham made an unexpected return to international football against Ireland in 1913 when Wales were a man short. And then in 1922 he was pressed into action by Cardiff City for a League game at Blackburn Rovers in 1922, aged 41, the oldest debutant in the Welsh club's history. A Welsh international half-back who was honoured in the Boer War, he was all set to join Everton, but a snow storm caused the abandonment of his trial game and he was never approached again. On leaving the Armed Forces in 1901 he rejoined Newtown and then spent seven years with Liverpool but made only 18 appearances. Capped for the first time against Scotland in 1905, Latham went on to win 10 at senior level and there is no doubt he would have won many more if he had played for a more fashionable club. After 'retiring' he served as Cardiff's official trainer for 21 years and was employed by Chester in the same capacity for five. During World War One he served as a captain in the 7th Battalion Royal Welsh Fusiliers on the Turkish front and earned the Military Cross. In the first battle of Gaza in March 1917 Latham's party of 40 men were successful in overpowering the Turkish line, only to learn that H.Q. had, the previous night, ordered the withdrawal on the basis of reports that around 7,000 Turkish re-inforcements were on their way. The line was abandoned and then reoccupied by the Turks, only for the RWF to be ordered to retake the position once again! He acted as manager to the Great Britain Olympic team in 1924 and also played an important role in Cardiff's sensational FA Cup Final victory over mighty Arsenal in 1927. In 1936 Latham was seriously injured in a cycling accident and ill-health later forced him to quit soccer and retire to his beloved Newtown where he sadly died a few months before the outbreak of World War Two. Latham, known as affectionately 'Gentleman George', did a terrific amount of charity work, raising hundreds of pounds for the Newtown Hospital where his mother was matron. It is said that during his time at Cardiff he never failed to send his mum a telegram after each match giving her the score.
NB: In his memory, Newtown's football ground is called Latham Park.

LAWTON, George

Goalkeeper: 1 app.

Born: Tunstall, Stoke-on-Trent, 17 December 1879.

Died: Stoke-on-Trent, March 1944.
Career: Burslem Port Vale (April 1896), Porthill FC (August 1898), POTTERS (July 1901), Porthill (March 1902), Tunstall (August 1903, retired 1912).

■ Third-choice goalkeeper George Lawton's only League outing for Stoke came in a 4–2 defeat at Bury three months after joining the club when he deputised for Tom Wilkes. After leaving The Victoria Ground he remained in football for the next 14 years, retiring at the age of 35, just prior to World War One. He made 17 first-team appearances for the Vale.

LAWTON, George

Outside-right: 17 apps. 3 goals.

Born: Stoke-on-Trent, 4 August 1862.
Died: Stoke-on-Trent, c.1930.
Career: Stoke St Peter's, POTTERS (July 1885), Burlsem Port Vale (January 1886), POTTERS (May 1886), Altrincham (January 1889), Belvedere FC (season 1889–90).

■ An orthodox right-winger, George Lawton had two spells with the Potters during the mid-1880s. He played in 13 of the 22 games in the first season of League football (1888–89), scoring in a 4–3 win over Burnley. He later scored three goals in 13 outings for Port Vale

LAWTON, John Kenneth

Forward: 9 apps. 3 goals.

Born: Woore near Newcastle-under-Lyme, 6 July 1936.

Career: Crewe Alexandra (amateur, July 1951), POTTERS (amateur, August 1952, professional, June 1954), Winsford United (August 1957).

■ John Lawton averaged a goal every three games for the Potters in 1955. A useful reserve, he moved on after failing to establish himself in the first XI.

LEE, James Thomas

Goalkeeper: 24 apps.

Born: Brierley Hill near Dudley, 12 April 1892.
Died: Dudley, May 1955.
Career: Cradley Heath St Luke's, Old Wulfrunians, Wolverhampton (1915), Army service with Grenadier Guards, Aston Villa (free transfer, March 1919), West Ham United (briefly, 1920), POTTERS (£750, August 1921), Macclesfield Town (July 1923–May 1924), later assisted Burton All Saints.

■ Sam Hardy's deputy during his short stay at Villa Park, Jim Lee (an ex-Grenadier Guardsman and one-time policeman) often relied on his long legs stopping the ball rather than using his hands! A good shot-stopper, nevertheless, he made 18 appearances for Villa during the first two seasons after World War One.

LEECH, William

Winger: 50 apps. 22 goals.

Born: Newcastle-under-Lyme, 1875.
Died: Leicester, 24 November 1934.
Career: Newcastle White Star, Newcastle Swifts, Tottenham Hotspur (July 1898), Burslem Port Vale (June 1899), POTTERS (May 1900), Plymouth Argyle (August 1903), Leicester Fosse (July 1906, retired, May 1910, became reserve-team coach and was later appointed trainer to 1915).

■ An out-and-out winger who could also occupy both wing-half and inside-forward positions, Billy Leech failed to make the grade with Spurs and returned to the Potteries to sign for Burslem Port Vale, making his debut against his future club Leicester Fosse. After a season there, when he made 36 appearances, he moved to Stoke (May 1900) and remained at The Victoria Ground until 1903, spending the latter campaign in the reserves. He helped Leicester win promotion in 1908 when he was an ever-present in their ranks. He scored once in 30 League and FA Cup games for the Vale.

LEES, Terence

Full-back: 21+8 apps.

Born: Stoke-on-Trent, 30 June 1952.
Career: POTTERS (apprentice June 1968, professional, July 1969), Cape Town, South Africa (on loan), Crewe Alexandra (on loan, March–April 1975), San Jose Earthquakes (on loan, May–July 1975), Port Vale (£3,000, August 1975), Sparta Rotterdam, Holland (£25,000, August 1976), Rhoda JC, Holland (season 1977–78), Kerkerade, Holland (season 1978–79), Birmingham City (July 1979), Newport County (August 1981), Morning Star, Hong Kong (on loan, summer 1982), Blackpool (trialist, late 1982), Dordrecht, Holland (early 1983), Altrincham (May 1983), Stafford Rangers (December 1983), Scunthorpe United (non-contract, September 1984–May 1985), Macclesfield Town (briefly), Hanley Town (manager, September 1985), Kidsgrove Athletic (manager, 1986–87), Meir KA (assistant manager, coach, late 1980s), Ball Haye Green (manager-coach, 1990, retired from football, summer 1993), later ran a sports shop in the Potteries.

■ Versatile full-back Terry Lees was understudy to more established players at each of the clubs he served in a longish career. After his exploits with Stoke, he made 47 appearances for Port Vale and spent three years in Dutch football before returning to England to sign for Birmingham City, who used him as a sweeper. Lees was also a useful club cricketer.

LEESE, Harold

Defender: 124 apps. 29 goals.

Born: Goldenhill, Stoke-on-Trent, 1884.
Died: Stoke-on-Trent, c.1957.
Career: Smallthorne FC, Goldenhill Villa, POTTERS (August 1909), Bradford City, POTTERS, Port Vale (May 1913), served in the Army during World War One,

demobilised in April 1919), Crewe Alexandra (July 1919), Goldenhill Wanderers (1920–21).

■ Harry Leese had two excellent spells with the Potters between 1909 and 1913. Strong and competitive, he was able to play in a number of positions including full-back and centre-half, but preferred the latter. He helped the Potters win the Southern League and Birmingham & District League titles in 1910 and 1911 respectively and, after leaving The Victoria Ground, scored five goals in 57 first-team games for the Vale.

LEIGH, Walter Harold

Outside-right: 70 apps. 14 goals.

Born: Lymm, Cheshire, June 1888.
Died: Winsford, c.1960.
Career: Aston Villa (professional, August 1906), Barnsley (September 1908), POTTERS (May 1909), Winsford United (August 1911). Did not play after World War One.

■ Harry Leigh was a reserve with Aston Villa (along with his brother Herbert) before joining Barnsley from where he moved to The Victoria Ground in 1909. He took over from Abe Hamnett on Stoke's right-wing and held his position for two seasons before losing his place in 1911. He helped the Potters win the Southern League and Birmingham & District League titles in 1910 and 1911 respectively, missing only two matches during the 1909–10 campaign.

LENAGHAN, John

Centre-forward: 37 apps. 10 goals.

Born: Liverpool, July 1888.
Died: Whitchurch, 1954.
Career: Maghull, Mardy FC, POTTERS (December 1911), Chirk (March 1913). Did not play after World War One.

■ 'Scouser' Jack Lenaghan served Stoke very well for 16 months, during which time he scored his fair share of goals. A strong, robust player, he had the pleasure of netting a hat-trick on his debut in a 4–3 home win over West Ham United in a Southern League game in mid-December 1911.

LENNON, George Ferguson

Full-back: 3 apps.

Born: Kilwinning, Scotland, 24 May 1899.
Died: Scotland, 1984.
Career: Kilwinning Rangers (1916), Third Lanark (1917), St Mirren (1918), Ayr United (1919), Luton Town (May 1920), POTTERS (£500, March 1923), Bristol Rovers (May 1925).

■ George Lennon was reserve to Bob McGrory at The Victoria Ground and as a result his chances of first-team football were limited. Earlier he played in over 50 senior games in Scotland, and prior to joining the Potters he made 107 League appearances for Luton.

LENNOX, Stephen John Martin.

Midfield: 1+1 apps.

Born: Aberdeen, 16 November 1964.
Career: POTTERS (apprentice, April 1981, professional, December 1981), Torquay United (on loan, December 1983–January 1984), Montrose (May 1984), Forfar Athletic, Peterhead (Highland League) East Fife.

■ Reserve midfielder Steve Lennox played in two League games for the Potters (one as 'sub') during the second half of the 1982–83 season. He had 11 outings on loan with Torquay before leaving The Victoria Ground for a career in his home county.

LEONARD, Arthur Ralph (also Arthur Leonard Bamford)

Inside-forward: 14 apps. 3 goals.

Born: Leicester, July 1874.
Died: Leicester, 1950.
Career: Served with the 17th Leicestershire Regiment (from 1892), Leicester Fosse (August 1895), Rushden Town (October 1895), Sheppey United (May 1897), Glentoran (July 1900), served in the Army during World War One, Birmingham (£120, November 1921), POTTERS (January 1904), St Bernard's, Edinburgh (November 1904), Reading (November 1905), Clapton Orient (September 1906), Plymouth Argyle (July 1908, retired, May 1909).

■ Inside-forward Arthur Leonard joined his first major club, Birmingham, in bizarre circumstances. The Blues had watched Leonard play for Glentoran and a few hours after the game signed him as a full-time professional. Also present at that same match were representatives of Leicester Fosse who recognised Leonard as their 'missing player' Arthur Bamford! When approached, Leonard ran off and was missing for several days, sending a telegram to his wife saying that he had gone to America. He later resurfaced in Bristol and was persuaded to return to Birmingham to see out the 1901–02 season, with the club paying Leicester a further £20 for the trouble caused. A real bag of tricks, able to use both feet, Leonard was a huge hit with the fans and stayed with the Blues until January 1904 (when he joined the Potters) having scored 26 goals in 75 appearances for the city club. He left The Victoria Ground without really making much of an impact and signed for Reading. He later scored 11 times in 37 games for Plymouth, helping the Pilgrims take the runners'-up spot in the Southern League in 1908. Before registering as a player with Leicester in 1895, Leonard had served in the Army and played several games for his unit. After 'deserting' Filbert Street he had spells in non-League football prior to going over to Ireland.

LESLIE, Steven

Midfield: 0+2 apps.

Born: Dumfries, 6 February 1976.
Career: West Park School (Dumfries), Motherwell (amateur), Clydebank (semi-professional, March 1991), POTTERS (full-time professional, March 1993, free transfer, May 1995), returned to Scotland.

■ A diminutive Scottish central midfielder, Steve Leslie's brief association with the Potters was limited to just two second-half substitute appearances, the first in the Anglo-Italian Cup tie against Ancona in September 1994 and the second versus Portsmouth in the League in February 1995. He was brought to the club by manager Lou Macari and at the end of his first season gained a Midland youth Cup winners' medal. Unfortunately, he was not retained and left the Potteries to continue his career in his homeland.

LESLIE, Lawrence Grant

Goalkeeper: 97 apps.

Born: Edinburgh, 17 March 1935.
Career: Newtongrange Star, Edinburgh (1954), Hibernian (professional, May 1956), Airdrieonians (£4,475, November 1959), West Ham United (£14,000, June 1961), POTTERS (£15,000, October 1963), Millwall (free transfer, July 1966), Southend United (free, June 1968, retired, May 1971, appointed club's trainer, coach to December 1972), later coached football in Hackney schools and was also involved in youth and sports club centres; employed as head sports-master at Homerton School for many years.

■ Lawrie Leslie was a very capable and brave goalkeeper who was good on his line and appeared in almost 100 senior games for Stoke over a period of two years during the mid-1960s. A Scottish League representative on three occasions, he also won five caps at senior level, the first as an Airdrie player against Wales in 1960. He was a Scottish Cup finalist with Hibernian (1956) and played in the League Cup Final for Stoke versus Leicester City in 1964. In all, Leslie made over 200 League appearances in his career. He was certainly a deservedly popular custodian.

LEWIS, Arthur Norman

Goalkeeper: 170 apps.

Born: Wolverhampton, 13 June 1908.
Died: Wolverhampton, 1972.
Career: Bushbury Park Council School, Wolverhampton, Sunbeam Works, Wolverhampton Wanderers (professional, July 1928), POTTERS (£250, May 1929), Bradford Park Avenue (£300, May 1936), Tranmere Rovers (£250, November 1936, retired, May 1942).

■ Another extremely capable goalkeeper, Norman Lewis served for the Potters for over six years, making 159 of his senior appearances in the Football League. One-time assembler on the shop floor at Sunbeam Works, he joined his home-town club, Wolves, at

the age of 20. After 30 appearances for the Molineux club he was signed by Stoke manager Tom Mather as cover for Dick Williams. Standing 5ft 10in tall and weighing over 12st, he eventually gained a regular first-team place at The Victoria Ground in 1930, but, after losing his place in the team to the former Huddersfield 'keeper Norman Wilkinson, Lewis later moved to Bradford. He appeared in 58 senior games for the Prenton Park club and helped them win the Third Division North title in 1938.

LEWIS, Frederick

Right-half: 2 apps.

Born: Handsworth, Birmingham, February 1886.
Died: Birmingham, 1949.
Career: Grove Lane School, Birmingham, West Bromwich Albion (May 1908), POTTERS (April 1910) Cradley St Luke's (May 1911), Dudley Town (1912) Brierley Hill Alliance (1913). Did not play after World War One.

■ Fred Lewis spent two seasons as a reserve at The Hawthorns before joining Stoke. He made just two appearances for the Potters before entering non-League football in 1911.

LEWIS, John E.

Half-back: 3 apps.

Born: Porthcawl, Glamorgan, June 1912.
Died: South Wales, c.1988.
Career: Merthyr Town, POTTERS (January 1934, retired through injury, August 1936).

■ A well-built defender, Jack Lewis was recruited to bolster up Stoke's reserve

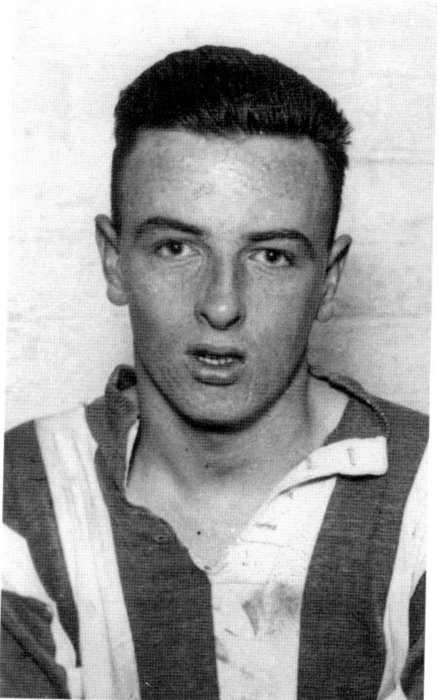

side. He made only three first-team appearances before injury forced him into early retirement in 1936. Lewis had done very well in Welsh football and was seen to be just the right type of player Stoke needed to develop. Sadly, his career was short-lived.

LEWIS, Kevin

Full-back: 0+1 app.

Born: Hull, 17 October 1970.
Career: POTTERS (apprentice, August 1986, professional, October 1987), Mansfield Town (trialist, 1988), Stafford Rangers (August 1989).

■ Injuries interrupted Kevin Lewis's career as a full-back with Stoke. His only senior game for the club came as a substitute against Millwall in April 1988 before entering non-League football with Stafford Rangers a year later. He is nephew to Kevin William Lewis.

LEWIS, Kevin William

Defender: 16 apps.

Born: Hull, 25 September 1952.
Career: Manchester United (apprentice, September 1968, professional, September 1969), POTTERS (free transfer, July 1972), Cape Town City, South Africa (on loan, March 1977), Crewe Alexandra (free, June 1979), Telford United (free, as player-manager, August 1982), Leek Town (during season 1983–84), later became licensee of the Dyer Arms, Leek.

■ Signed by Stoke boss Tony Waddington from Manchester United after having served a lengthy suspension, utility defender Kevin Lewis remained at The Victoria Ground for seven seasons, playing the majority of his football in the second team. A former England schoolboy international, he won a South African League Championship medal with Cape Town and he also fractured his right leg, sidelining him for almost two years. He made 122 League appearances for Crewe.

LIDDLE, Robert

Outside or inside-right: 314 apps. 64 goals.

Born: Gateshead, 11 April 1908.
Died: Billborough, Nottingham, 12 April 1972.
Career: St John's Roman Catholic School, Washington, Washington Colliery (from 1925), POTTERS (professional, January 1928, retired, 1945, club trainer until May 1953), later ran a newsagent's shop in Nottingham.

■ Discovered playing in the North East by an eagle-eyed Potters' scout, ex-miner Bobby Liddle was a star performer at The Victoria Ground for more than a decade. He joined Stoke at the age of 19 and the following season broke into the first team, firmly establishing himself in the side in 1929–30. He amassed an excellent strike-record prior to World War Two and collected a Second Division Championship medal in 1933. During the first-half of the war Liddle made a further 152 appearances (28 goals scored) before retiring to become the club's trainer, a position he held until 1953. In all, he gave Stoke 25 years' service. Standing 5ft 6in tall and weighing 10st 7lb, Liddle had Stan Matthews and Joe Johnson ahead of him as Stoke's regular wingers, so he was used effectively at inside-right and did extremely well, often performing with great zest both at home and away.

LIGHTBOURNE. Kyle Lavince

Striker: 100+30 apps. 25 goals

Born: Bermuda, 29 September 1968.
Career: Pembroke Hamilton FC, Bermuda, Scarborough (professional, December 1992), Walsall (free transfer, September 1993), Coventry City (£500,000, July 1997), Fulham (on loan, January–February 1998), POTTERS (£500,000, February 1998), Cardiff City (on loan, February 2001), Macclesfield Town (free, July 2001), Hull City (on loan, March–April 2002).

■ A Bermudan international, capped 22 times at senior level as well as winning youth honours, 6ft 2in striker Kyle Lightbourne was 24 years of age when he entered League football with Scarborough in 1992. He did superbly well with Walsall (84 goals in 198 games) and during his time with the Potters he produced some fine performances, netting some vital goals in the process, although he did have some dry spells when his form slumped. He helped the Potters win the Auto-windscreen Shield in 2000 and he struck his 100th League goal in 2003 (as a Macclesfield player). Besides representing his country at soccer, Lightbourne also played in several senior cricket matches.

LINDSAY, Alec

Left-back: 22 apps. 3 goals.

Born: Bury, 27 February 1948.
Career: Local junior football, Bury (apprentice, April 1963, professional, March 1965), Liverpool (£67,000, March 1969), POTTERS (on loan, August 1977, signed for £25,000, September 1977), Oakland Stompers, NASL (£7,000, March 1978), Toronto Blizzard (1980), Newton FC, North West Counties League (October 1982, retired, May 1983).

■ Blonde left-back Alec Lindsay played in 126 League games for Bury and 170 for Liverpool before joining Stoke. A very competent defender, who was capped four times by England at full international level as well as a youth team player, Lindsay won the UEFA Cup and First Division Championship with Liverpool in 1973 and the FA Cup the following year (having lost in the 1971 Final). He averaged a goal every three games for the Potters before moving into the NASL.

LISTER, Robert

Outside-right: 1 app.

Born: Glasgow, June 1901.
Died: Scotland, 1971.
Career: Heart of Midlothian (April 1918), Dunfermline Athletic (1922), POTTERS (October 1927), West Ham United (September 1929), Exeter City (May 1930), Rhyl (August 1931), Shrewsbury Town (August 1933, retired, May 1937).

■ Bob Lister was a nimble outside-left whose only senior appearance for the Potters was against Fulham in a Second Division game at Craven Cottage in November 1927, when he laid on two goals in a 5–1 victory.

LITTLE, Thomas Stewart Colquhoun

Inside-right: 21 apps. 1 goal.

Born: Ilford, Essex, 27 February 1890.
Died: Essex, December 1960.
Career: Ilford (1906), Southend United (August 1908), Bradford Park Avenue (November 1908), POTTERS (December 1920, retired through injury, May 1922).

■ Tom Little's only goal for Stoke came in a lukewarm 3–2 defeat at Clapton Orient in April 1921, his 15th outing for the club. Prior to joining the Potters he had netted 106 times in 232 League outings for Bradford and at one stage in his career seemed set to move to Manchester United.

LOCKER, William

Inside-forward: 1 app.

Born: Long Eaton, 18 February 1866.
Died: Nottingham, 1952.
Career Long Eaton Rangers, POTTERS (October 1889), Long Eaton Rangers (December 1889), Notts County (February 1890), Derby County (August 1892, retired 1893).

■ Bill Locker was another 'one game wonder' for Stoke, having his only outing for the club in November 1889, a 2–1 home defeat at the hands of reigning League and Cup double-winners Preston North End. He scored 12 goals in 21 League games for Notts County.

LOCKETT, Arthur Henry

Outside-left: 73 apps. 7 goals.

Born: Alsagers Bank near Stoke-on-Trent, 13 August 1877.
Died: Crewe, 1957.
Career: Crewe Alexandra, POTTERS (May 1900), Aston Villa (£40, April 1903), Preston North End (September 1905), Watford (July 1908), Port Vale (May–December 1912).

■ Regarded as a 'swift winger' with energy and pace, Arthur Lockett, an England international capped against Ireland in February 1903 (won 4–0), he also represented the Football League the following year. A player who loved to dribble with the ball, he struck five goals in 41 League games for Villa and five in 64 for Preston but failed to make the first XI with Port Vale.

LONIE, Thomas

Centre-forward: 9 apps. 4 goals.

Born: Dundee, July 1872.
Died: Dundee, Scotland, 1954.
Career: Dundee Harp (August 1890), Notts County (professional, January 1894), Darwen (July 1894), Dundee Wanderers (October 1894), Dundee (March 1895), POTTERS (October 1895), Leicester Fosse (August–October 1896).

■ Scotsman Tom Lonie never settled at The Victoria Ground or with four of his other senior clubs. One of six different centre-forwards used by the Potters in the 1895–96 season, he scored two of his four goals in a 4–2 home League win over Preston in mid-November.

LOWE, Kenneth, BSc

Midfield: 7+5 apps.

Born: Sedgefield, 6 November 1961.
Career: Hartlepool United (apprentice, April 1977, professional, November 1978), Billingham (briefly in 1984) Spearwood Dalmatic, Australia (1985), Gateshead (August 1986) Morecambe (October 1986), Barrow (March 1987), Scarborough (January 1988), Barrow

(April 1989), Barnet (£40,000), POTTERS (free transfer, August 1993), Birmingham City (£75,000, December 1993), Carlisle United (on loan, September 1994), Hartlepool United (on loan, August 1995), Darlington (non-contract, March–May 1977), Barrow (manager, seasons 2000–02).

■ A long-striding 6ft 1in midfield player, Kenny Lowe made a dozen appearances for Stoke in a four-month stay at The Victoria Ground. Born near the racecourse at Sedgefield, he started and ended his League career in the North East and played in more than 200 competitive games over a period of 19 years before moving into management.

LOWELL, Eric James

Inside-forward: 7 apps. 3 goals.

Born: Cheadle, March 1935.
Career: Derby County (amateur, April 1951, professional, March 1952), POTTERS (May 1955), Stafford Rangers (September 1956–May 1958), later worked for the Staffordshire Moorlands Council.

■ After a fairly lean time with Derby, inside-forward Eric Lowell, when called into first-team action by the Potters, scored two of his three goals in home and away League games against Bristol Rovers in August 1955. However, he failed to maintain that excellent form and left the club for non-League football with Stafford Rangers.

LUMSDEN, John Watson

Inside-forward: 2+4 apps.

Born: Edinburgh, 15 December 1960.
Career: East Fife, POTTERS (£40,000, January 1980), Doncaster Rovers (trialist, April 1982), returned to Scotland (August 1982).

■ Inside-forward John Lumsden was 19 when he moved from East Fife to Stoke in 1980. Unfortunately, he never settled in the Potteries and made only six appearances for the club before returning to Scotland after an unsuccessful trial with Doncaster.

LUMSDON, John David

Right-back: 26+2 apps.

Born: Newcastle-upon-Tyne, 30 July 1956.
Career: POTTERS (apprentice, July 1972, professional, August 1973), Port Vale (on loan, March–May 1978), Telford United (1978–80).

■ Right-back John Lumsdon graduated through the junior ranks at 'The Vic' and played 28 games in two years, never really holding down a first-team place.

McALINDEN, James

Inside-left: 36 apps.

Born: Belfast, 31 December 1917.
Died: Belfast, 18 January 1994.
Career: Milford School (Belfast), Glentoran (March 1934), Belfast Celtic (August 1936), Portsmouth (£6,500, December 1938), POTTERS (£7,000, September 1947), Southend United (£6,000, October 1948), Glenavon (player-manager, 1954–56), Distillery (player-manager, 1956–57) Drogheda United (player-manager, 1958–59), Glentoran (assistant manager-coach, 1959–61), Liverpool (scout, mid-1960s), also mine host of the 'City Lights' pub in Belfast for many years having taken the licence initially in 1946.

■ Stoke manager Bob McGrory signed Irishman Jimmy McAlinden for a club-record fee in 1947, believing him to be the right man to fill the problematic inside-left position. A tall, well-balanced player, McAlinden was, however, inconsistent at The Victoria Ground, and after scoring just twice he left the club for Third Division side Southend in 1948. A teetotaller and non-smoker, he had a fine career on the whole. After winning schoolboy and junior honours and representing the Irish League, he was capped six times at senior level (twice by Eire and on four occasions by Northern Ireland) and won an FA Cup winners' medal with Portsmouth against Wolves in 1939. He appeared in 306 League games during his career, 217 for Southend, scoring a total of 23 goals. As boss of Distillery, he nurtured Martin O'Neill.

McALLISTER, Samuel

Utility forward: 16 apps. 4 goals

Born: Kilmarnock, 1882.
Died: Scotland, 11 October 1957.
Career: Motherwell (briefly, as an amateur), West Ham United (1905), Grimsby Town (1906), Wrexham (1907), POTTERS (August 1908), Port Glasgow (May 1909).

■ Scotsman Sandy McAllister netted a goal every four games for Stoke in 1908–09 during his only season with the club. A reserve at West Ham, Grimsby and Wrexham, he failed to get into either club's first XI. His elder brother, Alex McAllister, played for Kilmarnock, Sunderland and Derby County between 1894 and 1905.

McARDLE, Peter

Outside-left: 7 apps. 1 goal.

Born: Lanchester, Durham, 8 April 1911.
Died: 1979.
Career: Trimdon Grange, Durham City (professional, August 1930), POTTERS (May 1933), Exeter City (August 1935), Carlisle United (March 1936), Barnsley, Stockport County (1937–38), Gateshead, Crewe Alexandra (August 1939), guested for Portsmouth during World War Two (retired, May 1945).

■ Orthodox left-winger Peter McArdle deputised for England international Joe Johnson during his two seasons with the Potters. A nomadic footballer, he scored 12 goals in 27 League games for Carlisle, three in 16 for Barnsley and five in 20 for Stockport but never really bedded down with any of his major clubs.

McAUGHTRIE, David

Defender: 56+4 apps. 2 goals.

Born: Newcummock, Ayrshire, 30 January 1963.
Career: Ayr Boys Club, POTTERS (July 1979, professional, January 1981), Carlisle United (July 1984), York City (June 1985), Darlington (July 1987), Northwich Victoria (August 1988), later with Bishop Auckland, Harrogate Town.

■ Potters scout Neville Briggs recommended Dave McAughtrie to the club after seeing him perform splendidly in a youth tournament for Ayr Boys Club. Standing over 6ft and weighing more than 12st, he certainly had the build for a defender, and after making steady progress – and gaining five youth caps for England – he was handed full professional status at Stoke by manager Alan Durban in 1981. A League debutant at the age of 17 against Nottingham Forest when a depleted Stoke side crashed 5–0, he failed to hold down a regular place in the side, his best spell in the first XI coming during the 1983–84 season when he played in 23 successive games. Then when Bill Asprey took over as manager, unfortunately McAughtrie became surplus to requirements. In 1988 he won both the Staffordshire Senior and mid-Cheshire Senior Cup Finals with Northwich. He made 182 League appearances for his four major clubs.

McCARTHY, Frederick

Inside-forward: 11 apps. 8 goals.

Born: Birkenhead, June 1890.
Died: before 1980.
Career: Tranmere Rovers (1909), Chester, POTTERS (July 1914), guest for Port Vale (1918) and Bury during World War One, Chesterfield (August 1919), Willenhall (1921), Stafford Rangers (August 1923, retired, May 1929).

■ Fred McCarthy, a thoughtful inside-forward, chose the Potters ahead of Middlesbrough, who had been interested in signing him for four months. A useful goalscorer, he netted eight times in only 11 games for Stoke in that last season before World War One. He worked in Liverpool as a teenager and opted for Stoke because he wanted to continue in his line of work. During his spell at The Victoria Ground he became something of a hero when, on returning home one weekend, he dived from the quayside at Liverpool docks to save a person in a suicide attempt.

McCLELLAND, John William

Inside-forward: 4 apps.

Born: Colchester, 11 August 1930.
Career: Colchester United (professional, September 1951), POTTERS (June 1952), Swindon (June 1954), Rochdale (June 1955–May 1956).

■ A reserve at The Victoria Ground for two seasons, Jack McClelland made 42 appearances in his five-year League career, scoring six goals. He played his best football with Rochdale.

McCLURE, Alexander

Defender: 31 apps.

Born: Workington, Cumbria, April 1894.
Died: Birmingham, 8 August 1973.
Career: Grangemouth Juniors, South Bank, Grangemouth Juniors, Birmingham (professional, August 1911), served in Royal Navy during World War One, guest for Bellis & Morcom (1916), Aston Villa (£1,000, December 1923), POTTERS (£300, October 1924), Coventry City (May 1926), Walsall (March–April 1928), Luton Town (player-coach, May–July 1928), Birmingham (youth team manager, August 1928, then assistant manager (1929–32), assisted Market Harborough (between August 1929 and May 1931 when registered at St Andrew's), Bromsgrove Rovers (coach), Market Harborough (coach), later worked for Rudge Motor Cycles, Birmingham, and also ran a successful haulage company in Small Heath, Birmingham.

■ A player with a fine physique and excellent positional sense, Alex McClure was the fulcrum of the Birmingham defence in almost 200 games in 11 years (1912–23), during which time he gained a Second Division Championship medal (1921) and twice represented the Football League. He spent only one season at Villa Park before switching his allegiance to Stoke. He gave the Potters good service prior to his transfer to Coventry in 1926. During his time at Kenilworth Road he coached Luton's colts team. His brother, Sammy, played for Blackburn Rovers while his nephew, Joe McClure, assisted Everton. He was sent off playing for Birmingham against Real Madrid in Spain in May 1923 for telling his goalkeeper, Dan Tremelling, to stand by an upright prior to a penalty being taken.
* As a sailor, McClure participated in the Zeebrugge Affair (one of the great military actions during World War One).

McCORMICK, Robert Fergus

Outside-right: 12 apps. 2 goals.

Born: Paisley, March 1864.
Died: Glasgow, 1940.
Career: Abercorn (April 1884), POTTERS (semi-professional, September 1889), Abercorn (December 1889, retired, May 1894).

■ Scottish international right-winger Bob McCormick, fast and clever, who relished the one off cut and thrust of Cup competitions, gained one full cap as an Abercorn player, lining up against Wales in 1886. He did reasonably well during his brief association with Stoke that lasted four months (the first half of the 1889–90 season). He helped Abercorn win both the Renfrewshire and local Charity Cups in 1886 and 1889 respectively.

McCOLL, James

Centre-forward: 27 apps. 5 goals.

Born: Glasgow, July 1895.
Died: Glasgow, c.1970.
Career: St Anthony's (Glasgow), Glasgow Celtic (August 1913), POTTERS (July 1920), Partick Thistle (May 1921), Hibernian (1922), Leith Athletic, Hibernian (again).

■ Another Scottish 'import', Jim McColl was a thick-set, robust centre-forward who had a useful career north of the border where he served with four major clubs, making well over 100 senior appearances. He had a reasonable season at The Victoria Ground, scoring a goal every five games before returning to his homeland.
* His uncle, Robert Smyth McColl, played for Queen's Park (Glasgow) and Newcastle United and gained 13 full caps for Scotland (1896–1902).

McCUE, John William

Full-back: 542 apps. 2 goals.

Born: Longton, Stoke-on-Trent, 22 August 1922.
Died: Longton, 19 November 1999.
Career: Longton Council School, POTTERS (amateur, August 1937, professional, April 1940), Oldham Athletic (September 1960), Macclesfield Town (1962–63).

■ John McCue had a fine career at The Victoria Ground. Proportionally right for a defender, he was strong in every department of full-back play, kicking long and true, a fine tackler and determined in every sense of the word. Not a dirty player, he never shirked a challenge and always gave 100 percent effort on the field. A great club man, McCue played in almost 550 senior games for the Potters (502 in the Football League, 40 in the FA Cup) as well as starring in 133 World War Two matches. He broke Bob McGrory's appearance record for the club and only Eric Skeels has played in more first-team games for the Potters than McCue, who made his debut against Mansfield Town in a regional fixture in September 1940. After establishing himself at the club, he remained a permanent fixture in the side for 14 years, eventually making way for Tony Allen. McCue was 38 when he left The Victoria Ground for Oldham Athletic. He made 56 appearances for the Latics in two years. A qualified PE instructor, McCue skippered the Potters several times and was indeed one of the finest players ever to don a red and white striped jersey.

McDAID. John

Inside-forward: 4 apps.

Born: Derry, Northern Ireland, 3 December 1909.
Died: before 1980.
Career: Drumcondra (1926), Heptonstall FC (1929), POTTERS (amateur, September 1930, professional, October 1930), Belfast Crusaders (free transfer, May 1932).

■ Irishman Jack McDaid played in just four League games for Stoke, making his debut in a 1–0 home win over Nottingham Forest in January 1931 when he deputised for Walter Bussey.

McDONALD, Edward

Wing-half: 2 apps.

Born: Newcastle-under-Lyme, June 1876.
Died: October, 1938.
Career: Newcastle FC, POTTERS (August 1893), Burlsem Port Vale (June 1894), POTTERS (August 1896), Burlsem Port Vale (May 1897), Notts County (£500, November 1897), Portsmouth (May 1904, retired, April 1909).

■ Reserve defender Ted McDonald, who could play in both wing-half positions, made two League appearances for the Potters, both against Lancashire clubs Preston and Bury in November 1896 when he deputised for Lucien Boullimier. A resourceful player, he made over 100 first-team appearances for the Valiants and gained a Staffordshire Cup winners' medal before joining Notts County for a substantial fee. During his career McDonald amassed 292 League appearances and scored 20 goals. His record with Pompey was 13 goals in 147 outings.

McDONALD, Michael Flynn

Goalkeeper: 9 apps.

Born: Glasgow, 8 November 1950.
Career: Clydebank, POTTERS (£20,000, October 1972), Hibernian (£22,000, June 1974), Dundee (briefly), Berwick Rangers (November 1980), St Johnstone (September 1982), later Gala Fairydean (manager).

■ In the autumn of 1972, following Gordon Banks's terrible car accident, Stoke manager Tony Waddington reinforced his goalkeeping availability by signing Mike McDonald instead of Bobby Clark, the Scottish international. McDonald, who had five youth caps to his name when he arrived at The 'Vic', went on to play in nine first-team games for Stoke in two seasons (1972–74) before returning to Scotland. He made over 200 appearances for Hibs.

McDONALD, William James

Inside-forward: 9 apps. 3 goals.

Born: Inverness, 1877.
Died: Dundee, 1950.
Career: Dundee (June 1898), Derby County (December 1898), POTTERS (August 1901), Dundee (May 1902).

■ A 'dashing' Scottish inside-forward, Billy McDonald spent one season with Stoke, averaging a goal every three games. Earlier, he had starred alongside Steve Bloomer for Derby County in their 1899 FA Cup Final defeat by Sheffield United.

* Some reference books have his surname spelt MacDoanld.

McGEACHAN, James

Defender: 6 apps.

Born: Edinburgh, February 1871.
Died: Edinburgh, March 1903
Career: Edinburgh Thistle, Hibernian (professional, March 1888), Bolton Wanderers (November 1894), POTTERS (£150, December 1897), Hibernian (February 1898), Bolton Wanderers (December 1899, retired through injury and poor health, May 1901).

■ A very talented but tempestuous centre-half, Jim McGeachan, nevertheless, had a very successful career both north and south of the border. He was playing exceedingly well for Hibernian when Celtic enquired about him at the start of the 1894–95 season. McGeachan certainly thought above a move to Parkhead but instead of joining the Scottish giants he chose Bolton Wanderers. Three years later he was suspended by the Wanderers' committee for failing to travel for an away game at Sheffield. This ban was lifted, but in the interim period he had lost his place in the team to Bobby Brown and was subsequently transferred to Stoke. He stayed at The Victoria Ground for just three months, making half a dozen League appearances for the Potters before being suspended for misconduct. He returned to Hibs and then, surprisingly, McGeachan had a second spell with Bolton (playing in the reserves) before retiring in 1901. He scored five goals in 81 appearances during his time at Bolton.

McGILLIVRAY, John

Centre-half: 25 apps.

Born: Broughton, Lancashire, c.1889.
Died: c.1960.
Career: Berry's Association, Manchester United (amateur, January 1907, professional, February 1907), Southport Central (August 1910), POTTERS (August 1911), Dartford (August 1912). Did not play after World War One.

■ Jack McGillivray joined Stoke in readiness for the start of the 1911–12 season. Having previously made four senior appearances for Manchester United, he spent just a season with the Potters before leaving the club after failing to agree terms of a new contract.

McGROARTY, James Martin

Outside-right: 8+1 apps. 2 goals

Born: Derry, Northern Ireland, 30 August 1957.
Career: Tammaherin Youth Club (Derry), Finn Harps (semi-professional, August 1975), POTTERS (£5,000, September 1977), Sligo Rovers (free transfer, May 1980), Finn Harps (May 1982), Glenavon (1984), Belfast Crusaders (1988), Dungiven Celtic (manager, 1993–95).

■ Reserve right-winger Jimmy McGroarty was a 'Potter' for almost three years, scoring twice in nine first-team appearances before returning to Finn Harps.

McGRORY, Robert

Full-back: 511 apps.

Born: Bishopton, Renfrewshire, 17 October 1891.
Died: Glasgow, 23 May 1954.
Career: Milngavie FC, Dumbarton (professional, April 1914), Burnley (£3,000, August 1920), POTTERS (April 1921, player-coach, July 1930, then player-assistant manager-coach, reserve-team manager, retired as a player, May 1935, manager, June 1935, resigned, May 1952).

■ Bob McGrory joined Stoke in 1921 and stayed at The Victoria Ground for the next 31 years, as a player and then manager. A Scot through and through, he was an apprentice joiner on Clydeside before taking up football. He never regretted that decision and had a fine career in the game, performing supremely well at right full-back for the Potters. A strong-tackler whose positional sense was second to none, he was hardly ever flustered, played the game wholeheartedly and was very rarely spoken to by the referee. McGrory went on to appear in over 500 League and Cup games for the Potters, having one unbroken League run of 101 games between March 1926 and September 1929, skippering the team for quite some time. He made his debut in May 1921 and played his last first-team game 14 years later in May 1935 when well past his 43rd birthday. In 1932 he had actually stepped down from regular first-team football to take over the running of Stoke's reserve team, but injuries meant that he was recalled to senior action much to the delight of his manager Tom Mather. After appearing in all 42 League games in his final

Robert McGrory

Jimmy McIlroy

season as a player (1934–35) McGrory took over from Mather at The Victoria Ground – doing so like like a duck to water. He made very few changes in the personnel at the club and gradually replaced the ageing players with younger ones as he steadily built up a useful side. One of his best buys was Tommy Sale. In the summer of 1952 McGrory stepped down as boss, handing over the reins to Frank Taylor, having managed the team in 192 League games of which 90 ended in victories. He guided the Potters to within two points of the League Championship in 1947 (they finished third behind Liverpool after losing their final game at Sheffield United). He remained in close contact with the club until his death at the age of 62.

McILROY, James

Inside-forward: 114+2 apps. 19 goals.

Born: Lambeg, Lisburn, Belfast, 25 October 1931.

Career: Craigavil FC (April 1947), Glentoran (professional, August 1949), Burnley (£8,000, March 1950), POTTERS (£25,000, March 1963, retired, January 1966), Oldham Athletic (manager, late January 1966, player-manager March 1966, resigned August 1968), POTTERS (chief coach, August 1968), Bolton Wanderers (chief coach, August–September 1970, manager, November 1970 for 18 days). After leaving football, he worked as a journalist for the Lancashire Evening Telegraph and spent nine years with the Burnley Express, he attended art school three days a week and achieved a handicap of 14 on the golf course.

■ One of the greatest inside-forwards of his time, Jimmy McIlroy, at times, could make the ball talk! A superb footballer who loved to play the passing game, he was the 'vital cog' in the Burnley midfield for 13 years, making 497 first-team appearances for the Turf Moor club and scoring 131 goals, besides making at least double that number for his colleagues. He began kicking a ball around from the age of three, encouraged by his father, Harry, a part-time footballer with Distillery, and his uncle, Willie, a professional with Portadown. McIlroy practised constantly, and on leaving school at the age of 15 he joined Craigavil FC near Bangor. Signing professional terms with Glentoran in 1949, he developed rapidly and Burnley signed him for a big fee a year later, giving him his debut against Sunderland in a First Division game in October 1950. He immediately established himself in the side and during his time at Turf Moor helped Burnley win the League title in 1960 and reach the FA Cup Final two years later, when he also finished runner-up behind his teamate Jimmy Adamson in the 'Footballer of the Year' poll. After being placed on the transfer list McIlroy was snapped up by Stoke boss Tony Waddington, He did a terrific job at The Victoria Ground, helping the Potters win the Second Division title by scoring six goals in 18 matches at the end of the 1962–63 season. He went on to appear in almost 120 games for the Potters before taking over as manager of Oldham in 1966, He came out of retirement to re-sign as a player within two months, while also retaining the position as team boss. Capped 55 times by Northern Ireland between 1951–65, McIlroy also starred for Great Britain against the Rest of Europe in 1955 and twice represented the Football League in 1960.

McILROY, Samuel Baxter, MBE

Midfield: 143+1 apps. 14 goals.

Born: Belfast, 2 August 1954.

Career: Ashfield School (Belfast), Manchester United (apprentice, August 1969, professional, August 1971), POTTERS (£350,000, February 1982), Manchester City (1985), FC Orgyte,

Sammy McIlroy

Sweden (on loan, 1986), Bury (March 1987), Modling, Norway (on loan, January–August 1988), Preston North End (player-coach, February 1990), Northwich Victoria (manager, July 1991–October 1992), Ashton United (manager, December 1992–April 1993), Macclesfield Town (manager, May 1993–January 2000), Northern Ireland (manager, February 2000–September 2003), Stockport County (manager, October 2003–04).

■ Midfielder Sammy McIlroy represented Northern Ireland schoolboys on four occasions as a 14 and 15-year-old before joining Manchester United. He developed quickly after that and made his League debut for the Reds as a striker against rivals Manchester City in front of 63,000 fans at Maine Road at the age of 17, scoring in a 3–3 draw. Soon afterwards he won the first of his 88 senior caps for his country, while slowly but surely clocking up an excellent individual appearance record for United. A determined competitor with an eye for goal, McIlroy helped the Reds win the Second Division Championship in 1975 and the FA Cup in 1977, while also playing in the two losing FA Cup Finals of 1976 and 1979. After scoring 71 goals in 419 appearances, he left Old Trafford following the arrival of Bryan Robson and went on to add a further 300 senior appearances to his tally, 276 in the Football League A record signing when he joined the Potters, manager Richie Barker having raised the cash from the sale of Adrian Heath to Everton for £700,000, despite playing in a struggling side for most of the time McIlroy notched 14 goals in 144 games for the Potters before his transfer to Manchester City. He later played in Sweden and Austria and his Football League career realised 510 appearances and 90 goals. Unfortunately, he didn't have much joy as a club or international manager.

McINTOSH, William Dowling

Forward: 27 apps. 6 goals.

Born: Glasgow, 7 December 1919.
Died: West Midlands, 1990.
Career: St Johnstone (1945–46), Preston North End (May 1946), POTTERS (£10,000, September 1951), Walsall (November 1952, retired, May 1953).

■ Scorer of a goal every four games for Stoke City in a little over a year, Billy McIntosh had claimed 46 goals in 91 League games for Preston, including two hat-tricks in a week in September 1946. After leaving The Victoria Ground he assisted Walsall.

MacKENZIE, Neil David

Midfield: 16+30 apps. 1 goal.

Born: Birmingham, 15 April 1976.
Career: West Bromwich Albion (apprentice, May 1992), POTTERS (apprentice, August 1995, professional, November 1995), Cambridge United (on loan, March–May 1999, signed for £45,000, October 1999), Kidderminster Harriers (free transfer, November 2000), Blackpool (free, July 2001), Mansfield Town (free, August 2002), Macclesfield Town (free, November 2004).

■ Blonde midfielder Neil Mackenzie broke into Stoke's first team during the 1996–97 campaign after playing intermediate and reserve-team football with West Bromwich Albion for two seasons in 1993–95. Two thirds of his senior outings for the Potters came as a substitute and his only goal came in the 2–1 home League win over Oxford United in February 1997. He was an Auto-Windscreen Shield winner with Blackpool in 2002.
* In December 2003 Mackenzie broke three fingers in a freak accident at home having just netted his first-ever hat-trick for Mansfield in an FA Cup win over non-League side Bishop's Stortford.

McKINLAY, Thomas Valley

Left-back: 3 apps.

Born: Glasgow, 3 December 1964.
Career: Celtic Boys' Club, Dundee (free, August 1981), Heart of Midlothian (December 1988), Glasgow Celtic (November 1994), POTTERS (on loan, January–March 1998), Grasshoppers, Switzerland (June 1999).

■ It seemed to be a master stroke when Potters boss Chris Kamara secured the services of Scottish international 'Tosh' McKinlay on a three-month loan spell early in 1998. The 33-year-old, who was in the running for a place in his country's World Cup squad, was quick to show his class, but a sending-off against Middlesbrough on his debut subsequently led to a three-match ban and that was it. He did make the World Cup, appearing in two group games as a substitute and thus taking his tally of full caps to 22, to go with those previously won at schoolboy, youth, 'B' and under-21 levels. He made 204 appearances for Dundee, 241 for Hearts and 141 for Celtic.

McLAREN, Douglas David

Inside-left: 1 app.

Born: Hanley, Stoke-on-Trent, 1870.
Died: before 1960.
Career: POTTERS (August 1892–March 1893).

■ McLaren played one game for Stoke as a late replacement for Wilmot Turner in the League game against Burnley in September 1892. A reserve inside-left, he spent just the one season with the club.

McMAHON, Gerard Joseph

Midfield: 44+17 apps. 3 goals.

Born: Belfast, 29 December 1973.
Career: Glenavon (March 1991), Tottenham Hotspur (£100,000, July 1992), Barnet (on loan, October–December 1994), Eintracht Frankfurt, Germany (trialist), Udinese, Italy (trialist), POTTERS (£300,000, September 1996), St Johnstone (February 1998).

■ A right-sided midfielder with good skills and an appetite for hard work, who regularly took the game by the scruff of the neck, Gerry McMahon joined the Potters from Spurs in 1996 after unsuccessful trials with German and Italian clubs, and he made his debut against Northampton Town in a Coca-Cola Cup tie 24 hours after signing. Capped by his country (Northern Ireland) at schoolboy, youth, under-21,

'B' and senior levels (on 17 occasions between 1995 and 1999), McMahon made just 20 first-team appearances in four years at White Hart Lane.

McMAHON, Hugh

Defender: 8 apps. 1 goal.

Born: Saltcoats, Ayrshire, September 1907.
Died: before 1990.
Career: Saltcoats FC, Cowdenbeath (professional, March 1927), Blackpool (May 1930), POTTERS (July 1931), Wrexham (May 1932), Workington (briefly), Doncaster Rovers (July 1936, retired, April 1937).

■ Although only 5ft 9in tall, Hugh McMahon was a well-proportioned

centre-half, good in the air and confident in the tackle. His only goal in his eight League games for Stoke was the winner on the opening day of the 1931–32 season against Chesterfield, which ended 2–1. Brought in as cover for the injured Arthur Turner, he held his position in the first XI for six games at the start of that season and then appeared twice in the inside-left position after Christmas. Never really settling at the club, he went on to appear in 165 senior games for Wrexham, gaining a Welsh Cup runners'-up medal and starring in the Racecourse Ground club's record 11–1 League win against New Brighton in a Northern Section Cup match in January 1934. He also captained Wrexham.
* Another player named McMahon, Patrick, (a goalkeeper and no relation) was also at Wrexham during seasons 1934–36.

McMANUS, Charles Eric

Goalkeeper: 4 apps.

Born: Limavady, County Derry, Northern Ireland, 14 November 1950.
Career: Coleraine, Coventry City (£8,000, August 1968), Notts County (£3,000, May 1972), POTTERS (£35,000, October 1979), Lincoln City (on loan, December 1979–April 1980), Bradford City (August 1982), Middlesbrough (on loan, January 1986), Peterborough United (on loan, March–May 1986), Tranmere Rovers (August 1986), Boston United (September 1987–May 1988), Bradford City (Football in the Community Officer, 1988–90), Walsall (Youth Development Officer from June 1990).

■ Eric McManus won amateur caps for Northern Ireland as a Coleraine player during the 1966–67 season. In all, he appeared in more than 450 senior

games, including 396 in the Football League, 229 with Notts County and 113 for Bradford. A tall and courageous 'keeper, he deputised for Peter Fox between the posts for the Potters.

McNALLY, Mark

Defender: 6+1 apps.

Born: Motherwell, 10 March 1971.
Career: Glasgow Celtic (apprentice, April 1987, professional, May 1989), Southend United (£100,000, December 1995), POTTERS (£120,000, March 1997), Dundee United (July 1998).

■ Despite playing under three different managers during his time with the Potters, sturdy defender Mark McNally was never given a meaningful chance in the first team. In fact, he spent most of the 1997–98 season in the reserves and jumped at the chance of returning to Scotland when the opportunity presented itself. Initially his move to Dundee United was set up for January 1998 but the deal fell through when Stoke demanded a transfer fee. He eventually left The Britannia Stadium on a free transfer. Capped twice by his country at under-21 level, McNally won the Scottish Cup in 1995 with Celtic, for whom he appeared in 152 senior games.

McREDDIE, Walter William

Inside-forward: 52 apps. 14 goals.

Born: Lochee, Scotland, 1871.
Died: Scotland, 1939.
Career: Lochee & Harp FC, Dundee Harp (1888), POTTERS (August 1889), Middlesbrough Ironopolis (January 1890), POTTERS (September 1893), Ardwick, Manchester City (August 1894), Bolton Wanderers (December 1895), Glasgow Celtic March, 1896, retired through injury, August 1896).

■ Wally McReddie had two spells with the Potters during the last decade or so before the turn of the century. The first lasted just five months and the second, a year. During his eight-year career he made just under 100 first-team appearances, producing his best figures by far with Stoke. He played in the same forward-line as the Welsh wizard Billy Meredith at Manchester City.

McSKIMMING, Robert

Centre-forward: 22 apps. 6 goals.

Born: Kilmarnock, June 1870.
Died: before 1960.
Career: Kilmarnock (briefly), Hurlford (1887), POTTERS (professional, July 1888), Burslem Port Vale (May 1889), joined Stone Town (May 1891, after

being released owing to business commitments), returned to Scotland before World War One.

■ One of Stoke's first real goalscorers, Bob McSkimming played in the club's opening League game against West Bromwich Albion in September 1888 and finished up as leading marksman that season. He scored plenty of goals for the Potters in friendly matches, but at senior level he managed only six in 22 appearances, later appearing in 17 first-team games for the Vale, scoring three goals. A fine sprinter, he competed at various Scottish athletics meetings, collecting a handful of medals.

McVAY, James

Defender: 12 apps.

Born: Wallsend, 1889.
Died: before 1950.
Career: Wallsend Swifts, POTTERS (February 1913), Barnard Castle (October 1913–May 1915), did not play after World War One.

■ Tall centre-half Jim McVay suffered with his health during his brief stay at The Victoria Ground. He made his debut for the Potters against Watford a week after joining the club and his last outing was against Croydon Common in September 1913, both games in the Southern League. Joey Jones took over his position.

MACARI, Michael

Striker: 15+19 apps. 3 goals.

Born: Kilwining, Scotland, 4 February 1973.
Career: West Ham United (juniors), POTTERS (apprentice, May 1991, professional July 1991, released, May 1998).

■ Mike Macari, the son of Stoke City manager Lou Macari, was a useful striker who made his debut for the Potters as a substitute against Barnsley in September 1996, having graduated through the junior ranks at Upton Park and then at The Victoria Ground after his father had become manager. He did well the following season but was released when a new management team arrived at the club.

MACARI, Paul

Striker: 0+3 apps.

Born: Manchester, 23 August 1976.
Career: POTTERS (apprentice, August 1992, professional, August 1993), Sheffield Wednesday (May 1998).

■ Brother of Michael Macari, Paul struggled with a back injury in 1998 at a time when he was looking to establish himself in the first team following a prolific goalscoring record in the reserves. He made his League debut against Charlton Athletic away in October 1997 but after that hardly figured in the action and was released at the end of the 1997–98 season.

MADDISON, John Arden Brown

Defender: 1 app.

Born: Chester-le-Street, 12 February 1900.
Died: Rugeley, Staffs, 19 August 1987.
Career: Usworth Colliery, POTTERS (professional, November 1923), Port Vale (October 1924), Oldham Athletic (May 1927), Mansfield Town (May 1929), Nimes, France (1930), Gresley Rovers (1932), Sutton United (1933–34).

■ Reserve defender Arden Maddison's only League appearance for the Potters was at left-half against Stockport at home in February 1924. Almost nine months later, after recovering from a fractured collar-bone, he was transferred to Port Vale, for whom he played in over 50 first-team games. He was sent off on his debut for Oldham in an ill-tempered encounter with Manchester City in October 1927.

MADDOCK, John

Right-back: 23 apps. 4 goals.

Born: Audley, Staffs, 24 November 1896.
Died: Normacot, Staffs, 27 October 1972.
Career: Bignall End, Audley FC, POTTERS (September 1916), Macclesfield Town (May 1921), Port Vale (trialist, July 1923, signed August 1923), Crewe Alexandra (July 1931), Nantwich Town, Audley.

■ After monitoring the progress of hard-kicking right-back John Maddock since he was a teenager, Stoke finally brought him to The Victoria Ground in 1916. He made over 40 appearances during World War One and then continued to impress throughout the 1919–20 League campaign. But then his form began to wane, and after a lean spell he found himself in the reserves where he stayed until leaving for Macclesfield. A fine penalty-taker – although he did miss a few times from the spot, including two in one game for Port Vale against Nottingham Forest in December 1926 – he went on to net 12 goals in 184 games for the Potters' arch-rivals.

MAGUIRE, Paul Bernard

Outside-left: 105+15 apps. 25 goals.

Born: Glasgow, 21 August 1956.
Career: Kilbirnie Ladeside, Shrewsbury Town (professional, August 1976), POTTERS (£262,000, September 1980), Tacoma Stars, NASL (free transfer, June 1984), Port Vale (June 1985), Northwich Victoria (player-assistant manager, May 1988, later player-caretaker manager, retired, May 1992).

■ A fast-raiding left-winger or wide midfield player, Paul Maguire packed a powerful shot, mainly in his left foot, and delivered marvellous corner-kicks. He was also a penalty expert as well as being a huge favourite with the fans at The Victoria Ground. He gave the Potters wonderful service, scoring a goal

every five games, including all four (two penalties) in an emphatic 4–0 home victory over Wolves in May 1984, this being his last game for the Potters before leaving for America. He returned to England a year later and helped Port Vale win promotion from the Fourth Division in his first season. After scoring 27 goals in 147 outings for Vale he entered non-League football with Northwich Victoria. During his senior League career, Maguire netted 81 goals in 373 appearances.

MAHONEY, John Francis

Midfield: 314+15 apps. 28 goals.

Born: Cardiff, 20 September 1946.
Career: Ashton United, Crewe Alexandra (professional, March 1966), POTTERS (£16,000, March 1967), Middlesbrough (£90,000, August 1977), Swansea City (£100,000, 1979), Bangor City (player-manager, September 1984–October 1987), Newport County (manager, August 1988–April 1989), Bangor City (manager, May 1991–June 1996).

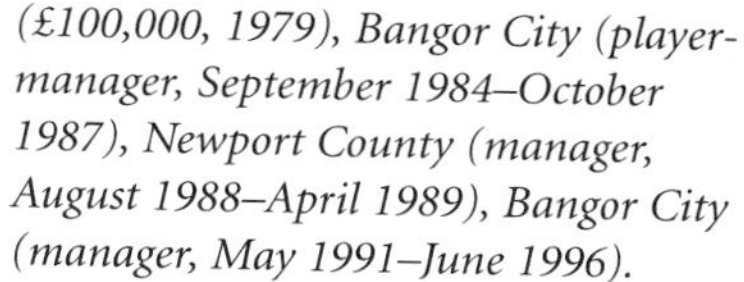

John Mahoney

■ During his 10 years at The Victoria Ground, bargain buy John Mahoney produced some excellent performances in midfield for Stoke City. He scored some cracking goals and gained a League Cup winners' medal in 1972, as well as becoming an established Welsh international, eventually winning 51 full caps (1968–83) plus three at under-23 level. Earlier he made 18 League appearances and followed up with 77 for Middlesbrough before adding a further 110 to his tally with the Swans. As player-manager of Bangor City, he led the non-League club into Europe via the Cup-winners' Cup after guiding them to a Welsh Cup Final victory in 1981. Mahoney, who served Newport until the Welsh club was wound up, also managed the Welsh semi-professional side against England and in fact played with his cousin, John Toshack, at Swansea. Mahoney, whose career was effectively ended after breaking his leg in a match against Brighton in March 1983, amassed a total of 489 League appearances for his four major clubs, and, in fact, was the first substitute to score for the Potters in a game against Leicester City in August 1968, three years after the 12th man was introduced.

* His father, Joe, was a rugby player in both Union and League.

MALKIN, John

Outside-right: 190 apps. 27 goals.

Born: Normacot, Staffs, 9 November 1925.
Died: Stoke-on-Trent, 19 May 1994.
Career: Queensbury Road School (Stoke), Army service (from 1941, played for the BAOR team from 1943), POTTERS (trialist, August 1946, then part-time professional, September 1946, professional, July 1947, retired, May 1956).

■ Diminutive right-winger Johnny Malkin was a very positive and popular player who was unlucky, in some respects, to have Stanley Matthews

vying for the number seven shirt during his time at The Victoria Ground. But when Matthews left for Blackpool in 1947 Malkin took over on the wing and did exceedingly well. He didn't play football in earnest until he was in the Army. Spotted in the BAOR team, word got back to Stoke boss Bob McGrory and almost immediately the impressive Malkin was signed as a semi-professional, his progress being monitored until his demob from the Army. Unfortunately, he damaged knee ligaments in a game at Filbert Street in October 1955 and, on the advice of a leading orthopaedic surgeon, announced his retirement at the end of that season, aged 30. He later had a joint testimonial with full-back George Bourne and received £855 plus an extra grant from the club.

MALONEY, Timothy George

Outside-left: 8 apps. 1 goal.

Born: South Bank, Middlesbrough, July 1908.
Died: Middlesbrough, 1956.
Career: Grangetown, Middlesbrough (professional, August 1926), Hull City (March 1928), Darlington, (August 1928), POTTERS (July 1931), South Bank (June 1932).

■ A useful left-winger from the north-east of England, Tim Maloney's only League goal for the Potters proved to be the winner against Bury at Gigg Lane in March 1932 when he replaced Bobby Liddle. Initially signed as cover for Bobby Archilbald, he never settled and returned home after spending just the one season with Stoke. He did not play in the first team for Middlesbrough or Hull City.

MARSH, John Henry

Full-back: 424+9 apps. 2 goals.

Born: Newcastle-under-Lyme, 31 May 1948.
Career: POTTERS (apprentice, May 1963, professional, June 1965), Los Angeles Aztecs, NASL (1978–79), Bulowa, Hong Kong (May 1979), Northwich Victoria (August 1980, retired, May 1984), now lives in Stoke and works as a sales representative.

■ Jackie Marsh followed a number of local born players of his generation to The Victoria Ground, and, like Bloor, Pejic and Smith, he went on to the ultimate accolade of gaining a League Cup winners' medal in 1972. An exceptionally fine full-back, his deep crosses were a feature of his play in the 1960s and 1970s, and, indeed, he played an important role in the club's success. He made his League debut against Arsenal at Highbury in August 1967 – the first of more than 400 senior appearances for the club. His last game in a red and white striped shirt came in March 1979, and he currently lies in

eighth place in the club's all-time appearance list.
* So secretive was manager Waddington when he drafted Marsh into the team for his senior debut against Arsenal in 1967 that not even the announcer on the Highbury tannoy system knew who the Potters' right-back was!

MARSHALL, Gordon George Banks

Goalkeeper: 13 apps.

Born: Edinburgh, 19 April 1964.
Career: Broxburn Juniors, Tynecastle FC (juniors, 1979), Glasgow Rangers (apprentice, January 1980, professional,

May 1981), East Stirlingshire (on loan, August–November 1982), East Fife (December 1982), Falkirk (March 1987), Celtic (August 1991), POTTERS (on loan, November 1993–January 1994), Kilmarnock (August 1998).

■ On loan 'keeper Gordon Marshall had a nightmare debut for Stoke, conceding six goals away at Luton in a First Division League game in November 1993. He played in a further 12 senior games for the club after that before returning to Parkhead. A Scottish international, capped against the US in 1992, he appeared in well over 500 games at club level and made 136 for Celtic before transferring to Kilmarnock. Marshall's father, Gordon, also a goalkeeper, played for Hibernian, Celtic and Aberdeen and cousin, Scott, a defender, served with Arsenal.

MARTEINSSON, Petur

Utility: 13+7 apps. 2 apps.

Born: Reykjavik, Iceland, 14 July 1973.
Career: Leftur, Iceland, Fram, Iceland (August 1994), Hammarby, Sweden (July 1996), Stabaek IF, Norway (February 1999), POTTERS (free transfer, January 2002), Hammarby (September 2003).

■ Able to play in defence or midfield, Petur Marteinsson, 6ft tall and 12st 4lb in weight, was an Icelandic international with 24 full, 19 under-21 and four youth caps under his belt and he spent four months with the Potters. Unfortunately, an injury to his right foot in training delayed his debut in English football and soon afterwards he suffered a damaged ankle, thus bringing his season to a premature end. He returned for the 2002–03 campaign but fans were mystified as to why he was given so few outings (only 14). After a handful of games at the start of the following season he returned to his former club, Hammarby. Prior to joining the Potters had had appeared in almost 200 games in Scandinavian football (165 at League level).

MARTIN, James Colin

Forward: 16 apps. 1 goal.

Born: Basford, 2 December 1898.
Died: Stoke-on-Trent, 27 June 1969.
Career: Stoke St Peter's (from 1912), POTTERS (£750, July 1916), Aberdare Athletic (June 1921), Wolverhampton Wanderers (September 1923), Reading (July 1924), Aberdare (again, June 1925),

Bristol City (May 1926), Blackpool (February 1928), Southend United (February 1929), Halifax Town (July 1929), Congleton Town (August 1930, retired, May 1931).

■ Scorer of just one goal for Stoke in a 2–0 League win over Nottingham Forest away in January 1920, Jimmy Martin was a decent enough player, fast over the ground with a big heart. He served as cover for all three central forward positions during his time at The Victoria Ground. In a professional career that spanned 15 years he netted 82 goals in a total of 225 league games, having his best spell with Aberdare (34 strikes in 76 outings).

MARTIN, John Alan

Utility: 115 apps. 6 goals.

Born: Smallthorne, Stoke-on-Trent, 23 November 1923.
Died: Stoke-on-Trent, 18 October 2004
Career: Nettlebank Villa, Port Vale (amateur, February 1941, professional, December 1942), POTTERS (exchange deal involving Albert Mullard plus £10,000, September 1951), Bangor City (March 1955), Port Vale (part-time professional, July 1957, free transfer, May 1959), Nantwich Town (player-manager, 1959–61), Port Vale (coach to juniors), his death came after a lengthy struggle against Alzheimer's disease.

■ A versatile half-back or inside-forward, Alan Martin was a regular member of Port Vale's League side from March 1947 and was an ever-present in 1947–48 and 1948–49. After moving across town he then gave the Potters excellent service before entering non-league football and later having a second spell with the Valiants, for whom he scored 30 goals in 201 appearances covering eight different positions.

MASKERY, Christopher Paul

Midfield: 96+12 apps. 5 goals.

Born: Stoke-on-Trent, 25 September 1964.
Career: POTTERS (April 1980, professional, September 1982), Stafford Rangers (free transfer, May 1988, retired, October 1990), joined the fire service.

■ Midfielder Chris Maskery actually retired from football twice! He joined the Potters as a youngster, turned professional on his 18th birthday and made his League debut in December 1982. Initially, he retired through injury in 1987 but came back and moved to Stafford Rangers. However, in 1990 he swallowed his tongue and at that juncture decided to call it a day again, this time at the age of 26. Called 'Mask' on the training pitch, he was granted a testimonial by Stoke for his service to the club.
* As a teenager Maskery won a penalty shoot-out competition at The Victoria Ground, and as a result he was signed by the Potters.

MASSEY, Alfred Woolley

Right-half: 2 apps.

Born: Normaton, Stoke-on-Trent, 16 October July 1918.
Died: before 2000.

Career: Congleton Town, POTTERS (professional, October 1938, retired, April 1944), returned with Stafford Rangers (May 1945–April 1950).

■ Alf Massey's two League appearances for the Potters were made early in 1939, against Manchester United away in January and at home to Blackpool a month later, each time deputising for Jock Kirton, allowing Frank Soo to switch to the left-half in a readjusted middle-line. A strong tackler, his League career was unfortunately cut short through injury in 1944 after he had played in 18 World War Two games.

MATTHEWS, Graham

Utility forward: 20 apps. 5 goals.

Born: Newcastle-under-Lyme, Staffs, 2 November 1942.
Career: POTTERS (amateur, April 1958, professional, November 1959), Walsall (August 1963), Crewe Alexandra (August 1965–May 1967).

■ No relation to Sir Stanley, Graham Matthews joined the club as a teenager and turned professional on his 17th birthday. He scored a goal every four games for the Potters before moving to Walsall after failing to hold down a regular place in the first team. In his League career as a whole, Matthews netted 43 goals in 139 outings.

MATTHEWS, Sir Stanley, CBE

Outside-right: 355 apps. 62 goals.

Born: Hanley, Stoke-on-Trent, 1 February 1915.
Died: Stoke-on-Trent, 5 May 1999.
Career: Wellington Road School (Hanley), Stoke St Peter's (1927), POTTERS (amateur, July 1930, professional, February, 1932), guested for Airdrieonians, Arsenal, Blackpool, Crewe Alexandra, Manchester United, Greenock Morton, Glasgow Rangers and Wrexham during World War Two, Blackpool (£11,500, May 1947), Toronto City, Canada (summer 1961), POTTERS (£2,500, October 1961–May 1965), Toronto City, Canada (June–September 1965, retiring on his return to England), later travelled the world, coaching in many countries, including Egypt, Soweto (South Africa) and the Middle East, Port Vale (general manager, July 1965, taking over as team manager, May 1967–April 1968), Hibernians, Malta (manager, April 1970–71), later coaching in Canada before returning to the Potteries to become Stoke City president, a position he held until his death in 1999.

■ Stanley Matthews – 'The Wizard of Dribble' – was a superbly gifted right-winger and one of the greatest footballers to grace the world stage. Blessed with dazzling skills, wonderful ball control, a magnificent body-swerve and speed off the mark (he would easily beat most defenders for pace over 25-30 yards), he could centre with pin-point accuracy. He also scored some splendid goals. His close control was, at times, mesmerising, and he regularly bemused and bewildered the toughest of opponents and the tightest of defences. He represented England schoolboys in 1929 and four years later won a Second Division Championship medal with the Potters, making his full international debut in 1934 against Wales and celebrating the occasion with a goal in a comprehensive 4–0 victory. In 1937 he netted a hat-trick for his country in a 5–4 win over Czechoslovakia, and when World War Two broke out he had already appeared in 17 matches for England. During the hostilities, as well as playing in several services matches and in 24 Wartime and five Victory internationals, he won a League North Cup winners' medal with Blackpool in 1943. Injuries, however, started to interrupt his performances, and as a result he found himself out of favour at Stoke. Despite vigorous protests from the Potters supporters to keep him, he was sadly sold to Blackpool where he renewed his England partnership with Stan Mortensen. The Bloomfield Road club began to attract huge crowds wherever Matthews played, and Blackpool reached two FA Cup Finals in four years, losing them both, in 1948 and 1951. But then in 1953 the Seasiders made it third time lucky as they triumphed 4–3 over Bolton Wanderers, courtesy of some of the finest wing play ever seen on a football pitch and a Mortensen hat-trick. With 20 minutes remaining, Blackpool were 3–1 down and struggling. Then Matthews layed on the winning goal for Bill Perry right at the end after a brilliant piece of dribbling out on the right-wing. Three years later he starred in the Blackpool team that finished runners-up in the First Division to Manchester United's Busby Babes. In 1957, at the age of 42, the oldest footballer ever to play for England, Matthews won his 54th and last senior cap – it should have been many more. He scored 11 goals at full international level. Surprisingly, he played in only one game in the 1950 World Cup Finals, two in the 1954 Finals and was left behind in 1958, to the dismay of the public. In 1961 he returned to relegation-threatened Stoke City and the crowds at The Victoria Ground immediately increased ten-fold, leaping from 8,400 to 36,000. Within a year the Potters had escaped the drop and won the Second Division title. Matthews made his final League appearance in 1965 at the age of 50 years and five days, having served the Potters, in two spells, for a total of 19 years. Soon afterwards he received a Knighthood to add to the CBE, which had been awarded to him in 1957. He was voted 'Footballer of the Year' in 1948 and 1963 and received the accolade of 'European Footballer of the Year' in 1956. Matthews appeared in almost 800 competitive matches at club level, 701 in the Football League (332 with Stoke and 369 with Blackpool). He scored 80 goals. Besides

Stanley Matthews

his record at senior/competitive level for the Potters, he also appeared in 69 World War Two games and netted a further eight goals. The son of Hanley's famous boxing-barber Jack Matthews, he did general office work with a local firm while also on the groundstaff at The Victoria Ground. He made his League debut for Stoke on 19 March 1932 at Bury, but it was a further two years before Matthews established himself in the Potters' first team. Prior to an FA Cup tie between Stoke and Sheffield United in 1946 Matthews went down with the flu. A doctor prescribed two capsules – similar to those used by Luftwaffe crews on bombing missions during the War! These worked perfectly as Matthews recovered and helped Stoke win 1–0. Matthews played League football for 32 years and 324 days from his debut for Stoke in 1932 to his last Potters outing on 6 February 1965. His international career spanned almost 23 years, and he is the oldest player ever to win a full England cap, aged 42 years and 103 days, against Denmark in May 1957. The record books show that Matthews played in at least 2,000 football matches during a tremendous career, including 1,127 at a competitive level.

MAWSON, Joseph Spence

Centre-forward: 93 apps. 50 goals.

Born: Brandon Colliery, County Durham, 26 October 1905.

Died: Stoke-on-Trent, 10 September 1959.

Career: Brandon Colliery, Crook Town (amateur, November 1921), Durham City (1925), Washington Colliery (1927), POTTERS (professional, January 1929), Nottingham Forest (September 1933), Stockport County (September 1935), Linfield (December 1935), Crewe Alexandra (August 1936, retired through injury, May 1937).

■ 'No frills' centre-forward Joey Mawson was a miner who played his early football in the vicinity of coalfields before moving south to sign professional forms for the Potters in 1929. He made his League debut a month later, scoring in a 3–3 draw at Swansea, the first of 50 he netted for the club in less than 100 senior matches covering four years. Top-scorer in 1931–32 and 1932–33, he gained a Second Division Championship medal in the latter campaign before transferring to Nottingham Forest.

MAXWELL, Allan

Centre-forward: 37 apps. 6 goals.

Born: Glasgow, Scotland, April 1870.
Died: before 1960.
Career: Cambuslang Rangers (August 1888), Everton (professional, October 1891), Darwen (November 1893), POTTERS (February 1896), St Bernard's, Edinburgh (April 1897–1900).

■ Allan Maxwell joined Stoke in exchange for a set of wrought iron gates! The Scottish striker, sharp and decisive with clever footwork, had an excellent spell at The Victoria Ground. His first game was a 5–2 defeat at Aston Villa, but he quickly hit the mark by scoring on his home debut three weeks later in a 5–0 win over Sunderland in March 1896. Earlier he had scored 16 goals in 53 games for Everton and 22 in 60 outings for Darwen.

MAXWELL, James Frederick

Left-half or outside-left: 10 apps.

Born: Glasgow, 1900.
Died: Scotland, c.1980.
Career: Neilston Victoria (1917), Arbroath (professional, 1919), POTTERS (July 1925), Watford (March–May 1927).

■ Reserve Jimmy Maxwell deputised for Sam Johnson in each of his 10 first-team outings for the Potters, all in season 1925–26. He later played in four League games for Watford, scoring one goal.

MAXWELL, William Sturrock

Inside-left or centre-forward: 173 apps. 85 goals.

Born: Arbroath, Scotland, 21 September 1876.
Died: c.1940.
Career: Arbroath (amateur, August 1892), Heart of Midlothian (amateur, 1893–95), POTTERS (professional, August 1895), Third Lanark (£250, August 1901), Sunderland (July 1902), Millwall Athletic (May 1903), Bristol City (August 1905), retired, September 1909), Leopold FC, Belgium (coach, January 1910–May 1915), later coached the Belgium national team (1920s).

■ Willie Maxwell was a solicitor's clerk, working in Dundee and playing for Heart of Midlothian when he decided

that he wanted to move to the Potteries to take up a similar position and also sign for Stoke. This was in the summer of 1894. Twelve months later he finally arrived at The Victoria Ground and went on to give the Potters excellent service, scoring on average a goal every two games and gaining one full cap for Scotland against England in 1898. He also twice represented Angus in county matches. A tall man, standing at around 6ft, at times he was brilliant in both his chosen positions. A dashing type of player, he had a knack of scoring goals out of nothing with boot feet and head, and during his career he netted well over 200 goals at various levels, including 62 in 128 outings for Bristol City, whom he helped win the Second Division Championship in 1906, three years before announcing his retirement at the age of 33.

MAYER, Wilfred

Forward: 1 app.

Born: Etruria, Stoke-on-Trent, 18 February 1912.
Died: Stoke-on-Trent, 5 April 1979.
Career: Newcastle PSA, Downings Tileries, POTTERS (August 1932), Southampton (£650, March 1937), Wellington Town (August 1938, retired, May 1943).

■ Reserve Wilf Mayer's only League game for the Potters was at inside-right in a 1–0 home defeat at the hands of Chelsea in March 1935 when he deputised for Freddie Steele during an injury crisis. He later appeared in 14 League games for Saints, occupying a number of forward positions. Two years after joining Wellington he gained a Welsh Cup winners' medal.

MEAKIN, Harry

Full-back: 41 apps.

Born: Stoke-on-Trent, 8 September 1919.
Died: Cheshire, 1986.

Career: Summerbank FC (Staffs), POTTERS (professional, November 1945), Northwich Victoria (May 1950).

■ Harry Meakin was a very competent defender who possessed a fair degree of doggedness. It was a pity there were two other excellent full-backs – Billy Mould and John McCue – at The Victoria ground at the same time. He had his best season in 1947–48 when he played in 24 League and Cup games.

MEAKIN, Samuel Stanley

Left-half: 1 app.

Born: Fenton, Stoke-on-Trent, February 1864.
Died: before 1945.
Career: Tunstall (1884), POTTERS (September 1887), Burslem Swifts (April 1888).

■ Sammy Meakin spent just one season with Stoke, playing in the FA Cup tie against Burlsem Port Vale in October 1887, which the Potters won 1–0.

MELLOR, Harold Halden

Inside-forward: 35 apps. 4 goals.

Born: Stoke-on-Trent, March 1878.
Died: Stoke-on-Trent, c.1950
Career: Burslem Port Vale (briefly, 1885), Dresden United, POTTERS (July 1897), Grimsby Town (June 1901, retired, May 1902), returned briefly with Brighton & Hove Albion (October–December 1893).

■ Harry Mellor had a brief spell with Stoke's arch-rivals Burslem Port Vale and also assisted local side Dresden United before moving to The Victoria Ground in 1897. After leaving the club he appeared in 33 games for the Mariners, helping them win the Second Division title. After suffering a bad knee injury early in the 1901–02 season, Mellor announced his retirement and returned to the Potteries. An attempted comeback with Brighton proved abortive. His brother, James, also played for the Potters and Dresden United.

MELLOR, James

Outside-left: 1 app.

Born: Stoke-on-Trent, 1870.
Died: Stoke-on-Trent, c.1943.
Career: Dresden United, POTTERS (October 1894), Stone (April 1895).

■ Elder brother of Harry, Jim Mellor made one FA Cup appearance for Stoke, replacing Joey Schofield on the left-wing against Nottingham Forest in February 1895. He left for nearby Stone after spending less than a season at The Victoria Ground.
* It is believed that another Mellor brother played for Burslem Port Vale in 1883.

MELLOR, Sydney

Forward: 11 apps. 1 goal.

Born: Leek, Staffs, 1898.
Died: Cheshire, 1967.
Career: Leek Town, POTTERS (August 1920), Congleton Town (June 1922).

■ A reserve at The Victoria Ground for two seasons, Syd Mellor's only goal for the Potters in his 11 League games came from the inside-left position in a match against Derby County away in February 1922, when he deputised for Arty Watkin in a 4–2 win.

MELTON. Stephen

Defender/midfield: 0+7 apps.

Born: Lincoln, 3 October 1978.
Career: Nottingham Forest (apprentice, October 1993, professional, October 1995), POTTERS (free transfer, February 2000), Brighton & Hove Albion (free, August 2000), Hull City (on loan, November 2002, signed permanently, December 2002), Boston United (free, March 2004).

■ With chances limited at The City Ground, hard-working utility player Steve Melton moved to Stoke, but again he had to battle for first-team action and after seven games as a substitute moved to Brighton, with whom he won a Third Division Championship medal in 2001.

MEREDITH, Samuel

Full-back: 50 apps.

Born: Trefonen near Chirk, 5 September 1872.
Died: West Gorton, Manchester, 25 December 1921.
Career: Chirk (May 1894), POTTERS (May 1901), Leyton (June 1905, retired, May 1910), later mine host of the Jolly Forgeman, Newbridge, near Ruabon, and then worked as a landlord for Hardy's brewery.

■ Older brother of the great Welsh international wing wizard Billy Meredith, Sammy was, in contrast, a tough-tackling, ever-reliable full-back, who invariably got the ball away to safety with precise kicking and passing. He joined Stoke at the age of 28 and stayed at The Victoria Ground for four seasons. Already capped four times by Wales since 1900, making his debut in the unfamiliar right-half position, he appeared in a further three internationals as a 'Stokie' – being one of three players who together became the first Potters to represent the principality when he lined up with Mart Watkins and Richmond Roose against England in 1902. He starred in his eighth and last Welsh game in 1907, also against England, when registered with Leyton, for whom he played in over 100 first-team matches, including 94 in the Southern League. He would have surely gained many more honours had he been with a more fashionable club. He was forced to give up football after developing a wasting disease. He was 49 when he died on Christmas Day in 1921.

MERRITT, Wilfred

Goalkeeper: 5 apps.

Born: Leek, Staffordshire, 13 November 1864.
Died: Leek, c.1940.
Career: Leek, POTTERS (July 1888), Leek (August 1891).

■ Understudy to Billy Rowley for three seasons in 1888–91, goalkeeper Wilf Merritt played in only a handful of senior games for Stoke, one in the FA Cup when Wolves won a 'replayed' tie 8–0 in February 1890.

MESTON, Samuel

Half-back or inside-forward: 19 apps. 4 goals

Born: Arbroath, Scotland, 16 January 1872.
Died: Ashurst, Hampshire, 14 August 1948.

Career: Arbroath Victoria, POTTERS (January 1894), Southampton St Mary's (April 1895), Salisbury City (May 1906), Croydon Common (player-trainer, July 1907), Salisbury City (April 1909), Chandlers Ford (1911), Eastleigh Athletic (1913, retired 1915), later Bishopstoke Working Men's Sports Club (trainer, 1923–25), during the 1920s, when working as a brake-fitter's mate at Eastleigh Railway Works, Meston played in several charity games for an ex-Saints XI.

■ A gargantuan figure, the versatile Sam Meston was 6ft 2in tall, weighed 14st 10lb and was known as 'Long Tom' for his long-range shooting. He made his debut at centre-half for the Potters in a 3–1 home League win over Newton Heath (Manchester United) in March 1894 and the following season lined up in four different positions including that of centre-forward. He scored two of his four goals in a 3–2 FA Cup win over Newton Heath in February 1895. As a Southampton player, he won six Southern League Championship and two FA Cup runners'-up medals, and made 288 Southern League appearances for the Saints, scoring 20 goals, the second highest tally for the club behind Bert Lee. Only Terry Paine and Nick Holmes appeared in more FA Cup games for Saints than Meston. His son, Samuel William Meston, joined the playing staff at The Dell in 1922.

MILARVIE, Robert

Outside-left: 15 apps. 5 goals.

Born: Pollockshilds, Scotland, April 1864.
Died: Gorton, Manchester, November 1912.
Career: Pollockshields FC, Hibernian (1887), POTTERS (October 1888), Derby County (August 1889), Burlsem Port Vale (September 1889), Derby County (October 1889), Newton Heath (August 1890), Ardwick, Manchester City (June 1891, retired, May 1896).

■ Bob Milarvie was a useful left-winger who did reasonably well with the Potters, averaging a goal every three games. He then signed for neighbours Port Vale for whom he made only one friendly appearance, against Halliwell, before the club was censured by the Football Association for playing him illegally as he had earlier signed for Derby. The Rams subsequently won the battle to secure his services. He scored 26 goals in more than 120 League and Cup games during his career.

MILES, John Francis

Midfield: 0+1 app.

Born: Bootle, 28 September 1981.
Career: Liverpool (apprentice, April 1997, professional, April 1999), POTTERS (free transfer, March 2002), Crewe Alexandra (free, August 2002), Macclesfield Town (free, March 2003).

■ An enthusiastic yet skilful midfielder who failed to get a game with Liverpool, John Miles made just one substitute appearance for the Potters in the 1–1 draw at Bristol City on the final day of the 2001–02 League season.

MILLER, W. Albert Bertrand

Goalkeeper: 11 apps.

Born: Newcastle-under-Lyme, Staffs. 1880.
Died: Stoke-on-Trent, 1953.
Career: Tunstall Park, Newcastle St Giles, Newcastle Swifts, Cross Heath, Burlsem Liverpool Road, Port Vale (trialist, 1902), Blackpool Etrurians, Stafford Rangers, Stone Town, Norwich City, POTTERS (July 1908), Leek United (April 1909, retired, April 1912).

■ An amateur throughout his career, Bert Miller, a smart, upright goalkeeper, helped introduce the May Bank Cup competition to the Potteries area, as well as being a plethora of other local League appointments. He qualified as a solicitor's clerk in 1907. As a youngster he helped Tunstall win the North Staffs District Premier League Championship, and when taking over from Arthur Box he made his debut for the Potters against Aston Villa reserves in the opening Birmingham & District League game of the 1908–09 season, which was won 5–3.

MILLER, Thomas John

Outside-left: 63 apps. 5 goals.

Born: Hednesford, 1875.
Died: Wolverhampton, 1949.

Career: Hednesford Town, Wolverhampton Wanderers (£100, September 1895), POTTERS (£400, August 1905), Willenhall (May 1907–April 1910), later a licensee in Wolverhampton.

■ Physically strong, moustachio'd left-winger Jack Miller was a fine, all-action footballer who gave Stoke good service for two years, during which time he produced some terrific performances, having his best spell during the 1905–06 campaign when he missed only two games. He scored 49 goals in 249 games for Wolves, being virtually an ever present for the Molineux club for eight seasons.

MILLS, Rowan Lee

Striker: 7+4 apps. 2 goals.

Born: Mexborough, Leicestershire, 10 Luly 1970.
Career: Stocksbridge Park Steels FC, Wolverhampton Wanderers (professional, December 1992), Derby County on loan, February 1995, signed for £400,000, March 1995), Port Vale (£200,000, in deal involving Robin Van der Laan, August 1995), Bradford City (£1 million, August 1998), Manchester City (on loan, March–April 2000), Portsmouth (£1 million, August 2000), Coventry City (on loan, November 2001, signed free transfer, January 2002), POTTERS (on loan, January 2003, signed free, February 2003), Telford United (July 2003), Hereford United (free, August 2004).

■ Striker Lee Mills was one of the last signings made by Potters manager Tony Pulis during the latter stages of the 2002–03 season. Although he scored

some vital goals, he was subsequently released as the senior squad was reconstructed in the summer. Mills scored 106 goals for his eight League clubs before entering the Conference with Telford United. He later helped Hereford reach the Conference play-offs.

MILLS, Michael, Denis, MBE

Full-back: 44 apps.

Born: Godalming, Surrey, 4 January 1949.
Career: Portsmouth (apprentice, May 1964), Ipswich Town (professional, February 1966), Southampton (£100,000, November 1982), POTTERS (player-manager, June 1985, retired as a player, May 1988, resigned as manager, November 1989), Colchester United (manager, January–May 1990), Middlesbrough (scout, July 1990), Coventry City (assistant manager, November 1990–November 1991), later Birmingham City (assistant manager, May 1996–May 2001).

■ Mick Mills was Stoke City's manager for four and a half years, and during his

time in charge of the Potters he played in over 200 competitive games, 190 in the Football League, of which Mills himself appeared in 38. As a player Mills occupied, in the main, the left-back position and made a club record 741 League and Cup appearances for Ipswich during his 16 and a half years at Portman Road, having been rejected as a teenager by Portsmouth. He won FA Cup and UEFA Cup winners' medals under manager Bobby Robson and gained 42 full and five under-23 caps for England, skippering his country eight times at senior level, including matches in the 1982 World Cup Finals. He added another 123 first-team appearances to his tally with the Saints before moving to Stoke as a player-manager, retiring as a player in 1988. With hardly any money to spend, Mills was unable to bring quality players to the club and this led to him quitting his position at The Victoria Ground after a run of poor results and performances that saw crowds drop alarmingly.

MILLWARD, Douglas

Forward: 1 app.

Born: Stoke-on-Trent, 1866.
Died: c.1934.
Career: Stoke Priory, POTTERS (September 1887), Leek Town (May 1888).

■ A utility forward, Doug Millward's only game in Stoke's colours was at inside-left in a fifth-round FA Cup tie against West Bromwich Albion in January 1888.

MILLWARD, Ernest Foster

Outside-left: 78 apps. 25 goals.

Born: Hartshill, Stoke-on-Trent, August 1887.
Died: Bournemouth, 23 June 1962.
Career: Cobridge Church, Biddulph Mission, Glossop North End (1905), Hanley Swifts, POTTERS (October 1907), Wrexham (November–December 1907), Port Vale (january 1908), POTTERS (August 1908), Huddersfield Town (May 1910), Glossop North End (1911), Crewe Alexandra (May 1913). Did not play after World War One.

■ No relation to Doug, Ernie Millward was an amateur left-winger who had a useful career in the game. Failing to establish himself during his initial spell at The Victoria ground, he returned a year later and was a regular in the first XI for two seasons. He struck home some wonderful goals while also creating several scoring opportunities for his colleagues with his precise and often dangerous crosses. He made just two appearances for the Vale.

MILNE, Alexander James

Left-back: 276 apps.

Born: Hebburn-on-Tune, 29 September 1889.
Died: Doncaster, 1970.
Career: Hebburn Old Boys, Hebburn Argyle (1909), POTTERS (October 1912), Doncaster Rovers (May 1926, retired, May 1930).

■ A solid performer, Alex Milne always looked the part. He was a rugged, no-nonsense tackler with a strong kick who was recruited by Stoke at the age of 23 as manager Alfred Barker started to rebuild a side capable of regaining Football League status. Milne made his debut for the club at left-half away at West Ham in a Southern League game on Christmas Day in 1912. Unfortunately, he didn't have a very happy debut as the Hammers won 5–0.

He was switched to right-back after seven games and established himself in the side during the second-half of that season. Moving across to the left-flank to accommodate George Turner on the right, Milne was the recipient of a Southern League Championship medal in 1915 when he was an ever present. He didn't play much during World War One after being called back to the North East to work on munitions. However, he returned after the hostilities and continued in the game until he was almost 41 years of age.

MITCHELL, Albert James

Forward: 10 apps. 2 goals.

Born: Stoke-on-Trent, 22 January 1922.
Died: Stoke-on-Trent, 1997.
Career: Burslem Albion, POTTERS (professional, May 1941), Blackburn Rovers (£1,500, February 1948), Kettering Town (briefly), Northampton Town (May 1949), Luton Town (July 1951), Middlesbrough (September 1954), Southport (August 1956) Wellington Town (May 1957), Kidderminster Harriers (1958), Stafford Rangers (as a player, 1959, later manager 1960–61).

■ Bert Mitchell had a useful career as a utility forward. He gained one England 'B' cap and was listed as a reserve during his time at The Victoria Ground, appearing in just 10 senior and 10 World War Two games, scoring two goals, for the Potters. He scored twice on his first-team debut against his future club Middlesbrough in January 1947 when he deputised on the left-wing in place of Alex Ormston. He netted 73 goals in a career total of 266 League games, including 41 in 106 outings for Luton.

MOHAN, Nicholas

Defender: 115+6 apps. 7 goals.

Born: Middlesbrough, 6 October 1970.
Career: Middlesbrough (junior, April 1986, apprentice, July 1987, professional, November 1987), Hull City (on loan, September–October 1992), Leicester City (£330,000, July 1994), Bradford City (£225,000, July 1995), Wycombe Wanderers (on loan, August–September

19987, signed permanently for £75,000, October 1997), POTTERS (free transfer, March 1999), Hull City (free, July 2001), Gateshead (October 2002).

■ An Auto-Windscreen Shield winner in 2000, Nicky Mohan gave the Potters two years' excellent service. Tough and resolute, his strength lay in his determination, competitiveness and the ability to organise his fellow defenders. He netted some vital goals for the club, including the winner at home to Bristol City in November 1999, which ended 1–0. Later, he was reunited with his former manager, Brian Little, when he returned to Hull City in 2001. Appointed captain in the absence of another ex-Potter, Justin Whittle, Mohan eventually entered non-League football at the age of 32 with a total of 482 senior appearances safely under his belt.

MOLYNEUX, Frederick

Centre-forward: 16 apps. 5 goals.

Born: Bolton, 1878.
Died: before 1960.
Career: 3rd Batallion, Grenadier Guards, POTTERS (February 1898), Bristol City (March 1899), Berwick Rangers (August 1900), Luton Town (season 1901–02).

■ Fred Molineux was a capable goalscorer at Southern League level.

MONTFORD, Edgar William John

Defender: 7 apps.

Born: Knighton near Welshpool, 1861.
Died: Knighton, 22 November 1940.
Career: Newtown (1879), POTTERS (professional, August 1885), Leek Town (July 1890), after retiring from football he became a collector of taxes for Hanley, Stoke and Fenton, and was clerk to the Mucclestone Parochial Church Council, living in Knighton.

■ A reliable reserve defender, able to play as a full-back or wing-half, Edgar Montford, one of Stoke's first full-time professionals, made only a handful of senior appearances for the Potters during his five years with the club. He joined his brother at Leek Town.

MONTFORD, Harold Ernest

Inside-left: 2 apps.

Born: Newtown, 1865.
Died: Bucknall, Stoke-on-Trent, 26 May 1947.
Career: Newtown (1882), POTTERS (professional, August 1888), Leek Town (May 1889).

■ Harry Montford, younger brother of Edgar, also assisted his home-town club before joining Stoke for the club's first

season in the Football League in 1888–89. He played for the first team twice, lining up in a League game against Accrington in the September and in the FA Cup defeat by Warwick County a month later.
NB: The Montfords were the first set of brothers to represent Stoke at football.

MOONEY, Thomas John

Forward: 11+1 apps. 3 goals.

Born: Billingham, County Durham, 11 August 1971.
Career: Aston Villa (apprentice, August 1987, professional, November 1989), Scarborough (free transfer, August 1990), Southend United (£100,000, July 1993), Watford (free, March 1994), Birmingham City (free, July 2000), POTTERS (on loan, September–December 2002), Sheffield United (on loan, January–February 2003), Derby County (on loan, March–May 2003), Swindon Town (free, July 2003), Oxford United (free, June 2004), Wycombe Wanderers (June 2005).

■ An enthusiastic performer wherever he played, Tommy Mooney never gave less than 100 percent out on the field. Strong and mobile, he failed to make the first team at Villa Park, but after leaving he certainly made up for lost time. He had already appeared in 477 League and Cup games and scored 125 goals before having a decent loan spell with the Potters in 2002. A Second Division Championship winner with Watford in 1998, he played in the Premiership with both the Hornets and Birmingham City.

MOORE, Albert Edward

Inside-forward: 1 app.

Born: Longton, Stoke-on-Trent, 1898.
Died: Stoke-on-Trent, 1975.
Career: Normacot, POTTERS (season 1921–22), Burslem Swifts (seasons 1922–25).

■ Bert Moore remained an amateur throughout his playing career, which he spent entirely in the North Staffordshire area. His only appearance in the Football League was for the Potters against Bradford Park Avenue in November 1921, which they lost 1–0.

MOORE, John

Half-back: 13 apps.

Born: Liverpool, 9 September 1945.
Career: Everton (apprentice, April 1961), POTTERS (professional, July 1963) August 1968), Swansea City (January–May 1973).

■ John Moore played all his senior games for Stoke City during the 1967–68 season. A very useful reserve-team player, he remained at The Victoria Ground for five years before transferring to Shrewsbury Town, for whom he made over 150 appearances.

MOORE, Thomas

Centre-forward: 1 app.

Born: Arbroath c.1864.
Died: before 1945.
Career: Arbroath, POTTERS (August 1888), Arbroath (January 1889).

■ Tom Moore made one League appearance for Stoke in the very first season of the competition, participating in the 2–1 defeat at Bolton in October 1888. He failed to settle down (or impress) in England and returned home after four and a half months.

MOORE, William

Half-back: 4 apps.

Born: New Washington, County Durham, March 1916.
Died: 1982.
Career: Walker Celtic, POTTERS (month's trial, July 1935, professional, August 1935), Mansfield Town (July 1938, retired during World War Two), Notts County (coach, 1946–53), Aston Villa (assistant manager-trainer, July 1953), Walsall (manager, December 1957), Fulham (scout, November 1963), Walsall (manager, February 1969, resigned, March 1972), later ran a hotel in Stafford.

■ Billy Moore was a useful footballer who was a reserve-team player with Stoke City for two seasons. Appointed coach at Meadow Lane by manager Eric Houghton, he nurtured such players as Jackie Sewell and Ron Wylie at Meadow Lane, and when Houghton became boss of his former club, Aston Villa, in 1953 Moore went with him as his assistant. He was spongeman at Wembley when Villa won the FA Cup in 1957. Later that year he became manager of Walsall and in 1960 guided the Saddlers to the Fourth Division Championship title and followed up 12 months later by leading them into the Second Division. When financial problems began to hit Walsall during his second spell there, he eventually quit after a disagreement with the coach, John Smith, who later took over the reins as team boss.

MOORES, Ian Richard

Striker: 57 apps. 15 goals.

Born: Newcastle-under-Lyme, 5 October 1954.
Died: Stoke-on-Trent, 12 January 1998.
Career: Staffordshire Schools, POTTERS (apprentice, April 1970, professional, June 1972), Tottenham Hotspur (£90,000, August 1976), Western Suburbs, Australia (on loan, summer 1977), Leyton Orient (£55,000, October 1978), Bolton Wanderers (on loan, July–August 1982), Barnsley (on loan, February–March 1983), Apoel Tel Aviv, Cyprus (1983–88), Tamworth (August 1988–90), Newcastle Town (briefly), Landskrona Bols, Sweden, Port Vale (trialist).

■ Over a period of 12 years Ian Moores, a gangling, sometimes awkward-looking striker at 6ft 2in tall and weighing over 13st, served with five different clubs, amassing a total of 225 League appearances and scoring 49 goals. He joined the Potters after playing for Staffordshire Schools and he was present at Wembley when the League Cup was won in 1972. Making his senior debut in April 1974, he went on to score a goal every four games for Stoke before leaving for Spurs in 1976 and scored the first hat-trick of his career for Spurs in a 9–0 Second Division win over Bristol Rovers during that season. He gained both Cypriot League and Cup winners' medals with Apoel before returning to England where he entered non-League football. Capped twice by England at under-23 level as a Stoke player, Moores helped Tamworth win the FA Vase in 1989, scoring a vital goal in the replay against Sudbury Town at Peterborough. He sadly died in a Stoke hospital at the age of 43.

MOORWOOD, John Edwin

Centre-half: 9 apps.

Born: Handsworth, Sheffield, 1896.
Died: before 1975.
Career: Chesterfield intermediate football, Army Service (World War One), Alfreton (1919–20), POTTERS (£300, July 1920), Wrexham (May 1921), Bangor City (May 1924).

■ Defender Jack Moorwood made all his senior appearances for Stoke during the second half of the 1920–21 season when he lined up across the middle with George Clarke and Dickie Smith. A strong tackler with good positional sense, he lacked that extra yard of pace that was required at top-class level, although he did appear in 65 League games for Wrexham.

MORGAN, Nicholas

Striker: 88+16 apps. 26 goals
Born: East Ham, London, 30 October 1959.
Career: West Ham United (apprentice, April 1976, professional, November 1977), Portsmouth (March 1983), POTTERS (£50,000, November 1986), Bristol City (£30,000, March 1990), AFC Bournemouth (on loan, October–November 1992), Exeter City (non-contract, February–April 1994).

■ Nicky Morgan had a fine career as an out-and-out striker. Although he spent over five years with the Hammers, he never really established himself in the first team. He did much better with Portsmouth, scoring 32 goals in 95 League outings, and then gave the Potters great value for money with some excellent displays. He spent three and a half seasons at The Victoria Ground, during which time he claimed a goal every four games before leaving to join Bristol City. In his League career as a

whole, Morgan netted 83 goals in 303 games. He was known at Fratton Park as 'Super Sub'.

MOULD, William

Defender: 194 apps.

Born: Great Chell, Staffs, 6 October 1919.
Died: Stoke-on-Trent, 27 September 1999.
Career: Summerbank, POTTERS (junior, July 1936, with Alec Ormston), Crewe Alexandra (free transfer, July 1952, retired, May 1954 to concentrate on his sports-outfitters business).

■ Billy Mould starred at full-back and centre-half for the Potters in almost 200 League and Cup games, while also making another 83 first-team appearances during World War Two. A very fine player, dedicated to the game, he replaced Arthur Turner at the heart of the defence and had over 100 outings in three seasons before injury and loss of form saw him slip into the second XI. He came back again in the early 1950s and played his last senior game for the club in mid-March 1952 in a 0–0 draw with Huddersfield Town, when he appeared at right-back as partner to Johnny McCue. During World War Two, Mould was wounded in the leg when serving with the Royal Artillery in Normandy and spent some time in Ireland with a handful of other 'Stokies', including Syd Peppitt and his good friend Ormston. Mould, who captained the Potters on several occasions, was a splendid club man.

MOUNTFORD, Frank

Utility: 425 apps. 24 goals.

Born: Askern near Doncaster, 30 March 1923.
Career: Bradley Junior School, Campsall Boys, POTTERS (schoolboy forms, July 1937, professional, April 1940), guested for Derby County during World War Two, retired, May 1958, POTTERS (trainer, from July 1958, then coach until 1978).

■ The versatile Frank Mountford had a fine career with Stoke City. He came down to the Potteries with his family at an early age and joined the club as a youngster in 1937, while still attending Bradley Junior School. Establishing himself in the first team in 1942, he held

down a regular place in the side for the next 13 years and eventually accumulated more than 600 appearances for the Potters, 183 coming during World War Two when he also netted an extra 54 goals, to go with those he scored at senior level. Only nine players have appeared in more competitive games for the Potters than Mountford and, indeed, only one man has amassed more than Mountford's tally of 608 (John McCue with 675). Able to play in a variety of positions, including those of full-back, centre-half and centre-forward, Mountford was a huge favourite with fans at The Victoria Ground. A totally committed footballer, he never shirked a tackle, produced nothing less than 100 percent effort out on the park, and one feels that if he had been with a more glamorous club (i.e Arsenal, Everton or Manchester United) he would surely have gained international honours. After hanging up his boots in 1958 he moved behind the scenes at Stoke, first as a trainer and then as coach, holding office until Alan Durban arrived as team manager. Mountford remained in close contact with the club and attended several of Stoke's home games right up until the mid-eighties.
NB: Mountford scored a record 14 penalties in peacetime League and Cup competitions for the Potters, as well as netting another six in World War Two football.

MOUNTFORD, George Frederick

Forward: 158 apps. 29 goals.

Born: Kidderminster, 30 March 1921.
Died: Kidderminster, 14 June 1973.
Career: Kidderminster Harriers (semi-professional, April 1938), POTTERS (£40, November 1942), Independiente Sante Fe, Colombia (May 1950), POTTERS (early October 1952), Queen's Park Rangers (£4,000 deal involving Des Farrow, late October 1952), Hereford United (1953), Kidderminster Harriers (1954), Lockheed Leamington (1935), after retiring worked as a post office engineer, based near his home in Kidderminster.

■ No relation to Frank, George Mountford played as an outside-right or inside-right, He scored 37 goals in 95 World War Two appearances for the Potters, playing mainly on the wing when Stanley Matthews was unavailable, and after the hostilities he became a regular member in the side, especially after Matthews had moved to Blackpool. Mountford made over 150 peacetime appearances for Stoke before going to play in Colombia with colleague Neil Franklin in 1950, outside the jurisdiction of FIFA. Known as 'Bald Arrow', Mountford was a star performer in the South American country and, during the 1950–51 season scored and created plenty of goals. On his return to England he was immediately suspended by the FA and after serving his punishment returned to The Victoria Ground, but was quickly off-loaded to Queen's Park Rangers by manager Frank Taylor. He played 38 games for Rangers before returning to non-League football.

MUDIE, John Knight

Inside-forward: 93 apps. 33 goals.

Born: Dundee, 10 April 1930.
Died: Hartshill, Stoke-on-Trent, 2 March 1992.
Career: Dunkeld Amateurs, Dundee Stobswell, Dundee (professional, July 1940), Blackpool (guest, 1945, professional, May 1947), POTTERS (£7,000, March 1961), Port Vale (£12,000 plus Ron Wilson, November 1963, caretaker-manager, February 1965, player-manager, March 1965, resigned May 1967), Oswestry Town (player-manager, 1967–68), Crewe Alexandra (assistant-coach), Eastwood (trainer-coach), Northwich Victoria (manager), Johanesburg Rangers, South Africa (scout 1970s), ran his own painting and decorating business in the Potteries for many years.

■ Jackie Mudie was a diminutive inside-forward who had an exceptionally fine playing career, which saw him amass a total of 463 League appearances, score 184 goals and win 17 full caps for Scotland. One of seven brothers, all of them footballers, Mudie played initially for two local teams in his home country before signing as a professional for Dundee. He then

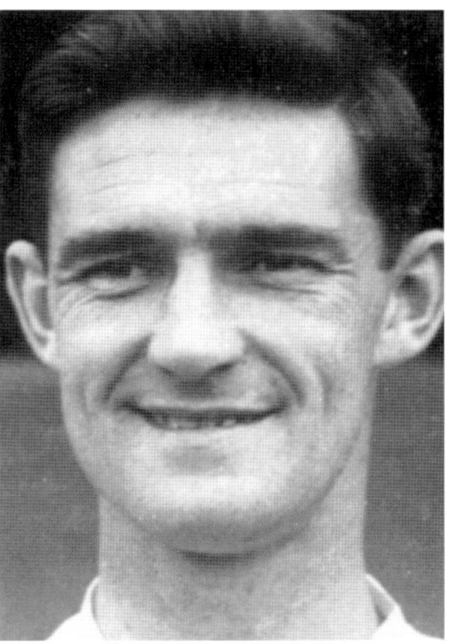

became a star with Blackpool, whom he helped win the FA Cup versus Bolton Wanderers in 1953 when he played in the same forward-line as Stanley Matthews. With Stoke manager Tony Waddington recruiting experienced footballers in an effort to win promotion from the Second Division, Mudie was lured to The Victoria Ground in 1961. He bedded in quickly and did a terrific job, appearing in almost 100 first-team games and scoring over 30 goals, while also helping the Potters win back their place in the top flight in 1963, having been reunited with his former Bloomfield Road teammate, Stan Matthews. Sold to rivals Port Vale soon after that promotion success, Mudie became caretaker-manager and then held the position of player-manager from March 1965. However, with the team doing badly, Mudie resigned his position for 'personal reasons' at the end of the 1966–67 season, having scoring 11 goals in 64 outings for the Valiants.

MUDIE, Leonard

Inside-forward: 3 apps. 1 goal.

Born: Forfar, Scotland, 1872.
Died: Scotland, 1948.
Career: Kirriemuir, Burnley (September 1888), POTTERS (September 1889), Dundee Wanderers (December 1889).

■ Len Mudie's only League goal for the Potters was scored against Notts County away in October 1889 when he was deputising for Arthur Edge. Earlier, he had appeared in just one League game for Burnley, ironically against Stoke in December 1888. A temperamental player, he never settled in the Potteries and, after an argument with the committee, left The Victoria Ground before the turn of the year and signed for Dundee Wanderers.

MUGGLETON, Carl David

Goalkeeper: 185+1 apps.

Born: Leicester, 13 September 1968.
Career: Leicester City (apprentice, September 1984, professional, September

1986), Chesterfield (on loan, September–November 1987), Blackpool (on loan, February 1988), Hartlepool United (on loan, October–December 1988), Stockport County (on loan, March 1990), POTTERS (on loan, August–September 1993), Celtic (£150,000, January 1994), POTTERS (£150,000, July 1994), Rotherham United (on loan, November–December 1995), Sheffield United (on loan, March 1996), Mansfield Town (on loan, September–October 1999), Chesterfield (on loan, December 1999–January 2000), Cardiff City (on loan, March–April 2001), Cheltenham Town (free transfer, July 2001), Bradford City (on loan, December 2001–January 2002), Chesterfield (free transfer, July 2002).

■ A fine shot-stopper, goalkeeper Carl Muggleton made 13 appearances for Celtic prior to rejoining the Potters in 1994, teaming up once more with manager Lou Macari, who had been his boss at Parkhead. Muggleton, who played in just nine senior games in his first spell at The Victoria Ground, was capped once by England at under-21 level and immediately claimed a regular place in the side on his return. However, he later had both Ronnie Sinclair and then Mark Prudhoe fighting it out with him for a first-team place and after several loan spells eventually moved to Cheltenham Town. Now a footballing nomad, he reached two career milestones in 2004 when serving with his 13th different League club, Chesterfield: 350 League appearances and 400 games in all competitions.

MULHOLLAND, George Rush

Full-back: 3 apps.

Born: Paisley, Scotland, 4 August 1928.
Career: Served with the Royal Navy during World War Two, POTTERS (amateur, August 1949, professional, July 1950), Bradford City (£1,000, part-time professional, July 1953, professional, July 1955), Darlington (free transfer, July 1960, returned to being a part-time professional, June 1962, retired, June 1963).

■ Resilient Scottish full-back George Mulholland developed through the junior ranks at The Victoria Ground, having moved to the Potteries at the age of two. He made only three League appearances for Stoke, all during the second half of the 1950–51 season. Unable to command a regular place in the side, he eventually left for Bradford City in 1953. He became an institution at Valley Parade and made 304 senior appearances for the Bantams in seven years (including 246 in succession between August 1953 and September 1958) before moving on to Darlington. He finally quit League soccer with more than 400 games under his belt, yet never scored a goal. Born into a family of swimmers, Mulholland now resides in Billingham, County Durham, and is believed to be one of the oldest former Stoke players alive today.

MULLARD, Albert Thomas

Utility: 23 apps. 5 goals.

Born: Tamworth, 22 November 1920.
Died: Bilston, 27 May 1984.
Career: Hinckley United, Walsall (professional, July 1938), Crewe Alexandra, POTTERS (August 1950), Port Vale (£10,000 plus Alan Martin, September 1951), Northwich Victoria (May 1956), later played Wednesbury Tube (Wolverhampton Works League).

■ Albert Mullard was an adaptable player who could do a good job as an half-back or as an inside or centre-forward. As strong as an ox, he was courageous, determined and totally committed to playing football. He scored almost a goal every five games for the Potters before switching to neighbours Port Vale, where he did very well, netting 23 times in 179 first-team matches and as an ever-present helped the Valiants reach the FA Cup semi-final and win the Third Division North title in the 1953–54 season. Having lost his place in the side in January 1956, he entered non-League football with Northwich Victoria at the end of that season. Mullard was a Prisoner of War for four years in the 1940s.

MULLINEUX, Ernest

Right-back: 186 apps.

Born: Northwood, Stoke-on-Trent, 12 March 1879.
Died: Bucknall, Stoke-on-Trent, 3 August 1960.
Career: Burslem Park, Port Vale (May 1900), Bury (£600, December 1904), POTTERS (July 1906); Wellington Town (season 1914–15). Did not play after World War One, he became a schoolteacher in Hanley and combined his educational work with that of playing football.

■ Ernie Mullineux played his early

football as a centre-half with Burslem Park before joining Port Vale. He did exceedingly well with the Valiants, making 132 appearances prior to his transfer to Bury in 1904. Two years later he returned to the Potteries with Stoke and made 19 appearances in his first season, 13 in his second and from then until 1912 was a regular member of the team, amassing almost 190 appearances in League and Cup action before winding down his career with Wellington Town. A skilful defender, strong in the tackle and known as 'White Nob' due to his silver hair, he scored a goal for Wellington from 60 yards with one almighty clearance.

MUNRO, Alexander Iain Fordyce

Full-back: 34 apps. 1 goal.

Born: Uddingston, Lanarkshire, 24 August 1951.

Career: Drumchapel Amateurs, St Mirren (professional, August 1968), Hibernian (£30,000, May 1973), Rangers (1976, in exchange for two players), Dundee United (briefly), St Mirren (£25,000, November 1977), POTTERS (£165,000, October 1980), Sunderland (£150,000, August 1981, retired as a player, May 1986), Hamilton Academical (manager, July 1986), later St Mirren (manager), then Raith Rovers (manager from September 1996).

■ A fine full-back on his day, Iain Munro was signed by Potters manager Alan Durban, who then secured his services again when he was in charge of Sunderland in 1981. Munro. who gained seven full caps for Scotland in 1979–80, appeared in 80 League games for Sunderland and more than 400 in his professional career. He was a polished, skilful and stylish footballer who, besides giving full value in the way of endeavour, could split a defence wide open with one measured 40-yard pass.

MURPHY, Joseph

Half-back or inside-forward: 56 apps. 2 goals.

Born: Stockton-on-Tees, July 1873.
Died: Scotland, c.1950.
Career: Hibernian (professional, 1893), POTTERS (August 1897), Woolwich Arsenal (£1,000, April 1899), Raith Rovers (£400, May 1900, retired through injury, April 1903).

■ A solid competitor, Joe Murphy always wore a wig on the field of play and was called 'Judge' by his teammates. He made over 50 appearances for the Potters before a big money transfer to Arsenal towards the end of the 1898–99 season. He appeared in 50 games for the Gunners in various competitions.

MYATT. Herbert Thomas

Outside-right: 4 apps. 2 goals.

Born: Stoke-on-Trent, 1884.
Died: before 1960.
Career: Stone Town, POTTERS (August 1908), Stafford Rangers (May 1909).

■ Reserve right-winger Bert Myatt, the son of former Stoke player Walter Myatt, scored twice on his debut for the Potters in a 5–3 home win over Aston Villa reserves in a Birmingham & District League fixture in September 1908. He spent only one season at The Victoria Ground.
* Herbert's brother, Harry Myatt (born in 1880), was part of a consortium of former Burslem Port Vale stalwarts who bought themselves into the new Port Vale club in December 1908. Later appointed to the board of directors, he then became vice-chairman of the club and held the position of team manager from October 1913 to May 1924. He later did excellent work in establishing Vale's supporters' club. He died at Sneyd Green in October 1967.

NAUGHTON, William Arthur

Outside-right: 101 apps. 25 goals.

Born: Glasgow, 1866.
Died: Edinburgh, c.1935.
Career: Celtic (1886), Carfin Shamrock (1888), POTTERS (August 1890), Southampton St Mary's (April 1895), Hibernian (May 1898).

■ Billy 'Chippy' Naughton, an inveterate practical joker, was suspended from football for playing as an amateur while receiving payments. This happened in mid-1891, a year or so after he had joined the Potters. Unable to gain a place in Celtic's first team, Naughton was nonetheless a useful right-winger who could cross a ball superbly well, almost inch-perfect. He spent five seasons at The Victoria Ground, during which time he averaged a goal every four games and followed up by netting 18 times in his 47 outings for Saints, whom he helped win the Southern League Shield in 1898.

NEAL, Lewis

Midfield: 35+47 apps.3 goals.

Born: Leicester, 14 July 1981.
Career: Leicester Schools, POTTERS (apprentice, April 1997, professional, July 1998).

■ Lewis Neal graduated through the Stoke City Academy and made his League debut as a second-half substitute

in a 4–1 home win over Bristol Rovers in March 2001. A willing worker with good sharp skills, he is predominantly left-footed and is now a key member of the first-team squad, having battled hard and long for four years.

NEWLANDS, Douglas

Outside-right: 34 apps. 8 goals

Born: Edinburgh, 29 October 1931
Career: Forres Mechanics (1947), Aberdeen (trialist, 1948), St Johnstone

(professional, October 1949), Aberdeen (October 1951), Burnley (£1,200, March 1955), POTTERS (£15,000, July 1959), St Johnstone (free transfer, September 1960) Airdrieonians (1962), later Forfar Athletic (player-manager).

■ Doug Newlands was a very positive right-winger who, after failing to make headway with any of his Scottish clubs, scored 23 goals in 104 games for Burnley before joining Stoke in 1959. He averaged a goal every eight games for the Potters prior to his release.

NGALULA, Gabriel (Junior)

Defender: new signing.

Born: Zaire, Belgian Congo, 1 June 1982.
Career: RSC Anderlecht, Belgium (professional, August 2001), AEC Mons, Belgium (loan, season 2004–05), POTTERS (June 2005).

■ A strong-limbed defender, 6ft tall and able to occupy a variety of positions, Junior suffered a set-back in 2003 when he fractured his right leg. He regained full fitness and spent the whole of the 2004–05 season on loan with AEC Mons, who were relegated after finishing bottom of the Belgian First Division before joining the Potters, for whom he made his senior debut against Sheffield Wednesday He has represented his country at both under-18 and under-21 levels.

NIBLOE, John Allister

Centre-forward: 23 apps. 5 goals.

Born: Sheffield, 1 June 1939.
Died: Stocksbridge, 12 November 1964.
Career: Sheffield United (amateur, July 1955, professional, August 1958), POTTERS (£33,000, October 1961), Doncaster Rovers (£5,000, October 1962), Stockport County (July 1964, until his death).

■ John Nibloe was a tough Yorkshireman who scored four goals in 25 League games for Sheffield United before transferring to the Potters in 1961. After just a year at The Victoria Ground he was sold to Doncaster. He was tragically killed in a car crash in 1964, aged 25, having netted 19 goals in a total of 102 career League appearances.

NICHOLAS, David Sidney

Outside-left: 58 apps. 4 goals

Born: Aberdare, Glamorgan, 12 August 1897.
Died: Aberdare, 7 April 1982.
Career: Aberdare Grammar School (1910), Merthyr Town (1912), Royal Navy (during World War One), Swansea Town (amateur, March 1918), Merthyr Town (professional, October 1918), Carmarthen Training College (November 1918, remaining a registered player with Merthyr Town), POTTERS (£1,000, March 1922), Swansea Town (November 1924–May 1930), Aberavon Athletic (August 1930, retired,

May 1931), later headmaster of Abernany School (Aberdare), also involved in the administration of schoolboy football, serving on the committee of the Welsh Schools FA.

■ After being capped by Wales at schoolboy level on 1912, Dai Nicholas was given trials by Merthyr but unfortunately World War One intervened and he was recruited to the Royal Navy. Towards the end of the hostilities he played several games as an amateur for Swansea before turning professional with Merthyr, only to enter the Carmarthen Training College to train as a teacher almost immediately. Said to have been a 'speedy left-winger', he performed well enough on the flank for the Potters before becoming homesick. He moved back to Swansea and secured a teaching appointment in his native Aberdare. He proceeded to score 13 goals in 150 games for the Swans before retiring in 1931. During his time at The Victoria Ground, Nicholas was involved in a serious motor cycling accident in 1923, which resulted in a fractured skull. He gained three full caps for his country, the first with Stoke against Scotland in 1923.

NIXON, William John

Outside-right: 2 apps.

Born: Stoke, 1886.
Died: France, 1916.
Career: Trentham FC, POTTERS (September 1911 until his death).

■ Amateur right-winger Billy Nixon appeared in two League games for Stoke in April 1912. He was killed in action serving with the British Army in France in 1916.

NOBLE, Daniel William

Goalkeeper: 2 apps.

Born: Hull, 21 September 1970.
Career: Hull Boys', POTTERS (apprentice, April 1987, professional, July 1989), Crewe Alexandra (free transfer, June 1991–April 1992).

■ After performing exceedingly well as a teenager for the Hull Boys' team,

reaching the English Schools FA Shield Final, goalkeeper Danny Noble was recruited as a junior by Stoke. He made rapid progress and signed professional forms in 1988, by which time he had also represented England at youth-team level. Unable to oust Peter Fox from Stoke's first team, he made just two senior appearances before being given a free transfer in 1991.

NOEL-WILLIAMS, Gifton Ruben Elisha

Forward: 83+8 apps. 23 goals.

Born: Islington, London, 21 January 1980. Career: Watford (apprentice, April 1996, professional, February 1997), POTTERS (free transfer, May 2003), Burnley (free, with Wayne Thomas, May 2005).

■ An England youth international, capped as a Watford player, Gifton Noel-Williams also helped the Hornets

win the Second Division Championship in 1998. He scored 41 goals in 193 first-team games for the Vicarage Road club before his move to The Britannia Stadium at the end of the 2002–03 campaign. He scored on his debut for the Potters versus Derby County and played in 44 games in his first season, producing some excellent displays to finish up as joint top-marksman. Able to hold the ball up, he loves to run at defenders and packs a powerful shot in his right foot.

NYAMAH, Kofi

Midfield: 10+9 apps.

Born: Islington, London, 20 June 1975. Career: Cambridge United (apprentice, June 1991, professional, May 1993), Stevenage Borough (on loan, March–April 1995), Kettering Town (June 1995), POTTERS (£25,000, December 1996), Luton Town (free transfer, August 1998), Kingstonian (December 1998), Cambridge United (non-contract, March 1999), Exeter City (free, August 1999). Stevenage Borough (June 2000).

■ A versatile left-footed player, able to occupy a midfield or striking position, Kofi Nyamah made his debut for the Potters as a substitute in the televised League game against Oxford United in February 1997. He scored three goals in 33 appearances for Cambridge in his first spell at the Abbey Stadium but failed to make an impact with Luton.

O'CALLAGHAN, Brendan Richard

Defender and forward: 284+10 apps. 47 goals

Born: Bradford, 23 July 1955. Career: Doncaster Rovers (apprentice, July 1971, professional, July 1973), POTTERS (£40,000, March 1978), Oldham Athletic (£30,000, February 1985), Newcastle Town (briefly in season 1990–91), after retiring he worked in the pottery industry in Stoke-on-Trent and was later Community Development Officer at The Victoria Ground, he worked for the PFA Management Committee, studied for a degree in business administration at the University of Dublin and also worked on a sports

Brendan O'Callaghan

programme for a local radio station near Stoke.

■ Brendan O'Callaghan gave Stoke City Football Club excellent service for almost seven years, scoring almost 50 goals in 300 senior appearances while occupying a variety of positions, including those of central defender and centre-forward! Alan Durban's first signing as Potters' manager, he proved to be a terrific bargain. He had already netted 77 goals in 212 games during his four and a half years at Belle Vue and was just the man Stoke needed to boost their attack. He made a superb start to his career at The Victoria Ground, coming on as a substitute against Hull City and scoring with his first touch in a 1–0 win, surely the fastest goal ever recorded by a Stoke player from the time he set foot on the pitch! O'Callaghan top-scored the following season with 15 goals, helping the team gain promotion to the First Division. In May 1979 he was called into the Republic of Ireland squad, making his international debut against West Germany in Dublin, the first of seven full caps he received. Standing almost 6ft 3in tall, 'Big Bren' was exceptionally good in the air and was no mean footballer on the ground either. A splendid target man, he was dangerous at set pieces and corner-kicks, especially those floated over by Paul Maguire. In his first game for the Latics he suffered a groin injury, which eventually ended his League career, although he did turn out for Newcastle Town in 1990.

O'CONNOR, James Kevin

Midfield: 209+2 apps. 22 goals.

Born: Dublin, 1 September 1979.
Career: POTTERS (apprentice, April 1995, professional, September 1996), West Bromwich Albion (tribunal set fee of £250,000, July 2003), Burnley (on loan, October 2004–February 2005, signed for £175,000, March 2005).

■ Capped by the Republic of Ireland at youth–team level, midfielder James O'Connor went on to appear in nine under-21 internationals during his time with the Potters, whom he helped win

the Auto-Windscreen Shield in 2000 and gain promotion to The First Division two years later. A totally committed performer and a firm favourite with the fans, his aggressive approach to any game has, over the years, earned him several yellow cards. A strong tackler, he appeared in more than 200 first-team matches for the Potters before moving to The Hawthorns, signed by his former boss Gary Megson. He made his Albion debut against Walsall on the opening day of the 2003–04 League programme and went on to play his part in helping the Baggies reclaim their place in the Premiership. However, he did not figure in Megson's plans at the start of the following season and was subsequently loaned out to Burnley, whom he later joined permanently.
* Stoke initially wanted £1.25 million for O'Connor, but a Football League transfer tribunal set the figures at a fifth of that sum.

OLDFIELD, David Charles

Forward or midfield: 57+17 apps. 7 goals

Born: Perth, Australia, 30 May 1968.
Career: Luton Town (apprentice, May 1984, professional, May 1986), Manchester City (£600,000, March 1989), Leicester City (£150,000, January 1990), Millwall (on loan, February–May 1995), Luton Town (£150,000, July 1995), POTTERS (free transfer, July 1998), Peterborough United (free, March 2000), Oxford United (free, August 2002, retired, June 2004).

■ Tireless, hard-working utility player David Oldfield was already an experienced campaigner by the time he joined the Potters in 1998, having scored 79 goals in 444 League and Cup appearances for his four previous clubs, while also gaining one England under-21 cap. He spent almost two years at

Stoke, playing in all 46 League games in his first season at The Britannia Stadium when he regularly donned the number 11 shirt and formed a very effective midfield combination with Graham Kavanagh and Kevin Keen. Six of his seven goals for the club came in that 1998–99 campaign, including a clincher in a 2–0 home win over York City in November. He reached the career milestone of 650 club appearances in August 2003 as an Oxford player.

OLDHAM, George

Left-back: 2 apps.

Born: Tintwhistle, 20 April 1920.
Died: Luton, June 1993.
Career: Montram Central FC, POTTERS (professional, 1938), guest for Aldershot and Stockport during World War Two, Newport County (September 1946), Hitchin Town (player-manager), Hebburn Town (coach), after retiring from football he lived in Luton.

■ Both of reserve full-back George Oldham's two League outings for Stoke came in December 1938 when he replaced Jack Tennant for the away games against Liverpool and Middlesbrough. Signed from a Manchester intermediate club, he drifted away from The Victoria Ground during World War Two and on his return signed for Newport, for whom he made 70 appearances before entering non-League football with Hitchin Town.

O'NEILL, James Anthony

Goalkeeper: 149 apps.

Born: Dublin, 13 October 1931.
Career: Bulfin United, Dublin (1947), Everton (trialist, season 1948–49, signed as a professional, May 1949), POTTERS (£5,000, July 1960), Darlington (March 1964), Port Vale (February 1965), Cork Celtic (loan, December 1966–January 1967, returned to Stoke and retired, May 1967), later ran his own taxi business on Merseyside.

■ Jimmy O'Neill enjoyed a very successful career. With a safe pair of hands, his commanding height made him a force whenever the ball was in the air and he was able to get down remarkably quickly to the low shot fired towards the corner of the net. After a successful trial at Goodison Park, he was taken on as a full-time professional but had to wait 12 months before making his League debut against Middlesbrough in August 1950. A regular in the side for five years, December 1951 to October 1956, he was rated one of the best 'keepers in Europe in 1955. Eventually replaced by Albert Dunlop, O'Neill won 17 caps for the Republic of Ireland before his transfer to Stoke, being one of a multitude of important signings made by manager Tony Waddington as he steadily assembled his team for a promotion push in the early 1960s. He helped the Potters win the Second Division title in 1963 and kept 48 clean sheets in his senior outings for Stoke. After leaving The Victoria Ground he made over 30 appearances for Darlington and almost 50 for Port Vale, whose manager at the time was former Stoke and England star Stan Matthews. O'Neill made over 450 appearances for clubs and country and he still makes the occasional visit to a Stoke City home match.

ORLYGSSON, Thorvaldur

Midfield: 106+4 apps. 19 goals.

Born: Odense, Denmark, 2 August 1966.
Career: KA Akureyri, Iceland, Nottingham Forest (£175,000, December 1989), POTTERS (free transfer, August 1993), Oldham Athletic (£180,000, December 1995, retired, June 1999).

■ An Icelandic international capped 41 times at senior level during his career, Toddy Orlygsson was an orthodox right-winger with his first club KA Akureyri and also with Nottingham Forest. However, after his transfer to the Potters he was successfully converted into an aggressive goalscoring midfielder. He had netted four goals in 45 outings for Forest, fading after making a decent start at The City Ground. He became a firm favourite with the Potters fans, and in the 28 months spent at the club he averaged a goal every six games before leaving for Oldham Athletic in 1995. When he quit competitive football in 1999 his record stood at 24 goals in 243 senior games (plus his international statistics).

ORMSTON, Alexander

Outside-left: 192 apps. 30 goals.

Born: Hanley, Stoke-on-Trent, 10 February 1919.
Died: Bentilee, Staffs, 12 July 1975.
Career: Wellington Road School, Hanley Boys, Stoke Schools, Summerbank FC,

POTTERS (professional, 1937), Hereford United (1951), Stafford Rangers, Runcorn, after retiring spent a short time in Loggerheads Sanitorium fighting poor health, later a publican in Hanley, worked in the colliery offices and for a Madeley pottery firm as well as assisting at The Victoria Ground in Stoke City's promotions office.

■ Alex Ormston, a diminutive but enterprising left-winger, joined the Potters as a 17-year-old from the club's nursery side, Summerbank, after trials with England schoolboys. He made his League debut in the inside-left position as partner to Frank Baker against Sunderland in November 1937, the first of almost 200 senior appearances for the Potters (plus 59 during World War Two with 19 goals scored). He eventually took over on the wing during the latter stages of the war and after the hostilities produced some excellent displays that earned him three outings with the Football League representative side. He lost his place in the side during the 1949–50 campaign when Baker, Johnny Malkin and Harry Oscroft were used by manager Bob McGrory.

OSCROFT, Harold

Outside-left: 349 apps. 107 goals.

Born: Mansfield, 10 March 1926.
Career: Mansfield Colliery FC (1941), Sheffield United (briefly, 1946), Mansfield Town (April 1947), POTTERS (£38,000 plus Verdi Godwin, January 1950), Port Vale (with Peter Ford and £2,000, in exchange for Dickie Cunliffe, September 1959, free transfer, May 1961), Brantham Athletic (player-manager, July 1961), Sutton United (1963–64), later moved to Manningtree near Colchester where he worked for a local plastics company.

■ Harry Oscroft was a terrific left-winger who effectively took over the number 11 shirt from Alex Ormston. He joined the Potters in a deal set up by

manager Bob McGrory and former Stoke City star Freddie Steele, who was then boss at Field Mill. Oscroft settled in quickly to his new surroundings at The 'Vic', and he went from strength to strength, scoring some vital goals on the way. He held his place in the side until the end of the 1958–59 season but, although still fit and keen to continue playing, he switched his allegiance to Vale Park, thus allowing Dickie Cunliffe to move in as his replacement. Oscroft's record of just under a goal every three games was a terrific return for an out-and-out winger. As a Vale player he added 12 more goals in 51 games to his tally before moving into non-League football with Brantham Athletic, whom he guided to victory in the Suffolk Senior Cup in 1962. He also starred in various local charity matches, eventually hanging up his boots in 1988 at the age of 62.

OULARE, Souleymare

Striker: 0+2 apps. 1 goal.

Born: Conakry, Guinea, 16 October 1972.
Career: Lycee Cbession, Guinea, Horoya, Guinea, Eeklo, Guinea, St Niklaas, Guinea, KSK Beveren, Belgium (June 1992), KSV Waregem, Belgium (July 1994), KAA Genk, Belgium (May 1996), Fenerbahce, Turkey (August 1999), Las Palmas, Spain (during season 2000–01), Fenerbahce (August 2001), POTTERS (free transfer, December 2001, released, September 2002).

■ The Stoke City management team worked overtime to bring experienced Guinea striker Souleymare Oulare to The Britannia Stadium. The former Belgium 'Player of the Year' had already scored 57 goals in 156 League games for his last four major clubs, including 37 in 84 outings for Genk, where he spent three seasons, gaining a Belgium Cup winners' medal in 1998. He had also suffered injury problems for 12 months and this allowed the Potters to secure his services on a free transfer. Unfortunately, after just one substitute outing, he contracted deep vein thrombosis and at that point life became miserable for the 29-year-old. However, he battled on gamely and was named in the squad for the Play-off semi-final with Cardiff City at the end of the season. He again came off the bench and scored with a deflected shot. But, unfortunately, the club wouldn't gamble on his fitness and he was released two months into the 2002–03 season.

OVERSON, Vincent David

Defender: 213+3 apps. 7 goals
Born: Kettering, 15 May 1962.
Career: Exeter Primary & Kingswood Grammar Schools, Kingswood Boys, Corby Town, Long Buckby, Burnley (apprentice, June 1978, professional, November 1979), Birmingham City (£235,000, June 1986), POTTERS (tribunal set fee of £55,000, August 1991), Burnley (free, August 1996), Shrewsbury Town (on loan, September–October 1997). Halifax Town (free, August 1998), Padiham FC, Lancashire (free, September 1998–May 2000).

■ Vince Overson was essentially a right-footed central defender, strong and uncompromising, whose battling qualities, particularly in the air, were always his strong points. Vince Overson turned professional at Turf Moor after representing England at youth-team level. As a regular member of the Clarets side, he helped them win the Third Division title in 1983 and went on to amass a fine record for the Lancashire club, appearing in 249 League and Cup games and scoring seven goals. After his move to St Andrew's he continued to perform with resilience, and in five seasons with the Blues he netted four times in 213 senior outings, helping the West Midlands club win the Freight Rover Trophy at Wembley in 1991 under manager Lou Macari. He then followed the Scotsman to The Victoria Ground a few months after that triumph and within 12 months he stepped out at Wembley again, this time for the Final of the Autoglass Trophy when he helped the Potters beat Stockport County 1–0. A year later he starred again as the Potters won the Second Division Championship. After well over 200 appearances for the Potters he completed a full circle by returning to Burnley in 1996, and when he quit top-class football in 1998 his appearance-tally had topped the 700-mark

* Overson played alongside his younger brother, Richard, in five League games for Burnley in season 1979–80.

OWEN, Alfred Sydney

Forward: 10 apps. 6 goals.

Born: Newcastle-under-Lyme, c.1883.
Died: Blackpool, 22 August 1925.
Career: North Staffs Nomads, Northern Nomads, POTTERS (January 1907), Stockport County (July 1907), Port Vale (guest, October 1907), POTTERS (April 1908), Leicester Fosse (August 1908), Port Vale (guest, September 1908), Middlesex Wanderers (April–July 1911), Blackpool (August 1911), POTTERS (November 1912, retired, April 1913), also played Newcastle Town, worked in a commercial capacity in Hungary in 1913–15, returned to England after World War One.

■ Brother of Walter and William Owen, Alf was a versatile forward who had three spells with the Potters. Each of his stays at The Victoria Ground were relatively brief, and in fact he made only 10 senior appearances all told, never really establishing himself in the team. An England amateur international, he also scored in a full international trial match at Anfield (Whites versus Stripes) in January 1910 as a Leicester player, and after leaving Filbert Street he toured Europe with Middlesex Wanderers, a team of selected amateurs.

NB: At Blackpool Owen was appointed the secretary of the Players' Union and took part in the first legal action around the League's retain and transfer system ('The Kingaby Case'). He resigned in February 1913 to take up a commercial appointment in Budapest, Hungary.

OWEN, Gareth David

Defender: 1+4 apps.

Born: Pontypridd, 21 September 1982.
Career: POTTERS (apprentice, April 1999, professional, July 2001), Oldham Athletic (on loan, January–May 2004), Torquay United (on loan, July–September 2004), Oldham Athletic (loan, March–May 2005, signed for £50,000, June 2005).

■ A tall, strong and confident central defender with a rugged, no-nonsense style, Gareth Owen made terrific strides via the Potters' Academy and reserve teams and made his senior debut as a

substitute against Wigan Athletic in October 2003. He also represented Wales at both under-19 and 20 levels before having an extended loan spell with Oldham during the last quarter of the 2003–04 season, and on his return to the club he signed a new contract.

OWEN, James

Centre-forward: 3 apps. 2 goals

Born: Manchester, September 1864.
Died: before 1945.
Career: Newton Heath, POTTERS (March 1890), Newton Heath (May 1890).

■ Jim Owen was 25 years of age when he scored on his senior debut for Stoke against West Bromwich Albion away in

March 1890. He added one more goal to his tally against Notts County at the end of that campaign, but he was not retained for the following season, returning to his former club Newton Heath (Manchester United).

OWEN, Walter Oscar

Forward: 6 apps. 4 goals.

Born: Newcastle-under-Lyme, April 1868.
Died: before 1945.
Career: Stoke St Peter's, POTTERS (October 1886), Long Eaton Rangers (September 1888).

■ Wally Owen, a utility forward, made all his senior appearances for the Potters in the FA Cup competition, scoring three of his four goals in consecutive games during the 1887–88 season.

OWEN, William Alfred

Defender: 2 apps.

Born: Newcastle-under-Lyme, c.1885.
Died: before 1945.
Career: North Staffs Nomads, POTTERS (August–October 1909), Northern Nomads, Manchester City (briefly), Port Vale (July 1911–February 1912).

■ Bill Owen was an amateur defender who deputised at left-half for Fred Tomlinson in two Birmingham League games in September 1909.

PAGE, Louis Antonio

Inside-forward or outside-left: 21 apps. 1 goal.

Born: Kirkdale, Liverpool, 27 March 1899.
Died: Prenton, Birkenhead, 11 October 1959.
Career: St Alexander Council School (Liverpool), Liverpool schoolboy football, Sudley Juniors, Everton (trialist), South Liverpool (August 1918), POTTERS (professional, August 1919), Northampton Town (November 1921), Burnley (£4,000 plus Jack Tresadern, May 1925), Manchester United (March 1932), Port Vale (October 1932), Yeovil & Petters United (player-manager, July 1933–May 1935), Newport County (manager, June 1935–September 1937), Glentoran (trainer-coach, December 1938), Carlton FC, Liverpool (manager, during World War Two), Swindon Town (manager, July 1945–May 1953), Chester (manager, June 1953–June 1956), Leicester City (scout to 1958).

■ Louis Page was one of four brothers, all of whom went on to play professional football and also represented their country at baseball. He excelled in Liverpool schoolboy soccer matches and scored 10 goals in one game from the inside-left position. Basically an inside-forward or left-winger, he worked hard without a great deal of success at The Victoria Ground but then did exceedingly well with the Cobblers, netting 22 goals in 122 League games. Page moved to Burnley in 1925, allowing Jack Tresadern to become player-manager of Northampton, and at Turf Moor, despite being on the losing side 10–0 away to Aston Villa on his debut, he became an instant hit with the supporters. Over a period of seven seasons he netted 115 goals in 259 appearances for the Lancashire club, claiming a double hat-trick from the centre-forward position when the Clarets beat Birmingham 7–1 at St Andrew's in April 1926, a victory that eased the fear of relegation. He was capped seven times by England (February–November 1927), scoring his only international goal in a 9–1 destruction of Belgium in Brussels in mid-May. In 1932, two years after Burnley had been demoted to the Second Division, Page was sold to Manchester United and later scored twice in his 19 outings for Port Vale. As manager of Swindon, he helped plan Burnley's downfall in the FA Cup in 1948. For three years up to 1956 Page managed Chester, after which he acted as senior scout for Leicester City. A painful illness interrupted his life and, sadly, he died in 1959, aged 60.

PAINTER, Ian John

Striker: 114+9 apps. 24 goals.

Born: Wombourne near Wolverhampton, 28 December 1964.
Career: POTTERS (apprentice, December 1980, December 1982), Coventry City (£75,000, July 1986, released, June 1990), coaching at non-League level, Bilston United (manager, 1995–99).

■ Ian Painter graduated through the junior ranks at The Victoria Ground and made his Football League debut 24 hours before his 18th birthday against Everton in 1982, the first of more than 120 senior appearances for the Potters. An England youth and under-21 international, injury unfortunately restricted his progress during the mid-eighties, and when Mick Mills took over as manager at The Victoria Ground Painter became surplus to requirements. At Highfield Road he was again plagued by more injury problems, and after four years of uneasiness he decided to quit the first-class game. He then did some part-time coaching while also running his own sports shop in his native Womborne. Painter returned to the game in 1995 as manager of West Midlands club Bilston United.

PALETHORPE, John Thomas

Centre-forward: 21 apps. 11 goals.

Born: Leicester, 23 November 1909.
Died: May 1984.
Career: Maidenhead United (1927), Crystal Palace (professional, August 1929), Reading (March 1931), POTTERS (£3,000, March, 1933), Preston North End (£4,000, December 1933), Sheffield Wednesday (£4,000, December 1934), Aston Villa (£3,500, November 1935), Crystal Palace (£1,000, October 1936), Chelmsford City (free transfer, August 1938), Shorts Sports FC (August 1939), Colchester United (briefly, retired 1946).

■ Jack 'S.O.S.' Palethorpe was a big, strong, bustling centre-forward who won promotion from the Second Division in successive seasons, with the Potters in 1933 and Preston in 1934. He then gained an FA Cup winners' medal with Sheffield Wednesday playing against West Bromwich Albion in 1935 before suffering relegation from the First Division with Aston Villa in 1936. He scored a goal every two games for the Potters, including two on his debut against Swansea Town in March 1933 when he lined up between Harry Ware and Tommy Sale in the front-line. The dressing room comic, Palethorpe gave up his job as a shoe-manufacturer to become a professional footballer in 1929. He had a fine career, netting 107 goals in 177 League appearances over a period of eight years, up to 1938. His nephew, Chris Palethorpe, played for Reading.

PALIN, Leigh Granville

Midfield: 21+2 apps. 3 goals.

Born: Worcester, 12 September 1965.
Career: St George's School (Worcester), Aston Villa (apprentice, September 1981, professional, September 1983), Shrewsbury Town (on loan, December 1984), Nottingham Forest (£20,000, November 1985), Bradford City (£25,000, October 1986), POTTERS (on loan, early September 1989, signed for £95,000, late September 1989), Hull City (£100,000, March 1990), Rochdale (on loan, October–November 1991), Burnley (non-contract, October 1992, retired, December 1992), Immingham Town (Promotion Manager, mid-to-late 1990s).

■ Midfielder Leigh Palin won England youth honours as a teenager but failed to make the first team at Villa Park. After a loan spell with Shrewsbury, with whom he made his Football League debut, he was transferred to Nottingham Forest but again failed to get into the senior side at The City Ground. Then, at long last, he finally came good with Bradford City, making almost 100 League and Cup appearances for the Yorkshire club in three years. He joined the Potters in 1989 but never really established himself in the team and left The Victoria Ground for Hull in 1990. Palin's career realised 153 League appearances.

PALMER, Calvin Ian

Full-back or wing-half: 196 apps. 27 goals

Born: Skegness, 21 October 1940.
Career: Skegness Town (April 1956), Nottingham Forest (professional, March 1958), POTTERS (£35,000, September 1963), Sunderland (£70,000, February 1968), Cape Town, South Africa (May 1970), Crewe Alexandra (October 1971, retired, January 1972).

■ Calvin Palmer spent over five years with Nottingham Forest, for whom he

made 106 appearances. In 1963 he became one of manager Tony Waddington's early season signings, recruited to boost the midfield as the Potters sought to establish themselves back in the First Division. At the end of his first season at The Victoria Ground he gained a League Cup runners-up prize. Palmer, who effectively replaced hard-man Eddie Clamp in the right-half berth, did a superb job during his four and a half years' stay with Stoke, appearing in almost 200 first-class matches. A heated argument with Maurice Setters on the training field in 1966 was perhaps blown up out of all proportions but it cost Palmer a place on Stoke's American tour. Fiercely competitive and very popular with the fans, Palmer was eventually transferred to Sunderland – a move that really didn't pay off for him – and after brief spells in South Africa and at Gresty Road he quit top-class football in 1972. He made over 350 appearances at club level and now lives in his native Skegness.

PALMER, Jermaine Ashley Clifton

Striker: 0+4 apps.

Born: Derby, 28 August 1986.
Career: POTTERS (apprentice, August 2002), Vikingur Stavanger, Norway (on loan, July–September 2004). POTTERS (professional, January 2005), Grimsby Town (free, May 2005).

■ The son of former Notts County full-back Charlie Palmer, powerful young striker Jermaine Palmer made his League debut for the Potters as a 17-year-old substitute against Rotherham United in April 2004. He played in two more games at the end of that season before spending the summer on loan to the Icelandic club Vikingur.

PARKER, Charles William

Centre-half: 79 apps. 5 goals.

Born: Seaham Harbour, County Durham, 21 September 1892.
Died: Durham, 1980.
Career: Seaham Albion, Hartlepool BD, Seaham Harbour, POTTERS (January 1914), Sunderland (£3.300, September 1920), Carlisle United (player-coach, May 1929), Chester City (briefly), Blyth Spartans (briefly), Chopwell Institute (May 1930, retired, April 1931).

■ Recruited from the North Eastern League football at the age of 21 in 1914, centre-half Charlie Palmer became one of the greatest defenders ever to pull on the red and white striped shirt of Stoke. Quickly establishing himself in the Potters Southern League side (gaining a Championship medal in 1915), he was capped by England in a Victory international against Wales at The Victoria Ground in October 1919. He also represented the Football League on one occasion. In fact, he had an outstanding 1919–20 campaign, being the cornerstone of the Potters team following the club's readmission to the

Football League after a break of 10 years. Many supporters, several players and indeed club officials were disappointed that Palmer never received full international recognition as he was a terrific player. After almost 80 senior appearances for Stoke (plus 120 more during World War One) he was at the peak of his career when sold to Sunderland for a fat fee by early standards. His move to Roker Park stunned the Potters faithful and for sometime afterwards his leaving caused a lot of debate. He spent nine seasons with the Wearsiders, for whom he made 256 first-team appearances. Unaffected by the lack of physical advantages most centre-halves enjoy, Parker was as brave as they come, never shirked a tackle and was totally committed throughout his career.

PARKES, David

Centre-half: 6 apps.

Born: Lye near Stourbridge, 17 June 1892.
Died: Cheshire, 1975.
Career: Brierley Hill Alliance (1908), Newcastle Town (1909), Brighton & Hove Albion (1911), Sheffield Wednesday (£250, March 1914), POTTERS (£120, May 1920), Llanelli (May 1921), Rochdale (August 1922), Macclesfield (May 1928, retired, April 1931).

■ David Parkes was born in the heart of the Black Country and was one of several centre-halves utilised by Stoke during the 1920–21 season. He made just half a dozen League appearances following his transfer from Sheffield Wednesday, for whom he appeared in 50 first-team games. He played in well over 300 games for Rochdale.

PARKIN, Derek

Left-back: 45 apps.

Born: Newcastle-upon-Tyne, 2 January 1948.
Career: Huddersfield Town (apprentice, April 1963, professional, May 1965), Wolverhampton Wanderers (£80,000, February 1968), POTTERS (free transfer, March 1982, retired, May 1983).

■ It was manager Richie Barker who secured the services of full-back Derek 'Squeak' Parkin from his former club Wolves on a free transfer in 1982. He had made a record 609 senior appearances (501 in the Football League) during his 14 years at Molineux, helping Wolves twice win the League Cup in 1974 and 1980 and the Second Division Championship in 1977, also gaining five caps for England at under-23 level and representing the Football League. Never a reckless tackler, he was a steady rather that enthusiastic defender who had an educated left foot. A player who always tried to use the ball rather than kick it long and aimlessly downfield, he spent just the one season at The Victoria Ground before announcing his retirement so that he could concentrate on a career in landscape gardening near Bridgnorth. A fine golfer, Parkin now resides in the same locality as Bert Williams and Willie Carr, two former Wolves players.

PARKIN, Stephen John

Full-back/midfield: 128+9 apps. 5 goals.

Born: Mansfield, 7 November 1965.
Career: Portland School (Worksop), Bassetlaw Schoolboys, Nottinghamshire Schools, POTTERS (apprentice, April 1981, professional, November 1983), West Bromwich Albion (£190,000, June 1989), Mansfield Town (free, July 1992, manager, September 1996–May 1999), Rochdale (manager, June 1999), Barnsley (manager, November 2001, sacked October 2002), Notts County (assistant manager-coach, August–December 2003), Rochdale (manager, December 2003).

■ After more than 10 years as a player, Steve 'Billy' Parkin entered management with Mansfield Town in 1996, becoming the youngest boss in League football at that time. Originally a wing-half, he played most of his 260 plus games as a full-back, first with the Potters, whom he served for six years, then West Bromwich Albion and finally Mansfield. He made his debut for Stoke in a 1–0 home league win over Nottingham Forest in March 1983. After leaving The Victoria Ground his first game for Albion was against Sheffield United when another ex-Stoke player, Brian Talbot, was manager at The Hawthorns, while former Potters winger Tony Ford was in front of Parkin at number seven. Halfway through the 1996–97 campaign Parkin appointed his former Stoke colleague Ford as his assistant at Field Mill. Capped five times by England at under-21 level, Parkin represented his country as a schoolboy and also played for the youth team.

PARKS, Anthony

Goalkeeper: 3 apps.

Born: Hackney, East London, 26 January 1963.

Career: Hackney & Inner London Schools, Tottenham Hotspur (apprentice, April 1979, professional, September 1980), Oxford United (on loan, October–November 1986), Gillingham (on loan, September 1987), Brentford (on loan, October 1987), Queen's Park Rangers (on loan, November 1987), Southend United (on loan, December 1988), Brentford (August 1988), Fulham (February 1991), West Ham United (August 1991), POTTERS (on loan, August–September 1992), Falkirk (October 1992), Blackpool (September 1996), Burnley (player-coach, August 1997), Doncaster Rovers (on loan, February–March 1998), Barrow (October 1998), Scarborough (early February 1999), West Bromwich Albion (goalkeeping coach, late February 1999, Halifax Town (player-goalkeeping coach, July 1999–2000).

■ The recipient of a UEFA Cup winners' medal with Spurs when he starred in the penalty shoot-out at the end of the two-leg Final against RSC Anderlcht in 1984, Tony Parks surprisingly spent by far his best years in Scotland, making 128 appearances for Falkirk and gaining a B&Q Cup winners' medal in 1994. His three outings for Stoke all came in September 1992 when he deputised for Ronnie Sinclair in two Second Division matches, which were both won, and a League Cup draw with Cambridge United.

PARSONS, Edward

Wing-half: 65 apps. 1 goal
Born: Stafford, January 1878.
Died: Stafford, 1956.
Career: Stafford Rangers, POTTERS (May 1896), Featherstone Rovers (May 1901), Brighton & Hove Albion (August 1902), later with Stafford Rangers. Did not feature after World War One

■ Hard-tackling right half-back Teddy Parsons, who was described in the local press as 'a player of vigorous stamp who used his weight', scored his only goal for the Potters against Staffordshire rivals West Bromwich Albion in October 1897. His best season at The 'Vic' was in 1899–1900 when he made 33 appearances.

PATERSON, George Frederick

Centre-forward: 7 apps. 4 goals.

Born: Lochgelly, Fife, April 1904.
Died: Scotland, 1983.
Career: Lochgelly United (1921), Kelty Rangers (1902), Lochgelly United (1923), POTTERS (professional, July 1925), Lochgelly United (December 1925), East Fife (March 1926), Rhyl Athletic (1930–31).

■ Centre-forward Jock Paterson had the pleasure of scoring a hat-trick on his Football League debut for Stoke against Middlesbrough at The Victoria Ground on 26 September 1925, when he was introduced into the attack in place of the injured Dick Johnson. A bold, aggressive Scotsman, Paterson joined the Potters from his home-town club, Lochgelly United, in 1925 but, unfortunately, a leg injury ruined his chances of making further progress with Stoke, and he returned to his homeland after just five months.

PATERSON, Martin Andrew

Striker: 0+3 apps.

Born: Tunstall, Stoke-on-Trent, 13 May.
Career: POTTERS (apprentice, May 2003, professional May 2005).

■ After some useful displays in the Academy and reserve teams (scoring 11 goals in 19 games and two in 14 respectively), Martin Paterson made his League debut for the Potters as a substitute in a 2–0 home League win over Plymouth Argyle in April 2005. He skippered the Potters Academy side and was voted Potters' Academy Player of the year in 2005.

PAXTON, John

Inside-forward: 3 apps. 1 goal.

Born: West Stanley, c.1890.
Died: before 1980.
Career: West Stanley, POTTERS (February 1911), Chesterfield (May 1911). Did not play after World War One.

■ Reserve Jack Paxton played only Birmingham League football for Stoke, scoring his only goal for the club in April 1911 against Stafford Rangers, which was won 4–0, when he deputised for Alf Smith.

PEACOCK, James

Half-back: 1 app.

Born: Stoke-on-Trent, 1871.
Died: Stoke-on-Trent, 1936.
Career: Dresden United, POTTERS (June 1896), Saltgates FC (May 1897).

■ Jimmy Peacock, a local-born player, appeared in just one League game for the Potters at home to Wolverhampton Wanderers in September 1896, which was won 2–1, when he stood in for the injured Bill Dickson.

PEART, John George

Centre-forward: 47 apps. 41 goals.

Born: South Shields, 3 October 1888.
Died: Paddington, London, 3 September 1948.
Career: South Shields Adelaide (August 1905), Sheffield United (professional, May 1907), POTTERS (July 1910), Newcastle United (£600, March 1912), Notts County (February 1913), guest for Rochdale, Barnsley and Leeds City during World War One, Birmingham (November 1919), Derby County (January 1920), Ebbw Vale (player-manager, August 1920), Port Vale (as a player, January 1922), Norwich City (July 1922), Rochdale (player-manager,

March 1923, retiring as a player, May 1924), Bradford City (manager, July 1930), Fulham (manager, May 1935 until his death in 1948).

■ Jack Peart was a prolific goalscoring centre-forward who found the back of the net on a regular basis throughout his lengthy career. His record with Stoke was quite superb, but it would have been much better if he hadn't been sidelined with a broken leg between December 1910 and September 1911, and, indeed, it was a pity he didn't stay at The Victoria Ground longer! A League Division Two Championship winner with Notts County in 1914, he represented the Football League once and the Southern League on three occasions. He actually transferred himself to Port Vale at the age of 34 but suffered injury problems and left for Norwich City after just four months. As manager of Fulham, he took them to the FA Cup semi-finals and was in office at Craven Cottage when he died in 1948.

PEJIC, Mel

Full-back: 1 app.

Born: Chesterton, Staffs, 27 April 1959.
Career: POTTERS (May 1975, professional, July 1977), Hereford United (June 1980), Wrexham (£27,000, January 1992, retired, May 1994, engaged as physiotherapist at The Racecourse Ground).

■ Mel Pejic's only League outing for Stoke City came in the home fixture against Ipswich Town in January 1980 when he deputised for Ray Evans. Younger brother of Mike, he joined the Potters straight from school and spent the last three seasons of his career with Stoke playing in the second team before transferring to Hereford United in 1980. At Edgar Street he did supremely well, and over a period of 11 and a half seasons he appeared in 412 senior matches for the 'Bulls', which still remains as a club record.

PEJIC, Michael

Full-back: 336 apps. 8 goals.

Born: Chesterton, Staffs, 25 January 1950.
Career: Chesterton & North Staffs Schools, Corona Drinks FC, POTTERS (apprentice, June 1966, professional, January 1968), Everton (£135,000, February 1977), Aston Villa (£225,000, September 1979, retired through injury, May 1980), became a farmer (unsuccessfully), Leek Town (manager, 1981–82), Northwich Victoria (manager, 1982–83), Port Vale (Youth coach, July 1986, senior coach, December 1987–March 1992), FA Coach & Player Development Officer, Kuwait (coach), Chester City (manager, 1994–95), POTTERS (Youth coach, 1995–99).

■ Son of a Yugoslav miner, aggressive full-back Mike Pejic was a thoughtful player who cleared his lines precisely, covered well, was totally committed and some say he was arguably the fiercest tackler seen at The Victoria Ground for a number of years. During a fine career he won four full caps for England, appeared in eight under-23 internationals and helped the Potters win the League Cup in 1972. He made well over 400 appearances during his career and actually made his debut for Everton against his former club Stoke in February 1977, but missed that season's League Cup Final, having already played in the competition with the Potters. Injuries interrupted his spells at both Everton and Aston Villa.

PENTLAND. Frederick Beaconsfield

Centre-forward or inside-left: 12 apps. 6 goals.

Born: Wolverhampton, 18 September 1883.
Died: 1962.
Career: Willenhall Swifts, Avondale Juniors, Small Heath, Birmingham (August 1900), Blackpool (June 1903), Blackburn Rovers (December 1903), Brentford (May 1906), Middlesbrough (June 1908), Halifax Town (August 1912), POTTERS (February 1913), Halifax Town (December 1913, retired August 1915), later coach in France (seasons 1919–21), Atletico Bilbao, Spain (1921–36), Brentford (1936–37), Barrow (manager, January 1938–September 1939). Did not feature in football after World War Two.

■ In May 1914 Fred Pentland secured what was considered at the time to be an important position with the German Olympic Council. Stationed initially at Karlsruhe, Baden, he was to assist with the coaching of the German athletes in readiness for the Olympic Games of 1916, scheduled to be held in Berlin. However, the Great War prevented them from taking place and Pentland's efforts were wasted! After the hostilities, and a spell in France, he coached the Spanish side Atletico Bilbao for 15 years before leaving at the outbreak of the Civil War in 1936. An exceptionally fine footballer in his own right, Pentland was capped five times by England in 1909. All five games ended in victory but he failed to score in his country's total of 24 goals. He appeared in his last professional game for Halifax in April 1915 in the Bradford Charity Cup semi-final replay at Heckmondwike where he received a bad knee injury that eventually forced him to retire. All told, his playing career realised more than 350 first-class appearances of which 151 came in the Football League. He played his best football with Middlesbrough (11 goals in 95 outings).
NB: Pentland was the son of a former Lord Mayor of Birmingham who was a fond admirer of Benjamin Disraeli, Earl of Beaconsfield, after whom his son was named! He was in Yorkshire at the start of World War One, in Spain when the Civil War commenced and in Cumbria at the outbreak of World War Two.

PEPPITT, Sydney

Utility forward: 106 apps. 29 goals

Born: Hanley, Stoke-on-Trent, 8 September 1919.
Died: Stoke-on-Trent, 25 December 1992.
Career: Cannon Street School (Hanley), POTTERS (amateur, September 1934, professional, September 1936), guest for Linfield during World War Two, Port Vale (£4,000, May 1950), Worcester City (1951, retired 1953).

■ Syd Peppitt won three England schoolboy caps in 1934 and turned professional with the Potters at the age of 17. Despite having to battle for a place in the first team with Stan Matthews and Freddie Steele, plus a few others, he worked perilously hard and went on to give the club excellent

Mike Pejic

service for 14 years. In that time he scored 60 goals while making 161 War and peacetime appearances, averaging a goal every four games at senior level. He spent quite sometime in Ireland during the hostilities when he assisted Linfield. And in 1950, after languishing in the reserves for six months, he was transferred to Port Vale, but an injury hindered his performances with the Valiants, and he left Vale Park after just one season, having scored three times in his 11 League outings.

PESCHISOLIDO, Paolo Pasquale (Paul)

Striker: 73+8 apps. 24 goals.

Born: Scarborough, Ontario, Canada, 25 May 1971.
Career: Toronto Blizzard, NASL, Kansas City Comets, NASL (1990–91), Toronto Blizzard, NASL (1991–92), Birmingham City (£25,000, November 1992), POTTERS (£400,000, player-exchange deal involving David Regis, August 1994), West Bromwich Albion (£600,000, July 1996), Fulham (£1.1 million, October 1997), Queen's Park Rangers (on loan, November–December 2000), Sheffield United (on loan, January–March 2001), Norwich City (on loan, March–April 2001), Sheffield United (£150,000, July 2001), Derby County (free, March 2004).

■ Canadian international Paul Peschisolido, an exciting, nimble, all-action, industrious utility forward, certainly made a big impact at The Victoria Ground, and there is no doubt that fans were bitterly disappointed when he was sold to West Bromwich Albion in 1996. At 5ft 5in tall he was one of the smallest forwards ever to wear a Stoke City shirt. 'Pesch' made his debut for the club in the home League encounter with Tranmere Rovers in August 1994, which they won 1–0, and netted his first goal a month later in a 4–1 win over Southend United. He finished up as leading scorer that season with 15 goals. He continued his goalscoring exploits after leaving the Potters and in 1998–99 helped Fulham win the Second Division Championship. He then played in the Sheffield United side that reached the semi-final in both the FA Cup and League Cup competitions in 2002–03 and also appeared for the Blades when they lost to Wolves in the First Division Play-off Final that same season. Capped 51 times for Canada having earlier starred for his country in 11 under-21 matches and in several under-16 and under-17 games,

'Pesch' was voted the US Major Indoor Soccer League's 'Newcomer of the Year' in 1990 and seven years later was named Canadian 'Footballer of the Year'. During the 2004–05 season he reached the personal milestones of 450 League and Cup appearances and 125 goals in English football. He helped Canada qualify for the 1996 World Cup Finals in France.
* He is married to the Birmingham City Managing-Director Karen Brady.

PETTY, Benjamin James

Defender or midfield: 40+25 apps. 1 goal.

Born: Solihull, 22 March 1977.
Career: Aston Villa (apprentice, April 1993, professional, May 1995), POTTERS

(free transfer, November 1998), Hull City (free, July 2001), Stafford Rangers (December 2002), Burton Albion (March 2003), Moor Green (December 2003).

■ Ben Petty, a right-footed defender or midfielder, failed to make the breakthrough at Villa Park. However, following his transfer to the Potters, he developed into a worthy performer and gave the club good value for three years before switching his allegiance to Hull City, signed by his former manager Brian Little. However, after a decent start with the Tigers, he fell out with new boss Jan Molby and halfway through the 2002–03 season drifted into non-League football.

PHILLIPS, Hugh

Defender: 7 apps.

Born: Lanark, Scotland, 1864.
Died: before 1945.
Career: St Bernard's, Edinburgh, POTTERS (September 1890, retired through injury, April 1892).

■ Hughie Phillips, normally a centre-half, kept goal for Stoke in a Football Alliance game against Crewe Alexandra at The Victoria Cricket Ground in November 1890 when regular 'keepers Billy Rowley and Wilf Merrett were unavailable. He had arrived at the club as deputy to Hughie Clifford and appeared in just seven games (all in the Alliance) before he was forced into early retirement through injury at the age of 28.

PHILLIPS, Wilfred John

Inside-forward: 14 apps. 3 goals.

Born: Brierley Hill, 9 August 1895.
Died: Penzance, Cornwall, 25 February 1973.
Career: Bilston United (1914), served in Army during World War One, POTTERS (May 1919), Ebbw Vale (May 1920) Darlaston (1921), Bilston United (1922), Bristol Rovers (May 1923–November 1925), Millwall (£500, November 1925), Thames Association (June 1930), West Ham United (£500, June 1931), Clapton Orient (June 1932), Stourbridge (August 1933, retired, May 1934), became a licensee in Stourbridge before moving to Cornwall.

■ Wilf 'Peanuts' Phillips had a nomadic career that spanned 20 years, during which time he appeared in well over 300 games for eight different clubs. He joined Stoke for the first season after World War One but stayed at the club for just one season, becoming surplus to requirements. Phillips was a player who took on defenders, choosing to dribble past them if possible. He scored 35 goals in 92 games for Bristol Rovers and 72 in 134 for Millwall, with whom he won a Third Division South Championship medal and London Cup winners' medal.

PHILPOTT, Alan

Utility: 52 apps. 2 goals.

Born: Stoke-on-Trent, 8 November 1942.
Career: Stoke Schoolboys, POTTERS (amateur, April 1958, professional, November 1959), Oldham Athletic (£7,500, November 1967), Stafford Rangers (February 1969), Eastwood, Hanley (player-coach, 1970–71), Port Vale (youth team coach, 1970s), later managed Leek CSOB and Tittensor, also a useful club cricketer with Stoke MO in the North Staffs League.

■ Alan Philpott graduated through the junior ranks at The Victoria Ground to give Stoke City eight years' service as a utility player, occupying every outfield position except centre-half. He turned professional at The Victoria Ground on his 17th birthday and appeared in over 50 senior games before moving to Oldham Athletic, signed by former Stoke player and then Latics manager Jimmy McIlroy. He left Boundary Park when Jack Rowley returned as manager.

PICKERING, Albert Gary

Right-back: 93+2 apps. 1 goal.

Born: Manchester, 22 June 1967.
Career: Buxton (semi-professional, 1986), Rotherham United (£18,500, full-professional, February 1990), Coventry City (£80,000, October 1993), POTTERS (£280,000, August 1996), Burnley (free transfer, December 1998), Radcliffe Borough (free, July 1999), Cambridge United (free, December 1999), Chester City (free, January 2000), Hyde United (March 2000).

■ Ally Pickering was signed by Potters manager Lou Macari in 1996 to replace Ian Clarkson, who had left the club to join Northampton Town. A player who added attacking flair to his defensive game, he was quick in recovery and always seemed to choose the right time to get forward. Pickering made 110 appearances for Rotherham, 75 for Coventry, 21 for Burnley and eight for Chester, failing, however, to appear for Cambridge.

PICKUP, Reginald John

Inside-left: 1 app.

Born: Stoke-on-Trent, 6 September 1929
Career: POTTERS (amateur, July 1946), played for Staffordshire Boys (1946–47), National Service with the RAF, POTTERS (professional, August 1949), Stafford Rangers (part-time, May 1954–May 1955).

■ During his service with the RAF, Reg Pickup played in various challenge matches. He signed professional forms at The Victoria Ground on being demobbed and made his only first-team appearance for the Potters against Huddersfield Town at home in a First Division match in November 1949. A nasty knee injury, suffered while in action against Blackpool reserves later that season, seriously hampered Pickup's career and after 18 months of playing and breaking down, he was forced to have cartilage removed. The operation was not a complete success and, although he remained at Stoke for quite a while, he eventually retired from competitive football in 1954, joining Stafford Rangers on a part-time basis. He managed to struggle on for a further 12 months but was forced to quit the game altogether in 1955.

PITT, Albert Edward

Half-back: 52 apps. 5 goals.

Born: Shardlow, Staffs, 1880.
Died: Stoke-on-Trent, August 1961.
Career: Stone Town (1900), POTTERS (August 1903), Birmingham University (March 1905), Canterbury Provinces,

New Zealand (1906), POTTERS (August 1908), Canadian football (May 1909), Trentham (1911), POTTERS (September 1912), Norton Bridge FC (January 1913). Did not play after World War One.

■ One of the few players who had three separate spells with Stoke, Bert Pitt was a capable half-back who remained an amateur throughout his career. He averaged a goal every 10 games during those three stints at The Victoria Ground.

PONSONBY, Joseph

Right-half: 5 apps.

Born: Dumbarton, Scotland, May 1876.
Died: Belfast, 1962.
Career: Distillery (August 1893), POTTERS (September 1897), Distillery (February 1898–May 1908).

■ Irish international right-half Joe Ponsonby, who gained nine full caps between 1895 and 1899, three each against England, Scotland and Wales, all with Distillery, was recruited soon after the start of the 1897–98 season. He played in only a handful of first-team games for the Potters before returning to his former club. Surprisingly, he was born in Dumbarton of Irish parents.

POOLE, William Arthur

Defender or forward: 12 apps.

Born: West Bromwich, 1902.
Died: Walsall, 1967.

Career: Kidderminster Harriers (August 1919), Merthyr Town (April 1921), POTTERS (May 1920), Watford (£250, July 1923), Coventry City (1925), Kidderminster Harriers, Yeovil & Petters United, Merthyr Town (1928), Wellington Town, Stourbridge, Walsall (May 1931), Dudley Town (January 1932, retired through injury, May 1934).

■ Billy Poole joined Stoke as a reserve defender in 1920. A reliable footballer, he made a dozen League appearances in three seasons before moving to Watford. Thereafter, he ventured around the country, and during his nomadic career when he also played as an attacker, he assisted 10 different clubs at various levels.

POTTER, Graham Stephen

Midfield: 53+5 apps. 1 goal.

Born: Solihull, 20 May 1975.
Career: Solihull schoolboy football, Birmingham City (apprentice, June 1991, professional, July 1992), Wycombe Wanderers (on loan, September–October 1993), POTTERS (£75,000, December 1993), Southampton (£250,000, July 19965), West Bromwich Albion (£300,000, February 1997), Northampton Town (on loan, October–November 1997), Reading (on loan, December 1999–January 2000), York City (free, July 2000), Boston United (August 2003), Shrewsbury Town (on loan, November–December 2003), Macclesfield Town (free, February 2004).

■ A former England youth international who later gained one under-21 cap, 6ft 1in Graham Potter has been a very useful footballer who prefers to play down the left-hand side of the pitch. He has a good technique, fair pace and delivers a telling cross, given the time and space. He also packs a powerful shot when allowed to swing his boot. He had to work for his money with Stoke, and although never really a regular in the side he always produced a sturdy performance when called into action. Manager Ray Harford's first signing for West Brom, he suffered with injuries during the second half of his three-year spell at The Hawthorns but after regaining full fitness and his appetite for the game, he played 125 times for York City and later did very well with Macclesfield. He reached the career milestone of 350 club appearances in 2005. He scored his only goal for Stoke in a 4–1 Staffordshire derby win at Wolves in October 1996. He also tasted Premiership football with Southampton.

POWELL, Edgar Frederick

Inside-forward or outside-left: 2 apps.

Born: Cardiff, 6 January 1899.
Died: Cardiff, 1962.
Career: Barry Schools, Barry FC, Denaby United, Huddersfield Town (May 1923), POTTERS (May 1924), Accrington Stanley (1925), Merthyr Town (August 1927), Barrow (July 1928–May 1929).

■ Ted Powell played in only two senior games for the Potters before going on to score 17 goals in 65 League games for Accrington. The recipient of a Welsh schoolboy international cap against England in 1913, he started his career as a left-winger but ended it as a very consistent inside-left. He was seriously injured playing for Accrington in the Lancashire Senior Cup semi-final with Manchester City at Bury in May 1926 and missed the final showdown with Bolton.

PRESSMAN, Kevin Paul

Goalkeeper: 6 apps.

Born: Fareham, 6 November 1967.
Career: Sheffield Wednesday (apprentice, April 1984, professional, November 1985), POTTERS (on loan, March–April 1992), West Bromwich Albion (on loan), Leicester City (free transfer, June 2004), Leeds United (non-contract, January–May 2005).

■ A competent goalkeeper with an excellent left foot, Kevin Pressman fancied his chances as a striker after scoring for Sheffield Wednesday in a penalty shoot-out against Wolves in 1995. He joined the Hillsborough staff as a youngster and turned professional on his 18th birthday. After battling for a first-team place with England's Chris Woods, he eventually claimed the number one spot for the Owls in 1993 and over the next 11 years or so appeared in 478 first-class matches (404 in the Football League & Premiership). Capped by England at schoolboy, youth, 'B', under-19 and under-21 levels, his outings for the Potters came towards the end of the 1991–92 season when he stood in the injured Ronnie Sinclair. Two of his appearances were in the Autoglass Trophy when Stoke beat Leyton Orient 1–0 in the Southern Area Final and drew 3–3 with Peterborough United in the first leg of the semi-final. Peter Fox played in the return leg and also in the Final against Stockport.

PROCTOR, Edward

Inside-forward: 3 apps. 2 goals.

Born: Barlaston 1870.
Died: Stoke-on-Trent, c.1950.
Career: Sheffield United (briefly, 1889), Leek Town (1890), Royal Dublin Fusiliers (1891), POTTERS (professional, October 1895), Port Vale (October 1896, released, May 1897).

■ Ted Proctor, brother of John Proctor, was a hard-working, efficient and indeed courageous inside-right who played Army football with the Royal Dublin Fusiliers before signing for Stoke. He found the net in his second game for the Potters against Preston North End at Deepdale, which was won 1–0, and also scored on his debut for Port Vale – the first of four goals in 17 games for Stoke's rivals.

PROCTOR, John

Centre-half: 52 apps. 1 goal.

Born: Barlaston, 3 November 1871.
Died: Fenton, 8 November 1893.
Career: Fenton, Dresden United, POTTERS (professional, August 1891, until his death).

■ Jack Proctor was a solid centre-half who quickly gained a place in Stoke's first XI after moving out of non-league football at the age of 20. However, during the early part of the 1893–94 season he became ill and sadly died of pneumonia.

PROSSER, Benjamin

Centre-forward: 1 app.

Born: Yorkshire, 1878.
Died: before 1945.
Career: Leeds FC, POTTERS (January 1903), Bradford City (May 1903).

■ Unknown amateur centre-forward Ben Prosser played in one League game for Stoke at Derby in March 1903. He later scored five times in 19 games in his one season at Valley Parade.

PRUDHOE, Mark

Goalkeeper: 38 apps.

Born: Washington, County Durham, 8 November 1963.

Career: Washington County Youths, Sunderland (apprentice, June 1980, professional, September 1981), Hartlepool United (on loan, November 1983), Birmingham City (£22,000, September 1984), Walsall (£22,000, February 1986), Doncaster Rovers (on loan, February 1986), Grimsby Town (on loan, March–May 1987), Hartlepool United (on loan, August–September 1987), Bristol City (on loan, November 1987), Carlisle United (£10,000, December 1987), Darlington (£10,000, March 1989), POTTERS (£120,000, June 1993), Peterborough United (on loan, September–October 1994), Liverpool (on loan, November–December 1994), York City (on loan, February–May 1997), Bradford City (£70,000, July 1997), Southend United (free transfer, November 1999), Carlisle United (trialist, October 2000, retired as player, May 2001), Bradford City (reserve team coach, June 2001).

■ A well-built goalkeeper with fine shot-stopping technique, Mark Prudhoe became one of soccer's great wanderers. Prudhoe began his career as an apprentice with Sunderland, turning professional at Roker Park in September 1981. During his four seasons at The Victoria Ground he had to battle for a place between the posts with Carl

Muggleton and Ronnie Sinclair, and at one stage Gordon Marshall. But a fighter to the last, he stuck in there and went on to appear in 38 games before his departure to Bradford City in 1997. Under future Stoke manager Brian Little, he helped Darlington win the Vauxhall Conference title in 1990 and the Fourth Division Championship the following year. He made well over 400 senior appearances while serving with 15 different clubs, having his best years with Darlington, for whom he had 169 outings in League and Cup games plus another 34 in the Conference during his four years at Feethams. Yes, indeed, a real soccer nomad.

PUCKETT, David Charles

Midfield: 7 apps.

Born: Southampton, 29 October 1960.
Career: Merry Oak School (Southampton), Southampton (apprentice, March 1977, professional, November 1978), Nottingham Forest (on loan, October–November 1983), AFC Bournemouth (July 1986), POTTERS (on loan, March–May 1988), Swansea City (on loan, November 1988), Aldershot (on loan, January 1989, signed permanently for £25,000, April 1989), AF Bournemouth (free transfer, March 1992), Woking (free, June 1993), Newport-Isle-of-Wight (1996–97).

■ A midfield player with good vision and a terrific engine, David Puckett struggled to maintain a degree of consistency, hence his association with so many different clubs. He did suffer a lot with injuries during his career but always bounced back. Something of a penalty expert, he once had a run of 19 consecutive conversions from the spot. He was the first Southampton player to top 50 appearances as a substitute, and he actually came off the bench on 65 occasions during a career total of 309 first-team appearances. He took responsibility in Stoke's midfield when both Gerry Daly and Carl Beeston were sidelined. He helped Woking reach the Final of the FA Umbro Trophy in 1995.

PUGH, David Henry

Utility forward: 20 apps. 1 goal.

Born: Wrexham, 1875.
Died: Waddington, Lincolnshire, 26 May 1945.
Career: Wrexham Grosvenor, Wrexham (May 1895), POTTERS (May 1897), Lincoln City (March 1898, retired, May 1902), played cricket for St Andrew's CC (Lincoln) and made 1 appearance for Lincolnshire in the Minor Counties competition (1909).

■ A Welsh international (seven caps gained between 1896 and 1901, four against Scotland), Dai Pugh had good dribbling ability and, at times, was described as 'a brilliant footballer with plenty of pluck, even when roughly handled'. He was basically an orthodox outside-right but was played in the inside-right berth by the Potters. He won a Welsh Cup winners' medal with Wrexham in 1897, having gained a runners'-up prize 12 months earlier. His only goal for the Potters was a beauty, struck home with power in a 2–1 League defeat at Bolton in November 1897.

RAISBECK, Alexander Galloway

Utility: 8 apps. 1 goal.

Born: Polmont, Stirlingshire, 26 December 1878.
Died: Liverpool, 12 March 1949.
Career: Blantyre Boys' Brigade, Larkhall Thistle, Royal Albert, Edinburgh Hibernian (May 1896), POTTERS (March 1898), Liverpool (£350, May 1898), Partick Thistle (£500, June 1909), Hamilton Academical, secretary-manager, April 1914, retired to become a director, 1917, also manager), Bristol City (manager, December 1921–June 1929), Halifax Town (secretary-manager, July 1930–May 1936), Chester (manager, June 1936–April 1938), Bath City (manager season 1938–39), Liverpool (scout from 1945 until his demise).

■ Alex Raisbeck was a class performer, able to play in a number of positions, including full-back, centre-half, outside-right (where he began his career) and as an inside-forward. One of the few footballers ever to wear spectacles out on the field, he was one of seven brothers and played junior and intermediate football in and around Stirlingshire as a teenager, and in 1897 represented the Scottish League against The Football League. He joined the Potters at the age of 19 and appeared in eight games at the end of the 1897–98 season, and his presence in the four vital Test Matches certainly went a long way in helping the team retain its First Division status. Then, surprisingly, he chose to leave The Victoria Ground for Liverpool, and while at Anfield he won the first of eight full international caps (seven against England) and also collected three more Inter-League XI caps. He helped the Merseysiders win two League Championships in 1901 and 1906, also gaining a Second Division winners' medal in 1905. He scored 21 goals in 340 League and Cup games for the 'Reds' in 11 tremendous seasons at Anfield before returning to Scotland. During World War One he became a Director and team manager of Hamilton and later moved back to England to manage teams in lower Divisions. He unfortunately fell out with the board of Directors at Chester, and after a brief spell with Bath City he became a scout for Liverpool, a job he held until his death. In his book, *Liverpool – A Complete Record*, Brian Pead's pen-picture on Raisbeck stated 'Restless energy marked him as a dedicated professional. He was an aggressive but fair player, a hard tackler, swift to recover.' One contemporary soccer writer described Raisbeck as 'an intelligent automation… pulsating in his finger tips with the joy of life.'

RALPHS, Bertram Victor

Wing-forward: 96 apps. 6 goals.

Born: Handsworth, Birmingham, November 1896.
Died: Stoke-on-Trent, c.1973.
Career: Dennisons FC (Birmingham), Reading (May 1914), Nuneaton Town (1915), guest for Blackpool (1917–18), Blackburn Rovers (£1.500, January 1921), POTTERS (£400, July 1922), Chesterfield (July 1926), Crewe Alexandra (August 1927), Stafford Rangers, (June 1929, retired through injury, May 1930), later ran a tailoring business in Stoke.

■ Bert Ralphs had an interesting career as a 'fast and enterprising' winger who occasionally played as an inside-forward. He gained experience by making 13 appearances for Blackpool during World War One and then scored six goals in 41 games for Blackburn prior to his transfer to the Potters. His best spell during his four years at The Victoria Ground came in 1924–25 when he was an ever-present, scoring twice. He eventually lost his right-wing position to Josh Williams (signed from Huddersfield Town). He made 224 League appearances during his career (23 goals).

RAMSEY, David Robert

Utility: 47 apps. 5 goals.

Born: Stoke-on-Trent, 1864.
Died: before 1945.
Career: Burlsem Port Vale (April 1886), POTTERS (August 1888), Newton Heath, West Manchester, Northwich Victoria, Burslem Port Vale (October 1893, released, May 1894).

■ The versatile Bob Ramsey joined the Potters just in time to start the first season of League football. Initially a full-back, he lined up at right-half in Stoke's opening game in the 'new' competition against West Bromwich Albion, which was lost 2–0, and the following season had the pleasure of scoring the Potters first-ever League hat-trick in a 7–1 home win over Accrington on 1 March 1890. He actually played in every outfield position for the club. His career ended following his release by Port Vale in 1894 because a knee joint kept slipping out of place. He claimed just one goal in 90 outings for the Valiants.

RANDALL, Paul

Utility forward: 41+10 apps. 8 goals.

Born: Liverpool, 16 December 1958.
Career: Bristol Rovers (apprentice, April 1976), Frome Town (October 1976), Bristol Rovers (professional, August 1977), POTTERS (£180,000, December 1978), Bristol Rovers (£55,000, January 1981), Yeovil Town (free transfer, March 1986), Bath City (1989–90), became groundsman at Tor Leisure Centre, later worked in industry, now lives in Glastonbury, Somerset.

■ Paul Randall, although born on Merseyside, moved south to start his career, eventually entering League football with Bristol Rovers at the age of 18, having been rejected by the Eastville club as an apprentice. He scored on his debut for Rovers against Cardiff City and netted 35 goals in 56 games for the Pirates before transferring to Stoke for a record incoming fee for the West country club. He immediately helped the Potters achieve promotion to the First Division but his chances were few in the top flight and he decided to return to Rovers after just two years at The Victoria Ground. He went on to score a total of 105 goals in 258 senior games for the Bristol club.

RANDLES, Thomas

Inside-forward: 2 apps.

Born: Blackpool, 13 October 1940.
Career: Ellesmere Port, POTTERS (£1,500, February 1960), New South Wales, Australia (May 1960), later with Canterbury, New Zealand (1965).

■ Stoke City manager Tony Waddington signed inside-forward Tommy Randles to boost his first-team squad. He remained in the reserves for practically all of his stay at The Victoria Ground, appearing in just two senior games, both in April 1962, his second away at Liverpool in front of 41,000 fans.

RATCLIFFE, Donald

Forward: 260 apps. 19 goals.

Born: Newcastle-under-Lyme, 13 November 1934.
Career: POTTERS (amateur, April 1950, professional, November 1951), Middlesbrough (£30,000, September 1963), Crewe Alexandra, Northwich Victoria.

■ The versatile Don Ratcliffe had an excellent career with Stoke City, playing in all five forward-line positions while

appearing in more than 250 first-team matches. He gained a regular place in the first team in 1957 and was a member of Stoke's 1963 Second Division Championship-winning team. Ratcliffe gave the fans an enormous amount of pleasure with his performances, both at home and away, as he was a marvellous competitor.

RATHBONE. Frederick

Goalkeeper: 32 apps.

Born: Meir, Stoke-on-Trent, 3 August 1885.
Died: before 1960.
Career: May Bank Sunday School, Newcastle Rangers, POTTERS (professional, August 1906), Whitchurch (October 1908), POTTERS (December 1908), Winsford United (May 1912). Did not play after World War One.

■ Fred Rathbone had two spells with Stoke. He joined the club on his 21st birthday, having earlier played church football like so many other players at that time. He had to contest the number one spot initially with Welshman Dicky Roose and Ike Turner and then with the likes of Arthur Box, Bert Miller, Fred Wain, Harry Cotton, Jack Robinson, Tom Baddeley, Jack Baxter and Horace Bailey. When Dick Herron was introduced between the sticks in 1910–11 Rathbone's career at Stoke was over. Indeed, he never got much activity in the first XI until the second half of the 1908–09 campaign when he made 18 appearances – this after having had a brief sojourn away from the Potters with Whitchurch.

RAYNOR, Albert Edward

Wing-half or Inside-forward: 4 apps.

Born: Salford, 18 August 1932.
Career: Northwich Victoria, POTTERS (May 1955), Chelmsford Town (May 1960).

■ Reserve forward Ted Raynor made just four appearances for the Potters in a five-year stay at the club in 1955–60. His League debut was against Grimsby Town in August 1956 when he deputised for Johnny Sellars at right-half. His last two were on the left-wing at the end of the 1959–60 season.

REECE, Paul John

Goalkeeper: 2 apps.

Born: Nottingham, 17 July 1968.
Career: POTTERS (apprentice, July 1984, professional, July 1986), Kettering Town, Grimsby Town (July 1988), Kettering Town, Doncaster Rovers (non-contract, September 1992), Oxford United (free, October 1992), Notts County (August 1994), West Bromwich Albion (free, August 1995), Ilkeston Town (on loan, March 1996, signed permanently, July 1996), Woking (February 1997), later with Cliftonville, Ireland (2000–02).

■ Surprisingly, during his 12-year professional career, goalkeeper Paul Reece, who was a fine shot-stopper on his day, made only 108 League appearances, including 54 for Grimsby Town and 39 for Oxford. Rather on the small side, standing a fraction under 5ft 10in tall, his two League games for the Potters,came in April 1987 when he replaced Peter Fox against Shrewsbury Town and Barnsley, saving a penalty against the Tykes. He teamed up with Hans Segers at Woking.

REGIS, David

Striker: 62+16 apps. 20 goals.

Born: Paddington, London, 3 March 1964.
Career: Dunstable Town (1982), Fisher Athletic (1984), Windsor & Eton (1985),

Barnet (1986), Notts County (£25,000, September 1990), Plymouth Argyle (£200,000, November 1991), AFC Bournemouth (on loan, August 1992), POTTERS (£100,000, October 1992), Birmingham City (£400,000, exchange deal involving Paul Peschisolido, August 1994), Southend United (September 1994), Barnsley (February 1996), Peterborough United (on loan, October 1996), Notts County (on loan, February 1997), Scunthorpe United (on loan, August 1997), Leyton Orient (non-contract, October 1997), Lincoln City (non-contract, December 1997–January 1998), Scunthorpe United (non-contract, February 1998, retired, March 1998), later with Notts County (School of Excellence), Nottingham Forest (Academy), now a director in a company that organises sports and business scholarships in the US and Canada.

■ Brother of the former England international Cyrille Regis, Dave Regis was also a well-built striker at 6ft 3in tall with good speed and a strong shot. After serving with seven clubs he became manager Lou Macari's record buy when he joined the Potters in 1992. Regis scored some cracking goals during his stay at The Victoria Ground and gained a Second Division Championship medal (1993) before moving to St Andrew's at the start of the 1994–95 season. He spent only a month with the Blues, moving to Southend where he was sidelined for 12 weeks after a cartilage operation. He failed to hold down a regular place in the side at Oakwell and was loaned out by manager Danny Wilson to three different clubs before joining Orient in 1997. 'Big Dave' scored 64 goals in a career total of 259 League and Cup games. He was a ClubCall Cup-winner with Barnet in 1989.
* Another cousin, John Regis, was a champion and Olympic athlete with Great Britain, and striker Jason Roberts (Wigan Athletic) is his nephew.

RENNIE, Paul Andrew

Full-back or centre-half: 5+1 apps.

Born: Nantwich, Cheshire, 9 May 1970.
Career: Crewe Alexandra (apprentice, May 1986, POTTERS (trialist, June 1990, signed for £20,000 as a full-time professional, May 1990), Wigan Athletic (on loan, March 1993, signed, free transfer, August 1993, released, May 1995).

■ Paul Rennie completed his two-year YTS apprenticeship at Gresty Road, and after 21 games he went for trails with Stoke City. He did well and was taken on as a full-time professional at The Victoria Ground in 1988, with a fee going to the 'Alex' and an agreement was made for a further cash payment to go to Crewe in respect of appearances and a percentage of any subsequent sale. There was to be no further cash adjustment as Rennie was restricted to just six first-team outings owing to the presence, in the main, of John Butler, and he left the club for Wigan on a free transfer in 1993.

REVILL, Thomas Frederick

Forward: 74 apps. 24 goals.

Born: Bolsover, Derbyshire, 9 May 1892. Died: Mansfield, 29 March 1979. Career: Chesterfield, POTTERS (January 1912), Chesterfield (April 1914). Did not play after World War One, also played for Derbyshire CCC (1913–20).

■ One of the few cricketer-footballers to play for Stoke, Charlie Revill served Derbyshire as a middle-order batsman and occasional leg-break/googly bowler for seven years either side of World War One, scoring 231 runs in 20 innings with an average of 14.43. He was a useful footballer too, and netted a goal every three games for the Potters before returning to the Spireites. Standing only 5ft 6in tall, he gave as good as he got out on the pitch and missed only five competitive games during his time at The Victoria Ground.

RICE, Brian

Midfield: 18 apps.

Born: Bellshill, Lanarkshire, Scotland, 11 October 1963. Career: Bellshill & District Schools, Glasgow Youth Club, Whitburn Central, Hibernian (junior, 1979, amateur, 1980, professional, October 1980), Nottingham Forest (August 1985), Grimsby Town (on loan, October 1986), West Bromwich Albion (on loan, January–February 1989), POTTERS (on loan, February 1991), Port Vale (on loan, March–April 1991), Falkirk (August 1991), Dundee (August 1994), Dunfermline Athletic (October 1995), Clyde (August 1997), Morton (assistant manager-coach, March 2000–May 2002).

■ Red-haired Scottish youth and under-21 international midfielder Brian Rice, predominantly left-footed, made his debut for the Potters in a 1–0 League defeat at Southend in February 1991. He had gained a lot of experience north of the border, being introduced to League football by Hibs against Motherwell as a 16-year-old. A strong running player who preferred to occupy the left-hand side of the park, he gained one under-21 cap for Scotland.

RICHARDSON, Frank

Centre or inside-forward: 14 apps. 3 goals.

Born: Barking, 29 January 1897. Died: 19 May 1987. Career: Barking (1915), served in the Army during World War One, Plymouth Argyle (May 1921), POTTERS (March 1923), West Ham United (March 1924), Swindon Town (June 1925), Reading (August 1926), Swindon Town (May 1930), Mansfield Town (May 1931, retired through injury, September 1931).

■ Frank Richardson had a fine scoring record as a professional, netting 132 goals in 271 League games while serving with five major clubs. He made a terrific start to League football, hitting a hat-trick on his debut for Plymouth, and claimed 31 goals in his first season at Home Park. He scored only once in his first 12 games for the Potters. He was 90 when he died in 1987.

RICHARDSON, Frazer

Right-back or midfield: 12+1 apps. 1 goal.

Born: Rotherham, 29 October 1982. Career: Leeds United (apprentice, April 1998, professional, November 1999), POTTERS (on loan, January–February 2001 and November–December 2003).

■ An England youth international, Frazer Richardson's opportunities were limited at Elland Road and he benefited his career by having two decent loan spells with the Potters, for whom he scored his only goal in a 1–0 League win at West Ham in December 2003.

RICHARDSON, Paul

Midfield: 137+5 apps. 11 goals.

Born: Shirebrook, 25 October 1949. Career: Nottingham Forest (apprentice, August 1965, professional, August 1967), Chester (October 1976), POTTERS (£50,000, June 1977), Sheffield United (£25,000, August 1981), Blackpool (on loan, January 1983), Swansea City (non-contract, September–December 1984, retired as player, January 1985), Gloucester City (manager, seasons 1985–87), Fairford FC (manager, 1988–89), now works for British telecom.

■ Paul Richardson was a splendid midfielder, tall and stylish, who could score goals as well as make them. He spent 10 years at The City Ground, during which time he scored 21 goals in 248 appearances. After just one outing for Chester, Stoke manager George Eastham moved in and brought him to The Victoria Ground in 1977, and it proved to be money well spent as Richardson gave the Potters great service, scoring the vital promotion-clinching goal at Notts County on the last day of the 1978–79 season. He took charge of Fairford FC while also working for British Telecom. The

recipient of four England youth caps, Richardson amassed a League record of 435 appearances (32 goals).

RICKETTS, Michael Barrington

Striker: 1+10 apps.

Born: Birmingham, 4 December 1978.
Career: Walsall (apprentice, April 1995, professional, September 1996), Bolton Wanderers (£500,000, July 2000), Middlesbrough (£2.2 million, January 2003), Leeds United (free, July 2004), POTTERS (on loan, February–May 2005).

■ An England international, capped against Holland in February 2002, Michael Ricketts scored 15 goals for

Walsall and 46 for Bolton, but then found it hard going in the Premiership with Middlesbrough after manager Steve McClaren had secured the services of Jimmy-Floyd Hasselbaink and Mark Viduka, with Josephe-Desire Job already at the club. A League Cup winner in 2004 as a substitute, he is a positive front-runner, keen and aggressive, who made his debut for the Potters against Leicester (won 3–2).

RIPLEY, Stanley

Half-back: 1 app.

Born: Seaham, County Durham, 1893.
Died: France, 1916.
Career: Seaham Harbour (1911), POTTERS (August 1914 until his death).

■ Sadly, Stan Ripley, a keen tackling half-back, was killed in action while serving in France in 1916. He played in one Southern League game against Brentford in December 1914 when he deputised for Charlie Parker, allowing Joey Jones to switch to centre-half.

RISOM, Henrik

Midfield: 16+18 apps.

Born: Denmark, 24 July 1968.
Career: Vejle Boldklub, Denmark (professional, March 1986), Lyngby FC, Denmark (August 1991), 1 FC Dynamo Dresden, Germany (January 1994), Odsense Boldklub, Denmark (November 1994), Silkeborg Idraets Forening, Denmark (October 1995), Vejle Boldklub (December 1997), POTTERS (August 2000), Aarthus Gymnastik Forening, Denmark (July 2001).

■ A Danish international capped nine times at senior level, Henrik Risom was a holding midfielder, vastly experienced, whose main strengths were his passing and deliveries from set pieces. Signed at the age of 32, he spent just the one season at The Britannia Stadium before being released by manager Gudjon Thordarson. Prior to joining the Potters, Risom had appeared in 345 League games for his previous clubs.

RITCHIE, John

Striker: 332+11 apps. 171 goals.

Born: Kettering, 12 July 1941.
Career: Kettering Town (August 1958), POTTERS (June 1962), Sheffield Wednesday (November 1966), POTTERS (£25,000, July 1969), Stafford Rangers (May 1975, retired, January 1976), opened a pottery business in Stoke-on-Trent selling crockery to hotels and restaurants.

■ Stoke City's champion marksman of all-time, John Ritchie scored a goal every two games for the club during two spells at The Victoria Ground. Signed for just £2,5000 in 1962 – manager Tony Waddington gambled on a footballer he had never seen play! That gamble paid off in a big way. He made only five senior appearances in his first season at The 'Vic' as Stoke won the Second Division title. But from then on, after hours of hard work on the training ground, he developed into a terrific goalscorer. He became a regular in the side during the following campaign when he netted 30 times in 42 games as Stoke reached the League Cup Final. Performing alongside the experienced professionals Dennis Viollet, Jimmy McIlroy and Peter Dobing boosted Ritchie's confidence no end, and it came as a massive shock to everyone associated with Stoke City football club when he moved to Sheffield Wednesday in 1966 without there being an adequate replacement in the camp. Manager Waddington publicly admitted that he had made a big mistake by selling Ritchie, and two and a half years later he bought the big fella back 'home' for a cut-down price of £25,000. The Potters favourite striker had done very well at Hillsborough, gaining Football League representative honours against the League of Ireland in Dublin in November 1967, when he scored twice in a 7–2 win while claiming 45 goals in 106 outings for the Owls. Ritchie immediately began to hit the net once again for Stoke, securing 16 goals in his first season 'back in the fold'. Wearing the blessed number 9 shirt, he was a constant threat for defenders up and down the country. He certainly played his part as Stoke reached successive FA Cup semi-finals in 1971 and 1972, while also in the

John Ritchie

latter year he was as proud as anyone as he helped the Potters win their first-ever major trophy, beating Chelsea 2–1 in the League Cup at Wembley. A complicated double fracture of the leg effectively ended his playing career, although after leaving Stoke he did have a handful of games for Stafford Rangers. On retiring, Ritchie concentrated on his pottery business based near to The Victoria Ground. His son, David, was on Stoke City's books for a short time, under manager Alan Ball, but was transferred to Stockport County for £10,000 without making the Potters first XI.
NB: Coming on as substitute for the Potters in their away UEFA Cup game with Kaiserslautern in Germany in 1972, Ritchie was sent-off after just 29 seconds for throwing a punch at an opponent. He never touched the ball and this is regarded as one of the fastest dismissals in football history from the time a player took to the field.

ROBERTS, Arthur

Inside-forward: 2 apps.

Born: Newcastle-under-Lyme, c.1876.
Died: Stoke-on-Trent, c.1950.
Career: Newcastle Casuals, POTTERS (January–May 1900), Tunstall Rangers (August 1900).

Reserve inside-forward Arthur Roberts spent just over four months at The Victoria Ground, playing in the League games against Derby County and West Bromwich Albion in March 1900 in the absence of Love Jones.

ROBERTS, Stuart William

Goalkeeper: 5 apps.

Born: Chirk, 25 March 1967.
Career: Chirk Council School, Newtown, Oswestry Town (1982), POTTERS (apprentice, April 1983, professional, March 1985), Derry City (May 1986).

■ After developing through the intermediate and reserve-team ranks at The Victoria Ground, 6ft 2in goalkeeper Stuart Roberts went on to appear in three First Division matches and two FA Cup ties for the Potters in season 1984–85. In fact, he became the club's youngest-ever 'keeper, at the age of 17, to play in the senior side when he made his debut against Ipswich Town on 8 December 1984. As a teenager, he won youth international honours for Wales.

ROBERTSON, James

Inside or centre-forward: 68 apps. 21 goals.

Born: Dundee, July 1868.
Died: Scotland, c.1950.
Career: Dundee United, POTTERS (August 1892), Ashton North End (March 1895), Ardwick (March 1896), Dundee Wanderers (September 1896–1900).

■ Scottish utility forward Jimmy Robertson was a useful marksman who had a good scoring record with the Potters. He was injured during the 1894–95 season and played in only 10 first-team matches. He helped Ardwick (Manchester City) clinch the runners-up spot in the Second Division during his brief stay with the Lancashire club.

ROBERTSON, James Gillen

Outside-right: 121+18 apps. 14 goals.

Born: Cardonald, Glasgow, 17 December 1944.
Career: Middlesbrough, Celtic (March 1959), Cowdenbeath (amateur, August 1959), St Mirren (professional, April 1962), Tottenham Hotspur (£25,000, May 1964), Arsenal (£55,000 plus David Jenkins, October 1968), Ipswich Town (March 1970), POTTERS (June 1972), Seattle Sounders, NASL (summers of 1976 and 1977), Walsall (September 1977), Crewe Alexandra (September 1978, retired, May 1979), later worked for the Task Force Group, a computer insurance company.

■ A fast-raiding, skilful and highly effective right-winger, Jimmy Robertson had been on schoolboy forms at Middlesbrough and a part-time player with Celtic before signing for Cowdenbeath in 1959. He made his Scottish League debut as a 16-year-old and won both youth and Amateur caps for his country before being taken on as a professional by St Mirren in 1962. Three months after winning the first of four under-23 caps, he moved to Tottenham Hotspur. He became a huge favourite at White Hart Lane, scoring 43 goals in 215 appearances for Spurs in four and a half years with the club, gaining his only full cap against Wales in 1964 and collecting an FA Cup winners' medal against Chelsea in 1967. In the autumn of 1968 Robertson made the short trip across North London to Arsenal in a cash/exchange deal that saw David Jenkins travel in the opposite direction. It was not one of Bill Nicholson's best decisions as Spurs boss, as Robertson still had plenty of football left in him. He spent two years with the Gunners, scoring seven goals in 46 League games before going on to net 10 times in 87 First Division outings for Ipswich. He then gave the Potters five years' excellent service, appearing in almost 140 senior games while also spending two summers playing in the North American Soccer League. After leaving The Victoria Ground he assisted in League appearances for Walsall for a season and ended his career at Gresty Road. On retiring from competitive football in 1979, Robertson become involved with a computer insurance company, of which he later was made a Director.

ROBERTSON, John Thomas

Defender: 100 apps. 2 goals.

Born: Newton Mearns, Renfrewshire, 1877.
Died: Hove, Sussex, 1948.
Career: Newton Thistle, Edinburgh St Bernard's (1891), Hibernian (professional, May 1894), POTTERS (£90, May 1897), Liverpool (April 1900), Southampton (May 1902), Brighton & Hove Albion (June 1904, retired, May 1906), stayed in Hove where he ran a pub for many years.

■ Stoke imported several Scottish players during the late 1890s/early 1900s and rugged defender Jack Robertson was one of them. A brave and daring player, he could play at right-back or centre-half and made an impact in his first season at The Victoria Ground, appearing in 25 League games. He continued to impress and scored two penalties in his last campaign in away games against Notts County (won 3-1) and Aston Villa (lost 4-1). Prior to joining the Potters, he was the recipient of a Scottish Cup runners'-up medal with Hibs in 1896 and made over 40 senior appearances during his association with the Edinburgh club. In his first season at Anfield he helped Liverpool win the Football League title and afterwards skippered the reserves. He later won two Southern League Championship medals with the Saints in 1903 and 1904.

* Some reference books have the playing careers and statistics of James Robertson and John Thomas Robertson mixed up.

ROBERTSON, William Harold

Goalkeeper: 250 apps.

Born: Crowthorne near Reading, 25 March 1923.
Died: Reading, 1973.
Career: Crowthorne Boys' Club, Camberley Auxillary Training Corps, Aldershot (August 1938), RAF Lossiemouth (from 1940), Chelsea (professional, October 1945), Birmingham City (£2,500, November 1948), POTTERS (£8,100, June 1952, retired, May 1960), later ran a newsagents in Bucknall, Stoke-on-Trent, before moving back to his roots in Berkshire.

■ Bill Robertson, 6ft 1in tall and 14st in weight, was a centre-forward before joining the forces. He top-scored for ATC (Camberley) when they won the Aldershot Minor League in 1938, his only prize in football. He was persuaded to take up goalkeeping during World War Two, and the decision proved right as he developed into a quality performer, being a fine shot-stopper with good reflexes, although it seems he was a shade hesitant at times. He made his senior debut for Chelsea against Leicester City in a third-round FA Cup tie in January 1946, and played 27 games in the League South that season before sharing the number-1 spot with Harry Medhurst during the next two campaigns. Said to have had a pair of hands larger than any other goalkeeper in the land, Robertson made just three appearances for Birmingham City before giving the Potters grand service for eight years. After taking over from Dennis Herod, he accumulated 250 first-team appearances, a record for a Potters 'keeper at that time, later beaten by Peter Fox who surpassed it in the 1980s. He kept 58 clean sheets for the Potters, this after recovering from a broken leg suffered in 1953.

ROBERTSON, William Seymour

Right-half: 126 apps. 3 goals

Born: Falkirk, 20 April 1907.
Died: 1980.
Career: Third Lanark (professional, July 1924), Ayr United (May 1926), POTTERS (£1,500, October 1929) Manchester United (£750, March 1934), Reading (free transfer, January 1936, retired, May 1937).

■ Billy Robertson was a tenacious, stern-tackling right-half who worked for a bath manufacturer in his native Scotland while also playing for Third Lanark and Ayr United, helping the latter club win the Scottish League 'B' Division by a margin of nine points over his former club in 1928! When he signed for the Potters the following year he was regarded as one of the best half-backs north of the Border. A Second Division Championship winner in 1932–33, he made over 125 appearances during his four and half year stay at The Victoria Ground. He was also a success at Old Trafford, making 50 appearances for the 'Reds' before winding down his career with Reading.

ROBINSON, JOHN

Outside-right: 8 apps.

Born: Birmingham, 1887.
Died: before 1980.
Career: Aston Villa (1907), POTTERS (amateur, August 1911), King's Heath, Birmingham (May 1912). Did not play after World War One.

■ Jack Robinson was a regular reserve with Aston Villa before spending a season with Stoke, playing in eight first-team games between September and November 1911.

ROBINSON, John William

Goalkeeper: 67 apps.

Born: Derby, 22 April 1870.
Died: Derby, 28 October 1931.
Career: Derby Midland, Lincoln City (January 1889), Derby County (£200, June 1891), New Brighton Tower (£200, August 1897), Southampton (£400, May 1898), Plymouth Argyle (£250, April 1903), Millwall (£300, November 1905), Exeter City (£100, December 1905), Green Waves, Plymouth (free transfer, October 1906), Exeter City (free, November 1908), POTTERS (free, May 1909), Rochester, New York (free, October 1912, retired, 1914, aged 44), returned to England in 1915 to take over a pub in Southampton and later became an insurance agent in Turnditch near Derby. In December 1922 he was seriously injured when falling from an upstairs window of a house and as a result suffered from epilepsy

■ Jack Robinson, an agile and daring goalkeeper, had spent six excellent seasons with Derby County and broken into the England team when, in 1897, he rocked the club by joining New Brighton Tower. An FA commission, held in Manchester on 11 August, ruled that the registration was invalid as the club was not affiliated. Only after New

Brighton joined the FA via the Cheshire FA did the transfer go through and a blunt, contemporary report gave the opinion 'If Robinson thinks he can enhance his reputation by joining a mushroom organisation like the New Brighton club, whose purse may not always be so heavy as at present, he has done well to leave Derby.' It did not do Robinson any harm as he retained his England place and, a year later, joined Southampton. At The Dell he took his total of England caps to 11, played in two FA Cup Final defeats, by Bury in 1900 and Sheffield United in 1902, and was involved in three Southern League Championships in 1898–99, 1900–01 and 1902–03. He was 39 years of age when he joined the Potters. Nevertheless, he was still fit enough to appear regularly for two seasons before Arthur Cartilage and Dick Herron pushed him out. He was over 40 years of age when he played in his last game for the Potters against Reading in February 1911. He represented the Devon County Select XI in 1907–08.
* Robinson was reported to the FA in 1900 for allegedly trying to poach Steve Bloomer for Southampton. Two years later, in October 1902, he was suspended after an incident at New Brompton, whereby he struck a spectator in the face, and two months after that he was cautioned by the FA for an article in the press about the same incident. Then, in November 1910, when registered with Stoke, he was suspended again, this time for alleged insubordination after a Birmingham League match. He may have been a wayward character but for four years Robinson was indisputably the best goalkeeper in England. It was a pity Stoke didn't sign him sooner!

ROBINSON Marvin Leon St Clair

Forward: 3 apps. 1 goal.

Born: Crewe, 11 April 1980.
Career: Derby County (apprentice, May 1996, professional, July 1998), POTTERS (on loan, September 2000), Tranmere Rovers (on loan, November 2002), Chesterfield (September 2003–May 2004).

■ The career of England schoolboy international Marvin Robinson suffered a major setback when he joined the Potters on loan from Derby, suffering a broken leg in only his third game for the club against Rotherham United. A big, strong lad, he had got off to a great start by scoring on his debut versus Oxford United. Recovery from the severe injury took over a year and there were few chances for him at Derby. After his release in 2003 Chesterfield gave him a fresh start with a one-year contract.

ROBINSON, Philip John

Defender or Midfield: 61+10 apps. 2 goals.

Born: Stafford, 6 January 1967.
Career: Rising Brook High School (Stafford), Stafford & District Schools, Aston Villa (groundstaff aged 14, apprentice, June 1983, professional, January 1985), Wolverhampton Wanderers (£5,000, June 1987), Notts County (£67,500, August 1989), Birmingham City (on loan, March 1991), Huddersfield Town (£50,000, September 1992), Northampton Town (on loan, September 1994), Chesterfield (£15,000, December 1994), Notts County (£80,000, August 1996), POTTERS (free transfer, June 1998), Hereford United (player-manager-coach, August 2000), Stafford Rangers (manager, May 2002), also a qualified physiotherapist.

■ Equally adept in defence or midfield, red-haired Phil Robinson always gave a good account of himself. After scoring once in three senior games for Villa, he joined Wolves and went on to play in 90 first-team games for the Molineux club (nine goals), helping them win both the Fourth and Third Division Championships as well as the Sherpa Van Trophy at Wembley. He was a key member of Notts County's Third Division promotion-winning side in 1990 and helped Birmingham lift the Leyland DAF Cup at Wembley a year later. After giving Chesterfield, Notts County (again) and the Potters good service, Robinson ventured into physiotherapy while playing for Hereford, after succeeding his former Wolves boss Graham Turner as team manager. One of Brian Little's first signings for Stoke, he made his debut in a red and white striped shirt at right-back against Northampton Town at The Sixfields in August 1998, and during a lengthy career he appeared in 534 games at competitive level, scoring 51 goals.

ROBSON, Harold Robert

Full-back: 1 app.

Born: Gateshead, 15 April 1897.
Died: Gateshead, 22 September 1962.
Career: Usworth Colliery (County Durham), POTTERS (July 1923), Southport (£50, February 1926).

■ Reserve full-back Bob Robson's only League appearance for the Potters came in a 5–1 defeat away at Wolverhampton Wanderers in February 1926. He won the Military Medal in 1916 as a 19-year-old in the Battle of the Somme for attending to the injured while badly wounded himself.

ROBSON, William Paisley

Centre-forward: 14 apps. 6 goals.

Born: Newcastle-upon-Tyne, 14 January 1908.
Died: County Durham, 1974.
Career: Walker Celtic (1926),

Huddersfield Town (trialist, 1929, signed professional, August 1930), Washington Colliery (May 1932), POTTERS (August 1933), Burnley (October 1937–May 1938). Did not play after World War Two.

■ Reserve centre-forward Billy Robson played only 14 first-team games for the Potters during his a four years with the club. Neat and tidy in his ways, he lacked the necessary strength and commitment to make the grade at top-class level.

* His father, William Robson, played eight League games for Hull City in 1910–11.

ROCHE, George

Wing-half: 3 apps.

Born: Birkenhead, 1889.
Died: Liverpool, c.1973.
Career: Liverpool University (from 1907), Preston North End (February 1910), POTTERS (May 1911), Lancaster Town (1912).

■ A former Liverpool University graduate, George Roche appeared in three Southern League games for Stoke in March 1913 having joined the club almost two years earlier.

RODGER, Simon Lee

Midfield: 5 apps.

Born: Shoreham-by-Sea, Sussex, 3 October 1971.
Career: Bognor Regis Town (1988), Crystal Palace (£1,000, July 1990), Manchester City (on loan, October–November 1996), POTTERS (on loan, February 1997), Woking (free, May 2002), Brighton & Hove Albion (free transfer, October 2002).

■ A left-sided midfielder, signed on loan by Potters' manager Lou Macari in 1997, Simon Rodger made his debut in a 2–1 defeat at Southend. Prior to his arrival at The Victoria Ground, he had amassed over 140 appearances for the 'Eagles', whom he helped win the First Division Championship in 1993–94. He missed most of the following season with a back injury but regained full fitness in 1995–96 when Palace reached the Play-off Final at Wembley but were beaten by Leicester City. When he left Selhurst Park in 2002 his record for the club was impressive: 328 senior appearances and 13 goals.

ROGERS, Walter

Left-half: 1 app.

Born: Stoke-on-Trent, 1883.
Died: Stoke-on-Trent, c.1961.
Career: Burslem Port Vale (trialist, 1906), POTTERS (September 1907), Reading (August 1908).

■ A short, stocky player, Walter Rogers joined Stoke with five other players from Port Vale. He appeared in only one League game for Potters in February 1908 when he deputised for Arthur Sturgess against Glossop North End. He moved to Reading when Stoke went bust but returned to the Potteries just prior to World War One.

ROOSE, Leigh Richmond

Goalkeeper: 159 apps.

Born: Holt, Wrexham, Denbighshire, 27 November 1877.
Died: France, 7 October 1916.
Career: UCW Aberystwyth, Aberystwyth Town (1898), Druids (August 1900), London Welsh (soccer), POTTERS (amateur, October 1901), Everton (November 1904), POTTERS (September 1905), Celtic (September 1907), Sunderland (January 1908), Port vale (guest, April 1910), Huddersfield Town (April 1911), Aston Villa (August 1911), Woolwich Arsenal (December 1911), Llandudno Town (seasons 1912–14), joined the 9th Battalion Royal Fusiliers at the outbreak of World War One as a Lance Corporal, but was killed in action, aged 38.

■ The son of a Presbyterian minister, 'Dicky' Roose obtained his early education at the Holt Academy where he was taught for a short time by HG Wells. He took a science degree at the University College of Wales in Aberystwyth and learnt his goalkeeping skills with the town's football team, gaining a Welsh Cup winners' medal almost immediately in 1900. He was a sporting hero when playing for Druids before moving to King's College Hospital in London to train as a doctor, but despite his keen interest in bacteriology he never qualified and remained a perpetual student. On joining Stoke he thought nothing of travelling by train to the Victoria Ground, charging the cost to the club! He once took a horse and carriage to get to a game and on another occasion used someone's bicyle. H. Catton ('Tityrus' of the Athletic News) described Roose as '…dexterous though daring, valiant though volatile.' Another writer was more expansive, stating 'Few men exhibit their personality so vividly in their play as LR Roose. You cannot spend five minutes in his company without being impressed by his vivacity, his boldness, his knowledge of men and

things – a clever man undoubtedly, but one entirely unrestrained in word or action. On the field his whole attention is centered on the game, he rarely stands listlessly by the goalpost even when the ball is at the other end of the enclosure, but is ever following the game keenly and closely'. He was certainly a character and also a very wealthy man, as well as being a marvellously-gifted keeper, who thought nothing of charging some 15-20 yards away from his goal to clear the ball if he thought his defenders were under pressure. He was unorthodox in style when dealing with shots hit straight at him, often double-punching the ball away or even heading it! After Stoke he went to Everton where he replaced the Irish international Billy Scott and played his part as the Merseysiders reached the semi-final of the FA Cup and runners'-up spot in the First Division in 1905. He certainly saved Sunderland from relegation during his time on Wearside and the club wanted to award him a Testimonial match for his efforts, but the FA stepped in and scotched the idea because of Roose's Amateur status. He had to settle instead for an illuminated address, presented to him by the Mayor. An inveterate practical joker, Roose once turned up for a match in Belfast with his hand heavily bandaged, moaning and groaning. With everyone in suspense, wondering whether he was fit or not minutes before kick-off, to the disbelief of the press, he shouted out 'I'm okay', quickly stripped off the dressing and went out and played a blinder! An erratic genius, he never took the field wearing a clean pair of shorts, his boots used to last him for years and generally he had a scruffy appearance about him – but what a star! He won 24 'senior' caps for Wales plus a handful at amateur level (it could and should have been far more in both instances). Quite often he would ask if he could stand down to allow eight times reserve Alf Edwards an opportunity to show his worth. But the FAW would have none of it! Roose was recruited by the Potters to fill the gap vacated by Tom Wilkes. He played in 159 games for the club and during his career amassed well over 300 appearances at club and international levels, and one suspects that he would have carried on longer had he lived.

* His only game for Port Vale was in a vital North Staffordshire District League match against Stoke reserves away on 3 April 1910. With time fast running out and Vale leading 2–0, the home fans swarmed onto the pitch. They surrounded Roose, jostling him to and fro before carrying him off towards the River Trent! Thankfully, stewards and police prevented a serious incident. The game was subsequently abandoned and later Roose agreed to turn out for the Vale 'if required', but alas he was never called into action.

ROUSE, Frederick William

Centre-forward: 73 apps. 26 goals.

Born: Cranford, Middlesex, 28 November 1882.
Died: Buckinghamshire, 1953.
Career: Bracknell & District Schools, Southall, High Wycombe (1900), Wycombe Wanderers (season 1901–02), Shepherd's Bush FC (briefly), Queen's Park Rangers (briefly), Grimsby Town (professional, March 1903), POTTERS (£150, April 1904), Everton (£750, November 1906), Chelsea (£850, October 1907), West Bromwich Albion (£250, May 1909), Croydon Common (September 1910), Brentford (1911–12), Slough Town (1913, retired, c.1915).

■ Described as a 'hefty attacker', Fred Rouse was astonishingly nimble for a centre-forward. He had good control, a useful shot and a witty sense of humour. He played for the Football League in 1905 and 1906 and during a good League career averaged a goal every three games, scoring 58 times in 154 outings. Rouse played his best football at The Victoria Ground, having an excellent 1904–05 season when he netted 12 times in 34 games. He also did well at Grimsby (15 goals in 39 starts). His career realised a total of 104 goals in Football League and Southern League action.

ROUSE, Alfred Valentine

Left-half: 94 apps. 2 goals.

Born: Hoddesdon near Harlow, 14 February 1898.
Died: Hereford, 1961.
Career: Pontypridd (from 1914), Wolverhampton Wanderers (professional, August 1921), POTTERS (£1,000, May 1922), Swansea Town (free transfer, May 1925), Port Vale (free, June 1926) Crewe Alexandra (free, May 1929), Connah's Quay (1930), Shotton (1932, retired, May 1933).

■ 'Vic' Rouse was born on St Valentine's Day, hence his Christian

name. A very efficient left-half, he was discovered by Wolverhampton Wanderers playing in the Southern League, but he failed to adjust to life in the First Division and made only five senior appearances during his brief stay a Molineux before transferring to Stoke. A gentleman on the field (and off it), Rouse quickly settled into the side and made almost 100 appearances for the Potters in three seasons before returning to South Wales. He revisited the Potteries a year later when he signed for Port Vale, for whom he made 103 appearances prior to his transfer to Crewe.

ROWLANDS, Walter

Centre-forward: 1 app.

Born: Hanley, Stoke-on-Trent, 1888.
Died: before 1980.
Career: Munton Juniors, POTTERS (September 1913), Stafford Rangers (April 1914). Did not play after World War One.

■ Reserve centre-forward Wally Rowlands played in only one Southern League game for the Potters versus Pontypridd (away) in April 1914.

ROWLEY, Arthur

Left-back or right-half: 62 apps.

Born: Leek, 1870.
Died: before 1960.
Career: Leek Town, Belfast Distillery, North Staffs Regiment, POTTERS (September 1895), Bristol Rovers (August 1899), Port Vale (September 1902, released, May 1904).

■ Arthur Rowley was a competent wing-half or full-back who left the Army to join the Potters at the age of 25. He appeared in 25 League games during the 1896–97 season, 20 more the following year and in 14 at the start of 1898–99, before he lost his place when Jack Eccles and Robertson established themselves in the two full-back positions and Jimmy Bradley bedded himself in at left-half. After just two outings in three years for Bristol Rovers, Rowley signed for Port Vale, for whom he scored four goals in 69 appearances.

ROWLEY, William Spencer

Goalkeeper: 143 apps.

Born: Hanley, Stoke-on-Trent, July 1865.
Died: US, 12 June 1939.
Career: Initially a postman, Hanley Orion, POTTERS (August 1883), Port Vale (April 1884), POTTERS (professional, August 1886, reclaimed amateur status, 1893, retired as a player, May 1896, appointed secretary-manager, May 1895–August 1897, staying in office as club secretary), came out of retirement to sign for Leicester Fosse (August–October 1898), became a licensee in Stoke-on-Trent before emigrating to the US.

■ Billy Rowley began as a centre-forward with Hanley Orion. Joining Stoke in 1883, he stayed with the cub for barely a season before moving to Burslem Port Vale. By now a goalkeeper, he nevertheless scored a goal for the Valiants in a 12–0 win over Ironbridge in the Final of the Burslem Charity Cup in March 1885. He was bored with having nothing to do so he ventured up field and, with one shot at goal, hit the target. In the midst of controversy, he was transferred back to Stoke at the start of the 1886–87 season. However, there followed a legal hearing at Burslem County Court in the November where it was claimed that Rowley (and George Bateman) had both joined the Potters despite having signed binding contracts with the Vale. Vale's claim was upheld and Stoke were ordered to pay £20 to a Burlsem Charity. The Potters subsequently released both players back to the Vale, only for the pair of them to say that they preferred to stay at The Victoria Ground. Rowley duly made his Potters senior debut on 30 October 1896 in the home FA Cup tie against Caernarvon that resulted in a 10–1 win. A fine and fearless 'keeper, Rowley had an enormous kick, he handled the ball well, and was never afraid to go in where it hurts (when the legs and boots were flying). Consequently, he suffered a lot of injuries, and although he remained as a player with the Potters until his retirement in 1897 he made less than 150 first-team appearances. After starring for Staffordshire in several County matches, he played for the Football League representative side and gained two full England caps – the first in 1889 in a 6–1 win over Ireland, the second, also versus Ireland, in 1892. In the latter game his full-back colleagues were also Stoke players: Tommy Clare and Arthur Underwood. Rowley also helped Stoke win the Football Alliance Championship in 1891. Four years later, and by now registered as an amateur player, Rowley was appointed secretary-manager of Stoke, a position he held until August 1898 when he stepped down in favour of Horace Austerberry. Prior to his resignation, Rowley was involved in an unusual incident whereby he transferred himself to Leicester Fosse for a small signing on fee. He made only one appearance for the 'Foxes' when the FA stepped in and cancelled the transaction.

Fosse were fined £10 for their part in the deal and both Rowley and Leicester's secretary, William Clark, were suspended by the FA Commission for 12 months. A postman by trade, Rowley later became a publican, taking over the Cock Inn in John Street, off Liverpool Road, Stoke-on-Trent.

NB: Rowley had over 60 games for Vale and fractured his right leg playing in a friendly against Stoke, sidelining him for four months. As manager, he saw the Potters win 26 of the 60 League games played during his two seasons in charge.

ROWSON, David Andrew

Right-back or midfield: 11+7 apps.

Born: Aberdeen, 14 September 1976.
Career: FC Stoneywood (Aberdeen), Aberdeen (professional, October 1994), Livingston (on loan, March–April 2000), POTTERS (free transfer, July 2001), Partick Thistle (free, January 2003).

■ A holding midfield player who could also occupy the right-back position, David Rowson made 161 League and Cup appearances for the Dons and another six on loan with Livingston before entering English football with the Potters at the age of 24. It took quite a while for him to establish himself in the side and then, once in, injuries rocked him severely and halfway through the

2002–03 season he moved to Partick Thistle.

ROXBURGH, John Alexander

Inside or outside-left: 14 apps. 1 goal.

Born: Granton, Edinburgh, 10 November 1901.
Died: Sheffield, 1965.
Career: Edinburgh Emmett, Rugby Town, Leicester City (June 1920), Aston Villa (October 1922), POTTERS (February 1924), Sheffield United (August 1925), Sheffield FC (1927–28).

■ John Roxburgh was selected for an England amateur international before his birthplace was confirmed– it was Scotland not Rugby! A winger, full of vim and vigour, he made his League debut for Leicester at the age of 18 in a match against West Ham and went on to score three goals in 50 senior games for the Foxes before moving to Villa Park. He had a useful half-season with Villa after scoring twice on his debut against his future club Stoke, with whom he spent 18 months (14 games) before having a spell at Bramall Lane. Elder brother, Andrew Roxburgh, also played for Leicester Fosse (1920–21) and a third Roxburgh sibling, Walter, had trials at Filbert Street in 1921–22.

RUGGIERO, John Salvatore

Inside-forward: 9 apps. 2 goals.

Born: Blurton, Stoke-on-Trent, 26 November 1954.
Career: POTTERS (apprentice, April 1971, professional, May 1972), Workington (on loan, January–February 1976, Brighton & Hove Albion (£30,000, June 1976), Portsmouth (on loan, December 1977–January 1978), Chester City (April 1979), Telford United (1980), Cape Town City, South Africa (1981–82).

■ Despite his Italian-sounding name, John Ruggerio was born in Stoke and played the Potters as a youngster before turning professional at the age of 17. He was never quite able to establish himself in the first team despite some enterprising displays in the second XI, and after six years at The Victoria Ground he switched his allegiance to Brighton & Hove. He made only 37 League appearances during his career.

RUSSELL, Colin

Centre-forward: 11 apps. 2 goals

Born: Liverpool, 21 January 1961.
Career: Liverpool (apprentice, April 1976, professional, April 1978), Huddersfield Town (£15,000, September 1982), POTTERS (on loan, March–May 1984), AFC Bournemouth (£10,000, August 1984), Doncaster Rovers (£7,000, July 1986), Scarborough (on loan, October 1987, free transfer, November 1987), Wigan Athletic (free, July 1988), Colne Dynamos (May 1989), Bangor City (1991) Morecambe (1992), Droylesden (1993), Warrington Town (1994).

■ Something of a soccer nomad, Colin Russell was an orthodox centre-forward whose career realised 49 goals in 210 League games, having his best spells with Huddersfield and Bournemouth. He scored his first goal for Stoke against his former club Liverpool in a 2–0 win in April 1984.

RUSSELL, Darel Francis Roy

Right-back or Midfield: 97 apps. 6 goals.

Born: Stepney, London, 22 October 1980
Career: Norwich City (apprentice, April 1997, professional November 1997), POTTERS (£125,000, August 2003).

■ An England youth international, Darel Russell made almost 150 senior

appearances for Norwich before moving to the Britannia Stadium. A competitive midfielder with a terrific engine, he is quick, has a good first touch and, after being an ever-present, was duly voted Potters' 'Young Player of the Year' by the fans for 2003–04, appearing in all 50 matches. An adaptable player, he has performed as an orthodox full-back, wing-back and as a central or right-sided midfielder, his natural role. Russell is a huge fan of American filmstar Samuel L. Jackson.

RUSSELL, Kevin John

Midfield: 45+11 apps. 7 goals.

Born: Brighton, 6 December 1966.
Career: Brighton & Hove Albion (apprentice, April 1983), Portsmouth (professional, October 1984), Wrexham (£10,000, July 1987), Leicester City (£175,000, June 1989), Peterborough United (on loan, September–October 1990), Cardiff City (on loan, January–February 1991), Hereford United (on loan, November–December 1991), POTTERS (on loan, January–February 1992, signed for £95,000, July 1992), Burnley (£150,000, June 1993), AFC Bournemouth (£125,000, March 1994), Notts County (£60,000, February 1995), Wrexham (£60,000, July 1995, appointed player-coach, March 2003, retired as a player, June 2003, assistant-manager, August

2004, then player-assistant manager, 2004–05).*

■ Easily spotted by his bald head, Colin 'Rooster' Russell was a midfield grafter and a tireless performer who worked his socks off every game he played in. During a wonderful nomadic career he amassed a total of 551 senior appearances at club level and scored 95 goals. His best performances came with Wrexham, for whom he netted 70 of his goals in 340 games over a combined period of 10 years. An England youth international (capped when with Brighton), he helped Stoke win the Second Division title in 1993.

SALE, Mark David

Striker: 0+2 apps.
Born: Rugeley, Staffs, 27 February 1972.
Career: POTTERS (apprentice, April 1988, professional, July 1990), Yeovil Town (on loan, March–May 1991), Cambridge United (July 1991), Stafford Rangers (trialist, August–September 1991), Rocester (October 1991), Birmingham City (March 1992), Torquay United (March 1993), Preston North End (August 1994), Mansfield Town (£50,000, July 1995), Colchester United (March 1997), Rushden & Diamonds (July 1999), Doncaster Rovers (May 2001), Alfreton Town (2003).

■ Lanky 6ft 5in striker Mark Sale made just two substitute appearances for Stoke. He joined the club as a youngster and turned 'pro' at the age of 18. Unable to establish himself with any of his three League clubs, he had a trial with Stafford Rangers before moving to Rocester, only to return to Football League action with the Blues in 1992.

SALE, Thomas

Centre-forward or inside-left: 223 apps. 103 goals

Born: Stoke-on-Trent, 30 April 1910.
Died: Stafford, 10 November 1990.
Career: Stoke St Peter's, POTTERS (amateur, August 1929, professional May 1930), Blackburn Rovers (£6,000, March 1936), POTTERS (March 1938), Northwich Victoria (June 1947), Hednesford Town (August 1948, retired, July 1949).

■ Tommy Sale accumulated a superb scoring record with the Potters. In 483 first-team appearances in two spells with the club he netted 282 goals – 98 in 204 League games, five in 19 FA Cup matches and 179 in 260 World War Two fixtures. He worked in a pottery factory as a 14-year-old, playing for Stoke's adopted nursery (St Peter's) before signing for the Potters in 1929. He made his League debut on Christmas Day versus Bradford City a year later and quickly established himself in the first team, helping the Potters win the Second Division Championship in 1932–33 when he netted 11 goals in 21 matches. The following season he topped the club's scoring list with 17 goals and repeated that feat in 1934–35 with 24 strikes and again in 1935–36. Then, perhaps surprisingly, Stoke manager Bob McGrory, knowing that Freddie Steele was about to hit the headlines as a marksman, transferred Sale to Blackburn in 1936. However, after spending two years at Ewood Park he returned to The Victoria Ground to

the delight of the supporters. With Steele, Sale responded magnificently, scoring five goals (including a hat-trick) in three games. He held his place in the side, bagged 18 more goals in 1938–39 and then went goal-crazy during the hostilities when he gave defenders up and down the country heart failure. In 1941–42 he weighed in with 56 goals and hit a total of 64 over two seasons: 1943–44 and 1944–45. He claimed hat-tricks galore and scored six in an 8–0 Cup victory over Walsall. A penalty specialist, he hardly ever missed from the spot and, indeed, it is believed he only fluffed one 12-yard kick in his entire professional career! By the time World War Two was over Sale was coming to the end of a terrific career and his last appearance for the Potters was on 8 April 1946 in a transitional League North game against Sheffield United at The Victoria Ground. In 1947 he joined Northwich Victoria and his swan song came with Hednesford Town in 1949.

SALMON, Henry

Defender or centre-forward: 3 apps.

Born: Fenton, Stoke-on-Trent, 14 March 1910.
Died: Caen, France, 30 July 1944.
Career: Stoke St Peter's (August 1926), Longton Hall FC, Macclesfield (1928),

POTTERS (amateur, April 1930, professional, May 1932), Millwall (May 1934), Wellington Town, Southport, Shrewsbury Town (retired during World War Two).

■ Ex-electrician Henry Salmon was a versatile player who lined up in both the centre-forward and centre-half positions and once netted five goals for the Potters in a reserve-team game before turning professional. He was sadly killed in action while serving as a sergeant with the Royal Warwickshire regiment in 1944. He is buried in Fonteney-le-Pesnel Cemetery, France.

SALMONS, Geoffrey

Midfield: 131+3 apps. 16 goals.

Born: Mexborough, 14 January 1948.
Career: Sheffield United (apprentice, April 1964, professional, January 1966), POTTERS (£160,000, July 1974), Sheffield United (September 1977), Leicester City (£45,000, October 1977), Chesterfield (August 1978–May 1981), Gainsborough trinity (1980s).

■ Midfielder Geoff Salmons, predominantly left-footed, had been a constant threat to Stoke City before finally joining the Potters, becoming a vital piece to manager Tony Waddington's jigsaw. As an ever-present, he had an excellent 1974–75 season, helping the team gain fourth place in the First Division. A man with a great sense of humour, he was the joker of the pack, and in his first spell with Sheffield United he netted eight times in 180 League games. He eventually quit top-class football in 1981 with 449 League appearances in his locker and 41 goals. He assisted Gainsborough Trinity while also running a pub in his native Yorkshire.

Geoff Salmons

SALT, Herbert Arthur

Goalkeeper: 1 app.

Born: Stoke-on-Trent, 1880.
Died: before 1960.
Career: Newcastle St Peter's (1899), POTTERS (November 1902), Stafford Rangers (May 1903).

■ Not the tallest of goalkeepers, Herby Salt's only League outing for Stoke came in a 3–0 home win over West Bromwich Albion in April 1903 when he deputised for Tom Wilkes.

SANDFORD, Lee Robert

Defender or midfield: 321+3 apps. 14 goals.

Born: Basingstoke, 22 April 1968.

Career: Portsmouth (apprentice, May 1984, professional, December 1985), POTTERS (£137,500, December 1989), Sheffield United (£500,000, August 1996),

Reading (on loan, September–October 1997, retired, May 1998).

■ A tall, left-sided player, strong in the tackle and in the air, Lee Sandford was able to occupy the full-back, centre-half and midfield positions, but preferred the first. He gave the Potters excellent service for six and a half years, helping them win the Autoglass Trophy at Wembley in 1992 and the Second Division Championship the following season. An England youth international as a teenager, he appeared in 90 first-team matches for his first club, Portsmouth, keeping goal twice when Alan Knight was injured, this after suffering a serious spine injury in 1987, which sidelined him for over five months. Former 'Stokie' Howard Kendall signed him for Sheffield United in 1996. Sandford retired from competitive football in 1998 with 478 senior appearances under his belt.

SANDLAND, Edward Tinsley

Inside-forward: 13 apps. 3 goals.

Born: Hanley, Stoke-on-Trent, 1870.
Died: before 1960.
Career: Newcastle Swifts (1892), POTTERS (professional, July 1894), Congleton (February 1897).

■ A bustling player with an eye for goal, Teddy Sandland spent two and a half years with the Potters, making 10 of his senior appearances in succession between September and mid-December in 1894. Two of his three goals were scored in a 3–1 home League win over Liverpool in his sixth game.

SAUNDERS, Carl Stephen

Striker: 151+41 apps. 31 goals.

Born: Marston Green, Warwickshire, 28 December 1964.
Career: POTTERS (apprentice, April 1981, professional, March 1983), Bristol Rovers (£70,000, February 1990), Oxford United (non-contract, December 1993), Walsall (non-contract, February–March 1994).

■ Carl Saunders was a useful goalscorer who always looked likely to

breach even the soundest of defences. He graduated through the junior and youth ranks at The Victoria Ground and turned professional in 1983. However, he took time to establish himself in the first team, having made his debut as a 'sub' against Everton at Goodison Park a month after signing 'pro'. But during the 1984–85 season he finally made it on a regular basis and scored three goals for a struggling team. An adaptable performer, who could also play at full-back, midfield and on the wing (in fact, he wore every outfield shirt for the Potters), Saunders formed a fine partnership in attack with Nicky Morgan before transferring to Bristol Rovers in 1990. Ironically, at the end of that season Rovers took Stoke's place in the Second Division!
NB: Three members of Saunders's family played for the Birmingham Basketball team.

SAVAGE, Albert George

Centre-forward: 9 apps. 4 goals.

Born: Warwick, 1888.
Died: before 1980.
Career: Nuneaton, POTTERS (March 1911), Bulkington (May 1911). Did not play after World War One.

■ Scorer of a hat-trick in a 10–0 Birmingham League win over Halesowen in April 1911, when he partnered the two Smiths (Alf and Billy) in attack, Bert Savage was brought to the club during an injury crisis. He was the ninth player to be used in the centre-forward position by the Potters that season.

SAVAGE, Robert James

Full-back or midfield: 5+2 apps.

Born: Liverpool, 8 January 1960.
Career: Liverpool (apprentice, April 1976, professional, January 1978), Wrexham (on loan, October 1982–May 1983), POTTERS (July 1983), AFC Bournemouth (December 1983), Bradford City (December 1986), Bolton Wanderers (September 1987, retired May 1990).

■ Robbie Savage's senior career ended in 1990 after breaking his leg. Prior to that he had done very well as a full-back or midfielder in competitive football, accumulating around 250 League and Cup appearances at senior level. Unfortunately, he failed to get a game with Liverpool where, in the main, he was reserve to Phil Neal and Alan Kennedy.

SAWERS, William

Inside-forward: 20 apps. 5 goals.

Born: Bridgton, Glasgow, 13 June 1871.
Died: 20 October 1960.
Career: Clyde (1890), Blackburn Rovers (May 1892), POTTERS (August 1893), Dundee (May 1894), POTTERS (August 1895), Dundee (September 1895, retired through injury, December 1895), later ran a sports shop in Eglington Street, Glasgow, for many years.

■ Strong in both feet, Bill Sawers could play on both sides of the pitch and, indeed, he occupied every position in the forward-line during his short career, which was brought to an abrupt end through injury. Capped by Scotland against Wales at Wrexham in 1895, he never really settled in the Potteries despite returning for a second time to The Victoria Ground.

SAYER, James Bernard

Outside-right: 24 apps. 3 goals.

Born: Mexborough, Yorkshire, 1862.

Died: Stoke-on-Trent, 1 February 1922.
Career: Mexborough, Heeley FC (Sheffield), Sheffield Wednesday, Sheffield FA, POTTERS (August 1883), Mexborough Town (May 1890–94), later became a secretary and then director of Fielding Limited, makers of Devon pottery at Stoke.

■ Jimmy Sayer's outstanding virtue was his blistering pace over 30-40 yards. An England international, capped once in a 7–0 win over Ireland in February 1887, he was known as 'the greyhound' by the fans who appreciated his speed and aggression down the flank.

SCATTERGOOD, Kenneth

Goalkeeper: 4 apps.

Born: Riddings, Bradford, 6 April 1912.
Died: Chesterfield, 10 June 1988.
Career: Derby County (trialist, 1929), Sheffield Wednesday (April 1931), Wolverhampton Wanderers (August 1932), Bristol City (May 1933), POTTERS (£500, August 1934), Derby County (July 1935, released, May 1938), did not play after World War Two.

■ Son of former England goalkeeper Ernald, Ken Scattergood followed his father as a professional footballer. He failed to make a League appearance for either Wednesday or Wolves, played in 39 games for Bristol City and played in

the first four League games for the Potters at the start of the 1934–35 season, following the departure of Roy John, before being dropped after conceding a total of nine goals. He languished in the reserves for the remainder of that campaign before joining Derby County. Things didn't get much better for Scattergood as he conceded seven goals on his debut for the Rams against Everton at Goodison Park on Christmas Day in 1935.

SCHOFIELD, Joseph Alfred

Outside-left: 230 apps. 94 goals.

Born: Hanley, Stoke-on-Trent, 1 January 1871.
Died: Hartshill, Stoke-on-Trent, 29 September 1929.
Career: Hanley Hope Sunday School, POTTERS (August 1891, retired, April 1899, joined office staff, appointed a director in 1908, secretary-manager, 1915), Port Vale (secretary-manager, January 1919, manager March 1927).

■ Joey Schofield had the distinction of being secretary-manager of both Stoke and Port Vale and was also a Director at The Victoria Ground. A very clever, enterprising left-winger who won three full England caps, the first in March 1892 versus Wales at Wrexham, and twice represented the Football League while a 'Potter', he was a schoolmaster by profession, teaching at Broom Street School, Hanley. Unfortunately, he was plagued by ill-health during his career, which finally resulted in him quitting the game (as a player) after scoring almost 100 goals in 230 competitive games for the Potters. He made his senior debut against Sunderland in October 1891 and was a regular in the side until April 1899, scoring in his final game against Wolverhampton Wanderers. At this juncture, Schofield entered the administration side of the club, and when Stoke hit financial trouble he was one of the men who helped pull things round. He duly became a director in 1908 when the club was reformed and entered the Birmingham & District League after losing Football League status. During World War One Schofield took over the secretarial and managerial

duties at The Victoria Ground. He chose to leave Stoke for Port Vale early in 1919, immediately taking over responsibility for internal office duties as well as team selection in conjunction with the club captain and vice-skipper. It is said that he was a man with 'well-balanced judgement' when it came to discovering talent, and he was also a player's 'friend', confidant and counsellor. He saw the Vale record victories in the Staffordshire Infirmary Cup Finals of 1920 and 1921 but was then fined £25 in June 1925 for being involved in the illegal payment of bonuses to 17 players. Two years later he was upgraded to full-time team-manager of Vale, but, after becoming a Poor Law official, he sadly passed away at Hartshill when the Vale were sitting at the top of the Third Division North table.

SCHREUDER, Jan-Dirk

Midfield: 0+2 apps.

Born: Holland, 12 August 1971.
Career: RKC Waalwijk, Holland (1994), POTTERS (Bosman, free transfer, July 1997), Helmond Sport, Holland (May 1998).

■ A Dutch under-21 international, spotted by Chic Bates who was on a scouting mission to Holland, Dick Schrueder joined the potters on a Bosman transfer ruling prior to the start of the 1997–98 season. Unfortunately, an niggling ankle injury ruled him out of contention and after returning 'home' for treatment he returned to Stoke, but was eventually released after appearing only twice for the first XI as a substitute.

SCOTT, Geoffrey Samuel

Defender: 86+2 apps. 3 goals.

Born: Birmingham, 31 October 1956.
Career: Aston Villa (apprentice, April 1973), Solihull Borough (1975), Highgate United (1976), POTTERS (professional, April 1977), Leicester City (£80,000,

February 1980), Birmingham City (on loan, February 1982, signed for £50,000, March 1982), Charlton Athletic (£40,000, October 1982), Middlesbrough (trialist, June–August 1984), Northampton Town (September 1984), Cambridge United (July 1985, contract cancelled March 1986), Solihull Borough (August 1986), Moor Green (January 1987), Highgate United (manager, July 1988, resigned, August 1989).

■ A tall, blonde defender, Geoff Scott had a long and interesting career, spending three years at The Victoria Ground, during which time he appeared in almost 90 first-team matches. At times his play was characterised by a series of errors but on his day he was certainly a very useful performer who accumulated 176 League appearances all told. He joined Birmingham immediately after scoring an own-goal for them while playing for Leicester. He was badly injured in his last game for Cambridge in December 1985 and after months of treatment his contract was cancelled.

SCOTT, Ian

Full-back or midfield: 28+10 apps. 2 goals.

Born: Radcliffe, 20 September 1967.
Career: Manchester City, POTTERS (£175,000, July 1989), Crewe Alexandra (on loan, March 1991), Bury (on loan, August 1992, signed on a free transfer, September 1992).

■ Ian Scott, an England schoolboy international (five caps won), played in 24 League games for Manchester City before moving to The Victoria Ground in 1989. He signed the appropriate transfer forms on his return from holiday at Manchester airport after being met by Stoke boss Mick Mills. Unfortunately, he could never hold down a regular place in the first team and left on a free transfer to Bury for whom he scored on his debut. He did not impress Crewe boss Dario Gradi.

SCOTT, Keith

Striker:24+4 apps. 4 goals.

Born: Westminster, London, 9 June 1967.
Career: Hinckley Athletic, Bedworth United, (1987–88), Hinckley Athletic (August 1988), Leicester United (July 1989), Leicester City (trialist, September 1989), Lincoln City (£22,500, March 1990), Gateshead (on loan, October 1990), Boston united (on loan, February 1991), Wycombe Wanderers (on loan, March 1991, signed for £30,000, plus share of a future fee, July 1991), Swindon Town (£375,000, November 1993), POTTERS (£300,000, November 1994), Norwich City (£450,000, in player-exchange deal involving Mike Sheron, November 1995), AFC Bournemouth (on loan, February–March 1996) Watford (on loan, February 1997), Wycombe Wanderers (£55,000, March 1997), Reading (£250,000, March 1999), Colchester United (on loan, October–November 2000, signed, free transfer, March 2001), Dover Athletic (April 2001).

■ When he moved to Carrow Road in 1994, striker Keith Scott, a former bank clerk, was valued at £300,000 against Sheron's £250,000...it was Stoke who got the better deal! Standing 6ft 3in tall and weighing over 14st, Scott found it difficult to adjust to the faster pace of League football having spent several seasons at a lower level. He helped Wycombe win the Vauxhall Conference and FA Trophy in 1993 before his big-money transfer to Swindon, who at the time where in the Premiership. Perhaps surprisingly, his career lasted far longer than expected, and when he returned to non-League football in 2001 (shortly before his 34th birthday) he took with him a pretty sound record of 303 senior appearances and 76 goals, having his best return with Wycombe, for whom he netted 22 goals in 99 outings in two spells at Adams Park.

SCOTT, Lewis

Goalkeeper: 22 apps.

Born: Sunderland, 1898.
Died: Lancaster, 1972.
Career: Fulwell FC, Sunderland (1913), POTTERS (July 1922), Preston North End (July 1923–April 1924).

■ Lew Scott played all his games for the Potters in season 1922–23 after the club had utilised five different men between the posts since August 1920. He had earlier made 100 appearances for Sunderland. Following the introduction of Kenny Campbell and the arrival of Bob Dixon, he left The Victoria Ground for Preston North End after spending just 12 months with Stoke.

SCRIMSHAW, Charles Thomas

Full-back: 130 apps.

Born: Heanor, Derbyshire, 3 April 1909.
Died: Smallthorne, Stoke-on-Trent, 4 June 1973.
Career: Hebden Bridge, POTTERS (amateur, December 1929, professional, February 1930), Middlesbrough £3,000, October 1938), World War Two guest for Port Vale (1939–40), POTTERS (1940) and Portsmouth.

■ Charlie Scrimshaw was a very reliable full-back, always steady in his play and extremely dedicated to the

game. Spotted playing for Hebden Bridge, he took quite some time before he became a regular in the Potters side owing to the presence of Arthur Beachill, Bob McGrory and Billy Spencer, who also played for Hebden Bridge. But like a true professional, he battled on and eventually took over from McGrory when he retired to become manager. During the second half of the 1939–40 World War Two season, he appeared in 10 regional games as a guest for the Potters. A bricklayer by trade, Scrimshaw skippered Stoke's reserve team during his early years at the club and later became senior vice-caption. He had the misfortune to break his left leg playing against Portsmouth in September 1937 and was out of action for five months.

SCULLY, Anthony Derek Thomas

Midfield or winger: 7 apps.

Born: Dublin, 12 June 1976.
Career: Crystal Palace (apprentice, July 1992, professional, December 1993), AFC Bournemouth (on loan, October–December 1994), Cardiff City (on loan, January–March 1996), Manchester City (£80,000, August 1997), POTTERS (on loan, January–March 1998), Queen's Park Rangers (£155,000, March 1998), Cambridge United (free transfer, July 2001), Southend United (on loan, November–December 2002), Peterborough United (on loan, March–April 2003), Dagenham & Redbridge (September 2003), Barnet (late 2003), Tamworth (briefly), Notts County (February 2004).

■ A Republic of Ireland international at schoolboy, youth, 'B' and under-21 levels, winning 10 caps in the latter category, Tony Scully has had a very interesting career, during which time he has served with 13 different clubs while making more than 200 League and Cup appearances. He didn't do a great deal with any of his major clubs, having his best spell with QPR (46 games). A skilful player on his day, he joined the Potters on loan following an injury to Paul Stewart and was never on the winning side during his time at the club.

SEGERS, Johannes

Goalkeeper: 1 app.

Born: Eindhoven, Holland, 30 October 1961.
Career: PSV Eindhoven, Holland (amateur, November 1977, professional, October 1978), Nottingham Forest (£50,000, August 1984), POTTERS (on loan, February 1987), Sheffield United (on loan, November–December 1987), Dunfermline Athletic (on loan, March–May 1988), Wimbledon (£180,000, September 1988), Wolverhampton Wanderers (free transfer, July 1996), Woking (free, February 1997), Tottenham Hotspur (free, August 1998, later appointed goalkeeping coach at White Hart Lane).

■ Agile and daring Dutch goalkeeper Hans Seger's only game for the Potters, while on loan from The City Ground, came in a 4–1 defeat at West Bromwich Albion. In his eight years with the 'Dons' he played in 322 matches and during his career amassed over 600 appearances at competitive level.
NB: In January 1997 Segers, along with goalkeeper Bruce Grobbelaar, who also played on loan with Stoke, former Wimbledon and Aston Villa striker John Fashanu and a Malaysian businessman, Heng Suan Lim, appeared at Winchester Crown Court, charged with match-rigging.

SELLARS, Harold

Left-half or inside-left: 394 apps. 21 goals

Born: Beamish, County Durham, 9 April 1902.
Died: Stoke-on-Trent, 30 December 1978.
Career: Ledgate Park, POTTERS (December 1923, player-assistant manager, 1936), Port Vale (July 1937), Drumcondra (1939–40).

■ Harry Sellars was brought to The Victoria Ground in 1923 at the age of

21. It was the start of a long association for the Sellars family with Stoke City FC as later Harry's son, John, joined the Potters and remained at The Victoria Ground until 1959. Sellars senior was a miner who could play at left-half or inside-left. His great strength was his passing and he was also a fine defender under pressure. A 100 per-cent performer every time he took the field, Sellars appeared in almost 400 League and Cup games prior to his transfer to neighbours Port Vale. He won a Second Division Championship medal in 1933 and was assistant manager to Bob McGrory for a short while before leaving The Victoria Ground

SELLARS, John

Left-half: 413 apps. 15 goals.

Born: Trent Vale, Stoke-on-Trent, 28 April 1924.
Died: Stoke-on-Trent, 1985.
Career: POTTERS (part-time professional, November 1942, retired, May 1959).

■ Johnny Sellars was a formidable athlete who often competed in the famous Powderhall Sprint events in the 1950s. He was brought to The Victoria Ground by his father, Harry, in the 1930s and vowed that he would eventually wear the famous red and white striped shirt, and he did just that. With war clouds hovering over England, Sellars bided his time and eventually signed as a part-time professional for Stoke during the 1942–43 season. Never a full-time professional, he became a regular in the side in 1947–48, and, as a hard-working left-half who occasionally lined up at centre-forward and even full-back, he gave the Potters great service, accumulating more than 400 senior appearances. A serious eye injury forced him to quit sport altogether in the summer of 1959. Sellars divided his time between playing soccer and that of being a quality shoe designer, working for the Lotus Shoe Company in Stone.

SETTERS, Maurice Edgar

Defender or midfield: 97 apps. 5 goals.

Born: Honiton, Devon, 16 December 1936.
Career: Honiton & Cullompton Schools, Bridport Juniors, Exeter City (amateur, June 1952, professional, January 1954), West Bromwich Albion (£3,000, January 1955), Manchester United (£30,000, January 1960), POTTERS (November 1964), Coventry City (November 1967), Charlton Athletic (January 1970, retired as player, May 1971), Doncaster Rovers (manager, July 1971–November 1974), Sheffield Wednesday (coach, August 1980), Rotherham United (assistant manager-coach, 1982–84), Newcastle United (chief scout, 1984–85), Republic of Ireland (assistant manager-coach, June 1986–May 1989), now out of football, living in Bawtry, near Doncaster.

■ With his bandy-legs and crew-cut hair, Maurice 'mo-mo' Setters looked like what he was on the field of play: a real terrier, as hard as nails, determined, fearless and reckless at times. After winning schoolboy honours as a youngster, aged 15, he went on to gain one youth cap for England, a further sixteen at under-23 level and also played for the FA XI and Young England in 1958. He appeared in 11 games for Exeter City, 132 for Albion and 193 for Manchester United before spending three years at The Victoria Ground, where his all-action performances certainly boosted team morale. He ended his career with exactly 500 club appearances to his name, of which 436 came in the Football League. An FA Cup winner with Manchester United in 1963, he made his senior debut for Exeter in March 1954 and played his last competitive game 16 years later with Charlton. He occupied seven different positions during his playing days, but believed he performed best in midfield. He formed an excellent relationship with Jack Charlton, initially at Hillsborough and then with the Republic of Ireland, seeing the national team do superbly well in the 1990 World Cup Finals in Italy.
* After being sacked as manager of Doncaster Rovers in 1974, Setters subsequently received £1,340 compensation by the courts in July 1975 for unfair dismissal.

SHAFFERY, Jack

Outside-right or left: 5 apps.

Born: Hanley, Stoke-on-Trent, 1874.
Died: before 1945.
Career: Northwood Mission, POTTERS (August 1897), Hanley Swifts (May 1898).

■ Right-winger Jack Shaffrey spent one season as a reserve at The Victoria Ground, deputising for Joey Schofield on the left-wing once and playing on the opposite flank on four occasions in the absence of Freddie Johnson.

SHARDLOW, Paul

Goalkeeper: 4 apps.

Born: Stone, 29 April 1943.
Died: Stoke-on-Trent, 14 October 1968.
Career: Northwich Victoria, POTTERS (May 1966, until his death).

■ Sadly, promising young goalkeeper Paul Shardlow collapsed and died during a training session after suffering a heart attack in 1968 at the age of 25. He played in just four senior games before tragedy struck.

SHAW, Graham Paul

Striker: 124+41 apps. 29 goals

Born: Stoke-on-Trent, 7 June 1967.
Career: POTTERS (apprentice, July 1983, professional, June 1985), Preston North End (£70,000, July 1989), POTTERS (£70,000, player-exchange deal involving Tony Ellis, August 1992), Plymouth Argyle (on loan, August–September 1994), Rochdale (March 1995, released, May 1996).

■ Graham Shaw developed through the junior ranks at The Victoria Ground to sign professional forms in 1985. Four years later he was transferred to Preston, where he did very well, netting 42 goals in less than 150 outings, before returning to Stoke for a second spell in 1992 in a deal that saw fellow striker Tony Ellis move to Deepdale plus a cash adjustment. Unfortunately, Shaw did not do as well with the Potters as he had done the first time round, although he did help the team win the Second Division title. He quit top-level football in 1996 with 73 goals to his credit in 343 first-team matches. Shaw had the pleasure of scoring Stoke's first goal on a plastic pitch against Luton Town at Kenilworth Road in March 1988.

SHELDON, Frederick Lawrence

Goalkeeper: 8 apps.

Born: Tunstall, Stoke-on-Trent, 1871.
Died: Stoke-on-Trent, 1953.
Career: Stoke St Peter's, POTTERS (July 1896), Eccleshall (May 1897).

■ With Fred Latham not in the best of form and Billy Rowley edging towards retirement, Stoke called up amateur goalkeeper Fred Sheldon to play in the first team during the mid 1890s. He joined the playing staff at The Victoria Ground in the summer of 1896 but, unfortunately, he didn't perform too well for the Potters, conceding 15 goals in his first five outings, and was quickly pushed back into the reserves. He was called upon three more times during the next campaign but again failed to keep a clean sheet and was eventually released by the club in 1897. He did not keep one clean sheet for the Potters.

SHELDON, Kevin John

Outside-right or left: 15 apps.

Born: Cheddleton, Staffs, 14 June 1956.
Career: POTTERS (apprentice, July 1972, professional, June 1973), Wigan Athletic (July 1981), Port Vale (on loan, August–September 1982), Crewe Alexandra (non-contract, August 1983), Trowbridge Town (March 1984), later with Burton Albion, Leek Town, Telford United.

■ Reserve team player Kevin 'Bomber' Sheldon spent nine years at The Victoria Ground, during which time he was introduced on both flanks, making his League debut in April 1976 in a 1–0 home win over Birmingham City. He helped Wigan gain promotion from the Fourth Division in 1982.

SHERIDAN, James

Inside-left: 12 apps. 1 goal.

Born: Belfast, April 1884.
Died: before 1960.
Career: Cambuslang Hibernian (August 1901), Everton (professional, August 1902), POTTERS (October 1904), New Brompton (December 1904, retired through injury, summer 1906).

■ Recruited a month into the 1904–05 season, skilful inside-forward Paddy Sheridan made his debut for the Potters in a 2–1 home League win over Sheffield United. Unable to settle in the Potteries, he left the club for Southern League side New Brompton after just three months' service. Capped five times by Northern Ireland during his spell at Goodison Park, Sheridan added a sixth to his tally with Stoke against England in 1904, thus becoming the Potters' first capped Irishman. He was Everton's youngest international player until Wayne Rooney arrived.

SHERON, Michael Nigel

Striker: 71+5 apps. 39 goals

Born: Liverpool, 11 January 1972.
Career: Manchester City (apprentice, May 1988, professional, July 1990), Bury (on loan, March–April 1991), Norwich City (£1 million, August 1994), POTTERS (£450,000 player-exchange deal involving Keith Scott, November 1995), Queen's park rangers (£2.75 million, July 1997), Barnsley (£1 million, January 1999), Blackpool (free transfer, July 2003), Macclesfield Town (free, August 2004), Shrewsbury Town (free, March 2005).

■ Valued at only £150,000 when signed from Norwich in 1995, the Potters certainly got their money back (and more) as striker Mike Sheron rattled in his fair quota of goals (one every two

Mike Sheron

games) during his two years at The Victoria Ground. A purposeful footballer, direct in his approach and always looking for an opening, he gave defenders nightmares at times and was a huge favourite with the Boothen End supporters. An England under-21 international (16 caps gained), he was nurtured by Manchester City, and after a loan spell with Bury he joined Norwich for £1 million. He failed to settle down in Norfolk and subsequently moved to Stoke, where he became an instant success. Perhaps it was a surprise when he moved to QPR in 1997 but, on reflection, the offer made by the London club was too good to dismiss. In 2004–05 Sheron, who won the Auto-Windscreen Shield with Blackpool in 2004, reached the career milestone of 500 appearances in League and Cup competitions, scoring 146 goals.

SHERRATT, Brian

Goalkeeper: 1 app.

Born: Stoke-on-Trent, 29 March 1944. Career: POTTERS (amateur, June 1959, professional, April 1961), Oxford United (August 1965), Nottingham Forest (on loan, October 1968), Barnsley (free transfer, June 1969), Colchester United (August 1970–April 1971).

■ Brian Sherratt kept goal in one League game for Stoke City, lining up against Middlesbrough at The Victoria Ground in the Second Division on 21 April 1962 in place of Irish international Jimmy O'Neill. He performed well and helped City to a 2–0 win in front of 9,000 fans. Owing to the form of other 'keepers in the camp, he reluctantly left the club for Oxford United in 1965. Sherratt appeared in just 70 League games for his five major clubs, including 44 for Oxford.

PETER SHILTON, MBE, OBE

Goalkeeper: 120 apps.

Born: Leicester, 18 September 1949. Career: Leicester Schools, Leicester City (apprentice, June 1965, professional, September 1966), POTTERS (£325,000, November 1974), Nottingham Forest (£270,000, September 1977), Southampton (£300,000, August 1982), Derby County (£90,000, July 1987), Plymouth Argyle (player-manager, March 1992–December 1994), Wimbledon (non-contract, January–February 1995), Bolton Wanderers (non-contract, March 1995), Coventry City (July 1995), West Ham United (January 1996), Leyton Orient (November 1996–May 1997).

■ England's most capped footballer with 125 appearances for his country, Peter Shilton was rated among the world's best goalkeepers during the 1980s. He was the complete 'last line of defence'. Not a stylish 'keeper, he simply kept shots out whether by hand, foot or body, regularly and bravely diving at the feet of players to avert danger inside the penalty area. Possessed with superb positional sense, he was commanding in the air, courageous and, above all, added confidence to his defence. He was a Stoke City player for almost three years.

He made his debut for the club against Wolves at Molineux in November 1974, replacing John Farmer in a 2–2 draw. He was an ever-present the following season and missed only two League games out of a possible 112 before transferring to Nottingham Forest. Having won the Second Division Championship with Leicester in 1971, he then helped Forest win the League title in 1978, the League Cup in 1979, two European Cups in 1979 and 1980, the Super Cup also in 1979 and the FA Charity Shield in 1978. He was also voted PFA 'Footballer of the Year' in 1978 and 12 years later received the PFA Merit Award for services to football. In December 1996 Shilton became the first player in history to appear in 1,000 Football League games when he kept goal for Leyton Orient against Brighton & Hove Albion. He went on to make over 1,375 senior appearances in competitive football (club and country). His final League tally was 1,005 and he scored one goal – a long clearance downfield in a 5–1 win at Southampton, his future club, in October 1967. He made over 100 League appearances for five different clubs: Leicester – 286, Stoke – 110, Forest – 202, Saints – 188 and Derby – 211, a record never to be beaten! Besides his senior international appearances, Shilton also played in three under-23 games and as a teenager collected a handful of youth caps. As Plymouth's manager he failed to prevent the cash-stricken Devon club from dropping into the Third Division, having survived a crisis board meeting in February 1993 when chairman Dan McCauley criticised Shilton for spending far too much money (over £1 million) while he was earning £125,000 a year!
* Shilton's son, Sam, joined Plymouth Argyle as a trainee at the age of 16 in 1994.

SHIRLEY, John Arnold

Inside-forward: 30 apps. 11 goals.

Born: Crewe, 1903.
Died: Cheshire, 1985.
Career: Whitchurch, POTTERS (£500, April 1927, released, May 1930), Hednesford Town (August 1930), Macclesfield (1931–32).

■ Jack Shirley scored twice on his debut for the Potters in a 5–1 win at Fulham in November 1927. Two years later he was suspended by the club for breach of club rules and left The Victoria Ground at the end of the 1929–30 season, eventually signing for non-League side Hednesford Town.

SHORE, Albert Victor

Inside-forward: 3 apps.

Born: Handsworth, Birmingham, February 1897.
Died: before 1980.
Career: Dean's Works FC, Birmingham, Sunderland (professional, March 1920), POTTERS (free transfer, May 1921), Whitburn (August 1922).

■ Vic Shore began his playing career in Birmingham junior football before gambling by going 220 miles north to sign for Sunderland at the age of 23, but he failed to settle in the North East and after just five games for the Wearsiders he returned to the Midlands to join the Potters. He was troubled by a leg injury and poor form during his days at The Victoria Ground and managed only three appearances before entering non-League football following a disagreement with the club's directors when he refused to live in the Potteries. Stoke, in fact, demanded a fee for his transfer, having incurred a hefty medical bill in their efforts to get him match fit.
* His nephew, Ernest William Shore, played for West Bromwich Albion in 1914–15.

SHORT, Christian Mark

Defender: 38+3 apps.

Born: Munster, Germany, 9 May 1970.
Career: Pickering Town, Scarborough (professional, July 1988), Notts County (£100,000, September 1990), Huddersfield Town (on loan, December 1994–January 1995), Sheffield United (free, December 1995), POTTERS (free, July 1998, retired, ill-health, August 2000).

■ Chris Short, the younger brother of Craig Short of Scarborough, Notts County, Derby County, Everton and Blackburn Rovers fame, was in excellent

form when he was struck down with a mysterious illness during the 1999–2000 season. He went to see a world-renowned doctor in Canada, whom he thought would give him hope for the future, but sadly he was forced to give up competitive League football at the age of 30. Able to perform at right-back or centre-half, he made 53 first-team appearances for Scarborough, 115 for Notts County, seven for Huddersfield and 57 for the Blades before joining the Potters. He helped Notts County win promotion to the First division in 1991 and four years later was an Anglo-Italian Cup winner at Wembley with the Meadow Lane club.

SHORT, John

Full-back: 55 apps.

Born: Barnsley, 18 February 1928.
Died: Barnsley, May 1976.
Career: Wath Wanderers (1944), Wolverhampton Wanderers (professional, May 1948), POTTERS (June 1954), Barnsley (£3,000, October 1956, retired, May 1960).

■ Yorkshireman Jack Short moved to the Midlands as a youngster and played for Wolves' nursery side, Wath

Wanderers, during the latter stages of World War Two before signing professional forms at the age of 20. A steady, competent full-back, he waited patiently behind a possee of good defenders under the watchful eye of manager Stan Cullis before he finally made his League debut in the Black Country derby against West Bromwich Albion in December 1951. He went on to make 107 senior appearances for the club with two goals scored, both from the centre-forward position against Manchester City in an FA Cup tie. But with so much talent at Molineux, Short, who helped Wolves win their first-ever League title in 1954, was allowed to leave the club to sign for the Potters in June of that same year, manager Frank Taylor acquiring him to bolster up his defence. He played in more than 50 matches for Stoke, whom he served for just over two seasons. He then rounded off his career back home with Barnsley, adding a further 109 League appearances to his tally with the Tykes.

SHTANIUK, Sergei

Defender: 95 apps. 5 goals.

Born: Minsk, Belarus, 13 August 1973.
Career: Belaruis Minsk FC (professional, August 1992), Dinamo 93 Minsk (May 1993), Dynamo Minsk (September 1994), Dynamo Moscow (April 1996), POTTERS (£200,000, August 2001), Shinnik Yaroslavi, Russia (May 2003).

■ Capped 42 times by his country, Sergei Shtaniuk, 6ft 3in tall and 12st 11lb in weight, had two exceptionally fine seasons in English football, picking up several 'Man of the match' awards as well as being voted 'Player of the Year' in various polls. Strong, dominant in the air, good on the ball with a great attitude, he produced some brilliant displays at the heart of the Potters defence and it was perhaps a surprise that a bigger club didn't move in for him on transfer deadline day. However, he had to withstand a lot of pressure from his family who could not settle in England, and in May 2003 he reluctantly left The Britannia Stadium to sign for the Russian club Shinnik Yaroslavi. Prior to moving to Stoke he had appeared in almost 200 League

games in Belarus and Russia and gained both Cup and League runners'-up medals with Dynamo Moscow in 1996 and 1998 respectively.
* Stoke tried to sign Shtaniuk in the summer of 2000 but failed to obtain a work permit.

SHUTT, George

Defender: 30 apps. 2 goals.

Born: Stoke-on-Trent, 1861.
Died: Hanley, Stoke-on-Trent, 6 August 1936.
Career: Stoke Priory, POTTERS (August 1880, professional, August 1885), Hanley Town (May 1889), Burslem Port Vale (August 1891), Hanley Town (May 1893), qualified to be a Football referee (1891), later entered the licensing trade, keeping pubs in both Burslem and Hanley.

■ George Shutt could play in any of the three half-back positions, and it was in the centre-half berth where he gained his only England cap (as a Stoke player) when he lined up against Ireland in March 1886, playing superbly well in a 6–1 win. He also represented Staffordshire on at least 12 occasions, played for the Birmingham FA, The Players XI and The North of England (against the South) in an international trial. He qualified to become a Football League referee in 1891, yet surprisingly he never 'talked football' after hanging up his boots. An intelligent, sure-tackling defender, he and 'Father' Smith were the only players to appear in Stoke's first FA Cup tie versus Manchester in November 1883 and the first League game versus West Bromwich Albion in September 1888. In between times, he was one of a group of players who signed up as full-time professionals for the Potters.

SIDDALL, Alfred Brian

Forward:: 59 apps. 10 goals.

Born: Northwich, 2 May 1930.
Career: Witton Albion, Wolverhampton Wanderers (professional), Witton Albion, Northwich Victoria, POTTERS (February 1951), Bournemouth (January 1954), Ipswich Town (May 1957), Haverhill Rovers (June 1961), became a qualified FA coach, based in Ipswich, and also worked at Felixstowe docks.

■ Brian Siddall challenged Johnny Malkin for the right-wing berth in Stoke's first team for quite a while and in the end had some success, especially in 1951–52 and 1952–53 when he played in virtually half of the League games in each campaign. Five of his 10 goals were scored in 10 games in 1953–54 before his transfer to Bournemouth. A troublesome knee prevented him from making the grade at Molineux but, recovering full fitness in non-league football, he was signed by his former Wolves teammate Frank Taylor for the Potters, who pipped Arsenal for his signature by a couple of hours. Siddall, who could, in fact, occupy any forward position, was badly injured in his 60th and final game for Ipswich against Sheffield United in October 1960. He never started a League game again, finishing with a total of 203 and 30 goals scored. He only played occasionally for Haverhill Rovers.

SIDDALL, Barry

Goalkeeper: 20 apps.

Born: Ellesmere Port, Cheshire, 12 September 1954.
Career: Bolton Wanderers (apprentice, April 1971, professional, January 1972), Sunderland (September 1976),

Darlington (on loan, October 1980), Port Vale (August 1982), Blackpool (on loan, October 1983), POTTERS (on loan, December 1984, signed for £20,000, January 1985), Tranmere Rovers (on loan, October–November 1985), Manchester City (on loan, March–April 1986), Blackpool (August 1986), Stockport County (June 1989), Hartlepool United (March 1990), West Bromwich Albion (non-contract, August–September 1990), Mossley (October 1990), Carlisle United (November 1990), Chester City (July 1991), Northwich Victoria (August 1992), Preston North End (November 1992), Horwich Railway Mechanics Institute (December 1992), Bury (on loan, February–March 1993), Lincoln City (on loan, August 1994), Burnley (December 1994), Birmingham City (non-contract, March–April 1995), later employed as a freelance goalkeeping coach, associated mainly with Burnley.

■ Former England youth international goalkeeper Barry Siddall, 6ft tall and weighing 14st 4lb, travelled all over England playing League football. He commenced his professional career with Bolton in 1972 and took part in his last League game for Preston some 20 years later. He retired from the game in 1995 having amassed over 700 senior appearances, 606 in the Football League alone, 20 with the Potters, who held his registration for two years, during which time he deputised for Peter Fox while also having loan spells at Prenton Park and Maine Road. He underwent a cartilage operation at Port Vale, who he helped gain promotion from the Fourth Division in 1983.

SIDIBE, Mamady

Striker: new signing.

Born: Mali, 18 December 1979.
Career: Racing Club de Paris (1997), CA Paris (2000), Swansea City (July 2001), Gillingham (free, August 2002), POTTERS (May 2005).

Talented Mali international striker, 6ft 2in tall Mamady Sidibe scored eight goals in 35 games for Swansea and 13 in 115 for Gillingham before joining the Potters in 2005. He immediately made an impression at The Britannia Stadium and following his debut against Sheffield Wednesday.

SIGURDSSON, Hannes

Striker: new signing.

Born: Iceland, 10 April 1983.
Career: Viking Stavanger, Norway (2000), POTTERS (loan, August 2005).

■ Strong, purposeful player who was signed on loan to boost the first-team squad at the start of the 2005–06 season.

SIGURDSSON, Larus Orri

Defender: 226+2 apps. 7 goals.

Born: Akureyri, Iceland, 4 June 1973.
Career: Thor FC, Iceland (professional, July 1991), POTTERS (£150,000, October 1994), West Bromwich Albion (£325,000, September 1999, retired through injury, November 2004).

■ During his career, Larus Sigurdsson won 42 full caps for Iceland, plus 16 at under-21 level and five as a youth team player. A solid, right-footed blonde defender who effectively occupied the right-back or centre-half positions, he made 228 appearances for Stoke before joining West Brom. Known as 'Iceman' or 'Siggy', he helped the Baggies gain promotion to the Premiership in 2002, but a year or so later suffered a badly damaged cartilage in his left knee at Crystal Palace. He never made a full recovery from that injury and was forced to retire at the age of 31. In his prime he was a quality player who was attracting the attention of several Premiership clubs in the mid-1990s and was an ever-present in 1995–96 when the Potters reached the First Division play-offs. Strong and controlled in the tackle, he was also fast in recovery and read the game exceedingly well. He had the misfortune to get sent-off twice in the space of three months during his Hawthorns days.

SIMONSEN, Steven Preben

Goalkeeper: 31+2 apps.

Born: South Shields, 3 April 1979.
Career: Tranmere Rovers (apprentice, May 1995, professional, October 1996), Everton (£3.3 million, September 1998), POTTERS (free transfer, July 2004).

■ Goalkeeper Steve Simonsen, who has represented England at both youth and under-21 levels, made 42 senior appearances for Tranmere before his big-

money move to Goodison Park in 1998. After just three outings for Everton in his first two seasons on Merseyside he became a regular in 2001–02 but then slipped out of contention again and was happy to join the Potters when the opportunity arose, rejecting an offer of an extension to his contract with the Blues. A fine shot-stopper with a good pair of hands, he had to fight for his place in the first XI at The Britannia Stadium with Ed De Gouy.
* Possibly Everton's most expensive free transfer ever!

SIMPSON, Harry

Outside-right or inside-forward: 12 apps. 3 goals.

Born: Scotland, July 1864.
Died: before 1945.
Career: East Stirlingshire (1885), POTTERS (1889–90), Forfar Atheltic.

■ Harry Simpson had been playing competitive football in Scotland for four years prior to joining the Potters. A useful player with a strong right-foot shot, he could perform in practically any forward position and two of his three goals for the Potters were terrific efforts that came in a 7–1 home League win over Accrington in March 1890.

SIMPSON, Henry

Defender: 8 apps.

Born: Tunstall, Stoke-on-Trent, 1875.
Died: Liverpool, 1958.
Career: Crewe Alexandra, POTTERS (May 1895), New Brighton Tower (August 1897).

■ Harry Simpson was a sturdy centre-half whose eight League appearances for the club were all made in the space of nine weeks at the start of the 1896–97 season when he deputised for Jimmy Grewer.

SINCLAIR, Ronald McDonald

Goalkeeper: 94+2 apps.

Born: Stirling, 19 November 1964.
Career: Nottingham Forest (apprentice, April 1981, professional, October 1982), Wrexham, (on loan, March–May 1984),

Derby County (on loan, August 1984), Sheffield United (on loan, March–April 1986), Leeds United (£10,000, June 1986), Halifax Town (on loan, March 1987 and December 1988–February 1989), Bristol City (free transfer, September 1989), Walsall (on loan, September–October 1991), POTTERS (£25,000, November 1991), Bradford City (on loan, March 1996), Chester City (free transfer, July 1996, retired, November 1998), POTTERS (goalkeeping coach, then under-16 assistant-director and under-19 Academy coach, 2004).

■ After making almost 100 first-team appearances for the Potters, goalkeeper Ronnie Sinclair slipped out of favour with manager Lou Macari and thereafter was third choice behind Mark Prudhoe and Carl Muggleton. Brave and a useful shot-stopper, before joining Stoke he had been loaned out on six occasions, having two spells with Halifax Town, but failed to make an appearance for Derby County and Sheffield United. He never settled down at Elland Road and after 55 outings for Bristol City he joined Stoke three months into the 1995–96 season. A Scottish schoolboy and youth international, Sinclair helped the Potters win the Second Division title in 1993 and when he retired on his 34th birthday he had amassed a total of 283 senior appearances at club level.

SKEELS, Eric Thomas

Defender: 576+20 apps. 7 goals.

Born: Eccles, near Manchester, 27 October 1939.
Career: Stockport County (amateur, April 1955), POTTERS (trailist, July 1956, amateur, August 1956, professional, December 1958), Seattle Sounders (on loan, April–July 1976), Port Vale (September 1976), Leek Town (free transfer, May 1977, retired, May 1978), went into business in Newcastle-under-Lyme with another ex-Potter, Willie Stevenson, and later ran a pub in Stoke-on-Trent.

■ Eric Skeels took the liberty of writing to Stoke City manager Frank Taylor asking for a trial. He got one, and after being an amateur with Stockport County one week he was signed by Stoke City the next, becoming a professional at The Victoria Ground at the age of 19. He progressed through the intermediate and reserve teams and after 15 months hard work finally made his senior debut against Charlton Athletic in March 1960. He became a regular in the first XI the following season and over the next 16 years or so, up to September 1976, gave the Potters tremendous service. He was associated with the club for 20 years, having been a trialist as early as 1956. He appeared in a record 596 competitive games – 507 in the Football League, 44 in the FA Cup, 38 in the League Cup and seven 'others', including three in Europe. In fact, he

played in 606 first-team games altogether. A very consistent performer in either the full-back or left-half positions, and known appropriately as 'Mr. Dependable', he helped Stoke win the Second Division title in 1963, gained a League Cup runners'-up medal in 1964, but was out of the side when the same competition was won in 1972. A short spell on loan in the NASL with Seattle Sounders preceded his departure to neighbours Port Vale. After leaving Vale Park in 1977, he teamed up with Leek Town. Skeels later kept a pub in the Potteries area and still visits The Victoria Ground when time allows.

SLATER, George Alec

Inside-forward: 2 apps. 1 goal.

Born: Walsall, 1864.
Died: in the US.
Career: Hanley United, POTTERS (August 1888, retired from football in 1891 and emigrated to America).

■ Reserve forward George Slater scored his only goal for Stoke in his second game, a 2–1 defeat at Bolton in October 1888 when he was deputising for the injured Arthur Edge. He surprisingly retired at the age of 27 and emigrated to America.

SLOANE, James

Centre-forward: 11 apps. 1 goal.

Born: Glasgow, 1864.
Died: Glasgow, April 1942.
Career: Glasgow Rangers, POTTERS (August 1888), Glasgow Rangers (January 1889).

■ Jimmy Sloane's only goal for the Potters was scored on his debut in a 4–3 home League win over Burnley in October 1888. An aggressive player, he held his place in the side until the turn of the year when fellow Scotsman Bob Barr was preferred as leader of the attack. He made only two appearances in his two spells with Rangers.

SMALL, Bryan

Full-back: 47+5 apps.

Born: Birmingham, 15 November 1971.
Career: Aston Villa (April 1988, professional July 1990), Birmingham City (loan, September 1994), Bolton Wanderers (free transfer, March 1996), Luton Town (loan, September 1997), Bradford City (loan, December 1997), Bury (free transfer, January 1998), POTTERS (free transfer, July 1998 to May 2000), Carlisle United (trialist, August–September 2000), Brentford (trialist, October–November 2001), Walsall (non-contract, January 2001, retired through injury, July 2001).

■ Left wing-back Bryan Small, an England youth and under-21 international (12 caps won at the latter level), played in 45 League and Cup games in eight years at Villa Park and then over the next five made over 100, including 52 for the Potters. A strong, tenacious defender who preferred the left-back position, he was superb on the overlap but a series of injuries disrupted his stay at Stoke, although it must be said that he rarely found favour in the Gudjon Thordarson era.

SMALLEY, William

Forward: 1 app.

Born: Lancaster, 1864.
Died: Preston, 1933.
Career: Preston North End (August 1888), POTTERS (on loan, October 1888), Leyland (1889).

■ When Stoke visited Preston North End for a League game in October 1888 they arrived minus two players and asked the home club to loan them a couple to make up the team. One of them was utility forward Bill Smalley, the other was Archie Dempsey. Stoke lost the game 7–0. Smalley, surprisingly, never appeared in North End's first team. His brother, Robert Edwin Smalley, kept goal for Everton in 1888–90.

SMART, Allan Andrew Colin

Forward: 0+2 apps.

Born: Perth, Scotland, 8 July 1974.
Career: St Johnstone (amateur, August 1990, professional, July 1991), Brechin City (free transfer, December 1991), Inverness Caledonian Thistle (free, July 1993), Preston North End (£15,000, November 1994), Carlisle United (on loan, November–December 1995), Northampton Town (on loan, September 1996), Carlisle United (free, October 1996), Watford (£75,000, July 1998), Hibernian (on loan, August–September 2001), POTTERS (on loan, November 2001), Oldham Athletic (£225,000, November 2001), Dundee United (free, June 2002), Crewe Alexandra (free, August 2003), Milton Keynes Dons (July 2004, released, May 2005).

■ A well-travelled striker who had just two substitute outings while on loan to the Potters from Watford in 2001, Allan Smart reached the personal milestone of 200 club appearances in 2004, but it took him 14 years to do so. He had his best scoring spell with Carlisle in 1996–98 when he netted 17 goals in 54 games, also helping the Cumbrians win the Auto-Windscreen Shield in 1997.

SMART, George Winston

Full-back: 52 apps.

Born: Bristol, 1889.
Died: Stafford, 1941.
Career: Lodge Hill FC (Bristol), Kingswood Rovers, Treharris, POTTERS (with Joseph Jones, July 1911), served in the Army during World War One, Stafford Rangers (March 1920).

■ A well built, impetuous full-back, George Smart played with Joseph Jones at Treharris and Stoke. He was sent off playing against Derby in a wartime game in 1916. In fact, during the hostilities Smart was wounded but recovered sufficiently to continue playing for the Potters until 1920.

SMITH, Alfred

Inside-forward: 149 apps. 72 goals.

Born: Longton, Stoke-on-Trent, 1880.
Died: Stoke-on-Trent, 1957.
Career: Burton United, POTTERS (1904), Wrexham (May 1906), Crewe Alexandra, POTTERS (August 1910, retired, May 1915).

■ A teacher by profession, inside-forward Alf Smith had two spells at The Victoria Ground and assembled a fine scoring record of a goal every two games for the Potters. Signed initially in 1904, he made his League debut against Aston Villa in November 1905 but unfortunately failed to impress the management team and left for Wrexham. Four years later, after serving Crewe, he returned to The Victoria Ground, a much wiser and experienced

footballer who had gained England junior international honours. At this juncture he had the reputation of being an excellent marksman, a 'dazzling dribbler', adept at getting into scoring positions. He became a firm favourite with the supporters and in season 1910–11 rattled in 35 goals in 44 first-team appearances, including five in a 10–0 drubbing of Halesowen (Birmingham League) and hat-tricks in successive games against Wellington and Salisbury City at the turn of the year. He announced his retirement at the end of the 1914–15 campaign. Outside football, Smith was a fine all-round cricketer, acting as vice-captain of Longton CC for a number of seasons.

SMITH, Alexander Richard

Wing-half: 110 apps.

Born: Newcastle-under-Lyme, April 1890.
Career: Newcastle Town, POTTERS (April 1917, professional, August 1919, retired through injury, December 1922).

■ Sturdy wing-half Dicky Smith came to the fore with Newcastle Town and signed for the Potters during the end of the 1916–17 wartime season, when free from duties with the Army. He made his mark during the following campaign in 1917–18, appearing in 32 regional games, adding another 28 to his tally the following term. When peacetime football returned in 1919 he was regarded as a key member of the team and went on to appear in over 100 League and Cup games for the Potters before retiring through injury at the age of 32. He played his last game in August 1922.

SMITH, Andrew Walter

Inside-forward/centre-half: 5 apps.

Born: Camberwell, London, 4 April 1890.
Died: Poole, Dorset, 3 March 1968.
Career: Camberwell & Southwark Council Schools, Langley Green Juniors (Birmingham), Crosswell's Brewery (1907), Birmingham (amateur, August 1912, professional, April 1914), Manchester City (guest, 1914–18), Birmingham (free, August 1918), West Bromwich Albion (£100, July 1919), POTTERS (£1,500, March 1923), Wigan Borough (free, October 1923), Bournemouth (September 1924, retired, May 1925), later ran a catering business in Poole.

■ A smart, deliberate inside-right or centre-forward, Andy Smith could also do justice to the centre-half berth where he played as a 'Policeman'. He was a good, clean header of the ball and his ground work was competent and trusty. He won a First Division Championship medal with West Bromwich Albion in 1920 and scored both goals when the Baggies beat Tottenham Hotspur 2–0 in that year's FA Charity Shield game. He played over 80 games for Albion, 54 for the Blues but only five for Stoke, failing to settle at The Victoria Ground.

SMITH, Clement

Inside-forward: 25 apps. 7 goals.

Born: Wath-on-Deane, 1912.
Died: Yorkshire, 1993.
Career: South Kirby, Halifax Town, Chester, POTTERS (£2,000, March 1938), guest for Halifax Town during World War Two, retired from League football, August 1946.

■ Potters' manager Bob McGrory gambled when he signed Clem Smith, whose lack of height, at only 5ft 7in tall, went against him in the long run. McGrory had hoped he would aide and abet Freddie Steele up front but he never really got to grips with action in the First Division. He played most of his wartime football as a guest with his former club Halifax while Stoke retained his registration. In May 1946 he was released, collected his accrued benefit and duly retired, although he did occasionally turn out for various non-League teams until 1952. He scored 24 goals in a total of 109 League games up to the outbreak of World War Two and during the hostilities netted another eight in 16 games for the Potters. He also made almost 60 appearances for the Shayman as a guest.

SMITH, Denis

Defender: 481+1 apps. 41 goals

Born: Meir, Stoke-on-Trent, 19 November 1947.
Career: Queensbury Road School, POTTERS (apprentice, April 1965, professional, September 1966, player-coach, July 1981), York City, (player, March 1982, player-manager, May 1982, retired as player, April 1983), Sunderland

Denis Smith

(£20,000, manager, June 1987–December 1991), Bristol City (manager, March 1992–January 1993), Oxford United (September 1993), West Bromwich Albion (manager, December 1997–Janauary 1999), Oxford United (manager, February–October 2000), Wrexham (manager, October 2001).*

■ One of the greatest defenders ever to wear the red and white shirt of Stoke City, Smith was a terrific servant to the club for some 17 years, amassing almost 500 senior appearances. He overcame countless injuries and was a totally committed footballer, never shirking a challenge, boldly going where every defender should – firmly into a tackle – and he was as dedicated as any man to Stoke City Football Club. It was not until he was almost 21 that he made his senior debut, lining up against Arsenal at Highbury in a First Division match in September 1968. He made four League appearances that season but thereafter became a permanent fixture in the side, forming a fine defensive partnership with Alan Bloor. He won Football League honours, but unfortunately he failed to pull on an England shirt at any level. He did play at Wembley, though, helping the Potters win the League Cup in 1972, and the ever-reliable Smith scored over 40 goals in almost 500 senior games for the Potters (407 in the Football League). He had also been on the coaching staff at The Victoria Ground since the start of his last season. On leaving the Potters he became manager of York City, holding office at Bootham Crescent until 1987 when he took a similar position with Sunderland, staying at Roker Park for four years. In 1992 he took charge of Bristol City and after only a short time at Ashton Gate he was given the manager's job at Oxford United in September 1993. In 2005 he guided Wrexham to victory in the Final of the LDV Vans Trophy at Cardiff's Millennium Stadium but failed to keep the Welsh club in League One that same season.

NB: Only three players appeared in more first-team games for Stoke than Denis Smith, teammate Eric Skeels (596) and full-backs John McCue (542) and Bob McGrory (511).

* Sunderland paid York City £20,000 when Smith and Viv Busby left Bootham Crescent to take over as manager and assistant manager at Roker Park.

SMITH, Elijah Matthias

Wing-half: 31 apps.

Born: Stoke-on-Trent, 1860.
Died: Stoke-on-Trent, c.1935.
Career: Tunstall (1882), POTTERS (professional, August 1885), Stafford Road FC, Wolverhampton, May 1890).

■ Known affectionately as 'Father' Smith during his footballing career, this tough tackling wing-half played in just over 30 League and FA Cup ties for the Potters, covering a period of five seasons. Among the first group of players to sign professional forms at The Victoria Ground, he represented Staffordshire on several occasions and figured in Stoke's first League game against West Bromwich Albion in September 1888.

SMITH, Henry George

Left-back: 1 app.

Born: Cannock, February 1885.
Died: Walsall, c.1945.
Career: Walsall (professional, 1905), POTTERS, Walsall (1909, retired through injury, March 1910).

■ Rough and ready reserve defender Harry Smith played in one League game for Stoke against West Bromwich Albion in March 1908 when he deputised for the injured Charlie Burgess, Billy Cope moving across to fill in at right-back. He had earlier appeared in 38 matches for Walsall, the club he returned to on leaving The Victoria Ground. Unfortunately, injury prevented him from making any more first-team appearances for the Saddlers.

SMITH, Herbert John

Full-back: 3 apps.

Born: Witney, Oxon, 22 November 1879. Died: Oxford, 7 January 1951.
Career: Oxford Schools, Witney (1894), Richmond (April 1896), POTTERS (November–December 1902), Reading (January 1903), Oxford City (February 1903), Reading (August 1903), Derby County (guest, April 1907), Clapton Orient (1908), Richmond (1909), also assisted Oxfordshire & Beccles College, elected President of the Oxfordshire FA in 1912, a position he held until his death in 1951.

■ An England international, capped 17 times at amateur level and four times by the seniors, full-back Herby Smith also won a soccer gold medal for Great Britain in the 1908 Olympics. He was a major capture by Stoke in 1902 after being strongly recommended to the club. One of the finest amateur footballers of his day, Smith played for the losing side, Oxford City, in the 1903 FA Amateur Cup Final and in the same year represented The South versus The North in an international trial. Well-built, weighing over 13st, he had a trusty left-foot and was a very mobile player who could volley a ball supremely well. He only played in three League games for Stoke during the 1902–03 season. He was on a social visit to meet up with Derbyshire cricketer Bertie Lawton at Cromford Hall when he agreed to assist Derby County against the Wednesday, helping them to a rare victory in the Rams' first relegation season. Smith was one of Reading's greatest players. He skippered the side for several years and made over 150 appearances, the majority of them in the old Southern League

SMITH, Mark Alexander

Outside-left: 2 apps.

Born: Bellshill, Glasgow, 16 December 1964.
Career: Gairdoch United (1981), St Mirren (trialist, 1982), Queen's Park (September 1983), Celtic (June 1986), Dunfermline Athletic (October 1987), Hamilton Academical (on loan, September–October 1989), POTTERS (on loan, February 1990), Nottingham Forest (£75,000, March 1990), Reading (on loan, December 1990–January 1991), Mansfield Town (on loan, March–April 1991), Shrewsbury Town (£25,000, August 1991, released, May 1995).

■ Tidy left-winger Mark Smith played twice for the Potters on loan from Dunfermline Athletic, with whom he gained a Scottish League Division One Championship medal in 1989. During his senior career Smith appeared in 268 club matches and scored 20 goals, having by far his best spells with Queen's Park (87 outings) and Shrewsbury (93).

SMITH, Robert

Half-back: 1 app.

Born: Newcastle-under-Lyme, 1870. Died: before 1960.
Career: Newcastle Swifts, POTTERS (July 1891), Burlsem Port Vale (May 1892).

■ Bob Smith's only League outing for the Potters was against Wolverhampton Wanderers in September 1891 when he replaced the injured Davy Brodie at left-half in a 3–1 home defeat. He did not make Vale's first team.

SMITH, Terence Peter

Centre-forward: 3+1 apps. 1 goal.

Born: Cheltenham, 10 June 1951.
Career: POTTERS (apprentice, May 1967, professional, December 1968), Shrewsbury Town (on loan, February–March 1973), emigrated to Australia, autumn 1973.

■ Terry Smith spent four seasons as a reserve wing-half with Stoke City and scored on his debut when deputising for Jimmy Greenhoff in a 2–1 defeat away to FA Cup holders Chelsea in November 1970. After a loan spell with Shrewsbury Town he chose to leave the UK and play his football in Australia.

SMITH, William Ernest

Forward: 141 apps. 62 goals.

Born: Lostock Hall near Preston, 1886. Died: Preston, 1950.
Career: Leyland FC (1903), Darwen (1904), Nelson (1907), Bradford City (May 1908), POTTERS (May 1909), Preston North End (December 1914). Did not play after World War One.

■ Billy Smith developed into an exceptionally fine marksman who netted over 60 goals in more than 140 senior games in his five and a half years with the Potters. Having failed to make headway with any of his previous clubs, it was a gamble by Stoke when they engaged him as one of the first full-time professionals after the club had been reformed in 1908. He didn't let anyone down and made a terrific start to his career at The Victoria Ground by hitting over 50 goals in his first three seasons, including four on his debut in an 11–0 home Southern League win over Merthyr Town in September 1909. Unfortunately, after that he was plagued by injuries and managed only nine League outings in his last 30 months with the club. He subsequently moved to Deepdale in 1914.

* Another William Ernest Smith played League football immediately after World War One and some reference books have their respective records mixed up. The other Smith played for Hartlepools United, Huddersfield Town, Southend United, Rochdale, Halifax Town and Barrow between 1919 and 1928.

SMYTH, Samuel

Inside-forward: 44 apps. 19 goals.

Born: Belfast, 25 February 1915.
Career: Distillery (amateur, May 1942), Linfield (amateur, 1944), Dundela (professional, June 1947), Wolverhampton Wanderers (£1,100, July 1947), POTTERS (£25,000, September 1951), Liverpool (£12,000, January 1954), later worked as a bookmaker, ran his own sports shop and was also a representative for the sports company, Habro & Falcon, as well as becoming

President of the Clandeboye 36-hole golf complex near Belfast.

■ For five years, from 1942, inside-forward Sammy Smyth had played only amateur football in his native Northern Ireland, serving in the main with Distillery and Linfield, along with a handful of junior clubs. In the summer of 1947, after agreeing to become a professional, he signed for Dundella, thus allowing him to be transferred for a fee, which was effectively a big bonus for the Irish club. A schoolboy international trialist, he had gained several amateur caps for Ireland (with Distillery) and also represented the Irish League, and once at Molineux he quickly made an impact, netting eight goals in 30 games in his first season there. He was immediately upgraded to senior international football, collecting the first of nine full caps against England in 1948. At the same time he continued to impress at Wolves, taking his tally to 43 goals in 116 senior appearances. He gained an FA Cup winners' medal in 1949 when he scored twice in a 3–1 Final win over Leicester City, including a real gem, which was later declared one of the best individual efforts seen at the old Empire Stadium. He joined Stoke in 1951 and in that same year became the first 'Potter' to represent Northern Ireland, playing against England. He also netted a further 19 goals for Stoke City before switching to Liverpool in 1954. He spent just five months at Anfield, quitting competitive League football at the age of 29 to return home to Belfast where he got married and took a full-time job. Smyth scored 72 goals in 187 League games in England.

SOBIECH, Jorg

Midfield: 3 apps.

Born: Gelsenkirchen, Germany, 15 January 1969.
Career: Gelsenkirchen (1988) SG Wattenscheid 09, Germany (1991), NEC Nijmegen, Holland (1995), POTTERS (on loan, March 1998), Twente Enschede, Holland (April 1998).

■ A reliable Dutch contact put Potters manager Chris Kamara in touch with 29-year-old experienced German-born midfielder Jorg Sobiech who was brought to the club on loan for a small fee on transfer deadline in 1998. A wonderful crosser of the ball, he could also play in defence and loved to drive forward. He had an excellent debut, setting up both goals in a win over QPR before a tedious injury ruined his stay in Stoke.

SOO, Hong Yi (Frank)

Wing-half: 185 apps. 9 goals.

Born: Buston, Liverpool, 8 March 1914.
Died: Liverpool, January 1991.
Career: Liverpool Schools, Derby Boys' Club (Liverpool), Prescot Cables, POTTERS (professional, November 1933), guest for Brentford, Chelsea and Everton during World War Two, Leicester City (£4,600, September 1945), Luton Town (£5,000, July 1946), Chelmsford City (May 1950, retired, May 1951), coached the Israeli and Swedish National teams and also SC Padua, Italy (April 1950–June 1952), then coach to four clubs in Sweden: IF City Eskiltuna (July 1952), Orebro Sportklubb (February 1953), Djurgaardens IF (1954–56) and IF Kamraterna Oddevold (1956–59), Scunthorpe United (manager, June 1959–May 1960), St Albans City (manager, 1960–62), then to Sweden as coach to IFK Norrkoping (1962–63), IFK Stockholm (1963–65), AB Copenhagen (1965–66), also coached at various junior clubs in both Copenhagen and Malmo (1966–71), last appointment, Hoganas BK, Sweden (coach, 1972–73).

■ One of the finest wing-halves in the country during the late 1930s, Frank Soo, despite his name, was born and bred in Liverpool. He was working as an office clerk when Stoke City manager Tom Mather signed him at the age of 19. The first player of Chinese descent ever to appear in the Football League, he made his Potters debut at inside-left against Middlesbrough at Ayresome Park in November 1933 – the first of 185 competitive games for the club. Soo also played in 81 World War Two matches and added a further 17 goals to his tally. Strong and resilient, he was a very fair player, a crowd-pleaser who hardly ever put in a rash tackle. Rarely spoken to by the referee, he was part of

that tremendous Stoke middle-line of Tutin, Turner and Soo, and during the hostilities he won eight caps for England, figuring in the same side as fellow 'Stokies' Neil Franklin and Stan Matthews. He also played for the FA and RAF sides. In 1945 Soo moved to Leicester, signed by his former boss Tom Mather. He ended his playing career with Chelmsford City after a spell with Luton. After retiring he became one of the finest coaches in Europe, spending a huge amount of time in Swedish football while also taking time out to manage Scunthorpe United.

SOUTHALL, Neville

Goalkeeper: 12 apps.

Born: Llandudno, 16 September 1958.
Career: Llandudno Swifts, Conwy United, Bangor City, Winsford United, Bury (£6,000, June 1979), Everton (£150,000, July 1981), Port Vale (loan, January–February 1983), Southend United (loan, December 1997–February 1998), POTTERS (free, February 1998), Doncaster Rovers (July 1998), Torquay United (free, December 1998), Bradford City (free, February 2000, retired April 2000), later coached the Wales under-16 squad.

■ Goalkeeper Neville Southall made a club record 750 appearances for Everton, 266 consecutively between 1987–93, including 212 in the League, of which 207 were in the Premiership. He was an ever-present and in the 1984–85 season played in a record 62 senior matches for his club. His overall tally of first-team outings was made up as follows: 578 League/Premiership, 70 FA Cup and 65 League Cup (both records) 13 in European competitions and 24 'others'. He played in 41 Merseyside derbies (another record), helped win two League Championships in 1985, when he was an ever-present, and 1987, triumphed in two FA Cup Finals in 1984 and 1995 and was victorious in the 1985 European Cup-winners' Cup. A runner-up in two other FA Cup Finals, Southall who was voted the Football Writers' 'Player of the Year' in 1985, gained 92 caps for Wales (a record for a goalkeeper and, indeed, for an Everton player) and 15 months after leaving Goodison Park walked away with Torquay United's 'Player of the Year' trophy. On leaving school Southall took a job with the local council clearing gun emplacements built during the Second World War. Almost immediately he became one of the youngest players ever to appear in the Welsh League, aged 14, when placed in goal for Llandudno Swifts against Rhos Aelwyd in 1973. After a spell at the Ritz Café in Llandudno, he worked on several building sites as a hod carrier while trying to establish himself in the local side. He made good progress, and after playing for Conwy and Bangor City he was signed by John Williams, Winsford's shrewd manager. His solid and consistent displays in the Northern Premier League prompted Bury to take him into the Football League at the comparatively advanced age of 21. He never looked back after that – and what a tremendous servant he was to Everton – signed for what was a bargain fee by former Stoke player Howard Kendall, one of his first acquisitions after he took over the hot seat at Goodison Park. Southall played his first game for the Merseysiders in place of Jim Arnold at Ipswich in October 1981 and made his last appearance 16 years later against Spurs in November 1997. Standing over 6ft tall and weighing 13st 8lb, he was a courageous goalkeeper whose reflexes for a big man were quite exceptional. He was a fighter to the last, always urging on his colleagues and he once said 'If you don't believe you can win, there is no point in getting out of bed at the end of the day.' He was well past his best when he assisted the Potters in a dozen games in 1998 when he took over from Carl Muggleton. In his first outing he was tasked to keep a clean sheet in the Potteries derby against Port Vale.

SPEARING, Anthony

Left-back: 9 apps.

Born: Romford, Essex, 7 October 1964.
Career: Norwich City (apprentice, October 1980, professional, October 1982), POTTERS (on loan, November–December 1984), Leicester City (£100,000, July 1988), Oxford United (on loan), Plymouth Argyle (July 1991), Peterborough United (free transfer, January 1993–May 1997).

■ An enthusiastic player and England youth international, loan signing Tony Spearing took over at left-back from Tony Maskery (switched into midfield) halfway through the 1984–85 season. A fine player on his day, he made over 350

senior appearances during his 17-year career, having his best spell with Posh (132 outings).

SPENCER, John Samuel Thomas

Outside-right: 17 apps.

Born: Middlesbrough, 18 January 1902.
Died: Wallasey, 3 January 1987.
Career: Crook Town (amateur, April 1919), POTTERS (amateur, August 1921, professional, November 1921), New Brighton (July 1923), Mid Rhondda (June 1925), Aberdeen (November 1925), Bristol Rovers (June 1928), Newry Town, Ireland (March 1929), New Brighton (August 1931–June 1932), Winsford United (player-manager, September

1933–June 1935), scouted for several clubs before and immediately after World War Two, later appointed President of the Wirral Youth Football League.

■ Right-winger Sam Spencer was brought into the Potters' first team to replace Harry Crossthwaite and proved to be a useful competitor having played over 50 games for the amateur side Crook Town. In his latter years (1931–32) he appeared as a wing-half and he played competitive football in England, Scotland, Ireland and Wales.

SPENCER, William

Full-back: 354 apps.

Born: Nelson, 15 May 1903.
Died: before 1990.
Career: Hebden Bridge, POTTERS (amateur, December 1924, professional, April 1925), Crewe Alexandra (£750, June 1938, retired, September 1940).

■ Billy Spencer had a fine career at The Victoria Ground. An ex-mill worker, he was 'cool, calm and collected' as they say, and could occupy either full-back position. Very conscious of how the game was being played, he and Bob McGrory formed a wonderful partnership, playing together for close on 10 seasons and helping the Potters win the Second Division title in 1933. Spencer made his League debut in February 1926 against Portsmouth when Alex Milne moved over to right-back, and he played his final game for the Potters against Wolverhampton Wanderers in December 1935, before handing over the right-back jersey to Bill Winstanley. He remained at The Victoria Ground for two more seasons, playing reserve-team football when required.

SPROSON, Archibald

Inside-left: 1 app.

Born: Stafford, 1890.
Died: before 1980.
Career: Stafford Rangers, POTTERS (September 1912), Cannock (May 1913). Did not play after World War One.

■ One of the many one-match 'wonders' to appear in Stoke's senior side, Archie Sproson had his moment of glory when he lined up at inside-left in a 1–0 defeat by Coventry City in a Southern League game in January 1913, replacing the injured Alf Smith.

STAINROD, Simon Allan

Striker: 33+1 apps. 7 goals.

Born: Sheffield, 1 February 1959.
Career: Sheffield & South Yorkshire Boys, Sheffield United (apprentice, June 1974, professional, July 1976), Oldham Athletic (£60,000, March 1979), Queen's Park Rangers (£275,000, November 1980), Sheffield Wednesday (£250,000, February 1985), Aston Villa (£250,000, September 1985), POTTERS (£90,000, December 1987), Racing Club Strasbourg, France (December 1988–89), FC Rouen, France (1989–90), Falkirk (player, June 1990, later player-caretaker manager), Dundee (player-caretaker manager), Ayr United (manager).

■ Accomplished marksman Simon Stainrod bagged all four goals on his debut for Aston Villa in a 4–1 League Cup win at Exeter in September 1985. Capped by England at youth-team level, he could also be an aggressive striker, easily losing his temper, but he certainly had the knack of being in the right place at the right time to snap up the half-

chance that came his way. He spent only a year at The Victoria Ground, linking up mainly with Graham Shaw, making his first of 34 senior appearances in a 2–1 home League defeat by Ipswich Town on New Year's Day 1988. He had to wait until his 10th outing to claim his first goal, the winner at home to Swindon almost four months later. A runner-up in the 1982 FA Cup Final with QPR, he helped the London club win the Second Division title the following year, and during his lengthy and varied career he netted more than 125 goals in over 400 matches at competitive level. He did well on the European scene prior to his managerial appointments in Scotland.

STANFORD, Thomas Arthur

Defender: 1 app.

Born: Tunstall, Staffs, 1860.
Died: before 1945.
Career: Tuntsall park, POTTERS (September 1883), Congleton (August 1884).

■ Tom Stanford played in Stoke's first-ever FA Cup tie, lining up at right-back against Manchester at The Victoria Ground in the qualifying round in November 1883.

STANLEY, Jesse Walter

Full-back: 3 apps.

Born: Stoke-on-Trent, 1870.
Died: Stoke-on-Trent, 1941.
Career: Northwich Victoria, POTTERS

(December 1891), Northwich Victoria (August 1892).

■ All of Jesse Stanley's senior outings for the Potters came in March 1892 when he deputised for Tommy Clare. Every game was lost, including a 5–3 reverse against Blackburn Rovers.

STATHAM, Derek James

Left-back: 49 apps. 1 goal.

Born: Whitmore Reans, Wolverhampton, 24 March 1959.
Career: St Mary's Primary & St Edmund's Junior Schools (Wolverhampton), West Bromwich Albion (apprentice, July 1975, professional, April 1976), Southampton (£100,000, August 1987), POTTERS (£50,000, July 1989), Aston Villa (trialist, July 1991), Walsall (August 1991–May 1993), Telford United (briefly, 1993–94), King's Lynn (briefly), West Bromwich Albion All Stars (mid-to late 1990s/early 2000s), now running a café/bar in Marbella, Spain (near to John Gidman).

■ Derek Statham was perhaps the finest left-back in England during the early 1980's, but he had Arsenal's Kenny Sansom ahead of him at international level and gained only three full caps for England despite all his effort, skill and enthusiasm, against Sansom's tally of 86. In fact, Albion boss Ron Atkinson, at the time, said that Statham was miles better than Sansom, England caps or not. A cheerful, buoyant character with a biting tackle, he loved to attack when given the chance. Indeed, he was well up with his forwards when he scored past Peter Shilton on his Albion debut against the Potters in December 1976, which was won 2–0, having earlier that year helped the club's youngsters lift the FA youth Cup by beating Wolves in the two leg Final. Statham played for his country at youth-team level (seven caps gained), followed up with six appearances for the under-21 side and also represented England 'B' before breaking into the full England team under Bobby Robson's management in 1982. Midland Sportswriter's 'Young Player of the Year' in 1978, Statham struggled at times with injuries during his last two seasons at The Hawthorns. And it was certainly a surprise when, in 1987, a proposed £250,000 transfer to Liverpool was called off at the 11th hour following unfavourable medical reports on his fitness. He was transfer-listed at the end of that season and subsequently joined Southampton for a six-figure fee. He made 75 appearances for Saints before doing a solid job down the left for the Potters, taking over initially from Cliff Carr who later regained the number three shirt before Statham left 'The Vic' in 1991. His only goal for the Potters earned a point from a 1–1 draw at Bournemouth in September 1990.

STATON, Frank Edgar

Centre-forward: 4 apps. 2 goals.

Born: Hanley, Stoke-on-Trent, 1864.
Died: before 1945.
Career: Goldenhill Wanderers, POTTERS (August 1887), Stafford Road, Wolverhampton (May 1889).

■ Frank Staton played in each of Stoke's first four League games at the start of the initial campaign of 1888–89, scoring two goals. He had been with the club the previous season but failed to keep his place in the side.

STEEL, Frederick Leslie

Left-half: 3 apps.

Born: Stoke-on-Trent, 1884.
Died: before 1960.
Career: Ashwood Villa, POTTERS (August 1909), Lancaster Town (November 1910).

■ Amateur Fred Steel spent two months with Stoke, playing in the opening three games of the 1909–10 season when he took over from the previous season's regular left-half Arthur Pitt. He made his debut in the 11–0 Southern League win over Merthyr Town, having a hand in two of the goals.

STEELE, Frederick Charles

Centre-forward: 251 apps. 159 goals

Born: Hanley, Stoke-on-Trent, 6 May 1916.
Died: Newcastle-under-Lyme, 23 April 1976.

Career: POTTERS (amateur, July 1931), Downings Tileries (1931–33), POTTERS (as a professional, June 1933), guest for Sheffield United, Northampton Town, Notts County, Leicester City, Doncaster Rovers, Bradford Park Avenue, Leeds United, Arsenal, Nottingham Forest and Fulham during World War Two, Mansfield Town (£1,000, player-manager, June 1949), Port Vale (£1,500, player-

manager, December 1951, retired as a player, January 1953, resigned, January 1957, re-appointed as manager, October 1962, left club by mutual consent, February 1965).

■ Freddie Steele did splendidly in schoolboy football before joining the Potters in the summer of 1931, being told by manager Tom Mather that he would work in the offices and play for the club's nursery side, Downings Tileries, until he was old enough to turn professional. That's how confident Mather was that Steele would make the grade! Two years later the appropriate 'signing on' forms were produced and immediately Steele put pen to paper. In double-quick time he became a goalscoring supremo at The Victoria Ground – a big hit with the supporters. Nicknamed 'Nobby', he made his senior debut against Huddersfield Town in December 1934 and scored his first goal in a 3–0 home win over West Bromwich Albion shortly afterwards, on Boxing Day. Thereafter, the goals flowed thick and fast. He went on to claim a total of 220 in all games for the Potters: 140 in the Football League, 19 in the FA Cup and a further 81 in World War Two competitions. He appeared in 346 first-team matches (95 in World War Two) and was part or a terrific forward-line that also included Stan Matthews, Tommy Sale and Joe Johnson. In September 1936 Steele played for the Football League XI against The Irish League in Belfast, scoring in a 3–2 defeat. Three weeks later he won the first of his six full England caps and in April 1937 was one of three Stoke City players who lined up against Scotland at Hampden Park in front of 135,000 fans. Steele did well in that 3–1 reverse and went on to the end-of-season tour to Scandinavia, scoring twice in big wins over Sweden and Finland. In October 1937 he badly injured his knee in a collision with the Charlton Athletic goalkeeper Sam Bartram. This set him back and he lost his confidence and struggled to regain full fitness. When Europe went to War in 1939, at the age of 23 he stunned hundreds people by announcing his retirement, stating that he was suffering from depression! However, after being treated by a psychiatrist he subsequently made a successful return to football and scored 10 goals in his next five matches! Unfortunately, he played very little competitive football during the first part of the hostilities and when peacetime soccer returned he was 30 years old, but still eager to play in the First Division. Indeed, during the 1945–46 transitional campaign he scored 49 goals in 43 League and FA Cup appearances. Three years later, after having given the Potters magnificent service and by now suffering with a niggling knee injury, Steele left The Victoria Ground to become player-manager of Mansfield Town in 1949. He later had two spells in charge of Port Vale (the first as player-manager, when he built up a solid, uncompromising side of mainly local players). He concentrated on getting in place a string defence that became known as 'The Iron Curtain' and 'The Steele Curtain'. He guided his tough Vale side to both the Third Division North Championship and FA Cup semi-finals in the same season (1953–54) but three years later, with the team now struggling and deep in relegation trouble, he resigned. He returned for his second term of office in 1962 and despite spending a lot of money on new players in a hope of gaining promotion, he left Vale Park when the team was on the brink of slipping into the Fourth Division. He also spent a short time in South Africa and was the uncle of the late David Steele, the former Northants, Derbyshire and England Test cricketer. Steele and his Potters teammate Harry Ware guested for Northampton Town when they beat Stoke City 10–0 at The County Ground in a Regional League game in May 1942.

* When at the peak of fitness, Freddie Steele also hurdled for Staffordshire as well as competing in the men's 4 x 100 sprint relay. He could run the 100 yards in 11.5 seconds.

STEELE, Timothy Wesley

Wing-forward: 7 apps. 1 goal.

Born: Coventry, 1 December 1967.
Career: Shrewsbury Town (December 1985), Wolverhampton Wanderers (£80,000, February 1989), POTTERS (on loan, February–March 1992), Bradford City (free transfer, July 1993), Hereford United (January 1994), Exeter City (August 1996–March 1997).

■ Tim Steele played over 60 games on the wing (as a wide midfielder) for Shrewsbury Town before transferring to Wolves in 1989. Three years later, after losing his first-team place at Molineux, he was signed on loan by the Potters and scored once, in a 5–2 home win over Exeter City, in seven League games. After leaving Molineux he signed for Bradford City and later assisted Hereford United and Exeter, quitting League football in 1997 with 214 appearances under his belt and 18 goals.

STEIN, Mark Earl Sean

Striker: 134 apps. 72 goals.

Born: Cape Town, South Africa, 29 January 1966.
Career: Luton Town (apprentice, April 1982, professional, January 1984), Aldershot (on loan, January 1986), Queen's Park Rangers (£300,000, August 1988), Oxford United (£50,000, September 1989), POTTERS (£100,000, September 1991), Chelsea (£1.45 million, October 1993), POTTERS (on loan, November 1996–January 1997), Ipswich Town (loan, August–September 1997), Bournemouth (on loan, March–May 1998, signed, June 1998), Luton Town (free transfer, July 2000, reserve team player-coach, May 2001), Dagenham & Redbridge (July 2001).

■ Scorer of almost 200 goals (72 for the Potters) in 568 League and Cup games in a first-class career covering almost 20 years, Mark Stein was a lively striker with a knack of being in the right place at the right time. Capped by England at youth-team level as a teenager, he won the League Cup with QPR in 1988 and the Autoglass Trophy and Second Division Championship with Stoke in 1992 and 1993 respectively. He also had the pleasure of being one of only five 'Potters' to score at the old Wembley Stadium, obliging against Stockport County in that AGT victory. After a fine first season at Stamford Bridge niggling injuries began

to interrupt his game. He returned for a second spell at The Victoria Ground but by that time he was slowly winding down his senior career, although he did bounce back with Dagenham & Redbridge in 2001–02 by netting 24 goals to finish joint top-scorer in the Conference with Boston United's Daryl Clare. Dagenham were actually pipped for a place in the Football League on goal-difference by Boston. He added a further 21 goals to his tally the following season.

* Two of his brothers, Brian (Luton Town and Barnet) and Edward (Barnet), were also professional footballers.

STENTIFORD, George Robert

Half-back: 11 apps.

Born: Brentford, London, 7 May 1900.
Died: Guildford, 1 February 1976.
Career: Old Kingstonians, Huddersfield Town (May 1920), POTTERS (March 1923), Stockport County (October 1924), Guildford United (August 1926, retired, April 1932).

■ After failing to make the first XI at Leeds Road, tough-tackling half-back George Stentiford played in only 11 League games for the Potters during his 18 months with the club. He went on to make 45 appearances for Stockport before re-entering non-League football with Guildford.

STEVENSON, William

Wing-half: 94+13 apps. 7 goals.

Born: Leith, 26 October 1939.
Career: Edinburgh Schools, Edna Hearts (1955), Dalkieth Thistle (1956), Glasgow Rangers (November 1957), went to Australia (briefly), Liverpool (£20,000, October 1962), POTTERS (£48,000, December 1967), Tranmere Rovers (free transfer, July 1973), Vancouver Whitecaps, NASL (May–September 1974, retired on his return to England), went into business in Newcastle-under-Lyme with another former Potters player Eric Skeels.

■ Willie Stevenson was a stylish wing-half, exceedingly good in possession, a fine passer of the ball, a hard tackler when required and one of the few players sold by the legendary Bill Shankly to another First Division club! When he moved from Anfield to The Victoria Ground he had already appeared in over 200 games for the Merseysiders, whom he helped twice win the First Division title in 1964 and 1966 and the FA Cup in 1965 as well as gaining a runners'-up medal in the European Cup-winners' Cup (1966). After commencing his professional career in his native Scotland with the team he supported as a lad, Rangers, he quickly claimed a first-team place at Ibrox and went on to win both the League Championship in 1959 and the

Scottish Cup in 1960 with the 'Gers. Having previously represented his country at schoolboy level (captaining the side three years running), he added Scottish League honours to his collection while also appearing in 108 competitive games in the famous blue shirt. However, while still registered as a player at Ibrox he slipped over to Australia, hugely disappointed that his place in the side had gone to new signing Jim Baxter. Thankfully, he returned safe and sound and joined Liverpool for £20,000. He made well over 100 first-team appearances for the Potters but sadly missed the team's great FA Cup runs in the early 1970s, and he also sat out the 1972 League Cup Final win over Chelsea. A fractured leg disrupted his final year at The Victoria Ground, and in July 1973 he left the club, moving on a free transfer to Tranmere Rovers.

STEVENTON, Thomas William

Goalkeeper: 3 apps.

Born: Bunbury near Crewe, 8 September 1898.

Died: Wolverhampton, 5 March 1971.
Career: Worleston FC, Aston Villa (March 1915), served in the Army during World War One, POTTERS (March 1921), Wolverhampton Wanderers (May 1922).

■ Amateur reserve goalkeeper Ted Steventon made only three League appearances for Stoke, all at the end of the 1920–21 season when he replaced Percy Knott and kept a clean sheet on his debut against Bristol City. He joined Wolves as extra cover for Noel George.

STEWART, Paul Andrew

Forward or midfield: 25 apps. 3 goals.

Born: Manchester, 7 October 1964.
Career: Blackpool (apprentice, August 1980, professional, October 1981), Manchester City (£200,000, March 1987), Tottenham Hotspur (£1.7 million, June 1988), Liverpool (£2.3 million, July 1992), Crystal Palace (on loan, January–March 1994), Wolverhampton Wanderers (on loan, September–November 1994), Burnley (on loan, February–March 1996), Sunderland (on loan, August–September 1995, signed on free transfer, March 1996), POTTERS (free, June 1997), Workington (free, August 1998–May 2000).

■ In a splendid 20-year career, Paul Stewart scored over 150 goals in more than 650 club appearances (145 in 600 in major League and Cup competitions) as well as gaining three full, five 'B', one under-21 and three youth caps for England. He was also an FA Cup winner with Spurs in 1991 and the recipient of two Division One Championship winners' medals with Palace in 1994 and Sunderland in 1996, while helping Workington clinch the North-Western Trains League in the twilight of his career in 1999. A totally committed player, using both aggression (when called for) and quality, he was a top-rate finisher who certainly did well at Blackpool (225 games and 62 goals) and Spurs (172 outings and 37 goals). He was almost 33 when he joined the Potters but battled on to give the club good service for a season, netting the winning goal at Middlesbrough in his third League match.

STIRLING, John

Outside-right: 21 apps. 1 goal.

Born: Clydebank, Scotland, 1886.
Died: Kinross, Scotland, 1924.
Career: Clydebank (1906), Clyde (1909), Middlesbrough (July 1911), Bradford City (July 1914), Bradford Park Avenue (September 1914), served in the Army during World War One, POTTERS (July 1919), Coventry City (March 1920), Alloa Athletic (July 1920, retired due to ill-health, May 1922).

■ Right-winger Jock Stirling had an interesting career that spanned 15 years. He scored only one League goal for the Potters, the clincher against Stockport County at home in a 2–1 win in October 1919. He made over 100 appearances while at Ayresome Park and 34 for Park Avenue. He was only 38 when he died.

STOKOE, Graham Lloyd

Midfield: 0+2 apps.

Born: Newcastle-on-Tyne, 17 December 1975.
Career: Durham County Schools, Northumberland FA, Newcastle United (junior), POTTERS (apprentice, April 1992, professional, July 1994), Hartlepool United (on loan, February–March 1996, signed on a free transfer, August 1998), Blyth Spartans (June 1999).

■ Tall, rangy reserve midfielder Graham Stokoe had a brief spell with Newcastle United as a junior before graduating through the ranks at The Victoria Ground. He made his debut in League football while on loan with Hartlepool United in February 1996 and his first outing for the Potters was as a substitute against Portsmouth at Fratton Park nine months later.

STRONG, Gregory

Defender: 5 apps. 1 goal.

Born: Bolton, 5 September 1975.
Career: Wigan Athletic (apprentice, April 1992, professional, October 1992), Bolton Wanderers (September 1995), Blackpool (on loan, November–December 1997), POTTERS (on loan, March–April 1999), Motherwell (on loan, March–May 2000, signed permanently, July 2000).

■ An England schoolboy and youth team representative, big, powerful central defender Greg Strong made only 84 League and Cup appearances in eight years south of the border before joining Motherwell in 2000. He lined-up with Larus Sigurdsson, Nicky Mohan and Bryan Small in the Potters back-four during his loan spell at The Britannia Stadium.

STUART, Edward Albert

Centre-half: 71 apps. 2 goals.

Born: Johannesburg, 12 May 1931.
Career: Johannesburg Rangers, Wolverhampton Wanderers (professional, January 1951), POTTERS (£8,000, July 1962), Tranmere Rovers (£4,000, August 1964), Stockport County (July 1966), Worcester City (August 1968–November 1970, later team manager to 1972), Wolves Old Stars (1975–79).

■ South African-born defender Eddie Stuart was a very competitive footballer. As hard as they come, he was quick, robust, a tough no-nonsense tackler and a battler to the end, always giving 100 percent out on the park. He played intermediate football in his homeland before Stan Cullis signed him for Wolves in 1951. He went on to appear in well over 300 games for the Molineux club, surprisingly making his League debut in the centre-forward position against Black Country neighbours West Bromwich Albion in April 1952, scoring a goal to celebrate the occasion, his only one for the club. A full-back in the old gold and black strip, he helped Wolves win the First Division Championship in 1954, 1958 and 1959 and added an FA Cup winners' medal to his collection in 1960. In his first season at The Victoria ground, when he starred at centre-half, he skippered the Potters to the Second Division title, scoring two goals – the first an important one in a 2–1 home victory over Huddersfield Town in December 1962. Later he joined many other seasoned professionals at both Stockport and Tranmere, helping the Birkenhead side win the Fourth Division Championship in 1967. On retiring from competitive football with 510 League appearances under his belt, Stuart had an excellent spell with

Worcester City in 1968–70, for whom he made 110 appearances. Thereafter, he managed the non-League club and in the late 1970s/early '80s, when living in Tettenhall, he played in various charity matches for the Wolves Old Stars in and around the Midlands, as well as running a successful hairdressing business with shops in Wolverhampton, Codsall and Newcastle-under-Lyme. He returned to South Africa in 1996, leaving his daughter to continue to live and work in Wolverhampton.

* In 1952 Stuart had to go back home to Johannesburg after being infected by a 'mystery illness'. Thankfully, he responded to treatment and came back to England to continue his footballing career.

STURGESS, Albert

Full-back or left-half: 135 apps. 4 goals.

Born: Etruria, Stoke-on-Trent, 21 October 1882.
Died: Sheffield, 16 July 1957.
Career: Tunstall Crosswells, POTTERS (July 1900, professional, October 1900), Sheffield United (June 1908), served in the Army during World War One, Norwich City (August 1923, retired, April 1925), later ran a crockery shop in Sheffield.

■ A honest-to-goodness defender with a strong kick, superb anticipation and reliability, Albert Sturgess was

nicknamed 'hairpin' by his colleagues. After doing well in the Potters reserve side, he gained a first-team place in 1905 and quickly developed into a prime defender, going on to appear in almost 140 senior games for the Potters before transferring to Sheffield United in 1908. During his time at Bramall Lane he occupied every position on the field, including that of goalkeeper. He gained an FA Cup winners' medal in 1915 and was selected for two full internationals by England, lining up at left-half against Ireland in 1911 and right-half against Scotland in 1914. After serving his country during World War One he joined Norwich City, for whom he played until 1925. On retiring, Sturgess returned to Sheffield where he opened a crockery shop in Eccleshall Road. Also a fine crown green bowler, he was 42 years and 116 days old when he played his last senior match of his career, for Norwich against Millwall in February 1925.

STURRIDGE, Simon Andrew

Striker: 56+37 apps. 15 goals.

Born: Birmingham, 9 December 1969.
Career: William Cowper, Duddleston Manor & St George's Schools, Birmingham City (apprentice, June 1986, professional, July 1988), POTTERS (£75,000, September 1993), Blackpool (on loan, March 1999), Northampton Town (free transfer, August 1999), Shrewsbury Town (on loan, March–May 2000), released by Northampton Town (June 2000).

■ A fast-raiding striker with good technique and goalscoring ability, Simon Sturridge was one of several Blues players who found their way to The Victoria Ground under Lou Macari's management. He netted 38 goals in 186 appearances during his time at St Andrew's, gaining a winners' medal at Wembley after helping his side win the 1991 Leyland DAF Cup Final. In his first three campaigns at The Victoria Ground 'Studger' did well, netting 15 goals in 80 appearances, including an excellent hat-trick in a 4–2 win at Southend in November 1995. He

was injured early on in 1996–97 and was out of action all season, and he never quite regained his firepower as a 'Potter'. Sturridge's younger brother, Dean, played for Derby County Torquay United, Leicester City, Wolves and Sheffield United (1991–2005).

SUDDICK, Alan

Inside-forward: 9 apps. 1 goal.

Born: Chester-le-Street, 2 May 1944.
Career: Newcastle United (), Southport (on loan) Bury, Blackpool, POTTERS (December 1976–August 1977), now self-employed, living and working in Blackpool.

■ Alan Suddick was a very cultured footballer who was certainly unlucky not to have gained at least one full England cap, particularly when he was playing so well for Blackpool. Unfortunately, The Victoria Ground faithful never saw the best of his talents after manager Tony Waddington had cast his net far and wide in an attempt to bring in quality players for a relatively small fee when the club was trying desperately to raise cash in a bold effort to fend off the bank manager and, indeed, to avoid relegation to the Second Division – an object they failed to achieve. During his career Suddick scored 108 goals in 503 League games between 1961 and 1978, including 64

strikes in 310 outings with the 'Seasiders'. His only goal for Stoke came in the 3–1 League defeat at West Bromwich Albion in May 1977. He played twice for England's under-23 side and also represented his country at youth-team level.

SVARD, Sebastian

Defender or midfield: 10+4 apps. 1 goal.

Born: Hividovre, Denmark, 15 January 1983.
Career: FC Copenhagen, Arsenal (January 2000), FC Copenhagen (on loan, August–December 2003), POTTERS (on loan, January–May 2004).

■ Seb Svard, a Danish youth and under-21 international, capped seven times in the latter category, had failed to make a breakthrough with Arsenal and was loaned out to his former club before having a similar spell at the Britannia Stadium. A versatile player, strong and competitive, he netted a cracking goal against Sunderland in mid-March 2004 that earned his side a point at The Stadium of Light. He won a Danish under-20 cap during his short stay in the Potteries.

SWARBRICK, James

Outside-left: 3 apps.

Born: Lytham St Anne's, June 1881.
Died: Lancashire, c.1970.
Career: Blackpool Red Star (1896), Marton Combination (1898), Blackpool Etrurians (1899), Blackburn Rovers (professional, November 1901), Accrington Stanley (on loan, March 1902), Brentford (June 1903), Grimsby Town (July 1905), Oldham Athletic (May 1907), Southport Central (November 1909), POTTERS (July 1910), Port Vale (August 1911), Swansea Town (August 1912, retired May 1916), served in the Army during World War One.

■ Left-winger Jimmy Swarbrick entered League football with Blackburn at the age of 20. He then travelled around the country before joining the Potters just after his 29th birthday. He never really settled at The Victoria Ground, making only three appearances in place of Amos Baddeley in Southern League games against Ton Pentre, Chesham Town and Salisbury City. He set up two goals in a 6–0 win over the latter club. Two years after leaving Stoke he gained a Welsh Cup winners' medal with Swansea. Swarbrick was an exceptionally good ball-player who suffered a compound fracture of the leg playing for Oldham against Bradford City at Valley Parade in September 1907. The injury kept him out of action for over a year. He had made his Latics debut against Stoke earlier that month, scoring in a 3–1 win.
* His younger brother, Lewis Swarbrick, played for Blackpool (1903–04).

SWEENEY, Peter Henry

Winger: new signing.

Born: Glasgow, 25 September 1984.
Career: Millwall (apprentice, December 2000, professional, December 2002), POTTERS (June 2005).

■ Former Scottish Youth, 'B' and under-21 international, winning eight caps in the latter category, tall, pacy winger Peter Sweeney broke into Millwall's first team in October 2003 and went on to appear in 67 senior games for the Lions before joining the Potters.

TAAFE, Steven Lee

Striker: 4+5 apps.

Born: Stoke-on-Trent, 10 September 1979.
Career: POTTERS (apprentice, April 1995, professional, September 1996, released, May 2000).

■ Only 5ft 5in tall and weighing barely 9st, striker Steve Taafe was given very few opportunities to show his goalscoring prowess with the Potters as his senior outings were few and far between.

TAGGART, Gerald Paul

Defender: 45 apps. 2 goals.

Born: Belfast, 18 October 1970.
Career: Belfast junior football, Manchester City (apprentice, April 1987, professional, July 1989), Barnsley (£75,000, January 1990), Bolton Wanderers (£1.5 million, August 1995), Leicester City (free transfer, July 1998), POTTERS (on loan, December 2003–January 2004, signed on a free transfer, February 2004, signed a new one-year contract, August 2004).

■ A left-footed defender, rugged in his performances, Gerry Taggart was 33 when he joined the potters on loan from Leicester City, and he had already accumulated a fine set of statistics: 483 club appearances and 38 goals. He had also already gained 51 full caps for Northern Ireland plus two more at under-23 level, as well as representing his country in both schoolboy and youth internationals. A First Division Championship winner in 1997 and the recipient of a League Cup winners' prize

Gerry Taggart

in 2000, Taggart made a solid enough start to his career at The Britannia Stadium, playing in 21 games before injuries started to plague him halfway through the 2004–05 campaign.

TALBOT, Brian Ernest

Midfield: 61+3 apps. 7 goals.

Born: Ipswich, 21 July 1953.
Career: Ipswich & Suffolk Schools, Ipswich Town (amateur, July 1969, professional, July 1972), Toronto Metros (1971 and 1972), Arsenal (£450,000, January 1979), Watford (£150,000, June 1985), POTTERS (£25,000, October 1986), West Bromwich Albion (£15,000, January 1988, appointed caretaker-manager, October 1988, upgraded to manager, November 1988, sacked, January 1991), Fulham (non-contract, March 1991), Aldershot (non-contract, April 1991, later manager, 1991–92), Sudbury Town (player-manager-coach, 1992–93), Hibernians, Malta (player-coach, 1993–97), Rushden & Diamonds (guest,1996, manager, August 1997), Oldham Athletic (manager, March 2004, resigned, March 2004), Oxford United (manager, May 2005).

■ Brian Talbot was a well-balanced, hard-working yet very skilful midfielder who won six full England caps and was an FA Cup winner with both Ipswich Town and Arsenal in successive seasons, 1978 and 1979. He made 533 League appearances during his career, which spanned 22 seasons. Signed by Potters manager Mick Mills (a former teammate at Ipswich Town), he made his debut against Huddersfield Town in October 1986, which was won 2–0, and spent 15 months at The Victoria Ground before transferring to The Hawthorns, where he subsequently became manager. He lost his job after a shock home defeat by non-Leaguers Woking in the third round of the FA Cup in January 1991. Later, after returning to senior management, he guided Rushden & Diamonds into the Football League as Nationwide Conference winners in 2001 and a year later saw them reach the Third Division Play-off Final at The Millennium Stadium, beaten by Cheltenham Town. *Talbot is only one of a dozen footballers to play for and against the same club in a Wembley FA Cup Final (Ipswich and Arsenal).

TAPAI, Ernest

Forward: 0+1 app.

Born: Subotica, Yugoslavia, 14 February 1967.
Career: Melbourne Hungaria, Australia, Hellas (South Melbourne), Melbourne Hungaria (again), Footscray, Australia, Sunshine George Cross, Australia, Adelaide City, Austarlia, POTTERS (£40,000, October 1992), Grupo Desportivo Estoril Praia, Portugal (free transfer, March 1993).

■ After becoming a naturalised Australian, striker, Ernie Tapai went on to win over 30 full caps for his adopted country. He only made one substitute appearance for the Potters, coming in the second half against Crewe Alexandra in an Autoglass Trophy match in January 1993. He left The Victoria Ground for the Portuguese First Division side, Estoril, two months later.

TAYLOR, Henry

Outside-right or left: 26 apps. 11 goals

Born: Hanley, Stoke-on-Trent, 1912.
Died: c.1985.
Career: Hanley schoolboy football, Stoke St Mary's, POTTERS (amateur, February 1929, professional, June 1929), Liverpool (July 1932, released, May 1936).

■ Winger Harry Taylor had a fine scoring record with Stoke, netting on average a goal every two games over a period of three years. Initially a reserve to the two Bobbys, Archibald and Liddle, he had his best spell in the first team between Boxing Day and mid-March in 1931–32 when he had a run of 13 successive games, all but one on the left flank. He went on to score six goals in 69 appearances for Liverpool, occupying every forward position for the Merseyside club.

TAYLOR, Henry George

Forward: 10 apps. 4 goals

Born: Fegg Hayes, Stoke-on-Trent, August 1892.
Died: Manchester, 1968.
Career: North Staffs Schoolboys, Chell Heath, Fegg Hayes, POTTERS (July 1909), Huddersfield Town (May 1910), Port Vale (£30, May 1912), Manchester City (£300, June 1912, retired, May 1921, after serving in the Army during World War One).

■ After scoring four goals in 10 first-team games for the Potters, utility forward Henry Taylor joined Huddersfield Town for their first season in the Football League. A beefy player, he appeared in 16 games for the Yorkshire club, scoring 5 goals, before returning to the Potteries to sign for Port Vale. He never kicked a ball in earnest for the Valiants, who quickly transferred him to Manchester City four weeks after signing him! He netted 28 times in 101 League and Cup games for the Maine Road club.

TEMPEST, William

Outside-left: 217 apps. 30 goals.

Born: Stoke-on-Trent, 8 January 1893.
Died: before 1980.
Career: Trentham (1909), Huddersfield Town (August 1910), Trentham (February 1911), POTTERS (amateur, August 1912, professional, March 1913), Port Vale (£1,000, June 1924, retired through injury, May 1926).

■ Standing only 5ft 5in tall, Billy Tempest, who was released by Huddersfield during their first season in

the Football League, was a courageous footballer who occupied the left-wing with great zest and desire. A positive, attacking player, he was a huge favourite with the Stoke supporters and made 38 appearances in the Southern League prior to the outbreak of World War One. After the hostilities had ended he once more established himself on the left-wing and played on for another five seasons, finally leaving The Victoria Ground for neighbouring Port Vale after scoring 30 goals in more than 200 senior games for the Potters. He added a further 45 outings to his tally with the Vale before retiring in 1926.

* When Tempest was 'sold' to the Vale there was a dispute regarding the transfer fee and in the end the League stepped in and a mutual agreement was reached that £1,000 should be paid to Stoke.

TENNANT, John Willie

Full-back: 29 apps.

Born: Washington, County Durham, 3 December 1907.
Died: December 1978.
Career: Washington Colliery FC, POTTERS (professional, September 1930), Torquay United (July 1932), Liverpool (May 1933), Bolton Wanderers (£2,750, December 1935), POTTERS (£2,500, November 1938), guested for Liverpool, Southport and Wrexham during World War Two, retired, May 1946.

■ Willie Tennant, a former pit boy, began as a centre-forward and did well in that position before he was successfully converted into a full-back. Recruited by Stoke in 1930, he spent two years at The Victoria Ground but in that time made only one League appearance, in a 2–1 League defeat at Southampton a month after joining when he deputised for Bob McGrory. A year after moving to Torquay he signed for Liverpool and then assisted Bolton before returning to The Victoria Ground. Speedy and tactically aware, Tennant had an excellent three years with the Trotters, appearing in 102 competitive games plus another five during World War Two. He then happily returned to Stoke for a second spell in 1938 and added a further 28 senior appearances to his tally during that last pre-war season. He guested for three other clubs during World War Two and finally retired after struggling with injury throughout the hostilities.

THOMAS, Michael Reginald

Midfield: 113+7 apps. 22 goals.

Born: Mochdre, Powys, 7 July 1954.
Career: Mochdre & Newtown Schools, Welshpool District Boys, Pentre Youth Club (1968–69), Wrexham (amateur, August 1969, apprentice, July 1970, professional April 1972), Manchester United (£300,000, November 1978), Everton (£450,000, player/exchange deal involving John Gidman, August 1981), Brighton & Hove Albion (£400,000, November 1981), POTTERS (£200,000, August 1982), Chelsea (£75,000, January 1984), West Bromwich Albion (£100,000, September 1985), Derby County (on

Mickey Thomas

loan, March–May 1986), Wichita Wings, NASL indoor League, £35,000 August 1986), Shrewsbury Town (August 1988), Leeds United (£10,000, June 1989), POTTERS (on loan, March 1990, signed permanently, free transfer, August 1990), Wrexham (July 1991–May 1993), Conwy United (December 1994), Inter Cardiff (August 1995), Portmadoc (caretaker manager-coach, January 1995), Inter Cardiff (August–September 1996), later manager of a soccer coaching School near Wrexham (1997–2000), also worked as a soccer summariser for Century Radio, Manchester; Rhyl (Director of Football, 2000–02), after leaving Wrexham in 1993 he served an 18-month jail sentence for handling counterfeit money.

■ Mickey Thomas was a hard-working, industrious midfield dynamo who spent almost 21 years in top-class football, making his League debut for Wrexham in January 1972 and playing his last game for the same club in November 1992. He starred on 80 different League grounds, visited 15 countries and cost more than £1.5 million in transfer fees. A Welsh international at three levels, under-21 (2 caps), under-23 (one cap) and full (51 caps), he was a member of Manchester United's losing FA Cup Final side of 1979 and gained a First Division runners'-up medal in 1980. Earlier, with Wrexham, he won three Welsh Cup winners' medals in 1972, 1975 and 1978 and also helped the Robins win the Third Division Championship in 1978. He was a real live-wire in midfield when Chelsea gained promotion to the First Division in 1983–84, and two years later, in 1985–86, he helped Derby clinch promotion to Division Two. His efforts for Stoke were greatly appreciated and the fans certainly enjoyed his commitment. He certainly had an excellent first season in 1982–83 when he netted 12 goals in 46 games. When he returned for a second visit he was voted 'Player of the Year' for 1990–91 when, once more, he grafted hard and long in 45 games despite the fact that time was catching up on him. Sadly for the likeable Welshman, a jail sentence was handed out to him in 1993 for handling counterfeit money. Thomas amassed more than 450 appearances and scored over 50 goals in what was an exciting career. Thomas, who is one of only a handful of players who have had three separate spells with the Potters, was rewarded with a testimonial match when Wrexham played Wolverhampton Wanderers at The Recreation Ground on 30 July 1997.

THOMAS, Wayne Junior Robert

Defender: 215+2 apps. 8 goals.

Born: Gloucester, 17 May 1979.
Career: Gloucestershire Schoolboy football, Torquay United (apprentice, June 1995, professional, July 1997), POTTERS (£200,000, June 2000), Burnley (free, with Gifton Noel-Williams, May 2005).

■ Able to play in an emergency at right-back, Wayne Thomas prefers a more central defensive position, and during his five seasons at The Britannia

Stadium he has certainly given a good account of himself while at the same time becoming a huge favourite with the supporters. He made 143 appearances for Torquay before bedding himself down with the Potters. Strong in the tackle, sound and forceful in the air, he played his 200th first-team game for the club in a 1–0 defeat at Reading in November 2004. He also scored twice in a 3–2 home League win over Ipswich Town two months earlier.

THOMPSON, Thomas

Inside-forward: 46 apps. 18 goals.

Born: Fencehouses near Houghton-le-Spring, County Durham, 10 November 1929.
Career: Lumley YMCA (1944), Newcastle United (£15, August 1946), Aston Villa (£12,000, September 1950), Preston North End (£28,500, June 1955), POTTERS (£10,000, July 1961), Barrow (£5,000, March 1963, retired, May 1965), returned to Preston where he became a carpenter.

■ Inside-forward Tommy Thompson had a fine career, appearing in almost 450 League games and scoring 224 goals for his five major clubs. He was one of the finest players in the game during the 1950s, his delicate touches, speed off the mark and expert finishing being his hallmarks. Small and stocky, he failed to hold down a regular place in Newcastle's side and did well at Villa Park before being replaced by Jackie Sewell. He then teamed up with Preston where he formed a wonderfully exciting right-wing partnership with Tom Finney. Then, after leaving Deepdale for The Victoria Ground, he was subsequently paired with another great England winger, Stanley Matthews, having a fine first season when he top-scored with 17 goals. He only featured occasionally, however, when the Potters won the Second Division Championship in 1963. Capped twice by England against Wales in 1952 and Scotland five years later, he also represented the Football League side and England 'B'. Nicknamed 'Toucher' he was certainly a smart one-touch footballer who gave most of his clubs excellent service.

THOMSON, Kenneth Gordon

Centre-half: 302 apps. 7 goals.

Born: Aberdeen, 25 February 1930.
Died: Cleveland, 1969.
Career: Caledonian Thistle, Banks 'o Dee, RAF service, Aberdeen (professional, August 1948), POTTERS (£22,500, September 1952), Middlesbrough (£8,500, December 1959), Hartlepool United (October 1962–May 1963).

■ One of the finest centre-halves ever to don a Stoke City shirt, Ken Thomson made over 300 senior appearances for the club over a period of seven years during the 1950s. A craggy Scotsman, he was watched by Stoke scouts playing non-League football north of the border, but their efforts were in vain as he joined the RAF on National Service. Then, on his demob, he signed for Aberdeen as it was regarded as one of the finest pivots in Scotland at that time. Thankfully, Stoke boss Frank Taylor finally got his man in 1952. While at Pittodrie Park, Thomson came mighty close to gaining full international honours for his country (he was named reserve for Scotland on three occasions and once by the Scottish League). A strong, commanding defender, he made an immediate impact at The Victoria Ground, although his first season was marred by relegation to the Second Division. Indeed, it was Thomson who decided to take a vital penalty-kick against Derby County in the last game of that campaign. He missed from the spot, Stoke lost the match and they went down in place of Manchester City, with only a point separating the two teams. Nevertheless, he was a born leader who skippered the side from the word go, and it is said that he hardly ever had a bad game. At the age of 28 Thomson's eyesight started to fade and he had to wear contact lenses, but they failed to cure the problem. Consequently, late in 1959, Tony Waddington reluctantly transferred him to Middlesbrough. His stay at Ayresome Park was not without controversy, and after making over 80 appearances for 'Boro he wound down his career with Hartlepool United, retiring in 1963 with well over 400 competitive games behind him (390 in League action). Sadly, Thomson died of a heart attack on a golf course in 1969 at the age of 39.

THOMSON, Walter James Gordon

Full-back or centre-half: 9 apps.

Born: Chatham, 1870.
Died: Isle of Wight, 1940.
Career: Chatham FC, Strathmore (briefly), POTTERS (July 1892), Southampton St Mary's (March 1894), Cowes Isle of Wight (May 1896, retired, 1900).

■ Also known as 'Dave', 'Lachie' Thomson was one of the forerunners of the Stoke invasion to The Dell. A very popular player with the fans, he was a strong defender with plenty of pluck and commitment who, although highly regarded, failed to settle at The Victoria Ground. He went on to make 37 appearances for Saints and appeared for them in their first-ever Southern League game against his former club Chatham on 6 October 1894. He later helped Cowes gain entry into the Southern League in 1899.

THORDARSON, Stefan

Outside-left: 28+37 apps. 11 goals.

Born: Reykjavik Iceland, 27 March 1975.
Career: IA Akranes, Iceland (1993), Osters IF, Sweden (1996), BK Brann Bergen, Norway (1998), Bayer Uerdingen, Germany (1999), POTTERS (free transfer, June 2000), IA Akranes (August 2002).

■ A former Icelandic youth international, Stefan Thordarsson, the son of the Stoke City manager Gudjon, went on to gain five senior caps and eight at under-21 level before joining the Potters at the age of 25. He made an immediate impact in his new surroundings, impressing in a pre-season friendly when he scored with a scorching free-kick against Liverpool. He then netted another stunner in the League Cup tie at Charlton – the effort later being voted the club's 'Goal of the Season.' Unable to hold down a regular place in the side, the skilful Thordarsson, who had a very languid style, was plagued by a back injury throughout 2001–02 when most of his outings were made as a substitute. He returned to his home country after spending two seasons in English football.

THORLEY, Dennis

Defender: 11+4 apps.

Born: Stoke-on-Trent, 7 November 1956.
Career: Roebuck FC, POTTERS (apprentice, April 1973, professional, July 1976), California Surf, NASL (on loan, 1981), Blackburn Rovers (on loan, March–April 1980), retired through injury, May 1982.

■ In his six seasons with the Potters reserve defender Dennis Thorley started only 11 first-team games. He also played in the NASL and was signed on loan by former 'Stokie' Howard Kendall as his Blackburn Rovers side went for promotion from the Third Division. Unfortunately, Thorley was plagued by injury during his last season with the Potters and announced his retirement at the age of 25.

THORNE, Peter Lee

Striker: 173+16 apps. 80 goals.

Born: Manchester, 21 June 1973.
Career: Blackburn Rovers (apprentice, June 1989, professional, June 1991), Wigan Athletic (on loan, March–May 1994), Swindon Town (£225,000, January 1995), POTTERS (£350,000, July 1997), Cardiff City (£1.7 million, September 2001), Norwich City (June 2005).

■ In 1999–2000, 6ft striker Peter Thorne, a very popular Mancunian, became the first Stoke City player to score 30 goals in a season since Mark Stein's haul of 33 seven years earlier in 1992–93. Thorne's total included three League hat-tricks, four goals in one match against Chesterfield at home, followed less than a month later by a treble at Bristol Rovers and another three-goal bonanza at Bury in May. Always likely to hit, even find, the net, Thorne notched 32 goals in 91 games for Swindon before his move to the Potteries, this after failing to make much headway at Blackburn and having a rather disappointing goalless loan spell with Wigan. He was a Second Division Championship-winner with Swindon in 1996 and had the pleasure of scoring the winning goal for the Potters in the Auto-Windscreen Shield Final against Bristol City at Wembley in 2000. It was a bitter blow to the supporters when he left the club to join Cardiff City in 2001, being reunited with former 'Stokie' Graham Kavanagh at Ninian Park…and both players were in the Welsh club's line-up that lost to the Potters in the Play-off semi-final of 2002. He took his career goals total past the 160 mark during the 2004–05 season.

THORNTON, Thomas

Defender: 20 apps. 1 goal.

Born: Erdington, Birmingham, 1885.
Died: Birmingham, 1957.

Peter Thorne

Career: Kingstanding Swifts, Crewe Alexandra (April 1907), POTTERS (£50, July 1910), Newport County (1911–12).

■ When he was playing for Crewe, Tommy Thornton was regarded as one of the best defenders in non-League football. So much so that Stoke went out and secured his services for a small fee. He did well for the Potters, playing mainly at centre-half, and scored his only goal for the club in a 2–1 Birmingham League defeat at Stourbridge in October 1910.

TIATTO, Daniele Amadio

Left-back, outside-left: 11+4 apps. 1 goal.

Born: Melbourne, Australia, 22 May 1973.
Career: FC Baden, Switzerland, POTTERS (on loan, November 1997–April 1998), Manchester City (£300,000, July 1998), Leicester City (free, August 2004).

■ Potters loan signing Danny Tiatto, who can play as an orthodox left-back, a wing-back or outside-left, always gives an honest account of himself. He grafts hard and long and has now played in over 25 full internationals for Australia, having earlier represented his country at under-21 level. A First Division Championship winner with Manchester City in 2002, he made almost 150 appearances for that club before his transfer to The Walkers Stadium.

TOMLINSON, Frederick

Half-back: 22 apps. 3 goals.

Born: South Shields, 1886.
Died: before 1980.
Career: South Shields Primitive Methodists, Workington United, West Stanley, Barnsley (August 1907), POTTERS (May 1909), Washington Sentinel (August 1910).

■ Wing-half Fred Tomlinson spent just one season with the Potters, during which time he appeared in half of the team's scheduled fixtures. He netted twice on his debut in the 11–0 Southern League win over Merthyr Town. He scored once in 16 League games for Barnsley.

TOMPKINSON, William Vincent

Outside-right: 2 apps.

Born: Stone, 18 June 1895.
Died: Bamford near Rochdale, 26 July 1968.
Career: Wolverhampton Wanderers, POTTERS (November 1914), Aberdare Athletic (June 1920), Rochdale (June 1923), Stockport County (May 1928), Connah's Quay & Shotton FC (August 1930), Macclesfield Town (December 1930, retired, May 1931).

■ An industrious right-winger with a lot of ability, Billy Tompkinson played for Wolves reserves before joining Stoke in 1914. Owing to World War One (when he served in the Army), he only made two first-team appearances for the Potters, the first against Mid Rhondda (Southern League) in April 1915, the second versus Bury (Football League) in February 1920. Tompkinson, who represented the Welsh League as an Aberdare player, later spent five seasons with Rochdale, for whom he made over 170 senior appearances, scoring 51 goals. He ended his senior career by having two seasons with Stockport, for whom he struck another 27 goals in 82 League outings, including a hat-trick against Barrow in May 1929, which was won 3–2.

TOOTH, George Arnold

Outside-left: 5 apps. 2 goals.

Born: Cheshire, 1874.
Died: before 1960.
Career: Congleton Hornets (1898), POTTERS (September 1898), Stafford Rangers (March 1900).

■ Reserve left-winger George Tooth scored on his League debut for Stoke against Everton at home in April 1899 when he deputised for the injured Joe Turner.

TUDOR, John Arthur

Forward: 29+2 apps. 3 goals.

Born: Ilkeston, Derbyshire, 25 June 1946.
Career: Stanley Common Welfare, Cotmanhay United, Middlesbrough (amateur, 1961–62), associated briefly with Derby County, Sheffield United (trialist), Notts County, Chesterfield (reserves), Nottingham Forest, then Ilkeston Town (September 1964), Coventry City (apprentice, January 1965, professional, January 1968), Sheffield United (November 1968), Newcastle United (player-exchange deal involving John Hope, January 1971), POTTERS (£30,000, September 1976), KAA Ghent, Belgium (£10,000, August 1977, retired through injury, May 1978), North Shields (coach, July 1978, appointed manager, October 1979), Gateshead (coach, December 1980), Bedlington Terriers (coach, November 1982), Derbyshire Coaching School (1983), Minnesota Kicks, NASL (coach, June 1994–95), he was a publican in Bedlington when associated with that club.

■ Blonde striker John Tudor was an amateur with Middlesbrough and had been employed as a truck driver, welder and tile-maker before joining Jimmy Hill's Coventry City, then assisting Sheffield United. He played in a good, honest and professional manner for both clubs, gaining a Second Division Championship medal with the Sky Blues in 1967 when he struck eight vital goals in 16 games. He then teamed up with Malcolm Macdonald at Newcastle

where he became the perfect foil and strike partner to the England international. He netted 73 times in 220 first-team games for the Geordies, helping them win promotion to the top flight at the end of his first season and playing in the 1974 FA Cup Final defeat by Liverpool three years later. Initially he partnered Jimmy Greenhoff in Stoke's attack, but then was aided and abetted by Dave Goodwin and Garth Crooks before his switch to Belgium. During his senior career in England, Tudor hit 99 goals in 334 League games.

TUEART, Dennis

Wing-forward: 3+1 apps.

Born: Newcastle-upon-Tyne, 27 November 1949.
Career: Newcastle Boys, Sunderland (apprentice, April 1966, professional, August 1967), Manchester City (£275,000, March 1974), New York Cosmos, NASL (£250,000, September 1978), Manchester City (£150,000, February 1980), POTTERS (free transfer, August 1983), Burnley (free, December 1983, retired from competitive football, May 1984), became a successful businessman (in corporate hospitality) in Manchester, and was appointed a Director of Manchester City FC (December 1997).

■ Dennis Tueart played on both wings as well as inside-forward during a fine career that spanned 17 years (1967–84). He netted 137 goals in 420 League games but played only four times for the Potters. An FA Cup winner with Sunderland in 1973 and a League Cup winner with Manchester City in 1976 when he scored

a spectacular goal in a 2–1 win over Newcastle United, Tueart lined up for City in the 1981 FA Cup Final when they were beaten in a replay by Spurs. He won six full England caps plus one at under-23 level and also represented the Football League. One of the best forwards of his era, he was a fine striker whose polished play excited crowds wherever he played, but, alas, the Potters fans certainly didn't see much of him.

TUNNICLIFFE, John

Forward: 3 apps.

Born: Hanley, Stoke-on-Trent, 1866.
Died: before 1945.
Career: Longton, POTTERS (March 1890), Audlam (August 1889).

■ Reserve forward Jack Tunnicliffe, younger brother of William, played in three League games for the Potters during March 1891. He occupied three different positions in three defeats, two by 1–0 against Everton and a 5–3 reverse at Blackburn.

TUNNICLIFFE, William

Outside-left: 9 apps. 4 goals.

Born: Hanley, Stoke-on-Trent, 1864.
Died: before 1945.
Career: Hanley Town, POTTERS (March 1888), Middlewich (April 1889).

■ Sprightly left-winger Billy Tunnicliffe joined the Potters just prior to the introduction of League Football. He made nine appearances in the senior side, all in the first half of the 1888–89 season, making his debut in the club's first game against West Bromwich Albion. He netted two of his four goals in a 3–0 home win over Notts County a fortnight later, the Potters first in League football.
* Three relatives of the Tunnicliffe family played football in later years: Josuah and James for Port Vale and William Francis for Vale, Bournemouth, Wrexham and Bradford City.

TURLEY, Patrick

Half-back or inside-left: 5 apps.

Born: Newry, County Down, Ireland, 1908.
Died: before 1980.
Career: Newry Town (1927), POTTERS (March 1929), St Patrick's, Dublin (free transfer, May 1931).

■ Well-built, Irish-bred half-back Paddy Turley played in just a handful of League matches for the Potters over a three-year period. With his opportunities few and far between at The Victoria Ground, he left Stoke on a free transfer.

TURNER, Herbert Arthur Wilmot

Forward: 59 goals 22 goals.

Born: Cheshire, 1866.
Died: before 1945.
Career: Chester, POTTERS (August 1890), Ardwick, later Manchester City (January 1893, released, May 1893).

■ Bert Turner arrived at The Victoria Ground practically unnoticed at the start of the 1890–91 season. A useful forward, he helped Stoke win the Football Alliance Championship in his first season when he netted 11 goals in 20 appearances. He continued to score regularly and produced a fine record before moving to Ardwick, for whom he appeared in just one League game against Crewe Alexandra in February 1893.

TURNER, Arthur Owen

Centre-half: 312 apps. 17 goals.

Born: Chesterton, 1 April 1909.
Died: Sheffield, January 1994.
Career: Wolstanton PSA (1919), Downings Tileries (1922), West Bromwich Albion (amateur trialist, May 1927), POTTERS (amateur trialist 1929–30, amateur, October 1930, professional, November 1930), Birmingham (£6,000, February 1939), guest for Crewe Alexandra, Wrexham and the POTTERS during World War Two, Southport (£750, February 1948), Crewe Alexandra (player-manager, October 1948, retired as a player, May 1949, remained as manager until December 1951), POTTERS (assistant manager, August 1952–November 1954), Birmingham City (manager, November 1954–September 1958), Oxford United (manager, January 1959–February 1969,

then general manager to 1972), Rotherham United (chief scout, April 1972–November 1979), Sheffield United (chief scout, May 1980–July 1981).

■ Arthur Turner had a passion and thirst for the game and was no angel when it came to defending, being rock hard, fearless, aggressive and totally committed, always giving 110 percent each and every time he took the field. A local junior player, he worked as an upholsterer and was an amateur with West Bromwich Albion but failed to make the grade at The Hawthorns. When he lost his 'day job' he wrote to Stoke asking for a trial. He succeeded in getting one, was signed as an amateur and subsequently turned professional. He made rapid progress and established himself in the Potters XI during the 1931–32 season when he made 40 appearances after taking over at the heart of the defence from Hughie McMahon. The following season, and by now the cornerstone of the Potters rearguard, he guided the team to the Second Division Championship, being an ever-present in the side. Between 1935 and 1938 he played in 118 consecutive League games for Stoke (only full-back Tony Allen did better) and kept his place in the team until February 1939. He was then transferred to Birmingham after making over 300 senior appearances. Just over six months into his association with the Blues, World War Two broke out and Turner had to be content, along with scores of other players, with playing regional football for the next seven years. He came through unscathed, guesting for three clubs during the hostilities as well as amassing 186 wartime appearances for the Blues. When peacetime football resumed in August 1945 he continued to star in the Blues defence, gaining a Football League South Championship medal in 1946 while adding another 53 senior appearances to his tally before moving to Southport. Soon after retiring he was appointed manager at Gresty Road, a position he held for one season. There followed a three-year spell as assistant manager at The Victoria Ground before he took over as team manager at St Andrew's. In his four-year association with the Blues he won

promotion from the Second Division and reached the FA Cup Final in successive years, losing 3–1 to Manchester City in the latter. There followed a decade in charge of Oxford, during which time the U's twice won the Southern League title in 1961 and 1962, climbed into the Football League, gained promotion in 1965 and then took the Third Division Championship in 1968 with Ron Atkinson in the side. After leaving The Manor Ground he remained in football as a scout until 1981. Also a very capable cricketer, he played for Silverdale CC, for whom he scored five centuries.

TURNER, George

Full-back: 190 apps. 17 goals.

Born: Halmer End near Newcastle-under-Lyme, April 1887.
Died: Stoke-on-Trent, November 1958.
Career: Halmer End Gymnastics FC, POTTERS (August 1908), served in the Army during World War One (from October 1917), Podmore Hall FC (secretary, August 1920).

■ George Turner had a fine career at The Victoria Ground. Tall and quite quick for a defender, he possessed a timely fine tackle, kicked long and true and was always involved in the thick of the action. A professional athlete, he joined Stoke at the age of 21, became team captain and went on to appear in almost 200 first-team games for the club to April 1915 when League football was suspended due to war in Europe. During the early part of the hostilities, Turner made a further 72 appearances for Stoke before joining the Army, being

transferred to the 'battle front' in April 1918. Within a matter of weeks he was shot in the leg and sadly had to have the limb amputated. On returning to England he became secretary of Podmore Hall FC, a position he held for a couple of years.

TURNER, Isaiah

Goalkeeper: 8 apps.

Born: Netherton, Dudley, 8 July 1876.
Died: Dudley, 2 February 1935.
Career: Blowers Green School (Dudley), Netherton Boys' Club, Dudley St James's (1894), West Bromwich Albion (professional, May 1898), Stourbridge (July 1899), Dudley Town (1902), Kidderminster Harriers (April 1903), POTTERS (August 1906), Old Hill Wanderers (August 1907, retired, May 1911).

■ 'Ike' Turner was a well-built goalkeeper whose career was more pronounced with Stoke than it was with his other major club, West Bromwich Albion, for whom he made just one senior appearance.

TURNER, James Arthur

Half-back: 63 apps. 1 goal.

Born: Black Bull, Staffs, 11 January 1866. Died: Stoke-on-Trent, 9 April 1904. Career: Black Lane Rovers (Radcliffe), Radcliffe FC (briefly), Bolton Wanderers (professional, July 1888), POTTERS (September 1894), Derby County (£70, June 1896), POTTERS (£100, August 1898, retired through injury, May 1899).

■ Jim Turner was brought up in Lancashire and played his early football as an outside-right. Two months before the start of League football he signed for Bolton Wanderers and remained with the club for six years, during which time he scored 12 goals in 108 appearances. In 1893 he was involved in a fracas with fans during a Lancashire Cup tie at Bury and the following year was forced to miss the FA Cup Final through injury. A Football League representative, he was capped three times by England with three different clubs, winning his first cap against Wales at Stoke in 1893. He moved to The Victoria Ground in the summer of 1894. After 18 months and following a dispute with the club Turner was sold to Derby where he was converted into a dominant half-back, playing in the 1898 FA Cup Final against Nottingham Forest. Four months after collecting a runners'-up medal he patched up his differences with Stoke and returned to The Victoria Ground but was forced to retire from active football at the end of that season with a serious leg injury. Turner's only goal for the Potters came in a 3–1 League defeat at Blackburn in April 1896.
* His brother, Dick Turner, also played for Bolton Wanderers.

TURNER, Josuah

Left-half: 1 app.

Born: Tunstall, Stoke-on-Trent, c.1884. Died: before 1960. Career: Tunstall, POTTERS (August 1908), Tunstall (April 1909).

■ A capable half-back, Jim Turner's only first-team game for the Potters was against Aston Villa reserves in a Birmingham League game in January 1909 when he deputised for the injured Albert Pitt.

TURNER, Joseph

Outside-left: 60 apps. 15 goals.

Born: Burslem, Stoke-on-Trent, 12 March 1872. Died: Southampton, November 1950. Career: Newcastle Swifts, Dresden United, Southampton St Mary's (professional, August 1896), POTTERS (May 1898), Everton (April 1900), Southampton (May 1901), New Brompton (May 1904), Northampton Town (July 1906), Eastleigh Athletic, Farnborough Athletic, worked in a Stoke brewery until 1915, after World War One he returned to live in Southampton until his death at the age of 78.

■ After earning 30s (£1.50) a week with Southampton, pacy left-winger Joe Turner averaged a goal every four games for the Potters during his two-year spell at The Victoria Ground, representing the Football League in 1899. He failed to settle on Merseyside and quickly returned to The Dell (Southampton having by now dropped their title St Mary's). In his second spell with the Saints he picked up a runner's-up medal in the 1902 FA Cup Final. The scorer of 74 goals in 153 games in his two spells with Saints, he wound down his senior career with New Brompton (now Gillingham) and Northampton Town before rounding things off by assisting two non-League clubs in Hampshire.

TUTIN, Arthur

Wing-half: 198 apps. 3 goals.

Born: Coundon, County Durham, June 1907. Deceased. Career: Bishop Auckland (1924), Consett (1925), Chilton Colliery (1926), Spennymoor United (1927) Crook Town (1928), Sheffield Wednesday (trialist, 1930), Bradford Park Avenue (trialist, 1931), Aldershot (professional, May 1932), POTTERS (£250, March 1934), guest for Crewe Alexandra, 1939–40 (retired, May 1945).

■ For many years Arthur Tutin, a short, stocky wing-half, was part of an exceptionally well-organised and utterly reliable middle-line at The Victoria Ground, his two colleagues being Arthur Turner and Frank Soo. Earlier in his

career Tutin served with a string of northern-based amateur clubs including Bishop Auckland, Spennymoor United and Crook Town. Then, in March 1934, after unsuccessful trials with both Sheffield Wednesday and Bradford Park, Stoke boss Bob McGrory signed him as a straight replacement for Bill Robertson, who left The Victoria Ground for Manchester United. Developing into an exceptionally fine footballer, neat and tidy, he appeared in almost 200 senior games for the Potters up to the outbreak of World War Two. During the hostilities he added a further nine outings to his tally while also guesting for Crewe, near his work place. He retired in 1945, aged 38.

TWEED, Steven

Defender: 42+5 apps.

Born: Edinburgh, 9 August 1972. Career: Hutchison Vale Boys' Club (Edinburgh), Hibernian (professional, August 1990), Ionikis, Greece (July 1996), POTTERS (free transfer, August 1997), Dundee (£150,000, December 1998–May 2001).

■ After spending a season in Greek football, tall, central defender Steve Tweed joined the Potters via his agent, the former Spurs and Blackburn Rovers striker Steve Archibald. An astute piece of business, it seemed, by manager Chic Bates as he began the 1997–98 campaign

Steve Tweed

in terrific form. By Christmas he was already marked down as a strong possibility to make Craig Brown's Scotland World Cup squad. However, after being in the team that crashed to a 7–0 home defeat at the hands of Birmingham City, his form began to wane and, coupled with off-the-field problems, new boss Chris Kamara dropped him. But, thankfully, he had somehow found a new lease of life towards the end of the League programme and went on to appear in almost 50 games before moving to Dundee, for whom he appeared in over 100 games in two and a half years at Dens Park. Capped twice by his country at 'B' team level, he also played in three under-21 internationals and made 126 appearances for Hibs before moving abroad.

TWEMLOW, Charles Victor

Outside-right: 1 app. 1 goal.

Born: Macclesfield, 1900.
Died: before 1980.
Career: Congleton, POTTERS (September 1921), Macclesfield (June 1922–24).

■ Reserve right-winger Charlie Twemlow scored in his only League game for the Potters against Derby County in February 1922, which they won 4–2. No relation to William Twemlow, he played as an amateur throughout his career.

TWEMLOW, William Thomas

Full-back: 37 apps. 2 goals.

Born: Hanley, Stoke-on-Trent, 1892.
Died: Hanley, Stoke-on-Trent, 1 July 1933.
Career: Audley, Sandbach Ramblers, POTTERS (May 1915), served in the Army during World War One, Port Vale (August 1921), Macclesfield (July 1923), Oswestry Town (1924–25).

■ Bill Twemlow joined at the end of the last pre-World War One season after making a full recovery from a broken leg suffered playing at Cheddleton some 12 months earlier. That injury occurred shortly before he was due to go for a trial with Aston Villa but, owing to him being sidelined, the First Division club withdrew their interest. One of the many talented local footballers around at the time, Twemlow played in 70 games for Stoke during World War One, followed up by 37 senior outings after the hostilities. Five months into his career with neighbours Port Vale, he suffered a cartilage injury that required an operation. He failed to regain full fitness and was released at the end of the 1922–23 campaign. Twemlow, who later played for Macclesfield and Oswestry, was only 40 when he died in 1933.

UNDERWOOD, Alfred

Full-back: 131 apps.

Born: Hanley-on-Trent, August 1867.
Died: Stoke-on-Trent, 8 October 1928.
Career: Hanley Tabernackle FC, Etruria FC, POTTERS (July 1887, retired through injury, May 1893, remained at the club for another season).

■ Alf Underwood was a formidable full-back, a prodigious kicker and reliable to a degree, who occasionally tackled 'far too rashly'. Nevertheless, he was still a fine player who gave Stoke excellent service, appearing in more than 130 senior games prior to his premature retirement at the age of 24, although he was called upon to assist the club from time to time later on. A member of the Stoke side that won the Football Alliance title in 1891, he also gained two full caps for England, both against Ireland, in March 1891 and March 1892. He lined up with his fellow colleagues goalkeeper Billy Rowley and full-back partner Tommy Clare in the second international in Belfast. A potter by trade, Underwood suffered with his health over a number of years during the early 1900s and was practically an invalid. In July 1908 he was struck down with a serious illness and at the time was said to be destitute. A group of local notables led by Denny Austerberry, the Stoke secretary, established a fund to support him. Chronically ill, Underwood battled on for 20 years, eventually passing away at the age of 59.

URSEM, Loek Aloysius Jacobus Maria

Midfield: 36+8 apps. 7 goals
Born: Amsterdam, Holland, 7 January 1958.
Career: AZ '67 Alkmaar, Holland (professional, 1978), POTTERS (£85,000, July 1979), Sunderland (on loan, March–April 1982), FC Haarlem (July 1983), later with FC Wageningen FC, Holland and OSV Velsen, Holland, retired 1994.

■ The first Dutchman to play for the Potters, and indeed the club's first foreign import, blonde midfielder Loek Ursem made less than 50 first-team appearances for the club during his

four-year stay at The Victoria Ground. Capped by Holland at under-23 level prior to joining Stoke, he made his Football League debut against Coventry City at home on the opening day of the 1979–80 season and scored his first goal against Ipswich Town a year later. He had his best season in 1980–81 when he made 29 of his 44 appearances.

* Sven Larsson was all set to become the Potters' first foreign-born player after playing in a friendly for the club against Moscow Dynamo in 1965–66 but the deal fell through at the last minute.

USHERWOOD, Arthur

Outside-left: 6 apps. 1 goal.

Born: Congleton, Cheshire, August 1884.
Died: Cheshire, c.1961.
Career: Congleton Excelsior, POTTERS (July 1904), Ashton Town.

■ An amateur throughout his career, Archie Usherwood spent just the one season at The Victoria Ground when he was one of seven players who appeared on the left-wing as the Potters struggled to field a settled side.

VAN DEURZEN, Jurgen

Defender or midfield: 49+12 apps. 5 goals.

Born: Genk, Belgium, 26 January 1974.
Career: KFC Turnhout, Belgium, POTTERS (on loan, July 2001–May 2002, signed permanently, July 2002, contract cancelled, December 2002), KFC Dessel Sport, Belgium (January 2003), Patro Maasmechelen, Belgium (March 2003).

■ Initially signed on a season loan contract from Belgium football, Jurgen Van Deurzen acquitted himself very well to English conditions and formed an

excellent partnership with Clive Clarke in the Potters defence, making his League debut against QPR. A versatile player, he also occupied the full-back and midfield positions and was a huge hit with the supporters, who appreciated his committed style of play. With the team playing poorly, plus a change of manager, Van Deurzen's contract was paid up and he returned home to join a moderate Belgium Second Division club. It was unfortunate that he didn't remain at The Britannia Stadium longer.

VERNON, Thomas Royston

Inside-left: 93+3 apps. 24 goals.

Born: Ffynnongroew near Holywell, Flintshire, 14 April 1937.
Died: Lancashire, 4 December 1993.
Career: Rhyl Grammar School XI, Flintshire Boys, Mostyn YMCA Juniors, Welsh YMCA, Mostyn YMCA Seniors, Everton (trialist, 1953), Blackburn Rovers (amateur, May 1954, professional, March 1955), Everton (£27,000 and Eddie Thomas, February 1960), POTTERS (£50,000, March 1965), Halifax Town (on loan, January–February 1970), Cape Town FC, South Africa (briefly, mid-1970), Great Harwood (1970–72), later ran an antiques business but sadly in later life suffered with arthritis in the hip and spine.

■ Roy Vernon, a forceful inside-forward noted for his powerful and accurate shooting, scored 52 goals in 144 games for Blackburn Rovers and 111 in 203 for Everton before joining the Potters at the age of 27. He made his League debut as an 18-year-old in 1955 and three years later represented Wales in the World Cup Finals in Sweden. He went on to gain a total of 32 full caps for his country between 1957 and 1968 as well as picking up two at both youth team and under-23 levels. He played alongside future 'Stokie' Peter Dobing at Ewood Park, helping Rovers gain promotion to the First Division in 1958, before following his mentor and manager Johnny Carey to Goodison Park. He did all things right with the Merseysiders, top-scoring four seasons running in major competitions in 1960–64, notching 24 goals in 41 League games in 1962–63 when Everton won the Football League Championship. He also possessed a strong, precise shot, mainly left-footed, and was a fine penalty-taker, being successful with 23 out of 26 spot-kicks he took during his career, including 19 conversions from 20 for Everton (all matches). Without doubt a superbly gifted player with added pace, perception and dribbling

skills, he was the dressing room joker and probably the only player who could smoke a cigarette in the shower. He gave the Potters almost five years' service, having his best season in 1965–66 when he struck 11 goals in 36 outings. He ended his league career with 172 goals in 398 games.

VINER, Horace

Goalkeeper: 1 app.

Born: Chirk, mid-Wales, June 1880.
Died: Rhyl, North Wales, June 1955.
Career: Birkenhead, POTTERS (August 1903), Rhyl (July 1904).

■ Reserve goalkeeper Horace Viner's only outing for the Potters was in the home League game against Nottingham Forest in March 1904 when the visitors won 3–2 in front of 7,000 fans. Signed as cover for Welsh international Richmond Roose and Jack Benton, he was literally snatched from under the noses of both Everton and Liverpool. On his release at the end of the season he joined Rhyl, a club nearer his home. He later ran a caravan park in the seaside resort.

VIOLLET, Dennis Sydney

Inside or centre-forward: 206+1 apps. 66 goals.

Born: Manchester, 20 September 1933.
Died: US, 6 March 1999.
Career: Manchester Schoolboys, Manchester United (trialist, autumn 1947, amateur, summer 1949, professional, September 1950), POTTERS (£25,000, January 1962), Baltimore Bays (on loan, April 1967–September 1968), Witton Albion (January 1969), Linfield (player-coach, August 1969), Preston North End (coach, July 1970), Crewe Alexandra (coach, February 1971, manager August–November 1971), Washington Diplomats (coach, April 1974–June 1977), later coach at Jackson University and also Richmond, Virginia, remained in the USA until his death.

■ Inside-forward Dennis Viollet was quicksilver in and around the penalty-area: sharp, incisive and a wonderful chance-taker. He could read a situation seconds before a defender could and

that proved fatal to the opposition. Not only could he sniff out a goal, he could also create them with some wonderful deft touches. A superb partner to Tommy Taylor at Old Trafford, his 20 goals in 1955–56 helped United clinch the First Division Championship and his contribution of 16 goals the following season ensured that the title remained at Old Trafford. Thankfully, he survived the Munich air crash in 1958 and went on to collect a runners'-up medal in that season's FA Cup Final, having missed out on a final appearance the year before through injury. In 1959–60 he broke United's seasonal scoring record with 32 goals in 36 First Division matches and at the end of that campaign played in the first of two full internationals for England against Hungary, his second followed in 1961 against Luxembourg. He also lined up on three occasions for the Football League. Quite why the selectors did not select him to partner the superb Tommy Taylor is difficult to fathom. Viollet, positive in every aspect of attacking play, scored on average two goals every three games for United, weighing in with a total of 179 goals in 293 outings (all major competitions). It remains a mystery why he was allowed to leave Old Trafford in 1962, but as a Stoke City player he continued to find the net, and, teaming up with Stanley Matthews and Jackie Mudie, he helped the Potters win the Second Division title in 1963 while the following year he collected a League Cup runners'-up prize when Stoke were beaten by Leicester City. He later won the Irish Cup with Linfield in 1970. Viollet spent the last 25 years of his life in the United States as a highly-respected coach.

WADDINGTON, Steven

Outside-right or midfield: 53+3 apps. 6 goals.

Born: Nantwich, Cheshire, 5 February 1956.
Career: Crewe Boys, POTTERS (apprentice, April 1972, professional, June 1973), Walsall (£40,000, September 1978), Port Vale (July 1982), Chesterfield (July 1983), Cape Town City, South Africa (1984), later with Macclesfield Town (two spells), Northwich Victoria, Winsford United, Leek Town, Rocester (retired 1992).

■ The son of the Stoke City manager Tony, Steve Waddington was a smart right-winger with good skills who bided his time at The Victoria Ground before gaining a regular place in the first team in 1977–78. That season he made 41 League and Cup appearances and scored five goals, including two in a 5–1 home win over Orient. He went on to play in over 50 first-team games for the club, whom he served for six years before joining Walsall. He underwent a cartilage operation as a Vale player and in 1986 was involved in a car crash with other players on their way to a friendly at Macclesfield.

WADE, Shaun Peter

Striker: 0+1 app.

Born: Stoke-on-Trent, 22 September 1969.
Career: Newcastle Town (1990), POTTERS (non-contract, October 1994, released, May 1995).

■ Shaun Wade, who signed for the Potters on a non-contract basis in 1994, looked a pretty useful striker yet only appeared once in the first team, coming on as a second-half substitute in the 1–1 home draw with Sheffield United five days after joining the club. Soon afterwards he badly damaged his cruciate knee ligaments in a reserve-team game. Surgery was required and this unfortunately resulted in his departure from the scene. He was a bricklayer by trade.

WAIN, Frederick

Goalkeeper: 2 apps.

Born: Hanley, Stoke-on-Trent, April 1887.
Died: Stoke-on-Trent, 1962.
Career: Hanley St Jude's, Hanley Villa, Smallthorne United, Norwood Mission, Stone Town, POTTERS (July 1908), Stone Town (May 1909), Blurton Swifts, Hanley Town, Hanley Swifts.

■ Goalkeeper Fred Wain played in two Birmingham & District League games for Stoke in October 1908 while nursing a broken finger that was only diagnosed afterwards! A tall man, standing over 6ft tall, he was signed initially as cover for Bert Miller, but after recovering from his hand injury he became surplus to requirements. And, like so many other players around this time, left The Victoria Ground and returned to his former club. An amateur throughout his career, it is believed that Wain continued playing at non-league level until he was over 40 years of age.

WAINWRIGHT, Thomas

Inside-forward: 1 app.

Born: Stoke-on-Trent, 1864.
Died: Stoke-on-Trent, c.1940.
Career: Stoke St Jude's, POTTERS (August 1888), Stoke Priory (August 1889).

■ Tom Wainwright made his only senior appearance for the Potters at inside-left in a 5–1 League defeat away to Aston Villa in September 1888, when the forward line was adjusted following an injury to right-winger Jimmy Sayer.
* A relative, also named Tommy Wainwright, played for Burslem Port Vale (1900–01).

WALKER, John David

Wing-half: 36 apps. 1 goal.

Born: great Wyrley, Walsall, 1900.
Died: Walsall, 1971.
Career: Cannock Town, POTTERS (October 1924), Walsall (June 1926), Walsall Wood (1930), Hednesford Town (briefly).

■ Solid wing-half Jack Walker, an ex-miner, did well at The Victoria Ground for a couple of seasons. However, with relegation looming, he slipped into the reserves towards the end of the 1925–26 campaign and was transferred to Walsall soon afterwards as efforts were made to rebuild the team in an attempt to gain rapid promotion.

WALKER, Thomas Jackson

Inside-forward: 2 apps.

Born: Gosforth near Newcastle-upon-Tyne, 20 February 1952.
Career: Newcastle Boys, POTTERS (apprentice, April 1968, professional, July 1969), Burnley (August 1970), Yeovil Town (March 1971).

■ Tommy Walker's two League appearances for Stoke were made in April 1972. Both ended in away defeats at Chelsea and Manchester United when he partnered Jimmy Greenhoff in the attack. After an unsuccessful spell at Turf Moor he joined non-League Yeovil Town.

WALLACE, Bertram

Outside-left: 1 app.

Born: Stoke-on-Trent, 1880.
Died: c.1952.
Career: Stoke St Jude's (1899), POTTERS (August 1901), Stoke Town (May 1902), Stoke St Jude's (1905).

■ Amateur left-winger Bert Wallace's only first-team outing for Stoke came in November 1901 when he made his debut in a 3–1 League defeat away to Sheffield Wednesday. Reserve to Aaron Lockett during his brief association with the Potters, he spent only one season in League football.

WALLACE, James

Inside-forward: 8 apps. 1 goal.

Born: Birkenhead, 13 December 1937.
Career: POTTERS (amateur, April 1953, professional, October 1955), Northwich Victoria (August 1959), Doncaster Rovers (March 1963), Stafford Rangers (August 1963), Ball Haye Green Youth Club (1965, retired, 1966), later Eastwood Hanley (manager), Nantwich Town (manager), Leek Town (manager).

■ Scorer of just one goal in eight games for the Potters, Jimmy Wallace spent five years playing reserve-team football at The Victoria Ground. A useful-enough inside-forward, he was associated with football until he was 60.

WALLACE, Raymond George

Forward: 182+29 apps. 16 goals.

Born: Greenwich, London, 2 October 1969.
Career: Southampton (apprentice, April 1986, professional, April 1988), Leeds United (£100,000, July 1991), Swansea City (March 1992), Reading (March–April 1994), POTTERS (free transfer, August 1994), Hull City (on loan, December 1994–January 1995), Winsford United (June 1999).

■ One of three footballing brothers, all of whom played for Southampton (Rod and Danny being the others), Ray Wallace was perhaps the least known of the trio. He made almost 50 appearances for his first club,

Southampton, before his big-money transfer to Leeds United in 1991. Unfortunately, he failed to establish himself at Elland Road and after loan spells with Swansea and Reading he was transferred to the Potters. 'Razor', as the fans knew him, took time to settle in at The Victoria Ground and was actually loaned out to lowly Hull City before returning in a much better frame of mind. After that Wallace produced some outstanding performances as a hard-tackling, highly competitive midfielder, never giving less than 100 percent and getting annoyed with himself when he wasn't at his best or indeed when he was out of action. When he quit top-class football in 1999 his club record stood at 277 appearances and 16 goals.
* A fourth Wallace brother, Clive, was a trialist at Southampton but failed to make the grade.

WALTERS, Mark Everton

Winger: 9 apps. 2 goals.

Born: Aston, Birmingham, 2 June 1964. Career: Hampton Junior & Holte Grammar schools (Lozells, Birmingham), Aston & District Boys, Birmingham Schools, Aston Villa (apprentice, June 1980, professional, May 1982), Glasgow Rangers (£600,000, December 1987), Liverpool (£1.25m, August 1981), POTTERS (on loan, March–April 1994), Wolverhampton Wanderers (on loan, September–October 1994), Southampton (free transfer, January 1996), Swindon Town (free, July 1996), Bristol Rovers (free, November 1999), Ilkeston Town (free, July 2002), Dudley Town (September 2003), Glasgow Rangers All Stars (2004–05).

■ Mark Walters could occupy either flank. A very effective player with excellent pace, clever on-the-ball tricks and telling shot, he could centre with great precision, on the run or otherwise.

He possessed one favourite trick whereby he used to drag his foot over the ball before gliding past a defender. After representing England at both schoolboy and youth-team levels, he gained one full, one 'B' and nine under-21 caps. An FA youth Cup winner in 1980 and a European Super Cup winner two years later, he then won three Scottish Premier and two Skol League Cup winners' medals with Rangers before helping Liverpool carry off both the FA Cup and League Cup in 1992 and 1995 respectively. Walters spent just a short time on loan with the Potters but even then he showed what a fine footballer he was. His senior career realised over 750 appearances and almost 170 goals.

WARD, Derek

Outside-right: 61 apps. 8 goals.

Born: Stoke-on-Trent, 23 December 1934. Career: POTTERS (amateur, April 1950, professional, August 1952), Stockport County (£2,000, July 1961–May 1964).

■ Brother of Terence, Derek Ward was a skilful right-winger who could occupy an inside berth. He spent 10 years at The Victoria Ground, playing mainly in the second team before transferring to Edgeley Park in 1961. He had his best spell in the Potters senior side either side of Christmas in 1958–59 when he played in 12 League games, 10 on the right-wing when he partnered Frank Bowyer and Bobby Howitt. He netted 21 times in his 84 senior appearances for Stockport.

WARD, Gavin John

Goalkeeper: 100 apps.

Born: Sutton Coldfield, 30 June 1970. Career: Aston Villa (apprentice, June 1986), Shrewsbury Town (professional, September 1988), West Bromwich Albion (free transfer, September 1989), Cardiff City (free, October 1989), Leicester City (£175,000, July 1993), Bradford City (£175,000, July 1995), Bolton Wanderers (£300,000, March 1996), Burnley (on loan, August–October 1998), POTTERS (free, February 1999), Walsall (free, August 2002), Coventry City (August

2003), Barnsley (on loan, April–May 2004), Preston North End (July 2004).

■ After an uneasy start to his professional career, when he had only one senior outing (for WBA) in three years, goalkeeper Gavin Ward developed into a very capable goalkeeper. Although travelling round the country quite a bit, when the 2005 season ended, he had amassed some 350 senior appearances, gaining both Third Division Championship and Welsh Cup winners' medals in 1993 and an Autoglass Trophy winners' medal in 2000. He certainly gave the Potters good service. Taking over from Carl Muggleton, he was an ever-present in 1999–2000 and played in a third of the games the following season. Each time, however, he and the Potters suffered defeat in the Second Division Play-off semi-finals, firstly against Gillingham and then at the hands of his future club Walsall.

WARD, Terence

Right-back: 45 apps.

Born: Stoke-on-Trent, 10 December 1939.
Died: Stoke-on-Trent, 1963.
Career: POTTERS (amateur, April 1955, professional, March 1958, retired through ill-health, December 1962).

■ Terry Ward graduated through the junior ranks at The Victoria Ground to make his mark in the first XI during the 1960–61 season when he made 28 appearances when partnering England international Tony Allen at full-back. He and his brother Derek Ward were at The Victoria Ground at the same time.

WARD, Thomas Edward George

Right-half and centre-forward: 5 apps. 4 goals.

Born: Chatham, Kent, 28 April 1913.
Died: before 2000.
Career: Chatham (1931), Crystal Palace (August 1933), Grimsby Town (June 1934), Port Vale (June 1936), POTTERS (£500, player-exchange deal involving Harry Davies, February 1938), Port Vale (February 1939), Mansfield Town (July 1939, retired during World War Two).

■ Tom Ward was a rugged right-half

who was successfully converted into a centre-forward. He spent just 12 months at The Victoria Ground, making a handful of appearances and scoring on his debut in a 2–1 home League win over Chelsea before returning to the Vale. He had earlier top-scored for Vale in 1936–37 and netted 29 goals in 61 appearances during his two spells with Stoke's arch-rivals. Unfortunately, he was injured for most of his time at Blundell Park.

WARE, Harold

Outside-left or inside-forward: 57 apps. 15 goals.

Born: Birmingham, 22 October 1911.
Died: Stoke-on-Trent, 28 October 1970.
Career: Stoke St Peter's School, Hanley St Luke's, Cobridge Celtic, Stoke St Peter's, POTTERS (amateur, December 1927, professional, December 1929), Newcastle United (£2,400, September 1935), Sheffield Wednesday (£1,700, May 1937), Norwich City (free transfer, November 1937), served as a sergeant in the anti-tank platoon during World War Two when he also guested for Port Vale (1939–40 and 1944), Northampton Town (1940–42), POTTERS (1940–41), Crystal Palace (1942–43) and Watford (1942–44), Northwich Victoria (player-manager, November 1944, retired as player, July 1947, continued as manager until May 1948), EDO Haarlem, Holland (trainer-coach, August 1948), Northwich Victoria (manager, August 1950–January

1951), Port Vale (coach, November 1956), Crewe Alexandra (manager, June 1958–June 1960), POTTERS (assistant-trainer, June 1960, then reserve–team manager and finally scout from 1965 until his death in 1970), became an American citizen after marrying into a new Jersey family.

■ Encouraged all the way in various sporting activities by his father, who was a British champion boxer in the 1920s, Harry Ware also took to the ring as well as being a fine swimmer, table tennis star and, indeed, footballer. A burly player, physically strong with a powerful right-foot shot, he occupied both the left-wing or inside-forward positions. However, his early days with Stoke were spent in the reserves and, in fact, he was restricted to only a handful of senior outings due to the form of Tommy Sale and Harry Davies. Ware, though, battled on during his six years at The Victoria Ground and averaged almost a goal every four games, helping the Potters win the Second Division Championship in 1933 before transferring to Newcastle United in 1935, going on to assist Newcastle and Norwich prior to World War Two. After suffering a chest wound on a Normandy battlefield during the Overlord operation, he was forced to retire from competitive football and became player-manager of Northwich Victoria. There followed a decent spell in Holland, after which he took a coaching position at Vale Park and was manager of Crewe Alexandra when Spurs beat 'The Alex' 13–2 in an FA Cup tie in 1960. He returned to The Victoria Ground to become assistant-trainer and later acted as scout for the Potters, a job he held until his sudden death at the age of 59.

* Ware, along with his Victoria Ground teammate Freddie Steele, guested for Northampton when they beat Stoke City 10–0 in a Regional wartime game in May 1942.

WARE, Paul David

Midfield: 115+27 apps. 14 goals.

Born: Congleton, Cheshire, 7 November 1970.
Career: POTTERS (apprentice, April 1987, professional, November 1988),

Stockport County (free transfer, September 1994), Cardiff City (on loan, January–March 1997), entered non-League football in 1997.

■ A hard-working, efficient and competitive midfield player, Paul Ware did a good job in the centre of the park for the Potters. He appeared in more than 140 senior games and scored and created some vital goals. Indeed, he netted the winner against Peterborough United in the Autoglass Trophy semi-final encounter of 1992 to book the Potters a place in the Wembley Final against his future club, Stockport County, which Stoke won 1–0. A member of the Potters' Second Division Championship-winning team the following season in 1993, he made 66 appearances for Stockport and five for Cardiff.

WARHURST, Paul

Utility: 4+1 apps. 1 goal.

Born: Stockport, 26 September 1969.
Career: Manchester City (apprentice, April 1976, professional, July 1988), Oldham Athletic (£10,000, October 1988), Sheffield Wednesday (£750,000, July 1991), Blackburn Rovers (£2.7 million, August 1993), Crystal Palace (£1.25 million, July 1997), Bolton Wanderers (£800,000, November 1998), POTTERS (on loan, March–May 2003),Chesterfield (free transfer, October 2003), Barnsley (free, December 2003), Carlisle United (February 2004), Grimsby Town (free, March 2004), Preston North End (trial), Blackpool (free, November 2004).

■ The versatile Paul Warhurst, who would play in any position to get a game, was certainly a soccer wanderer who, in a lengthy career, accumulated over 400 senior appearances, scoring 30 goals. He spent his best years, without doubt, at Bolton, for whom he played in 106 games. An England under-21 international, capped eight times, he suffered his fair share of injuries over the years, including a broken leg, fractured ankle, dislocated elbow and twisted knee, but he always bounced back and produced some sterling performances in defence, midfield and occasionally as an emergency striker. As a loanee from Bolton, he scored his only goal for the Potters in a 2–0 home League win over Rotherham United in April 2003.

WATKIN, Arthur Edmund

Inside or centre-forward: 177 apps. 77 goals

Born: Burslem, Stoke-on-Trent, 1896.
Died: Stoke-on-Trent, 1965.
Career: POTTERS (semi-professional,

May 1913), served in the Army during World War One, Congleton Town (August 1923), POTTERS (July 1924, retired, May 1927).

■ The recipient of a Southern League Division Two Championship medal in 1914–15 when he netted 24 times, including five in a 10–0 win over Ebbw Vale, 'Arty' Watkin was an alert forward who would play in any forward position if required. Surprisingly, he never played serious football before joining Stoke as a 17-year-old in 1913, but within a matter of 12 months he was regarded as one of the best strikers in the game. After serving in the forces during the Great War, he was back in action in 1919. He shook a lot of people by turning his back on the club in 1923 to go and play for Congleton Town, but a season later manager Tom Mather enticed him back to The Victoria Ground where he was to stay for the next three seasons. In that time he netted some important goals and appeared in six matches when Stoke won the Second Division title in 1926–27. Watkin, whose brother Frank played for Stoke in the mid-1920s, retired after that last campaign and went full-time in the pottery business.

WATKIN, Cyril

Full-back: 90 apps.

Born: Stoke-on-Trent, 21 July 1926.
Career: Park Road, Packmoor FC, Sneyd Colliery, Port Vale (briefly, 1943), POTTERS (September 1944), Bristol City (£8,000, July 1952, retired, May 1953).

■ Cyril Watkin played his early football all round the Potteries area, and after a brief spell with Port Vale he joined the Potters towards the end of World War Two and made a dozen or so regional appearances before establishing himself in the first XI at The Victoria Ground in 1948. Including his wartime appearances, Watkin made exactly 100 starts for the club, including 10 in World War Two, before transferring to Bristol City in 1952. Unfortunately, his career was brought to an abrupt end when he broke his right leg in a League game against Reaading. He retired in 1953, aged 26.

WATKIN, Frank

Centre-forward: 5 apps. 3 goals.

Born: Stoke-on-Trent, 30 March 1904.
Died: Hartshill, Stoke-on-Trent, 26 January 1979.
Career: Congleton Town, POTTERS (professional, May 1925), Port Vale (£500, June 1929), Congleton (free transfer, April 1931).

■ Frank Watkin scored three important goals for Stoke as they closed in on the Third Division North Championship in 1926–27 when he was brought into the side in place of the injured Johnny Eyres. On leaving The Victoria Ground he joined neighbours Port Vale, for whom he scored five goals in a 7–1 League win over Rotherham in February 1930. His brother, Arthur Watkin, had two spells with the Potters either side of World War One.

WATKINS, Walter Martin

Inside or centre-forward: 139 apps. 62 goals.

Born: Llanwnnog, Montgomeryshire, 1880.
Died: Stoke-on-Trent, 14 May 1942.
Career: Caersws (1894), Oswestry Town (1986), POTTERS (August 1900), Aston Villa (£400, January 1904), Sunderland (October 1904), Crystal Palace (June 1905), Northampton Town (May 1906), POTTERS (May 1907), Crewe Alexandra (July 11908), Stafford Rangers (August 1909), Tunstall Town (player-coach, July 1910), POTTERS (August 1911, retired, May 1914).

■ Along with his brother, Ernie, Mart Watkins was brought up on a farm in mid-Wales. Both players gravitated via Caersws and Oswestry United and it was Marty who signed for the Potters at the age of 20. An adaptable forward, able to occupy most front-line positions, he was leading scorer for the club in 1901–02 with 16 goals and again in 1902–03 with 13. Described in 1901 as a 'smart player' with a powerful shot, Watkins marshalled his colleagues splendidly and always used his wingers to good effect. In January 1904 Manchester City offered £450 for his signature. The move did not materialise but later in the same month Watkins moved to Aston Villa for a lesser fee! He had only spent nine months there, appearing in five games, before switching to Sunderland. He never settled in the North East and spent only one season with Crystal Palace, eventually returning to The Victoria ground via Northampton Town. He stayed just one more term with the Potters before having a decent spell with Crewe Alexandra, spending a full season with Stafford Rangers also assisting Tunstall. He then returned to Stoke for the third time prior to the 1911–12 season, remaining until 1914 when he retired. All told, he scored a goal virtually every two games for the Potters, gained 10 full caps for Wales (his first in 1902 versus England, his last in 1908 against Ireland). Brother Ernie Watkins went on to play for Leicester Fosse, Aston Villa, Grimsby Town, Millwall Athletic and Southend United and won five Welsh caps.

WATSON, David Vernon

Defender: 64 apps. 6 goals.

Born: Stapleford, Notts, 5 October 1946.
Career: Stapleford Old Boys, Notts County (professional, January 1967), Rotherham United (£25,000, January 1968), Sunderland (£100,000, December 1970), Manchester City (£275,000 plus Jeff Clarke, June 1975), SV Werder Bremen, Germany (£100,000, June 1979),

Southampton (£200,000, October 1979), POTTERS (£50,000, January 1982), Vancouver Whitecaps, NASL (free transfer, April 1983), Derby County (free, September 1983), Vancouver Whitecaps (on loan, briefly), Fort Lauderdale Sun, NASL (free, May 1984), Notts County (free, player-coach), September 1984), Kettering Town (August 1985, retired, May 1986), later ran his own business in Nottingham.

■ Making the initial breakthrough as a professional with Notts County in 1967, Dave Watson quickly became a quality defender. He developed briefly under Tommy Docherty's management at Millmoor, carried on his rise to the top with Sunderland and then Manchester City before spending a season in the German Bundesliga with Bremen, returning to England to sign for Southampton. One of Richie Barker's best buys for Stoke City, secured halfway through the 1981–82 season, it was a disappointment when he left The Victoria Ground after just a season, choosing to go on an 'illegal' tour to South Africa, which never materialised! Instead he played in the NASL, returning after four months to sign for Derby County. He later went back to the States, wound down his League career with Notts County and retired at the age of 39 after a spell with Kettering. A determined, confident centre-half with an abundance of skill, Watson played in 65 internationals for England between April 1974 and June 1982. Indeed, he was capped while associated with five different clubs, a unique record among England players until Peter Shilton was picked for the first time as a Derby player. He amassed a grand total of 660 League appearances, 67 goals scored, for his eight English clubs spread over a period of 18 years. He won the FA Cup with Sunderland in 1973 and was a League Cup-winner with Manchester City three years later. He returned to The Dell in 1989 to play in the Steve Mills charity match.

WATSON, Harold

Centre-half: 4 apps.

Born: Wath-on-Deane, 13 March 1908.
Died: Worcestershire, 1982.
Career: Wath Wanderers (August 1927), Brighton & Hove Albion (July 1931), Kidderminster Harriers (1932–34).

■ Tall reserve defender Harry Watson, reliable and efficient, played in only four League games for Stoke during his three seasons at The Victoria Ground, deputising for the injured Tom Williamson.

WESTLAND, Douglas George

Goalkeeper: 6 apps.

Born: Aberdeen, 3 April 1909.
Died: Montreal, Canada, June 1998.
Career: Aberdeen Banks o'Dee (1925–27), Aberdeen (amateur, August 1933), POTTERS (trialist, July 1936, signed, professional, August 1936), guest for Portsmouth (1942–43) and Barlaston St Giles (1944–45), Raith Rovers (1946–47), emigrated to Canada.

■ Goalkeeper Doug Westland played in just six senior games for Stoke over a

period of two years leading up to World War Two. He made his first-team debut in that record 10–3 League win over West Bromwich Albion in February 1937, having joined the Potters with his brother, James, from Aberdeen in 1936, signed by fellow Scot Bob McGrory. He made three appearances for the Potters during the war.

WESTLAND, James

Inside or centre-forward: 64 apps. 16 goals.

Born: Aberdeen, 21 July 1916.
Died: Newcastle-under-Lyme, Staffs, February 1972.
Career: Inchgarth FC, Aberdeen (1930–31), Aberdeen Banks o' Dee (1932–33), Aberdeen University (from 1932), Aberdeen (amateur, August 1933),

POTTERS (trialist, July 1936, signed professional, August 1936), Mansfield Town (November 1946–May 1947).

■ Jimmy Westland, brother of goalkeeper Douglas, was a useful centre-forward. He was recruited to The Victoria Ground in July 1935 for a trial and impressed so much that he was signed on a permanent basis the following month. He spent the next 11 years as a registered player with Stoke, accumulating a useful set of first-class statistics while also appearing in four regional games during World War Two. An undergraduate from Aberdeen University, Westland could have become a professional dancer, but he chose the football pitch instead of the ballroom. He was only 55 when he died.

WESTON, Thomas

Full-back: 4 apps.

Born: Halesowen, 23 August 1890.
Died: Stourbridge, 1952.
Career: Red Hill School, Quarry Bank (1907), Old Hill Comrades (1908), Coombs Wood (1909), Aston Villa (professional, July 1911), served in the Army during World War One, POTTERS (August 1921–November 1922), Stourbridge (December 1922, retired, May 1924), later coached at schools in Stourbridge, Old Hill and Cradley Heath.

■ Some fans considered Tommy Weston to be rather impetuous at times, wanting him to show more caution in his play, but he was undoubtedly a very fine full-back, strong-willed, competitive and solid. He introduced an element of dash into Aston Villa's defence, forming an excellent partnership at full-back with Tommy Lyons before World War One when he gained FA Cup winners' and League runners'-up medals in 1913. During the hostilities he partnered another Tommy, Tommy Smart, and collected a second FA Cup winners' medal in 1920, having been badly wounded in Ervilliers, France, in 1918. He joined the Potters as experienced cover for Bob McGrory and Alec Milne, he had been close to winning England honours on a number of occasions but missed out after being named reserve for two internationals. He made 179 appearances for Aston Villa.

Doug and Jimmy Westland

WHARTON, Tancey Clifford Arnold

Half-back: 19 apps.

Born: Dawden, Shropshire, 1890.
Died: before 1980.
Career: Seaham Harbour (Durham), POTTERS (March 1913), Grantham (July 1914).

■ Left-half Tancey Wharton spent 15 months at The Victoria Ground and had his best spell in the first team between September and January when he accompanied both Joey Jones and Jimmy Bradley at the heart of the Potters defence. Unfortunately, a knee injury led to his departure.

WHISTON, Donald

Full-back or inside-forward: 36 apps. 5 goals.

Born: Stoke-on-Trent, 4 April 1930.
Career: Boys' Brigade football, POTTERS (amateur, June 1948, professional, December 1949), Crewe Alexandra (free transfer, February 1957), Rochdale (free, May 1958–April 1959).

■ Don Whiston was spotted by a Stoke City scout playing for a local Boys Brigade team and within 18 months had signed professional forms at The Victoria Ground. Described as a 'genuine all-rounder', it was as a full-back where he played his best soccer. A dedicated club-man, he remained a 'Potter' until early 1957, performing mainly in the reserves and having less than 40 first-team outings during that time. He left Stoke for Gresty Road on a free transfer.

WHITE, Robert Nelson

Outside-right: 3 apps.

Born: Walbottle, Tyneside, 11 August 1902.
Died: Durham, 1977.
Career: Prudhoe Castle (1919), Huddersfield Town (professional, April 1923), POTTERS (May 1924) Tranmere Rovers (March 1925), Yeovil & Petters United (1928), Wolverhampton Wanderers (August 1929), Watford (May 1930), Portsmouth (briefly, 1931), Carlisle United (July 1932), North Shields (September 1933, retired, April 1939).

■ Right-winger Bob White had a useful career serving a number of clubs. He was a reserve with the Potters, coming into the forward-line in place of John Evans for three League games in 1924–25. He netted 16 goals in 45 League games for Tranmere, 16 in 20 for Watford and seven in 20 for Carlisle – these being his best returns with individual clubs.

WHITEHOUSE, Frank

Inside or centre-forward: 95 apps. 24 goals.

Born: Newcastle-under-Lyme, Staffs, June 1876.
Died: before 1960.
Career: Bucknall, Burslem Port Vale (June 1899), POTTERS (May 1900), Glossop North End (June 1905), Wolverhampton Wanderers (retired, May 1908).

■ Frank 'Tinker' Whitehouse was a willing and purposeful player who joined Stoke from neighbours Port Vale shortly before his 24th birthday. He spent five years at The 'Vic' and had his best season there in 1902–03 when he scored nine times in 33 League and Cup games when partnering Fred Johnson on the right-wing. Following a brief spell in Wolves' reserve side, he quit football in 1908.

WHITEHOUSE, Jack

Half-back 2 apps.

Born: Swan Village, West Bromwich, 15 August 1878.
Died: Dudley, 1950.
Career: Great Bridge United, Tipton All Saints, Wednesbury Town (1897), Wolverhampton Wanderers (professional, July 1900), Stourbridge (on loan, March–April 1906), Halesowen Town (July 1906), POTTERS (October 1906), Stourbridge (August 1907), Bloxwich Strollers (August 1908), later with Darlaston, Cradley Town, Dudley Town, Gornal Wood (retired 1915).

■ A very stylish yet competitive half-back, the fair-haired Jack Whitehouse was a regular in Wolves' League side for five years from 1901. He made 155 appearances, scored one goal for the Molineux club and always gave 100 percent on the field of play, getting himself sent-off at least twice during his time with Wolves. Whitehouse, who had four brothers, two of whom were also footballers, was initially reserve to Ted 'Cock' Pheasant at Molineux before claiming a place in the first XI in 1901. He was forced to leave the club after a flare-up with two colleagues. His two League games for the Potters were against Everton and Blackburn Rovers in November 1906. He then went on to play for a number of Black Country sides before announcing his retirement in 1915.

WHITEHURST, Albert John

Centre-forward: 18 apps. 4 goals.

Born: Fenton, Stoke-on-Trent, 22 June 1898.
Died: Birkenhead, 1976.
Career: New Haden FC, POTTERS (June 1920), Rochdale (June 1923), Liverpool (May 1928), Bradford City (February 1929), Tranmere Rovers (June 1931, retired, May 1934).

■ Bert Whitehurst turned out to be a fine centre-forward who played League football from 1921 to 1934. He joined Stoke soon after his 22nd birthday in 1920 and made his League debut against Stockport County the following March, scoring his first goal for the club a week later in a game at Blackpool, which was lost 3–1. Unable to hold down a regular place in the side, he moved to Rochdale in 1923 and spent five excellent years at Spotland, netting 116 goals in 168 League North appearances, including 44 in 42 matches in 1926–27 when he headed that Division's scoring charts. That form took him to Liverpool, but, sadly for him, he failed to impress at Anfield, scoring twice in eight games. He then moved to Bradford City, whom he helped win the Third Division North title, hitting 24 goals in only 15 appearances, including seven in an 8–0 drubbing of Tranmere Rovers a month after joining. Ironically, when he moved from Valley Parade he joined Tranmere, who used him as a centre-half during the latter stages of his career. He retired with a record of 180 goals in 313 League games under his belt.

WHITEHURST, William

Centre-forward: 5 apps.

Born: Thurnscoe near Barnsley, Yorkshire, 10 June 1959.
Career: Retford Town, Bridlington Trinity, Mexborough Town, Midland League XI, Hull City (£1,800, full-time, professional, October 1980), Newcastle United (£232,500, December 1985), Oxford United (£187,500, October 1986), Reading (£120,000, February 1988), Sunderland (£100,000, September 1988), Hull City (£150,000, December 1988), Sheffield United (£35,000, February 1990), POTTERS (on loan, November–December 1990), Doncaster Rovers (on loan, February 1991, free transfer, March 1991), Crewe Alexandra (on loan, January–February 1992), later with Stafford Rangers, Hatfield Main, Glentoran, Ireland, Kettering Town (two spells), Goole Town, Mossley, South China, Hong Kong, Frickley Colliery (July 1993, manager, November 1994), Preston Macedonia, Australia (briefly) and Stalybridge Celtic.

■ An ex-bricklayer, 6ft 1in tall and 14st in weight, Billy Whitehurst was a tough, aggressive striker who had just five outings for Stoke when on loan from Sheffield United in 1990. He netted 79 goals in 388 League games up to 1994 when he entered non-League football. His only club prize was to collect an Associate Members Cup runners'-up medal with Hull in 1984, and he played for Oxford during their historic first season in the top flight.

WHITLEY, John

Goalkeeper: 38 apps.

Born: Seacombe, Cheshire, 20 April 1880.
Died: London, 1955.
Career: Seacombe Swifts, Seacombe YMCA (May 1897), Liskeard YMCA (briefly, 1898), Darwen (January 1899), Aston Villa (May 1900), Everton (August 1902), POTTERS (September 1904), Tottenham Hotspur (briefly, June 1905, registration cancelled, returned to Stoke), Leeds City (April 1906), Lincoln City (September 1906), Chelsea (June 1907, retired, May 1914, then trainer until May 1939), served in the Royal Flying Corps during World War One.

■ When Welsh international goalkeeper Dickie Roose left The Victoria Ground for Everton in the summer of 1904, Stoke went out and recruited Cornishman Jack Whitley from Goodison Park as his replacement. But after playing in 34 games for the Potters in his first season at The 'Vic', Whitley suddenly found himself in the reserves as Roose chose to return for a second spell with the Potters. A sound and competent custodian, he later appeared in almost 140 games for Chelsea, helping them win promotion to the First Division in 1912. After retiring he was appointed trainer at Stamford Bridge and became a father figure to generations of young players, and his bald head and flapping coat-tails (as he raced onto the pitch) were very much part of the Chelsea scene during the inter-war years. In all, he spent 32 years with the London club.

WHITTAKER, Enos

Outside-right: 18 apps. 1 goal.

Born: Nelson, Lancashire, 1888.
Died: Burnley, Lancashire, 1959.
Career: Exeter City (1910), POTTERS (August 1912), Clapton Orient (August–September 1913).

■ Right-winger Enos Whittaker attempted to make the grade with Exeter City but failed to get a first-team call up and joined Stoke in 1912. Replacing Archie Dyke, he did much better at The Victoria Ground before having an unsuccessful two-month spell with Clapton Orient in August–September 1913. His only goal for the Potters was, in fact, the club's first of the season, in a 3–1 Southern League defeat at Brighton.

WHITTAKER, Harvey

Outside-right: 4 apps.

Born: Congleton, Cheshire, 1875.
Died: before 1960.
Career: Congleton Hornets, POTTERS (August 1899), Newcastle Town (August 1900).

■ Reserve right-winger Harvey Whittaker spent one season at Stoke, making his debut in place of the injured Fred Johnson in a 2–0 League defeat at Derby in November 1899.

WHITTINGHAM, Robert

Centre/inside-forward: 18 apps. 8 goals.

Born: Goldenhill, Stoke-on-Trent, April 1884.
Died: Goldenhill, Stoke-on-Trent, 9 June 1926.
Career: Goldenhill Villa, Goldenhill Wanderers, POTTERS (amateur, September 1902), Crewe Alexandra (professional, May 1906), Blackpool (July 1907), Bradford City (January 1909), Chelsea (£1,300, April 1910), South Shields (March 1914), World War One guest for POTTERS (1915–19) and Port Vale (April–May 1919), Chelsea (March 1919), POTTERS (September 1919, retired on health grounds, April 1920), returned with Stoke United (December 1920), Macclesfield (February 1921), Scunthorpe and Lindsey United (June 1921), Wrexham (November 1922), Goldenhill Wanderers (December 1923, retired, May 1924).

■ Bob Whittingham's tally of 30 goals for Chelsea in the 1910–11 season set a new club individual scoring record that lasted longer than any other in the Football League, some 48 years until Jimmy Greaves surpassed it in 1958–59.

A big, strong, bustling type of player with a cracking right-foot shot, he was the scourge of goalkeepers and loved to collect a ball 30-40 yards from goal and set off towards his target, brushing defenders aside with his powerful frame. After a few games in Stoke's second team he scored on his League debut for Blackpool against Stockport County in 1907. He went on to net 28 times in 53 games for the Seasiders before moving to Valley Parade. He then did the business with Chelsea, for whom he notched 80 goals in only 128 appearances, helping them win promotion to the First Division in 1911–12 when he scored 26 goals in only 32 games. His career realised a total of 147 goals in 249 League and FA Cup games, accumulated over a period of 13 years. Taking into consideration his efforts outside the Football League (wartime), his overall strike-record was exceptional, 211 goals in less than 350 competitive matches. He appeared in 84 games for the Potters during World War One, scoring a staggering 86 goals, 32 of which came in 1917–18, including four in a 16–0 home win over Blackburn. Capped by England against Scotland in a Victory international at Stoke in October 1919, scoring in a 2–0 win, he also represented the Football League. One defender who opposed the powerful centre-forward quite often once said 'I'd rather face his Satanic Majesty than Whittingham!' Tragically, the well-liked Whittinghaam died of tuberculosis, aged 42.
* Whittingham's elder brother, Sam, played for Blackpool, Port Vale, Stoke (briefly as a reserve) and Huddersfield Town.

WHITTLE, Justin Phillip

Central defender: 73+17 apps. 1 goal.

Born: Derby, 18 March 1971.
Career: Army service (from 1989), Glasgow Celtic (professional, July 1994), POTTERS (free transfer, October 1994), Hull City (£65,000, November 1998), Grimsby Town (free, August 2004).

■ Standing 6ft 1in tall and weighing 12st 12lb, Justin Whittle was signed by manager Lou Macari from Celtic on a free transfer in 1994 – after Macari had

returned to The Victoria Ground following a spell in charge at Parkhead. Unfortunately, Whittle had struggled to get a look in at Celtic, although he did perform well in the reserves. He took time to settle in Stoke, but after Vince Overson had moved on and Ian Cranson was forced to retire, he stepped up and made the number five position his own during the 1996–97 campaign. He eventually gave way when Larus Sigurdsson and Steve Tweed were preferred at the heart of the defence. At that juncture he joined Hull City, with whom he gained promotion from the Third Division in 2005 while taking his career appearance record towards the 350 mark.

WILKES, Harry Theodore

Goalkeeper: 89 apps.

Born: Alcester, 19 June 1874.
Died: Stoke-on-Trent, 9 February 1921.
Career: Congregational Unity (Redditch), Redditch Town (August 1891), Aston Villa (professional, April 1893), POTTERS (on loan, March–April 1898), Aston Villa (April 1898), POTTERS (August 1899, retired, May 1903), later licensee of the Wharf Tavern (Stoke).

■ Agile and brave, 'Tom' 'Badger' Wilkes, 6ft 1in tall and 13st in weight, spent six years with Aston Villa, collecting an FA Cup winners' medal in 1895 and a League Championship medal the following season. After being replaced by Jimmy Whitehouse he moved to Stoke where he took over from George Clawley. He went on to make almost 90 first-team appearances

for the Potters, playing brilliantly in the four Test Matches when on loan, which helped them preserve First Division status and again during his first two seasons, following his permanent move to The Victoria Ground in 1899. In April 1913 a benefit match was arranged on his behalf after he'd fallen on hard times and was suffering with his health.
* His son, Tom, also kept goal for Stoke's second XI.

WILKINSON, Andrew Gordon

Defender: 2+4 apps.

Born: Stone, Staffs, 6 August 1984.
Career: POTTERS (apprentice, August 2000, professional, July 2002), Prtick Thistle (loan, July–October 2004), Shrewsbury Town loan, March–May 2005).

■ A strongly-built defender, quick over the ground, Andy Wilkinson graduated through the junior and reserve teams at The Britannia Stadium and was loaned out to Conference side Telford to gain

experience. He returned to make his senior debut as a substitute against Walsall and started his first game at home to already promoted West Bromwich Albion in the penultimate game of the 2003–04 season.

WILKINSON, Frederick

Half-back and inside-left: 3 apps.

Born: Bury, Lancashire, 1889.
Died: Suffolk, August 1971.
Career: St Augustus FC (1906), Lancaster City (summer, 1908), Norwich City (August 1910), Blackpool (July 1912), Darlington (August 1913), Newport County (1914), served in the Army during World War One, POTTERS (guest, November 1918), Stalybridge Celtic (August 1919), Watford (July 1920), POTTERS (August 1921), Bury St Edmunds (June 1922, retired, May 1926).

■ 'Sonny' Wilkinson was a well-built defender who was 32 years of age when he joined the Potters after appearing in 37 League games for Watford. He played in the first three matches of the 1921–22 season against West Ham (twice) and South Shields but then lost his place when Dickie Smith returned to the left-half position. He had one game as a guest for Stoke in 1918 when, in an emergency, he played at right-back in a 1–0 win at Preston.

WILKINSON, Norman

Goalkeeper: 198 apps.

Born: Tantobie, County Durham, 8 June 1910.
Died: Stoke-on-Trent, 18 May 1975.
Career: Tanobie FC, Tannfield Lea, West Stanley, Huddersfield Town (professional), POTTERS (£100, July 1935), guest for Sheffield Wednesday (November–December 1943), Oswestry Town (August 1952).

■ Norman Wilkinson served the Potters for 17 years and during that time appeared in 212 first-team matches: 186 in the Football League, 12 in the FA Cup and 14 during wartime. He was manager Bob McGrory's first signing when the former Potters full-back took over the reins from Tom Mather, costing just £100 from Huddersfield, having started his career as a centre-half. He switched to goalkeeping in an emergency and stuck to the job with

great effect. He became first choice at The 'Vic' almost immediately and held his position until the outbreak of World War Two. On his return from serving his country, he found that Dennis Herod had taken over the gloves but in 1949 was called back into the fray and made another 41 first-team appearances when he thought his career was over. He played in his last game for Stoke at the age of 41 years, nine months and seven days against his former club Huddersfield Town in March 1952.

WILLIAMS, Brett

Full-back: 2 apps.

Born: Dudley, West Midlands, 19 March 1968.
Career: Dudley & Brierley Hill Schoolboys football, Nottingham Forest (apprentice, June 1984, professional, December 1985), Stockport County (on loan, March 1987), Northampton Town (on loan, January 1988), Hereford United (on loan, September 1989), Oxford United (on loan, February 1992), POTTERS (on loan, August–September 1993), Oxford United (signed, August 1993–May 1994).

■ Brett Williams's two League appearances for the Potters were at the start of the 1993–94 season in away draws at Bolton and Portsmouth. One of his 49 outings for Forest (in nine years) came in the 1992 League Cup Final defeat by Manchester United at Wembley.

WILLIAMS, James

Full-back or half-back: 9 apps.

Born: Tunstall, Stoke-on-Trent, 1888.
Died: before 1960.
Career: Tunstall Swifts, Blackpool (November 1908), POTTERS (March 1909), Hanley Swifts (August 1911). Did not play after World War One.

■ Jim Williams was a sturdy defender who had a brief spell with Blackpool (no first-team appearances) before joining Stoke, primarily as a reserve. Six of his nine appearances for the Potters were at left-half.

WILLIAMS, John Nelson

Striker: 1+3 apps.

Born: Birmingham, 11 May 1968.
Career: Cradley Town, POTTERS (trialist, July 1991), Swansea City (£5,000, August 1991), Coventry City (£250,000, July 1992), Notts County (on loan, October–November 1992), POTTERS (on loan, December 1994–January 1995), Swansea City (on loan, February–March 1995), Wycombe

Wanderers (£150,000, September 1995), Hereford United (free transfer, February 1997), Walsall (free, July 1997), Exeter City (free, August 1997), Cardiff City (free, August 1998), York City (£20,000, August 1999), Darlington (free, December 2000), Swansea City (free, July 2001), Kidderminster Harriers (free, August 2003), Bath City (July 2004).

■ Potters boss Lou Macari acquired 6ft 2in striker John Williams in 1994 in a bold bid to boost his attack. He played in four League games (three as a substitute), failed to score and duly returned to Highfield Road. Initially a postman, playing non-League soccer for Cradley Heath, he entered the Football League with Swansea in 1991, this after he had been on trial with the Potters playing in a friendly against Worcester City. He adapted to top-class football very well and scored 11 goals in 46 games for the Welsh club before his switch to Coventry in 1992. Life wasn't so easy in the Premiership but Williams, big, strong and difficult to contain when running with the ball, battled on and netted another 11 goals in 86 appearances for the 'Sky Blues', while having loan spells at his former club, Swansea, Notts County and, of course, Stoke. He continued playing until he joined Bath City in 1994. His senior career realised 502 appearances and 83 goals.

WILLIAMS, Joshua Joseph

Outside-right: 86 apps. 17 goals.

Born: Rotherham, Yorkshire, 4 June 1902.
Died: York, 1986.
Career: Rotherham Town, Rotherham County (professional, August 1921), Huddersfield Town (July 1924), POTTERS (March 1926), Arsenal (£3,000, September 1929), Middlesbrough (March 1932), Carlisle United (May 1935, retired, May 1937).

■ One of the smallest players in League football during the 1920s, 'Josh' Williams, an ex-toolmaker, stood at only 5ft 5in tall and weighed barely 10st, but he was a useful player, occupying the right-wing position, who made almost 90 appearances for Stoke. He started his career with his home-town club, Rotherham County, before joining Huddersfield, with whom he gained a League Championship medal under manager Herbert Chapman. In 1926 he was transferred to Stoke, arriving far too late to save the club from relegation from the Second Division. But he was a key member of the side that won the Third Division North title at the first time of asking the following season. In September 1929 manager Chapman, who by now had moved from Leeds Road to Highbury, recruited Williams for Arsenal. The winger did reasonably well with the Gunners before rounding off his interesting career at Middlesbrough and Carlisle, finally hanging up his boots with 355 League appearances to his credit and 48 goals. He represented the Professionals versus the Amateurs in the 1929 FA Charity Shield game and toured South Africa with the FA party in that same year. Unfortunately, he missed Arsenal's 1930 FA Cup Final win over Sheffield United through injury.

WILLIAMS, Louis

Centre-half: 36 apps. 1 goal.

Born: Longton, Stoke-on-Trent, 1889.
Died: before 1980.
Career: North Staffs Nomads, POTTERS (August 1906), Bradford City (July 1908), Bristol Rovers (May 1909), Port Vale (June 1912–May 1913).

■ Lou Williams was a dogged defender with a ferocious tackle and good technique. He broke his leg in a reserve-team game soon after joining the Potters and was out of action until the start of the 1907–08 season. His only goal for Stoke earned his side a 1–0 home League win over Stockport County in February 1909 when he played as an emergency centre-forward when Fred Brown was out injured. After leaving The Victoria Ground when the club went bust, he had 10 League outings with Bradford City, 116 at senior level with Bristol Rovers and made his debut for the Vale in a 7–0 FA Cup win over New Brighton Tower Amateurs.

WILLIAMS, Mark Stuart

Defender: 5+1 apps.

Born: Stalybridge, Cheshire, 28 September 1970.
Career: Newtown (April 1988), Shrewsbury Town (professional, March 1992), Chesterfield (£50,000, August 1995), Watford (free transfer, July 1999), Wimbledon (free, July 2000), POTTERS (free, March 2003), Columbus Crew, US (June 2003), Wimbledon/MK Dons (free, February 2004 as player and youth-team coach, signed an extended contract, August 2004), Rushden and Diamonds (loan, March–May 2005).

■ Not the quickest of defenders, by the time he joined the Potters at the age of

32 Mark Williams had accumulated a useful record in senior club football of 28 goals in 427 senior appearances as well as gaining one 'B' and 30 full caps for Northern Ireland. He remained at The Britannia Stadium for just three months, in which time he played in six League games, one as substitute against his former and future club Wimbledon.

WILLIAMS, Richard

Goalkeeper: 62 apps.

Born: Newcastle-upon-Tyne, 15 December 1905.
Died: 27 May 1983.
Career: Jarrow, POTTERS (professional, March 1926), Reading (£250, July 1930), Chester (August 1931–April 1932).

■ Goalkeeper Dick Williams played in over 60 first-team games for Stoke over a period of three years, April 1927–April 1930. Spotted playing in the North East, he was enticed down to the Potteries as cover for Bob Dixon. After spending almost a full season in the second team he finally got his chance in the first XI, making his debut at Lincoln City in the penultimate League game of Stoke's Third Division North Championship-winning campaign of 1926–27, celebrating by saving a penalty in a 3–1 win. He eventually left The Victoria Ground following the emergence of Norman Lewis.

WILLIAMS, Terence John

Midfield: 8+9 apps.

Born: Stoke-on-Trent, 23 October 1966.
Career: POTTERS (apprentice, April 1983, professional, October 1984, retired through injury, February 1987).

■ Midfielder Terry Williams was forced to quit the game through injury when only 20 years of age. He joined the Potters as a teenager in 1982 and appeared in 17 first-team games before a spate of aggravating leg injuries halted his career. He played his last game against Brighton & Hove Albion in October 1986, just before he turned 'pro.'

WILLIAMSON, William Marcus

Outside-right: 8 apps.

Born: Longton, Stoke-on-Trent, 1884.
Died: before 1960.
Career: North Staffs Nomads, POTTERS (July 1905), Crewe Alexandra (April 1908), Leicester Fosse (May 1910), POTTERS (June–November 1911).

■ Billy Williamson, an orthodox right-winger and basically a reserve-team player, deputised for Ross Fielding in all of his eight senior appearances for the Potters. He did not play at all during his second spell at the club. His father, Bill Williamson senior, was a director of Stoke City FC.

WILLIAMSON, Thomas Robertson

Centre-half: 162 apps. 15 goals

Born: Dalmuir, Glasgow, 8 February 1901.
Died: Norwich, 1 April 1988.
Career: Kilbowie Ross Dhu, Kirkintillock Rob Roy, Blackburn Rovers (professional, May 1922), Third Lanark (March 1924), POTTERS (December 1926), Norwich City (July 1931), Frosts Athletic (July 1934, retired, May 1938), later mine host of the Rose Tavern, Norwich.

■ A ship's plater working on the River Clyde during the week, centre-half Tom

Williamson played junior football at weekends before signing for Blackburn Rovers. Unfortunately, he never fitted in at Ewood Park and made an early return to Scotland to sign for Third Lanark. Just before Christmas in 1926, Stoke moved in and persuaded the rugged defender to sign for them. He became a star performer, making over 160 appearances for the club in less than five years. Williamson was an attack-minded defender who loved to carry the ball forward, and it was he who led the rest of the Stoke players in asking for improvements in wages and conditions. He skippered Norwich and scored in his last League game for the Canaries against Clapton Orient in August 1933, prior to rounding off his career with Frosts Athletic. Williamson died tragically in a house fire in 1988, aged 87.

WILSHAW, Dennis James

Inside or centre-forward: 108 apps. 50 goals.

Born: Stoke-on-Trent, 11 March 1926.
Died: Stoke-on-Trent, 10 May 2004.
Career: Hanley High School, Packmoor

Boys Club, Wolverhampton Wanderers (semi-professional, April 1943), Walsall (guest, February 1946), Port Vale (guest, May 1946), Walsall (on loan, August 1946–October 1948), POTTERS (December 1957, retired through injury, May 1961), thereafter concentrated on his profession as a schoolteacher, rising to the Head of Service and Community Studies at Crewe and Alsager College.

■ Dennis Wilshaw was a natural goalscorer – a player who, in today's game, would have fitted into any forward-line superbly well. He was strong and determined, two-footed, and could unleash a powerful shot, and wasn't bad with his head either. After doing well in the North Staffordshire League, he signed for Wolves during the early part of World War Two, making his debut in the local derby versus West Bromwich Albion in September 1943. With the hostilities in full flow, he was subsequently loaned out to nearby Walsall, helping them reach the Final of the Third Division South Cup, and he also guested for Port Vale against Stoke at The Victoria Ground on 5 May 1946 when the Vale were beaten 6–0. Wilshaw returned to Molineux in 1949, and after a settling-in period in the reserves he scored a hat-trick on his senior debut for Stan Cullis' side against Newcastle United wearing the number 11 shirt. He finished that season with 10 goals to his credit in only 11 games but missed out on a place in the FA Cup Final, sitting in the stand as Wolves beat Leicester City 3-1. During his long association with Wolves, Wilshaw appeared in four different front-line positions, outside-right being the odd one out. He established himself in the Wanderers' first team in 1952 and two years later was a key member of the team that landed the First Division Championship when he formed a terrific partnership in attack with Roy Swinbourne. He went on to score 117 goals in 232 first-team matches during his time at Molineux. He also won two 'B' and 12 full caps for England, netting four times in an emphatic 7–2 win over Scotland at Wembley in April 1955, the first player to achieve that feat. He moved from Molineux to Stoke in December 1957 and was a vital cog in the forward-line for four years before breaking a leg against Newcastle United in an FA Cup tie in January 1961. It was ironic that he should play his first and last senior games for Wolves against the Geordies. He failed to recover from that injury and retired, having scored exactly 50 goals for the Potters. On leaving The Victoria Ground he concentrated on his profession as a schoolteacher and attended games regularly at Stoke right up until 1994.

WILSON, Brian Jason

Right-back: 2+6 apps.

Born: Manchester, 9 May 1983.
Career: POTTERS (apprentice, May 1999, professional, July 2001), Cheltenham Town (on loan, December 2003–January 2004), signed permanently, free, March 2004).

■ Able to play in midfield as well as right-back, Brian Wilson had to work hard for his first-team opportunities at Stoke, although he did produce some excellent performances in the second XI. He impressed during his loan spell at Cheltenham and was signed on a permanent basis two months after returning to The Britannia Stadium.

WILSON, Charles

Inside or centre-forward: 167 apps. 118 goals.

Born: Atherstone, Warwickshire, 30 March 1895.
Died: Stafford, May 1971.
Career: Army football (from 1915), Coventry City (briefly), Tottenham Hotspur (guest, May 1919, signed professional, June 1919), Huddersfield Town (November 1922), POTTERS (March 1926), Stafford Rangers (June 1931, taking over as licensee of the Doxey Arms at the same time), Atherstone Town, Wrexham, Shrewsbury Town, Alfreton Town (retired, May 1938), later mine host of the Noah's Ark, Stafford.

■ Charlie Wilson was a prolific marksman, one of the best Stoke have ever had. He netted almost 120 goals in less than 170 League and FA Cup appearances for the club over a period of five years. A reserve-team player with Coventry City before joining Tottenham Hotspur during the latter stages of World War One, he scored 48 goals in 80 first-team games for the London club, including a hat-trick against South Shields on his League debut in September 1919. Signed by the great Herbert Chapman for Huddersfield, he top-scored for the 'Terriers' in 1923–24 and 1925–26, helping them win the First Division Championship in successive seasons. After netting 57 goals in 99 League games for the Yorkshire club, he switched his allegiance to Stoke, his services being acquired on transfer deadline day in 1926. He hit three precious relegation-saving goals for the Potters at the end of that campaign and thereafter went from strength to

strength, rattling in goals from all angles, including a record 37 in only 44 games in the 1927–28 season as the Potters won the Third Division North title. In fact, he was leading scorer for the team in four of the five full seasons he spent at The Victoria Ground. Very powerful, he was difficult to knock off the ball, and when in sight of the goal-frame he always tried a shot. In his League career Wilson struck 194 goals in 310 appearances – a fine record. He left Stoke for Stafford Rangers, later playing for several non-league clubs before taking another pub in Stafford. NB: During the 1918–19 season, Wilson played in six games for Spurs. In four he used the name of C. Williams (and was described as a 'colt from the Midlands'), in another the pseudonym of 'C. Forshaw' and in only one did he call himself Charlie Wilson!

WILSON, Dennis James

Defender: 18 apps.

Born: Bebington, Birkenhead, 30 April 1936.
Career: Wrexham (amateur, May 1951, professional, July, 1954), Rhyl (August 1955), POTTERS (free transfer, August 1959), Bangor City (free, May 1961).

■ Dennis Wilson played in both full-back and centre-half positions for the

Potters, and despite being only 5ft 9in tall he was always a match for the bigger and stronger opponents. He failed to make Wrexham's League side, did quite well with Rhyl and played in 18 games for Stoke in two seasons before joining Bangor City.

WILSON, Edward James

Inside-left: 1 app.

Born: Fenton, Stoke-on-Trent, December 1855.
Died: before 1945.
Career: POTTERS (August 1882–April 1884).

■ Ted Wilson was inside-left for Stoke in their first-ever FA Cup tie against Manchester in November 1883. This was his only senior appearance for the club, although he did participate in several friendly matches during his two seasons at The Victoria Ground.

WILSON, Mark Antony

Midfield: 4 apps.

Born: Scunthorpe, 9 February 1979.
Career: Manchester United (apprentice, April 1995, professional, February 1996), Wrexham (on loan, February–May 1998), Middlesbrough (£1.5 million, August 2001), POTTERS (on loan, March–April 2003), Swansea City (on loan, September–November 2003), Sheffield Wednesday (on loan, January–February 2004).

■ Capped by England at three different levels, schoolboy four times, youth twice and under-21 twice, Mark Wilson had 11 senior outings for Manchester United, teaming up with the likes of Paul Scholes, Nicky Butt, Roy Keane and David Beckham in midfield. Skilful, with vision and tact, his loan spell with the Potters produced three 0–0 draws and a 2–1 win.

WILSON, Ronald

Full-back: 11 apps.

Born: Edinburgh, 6 September 1941.
Career: Tynecastle Athletic, Musselburgh Athletic, POTTERS (professional, August 1959), Port Vale (£12,000 deal including Jackie Mudie, November 1963), emigrated to South Africa in December 1970, assisted Hellenic FC (1971–72), later returned to England to play for Caverswall FC and Lambourne FC.

■ Ron 'Chunky' Wilson spent four years at The Victoria Ground, acting as reserve to Tony Allen. He had just 11 League outings for the Potters before moving to neighbours Port Vale, for whom he amassed 293 appearances (5 goals). Voted Vale's 'Player of the Year' in 1968–69, he was a member of their 1969–70 promotion-winning side two seasons later. He emigrated to South Africa in an attempt to cure his son's severe asthma and while out there played for Hellenic.
* When sitting on the sub's bench for Vale, Wilson always wore a lucky overcoat – until it was stolen at a Christmas party on 22 December 1969.

WINSTANLEY, Ira William

Right-back: 53 apps.

Born: Prestwich, Manchester, 26 October 1906.
Died: before 1980.
Career: Altrincham, POTTERS (trialist, July 1933, signed permanently, August 1933), Trafford Park FC (June 1939), did not play after World War Two.

■ Bill Winstanley was a professional at The Victoria Ground for the six seasons

leading up to World War Two. Initially understudy to Bob McGrory, he appeared in over 50 first-team games as well as skippering the reserves in 1937–38. A clean kicker of the ball, his best spell in the first team came during the second half of the 1935–36 campaign when he partnered Charlie Scrimshaw in 24 League games.

WOOD, Alfred Josiah Edward

Utility: 134 apps. 10 goals.

Born: Smallthorne near Burslem, Stoke-on-Trent, 30 June 1876.
Died: Bradford, 5 April 1919.
Career: Smallthorne Albion, Burlsem Port Vale (December 1892), Southampton (July 1895), POTTERS (October 1895), Aston Villa (March 1901), Derby County (May 1905), Bradford Park Avenue (May 1907, retired through injury, May 1908).

■ Alf Wood could play on the left-wing, at inside-forward and in all three half-back positions. He made 65 appearances for Port Vale before spending six years at The Victoria Ground, during which time he produced some exquisite performances, especially after converting from a forward into a defender. His form attracted the attentions of several leading clubs and it was Aston Villa who acquired his services, signing him as direct cover for Scottish international James Cowan. He occupied the left-half berth in his first full season in 1901–02, alongside Tom Perry and Albert Wilkes. He later reverted to the pivotal role before transferring to Derby, having helped Villa take the runners'-up spot in the First Division in 1903. He made 58 League appearances for the Rams and four for Bradford before retiring in 1908.
* When Wood signed for Southampton, there was a dispute about his transfer from Vale. A commission cancelled the deal without Wood ever playing a single game for Saints.

WOODALL, Arthur John

Outside-left: 1 app.

Born: Stoke-on-Trent, 4 June 1930.
Career: Tunstall Park, POTTERS (1950), Altrincham (August 1954).

■ Left-winger Arthur Woodhall was blessed with good pace and strong shot. However, his chances were limited at the club and his only senior appearance was against Oldham Athletic in March 1953 when he deputised for Harry Oscroft in a 1–0 home defeat.

WOODS, Stephen John

Defender: 39+1 apps.

Born: Northwich, Cheshire, 15 December 1976.
Career: POTTERS (apprentice, April 1993, professional, August 1995), Plymouth Argyle (on loan, March–April 1998), Chesterfield (free transfer, July 1999), Torquay United (free, August 2001).

■ After serving a long apprenticeship in the Potters intermediate and reserve teams, Steve Woods was finally rewarded for his patience by manager Chris Kamara with his senior debut as a substitute against Huddersfield Town in March 1998. After that he gained further experience on loan with Plymouth (5 games) before new boss Brian Little gave him another chance in the first XI, which he grabbed with both feet, producing some fine displays. Surprisingly released on a free transfer at the end of the 1998–99 season, he was a near ever-present for Torquay in 2001–02 and was in sight of a personal milestone of 200 senior appearances in 2005.

WOODS, Samuel Byron

Inside-forward: 1 app.

Born: Glasgow, February 1871.
Died: Scotland, 1933.
Career: Greenock Morton, POTTERS (October 1896), Greenock Morton (December 1896).

■ Potters management team gambled when they brought Scottish inside-forward Sammy Woods in 1896. The gamble didn't pay off as Woods, a clever ball player, never really fitted into the team's style of play and returned to Morton after just one League game, a 4–0 defeat at Bolton a week after joining.

WOODWARD, John

Striker: 10+1 apps. 1 goal.

Born: Tunstall, Stoke-on-Trent, 16 January 1947.
Career: Tunstall Park, POTTERS (apprentice, June 1962, professional, October 1964), Aston Villa (£27,500, October 1966), Walsall (free, May 1969), Port Vale (£2,250, February 1973), Scunthorpe United (July 1975), Ostende FC, Belgium (May 1977), Kidderminster Harriers (August 1978–May 1979).

■ After just 11 senior outings for the Potters, the first in a 2–0 home defeat by Chelsea in February 1965, which they lost 2–0, swashbuckling striker John 'Woodie' Woodward looked like being a terrific marksman in the First Division with Aston Villa until he suffered a severe ankle injury during a game against West Bromwich Albion in October 1966. This knocked him back considerably, and although he recovered full fitness he was never able to establish himself in the Villa side again. He later notched 29 goals in 145 appearances for Walsall and 32 in 95 outings for Port Vale. He also did well in Belgium. He made more than 400 senior appearances during his career and netted over 80 goals.

WOOLLISCROFT, Ashley David

Defender: 1+1 apps.

Born: Stoke-on-Trent, 28 December 1979.
Career: POTTERS (apprentice, August

1995, professional, February 1997, released, June 2001).

■ Reserve defender Ashley Woolliscroft's League debut for the Potters was as a second-half substitute against promoted Walsall at The Britannia Stadium at the end of the 1998–99 season. His other outing was in the FA Cup tie against Blackpool the following season, before becoming surplus to requirements.

WOOTTON, Harold

Half-back: 1 app.

Born: Hanley, Stoke-on-Trent, 7 July 1896.
Died: Stafford, August 1964.
Career: Stafford Rangers, POTTERS (August 1919), Stafford Rangers (May 1920), Crewe Alexandra (April 1923), Stafford Rangers (July 1927), later appointed trainer by Port Vale (1930s).

■ A reserve half-back at The Victoria Ground, Harry Wootton's only League game for Stoke was against Nottingham Forest at home when they were beaten 2–0 in January 1920, when he was introduced into the half-back line as Dickie Smith was out injured. He made 132 League appearances for Crewe Alexandra.

WORDLEY, Edward Henry

Wing-back or inside-left: 10 apps.

Born: Stoke-on-Trent, 17 October 1923.
Died: Stoke-on-Trent, 1989.
Career: POTTERS (semi-professional October 1941, professional, August 1946), Bury (June 1950–February 1951).

■ Ted Wordley played in 10 senior games as a half-back or inside-left for Stoke during a brief spell at the club immediately after World War Two, making his League debut in a 5–0 home win over Preston North End in February 1947. He signed for the club during the hostilities and appeared in three regional games, but failed to make the first XI with Bury.

WORSDALE, Michael John

Outside-right: 4 apps.

Born: Stoke-on-Trent, 29 October 1948.
Career: POTTERS (October 1964, professional, November 1965), Lincoln City (May 1971), Worksop Town (July 1974), Gainsborough Trinity (July 1976), Skegness Town (June 1977), later worked in a Lincoln sports centre.

■ Four appearances were all right-winger Mick Worsdale made for the Potters during an eight-year association with the club. He later netted nine goals in 69 games for Lincoln City, regularly under manager and former Potters player David Herd, before drifting into non-League football.

WORTHINGTON, Nigel

Left-back: 15 apps. 1 goal.

Born: Ballymena, Northern Ireland, 4 November 1961.
Career: Ballymena (1978), Notts County £100,000, August 1981), Sheffield Wednesday (£125,000, February 1984, Leeds United (£325,000, July 1994), POTTERS (free transfer, July 1996), Blackpool (free transfer, as player-manager, July 1997, retired as a player, January 1998, remained as manager until December 1999), Norwich City (manager, January 2001).

■ Northern Ireland international left-back Nigel Worthington was signed on a free transfer from Elland Road to replace Lee Sandford who was sold to Sheffield United. Prior to joining the Potters, Worthington had appeared in 82 games for Notts County, 417 for Sheffield Wednesday, with whom he gained a League Cup winners' medal in 1991, and 55 for Leeds. Capped by his country at youth-team level, he played in 66 full internationals for Northern Ireland

(twice as a Potter) and during his first season at The Victoria Ground added two more to his tally. Worthington, who also played in midfield and on occasion at the heart of the defence, was an Irish League representative with his home-town club before moving to Meadow Lane. A steady, no-nonsense player, he had a sweet left foot and always enjoyed a flourish down the flank when the opportunity presented itself. He later did himself proud as a manager, guiding Norwich City into the Premiership in 2004.

WRIGHT, Ian Matthew

Defender: 8+1 apps.

Born: Lichfield, 10 March 1972.

Career: POTTERS (apprentice, April 1988, professional, March 1990), Corby Town (on loan), Bristol Rovers (£25,000, September 1993), Hull City (free transfer, July 1996), Hereford United (June 1998).

■ Reserve centre-half, well over 6ft tall, Ian Wright was given just nine outings by Stoke during the early 1990s. He later made 65 appearances for Bristol Rovers and 87 for Hull before entering non-League football with Hereford United.

XAUSA, Davide

Forward: 1 app.

Born: Vancouver, Canada, 10 March 1976.
Career: Vancouver Whitecaps (1995), Port Vale (trialist), POTTERS (February 1998), St Johnstone (March–May 1998).

■ Davide Xausa, 6ft tall and a Canadian Junior international, spent barely three weeks with the Potters, one of the shortest careers with the club. In that time he made just one League appearance, selected by manager Chris Kamara against Bury during an injury crisis.

YATES, John

Inside-right: 1 app.

Born: Stoke-on-Trent, c.1863.
Died: before 1945.
Career: POTTERS (September 1883–May 1884).

■ Jack Yates was registered with the Potters for one season and played in the club's first-ever FA Cup tie, a qualifier against Manchester in November 1883, which they lost 2–1.

YOUNGER, Thomas

Goalkeeper: 10 apps.

Born: Edinburgh, 10 April 1930.
Died: Edinburgh, 13 January 1984.
Career: Hutchison Vale FC, served in the Army during World War Two, Hibernian (1946), Liverpool (£9,000, June 1956), Falkirk (June 1959 in exchange for Bert Slater, appointed player-manager, October 1959, retired, February 1960), returned with the POTTERS (March 1960), Leeds United (September 1961, retired again, October 1962, appointed scout at Elland Road), Toronto City,

Canada (coach), Hibernian (October 1969, as Public Relations Officer, later joined the Board of Directors at Easter Road), he became a successful partner in a vending machine business in Scotland and was president of the Scottish Football League (until his death).

■ Goalkeeper Tommy Younger played for the BAOR XI while serving with the Royal Scots Greys in Germany during World War Two. After the hostilities he signed for Hibernian, with whom he gained the first of his 24 full caps for Scotland while also collecting two League Championship winning medals in 1951 and 1952 and a Scottish Cup runners'-up medal. He moved to Liverpool in 1956 when they were in the Second Division and spent almost three years at Anfield, gaining further international honours as well as representing the Football League and appearing in 127 senior matches for the 'Reds'. Transferred to Falkirk in exchange for Bert Slater in 1959, Younger retired with a severe back problem early in 1960 but, surprisingly, the following month joined the Potters – ironically after Geoff Hickson had conceded five goals in a League game at Anfield! An agile and dependable 'keeper, ever alert with good reflexes and a clean pair of hands, Younger played in 10 Second Division games for the Potters before being replaced between the posts by Irishman Jimmy O'Neill for the 1960–61 season. He later added a further 37 League appearances to his tally with Leeds before retiring for a second time. After becoming a successful businessman, he was voted on to to the Board of Directors at Hibernian.

Wartime Players

The Potters, like every major club in the country, utilised 'guest' players during the First and Second World Wars. They also engaged several local amateurs during both periods to make up the team. At the same time, many Stoke players, when available, guested for other clubs.

Here are details of most of the known players who made appearances for the Potters in wartime football, with the club they were officially registered with at the time, if known, given in brackets:

1915–19

■ Arthur Allman (Manchester United) was a full-back who also served with Shrewsbury Town, Wolves (1912–13), Swansea Town, Millwall, Port Vale (trialist) and Crewe Alexandra.

■ Centre-half Alf Bishop (Wolverhampton Wanderers) made 357 senior appearances during his time at Molineux (1906–20), collecting an FA Cup winners' medal in 1908. He also guested for Merthyr Town during the war and later assisted Wrexham, retiring in 1923.

■ Sid Bowser (West Bromwich Albion), an England international who played at centre-half and inside-left, won a League Championship medal with Albion in 1920. He scored 72 goals in 371 competitive games for the Baggies in two spells. He also played for Walsall.

■ Versatile forward Billy Briscoe (Congleton Town) played for Port Vale as a guest before joining the Valiants on a full-time basis in 1919. He scored a total of 60 goals in 331 games in three separate spells with the club. In 1931 he joined Congleton for a third time.

■ Winger Sammy Brooks (Wolverhampton Wanderers) scored 53 goals in 246 appearances for Wolves between 1910–22. He started out in non-League football in the Black Country and after leaving Molineux served with Tottenham Hotspur, Southend United and Kidderminster Harriers. He was known as the 'Little Giant.'

■ Robert George Brown (amateur) scored 12 goals in 10 games for the Potters in 1918–19. After the war, he joined Bradford City in 1921 and went on to assist Accrington Stanley and Rotherham County.

■ George Cameron (Queen's Park) was a Scottish-born right-back who also played for Heart of Midlothian.

■ Full-back Arthur Cook (West Bromwich Albion) played in the 1912 FA Cup Final for the Baggies. He also served with Wrexham and Swansea Town. Cook died in tragic circumstances, falling out of his pub window when sleep walking in 1930.

■ George Garratly (Wolverhampton Wanderers) played for Walsall before moving to Molineux in 1909. A full-back, he made 232 appearances for Wolves up to 1920 when he joined Hednesford Town.

■ Centre-half Albert Groves (Wolverhampton Wanderers) appeared in 200 League games during his 10 years at Molineux (1909–19). Rather on the small side for a defender, he later played for Walsall.

■ Centre-forward Harry Hampton (Aston Villa) gained two FA Cup winners' medals in 1905 and 1913, a League Championship medal in 1910 and played in four internationals for England. He scored 242 goals in 376 appearances for Villa between 1904 and 1920, then he moved to Birmingham, helping the Blues win the Second Division title in 1921.

■ Left-half George Handley (Barrow) also assisted Chesterfield, Bradford City (two spells), Southampton, Goole Town and St Gallen (Switzerland) in a lengthy career that spanned from 1904–23.

■ Right-winger Billy Harrison (Wolverhampton Wanderers) won the FA Cup with Wolves in 1908. He scored 49 goals in 345 appearances during his 13 years at Molineux from 1907. He played initially for Crewe Alexandra and joined Manchester United in 1920, later assisting Port Vale and Wrexham.

Henry Howell (Wolverhampton Wanderers) also played Test cricket for England and county cricket for Warwickshire. An inside-forward, he played football for Wolves, Southampton (trialist), Port Vale (guest) and Accrington Stanley. He played in 198 first-team games for Warwickshire, scored 1,679 runs (average 7.80) and captured 975 wickets (average 21.23). He took 10-51 versus Yorkshire in 1923 and secured 100 wickets in a season on six occasions.

■ Howard Humphries (Aston Villa) also played for Crystal Palace (guest), Southend United and Rotherham County and was reserve to Clem Stephenson at Villa Park.

■ Alec McClure (Birmingham) joined the Potters on a full-time basis in October 1924.

■ Centre-forward Aaron Lockett (Port Vale) also played for Stafford Rangers and scored 14 goals in 34 games for the Vale, whom he served before, during and after the war.

■ Outside-left George McGregor (St Mirren) played for Sunderland and Norwich City after the war.

■ Centre-half Fred Parker (Manchester City) joined Nottingham Forest in 1919 and ended his career with Southport in 1927. He helped Forest gain promotion from the Second Division in 1922.

■ Centre-forward Jack Peart (Notts County) had played for Stoke between 1901–12.

■ Teddy Peers (Wolverhampton Wanderers) was a Welsh international goalkeeper (gaining eight full and two Victory caps) who made 198 appearances between 1911 and 1921. He also played for Shrewsbury Town, Port Vale, Walsall (as a guest) and Hednesford Town. He won both the Welsh Cup and Welsh Amateur Cup with Connah's Quay before joining Wolves.

■ Right-half or inside-forward Jack Shelton (Port Vale) made almost 100 senior appearances for Wolves before joining the Valiants in 1911.

■ Right-back George Smart (Treharris)

joined Stoke as a full-time professional immediately after the war.

■ Wing-half Herbert Tierney (Goole Town) played for Bolton Wanderers, Exeter City, Darlington, Lincoln City and Castleford Town prior to 1914 and after the war he served with Rochdale, for whom he had assisted as a guest (1916–19).

■ Full-back Tom Weston (Aston Villa) joined the Potters in August 1921 after spending 10 years at Villa Park.

■ Centre-forward Bob Whittingham (Chelsea) joined the Potters from Stamford Bridge in September 1919.

1939–46

■ Wing-half Edwin Blunt (Northampton Town) also played for Port Vale and Accrington Stanley and guested for Bury, Crewe Alexandra, Wrexham, Charlton Athletic and Wolves.

■ John Boothway (Manchester City) was a centre-forward who played for Wrexham and Crewe Alexandra after the hostilities.

■ P. Bridges (local football) appeared in 19 games during the 1939–41 seasons.

■ Sid Clewlow (Wolverhampton Wanderers), a half-back, was born in Wallasey in 1919 and died in 1989. He scored twice in six games and also played for New Brighton (two spells) and Aberdeen as a World War Two guest.

■ Arthur Cunliffe (Hull City) had earlier played on the left-wing for Blackburn Rovers, Aston Villa, Middlesbrough and Burnley and later assisted Rochdale. He scored over 90 goals in more than 300 appearances in senior football between 1928 and 1947.

■ Charles G. Curtis (Boston Town) was a pre-war amateur with the Potters in 1933–34 and had one game as a guest.

■ Jack Edwards (Rotherham United) made three appearances for the Potters and was born in Wath-on-Deane in 1921.

■ Centre-half Harry Griffiths (Port Vale) played for Everton (1932–35) and made over 100 League appearances for the Valiants.

■ Full-back Jack Griffiths (Manchester United) played for Wolves and Bolton Wanderers before moving to Old Trafford in 1934. He also guested for Notts County, West Bromwich Albion, Derby County and Port Vale during the war.

■ Full-back Lol Hamlett (Bolton Wanderers) appeared in 72 League games for the Burnden Park club and followed up by playing in 109 for Port Vale (1949–52).

■ Eric Hayward (Blackpool) started his career with Port Vale in 1934 before transferring to Bloomfield Road in 1937. He made 269 League appearances for the Seasiders (up to 1952).

■ Outside-left Eric Longland (local) played for the Potters in seasons 1940–41 and 1941–42.

■ Paddy McMahon made three appearances in 1939–40.

■ Goalkeeper George Marks (Arsenal) had two spells with the Gunners and also played for Blackburn Rovers, from 1946, and Reading while guesting for West Bromwich Albion in 1943.

■ Left-half Les Micklewright (Stafford Rangers) appeared in one game versus Walsall in February 1943.

■ James Oakes (Charlton Athletic) served Port Vale as a left-back in 316 games at various levels between 1923 and 1933 when he moved to The Valley. In 1940 he guested for his former club, Vale, and in four games for the Potters.

■ Edinburgh-born left-winger Tom Pearson (Newcastle United) also played as a guest for Hearts, Blackburn Rovers, Birmingham, Blackpool, Bolton Wanderers, Liverpool, Tottenham Hotspur and Walsall. He joined Aberdeen in 1948 and was manger at Pittodrie Park from 1959–65. He scored 62 goals in 279 appearances for Newcastle (1933–48).

■ Centre-forward Billy Pointon (Port Vale) scored 53 goals in 119 first-team games for the Valiants between 1941 and 1949. He also guested for Portsmouth and Brighton & Hove Albion and later played for Queen's Park Rangers and Brentford.

■ Inside-forward Jim Simpson (Chesterfield) played in only three League games for the Spireites in the first post-war season of 1946–47.

■ George Stevens (Crewe Alexandra), ex-New Brighton, Everton, Southend United and Stockport County centre-forward, whose League career (1930–39) realised 110 goals in 181 games, was born in Wallasey in 1910 and died in 1987.

■ Outside-left Billy Tunnicliffe (Bournemouth) started his career with Port Vale in 1936. After the war he played for Wrexham and Bradford City and during his career made over 300 senior appearances, 381 in the Football League, scoring 102 goals.

■ Full-back Emlyn Williams (Preston North End) started his League career with Barnsley in 1936. After leaving Deepdale in 1948 he rejoined Barnsley and later assisted Accrington Stanley, retiring in 1949 with 182 League appearances to his credit.

■ Winger Sid Williams (Bristol City) scored 11 goals in exactly 100 League appearances during his six years at Ashton Gate (1946–52), having signed for City during the war.

■ Horace Wright (Wolverhampton Wanderers) was an inside-forward who scored once in eight League games during his pre-war Molineux days and afterwards netted 11 times in 56 Third Division South games for Exeter City (1946–48).

■ Four former players at The Victoria Ground were also engaged as guests: Doug Jones (Carlisle United), Charlie Scrimshaw (Middlesbrough), Arthur Turner (Birmingham) and Harry Ware (Norwich City).

■ Other players who appeared for the Potters at first-team level included: A.E. Basnett (3 apps, 2 goals), P. Bates (17 apps), H. Craddock (2 apps), R. Crossley (2 apps), D. Dunn (1 app), S. Glover (56 apps), W. Gould (1 app), S. Harrison (16 apps), T. Holden (3 apps), L. Howell (2 apps), W. Kinson (36 apps), J. Mannion (5 apps, 1 goal), E. Podmore (19 apps), G.H. Poulton (8 apps, 4 goals, later with Gillingham and Leyton Orient), F. Sherratt (4 apps), R. Shuffllebotham (1 app), C. Topham (12 apps), T. Vallance (3 apps, 1 goal. He was an RAF pilot in Transport Command, flying to and from India. He was an amateur outside-left later with

Torquay United and Arsenal, broke his leg in 1949 and never played first-team football again. He was born in Stoke-on-Trent in 1924 and died there in 1980 and was the son of Jimmy, Potters trainer), K West (1 app), R Windsor (2 apps, outside-right, later with Lincoln City, Wellington Town and born in Stoke-on-Trent in 1926).

■ Stoke players who guested for other clubs included: George Antonio (Aldershot, Leeds, Nottingham Forest, Notts Co. and Wrexham), Frank Baker (Linfield and Wrexham), Alf Basnett (Crewe), Fred Basnett (Derry City and Northampton), Frank Bowyer (Derby Co.), Harry Brigham (Derby Co. and Wrexham), Jack Challinor (Derby Co. Doncaster, Leeds, Nottingham Forest and Notts Co.), Neil Franklin (Wolves and Wrexham), Sid Fursland (Cardiff and Swansea), Patsy Gallacher (Charlton, Crystal Palace, Dundee, Fulham, Luton and Notts Co.), Eric Hampson (Fulham), Dennis Herod (Wrexham), Jock Kirton (Leeds, Nottingham Forest and Notts Co.), Stan Matthews (Blackpool and Wrexham), Billy Mould (Linfield), Frank Mountford (Derby Co.), George Mountford (Crewe and Kidderminster Harriers), George Oldham (Derry City), Alec Ormston (Linfield and Middlesbrough), Syd Peppitt (Linfield, Middlesbrough and Newcastle), Tommy Sale (Wrexham), Clem Smith (Arsenal, Charlton, Clapton Orient, Crewe, Fulham, Halifax, Leicester, Rotherham, Southampton, Watford, West Ham and Wrexham), Frank Soo (Blackburn, Brentford, Chelsea, Everton, Millwall, Reading and Wrexham), Freddie Steele (Bradford Park Avenue, Doncaster, Leeds, Leicester, Northampton, Nottingham Forest, Notts Co. and Sheffield United), Jack Tennant (Southport and Wrexham), Arthur Tutin (Crewe and Wrexham), Doug Westland (Nottingham Forest and Raith), Jim Westland (Doncaster) and Norman Wilkinson (Doncaster Rovers, Sheffield Wednesday and Nottingham Forest).

Stoke Managers

Prior to 1874, Stoke Football Club was run by a committee, comprising a chairman, vice-chairman, four other members and at least two players, one being the captain.

The first 'manager' to take office was Tom Slaney in 1874. Here is a full list of Stoke's managers from 1874 to 2005.

Thomas Charles Slaney	August 1874 – May 1883
Walter Cox	June 1883 – April 1884
Harry Lockett	April 1884 – August 1890
Joseph A. Bradshaw	August 1890 – January 1892
Arthur Reeves	January 1892 – May 1895
William Spencer Rowley	May 1895 – August 1897
Horace Denham Austerberry	September 1897 – May 1908
Alfred J. Barker	May 1908 – April 1914
Peter Hodge	June 1914 – April 1915
Joseph Alfred Schofield	May 1915 – January 1919
Arthur John Shallcross	February 1919 – March 1923
John Rutherford	March – April 1923
Thomas Mather	October 1923 – June 1935
Robert McGrory	June 1935 – May 1952
Frank Taylor	June 1952 – June 1960
Anthony Waddington	June 1960 – March 1977
George Edward Eastham, OBE	March 1977 – January 1978
Alan A' Court*	January 1978
William Alan Durban	February 1978 – June 1981
Richard J. Barker	June 1981 – December 1983
William Asprey	January 1983 – May 1985
Michael Dennis Mills, MBE	May 1985 – November 1989
Alan Ball, OBE	November 1989 – February 1991
Graham Charles Paddon*	February – May 1991
Luigi Macari	May 1991 – November 1993
Joseph Jordan	November 1993 – October 1994
Luigi Macari	October 1994 – May 1997
Philip Desmond Bates*	May 1997 – September 1997
Philip Desmond Bates	September 1997 – January 1998
Christopher Kamara	January 1998 – April 1998
William Alan Durban*	April 1998
Brian Little	April 1998 – July 1999
Gary Megson	July 1999 – November 1999
Gudjon Thordarson	November 1999 – May 2002
Steven Cotterill	May 2002 – October 2002
Anthony Pulis	November 2002 – June 2005
Johannes Boskamp	June 2005 to date

* Caretaker manager.

■ Slaney, secretary-manager of Stoke from August 1874 to May 1883, was born in the Potteries in 1852 and died in Stoke-on-Trent in 1935. He trained as a schoolteacher and was a leading light both at The Victoria Ground and to local football in general for a number of years. He played for Stoke while in office and, in fact, skippered the side for seven seasons from 1875–1882. It is believed he scored nine goals when the Potters beat Mow Cop 26–0 in a Staffordshire Cup tie in 1877–78. Along with Harry Allen, he helped form the Staffordshire County FA, of which he was also secretary. Slaney became a referee when his playing days ended.

■ A local man, born in the Potteries, Cox was another ex-Stoke player who appeared in over 25 games in the club's early years, before the introduction of the League and FA Cup competitions. His reign was comparatively short.

■ Lockett, Stoke's manager from April 1884 to August 1890, took the club into the Football League in 1888 and was also in charge when professionalism was introduced, agreeing to pay the better, more established players at the club the princely sum of two shillings and sixpence a week (13p). It was Lockett who represented Stoke at a meeting called at Anderton's Hall Hotel on 23 March 1888 to discuss the formation of the Football League proposed by Aston Villa's chief, William McGregor. Lockett later became the Football League's first secretary, having his headquarters at number 8 Parker's Terrace, Etruria (later renamed 177 Brick Kiln Lane). Initially the post of League secretary was an elected position, but eventually Lockett became a full-time pad employee of the 'League', merging the job with that of treasurer. Lockett held the secretarial positions simultaneously with both Stoke and the Football League, but in the end he relinquished the appointment at The Victoria Ground to concentrate solely on his League duties.

■ Bradshaw, another local man, born in 1850, led Stoke to the Alliance title in his first season in 1891. This led to the club regaining its Football league status, but in January 1892 Bradshaw stepped down.

■ Reeves took over as Stoke's secretary-manager from Bradshaw. He got the team playing reasonably well, especially after introducing several local-born players to join the more experienced professionals already in the team, recruiting several stars from Scotland. However, in May 1895 he was replaced by former player Billy Rowley, having seen the Potters win 35 League games out of 97 under his control. A Staffordshire man, born in 1837, Reeves died in 1915 at the age of 78.

■ Rowley became Stoke's manager at the age of 30 when the club became a Limited Liability Company in 1895. (See ROWLEY, William Spencer).

■ Austerberry was assistant-schoolmaster to Slaney at St John's School, Hanley. Known as 'Denny', he spent 11 years in charge, taking Stoke into the FA Cup semi-finals. Stoke won only 134 games out of the 382 they played at League level when he was in charge of team affairs. A strict disciplinarian, he once suspended three players for drinking champagne in breach of club rules. Nevertheless, he had a 'good eye' for talent and brought many fine players to the club. He quit as manager to become a journalist, reporting on Stoke games, and later ran his own news agency. He also rose to a high level in the Masonic movement and later became an Estate Agent in Longton. Born in Hanley in February 1868, he was 78 when he died in Stoke-on-Trent in April 1946.

■ Barker got the club back on its feet after it had gone into liquidation in 1908. He resigned in 1914 after doing an exceptionally fine job at The Victoria Ground. Born in the Potteries in 1873, and a former League referee, when he left The Victoria Ground his departure apparently left a sour taste in the mouth.

■ Peter Hodge, a native of Dunfermline, combined refereeing in the Scottish Second Division with soccer administration. He was involved with several clubs north of the border and was, in fact, Raith Rovers' first ever team manager (1907–12). He became Stoke's manager in June 1914 and did a fine job, steering the side to the Southern League Championship at the end of his first season in charge. He returned 'home' to his native Scotland during the War when he rejoined Raith Rovers, taking over Leicester Fosse in September 1919. He led the 'Foxes' to the Second Division title in 1925 but 12 months later was appointed manager of Manchester City, leading them out at Wembley for the FA Cup Final of 1926 versus Bolton Wanderers. In March 1932 Hodge signed Matt Busby for City, yet soon afterwards returned to Filbert Street as boss. He died in August 1934 while still in office at Leicester.

■ Schofield played for Stoke, was an England international and also managed Port Vale (See SCHOFIELD, Joseph Alfred).

■ Shallcross played for his native Leek and was also a match referee before taking over as secretary-manager of Stoke in February 1919. He never really hit it off with the supporters, especially after transferring star player Charlie Parker to Sunderland, but he did secure the services of Bob McGrory from Burnley. Under his control, the team had one or two good spells, yet only avoided relegation by the skin of their teeth in 1921. Twelve months later, however, things had turned around completely as he led the Potters to promotion to the First Division. Sadly, from his point of view, results then started to go wrong once more and relegation was suffered immediately. This eventually led to Shallcross resigning in March 1923. He was in charge of team affairs for 162 League games, of which only 56 were won. He died in Stoke in 1950, aged 74.

■ Rutherford spent barely a month in charge at Stoke. The former Newcastle United, Arsenal and England winger, who guested for Fulham and Chelsea during World War One, won three League Championship medals in the early 1900s with Newcastle as well as an FA Cup medal in 1910. After leaving Stoke, he made a brief comeback as a player with Clapton Orient and later coached non-League side Tufnell Park.

■ Tom Mather was Stoke's manager from October 1923 to May 1935. In those 12 years the Potters played almost 500 Football League games, of which 212 resulted in victories and only 167 in defeats. Born in Chorley in the summer of 1888, Mather worked as assistant-secretary at both Manchester City and Bolton Wanderers and later became club secretary and then secretary-manager at Burnden Park, taking the latter post in June 1915. Four of the next five years of football were, of course, marred by the Great War and then, in August 1920 he joined Southend United as their manager, holding office until his 'transfer' to The Victoria Ground. He took his time in revamping the playing side at Stoke and in 1926–27 the Third Division North Championship was won. After narrowly missing promotion again shortly afterwards, Mather finally guided the Potters into the top flight in 1933, having signed Bob McGrory (his successor in the manager's seat) as well as introducing Stanley Matthews to League action. Mather was a fine manager, working with little or no cash, and when he left The Victoria Ground for Newcastle United in May 1935 a lot of people were bitterly upset and disappointed at his departure. After the Second World War, Mather was appointed manager of Leicester City, and he stayed at Filbert Street for nine months before ending his soccer career in charge of the Scottish club Kilmarnock. He retired to the Potteries where he died on 29 March 1957, aged 68.

■ Bob McGrory was a fine defender with Stoke City before taking over from Mather as team manager. (See McGRORY, Robert).

■ Barnsley-born Taylor was manager of Stoke City for eight years, from June 1952 to June 1960. During his time in charge, the Potters played 336 League games, of which they won 138 and drew 69. He was a pre-war full-back with Wolverhampton Wanderers, making 54 senior appearances, one coming in the 1939 FA Cup Final defeat by Portsmouth. He also won an England cap during the war, playing against Scotland at Hampden Park in April 1944 before 133,000 fans. Forced to retire through injury at the age of 28, he was taken on the training/coaching staff at Molineux before taking over as manager of Scarborough in 1948. From there he became Major Frank Buckley's managerial-assistant at Hull City and did a similar job at Leeds United prior to his move to The Victoria Ground. Taylor was a track-suit manager who loved to be out on the field training with the players, and he was so keen that he placed a sign in the dressing room which read 'Are you 90 minutes fit? It's the last 20 minutes that count – train for it!' After suffering relegation at the end of his first season in charge, the Potters spent the rest of Taylor's reign in the Second Division before he was sacked by club chairman Albert Henshall in 1960. His brother, Jack Taylor, played with him at Molineux.

■ Waddington, without doubt, has been Stoke's greatest-ever manager, serving the club in that capacity for 17 years. Born in Openshaw, Manchester, on 9 November 1924, he was educated at St Gregory's School, Openshaw, and played his early football as an amateur with Manchester United prior to joining Crewe Alexandra. He made 179 post-war League appearances for the 'Alex' before a painful knee injury, received during his service in the Navy, forced him into an early retirement. In 1952 he was taken on at Stoke as a coach, and five years later was upgraded to assistant manager to Frank Taylor. When Taylor left in June 1966 Waddington took over as team boss and immediately set about rejigging the side in order to put in a stern challenge at gaining promotion back to the First Division. He got together a disciplined defence – known affectionately around Stoke as the 'Waddington Wall' – and then he concentrated on the midfield department and the attack. By recruiting the likes of 46-year-old Stan Matthews, Jackie Mudie, Eddie Stuart, Eddie Clamp, Dennis Viollet and Jimmy McIlroy, among others, he eventually assembled a very competent side, one full of experience, and the Second Division Championship duly came to The Victoria Ground in 1962–63. He worked well with his coaches and at one stage called in the local Fire Brigade to water the pitch just to suit his style of play! Not the most fashionable side in the land, Stoke, under Waddington's guidance, certainly in the late 1960s, was a workmanlike outfit that got results. There was little or no money to spend on new recruits, hence the signing of aged players. But Waddington did wonders in the transfer market and among his later acquisitions were Alex Elder, Roy Vernon, Jimmy Greenhoff, Peter Dobing, David Herd, John Ritchie, Harry Burrows, George Eastham and Gordon Banks, who cost just £52,000.

Several local-born players were also brought into the team, among them defenders Eric Skeels, Denis Smith and Alan Bloor, who between them amassed a combined total of almost 1,600 senior appearances for the Potters. In successive seasons, 1970–71 and 1971–72, Waddington's side reached successive FA Cup Finals, the teams also qualified for the UEFA Cup and in 1972 the first-ever major trophy was won, Stoke beating Chelsea 2–1 in the League Cup Final at Wembley. Two years later Waddington captured the services of one of the most talented footballers in the game – Alan Hudson from Chelsea. When goalkeeper Banks was badly hurt in a car crash he replaced him with Peter Shilton, who became a legend and the first footballer ever to appear in 1,000 League games.

Stoke finished fifth in the First Division in 1973–74 and again in 1974–75, and at this juncture Waddington believed he'd got the right bunch of players, was using the correct formula and had got the backing of both the Board of Directors and the supporters.

Unfortunately for all concerned, a financial cloud fell upon the club in around 1976 after a freak storm caused thousands of pounds worth of damage to the Butler Street Stand. Quality players left and as relegation loomed, amazingly, chants began to ring out round The Victoria Ground seeking Waddington's resignation – and in May 1977, after Stoke had lost their First Division status, 'Waddo' quit as Potters manager after serving the club for 25 years. He was out of football for two years yet still remained in contact with Stoke City. Between June 1979 and July 1981 he returned to the game as manager of his former club Crewe Alexandra, and 12 years later was appointed Associate Director at The Victoria Ground (summer 1993), a position he held until his death in Crewe on 29 January 1994. Tens of thousands of supporters, young and old, turned out for his funeral to pay their respects to Tony Waddington, 'Mr. Stoke City', the club's best-ever manager.

Under Waddington's management, the Potters played a total of 701 League games. They were undefeated in 438 of them, winning 241 and drawing 197.

■ A' Court was a left-winger with Liverpool, who also played for England at senior and under-23 levels. He was also manager-coach at Crewe Alexandra and assistant boss at Chester.

■ Eastham, an England international midfielder, played League football for both Newcastle United and Arsenal before joining Stoke City. (See EASTHAM, George Edward, OBE).

■ Durban had a fine playing career as an inside-forward or wing-half with Shrewsbury Town and Derby County, appearing in 554 Football League games between 1959 and 1978 and scoring 135 goals. He also gained 27 full caps for Wales. After retiring he managed the Potters for three years (1978–81). He then took charge of both Sunderland and Cardiff City and later returned to the Baseball Ground as assistant-boss before having a second spell at Stoke as caretaker-manager, having also been chief scout for Derby County (August

1994–May 1995) and Sunderland (from June 1995). He surprisingly quit his position at The Victoria Ground in 1981 saying 'I wish to manage a big club.' His record with the Potters (first time round) was 53 wins and 47 draws from 142 matches.

■ Barker, who was born in Derby on 23 November 1939, played for Moor Sports, Primo Hamilton in Canada (April 1965) before entering League football at the age of 28 with Derby County, whom he helped win the Second Division title in 1969. He later served with Notts County (gaining a Fourth Division Championship medal with the Magpies) but after breaking his leg playing for Peterborough he slipped down the ladder, assisting Enderby Town from August 1973 before moving into management, first as assistant to manager Alan Durban at Shrewsbury Town in February 1974. Then when Durban left for Stoke, Barker moved up to the manager's hot seat. Ten months later he went to Wolves as assistant-boss, in November 1978, before joining the Potters in 1981. Under his leadership the Potters won only 30 of their 101 League games (losing 48). He lost his job at The Victoria Ground in 1983 through player-power, despite making over £600,000 profit for the club during his reign in office. After that, he returned briefly to Meadow Lane as manager (November 1984–April 1985) and later coached the Greek club Ethnikos (1985–86) and the Egyptian team Zamalek (1986) prior to going on a scouting mission for Luton Town. Ron Atkinson's assistant at Sheffield Wednesday from February 1989, he was appointed Director of Football at Hillsborough, 1995–97, and served as chief scout with West Bromwich Albion from September 1977, acting as caretaker manager at The Hawthorns during December 1997. His last appointment in the game was that of assistant manager at Halifax Town (October 2000–August 2001).

■ Asprey was a fine player with Stoke City, making over 340 appearances for the club. (See ASPREY, William).

■ Mills was a full-back with Ipswich Town and Southampton before joining Stoke City as player-manager. He gained

Alan Ball

winners' medals in both the FA Cup and UEFA Cup Finals with Ipswich and also won 42 England caps, captaining his country several times. He played in more than 700 games as a professional and after leaving Stoke managed Colchester United, was assistant-boss at Coventry City (under his former teammate Terry Butcher) and acted as chief scout at Sheffield Wednesday before becoming Trevor Francis's assistant at Birmingham City in 1996 (See MILLS, Michael, MBE).

■ Ball, like Mills, had a fine playing career. A 1966 World Cup winner with England, for whom he won 72 caps, he also starred in midfield for Blackpool who he joined initially as an apprentice in 1961. He later assisted Everton, Arsenal, Southampton and Bristol Rovers, and also Vancouver Whitecaps and Philadelphia Fury in the NASL and Eastern Athletic in Hong Kong. He appeared in over 900 competitive matches (743 in the Football League, 170 goals scored). He had his first spell as manager with Blackpool in 1978–79 and eight years later guided Portsmouth into the top flight for the first time in 28 years. After serving as assistant to Mills at The Victoria Ground, Ball was given the manager's job at Stoke. He was in charge of the Potters for 58 League games, of which 15 were won and 23 lost. After leaving the club he had spells in charge of Exeter City (1991–94), his former club Southampton (1994–95), Manchester City (1995–96) and Portsmouth (again, 1998–99) and for a time was on the England coaching staff under Graham Taylor. When transferred from Everton to Arsenal for £220,000 in December 1971, he became the costliest footballer in Britain at that time.

■ Manchester-born Paddon played League football as an inside-forward (1968–82) for Coventry City, Norwich City (two spells), West Ham United and Millwall, making 415 appearances and scoring 38 goals. He also won one England under-23 cap.

■ Macari was born in Edinburgh on 7 June 1949 and played junior football with St Michael's Academy (Kilwinning), Kilmarnock Amateurs and Kilwinning Rangers. He was then a

professional with Celtic (June 1966–January 1963, for whom he netted 57 goals in 102 games) and after that served with Manchester United (January 1973–July 1984, scoring 97 goals in 404 appearances) and Swindon Town (May 1984–May 1985). In the early 1970s he won two League Championships, two Scottish Cup Finals and two League Cup Finals while with the Bhoys and then collected an FA Cup winners' medal with United in 1977. He was also capped 24 times by Scotland, having earlier represented his country at schoolboy, youth and under-23 levels. He started his managerial exploits as player-boss of Swindon Town in 1984–85, taking over as team manager after two seasons and holding office at The County Ground until 1989. He then served in the same capacity with West Ham United for 28 weeks in 1989–90 and Birmingham City in 1990–91 before being appointed manager of Stoke City (first time round). He left The 'Vic' for a brief sojourn with Celtic (from November 1993), returning to the Potteries in 1994 and later serving with Sheffield United (chief scout) and Huddersfield Town (manager, 2000–02). He guided Swindon to the Fourth Division title in 1986 and promotion to Division Two via the play-offs the following year. In 1991 he took Birmingham to victory in the Leyland DAF Cup Final at Wembley and followed up with success in the Autoglass Trophy with Stoke in 1992 and promotion from Division Two a year later. As a player, Macari scored almost 150 goals in over 600 competitive games (88 in 391 for Manchester United). At 5ft 6in tall, Macari is one of the smallest footballers ever to play for Scotland. In 1990 the FA charged him and the Swindon chairman, Brian Hillier, of unauthorised betting on a match involving Swindon Town FC.

■ Jordan managed Stoke City for just 10 months, from November 1993 to September 1994. He took over the reins from Lou Macari and duly handed them back to his fellow Scot when he left The Victoria Ground. Born in Carluke on 15 December 1951, Jordan was a robust striker, scoring goals, in turn, for Blantyre Celtic, Greenock Morton, Leeds United (1970), Manchester United (1978), AC Milan and Verona in Italy, Southampton (1983) and Bristol City. He netted over 140 goals in some 600 appearances at club level and also gained 52 caps for Scotland. He was player-manager at Ashton Gate towards the end of his spell with Bristol City, and in 1990 he took charge of Hearts, moving to Stoke from Tynecastle. Manager of Bristol City, again (re-appointed in November 1994), he was later employed by Portsmouth, initially as assistant manager-coach and then caretaker-manager, the latter between December 2004–January 2005 following Harry Redknapp's departure to

Southampton. He returned to his position as assistant-boss after that.

■ Bates was born in West Bromwich in 1949 and was a regular marksman for Stourbridge, Shrewsbury Town (64 League goals in two spells at Gay Meadow: 1974–78 and 1980–86), Swindon Town (15 goals) and Bristol Rovers (4 goals). He appeared in well over 400 competitive matches and halfway through his second spell with the 'Shrews' he was appointed player-manager. In 1987 he went back to Swindon as assistant to Lou Macari, later following the Scot to Birmingham City, then Stoke, Celtic and back to The Victoria Ground for a second spell as coach-assistant boss of the Potters. When Macari left Parkhead to rejoin Stoke, Bates stayed for a while as caretaker-manager at Parkhead.

■ Kamara had only one win in 14 matches during a disastrous spell in charge of the Potters. (See KAMARA, Christopher)

■ England international forward Little, as a player, scored 82 goals in 302 senior games for Aston Villa, whom he served from 1969 until 1982. Born in County Durham in 1953, he later returned to Villa Park as coach, held similar positions with Middlesbrough and at Molineux and was also manager of Wolves (1986), Darlington (1989–91), Leicester City (1991–94), Villa (1994–98), the Potters, West Bromwich Albion (1999–2000), Hull City (2000–02) and Tranmere Rovers (from 2003). During his time at The Britannia Stadium, the team finished eighth in the Second Division, missing the play-offs by two places and seven points.

■ Manchester-born Megson was a hard-working midfield player who served with Plymouth Argyle, Everton, Sheffield Wednesday (two spells), Nottingham Forest, Newcastle United, Manchester City, Norwich City, Lincoln City and Shrewsbury Town between 1977 and 1996, amassing over 500 senior appearances. After retiring he went into management and has been in charge of Blackpool (1996–97), Stockport County (1997–99), the Potters, West Bromwich Albion (2000–04, twice leading the Baggies into the Premiership) and Nottingham Forest (since 2005). He spent a relatively short time at The Britannia Stadium before moving on.

■ Thordarson, an Icelandic businessman and former player in his home country, took over from Megson when morale within the camp was rather low. He quickly established a new regime, signed some experienced and, indeed, quality players and guided the Potters into the Second Division play-offs three seasons running. After missing out in the first two, the team then gained promotion at the third attempt with a 2–0 win over Brentford at Cardiff's Millennium Stadium in May 2002. The Potters also won the Auto-Windscreen Shield in 2000. He was appointed manager of Notts County in May 2005.

■ Cotterill, who was born in Cheltenham in 1964, played as a forward for Wimbledon, Brighton & Hove Albion and Bournemouth between 1989–95, making just 73 League appearances and scoring 25 goals. He then did superbly well with Cheltenham Town (1997–2002) before his brief flirtation with Stoke City. After leaving the Potters he had a spell as assistant manager at Sunderland and became Burnley's chief in 2004.

■ Pulis, born in Newport, South Wales, in January 1958, appeared in a total of 313 League games (9 goals scored) during a career that spanned 16 years (1975–91). In that time he served as a defender or midfielder with Bristol Rovers (two spells), Newport County, Bournemouth (two spells) and Gillingham and also assisted the Happy Valley club in Hong Kong. He was manager of AFC Bournemouth (1992–94), Gillingham (1995–99), Bristol City (1999) and Portsmouth (2000) before taking over at Stoke. He was dismissed in June 2005 and was appointed manager of Plymouth Argyle in September 2005.

■ Johannes Boskamp, a former Dutch international, and coach of the Belgian League club RS Anderlecht, he also played club football with RWD Molenbeek, Belgium.

Assistant managers

Among the men who have held the position of assistant manager at Stoke City are (in A-Z order): former Shrewsbury Town, Bristol Rovers and Swindon Town striker Philip 'Chic' Bates (under Lou Macari); the Oxford United, Watford and Reading post World War Two player and former Wolves boss 'Sammy' Chung (under Mick Mills); Welsh international Alan Durban; the former Aston Villa, Leicester City and Scottish international defender Allan Evans (to Brian Little); ex-York City, Sheffield United and Brighton winger Walter Gould (assistant to both Alan Durban and Richie Barker); the Northern Ireland international and ex-Doncaster Rovers and Torquay United defender Len Graham (right-hand man to Tony Waddington); the ex-West Bromwich Albion, Manchester City, Everton, Nottingham Forest, Norwich City, Oldham Athletic, Stockport County and Scotland midfielder Asa Hartford (under Joe Jordan); ex-Ipswich Town and Welsh international wing-half Cyril Lea (under Alan Durban); the former Bristol Rovers and Torquay United defender Lindsay Parsons (to Tony Pulis) and three ex-Potters, Mike Pejic (under 'Chic' Bates), Harry Sellars (under Bob McGrory) and Arthur Turner (under Frank Taylor).

Chairmen

Stoke have had a chairman presiding over the Board of Directors ever since the club became a professional body in 1885. Here are details of the men who have held the position at The Victoria Ground:

1885–87	Mr A. Fleming
1887–97	Mr S. Barker
1897–99	Mr J.T. Fenton
1899–1908	Mr W.A. Cowlishaw
1908–14	Revd A.E. Hurst
1914–24	Mr E.B. Reynish
1924–36	Mr A.J.C. Sherwin
1936–51	Ald. H. Booth
1951–52	Mr T.A. Preece
1952–53	Mr E. Henshall
1953–55	Mr T.L. Duddell
1955–57	Mr G.W. Taylor
1957–59	Mr C.T. Salmon
1959–62	Mr A.A. Henshall
1962–66	Mr G.W. Taylor
1966–76	Mr A.A. Henshall
1976–80	Mr T. Degg
1980–83	Mr P. Axon
1983–85	Mr F. Edwards
1985–86	Mr S. Chubb
1986–98	Mr P. Coates
1998–2000	Mr K.A. Humphreys
2000 to date	Mr G. Thor Gislason

NOTES

Alderman Booth held office for the longest period of time, 15 years including a difficult spell during World War Two.

Mr A.A. Hernshall is the only man (so far) to have held the position of Stoke City Chairman on two separate occasions, covering a combined period of 13 years.

In the summer of 1919, 30-year-old John Slater, a former player and owner of both the Berryhill and New Haven Collieries, joined the Board of Directors at the Victoria Ground, bringing his knowledge of the game and business expertise to the club. An immediate move was made to promote Slater to chairman but this never materialised with Mr E.B. Reynish remaining in office until the summer of 1924.

Secretaries

The first appointed secretary of Stoke (City) Football club was John Witta Taylor who it is believed held office for six years, 1868 to 1874.

Tom Slaney then took over and thereafter, until 1935, the team manager also acted as the club secretary.

The first man to hold the title after that was Tom Hancock (from June 1935 onwards). He was followed by William (Bill) Williams and since 1977 there have only been two more club secretaries: Mike Potts (until his death in 1998) and Diane Richardson (February 1998 to date)

Mike Potts, who joined the staff at The Victoria Ground initially as a part-timer in 1959, was appointed as the club's assistant-secretary (to Bill Williams) and took over as secretary in July 1977, a position he held until his sudden death in 1998.

Diane Richardson joined the club as an office clerk in 1977. She was assistant secretary for a number of years before taking office early in 1998.

Significant Others

Dudley Henry John Kernick was Stoke City's commercial manager from 1970 to 1982, when he was succeeded by Mick Cullerton. Born in Cornwall in August 1921, he was a player with Tintagel FC, Torquay United, Northampton Town, Birmingham City, Shrewsbury Town, Kettering Town and Nuneaton Borough, retiring to become coach and then manager-secretary of the latter club. A qualified FA coach, he left Nuneaton to coach at Coventry City and from there he transferred to Stoke City as commercial manager. Although an Englishman, Kernick represented a Welsh XI against a Birmingham XI at St Andrew's in 1941 – chosen because Wales were a player short! On leaving Stoke, he quit football and wrote his autobiography titled *Who The Hell Is Dudley Kernick*. His son, Max, worked in American football for a number of years.

Mick Cullerton, who was born in Edinburgh in 1948, played as a forward for Port Vale from 1965 to 1969, while also having a loan spell with Chester. He then served with Derby County, Eastwood and Stafford Rangers before returning to Vale Park for £4,000 in 1975. Over the next three years he upped his record with the club to 58 goals in exactly 200 first-team games before joining Northwich Victoria after falling out of favour. Following a second spell with Stafford Rangers, he was then appointed commercial manager of Port Vale in 1982, holding office until 1985 when he took a similar position with Stoke City, continuing to attend Vale's home matches! He spent 10 years at The Victoria Ground.

Alan Ball senior, father of former Stoke City manager Alan Ball junior, was born in Farnworth near Bolton on 23 September 1924. An inside-forward with Bolton Boys' Federation, he then played for Southport (1945–47), Birmingham City (1947–48), Southport (again), Oldham Athletic (1950–52), Rochdale (briefly), Oswestry Town (player-manager, 1952–53) and Borough United (mid-1950s) before taking over as manager of Ashton United (1959–60) and then Nantwich Town. He was appointed Stoke City coach in 1972 and later managed Halifax Town (two spells), Preston North End (1973–74) and Southport (1974–75) before scouting for Blackpool (1980–81). He also managed and/or coached five clubs in Sweden, and he had just agreed a short-term contract with Vester Haringe (Sweden) before he was tragically killed in a motoring accident while on holiday in West Cyprus on 2 January 1982.

John Rudge played professionally as a winger for Huddersfield Town, Carlisle United, Torquay United, Bristol Rovers and Bournemouth between 1959 and 1977. Born in Wolverhampton in 1944, he was appointed Port Vale's coach in January 1980, was upgraded to assistant manager in December of that same year, was caretaker-manager from December 1983 and then was in charge at Vale Park for almost 15 years, from March 1984 until January 1999. In that time the Valiants gained promotion from the Fourth Division in 1986, from the Third Division in 1989 and from the (new) Second Division in 1994. He was also at the helm when Vale won the TNT Tournament in 1992 and the Autoglass Trophy (at Wembley) the following year. He is now Director of Football at The Britannia Stadium.

Fred Bradley never missed a match at The Victoria Ground in almost 43 years. He never saw one either – as he was the club's commissionaire from August 1924 until May 1967, always based at the front door of the main stand. He used to report for duty three hours before kick-off and leave when the final guest (or member of staff) went home afterwards.

Nick Hancock, an avid Stoke City supporter, hosts the TV programme 'Do You Think It's All Over' and also appears on TV adverts as well as being an accomplished after-dinner speaker – and indeed, comedian!

Former England Test all-rounder Dominic Cork, who played County cricket for Derbyshire, Gloucestershire and Lancashire, and took a hat-trick against the West Indies, has supported the Potters since he could stand up!

Tony Tams joined the Stoke City internal staff from Northwich Victoria in August 1984. He has held a number of positions at the club, including those of Lottery Manager, Matchday Services Manager and programme editor.

Stoke City's reserve goalkeeper Ben Foster helped Wrexham (under ex-Potters' defender Denis Smith) win the LDV Vans Trophy Final at Cardiff's Millennium Stadium in 2005 when on loan to the Welsh club.

Bibliography

I have referred to several books to clarify certain relevant statistics including facts and figures, individual players' details and, indeed, stories and match reports from past seasons regarding Stoke City Football Club. There are some conflicting facts, statistics and other information in these sources and I've made judgement as to what is likely to be correct.

The list (not including any of my previous publications on the club):

Martin, W. (1988) A Potters' Tale: The Story of Stoke City Football Club (Buckingham, Sporting & Leisure Press Ltd).
Martin, W. (1991–93) Master Potters of Stoke City FC (Sandbach, Sisyphus Books).
Hayes, D. (1997) Stoke City Football Club: An A-Z (Wilmslow, Sigma Books).
Davies, G.M. and I. Garland (1991) Welsh International Soccer Players (Wrexham, Bridge Books).
Farror, M. and D. Lamming (1972) A Century of English International Football: 1872–1972 (London, Robert Hale & Co.)
FA Yearbook (1951–2000, published annually) (London, The Football Association).
Gibson, A. and W. Pickard (1905–06) Association Football and The Men Who Made It, 4 vols (London, Caxton Publishing Company).
Goldsworthy, M. (1969) The Encyclopaedia of Association Football (London, Robert Hale & Co.).
Goldsworthy, M. (1972) We, The Champions (London, Pelham Books).
Horsnell, B. and D. Lamming (1995) Forgotten Caps (Harefield, Middlesex, Yore Publications).
Hugman, B.J. (ed) (1996) PFA Footballers' Factfile 1996–97 to 2000–01 (Hertfordshire, Queen Anne Press).
Hugman, B.J. (ed) (1996) PFA Footballers' Factfile 2001–02 (Basildon, AFS).
Hugman, B.J. (ed) (1996) PFA Footballers' Factfile 2002–03 to 2004–05 (Hertfordshire, Queen Anne Press).
Hugman, B.J. (ed) (1996) PFA Premier and Football League Players' Records: 1946–1998 (Hertfordshire, Queen Anne Press).
Johnson, F. (1935) Football Who's Who (London, Associated Sporting Press).
Joyce, M. (2002), Football League Players' Records: 1888–1939 (Nottingham, Tony Brown/SoccerData).
Rollin, J. (1985) Soccer At War: 1939–45 (London, Willow Books).
Andrews, G. (1989) The Datasport Book of Wartime Football: 1939–46 (Stratford-upon-Avon, Gardenia Books).
Lamming, D. and M. Farror (1972) English Internationals Who's Who: 1872–1972 (London, Robert Hale & Co.)
Lamming, D. (1982) Who's Who of Scottish Internationalists, 4 vols. 1872–1982 (Basildon, AFS).
Pringler, A. and N. Fissler (1996) Where Are They Now? (London, Two Heads Publishing).
Rollin, J. (1985) Soccer At War 1939–45 (London, Willow Books Collins).
Spiller, R. (ed.) (1990) AFS Football's Who's Who: 1902–03, 1903–04, 1907–08, 1909–10 (Basildon, AFS).
Williams, T. (ed.) (1992) Football League Directory: 1992–1995 (London, Daily Mail).
Turner, D. and A. White (1993) Football Managers (Derby, Breedon Books).

Other Publications
AFS Bulletins (various)
Rothmans Yearbooks: 1970–2005, vols. 1–35 (various editors).
News of the World Football Annual: 1946–2005.
Stoke City official matchday programmes and handbooks: 1946–2005.
Charles Buchan Football Monthly: 1951 to 1969.
Soccer Star (weekly magazine): 1963 to 1967.
Shoot (football magazine): late 1960s/70s.

I have also referred to scores of national and local newspapers (including the Stoke Sentinel), several club histories and selected Who's Who publications, autobiographies and biographies of players and managers and quite a number of statistical/record books for confirmation of certain factual points.